VIRGIL MICHEL AND THE LITURGICAL MOVEMENT

VIRGIL MICHEL

AND THE LITURGICAL MOVEMENT

BY
PAUL B.
MARX
O. S. B.

THE LITURGICAL PRESS

Published by

THE LITURGICAL PRESS

COLLEGEVILLE, MINNESOTA

AMERICAN BENEDICTINE ACADEMY. Historical studies. Biographies, no. 1.

This book was first published as a doctoral dissertation in sociology by The Catholic University of America Press.

Index by Joseph W. Sprug. *Art work by* Brother Placid, O.S.B.

Nihil obstat: John Eidenschink, O.S.B., J.C.D., *Censor deputatus. Imprimi potest*: ✠ Baldwin Dworschak, O.S.B., D.D., Abbot, St. John's Abbey. *Imprimatur*: ✠ Peter Bartholome, D.D., Bishop of St. Cloud. January 6, 1957.

Copyright 1957 *by* The Catholic University of America Press, Inc.

PRINTED BY THE NORTH CENTRAL PUBLISHING COMPANY, ST. PAUL, MINN.

To the Pioneers

of

the Liturgical Apostolate

PREFACE

DOM VIRGIL MICHEL, O.S.B., was, as his life, work, and writings indicate, a man of almost universal interests. To single out one facet of his varied labors would be difficult, since his many interests prove to be pathways to a single goal: bringing Christian social doctrine into vibrant life in the world of his time. Yet not everything in his crowded life can be treated here in detail. This study, therefore, is chiefly concerned with the American liturgical movement: its origins, development, and ramifications especially up to 1938, the year of Dom Virgil's death. His non-liturgical writings and activities are merely surveyed. It should likewise be kept in mind that the social, philosophical, and other movements discussed herein are confined to the period of Michel's lifetime, except where needed clarification made going beyond that date a necessity.

Perhaps, in tracing the background of the various movements in which Michel participated, other personalities and details should have been mentioned. But to say more of these would be to say less of Father Michel's thought and work, which of necessity had to remain the primary consideration. Due to Michel's breadth of view, a certain amount of repetition was unavoidable. Nor has the writer hesitated to quote Father Virgil's own words where these expressed more pointedly than paraphrase the message he had to deliver at important points.

So many have contributed to the completion of this study that it will be impossible to mention all. The first debt of gratitude, however, is due to the writer's superior, Abbot Baldwin Dworschak of St. John's Abbey, Collegeville, Minnesota, who allowed sufficient time and permitted the necessary travelling to complete the work. Were it not for the constant interest and encouragement of the chairman of the

vii

dissertation committee in the sociology department at the Catholic University of America, Father Paul Hanly Furfey, this book would not have become a reality. Monsignor John Tracy Ellis has recently spoken wisely about the need of Catholic scholarship; the many hours of consultation he generously granted have proved to this writer — if proof were needed — that he also practices what he preaches. To Dr. Mary Elizabeth Walsh, the third member of the committee, the writer is likewise grateful for valuable suggestions and observations.

In the very nature of the case the writer's confreres at Collegeville, Minnesota, were his severest critics. But precisely because their scrutiny was severe and yet kindly, it was invaluable, even if factual data forced the writer to disagree with his brethren in certain instances. Since the author of this volume may be given time to show them his gratitude personally, he will forbear a personal mention of their names. The list would be a long one. He also wishes to thank the staffs of the New York Public Library, St. John's University of Collegeville, the Mullen Library of the Catholic University of America, and the Widener Library of Harvard University. In this connection mention should be made of Mr. Eugene P. Willging, Director of the Mullen Library, of Father Henry J. Browne, archivist of the Catholic University of America, and of Father Victor Suren, Director of the Central Verein in St. Louis.

Hours of interviews were generously granted by a number of persons who knew and worked with Father Virgil; their names are mentioned in the Bibliographical Essay. To clarify certain points an extensive correspondence had to be carried on with many more. The writer hopes he may be correctly understood for saying here that the unstinted cooperation of all who have assisted him struck him as a kind of tribute to Dom Virgil. To every one he desires to express his sincere gratitude.

Paul Marx, O.S.B.

TABLE OF CONTENTS

VIRGIL MICHEL AND THE
LITURGICAL MOVEMENT

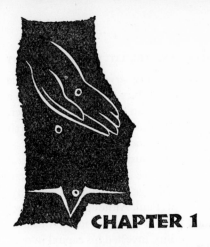

CHAPTER 1

EARLY LIFE AND WORK

INITIATION and development of the liturgical apostolate in various countries has been strikingly associated with a particular monastery and a particular personality. In France it began with Abbot Prosper Guéranger and Solesmes; in Belgium, with the Benedictine Lambert Beauduin and Mont César; in Germany, with Abbot Ildefons Herwegen and Maria Laach; in Austria, with the Augustinian Pius Parsch and Klosterneuberg. And in the United States the movement was to center largely around Dom Virgil Michel and St. John's Abbey. For this work Father Virgil had an interesting preparation and was gifted with unusual talents that found expression in a wide variety of activities. He first enrolled at the Catholic University of America for his doctorate in English and then at Columbia for courses in education; next he went to Europe to work for a doctorate in philosophy. He returned to the United States to spend his short but fruitful life chiefly in the task of organizing and leading the liturgical movement. Yet Michel's nervous energies were employed in so many other activities that Leo R. Ward, C.S.C., was prompted to say after his death, "I know of no one who has had more intellectual courage and enterprise." [1] What was this man's background?

George Michel was born the second of fifteen children into the well-to-do home of Mr. and Mrs. Fred Michel in St. Paul, Minnesota, on June 26, 1890, the year before Leo XIII issued his monumental *Rerum novarum*. His father had come to St. Paul in 1883 from Nieder-

3

marsberg, Westphalia, Germany, after having served as an apprentice in a textile store. George's saintly mother,[2] Mary Griebler, born into a pioneer family of St. Paul, was also of German extraction. Her father, a composer of music, had been the first organist at Assumption Church in that city and a teacher in its parochial school.

Fred Michel was joint owner with his cousin George of a general store, located at the southwest corner of Rice and Martin (now Central) Streets. The firm was known as George Michel and Company, and it grew to be one of the largest in St. Paul. Although Fred Michel had been a successful businessman, he sold his share in the business about 1900, and, looking for greater profits, invested his capital in opal and silver mines in Mexico. At one time these were valued at a half-million dollars. Thereafter the father of the family was to spend months each year on business in Mexico, away from his family, guiding his mining interests. To learn Spanish thoroughly, which he needed in his business, the elder Michel called in a Cuban tutor. His son George was later to gain proficiency in this language. With the Mexican revolution in 1910 Mr. Michel lost all his investments, except for a slight compensation which he received from the Mexican government. Meanwhile he had been nursing along a small real estate, loan and insurance business in St. Paul, and this he now expanded.[3]

Those who knew George Michel could see much of his father in him. Fred Michel was a rather unusual man, self-made and capable, adventurous and ambitious, to whom his son was deeply devoted and by whom he was without doubt, profoundly influenced. Prussian in temperament, the older man was aristocratic, conservative, and yet modern. He was a man of deep piety, strong faith, and ready charity — a father who, among other rules, insisted that his children attend Sunday vespers at their parish church of the Assumption, then in the hands of the Benedictines of St. John's Abbey. Mr. Michel was a perfectionist, a man of planned working routine, a voracious reader, and possessed of a mind inquisitive and curious about many things. All this went into the formation of the future Dom Virgil. Fred Michel was also alert to what was going on in the world; one of his daughters recalled that there was hardly anything new on the market which was not tried in the Michel home. As the father of a growing family, he was eager to have his children well-educated and cultured; they were not allowed to associate with children of a "lower" class; all had to take music at an early age.[4] Mrs. Michel, who played the piano, saw to it that there was frequent music and singing in a happy home.

To teach them to think on their feet and to acquire poise, the children were called upon at an early age to give impromptu talks in the home on a suggested topic. This may, indeed, have been the beginning of Father Virgil's distinct lucidity in expressing himself.

Besides his native German and dialects, the father of the family also spoke French, Spanish, English and Italian fairly well, and his work in the store made it necessary to have some familiarity with Polish, Bohemian, and Hungarian. In this way George early came into contact with foreign languages, of which he was ultimately to master five. After the death of the mother, the father and son did a certain amount of traveling. This seems to have left a deep impression on the boy.

It is doubtful whether he ever worked in his father's store. Beginning on July 6, 1900, and for the next nine years until he joined the Benedictines, George Michel spent nearly all his summers and even some of his Christmas vacations on his grandfather's farm in Scott County, near Jordan, Minnesota, with his closest boyhood and lifelong friend, Jack Schmitz. In fact, he was there so much that he was considered a member of the family. The Schmitz family was quite surprised at the way the city boy could adapt himself to life on the farm and take his turn at hard work and odd jobs in which he always acquitted himself in a resourceful, intelligent, and responsible manner.

His love of nature and the outdoors showed itself early. He loved to roam through the forests and fields; he did much target-shooting, hunting and fishing, swimming and skating. For the normal social activities of youth he had little time. Fond of history, he would read American history during the noon hour to his friend in the upper story of the corn crib, their favorite hideout. He likewise avidly read the daily newspapers, magazines and other reading materials that came into the Schmitz home.[5] These vacations on the farm gave him a familiarity with farm problems, people, life, and mentality that often came as a surprise to the leaders of the National Catholic Rural Life Conference, with which he later became associated.

A classmate at the Assumption School remembered George as "a very good student, lovable, very humble, with no mischievous traits." [6] In 1903, at the age of thirteen, he started his freshman year at St. John's Preparatory School, a small boarding school at Collegeville, Minnesota, conducted by the Benedictines of St. John's Abbey.[7] Although he took a classical course, the priesthood seems to have been far from his mind at the time. Rewards for scholastic achievement came easily to this promising student. But he did not receive all of the honors. In fact, the young man from St. Paul impressed his classmates and teachers more by his systematic and conscientious devotion to study than by his natural brilliance. A fellow student observed later, "Never did I realize that he had such a 'head' on him."[8] A classmate, and one of the closest of his many friends, had this to say:

He seemed through his lifetime never to be able to laugh as others do: his seemed a very forced one and surely was not attractive either. Yet I know as well as a close friend could that both the boy George and the religious Virgil spent his life joyously, carefreely, contented with what God's goodness allowed him in his unassuming way. . . . Everything he attempted broadened out into almost immediate success without *obvious* effort on his part. . . . He never really made an impression that he would one day set the world afire with his zeal for God and Church. . . . Of all my acquaintances I still see Father Virgil as the most generous type of unselfish, faithful friendship, one who wanted all to be his friends as true as was he. He sought to follow no human leader, however; nor did he seek to force others to go along his way.[9]

High school completed in 1907, George Michel returned for two years of college. He was a member of the editorial staff of the school paper, the St. John's *Record*, from 1906 to 1909, serving as editor-in-chief during his last year. Even as a student he could not refrain from putting his thoughts on paper, and in these three years he wrote eighteen poems, eight pieces of fiction, one play, and one sketch as well as numerous editorials and news articles.[10] George also took part in five stage plays and was an enthusiastic athlete, with a preference for baseball and tennis. Again, classmates remember him as interested in everything, energetic and alert — as one reading a book while waiting for his partner to arrive for a game of tennis or as one roaming through the woods, often with a book in hand.[11]

Only in his sophomore year in college, 1908-09, when he was nineteen years of age, did he start thinking seriously about the priesthood. Now he mentioned the possibility of becoming a priest in frequent letters to his boyhood friend, Jack Schmitz. The latter recalls that George was earnestly debating the question but had serious doubts and misgivings. About this time, as rector of the school, teacher in the classroom, or as moderator of the school paper, Father Alcuin Deutsch, O.S.B., the future abbot, had won George's confidence. Thus began a relationship which was to have a deep significance for St. John's Abbey and in a sense, for the Church in the United States.

Father Alcuin never underestimated his student's talents, and when the proper time came, he would see to their development. One day he asked Michel whether he had ever thought of the priesthood. The answer was: "Father Alcuin, if monasticism were what it once was, I would enter St. John's Abbey." By that he meant that Benedictine abbeys were once centers of spirituality, learning, and scholarship; it made no sense to Michel at that time to become a monk, be ordained, and then to spend one's life in a parish. For a time he seems also to have felt unworthy of becoming a priest and considered seriously entering religion as a lay brother with the hope that he could stay in the abbey and teach. Then again, the future Dom Virgil, with his budding interest in all human problems, also wondered whether one could do much good for the Church in a monastery hidden in the woods. And yet, monastic life appealed to him, and he loved to study. The future Abbot Alcuin apparently had no trouble solving his difficulties by assuring him there would be ample opportunity to study, to teach, and to promote the kingdom of God.[12] Having chosen the name of Virgil, George Michel entered the novitiate on July 4, 1909, with the strong hope of finding his life's work there. On September 26, 1913, he professed his solemn vows to God before Abbot Peter Engel.

It has happened that visitors have come to St. John's, and after talking to the Benedictine Fathers and working up enough courage, have timidly asked whether they could see the monks also. It may not be out of place, then, to say a few words here about Benedictine monastic life. Benedictines, of course, live by the ancient *Rule* of St. Benedict, which has withstood the viscissitudes of fourteen centuries. The father of western monachism aimed at no more than to set up "a school of the Lord's service," in which his sons were to "pray and work" in such a way that "in all things God may be glorified." As a religious family, as a community — through the liturgy living the life of Christ, whose visible representative is the abbot, the father of the monastic family — the monks confront the world, living apart from it but not apart from the common life of the Church, of which every abbey is, as it were, a miniature likeness, just as it is at once also the model of the truly Christian home. In a Benedictine house, peace and order are preserved not so much by a rigid discipline and blind obedience as by a mutual dependability, filial obedience, and fraternal love. Nothing is to be preferred to the "Work of God," that is, the common recitation and singing of the divine praises. In "the workshop of the monastery" the arts and sciences, sacred and profane, are cultivated; God is sought and served in the brethren, so that the peace and order of a well-regulated family and the light and life of praying and working and dwelling together may shine out before and into the world. In this way was western Christian civilization once saved. To this life Virgil Michel dedicated himself.

In the Benedictine clericate (seminary) his capacity for work and his versatility were fully tested.[13] Besides succeeding in his own studies, he taught at various times English, German, Latin and patrology. Moreover, taking violin lessons in Minneapolis, he also played in the small school orchestra. During the four years of his theological studies, 1912–16, he was prefect of discipline of Senior Hall, moderator of athletics, and coach of basketball in the winter of 1914–15. In his letters to his sisters he solved problems in Latin, German, mathematics, and theology, while commenting also on a wide variety of subjects. Among these were psychology, the morality of ouija boards, Shakespeare, and the problem of evil, which he confessed to have often "pondered" and which he thought his theology texts did not explain very well. He then set down his own closely-reasoned explanation.[14] He did not mention the liturgy, although there was a description of the profession of vows. During summers at the abbey he read much, especially in history, politics, and philosophy. After Michel's death, Abbot Alcuin stated that Father Virgil had read much of St. Thomas' writings by the time of his ordination.

Ordained on June 14, 1916, by the Most Reverend Joseph F. Busch, Bishop of St. Cloud, the young priest offered his first Mass at Assumption Church in St. Paul, with Father Alcuin as the preacher for the occasion.

In the summer of 1916, while Europe was beset by World War I, Virgil Michel outlined his academic plans for the Registrar of the Catholic University of America. He said:

I expect to work in English, Spanish, Latin, and in Dogmatic Theology or Apologetics if arrangements can be made. I also intend to take the examination for the S.T.B., to which I presume there are no objections on the score that I am to pursue studies in the course of letters.[15]

With a warning, often repeated, not to work too hard, Abbot Peter had sent his promising subject to the University in Washington to obtain a doctorate in English. He would get it in two years.[16] Correspondence indicates that the abbot had in mind a vaguely conceived plan to enlarge St. John's University and in this expansion Father

Virgil was to play a leading role. For this purpose, as well as to teach English, philosophy, and languages, he was to prepare himself. Nevertheless, it was about education, and to some extent philosophy, that Michel spoke in his letters.

While concentrating on English, he took his first minor in philosophy, the second in philology, for which he studied Latin, French, and Spanish. The various courses were apparently no challenge: "It may seem strange to you," he told his sister, "if I say that I do hardly any work for these classes." [17] Hence he studied English literature two hours a day on his own, spent special time on philosophy, which he knew he would have to teach upon his return, audited advanced Spanish, heard two dogma and apologetics lectures weekly and actively took part, as he said, "in the Seminar in American Church History, which is perhaps the most instructive class I am attending. In it we are introduced into the most thorough and the only method of true historical research, with some practical work to the point." [18] Never one to miss an opportunity to learn, he heard what he called "the best musical artists" and "some of the best speakers in the Senate and the House."

Marks for class achievement at the University were given percentage-wise, and Michel's were nearly all "99" and "100." His professors asked him to submit class papers to periodicals for publication, the first, as it happened, of many to follow. His professor of Spanish suggested that he drop the class and teach another, meanwhile convincing Bishop Thomas J. Shahan, the Rector, that Michel should be sent to Johns Hopkins University for a doctorate in Spanish in preparation for teaching it at the University later.[19]

Teaching philosophy at the Catholic University of America in these years were Fathers William Turner and Edward A. Pace. Pace did more than any one person to prepare the way for the future Scholastic revival in the United States. Michel described their seminar in philosophy as "*the thing*." Seminars that he later attended at Louvain only convinced him the more that this was the most effective teaching technique. In general, however, Father Michel was disappointed with philosophy courses at the University in Washington; he felt that Turner was "unscientific," and remarked that when they reached modern philosophy "the course ended."

While at the Catholic University of America Michel became very much interested in education. In view of this fact, it would be worth knowing how much Michel fell under the influence of Father Thomas

Edward Shields. Dr. Shields was the head of the Department of Education, inaugurator of the University's summer sessions, founder of Sisters' College, founder and editor of the *Catholic Educational Review*, and the outstanding American Catholic educational leader of his day. While Shields' thinking was far ahead of his time, he had made "the one explicit and avowed attempt" to formulate a Catholic philosophy of education with his text, *Philosophy of Education*. He had also a surprisingly early interest in, and an intuitive appreciation of, the liturgy. As his biographer correctly observed, "Long before the liturgical revival of our day, Professor Shields had been a pioneer in this direction."[20] True, one looks in vain for the doctrine of the Mystical Body in the writings of Father Shields. That had yet to be "rediscovered" and to be brought back into American Catholic consciousness, as will be shown. Nevertheless, when in chapter eighteen of his text Shields spoke of "the organic teaching of the Church," he was speaking of the liturgy. In the same chapter he showed himself aware of the values of active participation and of the educative values of the official worship of the Church. And in the four religion books of the Catholic Education Series for the primary grades, which he managed to publish before his untimely death in 1921, one finds evidence of an effort to imbue the instruction of children with the spirit of the Church as found in her prayers. In fact, Shields devoted the entire fourth book to the Mass. In the Christ-Life Series of grade school religion texts, Dom Virgil and collaborators were later to bring to maturity the ideas anticipated by Shields in his series.[21]

In these years an intellectual storm[22] over the educational theories of Dr. Shields was raging on the campus of the Catholic University. Turner and Pace — at least for a time — were collaborators with Shields and professors whose courses Father Virgil followed. In 1924 Father Virgil asked Mrs. Justine B. Ward, who had worked out the Gregorian Chant in Shields' books, to collaborate with him in the religion texts he had at that time already in mind.[23] Also, Dr. George Johnson, a student, protege, and successor of Shields, was a classmate of Michel's at the University, and the two became lifelong friends and collaborators. Parallels between the ideas of Michel and Shields, both in general Catholic education and in religious education in particular, could be readily established. It is hard to avoid the conclusion that Michel, intensely interested in education, intellectual controversies and movements, was at least somewhat influenced by Shields through the people who collaborated with the educator. And yet, there is not a single mention of Shields in his letters of this time. This much is certain : Dom Virgil was then primarily interested in education and philosophy, and not especially in the liturgy.

One is on surer ground when treating of Michel's choice of topic for his doctoral dissertation. It was significant that he should have chosen "The Critical Principles of Orestes A. Brownson" as his subject. In the preface to that volume he stated : :

Brownson's writings have been chosen as a subject for study because they are always thought-inspiring even when consent to the opinions expressed in them cannot be given, because they lend themselves admirably to thorough treatment, and because their almost total neglect at present, in striking contrast to the wide notice that was accorded them formerly, seems to indicate a rather undeserved fate.[24]

After running the gamut of modern philosophies and a number of religions, the stormy Brownson was converted to the Catholic faith and then became one of the most colorful defenders of the Church in the United States, a great champion of the truth but also largely a forgotten hero. The bulky twenty volumes of his writings are a veritable mine for American thought from 1830 to 1876. In that time there was hardly an intellectual, political, social, educational, philosophical, or religious movement in which Brownson did not take vigorous part by the spoken or printed word and which did not feel the strong impact of his influence ; his luminous and comprehensive mind was ever in pursuit of truth wherever it was to be found. Brownson had a rather clear concept of the Church and her role in the modern world,[25] and his writings on Church and State, in which he always vindicated the complete independence and freedom of the spiritual order, anticipated the pronouncements of Leo XIII almost fifty years later. The famous convert wrote much on the philosophical and religious bases for a healthy society. Never did he fail to point out the inadequacies of Catholic education. His writings on the relation between Catholicism and modern civilization have, perhaps, gone unsurpassed. Atheism and secularism traced in all aspects of American life — that was the heart of Brownson's contribution. In future years that became Michel's chosen task as well.

"My experience is that Brownson's profound philosophical thought seems to have cast its shadow upon all who study him," James M. Gillis, C.S.P., editor of the *Catholic World*, once told Michel.[26] Certainly Michel was no exception. He was profoundly influenced by his study of Brownson, for which he confessed to have read more than forty books and all that had been written about him in periodical literature.[27] References in his later writings to this controversialist, articles showing a familiarity with his thought, serious intentions while at Louvain [28] to write on Brownson the philosopher as his doctoral dissertation — all these indicated an abiding interest in the great controversialist. When the Friends of Brownson in the 1920's organized to arouse interest in Brownson's legacy as well as in public questions and their Catholic answers, Michel wrote in support of the cause, "The renewal of interest in the life and work of the great American convert . . . is long overdue. . . . It is difficult to explain the general apathy of Catholics towards this indomitable public champion of their views and beliefs." [29] And again somewhat later, to one of a number who asked him for help in their research, Dom Virgil said, "I am glad to note your interest in Brownson. Mine has little chance to function." [30] As late as 1937–38 Father Virgil seriously considered collaborating [31] in a definitive biography — still unwritten — of the convert who said in his autobiography that "all I have brought to the Church is my sins." In regard to his own mediocre dissertation, Michel later apologized for it. And yet, Joseph Donovan, C.M., a Brownson specialist, told the author that "the work itself is a piece of pioneering that you need not be ashamed of." [32]

In view of Michel's future work and manifold activities, it should be obvious how important and valuable was his research into the writings of a man with the stature and universal interests of the "uncompromising warrior," who has variously been called a "modern Augustine," the "Newman of America" and "America's foremost philosopher." From Brownson, Father Michel received his enormous interest in contemporary thought and modern philosophy. [33] Until he studied philosophy in Europe, Michel, like Brownson, was more interested in and certainly better acquainted with modern than Scholastic philosophy. In pointing out the absolute necessity of familiarizing oneself also with modern thought movements to meet the contemporary mind, Dom Virgil loved to refer to Brownson's famous passage in which he said, "The Scholastics are, as controversialists, far more influential in keeping men who have the truth from going astray than in recovering from error those who, unhappily, have yielded to its seductions." [34] The study of Brownson's philosophy of art and aesthetics gave Michel an intellectual appreciation which proved of value for his later writings on liturgical art. One wonders whether it was from this ardent convert that he likewise caught his deep-felt need for a Catholic intellectual apostolate in pioneer Catholic America as well as for a general Catholic revival, for which he came later to believe a knowledge and living of the liturgical life indispensable. Brownson could also have taught him the value of the written word, for in the conclusion to his doctoral dissertation Michel observed:

> His [Brownson's] outstanding viewpoint was that of a literature as a powerful agent in moulding the thought of readers. He recognized keenly the living force of the written word, its permanent and wide-spread influence for good or evil. For this Brownson cannot be commended too much. This side of literature is only too often not merely neglected but spurned and ridiculed. . . . Would that all . . . could catch the spirit of Brownson.[35]

In the same conclusion Michel almost seemed to have been describing himself and his future activities when he spoke of Brownson's

> absorbing enthusiasm with which he pursued any cause that he thought worth pursuing, and which seemed to control his entire being at such moments. . . . His concern for the betterment of society and for the uplift of the lower classes shows him to have been fully alive to the justice of the agitations going on in the United States. . . . He was not satisfied with reveling in abstract theories, however, and earnestly pleaded for practical application, an example of which we see in his sociological conception of literature.[36]

As early as the first years of his priesthood Dom Virgil showed himself a careful observer with a keen awareness of the conditions and needs of his times. His letters betray the growing foresight and vision that was to become an outstanding feature of his life. It was the time of a small and insignificant American Catholic press; Catholic letters and scholarship in the United States left much to be desired, and respectable Catholic journals of opinion and scholarship were all but non-existent. Thus, the *Sign* appeared only in 1921; the *Commonweal,* in 1924; *Thought,* in 1926; the *Catholic Biblical Quarterly,* in 1939; *Theological Studies,* in 1940; while the first Catholic book club was organized as late as 1928. He also thought deeply about the changing role of monasticism in the modern world, and what the Benedictine abbeys, true to their age-old ideals, might contribute. All this was evidenced when he told his superior:

> I always liked to write and shall keep up writing later, subject to your approval of course. Goodness knows how we need good Catholic writers in this country, and I am

of the Benedictine tradition. On the contrary, I think that the time has arrived when some of the abbeys can devote more energy to the work of giving missions and of being leaders in sound thought. So far there was too much necessity in other fields, fields that are closer to the heart of the servant of the Lord. But soon the time will come when we shall commence to emerge from that state which I always like to compare with the glorious work of converting Europe in the first centuries of our existence; and our attention must be directed also elsewhere soon if we do not wish to deteriorate. I think the best thing for us, especially with the nervous American spirit, is to see ahead of ourselves at all times at least double the work we can manage. [37]

But do not monks "leave the world?" Then how reconcile monasticism with an interest in current affairs, modern education, contemporary philosophy and thought? He went on with the answer to his own question, an answer which he himself lived:

If Father Master [the master of novices] heard me talk of keeping up with contemporary thought, he would think that I had become entirely worldly. . . . How such an opinion can be reconciled with the fact that we are educators, men who are pretending to fit out young men and priests for life's battles, I do not see. There is a big difference between knowing what goes on in the world and being worldly. I have always been interested in everything that goes on in the world, and I cannot say that I am not worldly. But I do know that this interest has never in the least lessened my yearning for monastic life, which was always strong in me, and the further I am from realizing it, the stronger it gets. [38]

Virgil Michel was first and last a monk. Nor does he seem ever to have had trouble thinking of his community first and always in terms of its future. [39]

While World War I was raging in Europe, Michel in the midst of his graduate studies at Washington volunteered for a chaplaincy in the army. "It is not that I care to go to war or anything like it . . ." he explained to Abbot Peter; "I know what a good chaplain can do." [40]

After gaining his doctorate he pleaded again:

I am hastening to put in my bid again. . . . I feel like two cents, as they say, sitting around and doing nothing to help along the greatest cause that was ever struggled for in the history of the world. . . . There is an immense field for work there, and work that is more important than anything else just now. . . . I feel ardently that the good of the cause ought to go above all other considerations. [41]

After making a third request, Dom Virgil learned that the abbot meant "no" the first time.

In the summers of 1917 and 1918 Michel attended sessions at Columbia University. This was his only experience in a secular educational institution, and it left him much impressed. Later, in the early 1920's, he unsuccessfully urged Abbot Alcuin to allow Father Mark Braun, O.S.B., to take a doctorate in education at Columbia. Father Michel had gone there, as he wrote, to "broaden out in the various lines I need most, . . . to observe the methods of others, their organization, etc.," and "to get in touch with other men." Besides auditing classes, he took courses in English, education, and advanced Spanish; he also did much reading and work in the New York Public Library. Father Virgil described his stay at Columbia as "most profitable and enjoyable." At the close of the summer school in August, 1918, he wrote to his superior:

I got a bird's-eye view of the educational question in this country, and think the field so large and important that one man ought to specialize in it. There is certainly going to be a reconstruction of ideas and ideals after this war in every line of thought and activity. And unless we Catholics are prepared to advertise (in a good sense) our views, we shall be missing a glorious opportunity. Nor will any Catholic's view count for much, unless he shows that he is acquainted with the best prevalent views and theories on any subject. This is only natural. [42]

Armed with a doctorate and a mind full of ideas on contemporary philosophy, education and other subjects, he returned home to labor and to apply them as professor, school administrator, and writer in the only way he knew how — indefatigably — for Dom Virgil had no half-interests.

Between 1918 and 1921 he taught English literature and a course in the history of philosophy. His students remember him as an excellent English teacher who believed in hard work and much writing. At times they sensed some sharpness in his remarks, a characteristic which left him with the passing years. In 1921 he took charge of philosophy in the seminary, but in this he was less successful. His interest in modern philosophy got in the way of his Thomism, in which he was himself inadequately prepared, having had only a few courses at the Catholic University of America besides his own reading and study of Aquinas. A student recalled how, after covering ancient and medieval philosophy rather quickly, Michel launched into contemporary philosophy, usually spoke above the level of student comprehension, and forever brought up his own numerous problems and difficulties. Later he admitted that both the content and manner of his teaching were a mistake.[43] At various times he taught Spanish, for two years the violin, and in 1918–19 directed the student orchestra. In 1921–22 Dom Virgil was Prefect of Studies, Dean of St. John's Prep School in 1922–23, and dean of the college until he left for Europe in February, 1924. As Dean of the Prep School he organized, with the help of a few confreres, a four-year high school religion course which received some national recognition.[44] Deeply interested in the improvement of religious education, he had in mind also to write a series of college religion texts.

On December 29, 1921, Prior Alcuin Deutsch was elected Abbot of St. John's, and with the election, Father Virgil's hopes of the college growing into a first-class school producing Catholic lay leaders soared. Subsequent correspondence between the abbot and Father Virgil showed the latter again and again urging his superior to build a four-year liberal arts program in an accredited college manned by a faculty of properly trained monks.

However, Abbot Alcuin was more a missionary than an educator. On a few occasions the abbot felt he had cause to remind Dom Virgil that the Benedictines were monks first and not educators primarily. Father Virgil had difficulty in seeing why they could not be both, as he looked out upon a distraught world and recalled what monasticism had once done for it. Had not Benedictine abbeys in past centuries been stable lighthouses for Christ in an unstable world, and had not this been their glory? With such views the abbot did not necessarily disagree, but he perhaps realized better than his subject that things could not be changed overnight. In the efforts that he made, he leaned heavily on Father Virgil.[45] But for this man of action, progress was too slow, and the apostolate of Catholic education was not moving along as it should — or could. By 1924 he had exhausted the inadequate local library,[46] and he was beginning to wonder if, perhaps, the missions which the community conducted in the Bahama Islands would not afford a better outlet for his impatient energies. There was wisdom in the observation the abbot recorded in his Diary under date of April 12, 1923:

Fr. Virgil left a note on my desk today, containing his application for the Bahama Missions. It is out of the question. I cannot spare him. I fear he is moved to ask because he is disgusted with conditions here. He is young, has high ideals and has not yet learned to be patient with the shortcomings of poor human nature. It is God's will that we become Christ-like by suffering patiently moral ills as well as physical. Unfortunately there are some who have little interest in their work and their monastic duties, and others probably appear indifferent to the more zealous. All in all, I am sure it is not worse here than in other places and probably better than in a great many.

Although carrying a heavy teaching burden and administrative duties in these years in addition to giving retreats, Michel still found time for some writing, chiefly on religious and secular education. In his writings at this time his call for a return to the greater use of the Bible in religious instruction was noteworthy, as well as his strong attack on the Smith-Towner Bill, which would have established a Department of Education with a secretary in the President's cabinet.[47] His essay, "Mission of Catholic Thought," was a lucid exposition of the need and role of Catholic thought and Scholastic philosophy in modern times.[48] While he was fundamentally interested in the liturgy, a deep and all embracing concern for the liturgical life had yet to be awakened. In the light of future events, it proved a momentous decision on the part of Abbot Alcuin to send Father Virgil to Europe in early 1924. On the first day of that new year Abbot Deutsch had confided to his Diary:

I have definitely decided, though after much hesitation, to send Father Virgil to Rome in February. It will be a great additional burden on me, as I must teach his classes in philosophy having nobody else to do it. But I think it most important for him and for the community that he should go. He is a good religious, thoroughly reliable, wasting no time, and of very good talent. He is widely read in modern philosophy, but I fear he has not a thorough grasp and appreciation of Scholastic philosophy and of the method of teaching it. I think it most important for the training of our candidates for the priesthood that he should have this. I will let him remain in Europe at least until next fall; if possible I will give him also the whole of the scholastic year 1924–25, or at least until I have to leave for Rome in the spring of 1925.

NOTES TO CHAPTER 1

[1] Archives of St. John's Abbey, Collegeville, Minnesota: Ward to Abbot Alcuin Deutsch, Notre Dame, Nov. 28, 1938. All unpublished sources hereafter referred to in this volume, unless otherwise stated, are in the Archives of St. John's Abbey.

[2] Mrs. Michel died in 1898, when her son was scarcely eight years old, and his father remarried in 1900; there were six children in the first family — George, the only boy — and nine children in the second; two of his sisters became religious, Sisters Eleanore and Virgil, members of the Sisters of St. Joseph of Carondelet in St. Paul; a half-brother is Father Bede of St. John's Abbey.

[3] Mr. Michel had the intention of making a million and at one time achieved a quarter of that. Part of his desire for profits was to help St. John's Abbey and to aid poor boys to the priesthood, which he had done all along. In 1924 he made a will and told his children, "You will all get a good, equal share." Meanwhile his business grew by leaps and bounds. Honest himself, he believed all others to be so, as he guaranteed every loan. Besides dangerous, perhaps naive, investments, there was also poor bookkeeping; the depression struck, and as with many other businesses of this kind, the crash came in 1931, and he lost all. To avoid legal difficulties, the father chose to leave his family permanently and departed for Mexico to live out his days, believing he had failed utterly and had disgraced his family. While in Mexico he still had ambitions of starting there all over again and so repay his debts. They were substantially paid later. He died broken-hearted at El Paso, Texas, in 1941. His father's financial debacle was a severe trial to Father Virgil, who was then in the Indian missions recuperating from overwork. He wrote to his father several times weekly at this time in an effort to encourage him.

[4] George started with piano lessons at seven or eight and took up the violin in high school; always an enthusiast for music, he practiced with characteristic thoroughness in high school, college, and seminary, although he played the violin more with mechanical proficiency than with an artist's touch. Even when at the Catholic University of America, 1916–18, he found time for frequent practice; when studying in Rome in 1924, he still occasionally practiced, as is evident from his Diary (Mar. 13, 1924).

18

[5] There was an air of education here and young Michel received considerable intellectual stimulation. Reading materials ranged from farm journals to Shakespeare, Schiller, and Goethe. Step-grandmother, Mrs. Schmitz, was a woman of culture and the daughter of a University of Bonn graduate. She used to read to George (ten-thirteen years old) and her own son interesting stories, travel experiences in strange lands, and accounts of stirring events from the early Christian era to modern times. Often they helped with the dishes to lengthen the reading period. "This condition at our home and more liberty and elbow room on the farm caused this brilliant young mind to prefer the life on the farm to the more crowded and more morally corrupt conditions of a big city. . . . I would say that as a boy of twelve or thirteen he could understand as much as average people understand when fully grown" (Jack Schmitz to the writer, Jordan, Jan. 26, 1953).

[6] Interview with Alfonse Schaffhausen, St. Paul, Minn., Sept. 12, 1952.

[7] In 1856 five monks came from St. Vincent's Abbey to plant a Benedictine community serving the Catholic immigrants of the upper Middle West. In 1903 the abbey conducted a seminary, a high school, and the equivalent of a small junior college, offering "commercial" and classical courses. The original community of five has now grown to more than 350 members. The hundred-year history of St. John's Abbey is ably told by Colman J. Barry, O.S.B., in *Worship and Work* (Collegeville: St. John's Abbey, 1956).

[8] Hyacinth Cismowski, O.S.B., to the writer, Graceville, Minn., Sept. 15, 1952. A collaborator with Father Virgil for some twenty-five years described his premonastic student years thus: "By nature richly gifted, with energy for three, George was insatiable in acquiring whatever worthwhile intellectual possessions came within his reach" (Basil Stegmann, O.S.B., "As We Knew Him," *Orate Fratres*, [1939], 97–98).

[9] Sylvester Harter, O.S.B., to the writer, Collegeville, Mar. 8, 1953.

[10] His student writings show a variety of interests and a vivid imagination. Only a few articles betray a "social" interest, although many deal with typical human events.

[11] Sister Eleanore recalls how he used to come home from school with a number of books and how — having read these and everyone else's — he then went down to the St. Paul Public Library for more. In a comparatively short time in his early youth he had read the thirty or more German volumes by the famous German writer of Indian stories, Karl May, and regretted there were not more. Although never in the United States, May wrote, á la Fenimore Cooper, graphically and realistically of the "noble savage." His reading of Karl May may help to explain in part why later, as a missionary among the Indians, Michel had such a sympathetic understanding of the Indians and their problems, and why the Indians cooperated with him as one familiar with their mentality.

[12] Abbot Alcuin gave a resumé of his conversations with George Michel in a eulogy preached to the student body on Sunday, Nov. 27, 1938, the day following Father Virgil's death. The writer heard this eulogy. "Sister Aloysia and I were ready to leave St. John's after the close of the session

[1929 liturgical summer school] and were having an interview with Abbot Alcuin prior to our departure. We mentioned what a magnificent person Father Virgil was and how his lectures had influenced our thinking. He then told us this in approximately these words: 'When Father Virgil was a sophomore in college I asked him whether he had ever thought of being a priest. He said, "Father Alcuin, if monasticism were what it once was, I would enter St. John's Abbey." I set about making our monastery the kind of place George was seeking, and what you see today is the result' " (Sister Estelle Cullings, O.S.B., to the writer, Canon City, Apr. 26, 1954). Grandmother Anna Griebler had lived in the Michel home from the beginning: "But I never knew what I owed to grandmother till later on. I had often wondered how God gave me the grace of a vocation, as I never did the least thing to deserve it, not even praying for it; after my novitiate grandmother told me that she had for years (in her eighties) prayed the rosary on her knees for my vocation. Hence I feel that, humanly speaking, I owe her everything that I am" (Michel to Abbot Peter Engel, Washington, May 17, 1917).

[13] In 1909, before entering the novitiate, he had received a "B.A. in Latin," having written a thesis on Prudentius. For his Ph.B. in 1912 he wrote another thesis, "On the Origin of the State"; for the M.A., such as it was at St. John's in 1913, he translated from the German Rauschen's *Grundriss der Patrologie*.

[14] Michel to Sister Eleanore, Collegeville, Jan. 27, 1915.

[15] Archives of the Catholic University of America: Michel to C. F. Borden, Collegeville, Aug. 23, 1916.

[16] At once he filed a request for dropping one year of graduate work because of the teaching done in past years, so that he could return to the abbey in two years with the doctorate. "The question is not whether I *can* finish in two years, but whether the faculty will let me, whether it will waive the rule of three years' graduate work in my case" (Michel to Engel, Washington, Oct. 24, 1916). There was considerable hesitation, but after the candidate for the doctorate submitted his translation of Rauschen's *Grundriss der Patrologie*, "the faculty examined the translation . . . pronounced it very good and voted that it should count as a year's graduate work in my Major subject" (*ibid.*). But in the spring of 1918, although the faculty had voted to allow him to take his degree in two years, some were still opposed and the issue was somewhat in doubt. "I have sent two articles . . . to magazines. . . . At all events my hope was that the articles would help me considerably in my prestige with the University and thus aid my cause regarding the degree" (Michel to Engel, Washington, Mar. 3, 1918). He received his S.T.B. on June 13, 1917 and the Ph.D. on June 12, 1918.

[17] Michel to Sister Eleanore, Washington, Nov. 19, 1916.

[18] *Ibid.*

[19] Michel begged the abbot not to permit such an eventuality, writing: "Ever since I joined the community, I have felt without a doubt that it would almost break my heart to be removed permanently from St. John's; and I do not think I'll ever change. My stay here has brought out this sentiment almost too much, so that I feel quite, . . . er . . . something

like homesick, very often"(Michel to Engel, Washington, Jan. 8, 1917; cf. Feb. 4, 1917; Apr. 8, 1917).

[20] Justine B. Ward, *Thomas Edward Shields* (New York: Scribners, 1947), p. 263.

[21] For a discussion and analysis, together with a comparison of the Catholic Education Series and the Christ-Life Series, cf. William Busch, "The Christ-Life Series," *Orate Fratres*, VIII (1934), 216–221; 253–260; 303–309.

[22] Ward, *op. cit.*, gives a complete account of this as well as of Pace's role in it.

[23] Diary, Dec. 27, 1924.

[24] *Critical Principles of Orestes A. Brownson* (Washington: privately printed, 1918), p. 1.

[25] Cf. an excellent treatise, Francis E. McMahon, "Orestes Brownson on Church and State," *Theological Studies*, XV (1954), 175–228. Speaking of Michel's articles on Brownson in the *Catholic World*, McMahon stated: "I want to express my sincere thanks and appreciation for the noble and opportune work that you are accomplishing" (Chicago, Sept. 2, 1927).

[26] Gillis to Michel, New York, Feb. 23, 1927.

[27] Michel to Sister Eleanore, Washington, Nov. 19, 1916, and Feb. 4, 1917.

[28] Diary, Oct. 28, 1924. "I spoke to Furfey about the Soc. and Econ. Views of Brownson as a subject for a thesis, and he said that if Fr. Michel recommended it, it must be worthwhile" (Martin Schirber, O.S.B., to Michel, Washington, Oct. 18, 1935).

[29] "Orestes A. Brownson," *Catholic World*, CXXV (1927), 499.

[30] Michel to John O. Riedl, Collegeville, Jan. 29, 1930, copy.

[31] With Verlyn William Ault, cf. Ault to Michel, Chicago, May 17, 22, 23 and June 4, 1937; Feb. 12, 1938: "Your letter . . . contained an excellent plan for a Brownson study."

[32] Webster Groves, Mo., Feb. 8, 1927 "Your discernment of a worthy thesis subject is going to be justified, I think" (*idem*). "Thanks to the efforts of such persons as the late Dom Virgil Michel . . . the stature of Brownson is being recovered" (Richard Deverall in reviewing Arthur M. Schlesinger, Jr., *Orestes A. Brownson's: A Pilgrim's Progress* [Boston: Little, Brown & Company, 1939], in *Christian Social Action*, IV [1939], 126.)

[33] Indicative of Michel's early consuming interest in modern philosophy, contemporary thought, current affairs and his already varied and wide interests is the permission he sought to subscribe to the following magazines: "*Philosophical Review* (bi-monthly); N. Y. *Times Book Review* (weekly); *Journal of Philosophy, Psychology, Scientific Methods* (fortnightly); *Bookman* (monthly); *New Republic* (weekly — the best general magazine on political, social, economic theories) . . . each covers a field and a need not supplied by any of the others." But the abbot was not to worry about their cost; Michel would write "an article or two for some publication. Since you encourage me so kindly, I intend to write occasionally anyhow" (Michel to Engel, New York, Aug. 12, 1918).

22   VIRGIL MICHEL AND THE LITURGICAL MOVEMENT

[34] Cf. "Brownson: A Man of Men," *Catholic World*, CXXV (1927), 761.

[35] *Critical Principles*, p. 102.

[36] *Ibid.*, pp. 101–102.

[37] Michel to Engel, Washington, Mar. 3, 1918.

[38] Michel to Engel, Washington, Mar. 3, 1918. Previously he had written, "I am glad to hear the question of colleges is still alive. In a few years we shall be going more and more into that kind of work and that of giving missions; and the time for preparing for these fields is the present. I often admire the foresight of Abbot Alexius in starting the large building at St. John's . . ." (to Engel, Washington, Nov. 15, 1917).

[39] These quotations from his letters to his superior give a glimpse of his monastic spirit, his devotion to his community, his interest in education, and his preparation for his future role in education: "Another year here, however profitable to myself personally, would hardly be worthwhile as far as St. John's is concerned" (Washington, Oct. 10, 1917). "Perhaps you remember that you gave me permission last summer to visit Belmont and Toronto, if I had an opportunity of doing so. I had figured on going to Belmont at the end of January during examination week, as I have nothing to do then. But it seems to me that travelling is not very monastic under present conditions. Much as I would like to see Belmont Abbey, and especially the workings of their military college at Savannah, the trip appears too much of a pleasure voyage for conditions; and the expense too, would be greater than under normal conditions. . . . The trip to Toronto I would be more loath to give up. I could stay with some Basilian friends at St. Michael's College. I am very anxious to see how the college stands in relation to Toronto University. This latter, you know, is in part made up of St. Michael's College and of some other denominational colleges" (New York, Dec. 24, 1917).

[40] Michel to Engel, Washington, Nov. 15, 1917.

[41] Michel to Engel, New York, July 28, 1918.

[42] Michel to Engel, New York, Aug. 12, 1918; cf. also, Washington, Mar. 25, May 17, Oct. 10, and 17, 1917.

[43] Referring to these days, he later wrote Deutsch from Louvain: "In a conversation a few days ago a professor told me how bad it is to put one's own difficulties before the class, etc. I never realized the difference between the professor's level and the students' until this year (by comparing with other students here). The little talk with the professor would some years ago have saved myself and others a good deal of needless trouble" (Jan. 18, 1925).

[44] Cf. *Experimental Courses in Religion*, Bulletin of the University of Notre Dame: Series XX, pp. 31–36. The course is described by Michel (anonymously) in the *Catholic Educational Review*, XXII (1924), 408–419; 472–486.

[45] Cf. Michel to Deutsch, Chicago, June 25, 1922; New York, July 19, 1922; Conception, Missouri, Aug. 1, 1923, etc.

[46] He spent over a month in the East studying educational problems in the summer of 1922; as was his wont, he used the occasion for working

also in libraries. "I put in two good days at the library [New York Public Library] so far. The library here has just about all journals, reports of societies, etc., on philosophy that come out in English, French or German. It makes me sick just to think of the opportunities that are out of reach" (Michel to Deutsch, New York, July 2, 1922).

[47] "The Smith-Towner Bill Again," *Educational Review*, LXI (1921), 70–79.

[48] *American Catholic Quarterly Review*, XLVI (1921), 657–664.

CHAPTER 2

IN EUROPE

EUROPE after World War I was in spiritual turmoil. At the heart of this unrest lay heated controversies over the liturgical and youth movements. Before he went to Europe, Virgil Michel's life had been a search for the solutions to life's problems. Now at last he was to discover some solutions to questions that had been troubling him for a long while. Broad horizons would open before him as he found in the doctrine of the Mystical Body, in the liturgy, and in Scholastic philosophy answers to many of his queries.

From his abbot's Diary it is clear that Father Virgil was sent to Rome in 1924 primarily to study philosophy under the well-known metaphysician Joseph Gredt at the International Benedictine College of St. Anselm.[1] Did the abbot also mean to expose him to the liturgical movement then beginning to flourish in Europe, following the pleadings of Pius X? There seems little doubt that Deutsch had that in mind.

Abbot Alcuin himself had been a student in Rome from 1897 to 1903, had traveled extensively in Europe, and had stayed at Maredsous, where he had come to know Dom Columba Marmion. He had also visited other Benedictine abbeys of the Guéranger tradition and in this way met the monastic liturgical revival.[2] Ever since his election as abbot in late 1921, he had made some efforts to interest his novices in the liturgy. He must have been at least vaguely aware of the later popular liturgical revival in Europe following the momentous *motu proprio* of Pius X in 1903. And he had been much impressed in 1920 by Romano Guardini's *Vom Geist der Liturgie*, which he handed to Michel. This seems to have been the beginning of Father Virgil's interest in the liturgy. At least, in later years Abbot Alcuin made a point of insisting that it was he who, by this gesture, interested Virgil Michel in what is today known as the liturgical movement. In their conversations before Father Virgil's departure for Europe, the superior and his subject most likely considered the possibilities of doing something to promote the liturgy outside the confines of the monastery. But just what seemed rather vague. This much is certain: Father Virgil in the next year and a half interested the abbot in the popular liturgical revival in Europe, convinced him of the great need of such a movement in the United States, and urged that St. John's undertake its leadership.

There is some evidence of this in Michel's first letter from Europe. He had gone at once to Louvain and then to the center of the Belgian liturgical movement, the Abbey of Mont César. In explanation of fifteen liturgical books sent to the abbot, he wrote:

The only "spending" I did was on books at the two liturgical centers (here and Mont César). . . . I really think we can do nothing better than commence by translating some of these books and spreading them in our world. St. John's would be a logical center for that. I was amazed at the manner in which people enter into the spirit of the liturgy — and they tell me all that was accomplished since the revival of the liturgical spirit in recent years. It is surely time for us to begin. . . . A new thought: How about offering the translated matter to the C.T.S. — at least the smaller pamphlets? [3]

Besides studying philosophy and observing things liturgical, Michel was determined to study European life from every point of view. Hence his interminable discussions with all kinds of people; interested in everything, he missed little. He was to spend a semester at St. Anselm's, travel and observe in various countries during the summer, go to Louvain for a year, and then occupy another summer in study trips in Europe, the Holy Land, and Egypt. This was an extremely important period of formation in his life.

Having seen the Louvre, churches, and other sights in Paris, and after a short stop at Versailles,[4] he arrived in Rome on March 1, 1924, ready to take up philosophical problems. "The asking of questions is an art whose full possibilities are never exhausted,"[5] he had written. It was characteristic of him, therefore, to have taken to Rome a notebook, on each page of which he had a question or an outline of a philosophical problem for which he wanted answers. While he had gone to Rome as a special student to audit Gredt's classes and those of others, he was there mainly to consult Gredt concerning philosophy in general and his book in particular, as well as to acquire a Scholastic pedagogical method. He was soon to be disillusioned by Gredt, his book, and his methods. Father Michel, who looked upon philosophy as a kind of apostolate, was seeking a living Thomism, slanted to modern problems. Soon he came to this conclusion:

Gredt is really no teacher at all—and *sub rosa*, it is here generally admitted. Gredt is simply his book, no more, no less. Having examined his book quite carefully, I found no reason whatever to change my mind either about his narrow limitations, his super-speculative (metaphysical in the modern sense) mental slant, or his real power of analysis in a *status quaestionis* . . . it is all *one* book; once you have mastered the profundities of that you know all of philosophy. . . . I answered Gredt that I had no difficulty understanding his meanings, but that there were a number of things that I could not agree with. . . . To make Gredt's course you must literally study him by heart . . . must be an intellectual slave. . . .[6]

Subsequent private sessions only confirmed this opinion. For a time he considered rewriting and revising Gredt's *Elementa Philosophiae* for American seminaries. "It would be doing a work," he wrote his superior, "that the Catholic Church is in great need of in our country."[7] He was thinking also of writing his own English manuals of Thomistic philosophy. In the following passage he gives his final judgment of Gredt, and in it one can see what he considered to be the role of Scholastic philosophy in the modern world:

Regarding philosophy I have little to add to my former letter except that Gredt is really a lovable personality, no teacher, really deep in metaphysical questions, and quite unique. But the general philosophy is Scholastic with a vengeance—so much so that there is hardly a hostile view worth distorting and then transfixing with a sharply pointed distinction. Scholastic philosophy here does not sally forth to make conquests. It shuts itself within its stronghold (whatever that is), it shuts all the loopholes with airtight theses and corollaries —and the result is that outside philosophies can shed no light on us and our problems. In fact, sitting within the hermetically sealed walls of our round tower we can see no enemies and so they do not exist. All we have to do is to raise an occasional glance at the different theses closing up the crevices of our fort, to see that they are still there. . . . Of course, we must know our own philosophical principles before we can combat the errors of others, but there is a way of imbibing those principles which develops no fighting spirit of zeal and only self-complacency.[8]

A colleague in philosophy at St. John's Abbey has expressed the opinion that Michel's grasp of the depths of metaphysics left something to be desired. Might not this be another reason why he did not appreciate Gredt? Father Virgil's philosophical competence lay mainly in ethics, psychology, and epistemology.

He had many private conferences with Gredt and attended classes at St. Anselm's and in the institutes of Rome. In addition he devoted himself to private study and reading in the whole realm of philosophy, especially the various schools of social, industrial, and economic ethics. Disappointed with the ethics textbooks in use in the United States, he now began his own notes on speculative ethics, to be published later. He also pored over the writings of Reginald Garrigou-Lagrange and often heard his lectures at the Angelicum.[9]

Teaching apologetics, ecclesiology, and liturgy at St. Anselm's was the renowned monk of Mont César, Dom Lambert Beauduin, whom a foremost scholar of the liturgy has recently called "one of the greatest figures of the Church in the twentieth century."[10] As a secular priest engaged for eight years in social work, Beauduin became profoundly convinced that the work of saving souls, to be truly effective, must be rooted in the liturgy. To make himself the instrument of its popularization, he became a monk, and soon he was one of the intellectual leaders of the liturgical movement in Europe. In 1909 Beauduin founded La Vie Liturgique, the popular little Missal that started the Belgian liturgical movement. In the early 1920's he took part in the Conferences of Malines, Désiré Cardinal Mercier's effort to bring back the Anglicans to union with Rome. In 1924 Beauduin was personally delegated by Pius XI to found a center at Amays (later moved to Chevetogne) in Belgium to train monks in the Eastern liturgical rites to work for re-union in Russia when the opportunity should present itself. It was Dom Lambert who, now in Rome and later at Mont César, fired Father Virgil's interest in the liturgy and in the doctrine of the Mystical Body. From his Diary and his letters it is clear that Michel found Beauduin's classes in the liturgy stimulating. Father Virgil had many private conferences with him, and soon would translate his celebrated *La Piété de l'Église*. No one in Europe influenced him more than this scholarly and zealous Belgian monk, possessed of "incomparable powers of persuasion." Here is Beauduin's statement of their meetings and his impressions of Dom Virgil:

I knew him well at Rome, and when he discovered that I was concerned with the liturgical movement at Louvain, we became quite friendly, and he often came to talk to me in private; but liturgy was not for him just a matter of study; it was above all a powerful means of doing apostolic work, by increasing the faith and devotion of the faithful.

His vocation for such work seemed part of himself. He asked me to arrange for him to spend his holidays in our monastery at Louvain, in order to become familiar with all the details of the organization of liturgical work. . . .

Later when he was organizing his liturgical work at Collegeville, he often wrote to me to tell me about the results of his efforts. In his letters he always showed the same enthusiasm for the liturgy.[11]

Noteworthy is the fact that all of Dom Lambert's interests became Father Virgil's interests, not the least of which was his work with Anglicans and Eastern Orthodox in the furtherance of Christian unity.

An endless stream of liturgical books, ideas, and pleadings that St. John's take some action to initiate the liturgical apostolate had already begun to flow to Abbot Alcuin, whom he urged to begin translating and writing — "How fine, if we could continue to work on these lines later!"[12] Michel had likewise interviewed Abbot Emmanuele Caronti, the Italian liturgical leader, and secured permission to translate his *La Pietà Liturgica*. Despite his conviction that the English-speaking world needed a liturgical movement, it was far from his mind that he should spend most of his later life in the liturgical apostolate. "As for myself: think how glorious it will be," he wrote to his superior, "to be working in philosophy with liturgical translations as a hobby, and no Dean's Office, prefecting, etc., to divide a man against himself! It is enough to make an Abbot jealous, eh?"[13] As it happened, philosophy became his "hobby," liturgical activity his lifework, and the Dean's Office an additional cross.

In sightseeing, of which he also did much both in and out of Rome, nothing seems to have escaped his careful eye. In his Diary he painstakingly recorded his pointed observations of people, customs, monks, buildings, clergy, and the hundred and one things

that never seemed to exhaust his curiosity.[14] This was his way of re-
membering them and learning from them. Meanwhile he kept up
with contemporary European and American periodical literature,
found time to review his Spanish for a study trip to Spain, and
wrote a lengthy philosophical treatise.[15]

But he was growing restive in Rome and the following plea to
go to Louvain won the Abbot's consent:

I think it would prove most
advantageous to the abbey and to myself if I should go to Louvain. I
could not think of staying in Rome next year and for instance attend
the Gregorianum instead of here. . . . Here . . . merely the *Elementa*. Imagine, nothing on St. Thomas. At Louvain I am attracted
particularly by the courses in Moral Philosophy, Social Ethics, General
Metaphysics (under Balthasar) and study of texts of St. Thomas (this
year parts of the Quaestiones Disputatae — any part of St. Thomas
will produce the same results) — besides the personal contact with the
university life as such and the different men who are very prominent.
By writing a thesis and passing an examination in all philosophy,
satisfactorily, I may be able to get a Doctorate in Louvain in one year
according to verbal advice and the conditions in the prospectus.[16]

Then came more than three months of planned trips with a confrere through Italy, Spain, and Germany — "the journey of study,"
he called it. "I'm after Benedictine life, churches and shrines, and
the ordinary people and their life," he wrote his abbot.[17] For almost
five weeks he journeyed and "studied" in Italy; two weeks were
spent in France, four in Spain, and four in Germany. He visited
churches, museums, libraries, public buildings, and religious houses.
He discussed philosophy with philosophers, farming with farmers,
and liturgy with liturgists. "But above all we took every opportunity
to live among the people," to observe them at close range while doing,
wherever possible, as people did, so as to get firsthand experience.
To be close to people and to save money, they traveled third class, in
Italy staying overnight in religious houses and monasteries; in France
and Spain, at small hotels; in Germany, for the most part in Benedictine abbeys.

In general, the apathy of the European clergy surprised Dom
Virgil. In France [18] he found many of the clergy far removed from
the lives of the people, and, on the whole, the faith lukewarm, with
only pockets of fervent Catholicism. In Spain, he deplored the cleav-
age between clergy and people; he had the strong impression confirmed by some enlightened priests that many boys became priests

because it would guarantee a comfortable living supported by state funds. In the common mind, the clergy belonged to the privileged class; they were identified with the monarchy, protecting the wealthy and doing nothing for the poor victims of social injustice. No wonder, he thought, there was an anticlerical spirit almost everywhere. He watched the endless Spanish religious processions, with all their external pomp and circumstance, and wondered to what extent they expressed a sound and healthy spirituality. It was contrary to his liturgical sense to see people receiving Communion before or after Mass without reason. During several days' stay at the famous Abbey of Montserrat, he was much impressed by the way the liturgy was celebrated there, and he described it in detail.[19]

It was quite a shock to enter churches elsewhere and to find Mass servers nonchalantly smoking cigarettes in the sacristy or to have a sacristan, cigarette in mouth, help him with the vestments. He could hardly believe that the Spanish clergy could be so self-satisfied, so uninformed in regard to actual spiritual and social conditions, taking little interest in the affairs and problems of the people — thus completely failing to see the handwriting on the wall. A religious priest whom he met on the train and who saw the glaring need of social and spiritual reform told him that there were certain areas in certain dioceses where the bishops had made no visitations for ten or fifteen years, that, traveling with a large retinue, they confirmed where it pleased them.

"Such conditions would be unbearable to me," Michel remarked and suggested what he would often do in the United States in the years to come. "Can you not write up these conditions and so stir up some fruitful discussions, thus bringing an awareness of actual conditions?"

"No," came the reply, "if I were to try such, my superior would have to silence me, else I would soon be thrown out of the country."[20]

Another Spanish clergyman, not so well informed, was amused when Father Michel gently predicted on the basis of observed conditions that the monarchy might fall within a year.[21] It fell seven years later, on April 14, 1931.

But Michel also found praiseworthy situations in Spain, among them an edifying family life in many areas and a strong Christian womanhood. It was heartening to note the genuine Catholicism of the Basques, unspoiled by this world, deep in faith, whose priests had the people's spiritual and social welfare at heart and whose religious houses overflowed with vocations.

Traveling from city to city in all parts of Spain and spending time in the countryside, he examined, it seems, everything from the Gypsy caves of Granada and bull fights to cathedrals and museums. According to his Diary, he talked with soldiers, policemen, maids, farmers, beggars, taxi drivers, laborers, young people, merchants, priests, sacristans, hotel men. He read the local papers and magazines and was careful to observe Spanish culture. He noted the extremes of wealth and poverty, the absence of a middle class. A religious made arrangements for a tour through the Spanish royal palace in Madrid.[22] In other places he saw employees mistreated, poorly paid, with no means of demanding justice. In the rich Andalusian farm lands, he was shocked to learn how landowners forced the peasants and their children to work on Sunday. The children did not learn to read and write, because they had to work so as to contribute to the family subsistence. Maids tearfully told him how they had to work twelve hours a day at poor pay and with no freedom or rest. Father Virgil admitted that such glimpses into the injustices of Spanish life aroused in him feelings akin to radical socialism.[23] "The employer had all the trumps in his hand. In Spain there was a labor problem only for the laboring people!"[24]

While Father Virgil rightly deplored the lack of social responsibility of the Spanish clergy and nobility, he was perhaps too little a social scientist to see or be aware of another dimension of the social problem in Spain, namely, the technological backwardness of a poor country.

Nevertheless, the fall of the monarchy, the Civil War, and the persecution of the Church came as no surprise to Michel. The situation in Spain was a frequent lecture topic from 1926 on, and he wrote from firsthand knowledge on the subject before and during the time of Spain's purgation. Thus he summarized his views of that country in 1924: "Spain was most interesting, and it was bristling exteriorly with policemen and interiorly with revolutionary ideas. It was ever a question with me when the twain would meet. . . . There is more trouble brewing for future Spain."[25]

When the debt-ridden *Commonweal* on June 24, 1938, editorially took a position of "positive impartiality" on the Spanish Question, and subsequently lost some 250 subscribers, Ed Skillin requested

Michel to write a letter for publication to the editor in defense of the journal's stand. Dom Virgil said in part: "As Catholics we agree on essentials of faith and morals. But there is no earthly (or heavenly) reason why we must all agree on every other question, including public questions. Quite the contrary. If, as some seem to hold, we should in spite of legitimate differences put on a 'united front,' pretending to agree on every other detailed question as much as we do on the above-mentioned essentials, would we not be as the scribes and pharisees whom Christ excoriated in no uncertain terms?"[26] In reacting against a totalitarianism of the left there is danger of stepping back into a totalitarianism of the right. The thinking Christian, intent upon social justice and charity and the truth that makes him free, need not choose between communism and fascism; a Christian social order does not entail setting up a theocracy. The eternal Church must not be identified with the fortunes of a particular political setup. How disconcerting, he used to say in the 1930's, that so many American Catholics raise not a finger to further a practical program of social action to ameliorate those conditions in the United States which, in Spain, made a Franco necessary or possible. Of course, Michel saw the communist threat and the sham of the so-called Loyalists for what they were, and he deprecated the almost total misrepresentation of the whole Spanish Question in the secular press. More on this later.

In describing the secular and sacred art and architecture of the various parts of Spain, Michel reveals a good understanding. In depicting historical places and remains, he includes details that indicate a wide knowledge of Spanish and European history. In Spain as well as in other foreign countries, he learned the danger of priests living too far removed from the people and taking no interest in their problems, and the horrible evils resulting from anticlericalism and social injustice. He must have resolved to remain close to the laity and to cooperate with them in every way, for this became an outstanding feature of his later life.

Back through southern France and into northern Italy "the journey of study" passed through Switzerland and Germany and on to Louvain, via the Abbeys of Einsiedeln, Engelberg, Ettal, St. Boniface in Munich, St. Ottilien, Beuron, and Maria Laach. "Our trip was a most delightful adventure," he wrote to Abbot Alcuin before starting the journey from northern Italy to Louvain without his confrere. "And spiritually, I think we also learned much. . . . Since June I have been in fourteen Benedictine monasteries and shall see about ten more in the next months. . . . I'm just dead eager to get down to work again. . . . I learned much." [27] And the pattern of the journey is the same: observing, studying, reading, discussing, recording impressions, visiting libraries, churches, museums, etc. At St. Ottilien he "studied" farming and gardening and at Beuron, art.[28] At Maria Laach, the center of the German liturgical movement, he conversed with eminent liturgists, pored over "a vast assortment of liturgical books," and made an outline of possible American publications. He urged Abbot Alcuin to send monks there "to imbibe the liturgical spirit." He wrote:

I had eyes and ears open here and at Beuron and was very much impressed by everything. I wonder if we will ever have public Office, etc., unto universal edification and the unified serious purpose of our life evident in the actions of individual and community alike. . . . I have been talking liturgical projects and pamphlets here with good results. . . . The project itself is developing in the realm of ideas, at least; it would be aided greatly later, if our life were an open living example of the liturgical life. But there our church is a great handicap. (By the way, don't approve any new church plan before reading Van Acken, *Christozentrische Kirchenkunst*.)[29]

"How nice it will be," he had written a week earlier, "to see the square at home beautified! How often I thought of that this summer and of the beautiful cloister we could have had there. We surely ought to get a unified plan of building and get it at once, even if we do not build now, and cannot complete it for a hundred years. And the corridors ought to be more ample and smiling, enough real cloisters, and a slight architectural 'kick' . . . visible everywhere. Why are we afraid to let a building stand incomplete for a few years?"[30] In 1953 the monks of Collegeville caught up with Michel's idea as they embarked on a comprehensive hundred-year building plan such as Father Virgil had suggested more than twenty-five years before.

Despite his past work in philosophy, it was an ambitious program that Michel outlined for himself for the one year the abbot allowed him at Louvain. The outline called for reviewing three years of course work, taking licentiate and doctoral examinations, and writing a doctoral dissertation. One gains an insight into real interests from his choice of a dissertation topic when he told Abbot Deutsch:

I made a hurried sketch yesterday of a possible dissertation: Industrial Labor, A Chapter in Ethics. It proposes to examine the industrial factors in the light of the theory of cause — with labor as the efficient cause, of course; to examine labor as a principal title of ownership; to examine the question from the standpoint of rational psychology, man's nature, intellect and will — rights, duties, responsibilities always in relation to labor; and the duty of society to regulate opportunities for work, to exact work, to demand social service from excessive riches, etc.; I showed it to the proper professor yesterday and he called it *très vaste*. I shall take the subject as suggested, which is also extensive enough for a Doctor's dissertation, while I am glad to leave the larger work to develop under the action of mature thinking during the future process of writing our Latin manual and the English books on Scholastic philosophy. Yesterday another thought came: after the above texts are written, the logical opus is an English dictionary of Latin Scholastic terms. . . .

The smaller subject I could probably finish almost wholly this year, though the task of studying up for all the courses given here in three years is a big one. . . . I shall be saturated with my hero, St. Thomas, when the year is over.[31]

Since what Michel set out to accomplish in one year was unheard of at Louvain, the faculty had to decide whether he would be permitted to proceed with his plan. Meanwhile he dug into his thesis while "some professors, the best here, had spoken of pushing through for me." In January the final decision came that he would have to spend half a year more at Louvain to get the doctorate. He informed his superior:

The good, solid, broad professors lost out; and the narrow, letter-of-the-law men won out. . . . There have been several indignant heads and hearts about the matter, but I can truly say that I am not among them. . . . I of course decided to chuck all examinations — in accordance with a previous permission of yours. But my philosophy program has for that improved.

I shall continue my research in St. Thomas (it is too profitable to give up) and can probably later publish his economic principles in English, or write a series of magazine articles. . . . I have gained about 75% of time for my own philosophical development and I intend to digest, with discussions at times with Profs., all that I have received in the past . . . all of which will constantly bring me to St. Thomas . . . and will give me a definite, coordinated series of my own notes on all these subjects. Of course, I also keep in mind at least unconsciously the apologetic and missionary possibilities of philosophy — I can never keep that apart from the *philosophia perennis*.

Since Christmas I had really been hoping that this might come about with no fault of mine, or failure to do what I could.[32]

To the prayers of Grandmother Anna Maria Griebler, Dom Virgil attributed his vocation. Only after ordination did he learn that for years she had said the rosary each night on her knees that God might call him into His vineyard.

Father Virgil's parents, Mr. and Mrs. Fred Michel.

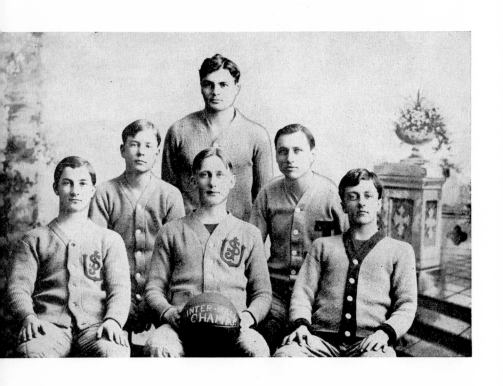

First Row, l *to* r: *Charles Kapsner (Father Celestine, O.S.B.),
Gustave Dierkes, George Michel (Father Virgil, O.S.B.).*
Second Row: *John Weckwirth (Father Urban, O.S.B.), Eu-
gene Lemire.*
Standing: *Nicholas Kopveiler.*

David at the Harp (George Michel), Jonathan (Theodore Harter — Father Sylvester, O.S.B.), Mephibosheth (Roman Steichen) and Juda (Carl George) (l & r), in the play, "King Saul."

Coach Ed Flynn and athletic director Virgil M.

Sister Eleanore and Father Virgil's father and
mother with him on the occasion of his first Sol
High Mass.

Student "Ducky" Meyers and Prefect Father
gil.

With no preparation for examinations to hamper productive thinking and no worries over a degree, ideas came fast, and plans for work in philosophy matured quickly; sketches for apologetico-philosophical articles multiplied; philosophical ideas and outlines were methodically catalogued; private conferences with professors increased, and there were the many discussions on philosophical questions with fellow students;[33] the stream of liturgical books, source materials, pamphlets, and brochures flowing to Collegeville widened to include a host of philosophical books and sources, including the volumes of *Lehrbuch der Nationalökonomie*, by Heinrich Pesch, whose Christian solidarism appealed to Michel.

All along he had believed there was a great need of an "apostolate of philosophy" in the United States:

I am daily becoming more convinced that philosophy is like liturgy a great means of apostolic work in the U.S., and for that reason I must expect to be doing continually less at the liturgical project after the first years. Others can jump into that work, while it takes all the preparation I have had in the last nine years, and more, even to commence the other work. Ideas have continued, and I have little sketches of about ten articles by now, made in order to get them out of the way. For two weeks no further inspirations came since the last too big to mature so fast, nothing less than a Prolegomena to a Scholastic Synthesis. It tackles what is really the biggest problem: the relation between philosophy and science, and metaphysics and the other parts, and epistemology. You may have noticed that these are approximately also the subjects of the Thomistic Week called by the Pope for this spring in Rome.[34]

For his English manuals in philosophy he had begun outlines.[35] In these plans his professors encouraged him and offered generous advice. "I had a great talk with Professor Noel two days ago on different philosophical subjects. I also mentioned the opportunity for philosophy in the U.S. He is about the best man here and *au courant* on everything philosophical. When I told him that sometimes the notions I get about the future in philosophy in the U.S. seem altogether too ambitious to me, he was as close to being excited as ever I saw him. He exclaimed, 'No, by all means not,' very emphatically, and almost waxed eloquent for once . . ."[36] To understand Michel's enthusiasm for philosophy in the United States, one must keep in mind that comparatively little had been done in this country in answer to Leo XIII's plans of 1879 to revive Scholastic philosophy. As early as 1921, Michel had called for a Scholastic movement.[37] The

American Catholic Philosophical Association was founded on January 5, 1926, and its official organ, *New Scholasticism,* appeared in January, 1927, while the Medieval Institute at Toronto was founded as late as 1929.

At Louvain, at last, Michel found the inspiration for a vital philosophy, what Jacques Maritain ten years later would call "a practical philosophy," that is, a philosophy that came to grips with critical problems of the day. For Father Virgil philosophical problems of former years were being resolved, and there "will not be so much groping in the dark as formerly." Thus he described his philosophical odyssey: "I suppose my philosophical *status quo* was definitely settled this year. It is that of a firm Thomist by conviction, no longer merely by faith. It now seems to me that my philosophy after the novitiate amounted to nothing (partly for avoidable reasons). Therefore the later period set in a feverish search in non-Catholic philosophy & superficial Scholastic sources; after that came a stage of negative Suarezianism, so to say, from which Gredt could not dislodge me (he perhaps lacked *time,* and something else) ; now the happy stage of positive Thomism has arrived." [38]

Meanwhile another apostolate was agitating his mind, that of getting people to perform properly their first duty and greatest privilege, the worship of God as intended by the Church and as called for by the popes, namely, the liturgical apostolate. Undoubtedly one of Michel's greatest discoveries in Europe had been the reality of the Church as the Mystical Body of Christ — a doctrine little stressed in the United States at this time — and the official life and prayer of that Body, the liturgy, which he now saw as the indispensable means of instilling the true Christian spirit into society by first permeating the lives of Christians. He began to perceive that a properly worshiping people, realizing that oneness in the Mystical Christ and actively contacting the living realities of the liturgy, could in time transform a whole society. If Catholics could be brought by active participation in the liturgy to think and pray and work with the Church and to live with her the life of Christ, they would soon also have the answers to many social problems, which in their roots, as the popes never tired of saying, were so often spiritual problems. Thus as early as in 1925, Virgil Michel considered the doctrine of the Mystical Body, the liturgy, and the non-individualistic liturgical movement as the providential means to counteract the new paganism compounded of individualism, naturalism, and secularism. Although primarily interested in Scholastic philosophy and believing that he would spend his life mainly in the apostolate of philosophy, he offered himself as organizer and editor of what he termed a "Popular Liturgical Library," which he suggested to the abbot in his early days in Europe. This was to consist of a series of liturgical books and pamphlets.

Many letters and much pleading were required to convince the abbot, still concerned chiefly with promoting the liturgy in monastic circles. But he was definitely interested, and he always encouraged his subject in his new-found apostolate, without, however, making decisions or giving assurances. With his superior's permission Father Virgil gathered information, read Europe's liturgical journals and publications, acquainted himself with the promotion of liturgical work, took copious notes, and sent home books and source materials. He became more and more convinced that a popular liturgical movement was a great need for the Church in the United States. American Catholics were then hardly aware of a liturgical movement in Europe or, if aware, they often had only the vaguest notions concerning it. But Michel had seen the effects of active participation and corporate worship in the lives of the people. Observations at Solesmes, Maredsous, Beuron, Maria Laach, Mont César, and other liturgical centers as well as long conferences with leaders, editors, and writers in the movement served to reassure him. The abbot would have to decide soon. Michel wrote on January 18, 1925:

The liturgical project got a good boost at Solesmes and has otherwise developed without a loss of time.[39] I am enclosing a tentative program of our Liturgical Library. Of course, these are the merest suggestions, but I am keeping my eyes open for all possibilities. The thing is growing in magnitude, but the grace of the Lord may be behind it. I (this is all suppositional) should do no more translating myself (the first two are almost done) but direct the whole matter, and make selections. I really anticipate no difficulty in getting men to do translations. . . . Just think how it would help to transform the mentality towards the liturgy at home, not to think of the possible providential work that lies before us in the whole English-speaking world.

Letters and pleas for action followed during the next two months and also more information, plans, and ideas. Why stop with translations ? Why not start writing on the liturgy ? Had not Pius X written as early as 1903 in his famed *motu proprio* that "the active participation in the most holy and sacred mysteries and in the solemn and common prayer of the Church" was the "primary and indispensable source" of the "true Christian spirit?" Were not these words clear, and were they not also meant for the English-speaking world? Why had so little been done to promote the liturgy in these countries? "And getting out our own books," Michel said, "will help better than translations. . . . (Of course, I am making no decisions or arrangements, only getting together information)." [40]

To promote interest and discussion and to unlock the treasures of the liturgy for the people, he now added to his former suggestions that a popular liturgical review be founded. The time had come for Abbot Alcuin to make a decision:

And our Popular Liturgical Library has kept pace with time, except that it still awaits your approval (in its general lines). But before that comes I must frankly warn you. While the whole thing may get to be one of the biggest events that struck the Catholic U. S. since the NCWC (I believe that very sincerely), it also may mean what every big thing means — *work* and manpower. The prospects for its growth as a movement of liturgical restoration are so big that I sometimes feel like backing out of the whole matter. And still there is the urge to go on, which apparently can only be checked by your word. Which way will your decision fall? There are many indications that a liturgical movement will be well received in the U. S. in many quarters — and that means going ahead once the start is made. That again means on our part the giving over of a few men to that work, the founding of a popular publication [41] (not immediately, of course), further books in the series (the *offer* has even been made by Mrs. Ward [42] to get the series out in school children caliber if that is at all feasible).[43]

During this time the Reverend William Busch, professor of church history at the St. Paul Seminary, was making similar requests to the abbot, as is evident from his own words to Michel: "During the past months while you were in Europe I had taken up with Abbot Alcuin both by letter and conversation the subject of the presentation to priests and people in this country of some of the excellent European literature on the liturgical movement. . . . The abbot told me that my first suggestion to him in this regard came to him just at the time when a similar one was made to him by yourself."[44]

Meanwhile Michel's urgings kept coming to the abbot: "I should be glad sometime to get a decision on the latest in the liturgical project . . . i.e., whether I should go on thinking in that direction or not."[45] After mature consideration Abbot Deutsch could hold out no longer. He not only gave his consent and approval but even suggested that the review might begin publication fairly soon. Father Virgil answered:

Your remark about the Review kept me awake for the greater part of two nights — with the result that practically all details of format, organization, departments, staff and resources of material, etc., are cleared up (in my mind). . . . After the two nights, also, I heard nothing the next morning & overslept; likewise — of all days! — on Good Friday! . . . The Liturgical Press (Pbl. Co.). . . . As Dom Berlière advised — have a year's matter in advance before beginning the Review. . . . My involuntary but pleasant nightly meditations (due to the obedience of the *sub*conscious to the abbot's suggestion) . . . netted a title, format, about 18 possible series of topics or articles, several permanent departments, a cover design, etc. I have thoughts put down for about one-half year for the "Editor's Corner" without having looked for them. — I have been bashful about suggesting the title, here it is: "Orate Fratres" — a Review that aims at fostering a deeper understanding and wider participation in the official prayer of the Church. Appearing every 2 weeks, 32 pp., $1.50 per year (or $2.00?). Neat appearance, eh?

Another result of those nights was a system of propaganda that was an inspiration (think of the Eucharistic Congress at Chicago!). Again, amid attempts (made from a sense of duty) to fall asleep, I went through a meditation on the Magnificat, on the mission of woman in the modern world, on the close contact between natural and the supernatural, and on the voice of reason in modern thought. And during the day, the surroundings here gave me many suggestions of how we could solve our building problem. . . . Besides the incomparable benefit of waking us up spiritually at home, and many also in the world, the Review might bring us many Mass intentions, and with the Popular Liturgical Library, also financial help. . . . You see, my excogitations have tried (unconsciously) to embrace all phases of the problem — even down to copyrights & imprimaturs . . . while the poor abbot will feel an itch in his fingers every time he sees a pen. I noticed that I have 18 names down on a slip (exclusive of outsiders), divided into: Contributors, Proof-readers; English Censors; Translators; Typists. . . . Then it would need only prudent guidance of the machinery. And what results, if 1st & foremost all do their share of praying! . . . But all coworkers must really live the liturgy, else it looks like slapping on spiritual plaster from the outside.[46]

What is so striking about these letters to Abbot Alcuin, in which Michel eloquently pleads for a liturgical movement, the Popular Liturgical Library, and *Orate Fratres,* is his consistent urging that, after these are established and organized, he devote himself almost exclusively to the apostolate of philosophy in order to promote the coming Scholastic movement in the United States. To this plan the abbot had agreed.

As philosophical ideas and plans matured, Father Virgil lost no opportunity to expand in the direction of the liturgy. He had urged the abbot to send monks to European monasteries for education and training "so that they could gradually imbibe the liturgical spirit." He had arranged for the compilation of the American supplement to Dom Gaspar Lefebvre's *St. Andrew Daily Missal*, just then being published by the monks of St. André![47] So, too, he had dispatched a lengthy preparatory article of new ideas to the *Catholic Educational Review*.[48] Finally, Michel was instrumental in Dom Ermin Vitry's going to St. John's to work in the liturgical apostolate. Dom Ermin, a chant expert, had been a disciple of Marmion and secretary to Beauduin. He has more recently edited *Caecilia*.[49]

With the abbot's consent and support assured, Michel read with renewed zeal Europe's liturgical periodicals, perused liturgical books, and familiarized himself with source materials, problems of publication and means of liturgical propaganda. A retreat at Mont César, a visit there every ten days for long discussions with Beauduin, Berlière, and Vandeur, talks with liturgists at Maria Laach and with Dom Lefebvre and his brethren at St. André, three weeks of Easter vacation at Maredsous,[50] a week at Solesmes,[51] and visits and consultations at other monasteries and liturgical centers — all these established invaluable connections and prepared him for his later work as leader and organizer of the liturgical movement in the United States. To all he listened, but when the time came to organize the liturgical apostolate in America, he would be realist enough to know that there could be no slavish imitation.

During his European sojourn, as during the rest of Michel's life, a constant cross-fertilization of ideas was going on in his unusually open and inquisitive mind. Also striking about this period is his early conception of ideas which would seem to have been the fruit of much later thinking, e.g., the mission of woman in the modern world (a frequent lecture subject at colleges for women), a series of religion texts liturgically oriented, the close relationship between natural and supernatural society, and the supreme need in the Church of an active laity.

Dom Virgil had not forgotten about the apostolate of Catholic

education. For twenty years Dom Virgil pleaded with his superior
for the educational development of St. John's Abbey. On September
22, 1924, he wrote to Abbot Alcuin:

The changes at St. John's were
really surprising, but mainly so on account of their occurring so soon.
The division of college and high school discipline was bound to come
and ought to help even our being accredited. I hope the accrediting of
at least the H.S. will come very soon. With the present men in office,
I do not think the Boards of Studies & Discipline will refuse to function, and the experiment ought to be really successful. Your letter has
also allayed all my 'trepidations,' and since its arrival I have been quite
free from a certain feeling of 'the futility of it all' which has been
persecuting me. I hope you'll not be disappointed in your hopes.

However, almost a year later, on August 6, he again regretted that
"there seems to be no systematic attempt to build up our college
faculty."

His days at Louvain were now coming to an end. On May 22,
he began with his father more than three months of carefully planned
study trips that took them into the important cities and places
throughout the length and breadth of Europe — through Belgium,
France, England, Holland, Germany, Spain, Switzerland, Italy,
Austria, as well as through Palestine and Egypt. With the same close
scrutiny as that of the previous summer's tours, Michel was out to see
life at firsthand, as lived by various people in various cultures, and to
study the social and spiritual conditions along with the needs of
people and Church. Meanwhile he visited monasteries, libraries, museums, and churches and attended plays, concerts, operas and other
interesting events along the way. And all of it entered his Diary in
detail.

After traveling through Belgium and France, the pair flew to
London for five days in England.[52] Then they took a plane to Holland
for four days of observation, spending the next ten days in Germany,
after which for a two-week period Father Virgil rechecked his impressions of the previous summer in Spain. From Italy they were off
to Palestine for two weeks. In Jerusalem, Bethlehem, Capharnaum,
and other places they relived the scenes of our Lord's life, drinking
in, meanwhile, the lore and culture of the Orientals.[53] After four days
in Egypt, they sailed back to the mainland, going through Italy,
Switzerland, Austria,[54] and again Germany, where from Bremerhaven they sailed for home on August 28, 1925.

The time spent in Europe, especially the study trips, was of inestimable value to Dom Virgil in the work that lay ahead. It gave him an insight into society and human needs and a rare vision of the Church and its role in the modern world. No one described this better than his good friend and collaborator, the late Frank Bruce, who said of Michel after his death:

No one had quite such an insight into the Church in all parts of the world as Dom Virgil Michel. His criticisms of the Church in Spain were so pointed and his analysis of the Church under persecution was so accurate that it was interesting beyond all expression to have such an exchange of ideas and such a basic understanding of the problems of the Church here in America and the world at large. . . .

I was at his funeral, and when we buried him, I thought that we buried one of the greatest Benedictines of all times. It is a great privilege in life to have a vision of your Church and of the Catholic and non-Catholic groups and then proceed to do something about it.[55]

Virgil Michel was the bridge over which the liturgical apostolate of Europe came to America. As H. A. Reinhold has said:

It is almost beyond human comprehension to grasp the completeness with which he absorbed everything that Austria, Belgium, and Germany had to offer. But greater yet was what he did with it. Instead of dragging his find across the border as an exotic museum piece, he made it as American as only an American mind can make it. He had seen the high sweep of German ecclesiology and sacramentalism; he had admired the Belgians for their clear grasp of a new spirituality and their critical awareness of all that stood in the way of liturgical, ecclesiastical piety from traditional carry-overs; he had learned in Austria what the common people could gather from the Church's treasure without fright, but he did not come back to force these foreign and incoherent moulds on the American church. Besides, his clear realism and his burning apostle's heart had one urge none of the great masters in Europe seemed to see: the connection of social justice with a new social spirituality. For Virgil Michel the·labor encyclicals of Leo XIII and the liturgical reforms of Pius X did not just by accident happen within one generation, but were responses to cries of the masses for Christ, who had power and gave the good tidings. They belonged together.[56]

How and why they belonged together will be the subject of much that follows.

NOTES TO CHAPTER 2

[1] Besides a complete file of letters to his abbot, containing the preliminaries of the liturgical movement in the United States as far as St. John's Abbey is concerned, there is also a Diary from the time Virgil Michel left St. Paul, February 11, 1924, until he sailed from Bremerhaven for home, August 28, 1925. There is also a series of thirty-six articles in German, "Streifzüge in Spanien," which appeared in *Der Wanderer,* December 2, 1926, to August 4, 1927. These articles record his impressions of Spain and other European countries. Written by Michel from his Diary, they were translated by editor Joseph Matt.

From the beginning he preferred to go to Louvain. Abbot Alcuin wanted philosophy to be taught in Latin in the seminary, Gredt to be introduced, and he wished Michel to acquire Gredt's method; but it was also his larger intention to permit him to audit classes at Louvain later. At once, then, Michel went to Louvain to see about such possibilities. He wrote, "After seeing the place and the atmosphere I am doubly eager to go there" (to Deutsch, Prieuré Sainte Marie, Feb. 27, 1924). Later he wrote from Rome to a confrere, "Suffice it to say that I am content to stay here until July. My coming here was an act of obedience, and why spoil it during Lent? But I am really getting something here at that — experience, and some other notions" (to Severin Gertken, O.S.B., Mar. 19, 1924).

[2] Cf. Deutsch, "Introduction," *Orate Fratres,* X (1936), 481.

[3] Prieuré Sainte Marie, Feb. 27, 1924. He wrote in his Diary, February 26, while at Mont César, "Great conversation on needs of American and Benedictine work. Mt. César is center of new liturgical movement. Had a half-hour French conversation in the recreation room after supper. 'Vous êtes plus fort en français.' "

[4] "I could think only of the condition of the people that were not beneficiaries of all this glory. No wonder that the lower hundreds of thousands revolted against the upper 400. Pictures and statues of Louis Quatorze everywhere. Was there ever a more self-loving and pampered man?" (Diary, Feb. 27, 1924). "On train met Lazarist & talked French; & artist from Torino & talked Spanish" (Mar. 1).

[5] "A High School Course in Religion," *Catholic Educational Review,* XXXII (1924), 485.

43

[6] Michel to Deutsch, Rome, Mar. 19, 1924. "In questions his final argument is: 'Das wuensche ich, koennten Sie so begreifen; es sind nicht viele die es koennen. Es wuerde mich freuen, wenn Sie koennten. . . .' God bless his soul" (Diary, Apr. 12). "Gredt the arguens. Got after the fellow unmercifully, but he was versatile" (May 21).

[7] Michel to Deutsch, Rome, Apr. 20, 1924. He soon abandoned the idea of revising Gredt but retained his original plan to get out a Latin manual of Thomistic philosophy for seminaries.

[8] Michel to Gertken, Rome, July 4, 1924. "I have discovered no pedagogical method except this one very simple principle: in using a textbook in class confine yourself as much as possible to the wording of said text. Emphasize merely by repetition of said phrasing, and only rarely forget yourself sufficiently to use other phraseology: Should that happen for several sentences, use your finger to lead you back to the phraseology of the book" (ibid., Mar. 19, 1924).

[9] "Getting tired of doing such concentrated work on Garrigou-Lagrange. At the end of the week will continue with about 20 pages a day" (Diary, Mar. 14). Of his lectures: "Slow, slowly dramatic and interesting" (Mar. 17), and again: "Whole could be boiled down to ten minutes" (May 24).

[10] Louis Bouyer, Liturgical Piety (Notre Dame, Ind.: University of Notre Dame Press, 1955), p. 59; cf. pp. 58-64 for a description of Beauduin's genius.

[11] Beauduin to writer, Chevetogne, Sept. 27, 1952. For a description of the almost incredible conditions prevailing in Belgium before Beauduin's liturgical work, cf. Belgian Benedictine, "Belgium-American-Liturgy," Placidian, IV (1927), 103-123.

[12] Michel to Deutsch, Rome, July 4, 1924.

[13] Michel to Deutsch, Rome, Apr. 20, 1924. "That quiet monastic cell of next year is infinitely appealing" (Louvain, Dec. 21, 1924).

[14] E.g., "To new part of Rome and had a great time strolling leisurely through and watching people and doings" (Diary, Apr. 28, 1924). "Then to St. Peter's and witnessed the saying of Office by the canons. Everyone shoots off at random and no two are alike in voice, time, position, etc. Most perfectly horrible and scandalous. Much talking going on during Office. Positions terrible. Turned down, sideways, arms suspended like wings on choir stalls, genuflections invisible, and bows a caricature. Reading of the homily lessons a veritable howl — response still worse . . ." (June 13, 1924). "Went to the Church of St. Croce in Jerusalem, and saw some real relics of nail, spikes, parts of real cross, and large beam of cross of good thief . . . believed myself for once undoubtedly in presence of something big and real. Lord, help my unbelief!" (Apr. 5, 1924).

[15] "On the Theory of Matter and Form," Ecclesiastical Review, LXXIII (1925), 241-263.

[16] Michel to Deutsch, Rome, Apr. 20, 1924.

[17] Ibid. The confrere was Roger Schoenbechler, O.S.B.

[18] "And France! A very fine country as far as I saw it! And it has some fine people too — but it is now on the direct road to Bolshevism; the

danger is REAL for 'Catholic' France — just think of it!" (Michel to Sister Virgil, Louvain, Nov. 30, 1924).

[19] "The solemn and majestic celebration of the liturgy had nothing theatrical about it; it was deeply religious, befitting the worship of God and all His glory." He wished American Catholics would witness it and become "convinced." He was also impressed by Montserrat's excellent up-to-date library, from which he found it hard to tear himself away, and by its Biblical museum, one of the best in Spain. And, of course, he had to examine closely the barn and shops, for "nothing was too small for our interest" (Der Wanderer, Feb. 27, 1927).

[20] Ibid., May 12, 1927.

[21] Cf. ibid.

[22] Michel has an interesting description of the royal palace. In the halls they saw paintings, expensive candelabra, priceless goblets covered with gold, all kinds of trinkets brought by pirates from colonies, marble statues, gold lamps, endlessly costly and wonderful things "one only dreams of." The irony was not lost: luxury here and starvation all over the land (ibid., June 9, 1927).

[23] Ibid., Apr. 14, 1927.

[24] Ibid., Jan. 27, 1927.

[25] Michel to Sister Virgil, Louvain, Nov. 30, 1924. Fifteen years later, referring to a conversation with Father Virgil about the Spanish Question, the general world situation, and the Church's role and mission, Jacques Maritain stated: "I was not long ago discussing these things with Father Virgil Michel, with whom I found myself so much in accord and whose so sudden death gave me intense distress. He told me how hopeful he was of the young American clergy. And we agreed in thinking that as far as the preparations for the achievement of a new Christendom are concerned, the United States, like France — and notable American Catholics like French Catholics — have a great vocation and great duties" ("Interview with Jacques Maritain," Commonweal, XXIX [1939], 398). Helen Iswolsky, Light Before Dusk (New York: Longmans, Green & Co., 1942), pp. 184–199, gives an excellent description of Maritain's views regarding the Spanish Question; it may well be taken as summarizing Michel's attitude also.

[26] Michel to Skillin, Collegeville, July 11, 1938, copy; Skillin to Michel, New York, June 8, July 1, Aug. 2, 1938; Harry Binsse to Michel, New York, Sept. 30, 1938. The letter was not printed.

[27] Michel to Deutsch, Milan, Sept. 10, 1924.

[28] Diary, Sept. 19, 1924. At St. Boniface: "As to French, German 're-vanche' seems certain to come some day" (Sept. 21). An example of his universal interests: at a monastery in Augsburg, "Saw Diesel engine at work in power room. It runs smoothly and occupies little space. Burns crude oil and needs no spark for ignition (heat of compressed air starts the 1st explosion — later sucks its own air). Heated water from cooling of engine flows into bathtubs for baths" (Sept. 24). "Got to work at my philosophy notes for several hours . . ." (Oct. 9). "In morning went to children's insane institute. . . . Very interesting to see how simplest

ideas had to be drilled in. . . . Some educable, others not. Some are
children of confirmed drunkards; some microcephalic, others macro —,
many of pronounced mongolian type — slant eyes, stub nose, very short
fingers, waterweb, etc. . . . In evening talked social and industrial conditions . . ." (Oct. 13). "Long talks on German student conditions . . ."
(Oct. 16).

[29] Maria Laach, Sept. 29, 1924. "Maria Laach is a wonderful place. The
whole monastery is imbued with the liturgical spirit; it is wonderful."
Here he did not fail to examine thoroughly also the small agricultural
school.

[30] Michel to Deutsch, Munich, Sept. 22, 1924.

[31] Michel to Deutsch, Louvain, Oct. 29, 1924. The proposed dictionary
appeared in 1948 under the title, *A Lexicon of St. Thomas Aquinas*
(Washington: Catholic University Press), edited by Roy Deferarri and
Sister M. Inviolata Barry, C.D.P. A real insight into the man: ". . . I
sometimes feel like rebelling at the dry technicality of preparing for
examinations. It prevents philosophical development in undeveloped
directions. It often stifles fertile thought. And I am doubting whether it
is better to work for the external appendage of a further degree, or to
make room for that truer intellectual development that is true education.
. . . If I were my own master, I should 'chuck' all chances for degrees
and examinations and just be educated through and through" (Michel to
Sister Eleanore, Louvain, Nov. 30, 1924).

[32] Louvain, Jan. 18, 1925. Out of this research came much of his later
writings. "Ideas are clarifying every day — also in relation with the
scheme of future textbooks, etc., (even the liturgical series)" (Michel to
Deutsch, Louvain, Dec. 31, 1924).

[33] American classmates at Louvain, some now bishops, were Fulton
J. Sheen, Thomas K. Gorman, James L. Connolly, Robert Kothen, Ru-
dolph Bandas and Gerald Phelan. A few years later one of Michel's class-
mates wrote to him, "I read those [philosophical] articles of yours. . . .
You are wonderful. I do not know how you succeed in getting everything
done. When I remember your eight-hour day in search of Sophia (wisdom
I mean of course) I just feel weak. Prosit" (James O'Mahoney, O.F.M.
Cap., to Michel, Louvain, n.d.).

[34] Michel to Deutsch, Louvain, Mar. 14, 1925. Typical Diary entry:
"Finished a vacation week reading James, Dewey, Fling, and Santayana"
(Mar. 1, 1925).

[35] "The projected series in philosophy now is as follows: Vol. I Philosophy of Nature (Inorganic and Organic). Vol. II Philosophy of Mental
Life. Vol. III Philosophy of the Knowledge of Being. Vol. IV Philosophy
of Being (In general, and Infinite Being). Vol. V Philosophy of Human
Conduct" (Michel to Deutsch, Louvain, Mar. 14, 1925).

[36] Michel to Deutsch, Louvain, May 16, 1925. Noel was president of
the institute and the successor of Cardinal Mercier.

[37] Cf. "Mission of Catholic Thought," *American Catholic Quarterly
Review*, XLVI (1921), 657–664.

[38] Michel to Deutsch, Louvain, Apr. 25, 1925. "In general I think that

I am beyond Louvain, certainly not merely imitating, and beyond Gredt in other ways" (Michel to Deutsch, Louvain, Mar. 14, 1925).

[39] Michel apologizes for spending so much time and thought on the liturgy, because the abbot had sent him to Europe to study philosophy.

[40] Michel to Deutsch, Louvain, Mar. 14, 1925.

[41] This is the first suggestion of founding a popular liturgical magazine; it became in 1926 the English-speaking world's pioneer liturgical organ, *Orate Fratres* (since 1952, *Worship*). Henceforth *Orate Fratres* will be indicated by the symbol *OF*.

[42] Michel met Mrs. Justine B. Ward, chant expert and one of the founders of the Pius X School of Liturgical Music in New York, at Solesmes. Here they agreed that what the chant in America needed was a liturgical movement. She invited him to give lectures on the liturgy at Pius X the following year. Michel, referring the request to Abbot Alcuin, also stated: "My head began working immediately — you know that is my chief trouble — and I divided 3 lectures into six headings: General Principles and Ideas; The Liturgical Cycle; The Liturgical Sacrifice; The Sacraments and Sacramentals; Liturgy and Sanctity; Liturgy and Modern Errors — and then divided each into about five main points. Since then the thing has been growing daily (really without loss of time). I think it is a disease in me — that of persecution by notions! Think what good could be done if the lectures were really good and were later published. I dare say it would be a revelation for many English-speaking people" (Michel to Deutsch, Louvain, Jan. 18, 1925).

[43] Michel to Deutsch, Louvain, Mar. 14, 1925.

[44] Busch to Michel, St. Paul, Sept. 28, 1925. As late as Mar. 25, 1925, Athanasius Meyer, O.S.B. — no doubt with the permission of Abbot Alcuin — by letter urged Busch to start the liturgical movement at the St. Paul Seminary. But at this time Busch was almost alone in his interest in the liturgy at the seminary. He had been interested in a liturgical movement before Michel, as early as 1919 (cf. Busch, "An Apostle of Liturgical Life," *OF*, XIII [1939] 102–103; "Past, Present and Future," *OF*, XXV [1951] 481–482).

[45] Michel to Deutsch, Louvain, Apr. 3, 1925.

[46] Michel to Deutsch, Maredsous, Apr. 25, 1925.

[47] "I went to St. André in particular to get firsthand evidence in regard to the English Missal that they are publishing. It was better and cheaper than I had been told, and so I accepted a copy from them as a present. Of course, I had mentioned that I should like to have one in order to use it for the Missal quotations in our coming Pop. Lit. Lib., and that we intend to recommend a good Missal in the series. If you now put a sudden end to the whole liturgical project, what a condition my conscience will be in!" (Michel to Deutsch, Louvain, Mar. 14, 1925). About this time Busch brought this Missal to the attention of the Lohmann Company in St. Paul, which then undertook the uncertain project of its sale.

[48] "A Religious Need of the Day," XXIII (1925), 449–456. Father George Johnson, editor of the *Catholic Educational Review*, had invited him to summarize his observations of European education, but "the ideas

. . . are not developing . . . and any attempt of mine to write them down would be rash."

49 "His coming would give us a logical man to direct the liturgical review [Orate Fratres], at least after its first year. And would give us someone for articles on religious instruction-based-on-the-liturgy, and especially a column regularly on chant, etc. It would help me to devote myself sooner exclusively to the philosophical apostolate. Judging from the utilitarian side, the chance of his coming seems to me nothing less than providential" (Michel to Deutsch, Louvain, May 16, 1925).

50 Here for twenty-two days, he intermittently left for "study-days" in other abbeys. At each place he described the liturgy and discussed liturgical projects with recognized leaders: "Good talk with Dom Berlière on Liturgical Review . . . with publisher of Collection 'Pax,' etc. Many views and counsels on publishing, Review, etc. . . . Notes on philosophy & Liturgy. . . . Continued work at Epistemology & Ethics. . . . Visited laundry and took notes" (Diary, Apr. 6-28).

51 Here he had the usual long discussions, including four talks with the abbot: "Good talk with abbot . . . on Liturgical Spirit." Very much impressed, he described the celebration of the liturgy in detail. He looked over old manuscripts, etc., and "gathered books from the Library and got busy on St. Thomas." After spending six days seeing the highlights of Paris, he returned to Louvain. "In Metro leafed thru Liturgica by Dom Lefebvre — excellent." During this Christmas vacation he also managed to read and "digest" four books in philosophy (Diary, Dec. 23-30).

52 Besides seeing the usual sights, this is significantly mentioned: "In evening took Cook's tour thru slum districts, etc. Interesting but too swift. Took subway to Wembley & saw exhibition. Walked all over. Saw all the Houses of the different Dominions with their scenic & industrial displays" (Diary, May 26-30).

53 "Our Holy Land trip was wonderful — including an 8-hour trip in the most desolate country I ever expect to see. . . . Saw some real oriental life of Jerusalem — bazaars, etc., garb & Turkish laziness . . ." (Diary, July 9-11, 1925).

54 Vienna: "In old regime — Church too closely identified with kingdom. In war priests promised victory 'if a just God exists, etc.' Now Church seems to have lost hold on people, esp. intellectuals. Vienna lost 40,000 Catholics since the war! — A sermon after Mass with few people listening. Communion before & after Mass — mostly old women." He was often shocked by the laxity of the clergy and monks; at Salzburg: "Met Abbot Peter . . . wears silverbuckled slippers and sent us to the best hotel (de Luse) . . ." He was fascinated by the culture and beauty of Berlin (Diary, Aug. 14-19, 1925).

55 To the writer, Milwaukee, Feb. 9, 1953.

56 National Liturgical Week: Proceedings (1947), p. 11; cf. "Denver and Maria Laach," Commonweal, XLV (1946), 86-88.

CHAPTER 3

THE LITURGICAL MOVEMENT

AS LATE as 1937 Dom Virgil wrote that it was a "telling confirmation of our general loss of liturgical sense that many persons think the liturgy is nothing but . . . rubrical prescriptions."[1] Ten years later, after defining the liturgy as the exercise and continuation of the priesthood of Christ in His Mystical Body through the Mass, sacraments, and the divine office, Pius XII expressly and forcefully rejected once and for all such a conception. In his encyclical, *Mediator Dei*, he said:

It is a total misunderstanding of the true meaning of the liturgy to regard it as the merely external element in divine worship, or as the outward splendor of ceremonial; it is equally wrong to see in it a mere catalog of the rules and regulations issued by the hierarchy of the Church for the conduct of sacred rites.[2]

And yet, this false conception seems still widespread. Michel used to say that by far the greatest obstacle to the liturgical movement was ignorance and misunderstanding as to its nature, aims, ideals, and scope. Even at the risk of later repetition it may be well, then, to consider here briefly the true nature of the liturgy and also to examine the dynamism of ideas that underlies the liturgical apostolate as conceived by Father Michel. Thus, naturally, this chapter will include much of what is to follow in later chapters, where what is merely broached here will there be further elaborated.

According to its etymology, *liturgy* means a public work or service which a civic-minded person performs for the benefit of the community.[3] The Catholic liturgy is the official, public worship which the community of the Mystical Body, Christ and members, offers up to God for His greater glory and for the sanctification of souls. Not only does the liturgy lead man to the proper worship of his Creator, but it also conveys to him God's grace. Our Lord entrusted His divine mission of glorifying the Father and of saving souls to His Church, to that fellowship of souls united in Christ and living the life of Christ and known as His Mystical Body. As Dom Virgil explained:

Now the acts by which she exercises her power of sanctifying the hearts of men through her sacrifice and sacraments, the acts by which she utilizes the great privilege conferred by the Redemption, namely, the power to offer to God an acceptable sacrifice of praise and glory — these acts constitute what is called her official public service or worship, her LITURGY. It is by means of her liturgy in particular that the Church is indeed the continuation of Christ, of the Savior of mankind.[4]

As must be evident, the Mystical Body and the liturgy are intimately related, in fact, inseparable. One cannot grasp the full import of the liturgy without a thorough understanding of the true, inner, spiritual nature of the Church as Christ's Mystical Body. Through the liturgical initiation of baptism men are incorporated into Christ, are united to Him and in Him with one another, are given a share in His life and priesthood. In *Mediator Dei* Pius XII shows that through baptism the faithful become "members of Christ the Priest." And even the baptismal rite speaks of having "part with Christ" in a context which can only mean part with Christ already here and now. This, then, is the beginning of the faithful's abiding in Christ and Christ in them — or better, Christ living His life in and through His members. Sanctifying grace is conceived of as incorporation in Christ and is spoken of as "the Christ-life."[5] Again, through baptism the children of Adam become living branches engrafted on the vine which is Christ. By this spiritual rebirth He becomes supernaturally their Brother, as they share in His very sonship and in His worship of the eternal Father. Together with Christ all the branches form a real, living, supernatural organism, permeated and vitalized by the indwelling Spirit of Christ. The Holy Spirit, as its vivifying soul, unites the whole organism into one living community of life. In this one living organism all are called to an active share, not only in the organic life and corporate worship of the undivided Mystical Christ

Chant pioneers and experts: Mrs. Justine B. Ward, Mother Stevens, Dom Mocquereau, and Dom Desrocquettes at Pius X School of Liturgical Music in 1922.

Mother Stevens with pupil at blackboard. Mrs. Ward and Father John Young, S.J., standing.

Father Virgil and his father traveling in Egypt in 1925.

Father and son were impressed by the beauty and culture of Berlin in 1925.

In this plane Dom Virgil and his father flew from Paris to London. In his Dairy for May 26, 1925, Dom Virgil described the trip: "Set out shortly after Mass & breakfast. Full hour's ride to Le Bourget Field. After due weighing, passports, etc., we entered the airplane. Baggage had been stored in for and aft. Propellors were whirling noisily. Ship-car had fine cane-cushioned parlor chairs. Each person had a window and a chair. Narrow aisle between. Suddenly purring grew deafening. We started slowly, gained speed and gracefully ascended. Roads, houses, farms passed by beneath us, as we went on, having little sense of height or speed. Farm plots, mansion gardens, city block were clearly discernible.

"I asked myself how I felt. There was no thrill, no emotion, no heartbeat. I told myself that an accident to the machine would be disastrous, but I could not warm up to anything. I took it like eating a breakfast, wondered at this phase of myself, and asked myself why I was so little human.

"There must have been quite a wind. The machine rocked like a ship at times — and then the elevator stomach sensation was far from pleasant. Several lurches sent thrills thru several passengers. But all were jolly, even if the noise made conversation impossible. After the 1st impression, I began to compare the travel with train travel & thought the latter more interesting. We were flying high, and ears hurt a little, but I did not use cotton. Scenery-horizon was almost too wide to be as varying as that in a train. Hence less interesting to me in the long run. But no.

"Clouds & rain appeared! It was most interesting to see us ascend or descend or switch to right or left, picking our way through the clouds. Bits of them often on one side of us, even beneath us. Steering thru the clear spots was a new adventure.

"Then sunshine came more regularly & with it the sea. We skirted along it for a while. It was calm & shallow. Then hopped across the channel & had beautiful English scenery before us — really very fine at times.

"Suddenly we came in sight of a vast expanse of buildings — it was London! But we saw also hangars & before we knew it, began turning around for our gradual descent.

"We had been 3000 ft. high at our best, at other times quite low. Sometimes men had looked like spots & we could not see plow horses move — they only bobbed up & down. In the moisture laden air there was no rocking of the ship — apparently the air was uniformly dense."

In these words Dom Virgil described the plane trip from London to Amsterdam: "Set out in due time. Delay of over an hour because of low thick clouds on the English coast. Set off in good style & soon rose higher & steered right & left to get between the clouds. Twice we dashed through a thin one which was pierced in a few seconds. Rose to above 4000 ft. & had some beautiful scenery of cloud mountains & of rolling fields of clouds stretching out indefinitely. Only twice for a few seconds was all sight of land lost & then we were piercing thin clouds. Closer to channel the pilot showed more skill still in avoiding clouds, going over or under, to rt. or lt. Stayed around 3–4000 ft. & went from 70–90 miles per hour.

"Over channel less cloudy. We gradually descended to ca. 1500 but could notice it only on the metre. At the end of channel we took on speed up to over 110 miles for a short moment. Whole coast of continent was foggy, & we flew so low that metre did not register altitude at all — only a few hundred feet high. We had to dash about more irregularly to get light. Sailed thus along whole French, Belgian, & most of Dutch coast. Near Amsterdam weather improved & we sailed higher — up to 1500 feet. Came upon our landing place as suddenly as at London. Landed in figure 8 form instead of spiral path & we seemed to be always upright while the earth turned about at angles of 45°" (Diary, May 30, 1925).

Inn of the Good Samaritan, Palestine, 1925.

— that is, His Church — but also to an active share, according to the status of each, in His work and mission as continued on earth by the Church.[6]

Now it is chiefly through the liturgy that the Mystical Body, in its entire organic life, prolongs the life and work and mission of Christ throughout the centuries. The liturgy is the exercise of Christ's priestly and sanctifying power through space and time. As Father Virgil stated:

It is the exercise of this power that constitutes the essential life of the Church on earth. . . . The liturgy can truly be called the life of the Church. Without the liturgy there would be no Church such as Christ has instituted. Without the liturgy there would be no Mystical Body of Christ, in which the divine mission of Christ continues. It is above all in the official liturgical acts of the Church that Christ himself lives and acts. In them He continues His active mediatorship between God and man, there He continues to offer to God His own all-sufficient Sacrifice of praise and atonement. It is through the liturgy that the redemption of Christ is extended over all time for the constant glory of God and the salvation of souls.[7]

To reject the liturgy is to reject the Church, Christ, and God. To this fact an increasingly disintegrating Protestantism has borne eloquent witness.

With Catholics, of course, there is no question of rejecting the liturgy. The Church has always had her liturgical life. Indeed, she could not have gone on without it. But the faithful can have a greater or smaller understanding of the primary and indispensable God-given means of living the Christ-life, and can thus more or less shape their spiritual lives under the inspiration of God's grace. "That in our age this has come to be done in a minimum degree," Michel observed, "is precisely the reason for the need of a movement that would again make the liturgy as vital in the actual lives of the children of the Church, the members of Christ, as it is officially in the Church herself, the bride and body of the same Christ." [8]

To give here Michel's explanation as to why and how a right understanding of the liturgy and, therefore, proper participation in it has been lost would take us too far afield. It is sufficient to realize that this has been the case and that the popes have called for a reawakening. Then also, as Michel always insisted, that the liturgical apostolate has met so much misunderstanding and even opposition seems only to prove its great need. Even if no Pope had ever called for or supported a liturgical revival, he asserted in 1926, organized efforts to grasp better the true nature of the Mass and the essential role of the sacraments in the Christian life would be in itself a most worthy cause.[9]

The very center and heart of the liturgy is the holy Sacrifice of the Mass, the wellspring of all liturgical life. "It cannot possibly be a depreciation of the other parts of the liturgy," Father Virgil commented, "to say that they radiate about the Mass as about their center, that they are in one way or another paths leading to or streams flowing from the Mass." [10] The Sacrifice of the Mass sums up all the mysteries of our Lord's redemptive life, "for as often as this memorial-sacrifice is celebrated, the work of our redemption is being enacted." [11] To the Mass the Church invites all the angels from the throne of God, in it she commemorates all the saints in heaven, remembers all the suffering souls in purgatory, and prays for all mankind. She joins the Redeemer of the world in offering to the Father His all-sufficient and most pleasing Sacrifice, and this becomes the Sacrifice of all His members, for Christ and His Mystical Body are one. The Mass is, indeed, corporate worship and the community Sacrifice of the Mystical Body, offered by all "by the hands of the priest" and "in union with Him [Christ]," as Pius XII expounded in *Mediator Dei*. Michel believed that there were very many Catholics for whom the Mass was "the exclusive function of the priest," the first, perhaps, but "just another devotion," the "means" to make Christ present and Communion "available" or — much worse — an obligation to be fulfilled under pain of sin. Christopher Dawson once spoke of individualistic and selfish Catholics who go to Mass to gather merits, as if God were their banker. The sacrificial character of the Mass, the Mass as sacrifice-sacrament, the participation in common sacrificial worship by all, the Eucharist as the memorial of the passion and as daily food — an understanding of this mystery and its implication for the whole Christian life the movement has always furthered.[12] And as Michel said: .

It is above all the general action of the Mass that should . . . inspire us. . . . There every action of our lives must be centered, and thence it must derive its inspiration. If we can learn again to offer our whole selves consciously on the altar of Christ's own sacrifice, our body and our soul, our actions and all the material possessions we have; if we can realize better that this offering is made in union with all our brethren, and is made by each for all and by all for each; and if we can learn to grasp by growing degrees the sublimer truth that this offering of ours is merged with the very sacrifice of Christ Him-

self — then, indeed, shall we be better able to assign to material goods
their rightful place in human life and no more; and then too, shall we
understand better that all we are and have is most solemnly dedicated
to the service of God, to Him directly, as well as to the service of Him
in all our fellowmen.[13]

The sacraments are of the very essence of the life of the Church and
so, of her liturgy. Through an infinite and loving condescension the
Son of God accommodated Himself to man by taking on human
nature, coming into the world in visible human form and accomplishing our redemption by visible actions and signs. After the Ascension
Christ's redeeming work passed into the sacramental order, and so,
through visible actions and signs, through the sacraments that is, the
Church now continues our Lord's redeeming acts and applies their
merits. Ranging around the Mass or the Eucharist as their central
sun are the other sacraments, living streams of the Christ-life to souls.
All the other sacraments are directed to the Eucharist, draw from it
the light and life that is Christ and are consummated in it. The sacraments are the actions of Christ reaching into souls and preparing
them for the more worthy offering of the supreme Sacrifice, for the
ever greater sharing in the fruits of that Sacrifice, and for the living
out of these fruits in all the aspects of life. In the fine expression of
Pius XII, "Christ acts each day to save us, in the sacraments and in His
holy Sacrifice." [14] Moreover, the sacraments are social [15] and have
as their whole purpose the building up of the Mystical Body of Christ,
the spreading of the Christ-life in the souls of men. Michel described
this when he said:

Baptism is the birth into this life; Confirmation
the attainment of maturity. Penance and Extreme Unction restore the
lost life or heal its wounds and strengthen its weakness. Holy Orders
and Matrimony provide for the propagation of the Christ-life on
earth; the former transmitting the spiritual powers for ministering
the divine life to men, the latter providing in a holy partnership with
God for the birth of children into the world so that these may in turn
be born anew into the life divine.[16]

Every participation in a sacrament is a dying to self, so that Christians
might live wholly for God, and for the greater service and love of
God's children, actual or potential fellow members in the Mystical
Body of Christ.

To the Catholic steeped in subjectivism and individualism, unaware that the Church's life is organic and her sanctity corporate, it
comes as something of a shock to realize for the first time that every

grace he receives is given also for the benefit of the fellowship; that all sin is social; that there is no spiritual isolation; that the Mystical Body is more or less holy, more or less effective, depending on how each member lives the Christ-life, and that "all members are co-responsible for the spiritual growth of the entire Mystical Body."[17] To understand the liturgy is to see it as eminently social, for the performance of the liturgy entails the operation of the whole Church. The liturgy is not only the external expression of the Church's inner, spiritual, organic life and action; it also includes this organic life and action. Through the liturgy the Church dispenses the gifts of God out of the common treasury of the merits of Christ and the saints. In the liturgical prayers she is constantly giving expression to the solidarity existing between the three-fold divisions of the communion of saints. In view of this, therefore, the liturgical movement may be termed a spiritual-social movement *par excellence*.

Intimately related to the sacramental life and fundamental in the ideology of the liturgical movement is the emphasis given to the participation of all the faithful in the priesthood of Christ. This again entails a right understanding of the Mystical Body, the very core-idea of the liturgy, just as it entails a correct understanding of the functional meaning of the sacramental characters in Christian worship and the apostolate. The Protestant reformers denied the ministerial or special priesthood of mediating human beings. They highlighted the common or general priesthood of all the baptized. To be sure, Catholic theologians reasserted in the polemics that followed what the reformers had denied, and played down what the latter had over-emphasized. In the course of time there passed out of Catholic consciousness to a very large extent an appreciation of the laity's share in the priestly power of Christ by virtue of the characters of baptism and confirmation. With the loss of this appreciation went the idea of active participation in the life and worship of the Church, and once that was lost, participation in the apostolate also lost its basis. Yet, only from the viewpoint of his general share in the priesthood of the God-man can the true role of the layman in the Mystical Body be properly understood.[18]

In the Mystical Body not all members have the same office. There is, indeed, a hierarchy of members. Not all are "other Christs" in the same way; still, each is a sharer in the whole Christ. All members possess the sacramental characters that make them sharers in the priesthood of Christ, even if not all share in this priesthood in the same way. The manner in which each member of Christ participates in His priesthood is specified by the characters received in the sacraments of baptism, confirmation, and holy orders. And the characters, says St. Thomas, "are nothing else than certain participations of Christ's priesthood derived from Christ Himself." Aquinas went on to explain that through participation in Christ's priestly power the "faithful are likened to Him by sharing a certain spiritual power with regard to the sacraments and to things pertaining to divine worship." [19] Pius XII stated this point very simply in a passage of *Mediator Dei* already referred to:

By reason of their baptism Christians are in the Mystical Body and become by common title members of Christ the Priest; by the character that is graven on their souls they are appointed to the worship of God, and therefore, according to their condition, they share in the priesthood of Christ.[20]

Life with the Church is life in and with Christ always and everywhere. Not only does Christ *give* us His life; He *is* our life. Perhaps nothing should remind Catholics so much of this as do the sacramentals, whereby the Church brings to bear the sanctifying powers of Christ upon all the phases of human existence.[21]

In the divine office the Church, ever filled with the life and love of Christ, lifts her mind and heart in glorious song and praise to God. As the official prayer of the Mystical Body this Sacrifice of praise "forms a setting for the daily Mass, of which it is a continued echo throughout the day." [22] As the radiation of the Mass the divine praises are intimately related to it and sanctify all the hours of the day and night. In the liturgical year time becomes a vehicle of grace, as the members of Christ relive in the liturgy of the seasons and feasts all the mysteries of His redemptive life.[23]

All that has been said thus far was summarized in Michel's answer to the pastor who challenged him: "Give us something that we can put across to the people in ten minutes and then we will all be with you":

No, Father, it can't be done! You can put something across to the people in ten minutes, only if you have put it across to yourself in many more minutes than a meagre ten. And no one can put the liturgical spirit across in ten minutes, no matter how many years he himself has been absorbing and living it.

For the liturgical spirit is just that — a spirit, a fundamental attitude towards the whole of Christian life, which will enter into and lend new and richer spiritual color to every angle of that life. It is not the learning of any new dogmas — God forbid! But it is the flourishing of a new spirit or, much better, the reflourishing of an old spirit. So Pius X characterized it: "Filled as we are with the ardent desire to see the true Christian spirit flourish again in every respect and be preserved by all the faithful." Here . . . pause and meditate on various phrases used by the Pope: *true Christian spirit — flourish — again — every respect — and be preserved — all the faithful.*

It is a change of spirit, or an enhancement of spirit, if you wish; not a change of dogma. Yet it may mean a shift of emphasis regarding the influence of some truths of our faith on our Christian life. . . . It will mean among other things a better understanding of the Mystical Body of Christ; Christian solidarity; the prayer-life of the Church; the priesthood of Christ, i.e., in Christ Himself, in the Church; in the ordained ministers, in all the faithful; the communion of saints; the life of grace, e.a. And it will mean not only a better understanding of these, in the sense of greater abstract knowledge about them, but an understanding of them as inspirational sources of a more intense spiritual life in and with Christ and His Church.[24]

Virgil Michel was first and last the practical apostle with his feet on the ground and both eyes wide open. This practical sense showed itself as well in his whole attitude toward liturgical reform. Here his spirit was: Let us first understand what we have, and above all, live it — then, we will be in a position to begin to think of and possibly suggest changes. It was an attitude remarkably similar to that of the humble genius from whom he learned so much in Europe, Dom Lambert Beauduin.[25] That certain reforms were desirable was a plain fact to Michel, but there was no point in urging them as long as "liturgy" meant "sanctuary etiquette." Besides, changes in the liturgy, precisely because the liturgy "is grounded mainly on the eternal bonds that unite the human to the divine and on the eternal needs of man as man," would always be slight and gradual even though the liturgy had developed considerably through the centuries and would continue to develop provided it became once again the Catholic's daily bread. In 1936 he wrote: "One of the effects of a wide liturgical revival in the Church will undoubtedly be that of considerable changes in her liturgy made in terms of the new conditions and needs of our day."[26]

The Collegeville Benedictine had a clear concept of the dynamic nature of the liturgy. In this connection it is important to emphasize that the liturgy was in Michel's words, "essentially the Christian faith prayed; it is dogma set to prayer." As certain Christian truths were questioned and were consequently more clearly formulated, or again, as certain Christian dogmas needed greater emphasis due to changing conditions, it was but natural that the liturgical forms and formulas, in which the earlier Christians gave living expression to their beliefs, should also change.[27] According to Michel, the liturgy, like tradition and above all the Church herself, is a living reality and not a static one. Times change and the Church, as a vital, living organism, adapts her unchanging doctrines to changing conditions; so, too, her worship, her liturgy, whereby she carries on the work of Christ. Obviously, the essential elements of the liturgy, those of divine origin and touching the substance of sacrifice and sacraments, must always be retained, whereas the external garb of the liturgy — that is, supplementary rites and ceremonies, actions and words — can change and develop so as to better carry out the work of redemption by making the liturgy more effective. Pius XII has restated this and more without mincing words.[28] Thus every century of Catholic living might have something to add to the official worship of the Church.

Father Virgil expressed his own strong desire when he wrote in 1937 that "not the least of the hopes among many modern liturgical apostles is for various changes in the liturgical forms and customs." [29] In the same year, pleading for the evening Mass, he expressed himself even more forcefully:

Not every concession to the conditions of a time or an age must be considered unchristian or even unliturgical. On the contrary, the basic principle of the entire liturgical worship, as of the continuation of Christ's redemptive mission in the Church — that is, the sacramental principle — is by its very nature a loving stooping down by God to the ways of man. The very manner of redemption chosen by God was an accommodation by divine love to the nature of man. And so also in the history of the Church, wherever accommodation to the exigencies of human nature and human life could be exercised without compromise of any basic principle, the Church herself has acted in imitation of God's own way with man. The very legitimate question therefore continues to impose itself: Why not an evening Mass? [30]

This suggests at once the question of the vernacular in the liturgy, a matter of importance in view of facilitating active participation. The question did not arise in the first years of the liturgical movement in the United States when all efforts were bent on effecting an understanding of the liturgy as being more than mere rubrics and ceremonial. However, as early as 1929 and 1930, Michel enthusiastically reported in *Orate Fratres* papal permissions for the use of the vernacular in European countries. While his earlier correspondence shows him to have favored it, only in 1938 did he think it prudent to make what seems to have been the first public call in the United States for the introduction of English into parts of the liturgy. While he would have retained the complete use of Latin in seminaries, colleges, convents, etc., he wrote that "we should be happy to see the Church go as far as she deems fit in introducing the vernacular into her liturgy." [31] He thus anticipated the words of the Holy Father nine years later, to the effect that the vernacular in certain parts of the liturgy "may be of great advantage to the people."

One could hardly be sympathetic with efforts to introduce the vernacular unless he appreciated the value of active participation, the very heart of the liturgical apostolate. Michel never seemed to tire of writing and talking about the nature and importance of this participation. Pius XI deplored in 1928 the fact that Catholics at Mass were so often what he called "merely detached and silent spectators." In *Mediator Dei* his successor exhorted, "Try in every way, with the means and helps that your prudence deems best . . . that the Christian people take such an active part in the Liturgy that it becomes a truly sacred action of due worship to the eternal Lord . . ." [32] Active participation is also the key-idea in the famous, oft-quoted words which make up the charter of the liturgical revival, spoken by the father of the movement, Pius X:

Filled as we are with a most ardent desire to see the true Christian spirit flourish in every way and be preserved by all the faithful, we deem it necessary to provide before aught else for the sanctity and dignity of the temple, in which the faithful assemble for no other object than that of acquiring this spirit from its foremost and indispensable fount, which is the active participation in the most holy mysteries and in the public and solemn prayer of the Church. [33]

As has been said, the liturgy is the exercise of the priesthood of Christ in the Church, "is the embodiment of God, who has in the liturgy descended from heaven and eternity into time and this earth of ours, and who abides and acts there throughout all time." [34] That Christ "abides and acts" in the Mass and sacraments *ex opere operato* is a supreme fact of Catholic faith. But the faithful must prepare themselves, cooperate, open their souls, as it were, if Christ's action is to have its full effect. The focal importance of the whole question of active participation, therefore, deals with the manner in which souls make contact in the liturgy with the priesthood of Christ, the source of all holiness. Obviously a minimal contact with the Church's liturgy is necessary for one even to become and to remain a Catholic. And it should be just as clear that the better he makes this contact, the more he partakes of the life of the Church, which is the life of Christ. But exactly what is the nature of this participation?

Active contact with the living sources of life in Christ, or active participation in the liturgy, entails contact and participation as rational creatures, a participation, therefore, of the rational faculties of understanding and will, first of all. The liturgy is not an efficient, impersonal technique or rigid apparatus to which the faithful must submit passively and mechanically, like automatons. According to St. Thomas, prayer is an act of reason. Sound and healthy religious life demands a rational and objective basis. Nor is genuine piety a matter of mere emotion or sentimentality. Rather, it is rooted in the dogmatic truths of divine revelation and redemption and requires the exercise of intellect and will according to the capacity of the worshipper. Men are not only physically but also intellectually and spiritually living beings, and life must either show itself in activity or perish. Since living membership in Christ is participation in divine life, this membership or divine life must likewise show itself in activity or die. This spiritual activity must be anchored and centered in Christ's eternal truth or become as unstable as an emotion. Now the Mass, like the rest of the liturgy, not only contains Christian truth and dogma but is dogmatic truth prayed, that is, acted and lived out in the prayer-action of the Church. To engage in this prayerful activity the liturgy ceaselessly invites the faithful. Again the Mass is, in Michel's words, "the concentrated embodiment of the whole scheme of redemption as well as of the whole of Christian truth and life." Against the rich background of the liturgical year, the Mass unfolds day by day the whole redemptive life and work of Christ. Thus the liturgy, taken as an organic whole, is one of the chief theological sources, or as Pius XI said, "the principal organ of the ordinary magisterium of the Church." The Mass is Christ worshipping the Father; ideally, at the holy Sacrifice each one and all together consciously offer and are offered with Christ to God. In this way does the church year become "the spiritual guidebook of the Christian's walking with Christ in the Mass."

To Michel's mind, what the Christian does in a concentrated form at Mass to cooperate and to associate himself with Christ instructing, sacrificing, praying, and offering praise to God so as to share His divine life in the Eucharist with each and all, that the participating Christian must continue to do from Mass to Mass in serving his neighbor. Obviously this requires some understanding of the inner spiritual, corporate nature of the Mass and some knowledge of the individual's part in it. Active and intelligent participation in the Mass, then, is "at once an instruction and an exercise of faith; it is a living contact with the channels of grace; it is eminently a living out of our faith." [35] That is why Pius XII urged the clergy to "promote a deeper knowledge among the people of the sacred liturgy so that they more readily and easily follow the sacred rites and take part in them with true Christian dispositions." [36] And what has been said of participation in the Mass applies in proper proportion to the other parts of the liturgy.

The liturgy calls into operation the whole man with all his faculties — mind, will, body, senses, and emotions. Like a wise mother who knows human nature, the Church draws upon the whole natural context of man's life and uses all the arts to penetrate the soul, to put it in touch with the divine redemptive action of Christ, to elicit wholehearted cooperation from man. Thus she employs symbols, chant, painting, sculpture, music, poetry, color, rites, gestures, ceremonies, words, vesture and edifice, the rhythm of the seasons, water, fire, and fruits of the earth. In Michel's words:

Therein lies the power of the liturgy, that it addresses itself to the whole man. It never moralizes without giving the intellectual reasons for the conduct to be followed; it never instructs without giving at the same time an inspiration to live the truths preached. Its appeal is not abstract but concrete, and is brought out in terms of past human achievement and present possibilities — it addresses and inspires the human person to a maximum of the Christ-life both in regard to prayer and to the service of God in the daily occupations and work. [37]

And yet, "the besetting sin of our Christian age," Michel maintained, "has been a self-complacent apathy and inaction," reflected in non-participation. This indifference begins at the altar in church and continues in the lives of should-be apostles in the world. "How was it possible at all for us to develop this trait so strongly, since it is above all else in veritable abomination before God? 'I would thou wert hot or cold. . . .'" Precisely this kind of hindrance the average Catholic presents to the operation of Christ in the liturgy. The failure to cooperate is in the supernatural order what passive resistance is in the natural order, "and such passive resistance or inaction is something which even the supreme love of God, humanly speaking, struggles against in vain."[38]

The benefits of joining Christ wholeheartedly in His prayer and Sacrifice should be evident to all. Not only does the Church enshrine the best of Christian tradition in her official prayer, but she also speaks to God in the liturgy chiefly in His own words. Active and intelligent participation would be the most practical and most effective way, thought Father Virgil, to bring the Bible back to Catholics. What was more, this would gradually effect a familiarity with God's Word according to the mind of the Church. Restoring to the faithful their active role in the worship of God through the Mystical Body would likewise, he believed, "restore to them their native right to a share in . . . theological knowledge and understanding, in place of the relegation of theology to an abstract science for experts."[39] This would aid in forming an enlightened and zealous laity prepared for the cause of God in the market place, because as they gave themselves with Christ to God at Mass, so this personal and corporate self-dedication would continue from Mass to Mass by serving God in one's neighbor. For the liturgy, Michel said, "is not only the primary fount of the grace of God, but also the first source at which the member of Christ must learn and must exercise active cooperation with this grace," and "because the prayers of the liturgical mysteries are the best expressions of the mind of Christ that the ages of Christianity have formed and passed on to us, active participation in them is an intelligent and voluntary steeping in the very mind of Christ."[40] In this way personal efforts at spiritual growth could be linked to the supernatural sources of that growth. Not only would the spirit of active and corporate participation thus become an antidote to a deadening formalism and routine in set forms of worship. It would also be a safeguard against that unchristian individualism and subjectivism in religion that inevitably produces spiritual selfishness.

But there are still other benefits that active contact with the living arteries of grace produce. Not the least among them would be the satisfaction of the soul's natural craving for true religious experience, for which the liturgy is again the divinely appointed means. This would not be an ephemeral religious experience of the moment, "the sudden conversion," nor a kind of social emotionalism, but the joyous realization of continuing transformation into Christ. As Michel phrased it:

Participation in the liturgy naturally produces in us the consciousness of our union with Christ and of our dignity as sharers in the divine nature. It brings us into contact with the many-sided aspects of the life of Christ, with the rich inexhaustible content of His life, and thus manifests the rich possibilities of our life in Him. It elevates our minds above the things of this earth and of self, broadens our spiritual outlook while deepening it, gives us a better sense of the truly beautiful and truly valuable, a better sense of unity with a sympathy for our fellow members of the body of Christ, a human family feeling for all mankind, and, being rooted in the wonderful condescension of God, a firmly founded optimism in regard to all the things that count in life.[41]

God can only act from infinite love, and the liturgy is filled with the spirit of God's love. To participate fully in this expression of divine charity is to gain "a personal experience of the best that has been spiritually achieved for man by none other than God Himself."[42]

To identify, then, the liturgy of the Church merely with its external aspects is to give evidence of misunderstanding the true nature of the Incarnation, the Church, and man himself. However, since the externals of the liturgy — gestures, vestments, song, postures, words — convey to man divine truth and life and are expressive of his interior sentiments of devotion and worship, they can in no way be unimportant. Hence the artistic aspects of the liturgical movement. The liturgy, like the Church and like Christ, has divine and human, external and internal, spiritual and material, visible and invisible, elements. As Christ lovingly adapted Himself to man's material-spiritual and social nature, so He has fashioned His Church, the liturgy, and the whole economy of redemption according to man's nature, constituted of material body and spiritual soul. Through the externals of the liturgy, therefore, the Church as the extension of Christ continues to mediate the Christ-life to men. "This general fact, that God has chosen to manifest Himself to men's minds through external visible things, and to act in human souls by means of material things, words, and actions," Michel explained, "is often called the Sacramental Principle,"[43] and is but the continuation of what Christ Himself, the first and greatest sacrament, did when carrying out the redemption on earth. Furthermore, man communicates with his fellows through actions, words, and signs. It is natural for him to express his thoughts, devotion, and sentiments visibly, through his body and by the use of external things. Only through this externalization can men join in corporate worship as members of a community and give expression to their common life in Christ. Consequently, not only are the external and visible elements of the liturgy the manifestations of the inner action of Christ, but also the external expression of the internal worship of the whole Christian community. As Father Virgil frequently stated, the liturgy is the best evidence of the Church's understanding of human nature.

But what is the relation between the official worship and prayer of the Christian community and private or non-liturgical prayers and devotions? According to Dom Virgil, "Nothing can be further from a true liturgical sense, which is above all eminently Catholic," than to condemn or minimize the importance of non-liturgical devotions and prayers. However, the liturgy, as the essential expression of the Church's spiritual life, is more important and efficacious: It is the infinite adoration and activity of Christ worshipping the Father, and by sharing in this activity the spiritual efforts of Christ's members take on the efficacy of the divine Redeemer and Mediator. Other religious devotions are ancillary and preparatory; though necessary, they must be properly subordinated. For the official worship of the Church is the model, norm, and inspiration of all other prayer; as such it lends proper perspective and balance. Therefore, Michel characterized it as "an intolerable abuse" [44] if non-liturgical practices prevent or even lessen proper participation in the official prayer life of the Church. "The right emphasis in the right place," Father Michel insisted, "and the most essential thing first and foremost, should be our universal rule." [45] He was always amazed how whole treatises on the spiritual life could be written with hardly a reference, or at most a casual one, to the liturgy. Such books, he said, gave the impression that holiness is chiefly to be attained through "purely private adventure." He added:

This is indeed an anomaly since there can be no truly Catholic life, least of all any such spiritual life, without the liturgy. The latter is *par excellence* the spiritual life of the Church and therefore officially also that of the faithful as members of the Mystical Body of Christ.[46]

This discussion began with the aim of defining the dynamism of ideas which underlies the liturgical apostolate as conceived by Dom Virgil. Occasionally deliberate reference was made to *Mediator Dei*.

The reader who examines Michel's liturgical writings today may be impressed by their accord with what Pius XII has officially laid down in *Mystici Corporis* and *Mediator Dei*, issued in 1943 and 1947 respectively. To some it may seem a strong statement, yet one need not hesitate to say that not a few times in his writings Michel's words foreshadowed the very words of the Pope. Moreover one can find scattered through Dom Virgil's writings nearly all the warnings and strictures that Pius XII enunciated almost twenty years later in *Mediator Dei*.[47] The remark of Michel's closest collaborator seems to the point, "He strove first of all to be correct and accurate."[48] In all of Michel's extensive correspondence, in his writings and in the volumes of *Orate Fratres* he edited, there is no trace of the allegations made — without stated evidence — by a writer in the *Homiletic And Pastoral Review* in answer to the question asked after the appearance of *Mediator Dei*, "Were Our Own Liturgists Afoul?"[49]

Liturgical piety, then, is the piety of the Church, a piety rooted in Christ because it is Mass-centered and sacramentally nourished, without neglecting the essential role of private prayer and devotions. Again, rooted in the very life of the Church and founded on dogmatic truth, this piety is corporate, organic and truly all-embracing. This, asserted Michel,

is eminently the view of that religion whose liturgy is at once the perfection of the individual and the union of the individual in a common fellowship, and whose liturgy is not the spasmodic exercise of isolated acts of worship but the spiritual source and inspiration of a life that is lived every moment of the day.[50]

Freed from a narrow, emotional subjectivism and from a confining, selfish individualism, the liturgical or Christian life was for Michel not so much a set of rules to be followed, a set of disparate spiritual exercises to be submitted to, a certain number of "acts" to be performed, as a constant living out of the Christ-life — more intensely at Mass and then all through the day — so all that the Christian does and engages in bears the mark of the glorious and joyous vocation to which he is called. As Dom Virgil recalled,

The early Christians were imbued with a strong sense of their dignity as Christians. This dignity they attained and fostered in the Church by active participation in her life of prayer, sacrifice and sacraments. It was there they found Christ. To be a Christian meant for them to continue to live in and for Christ.[51]

Conscious of Christ living in them, these Christians according to Michel brought about the greatest transformation of all time. What they were and did for their age, he urged, modern Catholics must be and do for their world. However, as he observed in 1936:

Nor is it difficult to understand to some extent what has been wanting, if one compares the spirit of the liturgy with that of ever so many well-meaning Catholics as exemplified in their religious life. They would be the first to be shocked, were they told that their spiritual life savors of the individualism, the subjectivism, even the selfishness of our day. Yet such is evidently the case.[52]

And after saying that praise is the culmination of all the acts which bind Christians to God, he continued:

How many are not spiritually indifferent to everything but their own needs, so that they pray much when they need something, and scarcely know how to pray to God except in a give-me terminology. . . . What if we were to be judged as to our faith by the kind of prayer we say? For how many Catholics would the judgment not have to be, that in their minds the world, with God included, exists only for the satisfaction of their own individual desires, and not they for the greater glory of God? . . . What of the many whose attendance is perfunctory and mechanical even on the Lord's own day. What can their faith be when judged by their actions? What again of those who consider their religious life as entirely their own individual affair, and who would laugh to scorn the idea that it has social aspects?

A storm of protest is wont to greet the person who speaks thus of his fellow Catholics. There is no denying that the faithful as a whole are well-meaning and sincere. But there is also no denying that many of them are individualistic in the extreme, even selfish, in their entire religious outlook. And so many of them are woefully ignorant about their faith and its practice far below the degree of their knowledge and intelligence in all other matters. . . . Often [they are] . . . faithful at Mass on Sundays but also quite like everyone else the rest of the week!

There is indeed something wrong. And it is something that was quite foreign to the early Christians, which they could not possibly have understood, which many of them, gazing down from above, possibly still view with amazement.[53]

In view of what has already been said, it may be superfluous to ask: why the inception of a liturgical movement in the 1920's? Surely the question cannot be fully answered here but must find a more adequate answer in what follows. "If the first purpose of the liturgical movement," Michel explained, "is to lead the faithful into more intimate participation in the liturgy of the Church, then the further objective must also be that of getting the liturgical spirit to radiate forth from the altar of Christ into every aspect of the daily life of the Christian." [54]

The liturgical apostolate is concerned with promoting the highest function of rational nature: the proper individual and corporate worship of the Creator. As such, Dom Virgil thought, it must always remain the primary apostolate, the heart of a Christian revival, the enlivening force behind all Christian activity. The liturgical revival represents a living return to the primary founts of a truly Catholic spirituality. Among its objectives are the unification of the individual and social elements of Catholic spiritual life, the healing of the chasm between religion and life, and the bringing closer together of clergy and people in worship and apostolic work. For the Church is much more than an organization with authority and obedience, bidding us to imitate Christ with the help of grace. Above all, therefore, apostles of the liturgy attempt to effect a right understanding of the Church as the Mystical Body of Christ, in which all baptized members are active, first at worship in church and by virtue of their baptismal character, and then active outside of church, in all of life, in the apostolate, by reason of the sacramental character of confirmation. This leaves no room for a kind of negative, moralizing, and joyless Christianity, "so frequent in our day, which does a minimum for God and a maximum for self, which measures its service of God by the rule of minimum obligation, only to give itself over all the more to a secular life in a secular way and to a maximum extent." [55]

In the 1920's, when the organized liturgical apostolate began, Virgil Michel frequently insisted that the world was at the end of an era, in an age of transition that is "questioning all its old beliefs and habits." [56] A pagan and unnatural individualism, in both secular and spiritual fields, had run its course. Extremes, he said, always breed extremes. The reaction had, he thought, already set in and the world was moving toward a new pattern of corporate life and spiritual unity. And a sick world would find these in a life lived in, with, and for Christ in the social solidarity of the Mystical Body, or it would continue to tend toward an all-devouring, godless collectivism that was certain to crush all human and spiritual values, even all human personality. What has happened since 1926 speaks for itself. The purpose of the liturgical apostolate, he stated thirty years ago, is to bring man, civilization, and culture back to Christ, after the apostasy that began with the Renaissance, received its great impetus in the Protestant Revolt, and developed with relentless logic through the successive eras of the enlightenment, deism, liberalism, and individualism to the secularism of his day.

NOTES TO CHAPTER 3

[1] *The Liturgy of the Church* (New York: Macmillan, 1937), p. 14.

[2] *Acta Apostolicae Sedis*, XXXIX (1947), 532.

[3] Cf. *The Liturgy of the Church*, p. 1; in the first four chapters of this survey of the liturgy of the Roman rite Michel gives, besides many definitions, a thorough explanation of the nature of the liturgy. "Liturgy and Catholic Life," a 263-page unpublished manuscript written in 1936–37 as a sequel to *The Liturgy of the Church* and meant to be published in 1938, contains his most mature thinking on the role and import of the liturgy in Catholic life. These, along with *Our Life in Christ* (Collegeville: Liturgical Press, 1939) and *The Christian in the World* (Collegeville: Liturgical Press, 1939), include his definitive liturgical thought. Parts of "Liturgy and Catholic Life" were published in separate articles in *Orate Fratres* in the years 1939–41; quotations will be taken from the original manuscript.

[4] *The Liturgy of the Church*, p. 29.

[5] Apostles of the liturgy have always made efforts to clarify and stress the life-aspect of grace, and hence, speak of "the Christ-life." Michel had words to the point: "The supernatural life is the life of grace. We can get some understanding of it only when we learn to know better what is meant by the life of grace, when we realize in what a sublime sense it is really LIFE. Is it too much to say that in this regard our ordinary teaching on grace has often missed the most important aspect of the life of grace, not merely by wrong emphasis but by omission? How frequently have we not learned simply that the state of grace is a state of soul in which we are made holy and pleasing to God? But why are we holy and pleasing when in that state? Because of the tremendous truth that God himself then dwells in our souls, that the Holy Ghost is then in a special way operative in us, that we are then truly temples of the Holy Ghost and bearers of God, living members of Christ. We have at times concentrated on what can be reduced to a mere utilitarian if not even selfish aspect of the life of grace, instead of emphasizing the much sublimer aspect, which has at all times been the true inspiration of ardent Christians, and which is in fact the cause and source of our being pleasing to God" ("Knowledge Requirement for Teaching the Mass," *Journal of Religious Instruction*, VIII [1938], 768).

[6] Michel has an illuminating discussion on the Mystical Body in "The True Christian Spirit," *Ecclesiastical Review*, LXXXII (1930), 128–142; cf. also *Our Life in Christ*, pp. 30–76.

[7] *Our Life in Christ*, pp. 50–51.

[8] "Liturgy and Catholic Life," p. 18.

[9] "Program for a Liturgical Movement," *America*, XXXIV (1926), 615.

[10] *The Liturgy of the Church*, p. 211.

[11] Secret, ninth Sunday after Pentecost.

[12] For how far removed this is from what was being taught on the Mass before the advent of the liturgical movement and in the religion textbooks for grade and high schools and other books in the 1920's and 1930's, cf. Paul Bussard, *The Vernacular Missal* (Washington: Catholic University of America, 1937), pp. 116–149; cf. also Michel, "Knowledge Requirement for Teaching the Mass," *Journal of Religious Instruction*, VIII (1938), 765–770.

[13] Apostolate, *OF*, XI (1937), 323–324.

[14] "Mediator Dei," *AAS*, XXXIX (1947), 533.

[15] For a convincing elaboration, cf. Michel, "Some Social Aspects of the Liturgy," *Catholic Action*, XVI (1934), 9–11; "Liturgy and Catholic Life," pp. 115–128; Michel's best explanation of the sacraments is found in *Our Life in Christ*, pp. 76–180; cf. also *The Liturgy of the Church*, pp. 210–252.

[16] "Philosophical and Theological Bases of the Liturgical Movement," unpublished manuscript, pp. 11–12.

[17] "Liturgy and Catholic Life," p. 139.

[18] Cf. Michel, "The Layman in the Church," *Commonweal*, XII (1930), 123–125.

[19] *Summa Theologica*, III, q. 63, a. 3 and 5.

[20] *AAS*, XXXIX (1947), 555.

[21] Cf. *Our Life in Christ*, pp. 181–189; *The Liturgy of the Church*, pp. 253–273. "The sacramentals are in a special manner designed for our intelligent participation. Yet it is just the idea of participation, of intelligent use of them, that has been forgotten in our day even by Catholics otherwise known for their intelligence. Almost the whole ensemble of the sacramentals is unknown to most Catholics. They are well nigh as ignorant of the great treasure of the Church's blessings and helps as are the unbaptized" (*ibid.*, 257–258).

[22] *Our Life in Christ*, p. 209; cf. pp. 209–212; *The Liturgy of the Church*, pp. 274–315.

[23] Cf. *The Liturgy of the Church*, pp. 84–90.

[24] "Making Converts to the Liturgy," *OF*, IV (1929), 18–20.

[25] Cf. Bouyer, *op. cit.*, pp. 58–64, for a striking similarity in methods and approach, even of personalities, as succeeding chapters of this volume on Michel may show.

[26] Cf. "Liturgy and Catholic Life," pp. 241–243, *passim*.

[27] Michel cites examples in *The Liturgy of the Church*, pp. 16–17.

[28] Cf. "Mediator Dei," *AAS*, XXXIX (1947), 541–543.

[29] *The Liturgy of the Church*, p. 7; cf. Apostolate, *OF*, II (1928), 316–318.

[30] "Why Not the Evening Mass?" *OF* (1937), 30. After outlining his ideas about the need for the evening Mass, Michel observed, "This may be an idle dream. But dreams may also be visions of constructive possibilities." Cf. Apostolate, *OF*, IV (1929), 190–191. Monsignor Joseph M. Corrigan had called for the evening Mass in a paper read at the International Eucharistic Congress at Chicago in 1926 ("Evening Mass," *Fortnightly Review*, XXXIII [1926], 418).

[31] "The Liturgy in the Vernacular," *OF*, XII (1938), 173. "I do think that some day the Mass of the Catechumens will be said in the vernacular (and, of course, it will have to come through the Holy See), but that may be 35 or 50 years from now, and I know of no indication to the effect that the Holy See is even aware of the possibility" (Michel to Theodore Vermilye, Collegeville, June 18, 1937, copy).

[32] *Acta Sanctae Sedis*, XXXIX (1947), 592.

[33] "Tra le sollecitudini," *ASS*, XXXVI (1903), 327–328.

[34] "Liturgy and Catholic Life," pp. 229–230.

[35] Michel, Apostolate, *OF*, IV (1930), 181.

[36] "Mediator Dei," *AAS*, XXXIX, (1947), 587. Note the agreement as to the nature and importance of active participation in the writings of Michel when compared to *Mediator Dei*: cf., e.g., "Liturgy and Catholic Life," pp. 19–23, *passim*; "Scope of the Liturgical Movement," *OF*, X (1936), pp. 486–487; "Meaning of the Church's Liturgy," *America*, XXXIV (1926), 386.

[37] "Liturgy and Catholic Life," p. 230.

[38] "Back to the Liturgy," *OF*, XI (1936), 10.

[39] Michel, "Scope of the Liturgical Movement," *OF*, X (1936), 488–489.

[40] "Back to the Liturgy," *OF*, X (1936), 10, 13.

[41] *The Liturgy of the Church*, pp. 60–61, *passim*.

[42] "Liturgy and Catholic Life," p. 234.

[43] *Our Life in Christ*, p. 77; cf. "Liturgy and Catholic Life," p. 18, *passim*.

[44] "Liturgy and Catholic Life," p. 230; cf. footnote 36; "Case for Private Piety," *OF*, XIII (1939), 354–360.

[45] "Advertising Our Wares," *OF*, IV (1930), p. 124. "Emphasizing essentials does not mean neglecting what is unessential or what is essential only in a secondary sense" (Michel, "Emphasizing Essentials," *OF*, IV [1930], 170).

[46] "Liturgy and Catholic Life," p. 223.

[47] Cf. Editor's Corner, *OF*, I (1926–27); editorials in Apostolate, *OF*, I–IV (1926–1931); also the many articles in the bibliography in which he explains the nature, aims, and scope of the liturgical movement.

[48] Busch, "An Apostle of Liturgical Life," *OF*, XIII (1939), 102.

[49] J. P. Donovan, C.M., in *Homiletic And Pastoral Review*, XXXIX (1949), 750–751.

[50] "Liturgy and Modern Thought," *OF*, XIII (1939), 209.

[51] *Liturgy and the Layman* (Collegeville: Liturgical Press, 1930), p. 22.

[52] "Liturgy and Catholic Life," p. 13.

[53] *Ibid.*, pp. 14–15.

[54] "Scope of the Liturgical Movement," *OF*, X (1936), 485. This article is Michel's best description of the liturgical movement.

[55] *Ibid.*, pp. 487–488.

[56] *The Liturgical Apostolate* (Collegeville: Liturgical Press, 1927), p. 7.

CHAPTER 4

STIRRINGS OF A MOVEMENT

AN OVER-ALL, definitive history of the liturgical movement, now more than a century old, has never been written.[1] Beyond a few historical sketches by various authors,[2] the story of how the organized movement began in the United States remains untold. Movements do not spring up over night, nor does one man start them. One should know something, therefore, of the situation in the United States before the first organized efforts for a liturgical apostolate began in 1926 with the establishment of the Liturgical Press and the founding of *Orate Fratres*, destined to be the organ of the liturgical movement in the English-speaking world. This general view of the American scene will best be appreciated in the perspective of the entire liturgical revival.

Never has there been a time in the history of the Church when some of her children did not have a profound appreciation of the liturgical life. So, too, there were always those who tried to spread this appreciation. Because the Protestant Revolt of the sixteenth century was specifically an anti-liturgical movement, the legislation of the Council of Trent contained and re-emphasized elements which were distinctly liturgical.[3] But the liturgical revival of our own day, now a conscious and organized endeavor, goes back to the second half of the nineteenth century. The way was prepared by theologians like Johannes Moehler, Matthias Joseph Scheeben, and Franz Staudenmaier, who rediscovered and restored the doctrine of the Mystical Body and

72

showed its central place in Christian theology and life. In England the writings and preaching of Cardinals Nicholas Wiseman and John Henry Newman, together with the Oxford Movement, broke ground for a liturgical renaissance. But no name looms so large as that of Abbot Prosper Guéranger (1805–75). In 1840 he began his monumental work of research and publication. His *Institutions liturgiques* (1840–51) showed the beauties of the Roman rite in contrast to some fifteen local, Gallicanized diocesan liturgies. His *l'Année liturgique* (1841–), translated into many languages, opened the glories and spiritual values of the liturgy to a large number of readers.[4]

The liturgical spirit and influence of Guéranger was carried into Germany by two brothers, Maurus and Placidus Wolter, students of Guéranger as well as founders of the Abbey of Beuron. In 1872 monks from Beuron came to Belgium to found the Abbey of Maredsous, the future home of Abbot Marmion and mother of the Abbeys of Mont César and St. André. In 1882 Dom Gerard van Caloen of Maredsous, one of the great pioneers, published his *Missel des Fidèles*, and a few years later the liturgical review, *Messager des Fidèlis*, to lead the clergy and faithful back to the official life and worship of the Church. "This," he said, "we believe to be the most efficient means of contributing towards the revival of the Christian spirit in the world." [5] The work of van Caloen and other pioneers found strong approval and support in the famed *motu proprio* on Sacred Music, issued on November 22, 1903, by Pius X, as well as in his decrees on early and frequent Communion and in the reform of Gregorian chant, calendar, and breviary. In this way Pius X gave the liturgical revival a new impetus and dimension. Since then the utterances of successive popes have given continued support to the aims and work of apostles of the liturgy, and have shown again and again the importance of the liturgy in Catholic life.[6]

After 1903 the inspiration of Pius X spread quietly and privately. Only in 1909 did a popular liturgical "movement" emerge, and this at Mont César through the efforts of Beauduin, who, as has been shown, so profoundly influenced Virgil Michel. From Mont César it spread to the other Belgian abbeys and to the secular clergy, led by a combined hierarchy under the leadership of Cardinal Mercier. Holland almost immediately felt its influence from Belgium, as did Portugal and Poland somewhat later.

Under the strong leadership of Abbot Ildefons Herwegen, the Abbey of Maria Laach of the Beuronese congregation inaugurated its liturgical activity in 1914 with the first liturgical week for laymen. In 1918 appeared Guardini's *Vom Geist der Liturgie*, the first volume of Maria Laach's famous *Ecclesia Orans* series, edited by Herwegen. Ever since that time Maria Laach has been more or less the intellectual leader of the movement, renowned for its profound liturgical scholarship.

While the German abbey addressed itself chiefly to intellectuals and scholars, Austria's Father Pius Parsch, an Augustinian canon, began his enormously effective popularization of the liturgy in the early 1920's. Dom Gaspar Lefebvre of St. André is second only to Parsch in his work of popularization. Since World War II the liturgical movement has made remarkable progress in France, chiefly under the guidance of the Dominicans. In the last thirty years the liturgical apostolate has circled the globe and has become a leaven in varying degrees throughout the Catholic world. The encyclicals *Mystici Corporis* and *Mediator Dei*, issued in 1943 and 1947 respectively, evaluated and confirmed what had developed, while also giving warnings about excesses and dangers.

In the United States the first proponent of liturgical reform was the father of the American hierarchy, Archbishop John Carroll. He had views and ideas about bringing the people into closer contact with the official channels of God's life that make some attitudes today very conservative by comparison. As superior of the American missions, the future first ordinary in the United States wrote in 1787 to an English priest-friend, the Reverend Joseph Berington, the following plea for the liturgy in the vernacular:

I cannot help thinking that the alteration of the church discipline ought not only to be solicited, but insisted on as essential to the service of God and benefit of mankind. . . . The great part of our congregations must be utterly ignorant of the meaning and sense of the public offices of the Church. It may have been prudent, for aught I know, to refuse a compliance in this instance with the insulting and reproachful demands of the first reformers; but to continue the practice of the Latin Liturgy in the present state of things must be owing either to chimerical fears of innovation or to indolence and inattention in the first pastors of the national Churches in not joining to solicit or indeed ordain this necessary alteration.[7]

Appointed first Bishop of Baltimore in 1789, Carroll was soon beset with the problem of lay trusteeism, rivalries between national groups and many other difficulties; the result was that he never realized his cherished ideals. In the first synod of Carroll's diocese in 1791 only minor concessions to the vernacular were made. But in a statement of Carroll and his three suffragan bishops in 1810, permission to employ a maximum of English in administering the sacraments — except for the sacramental form itself — was clearly implied, although at the same time the prelates deplored abuses in the use of the vernacular.[8] After a study of Carroll's role in these matters, the Reverend John Tracy Ellis concluded that

had he lived in a more disciplined age, . . . Carroll would have been in the vanguard of any movement to bring the sublime offices of the Church closer to the faithful and to those outside the fold by having as much as possible of the liturgical service performed in a language which they fully understood.[9]

The Most Reverend Ambrose Maréchal, the Sulpician third Archbishop of Baltimore, and John England, first Bishop of Charleston, unknown to each other but at about the same time conceived the need of a vernacular missal for the laity. Despite his many labors England edited this missal, which was largely a reprint of the British missal, to which he added a valuable hundred-page explanation of the Mass and vespers. It was published in 1822 and almost got Bishop England in trouble with the Holy See. Authorities in Rome at first understood that Bishop England's missal was a translation rather than a reprint; they were also concerned about England's explanation, until assured of its orthodoxy upon investigation. In the preface he stated the purpose of the missal, "The object of the present publication is to instruct the members of the Roman Catholic Church on the nature of the most solemn act of their religion. . . . Many well-disposed members of other communions might be greatly benefited by its perusal." Bishop England went on to say that he generally found "non-Catholics not only uninformed of the Catholic doctrines, but having on their minds the most extraordinary and erroneous impressions as to the belief of the Roman Catholics."[10]

England emphasized the sacrificial character of the Mass, remarking also that it was an action. One looks in vain, however, for the idea of active participation by the laity. Further editions of England's missal appeared in 1843, 1861, 1865, and 1867.

Nevertheless, this missal did not prevent the introduction of numerous prayerbooks "at times hardly orthodox," to use the expression of the American hierarchy assembled for the Third Plenary Council of Baltimore in 1884. In the words of the bishops:

Our Catholic people have in their hands almost numberless prayerbooks, too often the work of unskillful writers and which seem more and more to depart from the genuine and sound standard of prayer as laid down by the holy Church in her Liturgy.[11]

How far Catholic piety had strayed from the primary source of the true Christian spirit and of the Church's life can be seen from this frank and revealing declaration of the same Council:

That many Catholics know next to nothing of the Church's standard and form of prayer is indeed most deplorable. Hence, now that in their craving for the things of this world, men find it so hard to realize things divine, it is for clergymen a grave obligation to explain clearly and accurately . . . the rites and prayers of the Church. The holy Council of Trent requests parish priests, and all who have the care of souls, often to explain what is read at Mass and especially to dwell on the Mysteries of the most holy Sacrifice, so that the faithful, who have also a share in the Sacrifice of the New Law offered through the priest's ministry, may derive therefrom greater grace and spiritual benefits. Likewise, in order that the faithful may receive the sacraments with greater respect and devotion, the same Council demands that parish priests explain to the people with skill and piety, in the vernacular, the effects and ceremonies of the sacraments. . . . It is evident how profitable it will be for the faithful to have at their disposal prayerbooks containing an accurate translation of prayers and rites carefully chosen from those of the missal, the breviary, and the ritual. . . . And thus the beauties of the sacred liturgy will be offered to the mind of the readers, as it were a garden of delight.

It is a well-known fact that most prayers used by the faithful are anything but literary, and even at times hardly orthodox . . . and so we ordain that the aforesaid prayerbook shall contain a careful revision of all the prayers, hymns, psalms and canticles that are of frequent public use in the Church.[12]

The bishops' words constituted a plea for a return to fundamentals and essentials, to the holy Sacrifice, the sacramental life of the Church, and the divine office. In the *Manual of Prayers*, ordered by the Council and published in 1889, Catholics of the United States had an official prayerbook second to none for content in the whole Catholic world. It was a combination missal-breviary-ritual compiled for lay use. The hierarchy had charted the way with great vision. But priests were apparently not prepared to follow. The use and multiplication of prayerbooks containing inferior prayers continued. Concerning this Council the Reverend Godfrey Diekmann, O.S.B., wrote in 1946:

One of the tragedies of the Church's history in this country is that the resulting prayerbook was not as generally accepted and promoted as was the catechism of the same council, and that its legislation about popularizing the chant was not obeyed. Compliance with the injunctions of the Council would have anticipated the great reforms of Pius X; would have meant a liturgical movement in America a quarter of a century before such a movement made itself felt in any other country.[13]

As late as 1915 Archbishop John Ireland of St. Paul, after asking John J. Wynne, S.J., to compile a Sunday Mass book from the Roman Missal, stated that "what America needs is prayerbooks." [14]

Antedating the general liturgical revival was the chant movement. Here, too, the bishops had pointed the way — but again for the most part were not followed. As early as the Second Plenary Council of Baltimore in 1866, they had ordered that "elements of Gregorian chant be taught and exercised in the parochial schools." The Council of 1884 not only repeated this order but gave a reason for it in words which anticipated Pius X by nineteen years:

. . . in order that the number of those able to sing the psalms well may constantly grow larger, until gradually at least the majority of the faithful may, according to the custom of the ancient Church, still observed in some places, learn to chant Vespers and other services in union with the ministers and the choir.[15]

Among the few who in this time strove to restore the liturgy to the people was a Paulist, Father Alfred Young, choir director at St. Paul's Church in New York. His articles on congregational singing in the *Catholic World* and other publications were written with a view to convincing the priests and laity of his time that the true ideal of Catholic worship includes congregational song to God. "That was a very simple truth," he wrote in 1891, "yet what a number of people had never looked at it in that light." [16]

With two articles in the *Ecclesiastical Review* [17] Professor W. F. Stockley described vividly the conditions in matters liturgical and in regard to sacred music prevailing in the English-speaking world at the time that Pius X issued his *motu proprio* in 1903. Stockley's description almost taxes one's belief and furnishes a new estimate and appreciation of the reforms initiated by the pontiff. In view of conditions depicted, and in the light of the slow response to the reforms called for by the Pope, Stockley would not seem to have exaggerated when he stated, "Let us say it out boldly (if we are ready to follow the Pope), that we English-speaking Catholics of the New World have probably, in thus following him, the most troublesome journey to make of any Catholics on earth." [18] To present a long litany of abuses in the field of Catholic church music which continued despite papal pleas for reform would be a simple task. Suffice it to mention one instance: as late as 1928 Dennis Cardinal O'Connell strongly forbade the singing of secular hymns at divine services, in particular "The Beautiful Isle of Somewhere," at Catholic funerals in predominantly Catholic Boston.[19]

Archbishop Henry Moehler of Cincinnati and Bishop Bernard J. McQuaid of Rochester were among the first American prelates to urge congregational singing. Archbishop James Blenk, S.M., of New Orleans gave evidence of even wider vision. His was an unusual grasp of the reform Pius X had inaugurated. For Blenk it was much more than a reform of Church music, as so many had understood it. He warned his flock in a pastoral letter of November 22, 1907:

Once more let us remind you of the importance of this reform which concerns not merely the exterior of worship, as is sometimes supposed, but the very quality of that worship itself. It concerns most intimately the reverence due to God in His chosen dwelling upon earth. . . . This is the beginning of a great movement in the Church, and one whose real trend we have so far failed to grasp. We have thought of it as a reform in art, important in its way, but more or less external, affecting details rather than principles. This is a great mistake. . . . The Holy Father is insisting upon the supernatural.[20]

A year after coming to the United States in 1873, Sir John Singenberger founded from St. Francis Seminary in Milwaukee the Amerikanischen Cäcilien-Verein and its organ *Caecilia*, whose masthead read: "Monatschrift für Katholische Kirchen-Musik." [21] In an organized effort to improve church music throughout the country the Society of St. Gregory of America was organized at St. Mary's Seminary in Baltimore in 1913,[22] and two years later there appeared the official organ of the society, the *Catholic Choirmaster*. Because of their narrow concern with sacred music apart from its liturgical framework, one does these two publications no injustice, as Gerald

Ellard, S.J., also noted in 1929, in denying them an important role in the genesis of an organized liturgical movement.[23]

Much more significant was the work of leaders like the Reverends Thomas E. Shields and John Young, S.J., Mrs. Justine B. Ward, and Mother Georgia Stevens, R.S.C.J. Enough has been said of Shields, except to reiterate that his Catholic Education Series and his *Philosophy of Education* were distinct steps forward.[24] Converted to the Catholic faith in 1904, Mrs. Ward soon realized that "the Church has never confined herself to the spoken word in her formation of the human soul" but rather appeals "to all the faculties of men in their interrelation." [25] Before the urgent pleas of Pius X in 1903, the second and third Plenary Councils of Baltimore had made it clear that the chant could be restored only by teaching it to children, and that the trained children today would become the singing congregations of tomorrow. To effect this plan Mother Stevens and Mrs. Ward in 1916 founded Pius X School of Liturgical Music at Manhattanville College of the Sacred Heart in New York to train chant teachers. By 1925 the school had trained 1300 instructors.[26]

Some years before Pius X issued his *motu proprio* of 1903, Father John Young, S.J., who was Mrs. Ward's first chant tutor, had been experimenting with teaching chant to children and men as choirmaster at St. Francis Xavier church in New York. Long before Pius X ascended the throne of Peter this farsighted Jesuit had hoped and prayed that some Pope would do for music what Leo XIII had done for philosophy. Young worked out a system whereby children could read Gregorian notation through numbers. This system, brought into line with the principles of Solesmes, combined with Shields' pedagogy and put into books by Mrs. Ward, became known as the "Ward Method." This method was widely used in the United States and is still popular in Europe today.

Eloquent witness to the success of the Pius X School and the Ward Method was the Gregorian Congress held in New York on June 1–3, 1920, during which vespers, compline and high Masses were sung congregationally, with lectures on various phases of the liturgy, plus exhibitions and meetings. After directing nearly 5,000 children singing at high Mass in St. Patrick's Cathedral, the great Dom André Mocquereau exclaimed enthusiastically, "I realized that my dream had come true, and that through the medium of the children of America the great heritage of congregational singing will be restored to the Church." [27] The *Catholic News* for June 5, 1920, headlined the story, "The Silence of the Catholic Church Broken after Centuries." Yet Mocquereau's elation was premature. The silence in churches would be broken only here and there. Nevertheless, progress continued, as evidenced by the more than 60,000 children singing a high Mass at Soldier's Field in Chicago at the twenty-eighth International Eucharistic Congress in 1926. Unfortunately Mrs. Ward's projected establishment of a chant school at the Catholic University of America in the early 1930's never materialized. After a building had been erected at Mrs. Ward's expense, the donor and school officials could not agree as to who would head the school.[28]

In so far as Gregorian chant is the musical language of the Church and as such is a part of her liturgy, the chant movement was certainly an important factor in the genesis of the liturgical movement. But at this point a few distinctions and qualifications need to be made. As Michel defined it, "The chant is primarily the sung prayer of the Church, and not first of all music or art."[29] And in the words of Justine B. Ward, "The music must pray, the prayer must sing."[30] Choirmasters, Dom Virgil believed, had too often concentrated exclusively on the music and overlooked the prayer. In many instances they had trained choirs in the manner of specialists, almost as if for concerts, to the exclusion of congregational participation. Yet Pius X had warned in no uncertain terms, "In general, it must be considered a very grave abuse when the liturgy in ecclesiastical functions is made to appear secondary to, and in a manner at the service of, the music, for the music is merely a part of the liturgy and its humble handmaid."[31]

For this reason Michel urged Mother Stevens and Mrs. Ward to add lectures on the liturgy to their courses in chant at Pius X. He actually gave the first lectures there in 1926. Such lectures became a regular feature at Pius X.

As late as 1937 Father Virgil had reason to complain that "most of the diocesan promoters of the chant movement in our country have so far not envisioned it as part and parcel of the liturgical movement and so have often missed what must be the true soul of all their endeavors."[32] Before leaving the subject of chant, it is worthy of mention that in 1936, to help along the cause of active participation, Father Michel compiled with the help of confreres Norbert Gertken and Mathias Ethen, a small booklet of Gregorian chant Masses, *Parish Kyriale*, which has sold almost 2,000,000 copies.

One of the characteristic endeavors of apostles of the liturgy has been to make the Church thoroughly understood by the faithful and then sincerely loved. This is why interest in and exploration of the doctrine of the Church as the Mystical Body of Christ figures so prominently in the history of the liturgical movement. In both *Mystici Corporis* and *Mediator Dei* Pius XII credits the liturgical revival with playing a major role in bringing this doctrine to the fore. That such an influence was operative also in the United States seems hardly open to doubt. But the liturgical apostolate met with considerable opposition, apathy, misunderstanding, and even suspicion when attempts were made to awaken in American Catholics a consciousness of the Church as the continuation of Christ through time. In clarifying by his writings the Church as the Mystical Body of Christ, Michel did some pioneer work for the English-speaking world. As a confrere and theologian wrote to him from Europe:

I feel that we of St. John's cannot be grateful enough to you for opening the riches of this doctrine to us; and the whole U.S. owes a similar debt to St. John's. If it were possible to isolate this doctrine from the liturgy, it seems to me that the liturgical movement would have been fully justified, if it had done nothing else but arouse Christian consciousness to this teaching.[33]

In 1936 Father Virgil predicted that "we are fast approaching the day when the concept of the Mystical Body of Christ will again be for us in fact the traditional concept of the Church."[34] But what were the conditions a decade earlier when the liturgical apostolate became an organized movement? In 1926, Dom Virgil recalled, the comparatively few promoters of the liturgy used to wonder: "When would Catholics generally become more vitally conscious of the sublime truth of the Mystical Body of Christ? How long before the phrase would again be current?"[35] He described the true state of things in a lucid exposition of the Mystical Body in the *Ecclesiastical Review* for February, 1930.[36] This article, the clearest explanation in the periodical literature of the English-speaking world up to that time, drew wide attention and was in line with the future *Mystici Corporis.*[37] After long study Michel wrote it in an attempt to remove confusion and suspicion from the minds of priests concerning the liturgical apostolate. After explaining the doctrine of the Mystical Body of Christ as the traditional concept of the Church and the need of emphasizing the forgotten inner spiritual nature of the Church rather than merely her juridical aspects, he stated, "Many today have never heard of it; and for many who have heard of it, it is not a doctrine but merely a scriptural figure of speech." [38] Today "Mystical Body" is almost a household term among American Catholics; and this is somewhat of an "era of the Mystical Body" in theological science. It was not always so. How and why the concept of the Church through the liturgy was lost to the general Catholic mind, received only passing attention in older theological manuals and hence was overlooked or not emphasized by seminary professors need not detain us here.[39]

As has been pointed out, in the middle of the nineteenth century Moehler and Scheeben had made attempts to redefine the integral nature of the Church. The definition of the Church as the Mystical Body of Christ was on the agenda for the unfinished Vatican Council of 1869–70. Leo XIII, who attended the Council as Bishop of Perugia, freely used Mystical Body ideas in a number of documents, especially toward the end of his reign. Pius X made the doctrine of Christ's Mystical Body the motto of his pontificate: "To bring all things to a head in Christ." Again and again Pius XI spoke of it in his encyclicals.[40]

The nature and extent of current interest and discussion of theological topics for any given period is best measured by the content of periodical literature. According to the Jesuit Father Bluett's survey and complete bibliography of thought on the Mystical Body for the years 1890–1940,[41] it was found that only eight articles appeared in the more important English, Irish and American periodicals before 1926, when *Orate Fratres* was founded. Specifically for the United States: the *Ecclesiastical Review* had one; the *Homiletic And Pastoral Review*, two; the *Catholic World*, four.

Going back a little further, one finds that the *Catholic Encyclopedia* of 1911 had a half column bearing the strange title "Mystical Body of the Church." [42] In Pallen and Wynne's *New Catholic Dictionary* of 1929, which was based on contemporary Catholic life, the Mystical Body was not even mentioned in defining the Church; a purely legal definition was given. Virgil Michel ended his critical review of this book by saying, "As a record of the views with which we have so far been satisfied, as a final summary of an age that is passing, we think the volume cannot be surpassed." [43] Referring to a novena he preached in 1939 on the Mystical Body, Father William Leonard, S.J., of Boston College stated that "in 1939 that idea was very new in this country, and under considerable suspicion." [44] "I recall having heard in more than one gathering of priests in recent years," Abbot Columban Thuis told his audience at the 1943 National Liturgical Week, "objections raised against even using the term 'Mystical Body.'" [45] And at the National Liturgical Week of 1951 Monsignor Reynold Hillenbrand recalled that a retreatmaster that summer had preached that too much was being said about the Mystical Body and too little about the Church.[46]

Apparently even in seminaries the Church was explained for the most part merely as a visible, juridic organization or society. The Reverend John Gruden in his *The Mystical Christ*, published in 1936 and hailed as a "pioneer book," remarked, "The object of this book is to fill in the incomplete picture of the Church presented by catechisms and ordinary classroom manuals of theology." [47] This may explain in part why many priests in seminaries before 1925 rarely heard the term emphasized.[48] Only some years after the inception of the liturgical movement did the best theological treatises on the Mystical Body begin to appear in English.[49] In fact, the first complete treatise in English was published in 1931. This was *The Mystical Body of Christ*, a translation by John J. Burke, C.S.P., of a French work by Abbé Anger. In the same year appeared Monsignor Canon Myers' little book with the same title, the nineteenth volume in The Treasury of the Faith Series.

There was need for a popular and inspirational book in the 1930's. Monsignor Fulton J. Sheen attempted to supply it in 1935 with his volume entitled *The Mystical Body of Christ*, in which, by the way, he stated that "occasionally one hears it said that the doctrine of the Mystical Body is 'dangerous' and 'novel'." [50] Michel wrote a lengthy, highly critical review of Sheen's work.[51]

Even after Pius XII issued his magnificent encyclical, *Mystici Corporis*, in which he said that "Mystical Body of Jesus Christ" is the best definition of the Church, the American Catholic press seemed not to have caught its significance, or if it did, hesitated to express it. The encyclical was published in *Osservatore Romano* for July 4, 1943. Only two half-columns of the seventeen and a half full-length closely printed columns dealt with condemned erroneous tendencies. Yet, the national *Register*, basing itself on a report by the NCWC news service, announced the encyclical with a ringing headline, "Pope Condemns Errors on Mystical Body." [52] In *Humani Generis*, issued in 1950, Pius XII had this to say after expounding the importance of encyclicals, "Some say they are not bound by the doctrine, explained in our encyclical of a few years ago, and based on the sources of revelation, which teaches that the Mystical Body of Christ and the Roman Catholic Church are one and the same thing." [53]

It was hardly surprising, therefore, that the proponents of the liturgical apostolate in the 1920's and later met with both opposition and suspicion in explaining the Church as the Mystical Body of Christ, even though they were but attempting to revive the Pauline doctrine of the Church obscured by anti-Gallican and anti-Protestant polemics. They felt vindicated, therefore, when they read these words in *Mystici Corporis*:

Some through empty fear look upon so profound a doctrine as something dangerous and so they fight shy of it as of the beautiful but forbidden fruit of paradise. It is not so. Mysteries revealed by God cannot be harmful to men. Nor should they remain as treasures hidden in a field, useless.[54]

Actually, the genesis and evolution of the organized liturgical movement may be understood only in the light of the previous history of the Catholic Church in the United States. The liturgical apostolate may be regarded as a maturing of Catholic life. For many years the Church was preoccupied with establishing herself and winning a place in American life, and this not without untold sacrifice, heroic labor, and considerable opposition. As already noted, no sooner was Carroll appointed first bishop in 1789 than the spectre of lay trusteeism, lasting until the 1850's, showed itself. Nativist challenges began in the late 1820's and persisted until the War between the States. The 1830's were particularly a time of hate and opposition for the Church, with Maria Monk stories, convent burnings, and books like Samuel Morse's *The Foreign Conspiracy*. After the War between the States there were the Ku Klux Klan, Freemasonry, the American Protective Association, the growing evils of an expanding industrialism, and political corruption. Socialism had begun to rear its ugly head. Finally, there were internal tensions associated with so-called "Cahenslyism."

As one examines the national pastorals of the American hierarchy, he sees the constant preoccupation of the bishops with the serious shortage of clergy and religious, consequent losses to the Faith, problems of education, anti-Catholic liberalism, anti-Catholic propaganda, and the myriad dangers to the flock in a hostile pagan or Protestant culture. Between 1829 and 1884 seven provincial and three plenary councils were held to retrieve losses to the Church, prevent others, regularize discipline, and to meet the growing problems of an expanding Church in a missionary country.

Starting with 25,000 Catholics in 1789, the American Church grew phenomenally: from twenty countries of Europe came 9,318,494 Catholic immigrants between the years 1820 and 1920.[55] Integrating, democratizing, and Americanizing the newcomers was a gigantic task. And the fact that the rapidly increasing numbers spoke various languages, came from different cultures and backgrounds, and had varying degrees of education complicated the enormous task of supplying their needs. Churches, schools, seminaries, and charitable institutions had to be built, staffs trained, funds solicited, and priests secured from Europe. Native vocations were always far too few, despite shortened seminary courses. In general, the Church was in the brick-and-mortar stage. She was suffering from growing pains, and her energies were spent in defending herself and safeguarding essentials against a better day.

Until 1890 the predominant immigrant groups were German and Irish. From these two nationalities the main core of American Catholicism had to be forged. Each brought distinctly different traditions. For almost four centuries the heroic Irish had suffered from English persecution. Before Catholic Emancipation in 1829, the penal laws had been in effect for more than three generations. The Irish were denied schools and churches, Mass was celebrated in barns, on rocks, or behind hedges — always in secret. Among the Irish, love of and devotion to the Mass was second to none, but external worship corporately and actively expressed, the beauties normally associated with the worshipping Christian community pouring forth its homage to God — in fact, the whole external expression of Christian worship, art, and culture — passed out of Irish history.[56] Naturally private devotions and prayers multiplied. Only in 1954 did Ireland have its first Liturgical Week. Commenting on the approaching thirty-first International Eucharistic Congress in Dublin for June, 1932, John LaFarge, S.J., saw for the Irish a "providential opportunity" to effect a healthy correlation between the traditional forms of worship and private devotions. He wrote:

No country, in proportion to the fervor of her Catholicism, has suffered more cruelly by the breaks with her Christian past than has Ireland. Moreover, her missionaries, in carrying the Faith to the New World, were dependent on what eighteenth-century or early nineteenth-century France and Italy could afford of a badly weakened tradition of Christian forms.[57]

The Paulist pioneer, Father Young, gave added insight into the situation when he remarked, "I have met with some Irish peasants who thought that singing in Church was only a Protestant custom. They had never in all their lives seen or heard of a high Mass or Vespers."[58] Beauduin made this interesting observation of Abbot Marmion's early youth in Ireland:

During the 1914 war Dom Marmion collected together in a country house of his native land some monks who had been expelled from Belgium. We can still remember the wonder caused by the solemn celebration of the liturgy: an aged priest had never attended the singing of Vespers, and told us how amazed he was; the office which he had been reciting every day for forty years was then intended to be chanted solemnly in choir! . . . Such were the religious surroundings at the end of the nineteenth century, at the time of the youth and religious formation of Dom Marmion. If Benedictine life [in Belgium] later revealed to him all the riches of the liturgy, there was nothing in the memories of his childhood to awaken in him the desire for a liturgical apostolate in the parishes, or to make him foresee the effectiveness of such an apostolate among the general populace.[59]

It does not seem too much to say that it was with a penal-age Catholicism that the Irish settled, for the most part, in our large eastern cities, where they were plagued with the problems of winning their economic, political, and religious freedom in an anti-Catholic atmosphere. The tenacity with which they retained their faith and their contribution to the Catholic Church in the United States are too well known to need comment.

On the other hand, the German immigrants, fleeing revolution, conscription, and the Kulturkampf, came with a larger liturgical inheritance than the Irish, although they, too, had much to learn and unlearn. In general, they were better educated than other immigrant groups. Hampered by language difficulties, they settled in colonies, chiefly in the Middle West, and quickly built parish units, especially schools. Soon a vigorous Catholic German press flourished.[60] The Germans arrived with a strong community consciousness, with traditions of congregational singing, parish societies and social action, as was evidenced by the pioneer social action organization in the United States, the German Catholic Central Verein, founded in Baltimore, in April, 1855. "Their parishes," wrote Colman J. Barry, O.S.B., "were models of order, efficiency, and pronounced liturgical emphasis."[61] Furthermore, the Germans had benefited from the leaven created by

Moehler, Scheeben, Thalhofer, Staudenmaier, Guéranger, and others, and a bit later, by the enormously popular Schott missal.[62] It was small wonder that high Mass and vespers were more common among them than among the Irish. The earlier availability of liturgical literature for German American Catholics continued to modern times. After World War I, German priests were reading Guardini, and a little later, authors like Kramp and Parsch.

In the past the liturgical movement has sometimes been thought of in the United States as a German movement. This is, of course, erroneous. It was chiefly on the basis of Beauduin's plan in Belgium that Michel organized the liturgical movement for the English-speaking world. Moreover, one of the finest statements of principles underlying the liturgical apostolate was a paper delivered by the Irish-American church historian, Thomas O'Gorman, to the World Parliament of Religious held in connection with Chicago's Columbian Exposition in 1893.[63] Nevertheless, the liturgical movement won its first and strongest response in the United States from German priests and German Catholics. The Central Verein was the first American organization to endorse it. Unfortunately, this led at times to false impressions among some. For instance, Sister Antonia McHugh, C.S.J., President of the College of St. Catherine in St. Paul from 1929 to 1937, thought of the movement — at least so one of her community described it — as "this whole commotion . . . doubtless of German origin, reminiscent of Cahenslyism. She accorded little consideration to the Gregorian Chant, whatever Pius X had to say." [64] So too some priests of the eastern United States have at times looked upon interest in the liturgy as "a midwestern fad," reportedly characterizing the annual National Liturgical Week as "a meeting of a bunch of Germans out in the Midwest." [65]

But there were other reasons for this early response to the liturgical revival on the part of the Germans. Some of their priests had brought from Europe a dawning appreciation of the liturgy. The first articles on the liturgy amounting to more than rubrical discussions appeared in German periodicals, like *Pastoral Blatt* of St. Louis.[66] *The* pioneer of the American liturgical movement was a zealous German, the Reverend Herman Untraut of the Diocese of La Crosse. Untraut had been trained in the seminary of Eichstätt, where he had acquired a keen appreciation of the liturgy from the liturgical scholar, Father Valentine Thalhofer. As early as the 1880's, as pastor of a farflung territory and later as a hospital chaplain at Marshfield, he was contributing articles on various phases of the liturgy to German weeklies and periodicals. In 1901 Untraut published a prayer and hymn book liturgically oriented, and in the early 1920's he lectured to nuns and introduced the dialog Mass. At his own expense he published in 1925 a 109-page booklet, *Die liturgische Bewegung*, a work which shows an amazing grasp and comprehensiveness of view for those times. But it sold only a few copies, and Untraut was like a voice crying in the wilderness. Not without reason did he call himself "a martyr of the liturgical movement." When Michel arrived on the scene, he urged the Wisconsin priest to continue his apostolate of liturgical writing for German publications.[67]

There were other German priests with Untraut's background and spirit,[68] foremost of whom was a monk of St. Meinrad's Abbey, Father Bede Maler, who saw the need of a liturgical movement long before it was formally organized. In 1891 Maler had introduced into this country the Priests' Eucharistic League and was largely responsible for the founding of its official monthly, *Emmanuel*. Maler also edited St. Meinrad's eucharistic monthly *Paradiesesfrüchte*, which bore the earlier title, *St. Benedikts-Panier*. This Benedictine monk, a versatile writer and theologian, had some excellent suggestions and timely warnings for Virgil Michel, who, however, could not agree with him entirely.[69] What is of interest here is that Maler wanted to start a kind of liturgical movement at St. Meinrad's years before Michel had come on the scene. Maler's letters give a vivid picture of conditions touching liturgical observance and appreciation in Benedictine abbeys at that time. In response to Michel's articles in *Der Wanderer*, Maler wrote Abbot Alcuin in German:

It gives me great joy to learn . . . that your venerable Fathers are willing to take into their hands the promotion of the liturgical movement. Nothing better could be promoted for our Catholic life today. More than thirty years ago I attempted repeatedly to work in this direction in *St. Benedikts-Panier* and in the *Paradiesesfrüchte*, and it also was my plan to work for it systematically, a plan which I could not realize since in 1903 I broke down, exhausted by work. I am sorry to say that it was not possible for me to exert any influence on my successors as editors of *Paradiesesfrüchte*; now the publications of St. Meinrad are sailing in different directions, although they are still carrying the Eucharistic flag as a kind of camouflage. But I am old and miserable and not able to do anything but nag and criticize *more senum*. . . . Nor do I like the publication of the Sisters in Conception with its sweet devotions and strange asceticism. For that reason I will rejoice with all my heart when once again our people, *ex fontibus Salvatoris*, are given strong food and not this sentimental sugar-bread of awful, lovely devotions; what they need is the *cibus solidus unionis cum Christo et Ecclesia*.[70]

Recalling the strong opposition encountered at the National Eucharistic Congress of the Priests' Eucharistic League in Washington in 1895, Maler correctly predicted opposition for the liturgical apostolate. Meanwhile the league had disappointed its founder for narrowly promoting only adoration of Christ present in the Blessed Sacrament, thus isolating it from the Mass as Eucharistic Sacrifice. There were also other reasons for his disappointment. He continued:

It should be the main task of the . . . League to work for the liturgical movement. But it seems to me that there exists little prospect of this since the general direction of the League in N.Y. allows itself to be influenced in other directions. If Bishop Schrembs can be won over for it, there might be more hope for cooperation. . . . I expect absolutely nothing in this direction and also in other respects from the Congress in Chicago. . . . I know that Archbishop Glennon favors the movement.[71]

The enthusiastic Theodore Maynard has said that "Benedictine Abbeys have been focal points for the dissemination of liturgical practices, which are always flourishing where the Benedictines have their strongholds." [72] But it is a statement that needs qualifications. In regard to the American Benedictines Maler remarked:

I do not know whether steps have already been taken in order to win superiors in the Swiss-American Benedictine Congregation to a systematic promotion of the liturgical movement. If so, one certainly has to await what position they will take towards it. But I want to warn you, after long experience, against too great expectations in this respect (except for the Abbot of Subiaco, whom I do not know). . . . It would be nice if all the abbeys in the U.S. would unanimously participate in this work. But I have no such hope. As long as the Little Flower and St. Rita devotions and other private devotions, customs, observances, and litanies play the main role in our abbeys, the *Opus Dei* will necessarily remain unimportant (*nebensachen*).[73]

Obviously the liturgical mentality and observance in the Benedictine abbeys of the United States left much to be desired. It is a story that has not yet been told, and this is not the place to tell it. Maler's description, moreover, will surprise only those who forget that the monks had first come to this country in the 1840's, before the liturgical awakening in Europe and that thereafter they were overwhelmed with parish and mission work among German Catholic immigrants. Albert Kleber, O.S.B., wrote in his *History of St. Meinrad's Arch-abbey, 1854–1954* that "the daily life in a well-ordered Benedictine monastery is a constant liturgical movement in the best sense of the word." [74] This statement, however, would seem to demand some modification for the early days in terms of what Bede Maler had to say. In this connection it is of interest to note here that Abbot Deutsch contacted the abbots of the two congregations of Benedictines in an effort to win support for the liturgical cause. As far as could be determined, the abbots were cool to the proposition, with the exception of one or two.[75] Even Benedictine communities had to be awakened. And the next twenty-five years would slowly bring many changes in liturgical observance and a new appreciation of the liturgical life in most of the Benedictine houses of this country.

Meanwhile in the Church at large the process of spiritual matura-tion was steadily developing. On the hundredth anniversary of the founding of the American hierarchy in November, 1889, there were seventy-five dioceses. During the years 1907–1912 the monumental *Catholic Encyclopedia* appeared, the missionary status of the Church in the United States ended in 1908, and in 1911 Pius X appointed three American cardinals. By 1919, when the now famous *Bishops' Program of Social Reconstruction* was published, there were 100 flourishing dioceses. With twenty million adherents to the Faith, one-sixth of the nation was Catholic. The era of large-scale immigra-tion had ended, and the Church in the United States was coming of age.

"The issue between truth and error with regard to all that religion implies is now quite clearly drawn," the bishops had declared in their pastoral of September, 1919. With larger freedom from external interference the Church need no longer be on the defensive, apolo-getic, engaged and preoccupied with points of controversy. She could look upon herself, not as her enemies saw and hated her, that is, as a power structure merely teaching and ruling with an iron hand. Rather, she could gaze into her noblest and truest spiritual self, as the *Ecclesia orans*, living the life of Christ in His Mystical Body, active in all its parts and unceasingly leavening society. As John Cantwell, Bishop of Los Angeles, wrote Virgil Michel shortly after the founding of *Orate Fratres*, "It is a good sign of the times to see our priests specializing in matters that, in the rush of material construction, were overlooked." [76]

A far-visioned social program of action had been boldly outlined by the hierarchy. But did not this presuppose a new sense of Christian solidarity, a Christian social mentality, and communal piety to open minds to social needs and inspire wills to carry out the suggested social remedies and programs of action? Once before, in the Councils of Baltimore, the bishops had called for a return to the source of such a Christian mentality and piety. With these words, in 1919, they would do so again:

> And we therefore desire to impress upon parents, teachers, and pastors the importance and necessity of explaining to those in their charge, the origin, nature and value of the Holy Sacrifice, the meaning of the sacred rites with which it is offered, and the order of the liturgy as it advances from season to season. There is so much beauty in the worship of the Church, so much power to fill the mind with great thoughts and lift up the heart to heavenly things, that one who hears Mass with intelligent devotion cannot but feel in his soul an impulse to holier living.[77]

Would they be heeded this time?

The next five years would bring a pronounced liturgical awakening, an organized attempt at a spiritual renaissance, a liturgical movement. But from what did it move and what were the conditions that made such a spiritual renaissance necessary? To present the prevailing American Catholic attitudes toward the liturgical movement in the years immediately preceding 1926 is somewhat difficult. One may easily be accused of exaggeration. Human memory is too short and fallible to prevent persons living today from taking for granted what did not exist a generation ago. It was seen how the full concept of the Church as the Body of Christ was more or less overlooked in the ordinary theological seminary manuals, catechisms, and prayerbooks, even though that concept ran like a core-idea through all the liturgical books. And these pages have also given a glimpse into Benedictine abbeys and noted the development and shortcomings of the chant movement.

As one examines, for instance, the *Ecclesiastical Review*, the *Homiletic And Pastoral Review*, and the *Acolyte* for the five years preceding 1926, he finds practically no articles on the liturgy as generally understood today. Where such articles appear, or where the term "liturgy" is used, it is a question of rubrics, or at best, of the externals of ceremony. The idea of active participation by the laity seemed almost completely novel, except in a few contributions on congregational singing.[78] One looks in vain for the idea of the laity's share in the priesthood of Christ. By March, 1925, the *Ecclesiastical Review* had declined to publish original liturgical articles by the well known European writer of those times, Father Joseph Kramp, S.J. The *Homiletic And Pastoral Review* had ignored the offer, while the *Acolyte* had also refused any further "liturgical contributors," preferring somewhat later the largely rubrical treatises of "Peregrinus Gasolinus."[79] For two years the *Ecclesiastical Review* denied Michel access to its pages to explain the liturgical apostolate, and the *Homiletic And Pastoral Review* never granted him a page. In a few seminaries, where the course in the liturgy was for the most part a course on rubrics, *Orate Fratres* was at first forbidden reading. Priests in the seminary had studied "liturgy" from the celebrated volume by Innocent Wapelhorst, O.F.M., who had entitled his book dealing primarily with rubrics and ceremonial *Compendium sacrae liturgiae*.[80] So "liturgy" meant rubrics — and priests felt they already had enough of these.

The Liturgical Press of St. John's Abbey was established partly because no publishing house would risk the publication of popular treatises on the liturgy. After negotiating with several firms, Michel informed Father Busch:

Regarding publication, I had put out a feeler to the Extension Press, whose refusal was so absolute as to preclude any further negotiations. Between us: the total absence of any understanding of our pet ideas was astonishing to me. All the more need for us to get busy, eh?[81]

Dom Virgil had his eyes even more widely opened to the true situation in the summer of 1926 while lecturing to the nuns, priests, and laity at Pius X School in New York. Reflecting his experience in New York, he wrote Abbot Alcuin:

The audience I have is not very large, but it is really appreciative and therefore an inspiration. I am realizing more and more how utterly ignorant people are of the proper viewpoint in regard to the liturgy. Surely, in our Review, we shall hardly be able to become simple enough — SICUT PARVULI ought to be our motto.[82]

If today many priests still think of the liturgy as mere sanctuary etiquette, and of the liturgical movement as preoccupation with a sterile estheticism (with which the "practical priest" cannot disturb himself) rather than with the theology of the Mass and sacraments applied and exploited in daily Christian living, it is not difficult to picture the situation in 1925. One of Michel's closest friends, later the head of a large religious order, regretted that he was leaving the field of philosophy for what he termed "rubrics." He wrote, "You need not fear that I shall follow your bad example and go in for liturgy — two things I abominate and a third my soul despises — canon law and liturgy, and again liturgy." Obviously this man did not undervalue the Mass and sacraments, for Father Virgil, in answering him anonymously in an editorial later, called him "a really zealous and pious priest," but characterized him as the victim of a faulty conception of the Church, and hence also of the liturgy and canon law.[83] One of the original associate editors of *Orate Fratres* sent Michel this warning:

In December 1925 I spoke to the Apostolic Delegate in connection with the translation of Fr. Kramp's book. He was an interested listener, and did not seem to know where the impulse of the liturgical movement in this country was coming from. He warned me against such outward things as exaggerated "Gothic" vestments. This for your information.[84]

No doubt insights such as these caused Father Virgil to warn his collaborators that the fruit of their labors might show itself only in the next generation. "The future did not look very hopeful from the human standpoint," he reminisced later. "Even the word 'liturgy' was not quite understood by the generality of Catholics, educated and uneducated alike, although Webster's *New International*, e.g., was most explicit and orthodox in its definition." [85] By Michel's own admission the liturgy was at that time "looked upon as the 'pious sport' of some enthusiasts." [86]

In his encyclical on the liturgy, *Mediator Dei*, Pius XII stated that "the most pressing duty of Christians is to live the liturgical life. . . . The Mass is the chief act of divine worship; it should also be the source and center of Christian piety." [87] Michel frequently complained that the Mass was the great unknown for millions of Catholics. Sermons on the Mass in 1925, he recalled later, "were almost unheard of, and especially whole series of sermons preached from the same pulpit." [88] Today there are millions of missals in use, whereas in 1925 the vernacular missal was little used by the laity.[89] When the officials of the E. M. Lohmann Company of St. Paul approached

Archbishop Austin Dowling in 1925 as to his views concerning their securing the American agency for the sale of the *St. Andrew Daily Missal*, the archbishop was said to have

discouraged us from taking it over, mentioning that although it was a very fine thing and should be encouraged, the time was not ripe for it yet. He stated that a missal was a fine book for a priest or a nun, but it was expecting just too much of the laity to have them use a missal.[90]

Lohmann's sold 4,826 copies the following year, 12,800 in 1927 and then, as the liturgical movement progressed, the number rose by 1952 to a total for all years of "several million copies," according to the company. Today there are nineteen editions of English daily missals available in the United States.

According to the Michel Papers, Communion received outside Mass without an adequate reason and contrary to both the ritual and canon law was rather common in the 1920's. This practice was a clear indication of faulty understanding of the true nature of the Mass as sacrificial Eucharistic worship. But this could only have been the fruit of faulty teaching. For this was a time when the Prisoner-in-the-Tabernacle mentality was common. Let the reader examine Father Paul Bussard's critical analysis of how the Mass was taught in the most frequently used texts of the 1920's and early 1930's.[91] He will note the outlandish allegorical explanations of the Mass and the glaring lack of that difficult to define but important thing that Michel so often called "a liturgical sense." Bussard showed that in these texts sometimes only the external ceremonies were explained; that the idea of self-oblation at Mass was nearly always missing, and where mentioned, it was inadequately explained; that the text of the Mass was not even mentioned at times; that the celebrant's moving from the epistle to the gospel side at the altar represented Christ's passage from Pilate to Herod, while the kiss of peace at the Solemn High Mass symbolized Judas kissing Christ, and so on. Thus Bussard concluded: "Schools have been employing very inadequate instruments to teach the Mass and the use of the missal. This has probably been made necessary simply because there was no book which could even pretend to be adequate until quite recently. Of all the books which are actually being used today only three or four could merit approval even from generous critics." [92]

One final point should be mentioned to indicate the temper of the times out of which the liturgical apostolate emerged. In 1905 Pius X had decreed that the "faithful should be invited to partake of the sacred Banquet as often as possible, even daily." In 1910 Catholics the world over raised eyebrows when the holy pontiff lowered the age for reception of first Communion from the usual twelve or thirteen to the age when reason dawns. How long was it before pastors in the United States accepted the papal directive? It would be difficult to say exactly, but from all indications there was much neglect. For instance, Father Fidelis Busam, O.S.B., of St. Vincent Archabbey, complained in a letter to Michel on December 14, 1926, that "there are not many pastors who observe the decree of Pius X on frequent and daily Communion." Another pastor stated as late as 1929: I almost had to defend myself with a gun because I introduced the custom of taking the little ones to First Communion at the age set down in the decree of Pius X. I was besieged on all sides with arguments about the incapability of these little ones to understand what it was all about, not to say anything about their being capable of learning sufficient catechism.[93]

Such in general was the situation in regard to the liturgy in the United States down to the mid-1920's. What, then, could be done about it? The following chapters will attempt to show.

NOTES TO CHAPTER 4

[1] A few histories of the liturgical movement, covering various phases and periods, are available: Waldemar Trapp, *Vorgeschichte der liturgische Bewegung* (Würzburg: Richard Mayr, 1939). Dom Olivier Rousseau, *The Progress of the Liturgy*, trans. Benedictines of Westminster Priory (Westminster: Newman, 1951). Theodor Bogler, O.S.B., *Liturgische Erneurung in aller Welt* (Maria Laach: Verlag Ars Liturgica, 1950) is a comprehensive survey by twenty-one authors giving the present status of the movement in their respective countries. H. A. Reinhold contributed the account of the movement in the United States. Louis Bouyer, *Liturgical Piety* (Notre Dame: University of Notre Dame Press, 1955), is perhaps the best critique of the liturgical apostolate to date.

[2] E.g., Michel, "Liturgy and Catholic Life," pp. 8–12; Apostolate, *OF*, III (1929), 121–123. Gerald Ellard, S.J., "Die liturgische Bewegung in der Vereinigten Staaten," *Stimmen der Zeit*, CXVII (1929), 201–209.

[3] Cf. Dunstan Tucker, O.S.B., "The Council of Trent, Guéranger and Pius X," *OF*, X (1936), 538–544.

[4] Bouyer, *op. cit.*, 52–58, *passim*; Damasus Winzen, O.S.B., believes Bouyer is unduly critical of Guéranger's limitations ("Guéranger and The Liturgical Movement," *American Benedictine Review*, VI [1955–56], 419–426).

[5] Cf. Bernard Capelle, O.S.B., "The Liturgical Movement in Belgium among the Walloons," *OF*, V (1930), 376.

[6] A. Bugnini, C.M., editor of the foremost liturgical periodical, *Ephemerides Liturgicae*, made a study of papal documents promoting the liturgical revival from 1903 to 1953 in *Documenta Pontificia ad Instaurationem Liturgicam* (Rome: Edizioni Liturgiche, 1953). There were ten documents issued by Pius X, four by Benedict XV, twelve by Pius XI, thirty-one by Pius XII — a total of fifty-seven.

[7] Archives of the Archdiocese of Baltimore, Special C, C-1, Baltimore (1787), copy, as quoted by John Tracy Ellis, "Archbishop Carroll and the Liturgy in the Vernacular," *Worship*, XXVI (1952), 547–548.

[8] Peter Guilday, *Life and Times of John Carroll, Archbishop of Baltimore 1735–1815* (New York: Encyclopedia Press, 1922), II, 552.

[9] *Op. cit.*, p. 552.

[10] *The Roman Missal Translated into the English Language for the Use of the Laity* (Philadelphia: Eugene Cummiskey, 1843), iii. The editions of 1822 and 1843 are in the Mullen Library of the Catholic University of America. On England's missal, cf. Guilday, *The Life and Times of John England* (New York: America Press, 1922), I, 328–333. Paul Bussard, in *The Vernacular Missal in Religious Education* (Washington: Catholic University of America, 1937), pp. 1–39, has a valuable history of the vernacular missal.

[11] *Acta et Decreta Concilii Plenarii Baltimorensis* (Baltimore: John Murphy Co., 1886), n. 22, p. 120.

[12] *Ibid.*, n. 221–222, pp. 120–122. Cf. Busch, "The Voice of a Plenary Council," *OF*, XXI (1947), 452–458.

[13] "Lay Participation in the Liturgy of the Church," in *A Symposium on the Life of Pope Pius X* (Washington: Confraternity of Christian Doctrine, 1946), p. 147.

[14] Wynne complied and produced *The Mass* (New York: Home Press, 1915); the following year he and Edward A. Pace arranged and translated into English the Roman Missal under the title, *The Mass Every Day in the Year* (New York: Home Press, 1916). One should here also call attention to the missals in various forms (e.g. *The New Missal in English* and *The New Missal for Every Day* [New York: Benziger, 1916 and 1924]) compiled by F. X. Lasance. Besides the Mass texts, Lasance's "missals" also included many devotional specialties. Cf. Peter Moran, "Orate Fratres," *Commonweal*, III (1925), 103. The present writer was unable to trace the first publication of Benziger Brothers' *The Roman Missal* "adapted to the use of the laity from the *Missale Romanum*" . . . with appendices for English-speaking countries . . . and [with] a collection of prayers." The fifteenth edition appeared in 1910.

[15] *Acta et Decreta*, n. 119, p. 61.

[16] "On Congregational Singing," *Northwestern Chronicle*, April 17, 1891. Cf. Young's articles in *Catholic World*, "Church Music," X (1869–70), 402–413; 598–610; 743–754.

[17] "The Pope and the Reform of Church Music," XXX (1904), 279–292; 383–401.

[18] *Ibid.*, p. 279.

[19] Cf. Apostolate, *OF*, II (1928), 96.

[20] As quoted in Apostolate, *OF* (1929), 287–288.

[21] *Caecilia* eventually became an English periodical. Singenberger belonged to the Wagner School of Ratisbon. The sacred music he fostered was "churchly" and a kind of forerunner of the official chant. In 1954 the *Gregorian Review*, published by the Gregorian Institute of America (Toledo) and dedicated to "Studies in Chant and Liturgy," made its appearance.

[22] Prime movers in founding the society were the Rev. Leo Manzetti, the Rev. John Petter and Nicola A. Montani. J. Vincent Higginson summarized the history and purpose of the society in "The History of

the St. Gregory Society," *Catholic Choirmaster*, XXVI (1940), 57–59; 160–163. Gregory Huegle was the earliest Benedictine pioneer in the chant movement, giving a chant course for priests and Sisters with his confreres at Conception Abbey as early as the summer of 1906. Another pioneer, Vincent Donovan, O.P., had been associated with Pius X School since 1918. The Rev. Edgar Boyle was the pioneer on the west coast, heading San Francisco's Archdiocesan Music Institute, begun about 1925. John LaFarge, S.J., also had an early interest in the chant: cf. *The Manner Is Ordinary* (New York: Harcourt, Brace and Co., 1954), pp. 171–174, 289.

[23] Ellard, *op. cit.*, p. 203.

[24] On May 10, 1925, Ward wrote to Michel from Sablé, France: "All that you write of the awakening of interest in the Liturgy in America and of the approval of your Father Abbot of the beautiful plan for a 'Popular Liturgical Library' fills me with joy. I often think of what Rev. Dr. Shields said to me a few months before his death: 'We are all taking part in a movement that is much greater than any individual and is more far reaching than we imagine; it has all the characteristics of the great epoch-making movements in the Church.' I wish he could have lived to have seen the realization of your plan, but I know that he must be helping us from the other world."

[25] Ward, "Winged Words," *OF*, I (1927), 109. Mother Stevens, with whom Michel had a continuous correspondence, distributed 10,000 reprints of this article. She was also instrumental in distributing hundreds of sample copies of *Orate Fratres* and circulars and generously donated to Michel her official mailing list.

[26] The first convent to comply wholeheartedly with the *motu proprio* of 1903 was that of the Servants of the Immaculate Heart of Mary in Scranton. When their Marywood College began in 1915, it was the very first to include the study of sacred music for all students. Among the first of many chant experts teaching at the convent was the pioneer and ardent promoter of the Gregorian restoration in the Diocese of Rochester, Father John Petter.

[27] As quoted from the New York *Times* in J. Vincent Higginson, *op. cit.*, p. 159. For the Jesuit Young's work, cf. Ward, "Father J. B. Young, S.J.," *Catholic Choirmaster*, X (1924), 120–124.

[28] "I was sorry to hear of the end of the foundation at the Catholic University; I really do not see why the condition you have placed could not be complied with" (Michel to Ward, Collegeville, April 12, 1930, copy).

[29] "The Chant of the Church," *OF*, XI (1937), 363. "Christians, whole congregations are plodding along in the old rut as if Pius X, not to mention the present Holy Father, had never spoken" (*idem*). Cf. also "Modernism and the Chant," *OF* (1937), 463–465. In 1954 LaFarge wrote of "the vast *cultural* treasure of the Church's liturgical music; . . . The treasure is easily available and not over-mysterious; yet even to university-bred Catholics, it is practically a sealed book, many hardly knowing of its existence" (*op. cit.*, p. 173).

30 "The Reform of Church Music," *Atlantic Monthly*, XCVII (1906), 455.

31 *Op cit.*, p. 338.

32 "Liturgy and Catholic Life," p. 28.

33 Gregory Roettger, O.S.B., to Michel, Beuron, Aug. 16, 1936. Attention is called to the writings of Abbot Anscar Vonier, especially of his *A Key to the Doctrine of the Eucharist* (1925), which mentions the term five or six times.

34 "Natural and Supernatural Society," *OF*, X (1936), 293.

35 "Nine Years After," *OF*, X (1935), 2.

36 Cf. "The True Christian Spirit," *Ecclesiastical Review*, LXXXII (1930), 128–142. Thousands of reprints of this article were scattered throughout the country and used in study clubs. Francis Connell, C.SS.R., "Dogmatic Theology in the Ecclesiastical Review: 1889–1949," *Ecclesiastical Review*, CXXI (1949), 319, overlooked Michel's article in proclaiming " 'Mystical Body of Christ' and 'Catholic Church' Exactly Coëxtensive," by Joseph Bluett, S.J., in the same review, CIII (1940), 305–328, as the first article in line with *Mystici Corporis*. It seems that much of what impressed Bluett in the latter encyclical was already anticipated by Michel sixteen years earlier, in the article cited above. Cf. Bluett, "Theological Significance of the Encyclical 'Mystici Corporis'," Catholic Theological Society of America: *Proceedings* (1946), 46–60. For Michel's writings on Mystical Body, cf. first section of his bibliography.

37 In his later writings, however, Michel hesitated to declare himself on the relationship between the Mystical Body and the Communion of Saints. E.g.: "The doctrine of the Mystical Body is intimately connected with that of the Communion of Saints. In fact, exposition of the identity, or of the difference if any, between these two doctrines is but one of the many points in which the liturgical movement will result in doctrinal elucidation and clarification at some future time" ("Natural and Supernatural Society," *OF*, X [1936], 293); *Our Life in Christ*, pp. 55–58. Later he seems to have disagreed with John Gruden's identifying the Mystical Body with the Church militant, in the latter's book, *The Mystical Christ* (St. Louis: Herder, 1936). When the book appeared, Michel congratulated his friend. Gruden answered: "I deeply appreciate your words of congratulation. Coming as they do from one who has done pioneer work in this field of theology, they are very encouraging. There are certain points on which we disagree, but I am sure there is perfect harmony in realizing the need of preaching this doctrine in season and out of season" (St. Paul, Feb. 13, 1937). Most theologians now say that Pius XII settled (as Michel had predicted) the matter in *Mystici Corporis* and *Humani Generis* in favor of restricting the term Mystical Body to the Roman Catholic Church, although there is by no means total agreement as to some of the further ramifications.

38 "The True Christian Spirit," p. 131.

39 For an answer to this question and a short historical review of the

theology of the Church, cf. Gruden, *op. cit.*, 1–26; cf. also Emile Mersch, S.J., *The Whole Christ* (Milwaukee: Bruce, 1938), pp. 470f.

[40] Ellard traced the revival of the Mystical Body idea in theological manuals, encyclicals, and popular ascetical works in "The Liturgical Movement: In and For America," *Thought*, VII (1932), 475–479; cf. also his *The Mystical Body and the American Bishops* (St. Louis: Queens Work, 1939), pp. 22–23, and Gruden, *op. cit.*, 18–26, 325–326.

[41] "The Mystical Body of Christ: 1890–1940, A Bibliography," *Theological Studies*, III (1942), 262–289. Of some eighty-five articles, about twenty-five appeared in *Orate Fratres*; the content of this periodical, of course, presupposed the doctrine from the beginning.

[42] X, 663.

[43] *OF*, IV (1930), 239; cf. whole review for prevalent attitudes and conditions and for efforts to change them. While in New York in the summer of 1926, Michel had induced Wynne to include popular articles on the liturgy in the volumes of the Universal Knowledge Foundation and submitted seven such articles, four written by himself: in the two volumes that appeared the articles accepted for publication are mysteriously missing (cf. Wynne-Michel letters).

[44] "It Takes a While," *Action Now*, VIII (1955), 26. On the other hand, Ellard in his *Christian Life and Worship* (Milwaukee: Bruce, 1933), p. xiv, stated that some forty Catholic colleges and universities in the United States had introduced courses dealing with the Mystical Body or corporate worship or both. Another reason why the term "Mystical Body" was slow of acceptance may have been that some bandied the phrase about without understanding it and without applying it to their spiritual life, as Michel had occasion to regret in print. For more on opposition to, misunderstanding and evolution of, the Mystical Body doctrine, cf. the following: *OF*, V (1931), 430–431; VIII (1934), 305, 466, 525; X (1936), 94, 381–382, 491–421; XI (1936–37) 42–43, 183. "Liturgy and Catholic Life," pp. 40, 56. *Commonweal*, XXXIX (1944), 323–326. *Month*, CLIX (1932), 289–297. *Blackfriars* XIII (1932), 618–624.

[45] Discussion, National Liturgical Week: *Proceedings* (1943), 14.

[46] "The Priesthood and the World," National Liturgical Week: *Proceedings* (1951), 163.

[47] P. 15.

[48] This may be hard to verify; yet more than ten priests in the proper age group whom the writer questioned attested to it. A priest ordained almost fifty years was asked in 1952 what he had heard of the Mystical Body in his seminary days. The reply: "Mystical Body? Why, not even the Pope then knew there was a Mystical Body." Cf. the frank admission of a former professor of theology in Apostolate, *OF*, XI (1937), 138; also Busch, "Past, Present, Future," *OF*, XXV (1951), 485–487.

[49] E.g. Mersch, S.J., *The Whole Christ* (Milwaukee: Bruce, 1938); cf. footnote 40 and "100 Helpful Books," *Mediator*, I (1950), 4. Robert Hugh Benson, *Christ in the Church* (5th ed.; St. Louis: Herder, 1911)

seems to have been the first popular book in English with a good treatment of the doctrine of the Mystical Body.

[50] (New York: Sheed and Ward, 1935), p. 233.

[51] *OF*, X (1936), 285. Michel said later that he was so critical of the book because he was afraid theologians would condemn it and with it the liturgical movement, which had been propagating an understanding of the Mystical Body doctrine for a decade.

[52] July 11, 1943. The headline touched off a brief editorial skirmish between the editors of the *Register* and *Orate Fratres*. Cf. Apostolate, *OF*, XVIII (1944), 325.

[53] *AAS*, XLII (1950), 571.

[54] *Ibid.*, XXXV (1943), 197.

[55] Cf. Colman J. Barry, O.S.B., *The Catholic Church and German Americans* (Milwaukee: Bruce, 1953), p. 6, for two tables giving comparative statistics on immigration.

[56] Cf. Archbishop Richard J. Cushing, "Address of Welcome," National Liturgical Week: *Proceedings* (1948), pp. 1–5. J.J. Murphy, "A Call for Irish-American Honest Self-Appraisal," *Homiletic And Pastoral Review*, LIV (1954), 509–513. Stockley, *op. cit.* Theodore Maynard, *The Catholic Church and the American Idea* (New York: Appleton-Century-Crofts, 1953), pp. 132–133. Busch, "The Liturgical Movement," National Catholic Education Association: *Proceedings*, XXII (1925), 671. Thomas McDonagh, "Abbot Marmion and Glenstal," in *More About Dom Marmion*, eds. Monks of Glenstal (Westminster: Newman, 1948), pp. 129–134. Desmond Fennell, "Continental and Oceanic Catholicism," *America*, XCII (1955), 669–671. Joseph H. McMahon, "The Liturgy — Inspiration of Catholic Action," *Catholic Choirmaster*, XXIII (1937), 115–116. Donnchadh Ó Floinn, "The Integral Irish Tradition," *Furrow*, V (1954), 756–768, partially reprinted in *Worship*, XXIX (1955), 135–139, has a remarkable statement on early Irish liturgical life and tradition lost in the days of persecution.

[57] "With Scrip and Staff," *America*, XLIV (1931), 555.

[58] *Northwestern Chronicle*, Apr. 17, 1891.

[59] "Dom Marmion and the Liturgy," in *More About Dom Marmion*, eds. monks of Glenstal (Westminster: Newman, 1948), 67. The Benedictines returned permanently to Ireland only in 1927.

[60] Cf. Barry, *op. cit.*, pp. 36–37, 276, *passim.* A project of the Mullen Library at the Catholic University of America is currently gathering data on this early German Catholic periodical literature.

[61] *Ibid.*, p. 272.

[62] Cf. Rousseau, *op. cit.*, pp. 81, 100, 111. Ludwig Eisenhofer's *Handbuch Der Katholischer Liturgik* (2 vols.; Freiburg: Herder, 1932), was a revision of Thalhofer's earlier work, circulated among German priests in the United States as early as 1924.

[63] "Worship and Grace in Religion," *OF*, XX (1946), 495–502. Of the twelve founding associate editors of *Orate Fratres*, five were Irish, four, German. Father Edwin Ryan, of St. Joseph's Seminary, Dunwoodie, was

the first to call for a greater emphasis on the liturgy in seminaries in a paper, "The Teaching of Liturgy in the Seminary," given to the seminary section of the National Catholic Education Association: *Proceedings*, XVII (1920), 558–566. While Ryan's understanding was far in advance of that of his contemporaries, it was marred to some degree by an un-healthy rubricism and estheticism; cf. his definition of liturgy, p. 558, and also *Catholic News,* January 31, 1920.

64 Sister Helen Angela Hurley, C.S.J., *On Good Ground* (Minneapolis: University of Minnesota Press, 1951), 261. However it should be noted that while both were still students at Louvain, Michel invited Sister Jeanne Marie Bonnett, C.S.J. of the College of St. Catherine, to act as associate editor and subsequently sent her a prospectus of the coming *Orate Fratres*; she declined the editorship; "I received with great interest the prospectus. . . . Our Dean, Sr. Antonia, is wholly in sympathy with your under-taking, but feels that my duties as a teacher must occupy all my time (Sis-ter Jeanne Marie to Michel, St. Paul, Feb. 5, 1926). Subsequent letters show that the Sisters taught both the missal and the liturgy in their religion classes.

65 Murphy, *op. cit.*, p. 512. There is abundant evidence in the Michel Papers for such attitudes.

66 Cf., e.g., Chrysostomus Schmid, O.S.B., "Liturgie und Heiden-mission," Ildefons Herwegen, O.S.B., "Missa recitata," Joseph Löw, C.SS.R., "Der Kernpunkt der liturgischen Bewegung nach römischer Auf-fassung," *Pastoral Blatt*, LVII (1923), 55–58, 75–77, 139–142 respectively. Cf. also, (anonymous) "Liturgical Revival in France," *Catholic Choir-master*, VII (1921), 116–117; C. L. Dessoulavy, "Liturgical Worship," *ibid.*, VI (1920), 106–111.

67 Untraut's booklet, a collection of thirty-four newspaper reprints, carries the subtitle, "Ein Beitrag zu ihrer besseren Wuerdigung." For an appraisal of his work, cf. Bernard Laukemper, "Father Untraut, The Midwestern Pioneer," *OF*, XV (1941), 565–567. By 1927 Untraut had written ten articles for *Der Wanderer* of St. Paul, fifteen for *Excelsior* of Milwaukee, and "some" for *Der Ohio Waisenfreund* of Columbus (Un-traut to Michel, Jan. 18, 19, 22, 1927).

68 E.g., Fidelis Busam, O.S.B., of St. Vincent's Archabbey had written "monthly articles for several years for *Die Christliche Mutter"* (New York) to explain the Mass (Busam to Michel, Latrobe, Dec. 14, 1926). Others were the priests Holweck and Huelsman of St. Louis, Jasper and Hellriegel of O'Fallon, Laukemper of Chicago, to mention a few.

69 The somewhat eccentric Maler had a peculiar prejudice against the dialog Mass, and because the liturgical movement recommended it, it could not but "miscarry"; and strangely enough, he did not believe that sufficient subject matter could be found for a monthly magazine on the liturgy; Michel answered that the liturgy was an inexhaustible source of inspiration for liturgical writing. Michel feared his imprudence (Hellrie-gel to Michel, O'Fallon, Aug. 22, Oct. 16, 1926, and Sept. 18, 1929). "I am sorry in regard to Dom Bede Maler. His views must make him sad, they

can hardly have much effect elsewhere" (Michel to Hellriegel, College-ville, Sept. 21, 1929, copy).

[70] Evansville, Jan. 22, 1926. For data on Maler, cf. Albert Kleber, O.S.B., *History of St. Meinrad Archabbey, 1854–1954* (St. Meinrad: Grail, 1954), pp. 230–231; 389–394. For St. Meinrad's liturgical endeavors, cf. pp. 177, 244, 258–259, 426, 506–508.

[71] To Deutsch, Evansville, Jan. 22 and 31, 1926. By "congress" here Maler was referring to the forthcoming International Eucharistic Congress to be held in Chicago in 1926. In 1902 the Blessed Sacrament Fathers came to America and took over the League and *Emmanuel*. Both at the con-gress in Chicago and at the League's convention in Buffalo in 1927 Deutsch read papers pleading for the liturgical apostolate; for these papers, cf. "The Liturgical Movement," *Emmanuel*, XXXII (1926), 239–245, and "The Liturgical Movement as Related to the Mass and Sacramental Devotion," *ibid.*, XXXIII (1927), 299–307. In his summary of the Buffalo convention, Schrembs showed a typical understanding of the liturgy for that time, cf. *ibid.*, 307–310. Despite the efforts of Deutsch, Maler, Michel, and Hellriegel, Schrembs was never completely won over. Three years later, after the Liturgical Press had sent Schrembs sample copies of its publications, he replied, "I wish to thank you very sincerely. . . . I read them all with a great deal of interest and I can only say that I found them splendid and practical. I am sure that they are bound to do a great deal of good. I am going to call the attention of my Director of Schools and our teaching Sisterhoods to the outline and the little booklet. You are doing a splendid work at St. John's Abbey. Keep it within reasonable bounds so that it will not be looked upon as a hobby" (to Method Porwoll, Cleveland, Feb. 25, 1930).

[72] *Op. cit.*, p. 128. The Benedictine contribution to the liturgical move-ment has been exaggerated — or at least the work of others overlooked. In the interest of truth one must say that priests like Hellriegel, Busch, Ellard, Reinhold, Hillenbrand, and LaFarge have done more to spread liturgical understanding than a number of Benedictine abbeys. Doing outstanding work for the liturgy today are Conception Abbey, St. Mary's Abbey, and St. Meinrad's Archabbey.

[73] To Deutsch, Evansville, Feb. 4, 1926.

[74] P. 507. Maler was unable to suggest in 1926 an associate editor for *Orate Fratres* from St. Meinrad. In 1927 Benedict Brown, O.S.B., the editor of the St. Meinrad publication, *Grail,* asked Michel whether he could furnish him with a monthly column on the liturgy (Brown to Michel, St. Meinrad, July 22, 1927).

[75] Abbot Paul Schaeuble of St. Joseph's Abbey in Louisiana was cooper-ative; he wrote to Deutsch, "We shall be glad to do all within our power (subscribing and cooperating) to make the *Orate Fratres* a success. Our Doctor of Canon Law volunteers to write articles regarding the Laws of Liturgy" (St. Benedict, Feb. 20, 1926). Abbot Philip Ruggle of Concep-tion was not sympathetic: "He's none too favorable to the movement, as he told you, I think. He didn't even care to have me associate editor, and

consented only when I told him I was bound only for a year. By that time, I hope, he will have changed his mind" (Patrick Cummins, O.S.B., to Michel, Conception, Aug. 29, 1926). The attitudes of the abbots did change as the movement took root.

[76] St. John's *Record*, Mar. 17, 1927. Cf. *Acolyte*, Feb. 7, 1928.

[77] Guilday, *The National Pastorals of the American Hierarchy, 1792–1919* (Washington: NCWC, 1923), 278.

[78] E.g., Charles Bruehl's three articles under the general title, "Pastoralia," in the *Homiletic And Pastoral Review*, XXIII (1922), 1–7, 109–115, 221–228; the first article is not on congregational singing. "Amator Liturgiae" pleaded in a letter to the editor for "a concerted movement" in *Ecclesiastical Review*, LXVI (1922), 65–67. *Acolyte* began only on January 3, 1925. Cf. Apostlate, *OF*, I (1927), 189–190, II (1928), 186, 408–409.

[79] Leo Miller to Busch, Columbus, Mar. 30, 1925. Peregrinus Gasolinus, regretting the lightness of his style, wrote to Michel, "I found that the first and very serious articles on ceremonial . . . were not read, while P. G. became at once very popular. It's a pity, but it seems to be true, that one must 'sugar-coat' the ceremonial pill to induce the brethren to swallow it at all. That is the only reason why P.G. is P.G. (Michael Chapman to Michel, Huntington, Feb. 16, 1928). The *Acolyte* featured Dom Cuthbert Goeb's "The Liturgical Movement," in its issue for May 23, 1925, and again another article on the liturgy by this monk of St. John's Abbey for June 5, 1926.

[80] Cf. Michel, "Casual Comments," *OF*, IV (1929), 72–77, for the allegorical distortions in Wapelhorst's explanation of the Mass. The appearance of Stapper-Baier, *Catholic Liturgics* (Paterson: St. Anthony Guild Press, 1935), revised in 1940, resulted in some improved seminary liturgical instruction.

[81] Collegeville, Sept. 30, 1925, copy.

[82] New York, July 11, 1926.

[83] Cf. "Making Converts to the Liturgy," *OF*, IV (1929), 18–20. In this statement of what the liturgical apostolate stands for, Michel reveals that because liturgy was so misunderstood, some of his collaborators originally suggested abandoning the term: "But that would not do. It is for us to adjust our notions according to the concepts of the Church, and not *vice versa.*" When a group of Boston priests founded the liturgical quarterly, *Mediator*, in 1950, they thought it prudent to speak of the "sacramental" instead of the "liturgical" apostolate.

[84] Miller to Michel, Columbus, July 2, 1927.

[85] "Nine Years After," *OF*, X (1935), 2. This article is a good description of the situation when the movement began.

[86] Apostolate, *OF*, II (1928), 156.

[87] "Mediator Dei," *AAS*, XXXIX (1947), 591–592.

[88] "Nine Years After," *OF*, X (1935), 2.

[89] According to official statistics in the Michel Papers from companies concerned, Kenedy sold a yearly average of 4,000 missals for 1924–28; Macmillan for all of the 1920's sold a total of 7,000. Bussard estimated that

"there were well under 50,000 copies of the missal in English in the U.S.A." in 1928 ("They Want English," *OF*, XXV [1951] 465). For an interesting comparison between the 1920's and 1930's in missal sales, cf. Bussard and Jennings, "How Many Use the Missal for the Laity?" *Ecclesiastical Review*, CII (1940), 61–63. For the latest data on English daily missals, cf. John P. O'Connell, "English Daily Missals," *Homiletic And Pastoral Review*, LIII (1953), 809–819.

90 Cf. Diekmann, "The Primary Apostolate," in *The American Apostolate*, ed. Leo Ward (Westminster: Newman, 1952), p. 35.

91 Bussard, *Vernacular Missal*, pp. 116–149.

92 *Op. cit.*, p. 142. For the abuse of parallelism "found in some of its extremest forms in Wapelhorst, *Compendium sacrae liturgiae*, one of the classics of our seminary training," cf. Michel, "The Mass and the Life of Christ," *OF*, IV (1930), 72–77.

93 Ignatz Groll to Michel, Stoughton, Wis., June 19, 1929.

CHAPTER 5

LAUNCHING THE MOVEMENT

MORE than one plan was in Virgil Michel's mind as he returned from Europe to St. John's Abbey, September 12, 1925. Between that day and his death in 1938 so many ideas and plans were pressing for expression in lecture, print, or action that thirteen years of indefatigable activity would not exhaust them. Possessed of a good knowledge of the liturgy, well-versed in modern and Scholastic philosophy, particularly social philosophy, trained in languages, English literature, and to a degree in theology, with also some understanding and appreciation of sacred art and music, he was uniquely qualified to initiate the program of St. Pius X in the English-speaking world. Europe had opened his mind to many fields and still further widened the already broad periphery of his interests. This and the next chapter will treat of his life and work for the years 1925–30, going beyond them only where clarification demands it.

A slight digression is necessary before launching into the story of how the organized liturgical apostolate took root. This digression will lend perspective to Father Virgil's manifold activities in the next five years; without it, one might miss an important facet of the man. After all, he was never at work at just one project.

While torn between the apostolates of philosophy and liturgy, Dom Virgil kept a third, the apostolate of education, always dear to his heart. For a long time he had believed in the necessity of a vital Catholic education and scholarship. Often he had explained to Abbots

Peter and Alcuin that the American Benedictine abbeys should be, or at least strive to be, centers of intellectual, cultural, and spiritual endeavor as they were, or had once been, in Europe. It would not seem too much to say that no Benedictine abbey or college in the United States has yet realized the ideals and program he set before the National Benedictine Education Association in 1929 for the small liberal arts college.[1] The mission of the Benedictines through fourteen centuries had been to do the work of the Church, he explained, and Catholic higher education and scholarship were a very great need in the Church of the United States, just emerging from pioneer conditions in many areas.

If Catholic educational conditions throughout the country left much to be desired, they were even worse at St. John's — at least so thought Michel.[2] Again and again before going to Europe, he had pleaded for a fully accredited preparatory high school and college at the Minnesota abbey. This would help to remedy what he considered a great need: Catholic lay leaders, trained in the rich Benedictine tradition and prepared to take their place in the world as dedicated witnesses to Christ. His perfectionist tendencies permitted him never to be satisfied with anything but the best. This is reflected in his letter to Abbot Alcuin in Europe, September 19, 1925:

The reason of the protracted blues that I have been having is the condition of college and high school relative to our standing in the educational world, coupled with the fact that we must be suffering from an incomprehensible apathy in regard to this very critical question. Two and three years ago there were at least two men out during the year studying with a definite view to fulfilling requirements of standardization. . . .

The worst of it is that the fault is altogether ours, it seems to me. The demand for high school teachers with a recognized college degree is the most natural thing in the world. The demand could be foreseen and was foreseen, and it was mentioned more than once at St. John's by way of warning. We really ought to shut down entirely and do penance in Trappist fashion for the rest of our lives for thus neglecting the cause of God. . . . The change from the educated European atmosphere to the American did not affect me, but the unforeseen plunge from European apathy to American indifference was a shock almost too big. . . . (Think of the deluded ones of the future who think they are getting a recognized diploma!). . . . Forgive me, if this letter has marred your peace of mind. You will have enough mixed feelings when you strike rock bottom here after your triumphal march through Europe.[3]

Michel never ceased his efforts to improve the standards of education at Collegeville. A later chapter will discuss Michel's educational ideas further.

But now he had another apostolate for which monks should be prepared, the liturgical apostolate. In the next five years Abbot Alcuin sent some ten monks to Europe, including the present editor of *Worship*, Godfrey Diekmann, O.S.B., and Paschal Botz, O.S.B., currently editing *Sponsa Regis*.

Into the making of any movement flow many streams. While Michel was in Europe, the way for an organized popular liturgical revival was being prepared by Fathers William Busch, Martin Hellriegel, Augustine Walsh, O.S.B., and Gerald Ellard, then a Jesuit scholastic. The first public expression of interest in the promotion of the liturgy showed itself in letters to the editors of *America* and the *Commonweal*, in both of which Busch was the first to write pleas for a return to the liturgy, which he called "the reservoir of Christian spirituality."

After calling attention to the interest the young were taking in the liturgical awakening in Europe, Busch stated in *America* for August 30, 1924, that the liturgical movement "is making great strides in Europe but is almost unknown in America." He then pleaded, "Why withhold the liturgy from our young men and women in the United States?" Perhaps indicative of the times, the plea called forth only one letter. However, writing again on November 4, 1925, to the editor of the *Commonweal* and commending that magazine for its appeals for a "greater sense of Catholic solidarity and communal piety," Busch suggested the study of the liturgical movement in Europe, whose reports "are a distinct challenge to the Catholics of the United States." This letter brought a number of favorable replies. By far the clearest call for a liturgical movement, however, was that Busch made in an able address, remarkable for its vision and foresight, to the seminary section of the National Catholic Education Association meeting in Pittsburgh in the summer of 1925. Among other comments, the St. Paul Seminary professor remarked, "The liturgical movement is of immense importance, and I am tempted to say of supreme importance in the life of the Church in our country and particularly in seminary life." [4]

Meanwhile, with the help of several priests including the Reverend John Volz, editor of the *Catholic Bulletin*, weekly paper of the Archdiocese of St. Paul, Busch had actually been conducting a campaign [5] for a liturgical revival in that journal from September, 1924, to January, 1925. Articles on the liturgy continued thereafter under the editorship of Bernard Vaughan. For his early, consistent, and public efforts, Father Busch can be acclaimed the proto-evangelist of the liturgical apostolate in the United States.

On April 25, 1925, Ellard made a strong plea, "Open up the Liturgy," in the correspondence section of *America*. "The liturgy," he insisted, "is a whole world that to the ordinary Catholic has been singularly unexplored. . . . It is all but sealed. . . . Why not," he asked prophetically, "an American Journal of Liturgical Studies?" This call elicited several interested responses and so many personal requests for information that the author was prompted to survey for *America*, in its issue of July 11, 1925, what was being done in the schools to further liturgical understanding.[6]

Another early contributor to the liturgical awakening was Dom Augustine Walsh, former rector of the archdiocesan seminary of Cincinnati, professor of philosophy at the Catholic University of America and, with Dom Thomas Verner Moore and others, founder of St. Anselm's Priory in Washington in 1924. Walsh published an article, "Parish Life and the Liturgy," in the October, 1924, issue of the Priory's quarterly, the *Placidian*, which he edited. In it he pleaded for a return to the liturgy, remarking that there were signs of a revival. Exactly a year later, writing under the title "A Petition for Liturgical Restoration" in the same journal, Walsh called for a movement and asked interested readers to communicate with him. Hearing of Michel's plans and preparations, Walsh wrote to him on January 19, 1926:

I do not know the kind of work you plan — I have had plans of my own, and have some action groups in operation, in a quiet way. I think a meeting of interested persons — a small group — could clear up the whole matter. We have to escape extremists and dilettantes.

Michel's answer is interesting. It dates the first liturgical planning at St. John's, reveals his thought at this time, and indicates how quickly he set to work as soon as he returned from Europe:

It does not surprise me that you had not heard of our plans in regard to the liturgy. Although somehow or other various persons in the country interested in the liturgy got news of them, we tried to make nothing public until we should have a definite program established. The first ideas of our plans were penned in February, 1923, and by dint of slow correspondence the plans grew until they are now full-fledged. We commenced with the beginning of this year to publish as much of them as we intend to give to the public at present. An article was sent to *America*, similar ones to the leading German Catholic paper in the country, and our own students' paper has been spreading information locally. I am only waiting for the final return of assurance from the official collaborators of the coming review, before sending news to the press.

The review we are planning is not to be merely Benedictine in tone or scope. It will devote itself entirely to the liturgical movement, both theoretically and practically envisaged. Our editorial staff includes eleven persons outside of our monastery (one of these also a Benedictine) all but one or two of whom have for some time been well acquainted with the liturgical movements in Europe. We expect to launch the review with the beginning of the next ecclesiastical year. . . .

The Popular Liturgical Library will pursue the same aim as the review (the *Orate Fratres*, by the way), but by means of pamphlets. One pamphlet is now through the press and awaits the last touches. Another is with its printer, and a third is ready for press. Besides these three, eleven others are now in actual preparation.[7]

After *Orate Fratres* appeared, Walsh decided to withdraw the *Placidian*, founded to promote general Catholic scholarship, from the liturgical field. Walsh and Michel agreed to exchange articles and to collaborate henceforth in their respective endeavors.

While the writings of those mentioned above were published to generate a liturgical renaissance, priest-visitors had already been catching the liturgical spirit at O'Fallon, Missouri. Here Father Hellriegel, chaplain to the Sisters of the Most Precious Blood, and Father Anthony Jasper, pastor of the local church, had been quietly studying the liturgy and making the first efforts to bring the faithful back to active participation. Having made a study-visit to Maria Laach in the summer of 1922, Hellriegel in that same year introduced the dialog Mass at O'Fallon. In late 1924 his little Pax Press published two pamphlets, of which one was the first dialog Mass booklet in the United States.[8] In 1925 the July and August issues of *Central Blatt and Social Justice* carried two articles by Hellriegel and Jasper, "Der Schlüssel zur Sozialen Frage," a remarkable statement far in advance of its time on the social values of the liturgy as an aid in the solution of the social question.[9]

In *America* for December 12, 1925, Ellard enthusiastically described the liturgical efforts at O'Fallon, although there seem to have been at this time some undue preoccupation with externals and a touch of archaism, at least if one may judge from Ellard's approving description.[10] In any case, this resulted in a few controversial [11] letters to the editor and, according to the Michel Correspondence, caused some misunderstanding concerning the nature of the liturgical apostolate. Michel then submitted two articles explaining the movement with characteristic lucidity and prudence, and outlining a program. There is evidence to show that these two articles went a long way in arousing interest as well as allaying the fears and suspicions of those already interested, though also skeptical. These articles were the first of many Dom Virgil wrote in the next five years in an effort to win a hearing for the liturgical movement. "The initial stages," he assured the readers of *America*, "will be difficult and require patience and general good will. We have strayed so far from a real understanding of the liturgy that it is almost discouraging. There is so much to learn over for us." Having sketched a program based on that of Beauduin in Belgium, he continued:

The program thus outlined may seem ideal and at first sight unattainable, in some points even undesirable. Time, always a great weapon of the Church divine, will decide that question. It is for us to ask whether some of the aims mentioned do not express real general needs in the Church, and if so, to let those aims for the present be the object of our endeavors.[12]

Besides these men others were quietly at work.[13] Some of them will be cited later. But the above-named, along with Abbot Alcuin, were the first active pioneers in the movement back to the liturgy. Virgil Michel now employed his unusual talent for organization to unite these pioneers and others they mutually discovered, as well as his confreres, into an organized apostolate. The Liturgical Press would be the source of a much-needed literature, while *Orate Fratres* was to become the official spokesman for the liturgical movement in the English-speaking world.

There were all the pangs of launching a pioneer venture and a new form of journalism in a controversial field. "I am beginning to think," Michel wrote Walsh on January 25, 1926, "that editorially there can be no end of caution." On August 25, 1926, he told Donald Attwater, "I should caution against in any way giving the impression that we are trying to tell priests how to conduct their parishes. . . . [The] editing of our proposed section entitled 'The Liturgical Apostolate' will require all the wisdom of serpents."

In America there were no precedents to follow and no mistakes from which to learn, although Dom Michel learned much from the mistakes he had observed in Europe. Contemporaries are rarely kind to pioneers. The almost universal misunderstanding, the opposition, and even suspicion accorded those attempting to arouse interest in the public worship of God has already been recorded. This is not to say that the efforts of the pioneers and early promoters of the movement bore the mark of infallibility or even always of prudence. Where there are fallible human beings, excess remains a possibility to be reckoned with. Just as teachers of sacred music can become so engrossed in the music and forget the prayer for which the music is ancillary, so other artists can be so intrigued with the externals of the liturgy that they miss its inner soul, that is, its spiritual inner character, and thus become preoccupied with its mere shell. In every movement there are enthusiasts with narrow vision, a "lunatic fringe" some prefer to call them, who, hearing a new idea, want to change things overnight, only to pass on to other ideas that please their momentary fancy. Undoubtedly there were such. On the other side are those whose rigidity and self-satisfaction prevent them from seeing the changing needs of the apostolate; these are *ipso facto* against any kind of new approach, the more so if there is question of a "movement." How to steer a sound middle course that would avoid controversy and yet fully meet inevitable objections and misunderstanding — educating the while — that was the principal task at hand. As John LaFarge, S.J., remarked in summarizing his experiences as editor of *America*, one can start a controversy by commenting on the weather.[14] What must it have been like, then, to guide the first exclusively liturgical periodical in the 1920's?

The ground had to be prudently prepared, associate editors and collaborators carefully chosen; those had to be avoided with interests too superficial or exclusively artistic. But interest had to be aroused and apathy overcome. And there was much apathy in the "tumultuous twenties," a period of much complacency, a time which Monsignor John A. Ryan described as one "of thinly veiled materialism." [15] Therefore, after demonstrating that the status quo might not be all that it was thought to be, and after gradually uncovering the evils of subjectivism and individualism in religion, no opportunity could be missed to show the liturgical movement as "respectable," orthodox, Catholic, and concerned with the essentials of Christian faith and practice. The way to a return to the primary founts of Christian living had to be discreetly shown and systematically furthered. In the offing was a gigantic task of education, or better, re-education and "propaganda."

From the beginning Father Michel was convinced that the liturgical movement in the United States must be genuinely American, an emphasis that would also best assure its success in the whole English-speaking world. But this demanded a unique periodical and literature. The approach in some countries of Europe had often been too exclusively theoretical, or too often only narrowly scientific, and therefore removed from practical, everyday Christian living. Maria Laach had concentrated to excess on the elite and had neglected the practical and social aspects of the liturgy.[16] While impressed with Dom Odo Casel's "Mysterientheologie," Michel could not accept it uncritically. Both Maria Laach and St. André had mixed liturgical and monastic elements in their literature. Doing this in the United States would be a mistake, Dom Virgil believed, and would merely confirm the prevalent opinion that the liturgy at best was for monks and nuns. Moreover, in Europe much opposition and controversy had been needlessly stirred up. For instance, ill-advised attacks on private devotions had led some to believe that the liturgical apostolate was a revolution, a literal return to the past, rather than a gradual evolution guided by the best the past could offer and having in view legitimate historical developments and current needs, under the guidance of the Holy See. Finally, Michel's systematic plan called for a broad and practical program embracing as many priests, religious, and members of the laity as were or could be interested.

But it was time to set things moving. The year 1926 was a time of intense preparation. Michel made efforts to contact by letter or interview every priest and religious and some of the laity who had manifested an interest. In early 1926 the Liturgical Press began operations. But before this, Busch and Father Leo Miller offered to the public English translations of Kramp's *Eucharistia* and *Opfergedanke und Messliturgie*, respectively.[17] These two translations were landmarks because they were among the first attempts to show the spiritual character of the liturgy, and above all, the Mass as the Eucharistic Sacrifice in which all have part. Michel, on the other hand, prepared the way by translating from the French and adapting to American conditions Beauduin's famous statement on general principles of the liturgical apostolate, to which booklet he gave the significant title,

Liturgy, the Life of the Church. Abbot Caronti's explanation Michel translated from the Italian as *The Spirit of the Liturgy.* To clear the air still further Father Virgil asked a confrere to compile a *Liturgical Dictionary.* Another confrere arranged a lay *Ordo* and *Offeramus,* a dialog Mass booklet with explanations, intended to further active participation and to introduce the daily missal, especially the *St. Andrew's Daily Missal,* at this time superior to others for its liturgical notes. Michel's own pamphlet, *Why the Mass,* appeared in 1926. Somewhat later, when priests complained to Father Virgil about the dearth of liturgical sermon material emphasizing active and intelligent participation at Mass, he composed for them and others the booklet, *My Sacrifice and Yours.*[18] Leaflets, brochures, and circulars explaining the liturgical apostolate and announcing the Popular Liturgical Library and *Orate Fratres* were sent from Collegeville to all willing to support the cause. For years the conventual high Mass on Sundays was offered at St. John's Abbey for God's blessing on the liturgical apostolate.

Meanwhile, Dom Virgil was also at work organizing his staff of associate editors and contacting other collaborators. A few persons offered themselves as associate editors. For example, there was the gentleman, who, having assured Michel of his qualifications, added, "The liturgy has been a hobby of mine for years." But there were also some who refused, like the chancellor of the Diocese of Des Moines, Father Vitus Stoll, who recalled the controversy in *Das Pastoral Blatt* over whether it was better to receive Communion during, before, or after Mass and promptly declined collaboration, saying " a liturgical review is a hazardous proposition though undoubtedly necessary . . ."[19] Although he corresponded with a few American Franciscan and Dominican Fathers, Michel was not able to induce them to accept a place on the editorial board.

Besides Busch, Hellriegel, Ellard, and Miller, Father Virgil chose eight other associate editors: Mrs. Justine B. Ward, the chant expert; Father James O'Mahoney, O.F.M.Cap., of Ireland; Mother Mary Ellerker, O.S.D., of Duluth; Father Richard Power, of the Diocese of Springfield, Massachusetts; Father Jeremiah Harrington, professor of moral theology at the St. Paul Seminary; the Right Reverend F. Holweck of St. Louis; Patrick Cummins, O.S.B., of Conception Abbey; and Donald Attwater from England.

With England, Ireland, a Jesuit, a Capuchin, five secular priests, a Dominican prioress, a Benedictine monk, and two lay people, the board of associate editors composed a well-balanced and fairly catholic staff. This catholic character was unique for liturgical periodicals and brought considerable favorable comment in liturgical circles of Europe. As future events would show, the editors had been well chosen. While in Europe Dom Michel had enrolled Mrs. Ward. A classmate in philosophy at Louvain, he had interested Father O'Mahoney in the liturgy.[20] Today the latter is one of Ireland's best loved preachers and writers on religious subjects and the author of more than twenty books. Mother Ellerker was the author of the Corpus Christi Books, children's books of a liturgical nature. She had come to America from England to found a community of nuns for social work. In England she had known the great English liturgist, Adrian Fortescue. Attwater offered himself as collaborator, saying that he was as far as he knew, "the only person in England, clerical or lay, regularly concerned in popular liturgical writing."[21] He was the lay editor of Caldey Abbey's *Pax* and its *Notes for the Month*,[22] the first organized attempt in English at spreading a knowledge of the liturgy among the people. Attwater was later to show himself by his books and by articles in *Orate Fratres* an authority not only on things Catholic but also on the difficult subject of the eastern rites. The previous year in Rome, Michel had engaged Conception Abbey's Patrick Cummins, O.S.B., who had some training in theology and Scripture, and who had been the Rector of St. Anselm's College in the Eternal City. Michel discovered Father Power through correspondence. Holweck, vicar general of the Archdiocese of St. Louis and one of the most learned priests of his day, was an internationally known hagiographer with an archeological interest in the liturgy. He assured Michel that he wrote with a "furor teutonicus" and then proved it with forty-page articles for the thirty-two page *Orate Fratres*. Father Virgil had chosen him chiefly for his reputation.[23] Of all the editors, only Holweck was then widely known; the rest were young, unknown, and inexperienced. Michel himself was but thirty-six years of age.

It may be of interest to record the tidbits of advice and warning, inspiration and encouragement, Michel passed out to his associate editors and other co-workers. To what extent the organizer of the liturgical apostolate followed his own directives the reader can judge for himself. Fellow workers were always to remember, Dom Virgil insisted, that they were "engaged in an apostolate, NOT in a controversy."[24] And he cautioned them against iconoclastic tendencies: there were to be no attacks on private devotions, or existing conditions, no matter how objectionable. Emphasize the positive and constructive, he said, for in doing so "the negative criticism follows without our stating it." Even the polemical spirit, "such as would arouse opposition," was not to enter into their writing style. Hence they were to be more "apologetic" than "dogmatic." He asked them to "quote liturgical texts to illustrate basic Christian truths," thus showing the liturgy as meaningful, practical, beautiful. Never exaggerate, he admonished, never overstate — never state "anything which if challenged you cannot defend." Never to have to retract wins confidence. "Our movement will turn to naught if we are not constantly anchored to the theological truths." [25] The generality of priests, he assured them, "are not opposed — they only misunderstand." Objections would have to be met, but always in the spirit of charity. So, too, opposition must be expected, but "God's cause has always been opposed in this world." For a time they would have "to walk the winepress alone." But they were "sowing the fire of the Holy Spirit," and ". . . in the book of life" would "their zeal and their work be recorded." ". . . And if judgment day brings recognition," that would be "soon enough." After all, they were "working mainly for the coming generation," and "that will be for us a way of imitating just what Our Divine Master Himself did, . . ." and "we must not be less patient than our Lord." The liturgical spirit was a leaven; it penetrated slowly but unceasingly. While the primary role had to be accorded to instruction, the liturgical movement would be a "slow, peaceful evolution," "not so much a change of form as of spirit; not innovation, but restoration," and "as the liturgical movement reaches more and more souls, there will be many a small but not insignificant change wrought in not a few matters." [26]

Father Virgil's sound judgment, zeal, sincerity, the stark reasonableness of his approach, his grasp of the needs and temper of the times and, above all, his unshakable confidence that the liturgical movement was the stirring of the Holy Spirit in the Church — all these served to reassure his associate editors and other collaborators closing ranks behind him. To each of the editors a phase of the work was assigned. Because he knew the number of readers of *Orate Fratres* would be limited, he asked his official collaborators to contribute articles in other periodicals, and, especially, to be apostles in their own area and in all their contacts. For this purpose he furnished propaganda materials. While *Orate Fratres* was largely Michel's own planning, he had also the valuable assistance of his associates; and so by letter and prospectus combined advice made for combined decision, the editor-in-chief always having the last word and final responsibility. Under his leadership there evolved a remarkable agreement on essentials. As for the rest, Dom Virgil, blessed with an irenic personality and a democratic spirit, had a way of pouring oil on waters before they became troubled.

Michel benefited much from his immediate associates, particularly from Busch, Hellriegel, Power, Ellard, and Attwater. Busch was an unfailing guide. In fact, it would be difficult to overrate Busch's role in the founding and guidance of the American liturgical apostolate. From John A. Ryan he had acquired an appreciation of Catholic social thought, later enhanced by liturgical study. To the work he also brought the wisdom of a competent church historian, who had discovered nothing, as he once said, "in the history of the Church that seems . . . more important than the liturgy."[27] In Michel's own words, "In my notion you always had the position of chief worker and consultor."[28] Busch was certainly that. Many were his trips to Collegeville in those first years; never would Michel pass through St. Paul without a conference with him. It would seem that the St. Paul Seminary professor was a steadying influence on Michel, perhaps a bit inclined at times to rush in. And as one now reads the first liturgical writings, Busch and Michel were in these early days the most clear-minded on the liturgy.

Father Hellriegel, who had won the confidence and approval of Archbishop John J. Glennon as early as 1925, had made a personal study of the liturgical movement in several visits to Europe. He, too, was a sound advisor and most faithful worker. His suggestions were all the more valuable because they were based on practical experience. His words to Michel might well serve as a motto to all apostles of the liturgy: "Langsam, und die guten Sachenkeinen Schaden tun."[29] This is not the place to tell the story of Hellriegel's work, but when that is done — if one may judge from the Michel Papers — many will be surprised to know how much this one priest has done for the liturgical apostolate.

Father Power, a capable though self-made theologian and writer, at times corresponded with Michel every week. Their letters bristle with vigorous theological discussion, and more than once Power sent Michel to theological sources. Father Virgil had the highest regard for Power's advice.[30] The very popular sacramental series of pamphlets of the Liturgical Press, and what was for a long time considered the best translation of the ordinary of the Mass, now the basis of the Uniform Text, were the work of this indefatigable collaborator.

One year after his ordination in 1926, Ellard sailed for Europe, well supplied at his own request with letters of introduction and suggestions from Virgil Michel as to the best ways of familiarizing himself with the liturgical movement in Europe.[31] During his stay abroad, which lasted until 1931, he kept Michel informed as to the movement there; he also proffered many invaluable suggestions at a time when these were sorely needed. Ellard has been the most faithful researcher and writer of liturgical books in the United States. Along with William Puetter, S.J., and Daniel Lord, S.J., he deserves credit for bringing the liturgy, especially the dialog Mass, into the sodality movement.[32] It is evident from the Michel Papers that Ellard interested several Jesuits in the liturgical movement.

The quality of *Orate Fratres* was undoubtedly improved through the keen observations of Donald Attwater, who also relayed to Michel the helpful criticism of Eric Gill, with whom he frequently discussed the magazine. Attwater also did much to make *Orate Fratres* and Liturgical Press literature known in England; Michel once paid him the compliment of saying that Attwater was his idea of an alert and apostolic Catholic layman.

Not to mention those at St. John's Abbey who worked with Father Virgil during the first years would be unfair. First of all one must mention Abbot Alcuin. He always insisted on a sound monastic and liturgical observance. In addition he had the courage to give his support to a project even if he could not foresee all of its ramifications. Later, however, he seems to have demurred somewhat in his support. Fathers Basil Stegmann, Cuthbert Goeb, Ermin Vitry, Charles Cannon, and others [33] were among the first workers. One should think of Virgil Michel's accomplishments, therefore, as the result of the labors of a large monastic family toiling together under the abbot, as befits a Benedictine community.

In the summer of 1926 Father Michel explained his plans for the liturgical apostolate by letter to the Most Reverend Pietro Fumasoni-Biondi, Apostolic Delegate to the United States; Austin Dowling, Archbishop of St. Paul; and Joseph Busch, Bishop of St. Cloud. From all three prelates he received encouraging statements in praise of his endeavors, parts of which statements were later published in *Orate Fratres*. "I shall follow with interest your very commendable aposto-

late in the interest of the sacred liturgy," the Apostolic Delegate
stated, "and I earnestly hope it will bear great fruit among both clergy
and laity." [34] "Please do all you can to innoculate our seminarians,"
Bishop Busch told Michel.[35] Furthermore, Michel was convinced
that Pius XI favored the liturgical movement, as the Pope's later
statements abundantly proved.

Earlier that same year complaints had reached the Holy See concerning the orthodoxy of some of the teaching and practices of Maria
Laach. The Prior of that abbey, Albert Hammenstede, O.S.B., was
dispatched to Rome, where he was granted an audience with Pius XI
and other high officials in the Roman Curia. The Holy See had asked
for a memorandum thoroughly explaining the principles and aims
guiding the promotion of the liturgical movement at Maria Laach.
Abbot Herwegen composed a treatise on the liturgical apostolate
which Hammenstede presented to the Pope. The result was a vindi-
cation of the German abbey. Pius XI sent a letter [36] of congratulations
on April 29, 1926, to Herwegen, with praise for the work of his community and shortly afterward the abbey church at Maria Laach was
raised to the rank of a minor basilica by an apostolic brief in recognition of the liturgical apostolate fostered by that community.

Like Hellriegel, Michel received a complete report of the entire
Maria Laach episode from a number of sources, including one from
a confrere in Rome, Father Roger Schoenbechler, who relayed
Hammenstede's interview with Pius XI. The Pope had asked why the
monks had not sought the apostolic benediction upon their work
when it was begun in the days before World War I. To which Hammenstede responded that the work at that time was only preparatory,
and that it did not occur to them to seek such an honor. Whereupon
Pius XI is said to have answered, according to Hammenstede's report, that he "was always very greatly interested in liturgical activities,
and he wanted to know about them wherever they are." [37]

The Prior of Maria Laach at once suggested that Michel approach
the Holy See for a papal letter of approval through Raphael Cardinal
Merry del Val, secretary of the Holy Office, whom Hammenstede
had quoted as saying, "Maria Laach hat die grosse Linie Pius
X. gefunden." What a boon if *Orate Fratres* could appear with a
papal letter of approval! Michel — and the Prior of Maria Laach —
were naive in thinking that such a letter could be secured, but perhaps
Michel was even more naive in the manner he went about it. The

Abbot Primate, Fidelis De Stotzingen, through whom normally such matters were expedited, was to be absent from Rome for months. After some thought Michel wrote to his confrere:

This letter is being written to ask you to be the representative of the *Liturgical Press* of St. John's Abbey in Rome. . . . Would you kindly undertake to see the proper dignitaries in Rome, and to explain the nature of our projects to them? You know that there is nothing we should esteem more highly than to know that our undertakings have the approval and the blessing of His Holiness. With the assurance of that blessing, we should care little for the discouragements and the difficulties that lie in the path of any undertakings like ours. And nothing is further from our intentions than to desire to push on with our projects, if they are not fully in accord with the ideals and desires of His Holiness.

In presenting our plans, I would suggest to you that you stress two things: That we are aiming solely to awaken among both priests and laity a better practical understanding of the Church's liturgy as the real factor it should be in the spiritual life of every Catholic; and that in this, as in all else, we wish to be guided solely by what is established custom and approved by the official ecclesiastical pronouncements. . . .

Having presented these matters for us, will you humbly ask for the blessing of his Holiness upon the *Liturgical Press*, and upon its projected review, the *Orate Fratres*, giving the fullest assurance of our filial obedience and deep veneration for the chair of Peter? [38]

In the spring of 1926 Merry del Val had told Hammenstede on the occasion of the latter's audience with Pius XI, "We here in Rome know that the liturgical movement is something so great that it cannot be achieved in a short time. Go and continue our work." [39] Although manifesting interest in Father Roger's proposal some months later, Merry del Val declined to act as intermediary and sent him to the abbot primate. According to Father Roger's report to Michel:

The Cardinal claimed that there was already too much exaggeration in liturgical movements, referring to the war against devotions and the like. That I answered by meekly stating that our intention was nothing of the kind. . . . Now breathe freely, look alive, dig into the spurs anew!!! Don't know what sort of jolt this has been for you after all the other recent ones, but it is a pretty big one for me too. . . . The Prior of Laach was perhaps too enthusiastic when here & his extreme confidence in Cardinal Merry del Val somewhat deceived me. [40]

But that was not the end of the affair. Father Roger then approached

Giovanni Cardinal Bonzano, Apostolic Delegate to the United States from 1911 to 1922 and papal legate to the International Eucharistic Congress in Chicago in 1926. Bonzano, appearing to be very interested, offered to do all he could but only after a year. As Father Roger said:

Bonzano explained that the Holy See, cardinals, or bishops do not, out of policy, baptize or christen but rather confirm. . . . If after about a year (yes, he said a year) we were still flourishing with the movement, the review and the library, he would (and said he could) get a papal approval and would do so gladly.[41]

Three years later Abbot Alcuin presented Pius XI with the gift of the first three volumes of *Orate Fratres*, which at once brought the following letter:

The Vatican, Nov. 21, 1929

Right Reverend Father Abbot:

His Holiness has received the three volumes containing the numbers from November 1926 to October 1929 of the review of the Liturgical Apostolate, "Orate Fratres."

The Holy Father is greatly pleased that St. John's Abbey is continuing the glorious Benedictine tradition, and that there is emanating from this abbey an inspiration that tends to elevate the piety of the faithful by leading it back to the pure fountains of the sacred liturgy.

Wishing the movement a most abundant harvest of fruit, the Sovereign Pontiff thanks [you] for the expression of homage, and imparts to you, Right Reverend Father, and to all who collaborate with you in the publication of the review, the Apostolic Blessing.

I take pleasure on this occasion to call myself,

Yours most devotedly in the Lord,

[signed] P. Card. Gasparri

In the midst of his plans and labors in organizing the liturgical movement, Michel still entertained hopes of spending his lifework chiefly in philosophy. He was only a "dry philosopher" and "inadequately prepared in theology," as he said in one of his letters. In urging Abbot Alcuin to set aside monks for liturgical work, he reminded him of a previous agreement:

I simply MUST put 85% of my time to philosophy. The spirit is urging stronger than ever; especially since indications are that people read philosophical articles with real interest. And as far as things are left to me, I cannot think of starting the Review under conditions that may suddenly put the whole burden of the material on myself. I'm only to be the distant wirepuller, or organizer, whose name is not even known. Hence, we must definitely organize here at home and divide the burden (several months ahead of time). . . . And: Should the Review be printed here? I fear that most, since it may at any moment put all the work, editorial and mechanical, on my shoulders.[42]

What he feared more or less happened. He wrote more than a third of the first number of *Orate Fratres* and the first three publications of the Popular Liturgical Library came from his pen. Abbot Alcuin appointed him director of the Liturgical Press and its financial custodian. Because publishing was a new venture for St. John's Abbey, Michel almost overnight had to familiarize himself with the intricacies of the publishing field. The liturgical work ahead would be overwhelming. Virgil Michel "sacrificed" an absorbing desire to write and labor in what he thought of as the apostolate of philosophy in order to further an understanding and appreciation of the liturgy, seemingly because Abbot Alcuin could find no one with his talents to take his place. As for his lacking proper theological training, the abbot reminded him that he had a licentiate in theology from the Catholic University of America and had heard the lectures of eminent theologians in Rome. Besides, his practical good sense and natural prudence together with his grasp of Scholastic philosophy would preserve him from serious error in liturgical work.

To make philosophy merely his "pet hobby," as he later called it, could hardly have been easy. Attendance at the Sixth International Philosophical Congress at Harvard, September 13–17, 1926, fired his interest in philosophy anew.[43] Here the non-Catholic philosophers invited the collaboration of the dozen or so priests present. This was the very task Michel had always believed Catholic philosophers should be performing, that is, making themselves, Scholastic philosophy, and the whole realm of Catholic thought intelligible to the non-Catholic learned world. But this would also entail familiarizing themselves with non-Catholic philosophy and thought in order to grasp its elements of truth and to meet the non-Catholic mind. In view of the fact that he had opportunity to work in philosophy only at odd moments, his philosophical writings are considerable. No doubt it was providential, however, that a "dry philosopher," also intensely interested in the liturgy, should guide a controversial movement in its most critical stages — a movement that could, indeed, have gone in a number of wrong directions except for his prudent shepherding. At the end of his lectures at Pius X School in the late summer of 1926, two months before *Orate Fratres* appeared, and after he had stated that he had "again commenced reading in philosophy," he made his final plea to Abbot Alcuin, suggesting organization and division of labor as well as possible successors in liturgical work at Collegeville:

I believe I could find more work for myself in the liturgical apostolate than I could do in twenty-four hours per day, if I should go into it completely. But, you know, the intention, as you stated it also, was that I should later be able to continue exclusively with philosophy.[44]

As it happened, Virgil Michel never was given opportunity to do what he most wanted, and was best prepared, to do. The plan to write a series of philosophical texts had to be abandoned for the time being. Once he saw that, in the providence of God, his lifework would chiefly be the popularization of the liturgy, he made a systematic study of theology, concentrating on St. Thomas, Scheeben, and the Church Fathers. From his study of St. John Chrysostom's commentaries on the Pauline epistles he received his clear concept of the Mystical Body and of the essential role of the laity in the Church.

At this point *Orate Fratres* became a major concern of Dom Virgil's. The magazine was meant to reach the clergy, religious, seminarians, and the more educated laity, that is, those whose vocation it is to lead and teach others. Give it to leaders, Michel pointed out, and soon it will seep down into others. This was characteristic of all his activities. Above all, the review was not to be narrowly Benedictine but "Catholic in the full sense of the term." Launched upon the stream of Catholic life among the English-speaking people, *Orate Fratres* was to be essentially a review of the spiritual life. While based on sound scholarship, it was intended primarily to serve the apostolate. Its contents and approach were to be guided by the conditions of the time and the growth of the liturgical mentality. "He is not a leader," Michel liked to say, "who is too far ahead." Keeping readers informed of liturgical activities the world over, this pioneer liturgical periodical would cover all phases of the liturgy, eventually also the oriental liturgies. "Its invitation is extended to all Catholics of whatever rank," Father Virgil wrote in the first issue, "to cooperate in the liturgical apostolate by whatever means lie within the possibility of the individuals."[45] Each issue would contain a section entitled "The

Apostolate," which, he admitted, would be "an experiment without precedent in liturgical reviews," and meant for the discussion and furthering of practical projects in liturgical living.

The entire foreword to *Orate Fratres*, to which he would have occasion to refer many times in the future, is so lucid a statement of principles and ideals, presented with tact and rare vision, that it merits an extensive quotation:

Our general aim is to develop a better understanding of the spiritual import of the liturgy. . . . We are not aiming at a cold scholastic interest in the liturgy of the Church, but at an interest that is more thoroughly intimate, that seizes upon the entire person, . . . affect[s] both the individual spiritual life of the Catholic and the corporate life of the natural social units of the Church, the parishes, so properly called the cells of the corporate organism which is the entire living Church, the mystic body of Christ.[46]

"In some countries of Europe," he explained,

the liturgical movement has made its most striking headway in the realm of ideas. Theoretically the liturgical ideas were received wholeheartedly, but the practical aspects lagged behind, or were entirely neglected. Such a situation cannot be considered very satisfactory, to say the least. . . .

Some persons can absorb a great amount of theory, even theory connected with life, without having their practical life affected in the least by their knowledge. Others, seized with great enthusiasm upon acquiring some new idea, may rush headlong into practice with it, and find themselves confronted by circumstances that resist their efforts. For the liturgical life the true way must be a mean somewhere between these two, in which zeal and good sense are properly blended.[47]

But he warned,

Our hopes are therefore based, like our efforts, on the possibility that many persons may find in the liturgy the first answer to the intimate need of their souls for a closer contact and union with the spiritual and the divine.

Our hopes, indeed, do not exclude other aspects of the liturgy, all of which may combine and should combine to emphasize its essential function in the spiritual life. Many and varied interests meet in the liturgy. The latter is a great mine of the widest cultural life. There are the literary, musical, artistic, historical, even ethnological and archeological aspects, all of which are worth fostering, and all of which are replete with interest and value in life. Our hopes are also for a better appreciation of these aspects of the liturgy, but always in subordination to the more fundamental aspects, that of the spiritual import, which is its true essential nature. Should any of the secondary aspects and interests break away from their proper relation to the real nature of the liturgy, that is, should any one of them cease to be a way of leading to the latter or of revealing the latter, and should that result occur by reason of our efforts, we should have to confess the keenest disappointment of our hopes, if not complete failure.[48]

Thus the liturgical movement, with its aims clearly defined, was set on a broad base. No elements or phases of the liturgy were to be neglected, and all was to be subordinated to its spiritual character. Who could intelligently object to such a movement? "Ultimately the liturgical movement is bound to come," Michel insisted in the foreword. Already he foresaw the possibility of other reviews "more specialized and more profound" in their contents and purpose.[49] With such thoroughness did he guide the planning of *Orate Fratres* that in 1940, when most of the associate editors met for the first time at the first National Liturgical Week,[50] they unanimously agreed to continue the original policy. And, it may be added, *Worship* is still essentially the same magazine with the same aims and policy.

The Liturgical Press was to pursue the same ideals as *Orate Fratres* through the Popular Liturgical Library[51] and other publications. Michel's hope was that the Press would grow to a point where it would teach certain Catholic publishing firms that there are higher ideals than the making of money. Although most concerned in the first years with effecting an understanding of the inner spiritual nature of the liturgy, especially of the Mass, Father Virgil at the same time envisioned the day when more and more of the laity would join in the divine office, the prayer of the Mystical Body, as they had once done in past ages. His idea to publish some form of a shortened breviary for the laity, priests told him, was ludicrous.[52] But some had said that of the missal. To prepare for a better day, the Liturgical Press besides other liturgical literature published pamphlets for compline and prime. *A Short Breviary*, issued only in 1941, went through several editions within a short time of its publication. The Liturgical Press has sold to date more than 300,000 copies of its compline and prime booklets.

Michel had occasion early to outline his aims for the Liturgical Press for Benziger Brothers, with whom he had a lengthy correspondence and for whom, as with other publishers, everything suddenly became "liturgical." [53] The Liturgical Press, he said, was to supply a need not being supplied by other firms. The aim would be to print "books and pamphlets of a spiritual value" serving the liturgical apostolate, "quantity sales," and "no money-making." Moreover, the products of the Press were to exhibit the "finest workmanship" and a "beautiful make-up and type" according to the best canons of Catholic art.[54] In this way Dom Virgil established a tradition for which the publications of the Liturgical Press have often been commended. His confreres recall Michel's saying at this time that one could not write much on liturgical art since so many identified an interest in the liturgy with a fondness for art; but that the Liturgical Press, by presenting its publications with sound artistic format, could teach the lesson that nothing is too beautiful in the worship of the God of all beauty. It was surprising what pains he took in those busy days to meet his own ideals. "We want the Review to look as pleasing and artistic as possible," he pointed out to the manager of the Wanderer Printing Company. "Any suggestions you can give us towards that end will be most welcome." [55]

With a cover designed under the direction of Eric Gill, *Orate Fratres* made its initial appearance on November 28, 1926. The uncertainty of the whole venture was reflected in its foreword:

No human tongue can tell what are our prospects of success. Only one thing we know, and that suffices. The voice of Peter has spoken, and spoken repeatedly. And our effort in response to it shall be made as best we know how. Further questions of hope or success are distracting and useless.

The only commercial advertising, besides circularizing and distribution of informative materials through interested collaborators, was the sending out of 15,000 letters to the clergy. For the first issue there were only 800 subscribers, chiefly from the Middle and the Far West.[56] After seven numbers the list of subscribers had almost doubled; and before the end of the year, the magazine had readers scattered around the globe. By April of 1929 *Orate Fratres* and Liturgical Press publications were going to twenty-six countries. A surprising number of the original subscribers, as of those ever since, were members of the laity. One of the most peculiar phenomena of the American liturgical movement, and the continuing embarrassment of its proponents through the years, has been the fact that the laity have often evidenced more interest in promoting the liturgy than the clergy.

At the end of the first year of publication Michel commented editorially:

The editors, before commencing their projects, had taken the avowed position that if their undertakings were not of God they would and should perish, and that if they were God's work, they would continue by His grace. . . . The liturgical movement has evidently come to stay and to grow. . . . The main uncertainty in regard to the future centers rather about the extent and speed of growth, not at all about the fact of the growth of the liturgical movement.[57]

Work related to the liturgical apostolate soon outgrew available manpower at St. John's Abbey, a community which in many ways was itself emerging only then from pioneer conditions.[58] The burden, therefore, fell squarely on Michel's shoulders. In the first number of *Orate Fratres* he had stated that anyone was free to write to him about the liturgy. He probably little realized what he was inviting. In the next five years there would be an avalanche of letters which he answered with enormous personal labor and sacrifice, besides continuing his other labors. Keeping in contact with widely scattered associate editors was in itself a large task.

While yet in Europe, Dom Virgil had urged his superior that confreres be exclusively set aside for liturgical work. Since almost none of the monks were qualified to do liturgical research, to write, and edit, Michel in 1928 again suggested that in view of present and future needs a permanent staff of trained monks be gradually built up and that Donald Attwater, who had expressed a willingness to come to St. John's, be invited as literary editor of the Liturgical Press. However, Abbot Alcuin did not consider it wise or possible to act fully on these and other suggestions. Through the years, therefore, the liturgical work at Collegeville has been performed by men who were also engaged in other tasks.

Besides the work of organizing, writing, and editing, Dom Virgil also taught philosophy in the seminary, gave retreats, and lectured on various subjects. Because he had written realistically while in Europe about the role of monasticism in the modern world, his superior also gave him the time-consuming task of guiding the young monks as Prefect of Clerics for the years 1927-29. Many came to Collegeville to consult him on liturgical matters. Abbot Alcuin did not seem to realize what a response the initiation of the liturgical apostolate would bring and the work it would entail, though Michel himself, while somewhat underestimating it, had predicted the favorable reaction. In any case, he now clearly foresaw that his lifework would mainly be the promotion of what he always called the primary apostolate.

As a new periodical, *Orate Fratres* received a warm welcome from *America*, the *Commonweal*, and the *Catholic World*. What was even more heartening was the fact that within a year some fifteen bishops in the United States and Canada encouraged Father Virgil in the newly-founded apostolate. The message of Archbishop Dowling was typical:

I am sending you a little viaticum for the *Orate Fratres*. I have just looked over the second number. You have made a good beginning. Your monthly is interesting. It is modest. I wish it a full measure of success.[59]

Only in January of 1936 did Michel learn that at the time Dowling had also written to his sister and the community of religious to which she belonged to pray that the liturgical apostolate of St. John's Abbey would be blessed by God.[60] In fact, individual episcopal expressions of support were such as to prompt Michel in late 1929 to express the opinion that the day was not far distant when the combined American hierarchy would direct and sponsor the liturgical movement as the hierarchy of Belgium and Holland had done years before.[61] Father Virgil, however, wholly miscalculated the situation. After sponsoring the first two National Liturgical Weeks in 1940–41, the Benedictine Abbots comprising the Benedictine Liturgical Conference asked the Administrative Board of the National Catholic Welfare Conference to consider sponsoring the Week through the National Catholic Welfare Conference. Monsignor Michael J. Ready, General Secretary of the Conference, replied for the bishops on September 9, 1942:

Your letter of October 10, 1941 was presented . . . and has received the Board's study. . . . I write to inform the executive council of the Benedictine Liturgical Conference that the Board read your communication with interest but with the conclusion that the matter of the request from the Benedictine Liturgical Conference does not come within the ambit of the National Catholic Welfare Conference.[62]

Then, at the strong urging of Alcuin Deutsch, President of the Benedictine Liturgical Conference and Abbot-President of the American Cassinese Congregation, the Benedictine Liturgical Conference was dissolved on September 8, 1943. To take its place as sponsor of the annual National Liturgical Week, the Liturgical Conference was organized, with Monsignor Joseph P. Morrison as President, the late Reverend Joseph F. Stedman — who did so much to spread the missal — as Vice President, while Michael Ducey continued as Secretary.

However, in the same year that the Administrative Board had declined sponsorship, Archbishop Michael J. Curley of Baltimore said in his introduction to Ellard's *The Dialog Mass*:

To those who have watched the progress of the Liturgical Movement in the United States these last few years, it comes without surprise that the American hierarchy, through its corporate agency, the National Catholic Welfare Conference, will assume episcopal leadership in the Movement and integrate it into the ordinary framework of ecclesiastical affairs.[63]

While there have been many individual statements by bishops in support of the liturgical apostolate, in 1957 the American liturgical apostolate is still awaiting the episcopal leadership of the combined American hierarchy.

The liturgical movement had been successfully launched. It now had to be diffused. The labor was only beginning.

NOTES TO CHAPTER 5

[1] Cf. "Basic Need of Christian Education Today," National Benedictine Education Association: *Proceedings* (1929), pp. 34–45.

[2] The 1928–29 enrollment records for the Graduate School of the University of Minnesota show that 776 had come from the University's undergraduate school, 294 from seven Minnesota Protestant colleges and only 37, of whom a number were religious, from six Minnesota Catholic colleges. Of the 37 not one had attended St. John's University. The breakdown for Protestant colleges was as follows: Augsburg, 19; Carleton, 51; Concordia, 14; Gustavus Adolphus, 41; Hamline, 40; Macalester, 49; St. Olaf, 80. For Catholic colleges: St. Benedict, 3; St. Catherine, 23; St. Thomas, 8; St. Scholastica, 1; St. Teresa, 2; St. John's, 0 (Archives of St. John's University, an official release of 1929, University of Minnesota, bound in a volume entitled, "Relations with U. of Minnesota"). There would seem to be little reason to believe that the general conditions of Catholic education were better in other states.

[3] Speaking of organizing for the liturgical enterprise in a letter to the abbot in Europe, October 28, 1925, he wrote, "Hence the need of definite organization of our forces here. And that again brings in another consideration. Can we organize such an activity when there is a more supreme and pressing problem demanding all our energies — the problem of our college? All the many discussions of Catholic education in *Commonweal* and in *America* come to one point: We too are at the dividing point; now is the time, etc.; it is really DO OR DIE this time. If it is DO, can we think at all of entering upon any extra-scholastic activities? You being absent, the whole matter has seemed so oppressive at times that I asked myself what the use was of trying to do so much, . . . and I often felt the temptation to let things go and commence browsing in literature, etc., for myself and putting a minimum of time to all the perplexing problems around us, which we have to face with no feeling but that of our helplessness."

[4] "Liturgical Movement," NCEA: *Proceedings*, XXII (1925), p. 670.

[5] Busch's first plea for a liturgical restoration appeared in the *Catholic Bulletin*, July 28, 1922. Two preceding pleas for a liturgical movement were published by Arthur Preuss, "Notes and Gleanings," *Fortnightly*

Review, XXIX (1922), 233, and by Amator Liturgiae, To the Editor, *Ecclesiastical Review*, LXVI (1922), 65–67. The following helped Busch in his attempts to stir up liturgical interest: Joseph Kreuter and Alcuin Deutsch of St. John's Abbey, Father Jeremiah Harrington of St. Paul and William Sommerhauser, S.J. The latter discovered the liturgical renaissance in O'Fallon, Missouri — where Hellriegel was already active — and then wrote a series of five articles for the *Fortnightly Review*, beginning on Oct. 15, 1923, reprinted in 1924 in the *Catholic Bulletin* (Nov. 1, 8, 15, 22, 29). Busch summarized the earliest American liturgical efforts in the *Catholic Bulletin* for September 27, 1924, and thereafter led the campaign by signed and unsigned articles as well as by quoted items from various authors and translations from Kramp's *Eucharistia*.

⁶ Ellard first heard of the liturgical movement from Jesuits returning from Europe (interview, St. Marys,Kansas, Sept. 23, 1952). His interest, as well as that of other Jesuits including Daniel Lord and William Peutter, was enhanced by several "pilgrimages," the first made on Nov. 1, 1925, to O'Fallon, Missouri, where Hellriegel was already very active. In fact, according to the Michel Papers, Hellriegel gave the 120 Jesuit scholastics at St. Louis University at least six lectures on the liturgy between February, 1926 and May, 1927. During Christmas vacation, 1925, Hellriegel, Ellard, and Michel met at O'Fallon to discuss the organization of the liturgical movement. " 'The day would fail me' as I began to recall our golden days at O'Fallon. They shall stand out no matter what the future may bring" (Ellard to Michel, St. Louis, Jan. 1, 1926).

⁷ Collegeville, Jan. 25, 1926. From abundant internal evidence it is clear that Michel meant "February, *1924*."

⁸ Writing on September 23, 1925, Hellriegel told Michel that "over 12,000 copies of the *Holy Sacrifice of the Mass* are in use in various parts of the U.S.A." Before it went out of print in 1939, it had sold some 250,000 copies. Jasper died on June 26, 1925.

⁹ Translated into English by Busch and published as a pamphlet under the title the *True Basis of Christian Solidarity* by the Central Bureau of St. Louis, this brochure has sold thousands of copies. At first the *censor librorum*, John E. Rothensteiner, objected to it as "exaggerated"; today the ideas in it are more or less commonplace (cf. Frederick Kenkel to Michel, St. Louis, June 30, 1928).

¹⁰ Cf. "A Pilgrimage and a Vision," XXXIV, 201–203. "Everything unfamiliar at O'Fallon represents a bringing back of old customs" (p. 201). Michel received a number of letters referring to Ellard's article and deprecating "O'Fallonism." Among them was one from Walsh, to whom, as to others, Michel replied that he was being unfair to Hellriegel and that one must be patient in this as with all pioneer efforts. (Collegeville, January 16, 1926, copy.) Cf. Walsh's review of *Orate Fratres* in the *Placidian*, IV (1927), 79.

¹¹ Cf. *America*, XXXIV (1926), 241, 410, for three letters.

¹² "Program for a Liturgical Movement," *America*, XXXIV (1926), 615. The second article, "Meaning of the Church's Liturgy," appeared a week earlier, *ibid.*, p. 386.

[13] Busch, "Liturgical Movement," NCEA: *Proceedings* (1925), pp. 670–686, gave a summary of liturgical efforts up to 1925. For Michel's account as to pioneers, cf. Apostolate, *OF* (1929), 121–123; Ellard, "Liturgische Bewegung in den Vereinigten Staaten," *Stimmen der Zeit,* CXVII (1929), 201–209.

[14] *The Manner is Ordinary* (New York: Harcourt, 1954), p. 302.

[15] *Social Doctrine in Action* (New York: Harper, 1941), p. 149.

[16] For Maria Laach's justification of this, cf. Albert Hammenstede, O.S.B., "Reports on the Liturgical Movement in Germany," *OF,* VI (1932), 165–172. Cf. Reinhold, "Denver and Maria Laach," *Commonweal,* XL (1946), 87; *Social Forum,* December, 1938. The first popular German liturgical periodical, *Liturgische Zeitschrift,* appeared only in 1929. Parsch's *Bibel und Liturgie* was first published in Austria in 1926.

[17] Miller, professor of theology at the Pontifical College Josephinum, was another pioneer and one of the original associate editors of *Orate Fratres.* Busch and Miller's translations were published together as *Live the Mass* by the Catechetical Guild of St. Paul in 1954, a work that is now selling its second edition of 100,000 copies.

[18] It sold 12,000 copies. *Why the Mass* was a modest pamphlet, but novel in 1926, and since has sold more than 100,000 copies; Louis Traufler was co-author. *Offeramus,* set up by Cuthbert Goeb, O.S.B., went through six editions in two years, and in the twenty-three editions has since sold to date more than 400,000 copies. The *Liturgical Dictionary* was the work of Alexius Hoffmann, O.S.B. *Liturgy the Life of the Church* and *Spirit of the Liturgy* sold over 12,000 copies.

[19] Stoll to Michel, Des Moines, December 4, 1925. Stoll had done some liturgical writing based on Kramp and the *Ecclesia Orans* Series.

[20] O'Mahoney to writer, St. Bonaventure (Cork), Mar. 31, 1953; cf. O'Mahoney to Michel, Jan. 18, 1930.

[21] Attwater to V, Capel-y-ffin, May 13, 1926. In 1924 the English hierarchy appointed a committee to promote liturgical worship and active participation by the laity (cf. *Catholic Bulletin,* Aug. 30, 1924).

[22] It was begun about 1920, enlarged to twelve pages in 1927 and renamed, *Caldey Notes*; in 1929 it became a part of *Pax.*

[23] Holweck and Harrington died within a year. Appointed Visitor, Mother Ellerker reluctantly dropped out of the board of editors after the first year.

[24] Michel had a horror of controversy and to prevent it became almost an obsession with him. When, in 1934–35, Ellard and Michael Ducey, O.S.B., tangled in the *Homiletic And Pastoral Review* on the Mysterium Theory (XXXIV, 1026–1033; XXXV, 922–934; 1035–1042), Michel stopped the controversy by writing to Ducey's superior, "May I be bold enough to ask you to use your utmost influence to put an end to it in the general interests of the liturgical movement in this country?" (to Prior Adrian, Collegeville, June 5, 1935, copy). To Ellard, Michel stated that he agreed absolutely with his last pages but not entirely with "everything you said in the article." After explaining, Michel added: "But I do not wish to get into even private controversies at the present time. I do hope

that we can all continue to put forth our best efforts in the noble cause to which we have dedicated ourselves" (Collegeville, June 5, 1935, copy). Later Michel wrote to Ducey, "May I express my pleasure and satisfaction at your latest reply to Father Ellard? When the controversy first arose I was very doubtful of the advisability of starting an argument. At all events, I allowed myself to be persuaded to write to your Father Prior and request him to use his influence toward putting an end to the controversy. I see now that my fears were needless" (Collegeville, Aug. 12, 1935).

[25] Michel to Cummins, Collegeville, Jan. 17, 1928, copy.

[26] Apostolate, *OF*, IV (1930), 322; cf. Apostolate, *OF*, II (1927), 30; Michel to Charles Cannon, O.S.B., Collegeville, Mar. 18, 1929; "Program for a Liturgical Movement," *America*, XXXIV (1926), 614; many letters to associate editors and others.

[27] "Liturgical Movement," NCEA: *Proceedings* (1925), p. 685.

[28] Michel to Busch, Collegeville, Sept. 25, 1925, copy.

[29] Hellriegel to Michel, O'Fallon, October 26, 1926. Besides his lectures to the Jesuits at St. Louis University, Hellriegel also lectured a good deal to other groups in the years 1926–1927, and since. Pio Decimo Press is his inspiration. Like Michel, he was continually plagued with a large correspondence. Once, after a few months in Europe, he found 250 letters awaiting him "from all parts of the country, . . . as though I were an authority!" (cf. Hellriegel to Michel, O'Fallon, May 2, 1927; June 18, 1928, etc.). His work from 1918 to 1940 as chaplain to the Motherhouse of the Most Precious Blood Sisters with its thirty-two houses is not to be calculated. Hellriegel's guidance of the St. Mary's Institute conducted by the Sisters to improve Catholic art was an effort made long before others were even aware of the problem. Hellriegel was personally responsible for eighty subscriptions to *Orate Fratres* by 1929. Cf. John J. Glennon to Hellriegel, St. Louis, Oct. 14, 1925.

[30] "Nothing has been more stimulating to us than your letters, and so I must beg you to continue your vigilance. . . . There are many phases to our whole apostolate that I feel the need of discussing with you in particular since you are the most experienced scholar of our group" (Michel to Power, Collegeville, n. d., copy). Unfortunately, Power became ill about 1932 and could no longer be active. All his articles in *Orate Fratres* were given gratis. In 1928 he suggested that the title, *Orate Fratres*, be changed to *Worship*.

[31] "By Easter I shall have definite word about our proposal for a course of study in Europe" (Ellard to Michel, St. Louis, Mar. 1, 1927). "A task for your spare moments these next few months will be to set down a list of places that you think I should see in Europe, and . . . to prepare letters of introduction to some of the Abbeys in which you are acquainted" (Apr. 12, 1927).

[32] Cf. Ellard, "Tiptoe on a Misty Mountain Top," *OF*, IV (1930), 394–399; "Sodalists and the Dialog Mass," *OF*, XIII (1938), 5–10. Ellard also wrote a series of articles on the sodalist and the liturgy for the *Queen's Work* in 1926. Speaking of Lord's visit to O'Fallon, Hellriegel told Michel, "He left with great enthusiasm and the resolution to 'push

the liturgical apostolate.' He is a very *influential man.* Send him a little reminder now & then, please" (O'Fallon, Jan. 24, 1929). Michel did. The letters between Lord and Michel for the years 1928–30 indicate that they supported one another's projects.

[33] Michel had counted on Severin Gertken, O.S.B., as his chief collaborator at the abbey, but in 1926 the latter was appointed Abbot of St. Peter's Abbey in Canada. Michel wept when the news reached him in New York. But Abbot Severin took the liturgical movement to Canada, where he has done much to spread the apostolate, as his frequent letters to Michel show. In a lengthy interview at St. John's Abbey, August 22, 1952, Abbot Severin told the writer that his interest in the liturgy began with Michel's enthusiastic letters from Europe and his later conversations with him. Stegmann was Michel's chief worker at home; Vitry left to do chant work on the Pacific Coast in the summer of 1929. Goeb left St. John's on September 16, 1928, eventually to become Abbot of Assumption Abbey in North Dakota, although he continued to do some writing. Returning from Europe in January, 1928, Dunstan Tucker, O.S.B., helped with the liturgical work, as did Roger Schoenbechler, O.S.B., after September, 1928. There were others doing lesser and more mechanical tasks.

[34] Apostolate, *OF*, I (1927), 320.

[35] Bishop Busch to Michel, St. Cloud, n. d.

[36] Press Bulletin of the Central Bureau, vol. XIV, 9a, Aug. 25, 1926. An account of Hammenstede's audience and Herwegen's treatise was later published in part as "The Liturgical Movement as Approved by Pius XI," *OF*, XVIII (1944), 324–328.

[37] Schoenbechler to Michel, Rome, May 17, 1926.

[38] New York, Aug. 29, 1926, copy.

[39] "The Liturgical Movement as Approved by Pius XI," XVIII *OF* (1944), 325.

[40] Schoenbechler to Michel, Rome, Oct. 30, 1926.

[41] *Ibid.*

[42] Michel to Deutsch, Collegeville, Oct. 28, 1925.

[43] Cf. Michel's interesting account of this in "International Philosophical Congress," *Fortnightly Review*, XXXIII (1926), 459.

[44] Michel to Deutsch, New York, Sept. 9, 1926.

[45] Editor's Corner, *OF*, I (1926), 29.

[46] Foreword, *OF*, I (1926), 1–2.

[47] Apostolate, *OF*, I (1926), 31.

[48] Foreword, *OF*, I (1926), 2.

[49] While *Orate Fratres* itself became in many ways "more profound" and scholarly, the "more specialized" reviews to follow were: *Liturgical Arts* (1931); *Altar & Home* (1933); *Living Parish* (1940), since 1955, *Pio Decimo Tidings*; *Liturgy Bulletin* (1948), since 1950 *Mediator*.

[50] Apostolate, *OF*, XV (1940), 34.

[51] It consisted of three series, the first dealing with general ideas and principles of the liturgy; the second, with sacraments and sacramentals; the third, consisting of practical manuals.

[52] Cf. Busch, "Breviary for the Laity," *OF*, X (1936), 102–107. A few

of the laity were already reciting Abbot Fernand Cabrol's *Day Hours of the Divine Office* (London: Burns Oates and Washbourne), available since 1921. For Cabrol's other popular liturgical publications antedating the organized liturgical apostolate, cf. London *Tablet*, June 12, 1937. Attention is called to Lefebvre's *Catholic Liturgy*, first published in English in 1924.

[53] The joint publication of Haering's *Das Leben mit der Kirche*, translated by Rembert Bulzarik, O.S.B., and edited by Michel, the proposed Christ-Life Series in Religion texts, and Michel's insistence that he write all advertising copy for *Orate Fratres*, occasioned the correspondence, in which Michel frequently explained to Benziger, the Lohmann Company, and others the true nature of the liturgy and the proper meaning of the term "liturgical," applied by them to all kinds of devotional literature. For that reason some advertising was rejected. Michel must have chuckled when Benziger, referring to his writings, asked him to write a book on "rubrics" (Benziger to Michel, New York, Mar. 13, 1928). Cf. Apostolate, *OF*, VIII (1934), 562–563.

[54] Michel to Benziger, Collegeville, Apr. 15, 1929, copy.

[55] Michel to Alphonse Matt, New York, Aug. 23, 1926, copy. The Joseph Matt family, owners of the Wanderer Printing Company and for many years printers of *Orate Fratres* and many Liturgical Press publications, are deserving of commendation for the efforts that they made in this regard.

[56] The reason for the response on the Pacific Coast was due in good measure to the interest of Bishop John J. Cantwell of Los Angeles and the promotion of the liturgical cause by Edward J. Hanna, Archbishop of San Francisco, and his director of music, Father Edgar Boyle (cf. "Liturgy in California," *Commonweal*, III (1926) 661. The December 18, 1926, issue of the *Monitor*, official organ of the Archdiocese of San Francisco, reprinted articles from the first *Orate Fratres* and thereafter fostered the liturgical movement.

[57] Editor's Corner, *OF*, I, (1927), 407–408.

[58] On January 15, 1927, Michel wrote to A. Taggart, "As to our conditions here, we Benedictines are just emerging out of the days of strenuous pioneer life as missioners, and have still much of the rough-and-ready mentality of the pioneer about us. We are only now beginning to head in other directions (witness the liturgical apostolate); so far the mission work of building up parishes and dioceses drained all our forces."

[59] St. Paul, Dec. 14, 1926. The "viaticum" was a check of twenty-five dollars. Michel's answer: "The kind words you sent were both a joyous encouragement to the staff of *Orate Fratres* and a source of sincere gratification in so far as they are for us an assurance that we have not been unsuccessful in hitting upon a moderate tact and tone in the Review" (Collegeville, Dec. 16, 1926, copy.) Cf. Apostolate, *OF*, IV (1927), 133–134. No member of the American hierarchy supported the nascent liturgical apostolate more firmly than Dowling, unless it was John J. Glennon, Archbishop of St. Louis: "We welcome with all our heart a liturgical movement," wrote Hellriegel to Michel, quoting from Glennon's sermon

at the dedication of the Sisters' chapel at O'Fallon, (O'Fallon, Aug. 22, 1926).

[60] "The late Archbishop Dowling (my brother) was so interested in having you succeed he bid us keep this intention in our prayers the year you began the new work. Surely God has blessed the O.F." (Sister Mary Antonine Dowling, R.S.M., to Michel, Providence, Jan. 23, 1936).

[61] *Liturgical Movement* (Collegeville: Liturgical Press, 1930), p. 19.

[62] Ready to Michael Ducey, O.S.B., Washington, Sept. 9, 1942, Archives of St. Mary's Abbey, Newark.

[63] (New York: Longmans, 1942), vii. Since 1952, a bishop has been president of the Liturgical Conference, the Most Reverend William T. Mulloy of Covington having been the first.

CHAPTER 6

DIFFUSING THE MOVEMENT

BESIDES the apostolates of philosophy, education, and liturgy, Virgil Michel had a fourth activity that almost amounted to an apostolate — writing letters. It is an interesting phenomenon in his life: his unusual ability, by conversation or letter, to initiate projects and keep them going; to win the cooperation of others; of enthusing coworkers, arousing their interest and setting them to action; to instigate discussion among Catholics who, he once remarked, "too easily rest content with the norm of their own immediate past." Letters, letters, letters poured out to priests, religious, and lay people. This correspondence contains much of the story of the diffusion of the liturgical movement during the years 1925-30 throughout the English-speaking world. All the personalities, the opposition, and the difficulties are there recorded, as well as the triumphs and the joys. What follows is based chiefly upon that correspondence. There could hardly have been a liturgical project in this country for which Dom Virgil did not dispense advice, or in which he did not play some role. Interested European students have often wondered how the liturgical apostolate spread so rapidly in the United States. The present chapter will attempt to answer that question.

As early as the spring of 1927 a publishing firm, apparently sensing a new era in the Catholic Church of the United States, offered to take over the commercial end of the entire liturgical enterprise at St. John's. Because Michel thought of the liturgical apostolate as the cause of God and as an essential form of Catholic Action, the refusal was hardly surprising:

We refused because we feel that a commercialization of our efforts would detract from the dignity with which the apostolate is vested as a work of God, as an undertaking whose aim is the promotion of the cause of Christ and His Church. Nothing has been further from our minds than the use of modern methods of "putting across" an idea. Neither Christianity in its earlier days, nor conversions today, are "put across" by forcible methods of propaganda. Hence it was that we depended from the start on the good will and the cooperation of our friends and well-wishers. That this cooperation has not been wanting is attested by the steady progress the work of the apostolate is making.[1]

He submitted that the liturgical movement, like Christianity in the early centuries, must be spread by those who understood and valued its ideals and who were willing to be apostles for it. In the first issue of *Orate Fratres*, Father Virgil had thrown open the liturgical apostolate to all, clergy and laity alike, for the liturgy was the living heritage of all members of Christ's Mystical Body. Moreover, as he insisted, "a liturgical awakening must come through a sympathetic understanding on the part of the general faithful . . . is necessarily a collective event, and therefore needs the cooperation of many."[2] What they must be intent on doing, he advised the readers of *Orate Fratres*, was "to see a truly apostolic opportunity in every chance to bring anyone's knowledge of the liturgy closer to its true and rich meaning in the spiritual life of the Church."[3] Michel himself did just that. His guiding principle was: make a convert to the liturgy and you have an apostle. It might be a priest, a religious, or a lay person. But it is interesting to note that he would never strongly urge anyone to promote the liturgical apostolate until he had assured himself that the person had grasped its nature and ideals. "Our subscription list has never been large," he confessed a decade later. "We have never sought numbers. But we have endeavored to develop quality and spirit among our readers, for these are what count in any apostolate."[4] He particularly sought out lay leaders, because, as he remarked on one occasion:

The wider spread of the true understanding of and participation in the Church's worship by the general laity must come through the encouragement and example of the more educated among them. The latter exert a natural influence over their fellow Catholics and are unconsciously looked up to as setting the tone of what is good or better.[5]

The mission of Christ, he reminded lay leaders again and again, is primarily carried out through the liturgy, and in bringing to others a better understanding of the means whereby the Church chiefly continues the work of Christ, they were performing true Catholic Action. "Like the spread of early Christianity," he said in 1928, "the renewal of the 'true Christian spirit' is one whose first contacts are very frequently made by the lay apostle." [6]

Therefore, from lay apostles as from clergy and religious, he asked for names of persons who were or might become interested. To all he was ever ready to furnish booklets, explanatory leaflets, brochures, pamphlets, and sample copies of *Orate Fratres* as the need or occasion seemed to demand. In the section of *Orate Fratres* entitled "Apostolate" he encouraged, coached, and guided them, recording their efforts and results as examples to others. Meanwhile he attempted to reach various groups of the laity by lecture or printed word as, for instance, when very early he sent an article to Myles Connolly, editor of *Columbia*, in an effort to arouse the Knights of Columbus to the significance of the liturgical apostolate.[7]

Dom Virgil never tired of saying that once the liturgical life was thoroughly understood and fully lived, the apostolic life and apostolic movements would surely follow. In this connection he stated in 1930, "Thus will come a new vision. . . . What such a new vision and inspiration may mean for the Kingdom of God on earth only a future still veiled to our eyes can reveal." [8] The consistent response to papal calls for Catholic Action would come only in the 1930's, but its indispensable foundation was already being laid in the 1920's. By 1929 pronouncements on Catholic Action by Pius XI had already filled an Italian volume of 614 pages.[9] Michel suggested the translation and publication of this to Benziger Brothers, but before he could take up the translation, his health broke. It is at least a fair question to ask whether any American Catholic periodical in the years 1926–30 so consistently and strongly called for an active Catholic laity as did *Orate Fratres*. But it would seem an even fairer question to ask whether any one person in the United States, by his work, influence, and writings, during that time responded more faithfully to the pleas of Pius XI for Catholic Action than Dom Virgil.[10] When George Shuster cautiously wrote an editorial on Catholic Action in the *Com-*

monweal for February 13, 1929, Michel wrote to him rather inelegantly:

A layman (alas!) must still be very cautious in writing such an editorial, and this editorial could hardly have put things more diplomatically and yet tellingly. — My hearty congratulations! Some day an "official teacher" will have to re-utter the age-old Catholic doctrine that the layfolk are not merely trained dogs but true living members of the Church and in their own way true Apostles of Christ.[11]

Meanwhile, because the liturgy had "been too long a hidden spiritual treasure for many" and because the liturgical life is the basis of Catholic Action, the imperative task of the moment was to diffuse a greater understanding and appreciation of the liturgy. Only in this way could the Pope's program be best realized.

One of the most interesting liturgical projects with which Michel was associated was that among both the Europeans and Africans, mostly Zulus, in South Africa. Here a certain Dr. F. K. McMurtrie, a convert from Anglicanism and mission-doctor at Mariannhill in Natal, had written to him on November 10, 1926, "There is not much appetite for such fare [liturgical activity] so far in South Africa at present, but I hope it will develop." That was all Michel needed to furnish McMurtrie with "unstinted encouragement, help, and advice" in pushing the liturgical apostolate in South Africa. As a result, the convert-doctor became an agent for *Orate Fratres* and the Liturgical Press. An agency for the Liturgical Press was set up in 1928, from which circular letters were dispatched far and wide and regular liturgical propaganda was activated. Thousands of pamphlets were sold before 1940, when war conditions stopped operations. Inspired as he said by Father Virgil, McMurtrie lectured widely on the liturgy and organized a Liturgical Week in Durban, to which Pius XI sent a message. He likewise founded the Mariannhill Gregorian Society and the Natal Liturgical Society, trained several choirs in Gregorian chant, arranged for the translation of *Offeramus* in Zulu, and wrote many articles on the liturgy for the South African *Southern Cross, Clergy Review, Catholic News, Um-Afrika,* and *Marianna.*[12] The flow of liturgical literature from Collegeville to Africa has increased annually.

The liturgical revival had girdled the globe of the English-speaking world when Father Michel discovered the Reverend John T. McMahon, author, director of schools, and editor of the *Record,* the official paper of the Archdiocese of Perth, Australia. Dom Virgil asked McMahon to cooperate in spreading the apostolate in that distant continent and to act as associate editor of *Orate Fratres*, a post which the Australian editor accepted in 1928. "Our one aim," Michel explained, "is the cause of Christ, and the more apostles can work together in that cause, the better will it flourish." [13] On his side Father McMahon answered, "My chief part will be played in making *Orate Fratres* better known." Many Catholic papers in Australia began carrying liturgical items, several published reprints from *Orate Fratres*; an agency for the Liturgical Press was also set up. Father McMahon's liturgical work in Western Australia has been notably successful, although Australia had its first Liturgical Week only in 1953.[14]

In the last half of the 1920's Michel was also instrumental in stirring up similar liturgical beginnings in New Zealand, though on a lesser scale.

One can scarcely do justice to all those who helped Michel promote the liturgical revival in the United States. Nevertheless some merit special mention. There was, for instance, Ellen Gates Starr, convert, writer, social worker, and cofounder with Jane Addams of Hull House in Chicago in 1889. "It is very good of you," said Miss Starr early in 1927, "to let me collaborate in any smallest way in the work of extending knowledge and love of the liturgy. So, do not hesitate to make use of my small capacity in that direction, or to make any suggestions about the use of it." [15] As her capacity was not small, so Michel's suggestions were not few. To warn her against hurting the sensitivities of priests in her lecture audiences was typical of him. Her articles on the divine office, which Michel helped her to write for the first volumes of *Orate Fratres*, were well received, reprinted, and widely read. Miss Starr, in turn, interested Sara Benedicta O'Neill, a well known figure in Catholic library circles in Chicago. The two engaged in a number of projects under Michel's direction. At his behest Miss Starr wrote and lectured on the liturgy to various groups, campaigned for the lay recitation of the divine office, "scattered" Liturgical Press publications, and shared Michel's interest in Christian art, which, as she said, "needs talking about as much as liturgy." [16] She was in constant correspondence with Father Virgil, who also directed her philosophical readings. Only the Lord could tell how many received their interest in the liturgical apostolate, and the divine office in particular, from this tireless and effective lay apostle. Even as an invalid in her last ten years she managed to "scatter about" Michel's pamphlets and ideas. "You are conducting an apostolate all your own," he assured her, "and you will get your reward some day." [17]

Michel always believed that a liturgical revival would also eventually bring a much-needed revival of Catholic art. For the liturgical spirit, that is to say, the true Christian spirit, is an all-pervading spirit, and the aim of the liturgical apostolate is to restore all things in Christ. The Church has always used the arts in her worship to lead to and reveal the spiritual, and after all, said Dom Virgil, "nothing in its proper function to the sublime worship of the Church is really unimportant. As an aid and an expression of this worship true liturgical art is of utmost importance, . . . is . . . an integral element of that worship." [18]

To say that Catholic places of worship often leave much to be desired in this regard is a truism. As late as 1937 Peyton Boswell, writing editorially in *Art Digest*, spoke of "the blasphemy of ugliness" in Catholic churches, adding that "bad art continues to characterize the Catholic Church in America." [19] The artistic situation was considerably worse in the 1920's. [20] It was a condition remaining from pioneer days. Urging patience in the matter of liturgical reform, Archbishop Cushing remarked to the group assembled for the national Liturgical Week in Boston in 1948 that

architecturally, particularly in our older cities, the Church has in times gone by depended on builders some of whom had seen few Catholic churches and knew little about strict liturgical requirements. Vestments were more often than not the work of a pious seamstress who faithfully followed the only pattern she had ever seen. People who had never heard a proper choir carried on as best they could. God bless them all. [21]

On August 30, 1929, the late Father Matthew Britt, O.S.B., told Michel:

It will interest you to learn that Mr. Lavanoux's article in the July *Orate Fratres* furnished me an opportunity, for which I had been looking, to step on the tender toes of our altar builders. Among others the Daprato Company of N. Y. and Chicago, and the Da Prato Co. of Boston. The Daprato house became quite worked up over my gentle insinuation that in their great catalog they illustrated only one altar that apparently met the requirements of the Ritual. To make good they promised to prove that they really could make strictly liturgical altars and they promised to change all their advertisements in the *Ecclesiastical Review* and the *Homiletic Monthly*. They sent me advance proofs of the ad . . . promised to get out a booklet on the subject . . . and send a copy to every priest in the U. S. . . . Altar builders build the kind of altars that priests and bishops ask them to build. Why do not priests ask to have altars constructed that meet the prescriptions of the Ritual? For the simple reason that they have never seen such altars, and in most instances they have never heard of them. This is literally true. I doubt if there is a liturgically correct altar in the Diocese of St. Cloud. I know there is not a single one in this Province. . . . One of the best things your Review can accomplish is the spread of correct information concerning liturgically correct altars and the consequent elimination of the monstrous architectural nightmares from our sanctuaries.[22]

Michel, of course, agreed with Britt, suggested that he write an article on liturgically correct altars, but believing that art can be a good servant but a bad master, he warned:

In general, however, we shall continue fighting shy of too great emphasis on the externals . . . but shall continue to stress the inner nature of the liturgy above all. This is the source of greatest misunderstanding of the liturgy by bishops and priests, even Benedictines. Once the true inner spirit is caught, the externals will almost take care of themselves. On the other hand we might stress the externals without ever getting at the true internal spirit, and thus end by being mere esthetes and not true children of God.[23]

Father Virgil had brought home from Europe a better appreciation of liturgical art. And after his return he had kept up a correspondence with Dom Lefebvre [24] on the subject and gave lectures as well. These lectures on liturgical art would seem to have been the first given by a Catholic in this country. Speaking on this subject in 1927, he stated that "among the many [Catholics], almost all understanding has been lost." [25] In the foreword to *Orate Fratres* he had written that the secondary aspects of the liturgy, among them the artistic, would also be treated, but, he added, "always in subordination to the more fundamental aspect, that of the spiritual import, which is its true essential nature." Due to the conditions of the times, the first four volumes of *Orate Fratres* were primarily devoted to clarifying the spiritual nature of the liturgy. And yet, in the section entitled "Apostolate," he occasionally treated of art. These paragraphs plus a few short articles amounted to no more than ten pages.[26]

Meanwhile Dom Virgil lost no time making efforts to interest artists and architects in the liturgy. "The Christian artist," he pointed out, "perhaps more than many another Christian, is always a lay apostle, he is *ex professo* an apostle of the liturgical spirit in his very vocation." [27] Moreover, his ideal of making *Orate Fratres* and the products of the Liturgical Press "artistic" and "pleasing" examples of the "finest workmanship" brought him into contact with a number of artists. Among these was Maurice Lavanoux, then a draftsman in the architectural office of Maginnis and Walsh, later one of the founders of the Liturgical Arts Society, and at present the editor of *Liturgical Arts*. Lavanoux and his associates have done much to improve the beauty of God's house, in which, as Pius X stated, "nothing should occur . . . calculated to disturb or even merely to diminish the piety and devotion of the faithful." Lavanoux, it appears, had already been disturbed by architects who planned churches in total inadvertence to liturgical practices [28] when Michel wrote to him about his plans for *Orate Fratres*. The Minnesota Benedictine informed him that after the liturgy was better understood as the core of Catholic religious life, the magazine could then also publish articles on liturgical art. Father Virgil asked Lavanoux whether he would consider preparing himself to write them. It was the beginning of a correspondence which, except for the few years of illness, extended to the time of Michel's death.

Lavanoux remarked in reply to Father Virgil's first letter:

Even from the point of view of the artist, the stress on the spiritual significance of the liturgy is an excellent thing. Ofttimes, in the office, I have felt that the IDEA was lost in the attempt to copy old forms of architecture without realizing their real significance in the ages that gave them birth. . . .

Nothing would please me more than to contribute to your publication but I fear I am not up to the liturgical level; if a short article of architectural interest, as related to ecclesiastical architecture, should be of interest, I will gladly make the attempt.[29]

A continuous exchange of ideas and views on liturgy and art followed. "I find the field so vast," Lavanoux wrote later, "that I would welcome the assistance and guidance such as I presume your courses would offer. . . . In the meantime, to facilitate my studies and keep me on the right track, could you suggest the book that I might purchase, in English or in French?" [30] Distance made impossible Lavanoux's attendance at Michel's lectures on liturgical art and symbolism given in St. Cloud and Collegeville at the summer schools of chant and liturgy in 1928 and 1929.

The Liturgical Arts Society was chartered in 1928 and its quarterly, *Liturgical Arts*, first appeared in 1931.[31] Michel had nothing to do with the founding of either beyond offering requested suggestions and advice concerning the quarterly to both Lavanoux and L. Bancel LaFarge. He also assured both that Abbot Alcuin could easily be interested in this project.[32] On September 25, 1934, he lectured on the "Theological and Philosophical Bases of the Liturgical Movement," the first in a series of five lectures sponsored by the society.

During his many lecture tours in the 1930's as an "ambassador of the liturgical movement" (so Michel called him), Lavanoux was in continuous contact with Father Virgil, to whom he wrote more than fifty letters in that time. Lavanoux was typical of a number of persons with live ideas for whom Michel arranged lectures and afforded guidance so that Pius X's ideal might be realized, "I will that my people pray in beautiful surroundings." As Lavanoux stated, "We all relied greatly on Father Virgil's advice in the early years of the Liturgical Arts Society; his writings have always been of great help to me — as they have been to countless others." [33]

Mention has been made of a liturgical summer school, the first of its kind in the United States, which was organized at St. John's Abbey in the summer of 1929. While Michel planned the summer school as a permanent affair, he kept in mind that it might be moved to a more advantageous place. It is significant that in his very first talk to an enrollment of seventy-five largely composed of nuns, he should have said that, in furthering the liturgical apostolate, they would have to expect opposition.[34] In the syllabus one can see Michel's broad approach to the liturgical awakening: "The ultimate aim of the liturgical summer school will be to offer courses of instruction and lectures in all the phases of the liturgy in order to bring out the many vital contacts the liturgy of the Church has in our Christian life and civilization." [35] Hence courses were given in liturgy, pedagogy in religious instruction, church music, Christian art and symbolism. Michel lectured on the last two subjects. He hoped that the summer school would progress to include the teaching of all the sacred arts under the inspiration of the liturgy. Meanwhile, that he used the occasion to form apostles of the liturgy for the various religious communities represented, is evident from subsequent correspondence.

The following appraisal by a religious may be considered typical of the reaction of others present at the summer session:

I will say that

that summer session opened a new era in my own personal life in the Church. . . . The entire doctrine of the Mystical Body was a revelation to me, as well as the part we play in the Sacrifice of the Mystical Christ. . . . It was that idea that I carried back to Chicago and the *Ciscora News* the following year.[36]

The liturgical summer school closed on July 25 with the first National Liturgical Day held in the United States, attended by more than 400 persons from various parts of the country. The success of this first national gathering seems to have been one of the great joys in Michel's life.[37] This Day was meant as a prelude to a national Liturgical Week. However, such a Week was first organized in Chicago in 1940, two years after Dom Virgil's death. There the proponents of the liturgical apostolate professed discipleship to this pioneer, and the gathering was said to be "a living memorial to his tireless zeal." [38]

Ever since returning from Europe Michel had planned for an annual national Liturgical Week. As early as 1910 Liturgical Weeks had been held at Mont César. Again and again there is mention and discussion concerning such a Week in the United States in Dom Virgil's correspondence with associate editors during the late 1920's. At times Michel had worked out a whole program — site, speakers, topics, publication of proceedings, etc. — only to decide that the time was not ripe. To find a bishop who would sponsor it might be difficult. In the very nature of the case, the first Week had to be a success. "We have discussed the matter of a Liturgical Week very often," he told Father Henry Borgmann, C.SS.R., "and still feel that a public liturgical congress might be premature, especially if engineered by us." [39] Then, too, his letters reveal that he had some misgivings about a separately organized Liturgical Week. As with so many other national meetings, fine resolutions could be passed and high-sounding statements rendered, only to have the participants fall back into the same old routine — until the next Week. It would be better if apostles of the liturgy used existing diocesan centers, organizations and programs to promote the liturgy, showing its need and role in every spiritual endeavor and cause. "The liturgical life is not a life apart," he often explained, "but precisely parish life, diocesan life, in its purest form . . . not . . . a specific kind of action of its own; it is simply the primary Christian life and spirit." [40]

There is no evidence beyond an occasional reference in his letters to indicate that Michel seriously attempted to organize a Liturgical

Abbot Alcuin Deutsch, O.S.B.

Mr. Donald Attwater.

Rev. Gerald Ellard, S.J.

Rev. William Busch.

Mother Mary Ellerker, O.S.D.

Original board of associate editors of Orate Fratres.

Rev. Patrick Cummins, O.S.B.

Dom Virgil Michel.

Rev. Martin B. Hellriegel.

Rev. Leo F. Miller.

Rt. Rev. F. G. Holweck.

Rev. James E. O'Mahoney, O.F.M. Cap.

Original cover of Orate Fratres, *drawn under the direction of Eric Gill.*

INSTAURARE OMNIA IN CHRISTO

Rev. Richard E. Power.

Mrs. Justine B. Ward.

Week in the 1930's. Whether he still thought such a Week premature is a matter of speculation, but the fact is that he frequently expressed himself as very happy over the manner in which the liturgical apostolate was progressing. The first Liturgical Week, held at Chicago in 1940 and sponsored by the Benedictine Liturgical Conference, was organized chiefly by Michael Ducey, O.S.B., of St. Anselm's Priory, with the strong support of Abbot Patrick O'Brien of St. Mary's Abbey, and with the help of Father William Busch and Monsignor Joseph Morrison.[41]

As indicated, liturgical life in Benedictine abbeys before the liturgical awakening was not at all what one might expect. St. John's Abbey was no exception. In urging his abbot to give impetus to a popular liturgical revival Michel, while yet in Europe, had stated, "Just think how it would help to transform the mentality towards the liturgy at home." [42] Letters between Abbot Alcuin and Father Virgil frequently spoke of how the Abbey of St. John might be impregnated with the liturgical spirit. And the conclusion always was: form the young monks and thus provide for the future.

The way for Michel at St. John's had been prepared by Abbot Alcuin's efforts to effect a sound monastic and liturgical observance, and by the preliminary work of a deeply pious novice master, Athanasius Meyer, O.S.B., who at least as early as 1925 had his novices gather materials on matters liturgical. In the spring of 1925 he sent these papers to Father Busch with the exhortation that he organize the liturgical movement from the St. Paul Seminary. Father Athanasius explained:

> In order to forestall any misconceptions and misunderstandings, I beg to reiterate that the novices collected the material forwarded to you. They translated most of it from German sources. . . . My purpose in assigning such work to them is to confront them with the matter and to arouse an interest for the liturgy. I keep their gatherings on file and they may be of use to some future connoisseur. I am only an amateur, who has his future behind him.[43]

As it turned out, the real connoisseur would be Michel, whose unusual knack for winning the cooperation of others was, perhaps, never better tested and proven than in his own abbey. Through his gentle though insistent prodding of his fellow monks, they became interested, then involved, and before they knew it they were working. As Michel's closest collaborator at St. John's Abbey wrote after his death:

> With a practical sense of values he strove, not in a spirit of

competition, but with an unassumed challenge of excellence that never stirred up rivalry. He was destined to lead and inspire and not to cross the path of another's ambition. Whoever shared his tastes and interests, which seemed unbounded, profited by his generous support and prudent judgment and undaunted pertinacity of purpose.[44]

To certain confreres in parishes he wrote urging them to do what they could to bring the people back to active participation in the official worship of the Church and to make their parish communities models of liturgical life for others to imitate. While something was certainly done in this regard in Benedictine parishes, nevertheless, it is safe to say that today, in general, parishes conducted by the monks are not particularly distinguished for their liturgical observance. Such model parishes are in the hands of diocesan clergy. In 1929 Abbot Alcuin asked Dom Virgil to give a liturgical retreat to the monks of his own abbey. Michel at first shrank from the task, but he undertook it and the retreat was well received.[45] While there was not much active opposition, it would, nonetheless, be inaccurate to state that Deutsch and Michel won all the monks of the community to a sympathetic understanding of the liturgical movement. A few, in fact, thought the movement and *Orate Fratres* premature. Some expressed the opinion that the Jesuits would put an end to the whole commotion. Others did not like the cover design of *Orate Fratres*, even if Eric Gill had guided its drawing and the London *Catholic Times* had called it "admirable." A lay Brother feared that St. John's would become a place where there was "nichts als Liturgie und Disciplin."

Michel's monastic liturgical efforts, however, were by no means confined to his own abbey. Whenever opportunity presented itself, he tried to stir up interest in the liturgical revival among monks of other abbeys and to win their cooperation or even advice. For the Benedictine nothing is to be preferred to what St. Benedict called the "Work of God," by which he meant the right worship of the Creator through the liturgy. With this in mind Father Michel sought to bring St. Vincent Archabbey into the liturgical apostolate by inviting the collaboration of Fidelis Busam, O.S.B.[46]

When Dominic Scherer, O.S.B., chaplain to students of St. Anselm's College, Manchester, New Hampshire, expressed an interest in the liturgy, Michel urged him to do what he could to promote the cause in those parts. Using *Offeramus*, Father Dominic initiated the dialog Mass among the students, and at the same time the *St. Andrew*

Daily Missal was introduced and also made a part of religious instruction.[47]

At Conception Abbey in Missouri Father Patrick Cummins, O.S.B., was the prime mover in arousing liturgical interest. Father Patrick and Dom Virgil had discussed the future of the coming liturgical apostolate in the United States when both were in Europe in 1925. Father Virgil considered his articles somewhat impractical, too polemical, and controversial. After much coaching, Michel accepted seven articles from this associate editor, and then in part rewrote them. As Father Patrick humbly admitted, ". . . I have too much, unwittingly, of the pugnacious, defiant tone, that will antagonize readers, not merely interest them."[48] Cummins' many letters to Dom Virgil indicate that the courageous Conception pioneer met no small opposition in his own abbey, where he introduced the dialog Mass in September, 1926. He was in part responsible for a few confreres coming to St. John's Abbey in the 1920's for their theological training, among them Bonaventure Hirner and Bede Scholz. When the latter evinced an interest in the liturgical movement, Father Virgil made serious efforts[49] during the years 1926–30 to teach him the liturgy of the Church and thus to equip him for liturgical work at Conception Abbey. It was from this abbey that the third liturgical periodical in the United States, *Altar and Home*, emanated in 1933. Founding a popular liturgical weekly for the home and the ordinary Catholic, to whom the more scholarly *Orate Fratres* did not appeal, had been one of Michel's unrealized ambitions in the 1920's.[50] In an editorial after Michel's death Father Bede, who contributed eight articles to *Orate Fratres*, testified to Dom Virgil's intense interest in *Altar and Home*, stating too generously that "the founders of this periodical received their inspiration from this untiring monk."[51]

One of the unsung workers in the liturgical apostolate was Matthew Britt, O.S.B., of St. Martin's Abbey, who has already been cited for his successful agitation for altars built according to the prescriptions of the Ritual. He succeeded in persuading P. J. Kenedy & Sons to print a student edition of the Cabrol daily missal in the late 1920's, with the result that other publishers had to follow, and the price of missals was cut in half.[52] Unfortunately Father Matthew never found the time to do the spiritual essays on the psalms and other articles for which Michel had pleaded, nor did the psalter for the laity that they planned ever materialize. Yet Father Matthew was always a sound counselor and a strong encourager.

But by far the most faithful of Michel's disciples and workers in other abbeys was the well known retreat master and popular lecturer on the liturgy, Father Benedict Bradley, O.S.B., of St. Mary's Abbey. Without hesitation one can call him the Virgil Michel of St. Mary's Abbey. Bradley was his student when Michel lectured at Pius X School in the summer of 1926. Although that was not the origin of Bradley's interest in the liturgy, his superior, Abbot Patrick O'Brien, believed that Michel "influenced Father Benedict very much." [53] The many letters between them bear this out. Father Benedict frequently complained about his "limited education" and "deficient theological training" and so leaned heavily upon Father Virgil, to whom he sent his addresses and other writings for correction and approval. In fact, he made such demands on him that Michel on one occasion almost lost his characteristic composure. "I still marvel," he exclaimed, "at your power of throwing out requests that might need pages for answer." [54]

Both Bradley and Father Patrick O'Brien were the agents of the *St. Andrew Daily Missal* in the East and sold thousands of copies. While he did not write much, Bradley gave many liturgical retreats and numerous lectures on the liturgy to various groups, including several series of addresses on the liturgy over the Paulist radio station WLWL in New York City. The liturgical notes in *My Everyday Missal and Heritage*, edited by monks of St. Mary's Abbey, were largely his work. The efforts to promote the liturgical apostolate at the New Jersey abbey definitely began with Bradley's revamping the religion courses, and late in 1929 he told Michel:

The liturgy is scoring a triumph. Since the opening of the school in September, we have been drilling all the students in the use of the missal. It's a grand sight to see the 700 assisting at the Mass every morning with a missal. Jersey has never witnessed the sight before. I feel a pardonable satisfaction in the accomplishment — our first effort in that line. [55]

But Father Benedict is best known, perhaps, as the spiritual director of Sister Miriam Teresa Demjanovich, of the Sisters of Charity of St. Elizabeth, Convent Station, New Jersey, whose cause for beatification has been introduced in Rome. As Bradley asked Michel to help in her spiritual direction, to read, and to edit all the famous Conferences written by this theologically untrained and unusual novice and even suggested that the Liturgical Press publish them, comment on the matter is necessary here. Incidentally, with Bradley's blessing, the

Conferences had meanwhile been privately disseminated in convents throughout the world by the nuns.

While Michel never seriously doubted Sister Miriam's extraordinary holiness, he was skeptical from the very beginning about the "miraculous" character of her Conferences, remarkable as they were. But he was also impressed by the direct appeal they made to the soul and by the telling way of their exposition. After mature reflection, however, he discovered "many" theological inadequacies. He pointed out:

The fundamental view of the spiritual life is to my mind faultily conceived. For instance: "Without this continual hammering away at the seemingly-beautiful statue of EGO, *until it is completely destroyed, no spiritual progress is possible.*" The underlining is my own. We must of course keep a high ideal in mind; but to say no progress is possible until that ideal has been attained, is saying very much too much. And that attitude is at the bottom of many statements.[56]

The Conferences, he maintained, showed "many signs of an immature mind" and "not the slightest evidence of revelations." Writing to Bradley in April, 1927, he stated:

The Sister has evidently read a good many spiritual reading books, and absorbed their contents. That is sufficient explanation for the Conferences, it seems to me. To speak of more, or to make much of the Conferences, at present would be to my mind a big mistake. . . . From a distance it seems to me that the greatest danger at present is the nipping in the bud of a possible flower of spirituality, by extravagant guidance. Frankly, if you have put the Sister under any notion that she is receiving revelations (unless you are hiding many things from me), I am afraid you have something to make up for.[57]

Having warned Bradley against undue enthusiasm, Michel then declined to edit and publish the Sister's Conferences, suggested that Sister Miriam rewrite them at a later date and questioned the advisability of circulating them privately.[58]

Father Bradley often told Father Virgil how little nuns knew about the Mass and about the liturgy in general, and how urgent it was, therefore, that they be instructed in the liturgy. Michel never lost a chance to advance the liturgical cause among the sisterhoods by retreat, lecture, and letter.[59] He had repeatedly stated that "our main hope is in the young, in the growing generation. In Church and school and home . . . they must imbibe, along with their food, the spirit of Mother Church." [60] And what was given to the Sisters, Michel maintained, would be given to the children, who would take it into homes, out of which alone Christian communities can be formed. Inviting Michel to address the National Catholic Alumni Federation in New York, April 20–22, 1928, President Edward S. Dore stated, "The alumni and delegates . . . know next to nothing about the liturgy of the Faith, though many of them spent from six to eight years in Catholic colleges and universities in the United States." [61] The only way to improve a bad situation in the schools was to win the sisterhoods for the liturgical cause. No single group has done more to spread the ideals of the liturgical apostolate than these devoted religious women. And in this the Catholic colleges for women have far outshone colleges for men.

As is evident from chapter one, almost from the first years of his priesthood Father Virgil was dissatisfied with available religion texts. He threw himself vigorously into the catechetical movement which arose almost simultaneously with the liturgical revival. He had discussed ways and means of bringing the liturgy to children with Mrs. Ward in Europe, and he had hoped to do something in that line with Mother Ellerker.

In March, 1929, Sister Estelle Hackett, O.P., and Sister Jane Marie Murray, O.P., of the Dominican motherhouse of Marywood, Grand Rapids, Michigan, came to Collegeville to consult the editor of *Orate Fratres*, which they had been reading for advice and assistance toward a plan for the liturgical training of children. To Michel their coming was providential. "I shall never forget those days," Sister Jane Marie recalled later. "The clarity and conviction with which he laid out for us the central role of the liturgy in the life of the Christian and of the Church left us expressionless. A whole new world opened up to us." [62] But the Sisters were dumbfounded when Michel asked them to write out that night yet the first lesson for his analysis the next morning. Thus was born *With Mother Church*,[63] five small volumes of "Laboratory Manuals" based on the liturgical year, which were supplementary to grade and high school catechisms and had as their purpose to unlock the treasures of doctrine and practice enshrined in the liturgy.

Although in Michel's words *With Mother Church* "met with a most enthusiastic reception," it became increasingly evident that Sisters and others teaching religion at that time were sadly unacquainted with the liturgy. Even while working on these pioneering manuals, the authors began to realize that what was really needed was a completely new and basic series of religion texts, one book for each grade, for each year in high school, and eventually a college series. When the two Dominican Sisters protested that this was the work of priests, Dom Virgil at once retorted, "St. Dominic would not say that — let us get busy." He promised that he would guide their study of the liturgy and the intellectual preparation for the work. It marked the beginning of a stream of correspondence between St. John's and Marywood. In six weeks he wrote for their guidance one-half of his volume, *Our Life in Christ*, a positive treatise of Catholic dogma as revitalized in the liturgy. With it he also sent notes, outlines, and bibliography.

Actual work on the Christ-Life Series for the grades and the Christian Religion Series for high school began in October, 1929. Instead of attending a philosophical convention during Christmas vacation, Father Virgil went to Marywood to continue the work of organization. In a letter to Sister Estelle previous to the first of many such meetings, Michel revealed much about himself:

I expect to get to Marywood on Saturday. You need not bother about entertainment, there will be too much work to do. If you wish you may figure on two conferences a day, besides the organizing work. As to the latter, it would be good if one or two of the experienced Sisters could be assigned to each grade or book. We could have our first meeting as soon as I arrive, and after our first discussion the Sisters could plan out the individual lesson topics at once. In that way, the lessons should be outlined for all books by the time I leave. By outlining I here mean only designating the exact topic. I suppose we will have many meetings together about this, but I don't think I must be continuously in session with the Sisters. You know my forte is to make others do the work. I hope Reverend Mother will be able to attend some of our meetings.[64]

An analysis of the Christ-Life Series and the Christian Religion Series will be made in treating of the liturgy and religious education. Suffice it to say here that the Sisters of the large motherhouse embraced the liturgical apostolate. Mother Eveline Mackey, Prioress General of Marywood, sent sixteen of her subjects to the liturgical summer school at St. John's in 1929. Later she gave the following directive to her many subjects:

In the name of the Divine Victim of the Holy Sacrifice

of the Mass I beg you to take up the teaching of the liturgy at once.
. . . Let us pledge ourselves to do this work so that we may draw
down the blessing of heaven on ourselves and on the ten thousand
and more children who will, through our efforts, be brought closer to
our Lord on the Altar of Sacrifice. Heaven alone will reveal what
good must come from this to the souls of the children now in our
schools, to the souls of the children yet unborn.[65]

Besides the Marywood community in Michigan, Michel was in
contact with other religious communities, their schools and colleges,
especially the respective departments of religion, during the years
1925–30.[66] Outstanding among these and deserving special mention
were the Sisters of the Most Precious Blood of O'Fallon, Missouri, and
the Sisters, Servants of the Immaculate Heart of Mary, of Monroe,
Michigan, with their many schools, including Marygrove College,
which was moved to Detroit in 1927. There is perhaps today no better
liturgically trained sisterhood in the United States than the Sisters
of O'Fallon, thanks to Father Hellriegel's twenty-two years (1918–40)
of pioneer work as chaplain. The O'Fallon and Monroe Sisters[67] were
two religious communities primed for a liturgical movement in 1925.
From the Sisters at Monroe the first spark of liturgical interest had
spread to the Dominicans at Marywood in 1928, and no doubt eventually to other religious communities also.

Interest in the liturgy at Monroe had manifested itself in an enthusiasm among the religious for the missal several years before the
publication of *Orate Fratres* made them aware of an organized liturgical apostolate. Through Fathers Busch and Michel, this interest
grew into a strong and conscious cooperation with the liturgical
revival in 1927–28. In the summer of 1927 Mother Domitilla Donohue,
the Superior General, strongly urged the Sisters to take up the
liturgical apostolate by reading *Orate Fratres*, studying the liturgy,
teaching it in the schools,[68] and by using and spreading the publications of the Liturgical Press. On one occasion in a single order from
the Liturgical Press, she purchased fifty-eight subscriptions to *Orate
Fratres*, all the volumes of the Popular Liturgical Library for each
local convent and also 232 copies of Michel's *My Sacrifice and Yours*.
Worried about a $3,000,000 debt on Marygrove College, Mother Dom-
itilla assured her subjects that God would bless the community if
they furthered the liturgical apostolate. As her Sisters had done very
much to promote the *St. Andrew Daily Missal* in its first uncertain
years, so their large orders from the Liturgical Press in its infancy
were a similarly strong support.

Marygrove College required all freshmen to take a course in the liturgy. The college weekly, starting in 1926, fostered liturgical understanding by sponsoring essay contests and printing columns and articles on the official worship of the Church. Marygrove's unique Catholic liberal arts program, President George Herman Derry explained to Michel, centered "around the idea that we have selected as our college motto: 'What Matters is the Mass.' " [69] Chiefly through correspondence Dom Virgil was in continuous contact with the Marygrove program. "We have most of the schools in the Diocese of Detroit," said Sister Mary Judith Connelly before the program at Marygrove in Detroit had begun. "If we — as a body — established the liturgy in our schools, it would have a tremendous effect upon the future Catholic life of Detroit." [70] No doubt it did. In one of his many letters to her, Michel observed:

For me there is something prophetic in the way you are taking hold of the liturgy. You are a young order, are you not? And we are one of the oldest. Yet in Christ we meet and cooperate. . . . Marygrove is an interesting and edifying experiment to watch. The best of modern learning and an intense religious spirit pervading it. It is what our poor world has been aching for for a long time.[71]

No community of Sisters and no Catholic college did more, it seems, so early to propagate the liturgical apostolate than did the Sisters of the Immaculate Heart of Mary of Monroe, Michigan, and their Marygrove College in Detroit — unless it was the O'Fallon community.

The liturgical emphasis in these and other midwestern religious congregations in the 1920's explains further why the liturgical apostolate took early and firm roots in the Middle West. In the 1930's Michel's influence penetrated into some motherhouses and Catholic colleges for women in the eastern United States. But many of the personalities concerned are still living, and the full story cannot be told at this time. Regarding this phase of Michel's activities, one Sister remarked, "He was tireless in his efforts to help, and his contact with us in the eastern states was so much needed. His was a real, personal interest." [72] To those imprudent or impatient with their community's liturgical evolution, he had this to say, "People give up readily when they expect their own efforts to produce success, whereas all true success comes only through Christ, and He will not succeed in us unless we work with His way of charity, patience, long suffering and indomitable perseverance. True life that is sturdy will develop only after obscure germination." [73]

The criticism made by a writer in the *Homiletic And Pastoral Review* in 1938 to the effect that the proponents of the liturgical movement had made the mistake of appealing chiefly to the laity and neglected what was more important, winning the clergy, was wide of the mark.[74] In 1928 Dom Michel wrote a series of five articles entitled "The Priest and the Liturgy" for the 15,000 priest-readers of the *Acolyte,* articles which were well received because they exemplified the acme of prudence and tact. For instance:

If we take the term *liturgy* as embracing the sacrifice of the Mass, the sacraments, the sacramentals, and the divine office, and take the word *interest* to mean that which is a person's vital or professional concern in life, then one takes no risks in saying that the liturgy is *the* supreme interest of the priest. The liturgy is, in fact, the business of the priest, yes, his *raison d'etre.* Take away the liturgy, and the priest and Church alike will disappear.[75]

Months before *Orate Fratres* appeared, and again in 1928, Michel made systematic attempts by letter to reach seminary professors of liturgy, to win their support, and to obtain their suggestions. The response was so unrewarding that he soon gave up the effort, resting satisfied for the time being with contacting individual seminarians in the various seminaries, where students organized liturgy clubs or acted as agents for the Liturgical Press when this was permitted. Like others, seminarians found Michel the source of much encouragement. Only a part of this story can be told at this time.

On March 27, 1926, Hellriegel told Michel:

On March 10th I delivered my second lecture at St. Louis U. [to Jesuit scholastics], again before a very appreciative and enthusiastic audience. At the same time a person will find — and be this *salva reverentia* and *entre nous* — a pronounced helplessness in things liturgical. It is a condition which confronts us, nobody is to be blamed. But if this happens in the greenwood, what of the dry? — We must in all simplicity build slowly from the bottom up. A great task, but a noble work.

In 1927 a confrere summed up the attitudes towards the liturgical movement among student-priests and Sisters at the Catholic University of America when he wrote:

Priests and nuns mostly have the idea that it [liturgical movement] consists in a revolutionary movement in regard to chalices, vestments, monotony of plain chant, and the almost impossible recitation of Mass by the people. And I would add that these do not wish, whether consciously or unconsciously, to be convinced of any other viewpoint. . . . I recall one who came into my room and held out the red flag before him. "What's all this bunk about the chanted or recited Mass by the people? Where do you get your authority? The decrees forbid it." . . . He was a canonist ready for his J.C.D.[76]

Explaining the falling off of subscriptions to *Orate Fratres* at the Pontifical College Josephinum, Father Leo F. Miller, a member of the faculty and associate editor of *Orate Fratres*, wrote to Michel on December 30, 1927, that this resulted "partly because the students are not enlightened and taught to appreciate the Missal, and partly because their minds seem to gravitate toward church buildings and vestments when the liturgical movement is mentioned." Three years later, on January 10, 1930, he informed Michel that the dialog Mass had been dropped. "The liturgical movement here," he said, "seems to have collapsed completely, since the Rector declared that the recitation of the prayers [at the dialog Mass] disturbed him."

From Baltimore's St. Mary's Seminary Philip T. Weller wrote on January 20, 1930:

Since I last wrote to you, I have been striving my utmost to arouse an interest in *Orate Fratres* among the seminarians of St. Mary's. Just when I thought I was succeeding admirably in my efforts, my enthusiasm was quenched by the superiors' refusal to permit us to subscribe. There is a rule in the house that no periodicals, no matter what their nature may be, are to be received by the student. . . .

I have been successful, however, in making the magazine known to the student-body, almost all of whom had never heard of it before. Moreover, I have succeeded in winning over to our cause Fr. Lardner, the spiritual director of first-year theologians. At the half-hour conferences which we have every evening, Fr. Lardner has been reading articles from *Orate Fratres* and supplementing them with comments of his own on the liturgy.[77]

Seminarian Aloysius Wilmes, today Secretary of the Liturgical Conference, assured Michel from Kenrick Seminary in one of his letters, dated November 14, 1937, that "even a mere interest in the liturgical cause is as yet by no means universal here, . . ."

Monsignor Reynold Hillenbrand, rector of St. Mary of the Lake Seminary, had this to say on June 28, 1937:

I know very well that our

students were not becoming familiar with the liturgical literature that your Press issues. I acquired a good deal of it, which I made available for examination to the men who were ordained this spring. Next year we shall do things more systematically. I shall obtain the Christ-Life Series so that the men will know what it is before they leave. I should like to see much deeper interest in the *Orate Fratres*, and I think it will come in time. We are glad that you came to the Seminary; it did the students a lot of good.

No diocesan seminaries have done more to spread an understanding of the liturgy than the seminary of the Archdiocese of Chicago under the rectorship of Monsignor Reynold Hillenbrand, and through the years, the St. Paul Seminary, thanks to the quiet but effective influence of Father William Busch. Because the liturgical cause would achieve permanent results only if priests undertook its promotion, Michel to the last worked to win seminary professors and seminarians wherever opportunity allowed.

A word should likewise be said about the first dissertations on the liturgy and religious education that were written both at the University of Notre Dame and the Catholic University of America. At the latter school Michel's friend and classmate, Dr. George Johnson, was carrying on the tradition of his mentor, Dr. Shields, and guiding the pioneer work. One can see its pioneer character from Michel's words to one of several dissertation writers who appealed to him for help. "Your letter merely calls to my mind what I have been keenly aware of a long time: there is no material extant, at least not in English, on the question of the liturgy as a basis for education." Then, having mentioned a few foreign "completely pioneer" works, he explained, "All you can do, Father, is strike out for yourself. I can only suggest what you already know." [78]

Real forward steps for a movement back to the liturgy occurred in 1928–29, when the National Catholic Welfare Conference news service offered to syndicate a 500-word commentary on the Sunday and feastday Mass along with an *Ordo* for the week at Michel's suggestion. Beginning with advent, these commentaries appeared in more than eighty Catholic papers throughout the United States alone. These commentaries were written chiefly by monks of St. John's Abbey and edited by Michel. At its 1929 convention in Washington, the National Council of Catholic Women decided to make the liturgy the official program of study in its study club program. When these and other study clubs, which mushroomed in the late 1920's and 1930's, struggled with their subject "in some desperation because of lack of study direction," the Liturgical Press furnished pertinent reprints of basic articles in *Orate Fratres*, eventually six out-lines, and also special pamphlets. Thousands of these were used throughout the United States and Canada in the following years.[79]

Another project with which Michel was intimately associated was the *Leaflet Missal*. Parsch had been putting out Mass leaflets since the middle 1920's. They were an ingenious device for introducing the faithful to the prayers of the Mass and eventually to the larger missal itself. As early as March, 1928, Father Virgil considered publishing the Mass in leaflet form for each Sunday, but costs were forbidding and personnel lacking, and besides, he was also advised against it.[80] It was left for two young, far-seeing and enterprising priests of the Archdiocese of St. Paul, Fathers Paul Bussard and Edward Jennings, to make a genuine success of this project, with the strong support of Archbishop Dowling.[81] Jennings had been agent for the Liturgical Press at the St. Paul Seminary, while Bussard had been, after his ordination in June, 1928, one of Michel's most faithful collaborators, and eventually became an associate editor. Both had been among those at the seminary whom Father Busch interested in the liturgy. The two priests had offered the *Leaflet Missal* to the Liturgical Press, but Abbot Deutsch believed that the Press had neither the physical equipment nor the manpower to handle it. However, Michel offered generous help and advice in planning, launching, and publicizing it.[82] The *Leaflet Missal* appeared in January, 1930, with 1,500 sub-scribers. By the end of the year it had sold 429,600 copies — it still averages 100,000 per Sunday — and by 1955 an estimated 30,000,000 copies had been sold. Michel had correctly hailed it as a great step ahead in the progress of the liturgical movement.[83]

Shortly after Michel's death a theologian in Rome wrote to Abbot Alcuin of Michel's lifework, "What he did as organizer of the litur-gical movement would alone do great honour to one person's capa-bility."[84] These words might well be applied to the years 1925-30. Yet an injustice would be done Virgil Michel if at least some mention were not made of his non-liturgical activities during this time. "We cannot ignore our own age and its symptoms. The latter we must examine to their very roots," he insisted in 1921 in regretting there was as yet no Scholastic movement in the United States. How well he followed his own dictum is reflected in the articles on a variety of subjects that flowed from his pen. More will be said later about Michel's early realization of the need for economic and social reform and his efforts in that direction in the 1920's. The liturgical movement having by then been organized and the great depression having ruined the dreams of many, Dom Virgil's words in April, 1930, to Michael Williams, editor of *Commonweal*, were symptomatic of what was to follow from his pen in the next decade:

> Permit me to express my keen pleasure at the general tenor and substance of your article in the latest *Commonweal*. . . . I had been wondering for some time to what extent the *Commonweal* may become an instrument of fostering a new social order based on strict Catholic principles. . . . I was figuring on getting to New York late next summer and possibly broaching such a subject to you if we should be able to meet. I believe with you that it is most imperative for us to come out plainly and openly with our views else the future will be in the hands of Communism as much as the past has been in the hands of unbridled capitalism.[85]

Meanwhile seventeen articles of varying lengths, in many of which he often refuted the philosophical errors of the day, had appeared, chiefly in the *Philosophical Review, New Scholasticism,* and the *Fortnightly Review.* For the latter two he reviewed philosophical works in several languages besides writing anonymously for the *Fortnightly Review*: "In the last two or three years," he said, "I have contributed articles and book notes, signed and unsigned . . . gratis to almost every issue, sometimes several in one issue."[86] The editor, Arthur Preuss, like other editors, thanked him a number of times for his "very precious" and "unwearied and valuable collaboration."[87] The *Acolyte* published Michel's series of nine articles, "Our Modern Civilization," in which he lucidly analyzed the philosophical climate and *Zeitgeist* of the 1920's, taking as his cue the widely read *Whither Mankind*, a symposium edited by Charles A. Beard, and to which Bertrand Russell, John Dewey, the Webbs, Havelock Ellis, and others had contributed, often with unfavorable references to the Church. And when the national society, "Friends of Brownson," organized in late 1926 "to promote interest in the works of Brownson and to make his memory an inspiration for virile Catholicism in word and act,"[88] Dom Virgil sprang to the support of the cause with two lengthy articles in the *Catholic World*, in which he sketched the life and character of the great convert. Most of his seven articles on liberal arts and religious education appeared in the *Catholic Educational Review*. Finally, in the wave of religious bigotry that stirred the 1920's Father

Michel contributed his bit by answering an anonymous priest who wrote against the Church in the *Atlantic Monthly*.[89]

An attempt will be made hereafter to survey briefly Michel's purely social, educational, and philosophical thought, but a few remarks about his philosophical activities for the years 1925-30 are pertinent here, especially since he kept closely in touch with the philosophical world. In 1928 he made an important work available to the English-speaking world by translating Grabmann's *Thomas von Aquin*. He was chosen a member of the Medieval Academy of America in 1926 and was a member of both the American Philosophical Association and of the newly-formed American Catholic Philosophical Association, having been elected to the executive board of the latter in 1929. In the same year appeared his lithoprinted *Notes on Epistemology* and his *Notes on a New Philosophy of Conduct*, later revised. Asked by the Medieval Academy to contribute scholarly articles on the liturgy to *Speculum*, he answered that he had neither the time nor the training to write these.

In short, upon the completion of his European studies in September, 1925, he taught philosophy in the seminary, wrote on a variety of subjects, organized the liturgical movement, in collaboration with his community and others founded and edited *Orate Fratres*, established and directed the Liturgical Press, edited some twenty publications, translated Grabmann's *Thomas von Aquin*, lectured and conducted about a dozen retreats, acted as Prefect of Clerics (1927-29), carried on a large correspondence, organized the liturgical summer school and the first National Liturgical Day, directed and edited *With Mother Church*, and began an entirely new series of religion textbooks for the grades.

"The possibilities of doing good are almost overwhelming us," Michel told Bradley in 1929. By 1930 it had overwhelmed him. No matter how much he did, he always saw how much more could be done and needed to be done. But an indomitable will had worn out both eyes and nerves. Early in 1930 a kindly warning against overwork from one of his superiors brought only the characteristic response, "Did not God give us powers to use in His cause?"[90] In late April of that year his eyes had completely given out, and he was close to a nervous collapse; in the next month, while sitting in a dark hospital room unable to sleep and rest, he was the victim of such severe headaches that he thought he would lose his mind. And ironically enough, this promoter of the liturgy for months could not say Mass nor, for nearly two years, his divine office, and so was given three rosaries as his daily obligation. As a part of a program of recovery he was sent to the Indian missions in northern Minnesota to repair his eyes and to rest his nerves by engaging in a minimal amount of missionary activity, but, as it turned out, he embraced with zeal the apostolate to the Indian.

Before tracing that story, however, it is well to summarize briefly the progress and status of the liturgical apostolate by October, 1930, when Joseph Kreuter, O.S.B., founding editor of *Sponsa Regis*, took over the editorship of *Orate Fratres* for the next five years.[91] Certainly the movement had taken firm roots. Subscriptions to *Orate Fratres*, enlarged to forty-eight pages in 1929, had increased to some 3,000, and the Liturgical Press was out of the red. In 1928 the Liturgical Arts Society had been incorporated, and its organ, *Liturgical Arts Quarterly*, was on the planning boards ready to appear in 1931. The *Leaflet Missal* had been an immediate success. Articles on the liturgy which treated of more than rubrics and external ceremonialism had begun to appear and increased in number in the American Catholic press. "Booksellers tell us," *America* wrote, "that the sale of Missals and books on the Liturgy is astonishing."[92] Pius XI had blessed the American liturgical movement. The liturgy had entered religious education with *With Mother Church*, and theses on the liturgy were being written in two universities. Hundreds of study clubs were taking up the study of the worship of the Church, while the National Catholic Welfare Conference's news service was syndicating a weekly column on the Sunday liturgy. The dialog Mass was no longer a novelty, thanks also to the Sodality movement. Two National Liturgical Days had been held, and liturgical summer schools for liturgical music were on the increase. Several sisterhoods had embraced the liturgical revival. There had been liturgical beginnings in Canada, Australia, Africa, and New Zealand. No doubt an exaggeration and yet also indicative of the leaven that was quietly pervading the American Catholic body were the words of George Shuster, "*Orate Fratres* . . . has (though the fact is not widely realized) completely revolutionized devotional literature."[93] In view of conditions in 1925, progress over the five years had been remarkable.

The three years with the Chippewa Indians of northern Minnesota present an interesting interlude in the life of Virgil Michel. After leaving the hospital at the end of June, 1930, he spent the next three months trying to recuperate, visiting various missions and helping where he could. He had never been inactive, and he could not be so now. After September, when he could take on mission work on his own with headquarters at Cass Lake, he provided for the scattered missions at Federal Dam, Remer, Longville, and Tobique. Here he labored until September, 1931, when, against his will, he was called home to resume teaching philosophy. His eyes and nerves, however, were far from restored, and, for what was to be further rest, in January, 1932, he was appointed administrator of the missions at White Earth, where he stayed until August 1, when he returned for a lighter assignment to Cass Lake. This time he cared for a different set of five missions in outlying areas. At Cass Lake he took in an Indian family to live with him for a whole year, until called home to be made dean of the college in September, 1933, against strong protests.

Once sufficiently recovered to do some missionary work, he embraced the cause of the Indians in the same spirit in which he had taken up the cause of the liturgical apostolate. He lived with the Indians, hunted with them, ate their simple food, often prepared his own meals, worked and took his recreation with them. He felled deer with the best of them. He acquired a sufficient knowledge of the Chippewa language to hear the Indians' confessions in their own tongue. A fellow worker remembered that he "got after those living in invalid marriages like John the Baptist," hunting out the fallen-aways, both Indian and white. How he could adapt himself to primitive conditions and feel at home with the most ignorant and the most unlettered of men was extraordinary. When he wrote and spoke later of the curses of poverty and the blessings of a more simple life, he spoke from firsthand, personal experience.

During much of this Indian period chronic insomnia and headaches were a heavy cross; he suffered physically and also underwent mental depression. Letters at this time frequently ended with "In Passione Domini." But he never gave up work. There was some correspondence and some direction of the Christ-Life Series,[94] his only connection with the liturgical movement.

Always the glaring needs of the Indians challenged him. How could he be idle when there was so much to do? Michel's confreres remember him as doing much meditating during this time; he was allowed to read very little the first two years. In his letters he spoke of organizing ladies' aid societies, forming young people's clubs, organizing choirs, seeking out children and adults for instruction, settling family disputes, solving inter-mission difficulties, repairing churches and houses.[95] Michel's successor at White Earth indicated how active he was:

> When he came to White Earth in January, he was a sick man; he inherited a financial mess but straightened it out by August 1; he supervised the 300 acre mission farm having 50 head of cattle, 40 hogs, 500 chickens and big gardens. He took a complete census (200 families), got a confirmation class of 160 together (children and adults), organized a religion class for 30 children in the country, supervised the boarding school for 125 girls, etc. — all this in seven months.[96]

Interested in their culture, he studied the Indians and understood them. Allowing for what seems to have been some initial imprudent zeal in urging Indians living in sin to take marital vows, in a comparatively short time Michel grasped the problems of missionary work. The many letters between Father Virgil and his superior show that the abbot used him as a trouble-shooter, and that he depended heavily upon Father Virgil for advice in dealing with knotty mission difficulties. "His grasp of every situation made him an excellent counsellor," one missionary wrote, "and I loved to go to him to discuss problems, and we usually found the solution." [97]

Among the Indians, as elsewhere, Michel operated on the principle of working with certain leaders who were responsible for getting others to Mass and the sacraments. Thus on Thursday before first Fridays he would contact the leaders and remind them of their task. He had a theory that, if one remembered the Indians had the mentality of unsophisticated children due to their lack of education and to their general background, one would know where and how to make allowances. He rarely scolded them, but sought them out for private conversations and as a fellow missionary recalled, "with telling effect." [98] He had a way of touching their hearts. Needless to say, they became attached to him, as is evidenced also by the delegation that the red men sent to his funeral.

The twenty-third annual convention of the Catholic Chippewa Societies of northern Minnesota, which Michel organized at Cass Lake for June 21–25, 1933, was the largest that had ever been held. "It was a great religious spectacle and a real spiritual success," thus he proudly described it.[99] In his address to the more than 1,000 Indians assembled, he emphasized the importance of educating the children and the need for higher education of the young people. For this congress he composed after-communion thanksgiving prayers. These along with seven very short articles, chiefly on Indian lore and life, constituted the only writing in this period.

It is not correct, as some have written, that Dom Virgil re-organized the Indian missions and had a definite program of reconstruction for them. He was sent to the missions to regain his health; he was never at one place long enough to get the reaction to his initial enthusiasm. Thus a missionary observed:

Had he spent ten to fifteen years among them, no doubt something outstanding would have happened. He was intensely interested in Indian congresses and tried to arouse the young Indians and work out an Indian program, but his stay was cut short, and nothing became of it.[100]

Meanwhile a number of the monks of St. John's had been begging him to return and to lead the effort for the accreditation of the college: "You won't have to do any work — just come back," a delegation of three headed by Walter Reger, O.S.B., told him in December, 1932. His name and recognized scholarship, it was thought, would help to achieve accreditation. And *Orate Fratres* also could use his dynamic leadership. While his health was by no means fully restored, the abbot was determined to recall him. Michel admitted feelings of rebellion; he confessed that returning was the hardest act of obedience he ever had to make.[101] He was prepared to spend the rest of his days for the spiritual, social, and economic regeneration of the Indians. But there was another reason why he hesitated: Father Virgil and Abbot Alcuin had differed on the development of the college. He protested to his superior:

My going back to St. John's as Dean, seems like a huge joke to me, although a very grim one. . . . Once you wrote that I should pray that my health improve. I have found that almost impossible — and for two reasons. One is that I find it very difficult to pray for any temporal favors at all — it seems to degrade prayer when we want to insist on getting from God what does not belong to the One Thing Necessary. . . . The second reason is that I have come to believe that God does not want me to get better. And I had to come to this conclusion for my peace of mind. I have always preached to others that we see the will of God in the actions of our superiors. And when I applied that to myself in the present condition, I had to conclude that I am not to get better.[102]

To which Abbot Alcuin responded:

. . . Come then, leaving the future in God's hands. That you have not gotten better up to the present time is not an indication that it is God's will your health should not improve. . . . When your mind is again serene, you will sleep well and your eyes and your nerves will improve. If not, then I will look upon it as an indication that it is not God's will that you be here and I shall have other work for you. Strive to be humble and put yourself completely in God's hands. I know you try to do this.[103]

Home he came, but his heart remained with the Indians, and in the following summer he was allowed to return for one month to organize another large Indian congress. At that time he helped in directing seminarians in a summer program of catechizing the Indians. This only convinced him the more that he belonged with the latter. Once again he begged, "I surely wish I could stay all summer and direct the work and get the slack ones. So much good could be done here! . . . Why, oh why, did I ever have to go back to school work . . ."[104] But before he could get involved with the children of the forest, the abbot withdrew him. His health improved, and the next five years would be the most fruitful of his life.

NOTES TO CHAPTER 6

[1] Editor's Corner, *OF*, I (1927), 218.
[2] Foreword, *OF*, I (1926), 2–3.
[3] Apostolate, *OF*, IV (1930), 322–323.
[4] Apostolate, *OF*, X (1936), 29.
[5] Apostolate, *OF*, III, 1929), 186.
[6] Apostolate, *OF*, II (1928), 410. "A word here or there, a question rightly put, a casual conversation, or a more conscious plea for a proper understanding of the liturgy, will not infrequently gain new followers. There are many among the faithful who yearn for this light; and there are a few in close enough contact with them to show them where and how to find the light. . . . It seems to be the way in which every true cause of Christ spreads" ("On Being Apostles," *OF*, I [1927], 314–315).
[7] Connolly answered, "I like your informative article but feel *Columbia* is not the place for it. It is not the sort of article I can make my readers read" (New Haven, Oct. 4, 1927).
[8] "The True Christian Spirit," *Ecclesiastical Review*, LXXXII (1930), 141.
[9] *Pio XI e l'Azione Cattolica* (Rome: Via Dei Cestari, 1929).
[10] Cf., e.g., Editor's Corner, *OF*, I (1926–27); Apostolate, *OF*, I–IV (1926–30), esp. articles in I, 314–315; II, 123–126, 410; III, 186, 317, 427–428; IV, 18–21; 322–323. "Significance of the Liturgical Movement," *NCWC Bulletin*, X (1929), 6–8, 26; "The Layman in the Church," *Commonweal*, XIII (1930), 123–125; "The True Christian Spirit," *Ecclesiastical Review*, LXXXII (1930), 128–142. "The Liturgical Movement and the Catholic Woman," Catholic Central Verein of America: *Annual Report* (1929), pp. 57–62. One should mention in this connection a pioneer book by John Harbrecht, *The Lay Apostolate* (St. Louis: Herder, 1929).
[11] Collegeville, Feb. 13, 1929, copy.
[12] Above information in the many letters of Michel and McMurtrie between Nov. 10, 1926, and Mar. 4, 1930. Cf. McMurtrie, "Liturgical Propaganda in South Africa," *OF*, III (1929), 303–310. McMurtrie to the writer, Empangeni, Zululand, South Africa, Sept. 22, 24, and Dec. 10, 1954. In 1929 McMurtrie was given the Cross *Pro Ecclesia et Pontifice* for his zealous work in South Africa.

[13] To McMahon, Collegeville, Aug. 28, 1928. Cf. Apostolate, *OF*, III (1929), 429–430; IV (1930), 186.

[14] Cf. Apostolate, *Worship*, XXIX (1955), 360–362. *Worship* today has 67 subscribers in Australia, 27 in New Zealand.

[15] Gates to Michel, Chicago, Mar. 18, 1927.

[16] Gates to Michel, Suffern, Jan. 14, 1934.

[17] Michel to Gates, Collegeville, Jan. 31, 1929, copy. Above information in correspondence running from Aug. 23, 1926, to Dec. 7, 1937. She died in 1940. "When I was a new convert I used to marvel at the utterly unsocial and unliturgical habits of prayer: what people would be doing — anything but 'assisting' at Mass. Once, in Holy Week I asked my good and very dear laundress, 'May, what *do* the people do during those long Gospels?' 'Oh, some of 'em stands and some of 'em sits!'" (Gates to Michel, Suffern, Nov. 27, 1935).

[18] Apostolate, *OF*, II (1928), 221.

[19] "The Valiant Few," *Art Digest*, XI (1937), 3; cf. also quotation from a letter by Sister Esther Newport, S.P., to the editor, *ibid.*, p. 4.

[20] Cf. Ralph Adams Cram, "New School of Christian Arts," *Commonweal*, IX (1928), 196–199; also Maurice Lavanoux, letter to the editor, *ibid.*, p. 347.

[21] "Address of Welcome," Liturgical Week: *Proceedings* (1948), p. 5.

[22] Britt, originally a member of St. John's Abbey, was a monk of St. Martin's Abbey, Lacey, Washington, then in the ecclesiastical province of Portland. As to the altars in the Diocese of St. Cloud, Michel responded, "There *are* some good altars in this and the St. Paul Archdiocese, but all are of relatively recent origin. We just reconstructed the altars in our main Church here, and they are as correct as the old materials would permit" (Collegeville, Sept. 9, 1929, copy).

[23] *Ibid.*

[24] Having asked Michel to make known the newly founded *L'artisan liturgique*, first magazine devoted to liturgical art, Lefebvre wrote, "Unissons nos efforts sur le terrain liturgique et nous arriverons à les résultats surprenants" (to Michel, Nîmes, Apr. 7, 1927).

[25] Editor's Note, *OF*, I (1927), 182. As early as 1926, Michel and Attwater began discussing the possibility of articles on liturgical art (Attwater to Michel, Capel-y-ffin, June 15, 1926, etc.).

[26] For these, cf. the following: *OF*, I (1926–27), 2, 182; II (1928), 220–221, 409; III (1929), 217–218, 426; IV (1930), 170–171, 223–226.

[27] Apostolate, *OF*, XI (1937), 183.

[28] Recently Lavanoux wrote of Michel, "His ideas appealed to me since I found in them a justification for many of the misgivings I had entertained while working as a draftsman in the offices of Catholic architects" ("Collegeville Revisited," *Liturgical Arts*, XXII [1954], 44–45). Michel began his correspondence with Lavanoux when the latter had asked for a sample copy of "Sursum Corda" on November 27, 1926.

[29] Boston, Dec. 4, 1926. Lavanoux's first article: "An Architect's Dilemma," *OF*, III (1929), 277–281.

[30] Lavanoux to Michel, Boston, June 8, 1928.

[31] Cf. *Liturgical Arts Society* (New York: Liturgical Arts Society, n.d.); LaFarge, *op. cit.*, 290–293; Michel, Apostolate, *OF*, XI (1937), 182–184. LaFarge has been an inspiration for and chaplain to the Society from its formal incorporation. Editor of *Liturgical Arts* in its first year was Harry Lorin Binsse and first president of the Society, Charles D. Maginnis. The Catholic Art Association was organized in 1937 largely through the initiative of Sister Esther Newport, S.P., in which year its *Christian Social* (now *Catholic*) *Art Quarterly* made its first appearance.

[32] Cf. L. Bancel LaFarge to Michel, New York, Feb. 5, 1930; Michel to LaFarge, Collegeville, Feb. 14, 1930, copy; LaFarge to Deutsch, New York, Mar. 22, 1930. "May I ask — without indiscretion — the cost of printing *Orate Fratres?* A group of us here and in N.Y. hope some day to publish a magazine, most likely a quarterly, devoted to liturgical arts and other matters of interest to architects, sculptors, painters, etc. As I may be called upon to do most of the editorial work I am interested in costs. Give me the *dark* side of the question as I know that some of my confreres are optimistic in the matter" (Lavanoux to Michel, Boston, Feb. 9, 1930). Michel supplied details, and the projected quarterly became *Liturgical Arts*.

[33] "The Editorial Diary: XVII," *Liturgical Arts*, XXIII (1955), 159.

[34] Sister Estelle Hackett, O.P., to Michel, Marywood, Nov. 1, 1929. "The suffering has indeed been bitter and humiliating. . . . I am convinced that hell is astir . . ., but the effect of the liturgy will go on throughout all time" (*idem*). Stegmann was dean of the summer school. The origin of this school goes back to the previous summer, when at St. Cloud the liturgical apostolate of St. John's Abbey conducted a chant school under the direction of Ermin Vitry, O.S.B.

[35] Apostolate, *OF*, II (1928), 255; cf. pp. 253–256 for Michel's comprehensive plan and description of the liturgical summer school.

[36] Sister Estelle Cullings, O.S.B., to the writer, Canon City, Colorado, Apr. 26, 1954. The *Ciscora News* was the official organ of the Chicago Sodality Union.

[37] Cf. Michel's enthusiastic description, "First National Liturgical Day in the United States," *OF*, III (1929), 324–330. This must have been a most busy day for him; yet that very day he wrote letters! The other Liturgical Days were held at Collegeville in 1930 and at St. Cloud in 1931. As early as 1927 Michel had attempted to hold such a Day in St. Cloud (Michel to Charles Grunewald, Collegeville, Oct. 4, 1927, copy).

[38] Diekmann, Apostolate, *OF*, XV (1940), 32.

[39] Collegeville, Feb. 27, 1929, copy.

[40] Apostolate, *OF*, III (1928), 55–56.

[41] Cf. Apostolate, *OF*, XIV (1940), 368–372; an archdiocesan Liturgical Week had been held in Cincinnati in 1924. In "The National Liturgical Weeks and American Benedictines," *American Benedictine Review*, VI (1955), 156–167, Ducey gives an account of the meetings that eventuated in national Liturgical Weeks sponsored at first by the Benedictine Liturgical Conference.

[42] Michel to Deutsch, Louvain, Jan. 18, 1925.

43 Meyer to Busch, Collegeville, Mar. 25, 1925. In this letter Meyer wrote to Busch, "Dear Father, you will not take it amiss if I submit to you a few observations anent the genesis and aims of this liturgical movement. I even venture to offer some suggestions, which, in my humble opinion would assure success if they were carried out. These are, of course, *inter nos* — and not for public use. For if the prophets should find out that the animal spoke, they might put a halter on him. My old Irish teacher used to encourage me when I guessed the correct answer to his query by saying: "Well, once in a while a blind pig finds an acorn." In case I should have been lucky this time, too, in finding, you may throw the acorns where you think an awakening would be beneficial." The "observations" consisted of a six-page paper on the liturgical movement given shortly before, to the seniors of the abbey; these pages indicate a thorough grasp of the ideology of the liturgical apostolate; Meyer was certainly a pioneer. He successfully resisted all of Michel's strong pleas that he write.

44 Basil Stegmann, O.S.B., "As We Knew Him," *OF*, XIII (1939), 97–98.

45 "If you were abashed at the task of facing that heterogeneous audience at our retreat, you certainly disguised your feelings. You looked as though you enjoyed it immensely. I admired your grit." "Even during the silence of the recent retreat a few Fathers remarked to me that they wished they knew how to begin the liturgical work" (Charles Cannon, O.S.B., to Michel, Mahnomen, Aug. 27 and Sept. 9, 1929).

46 Busam to Michel, Beatty, Pa., Dec. 14, 1926. Busam was then eighty years old and so could not accept. In one of his letters he complained to Michel that the clerics at St. Vincent Archabbey were reciting the rosary instead of actively assisting at the conventual Mass.

47 Scherer to Michel, Manchester, Mar. 8, 1927. *"Et harum rerum omnium tu pars fuisti"* (*idem*). The correspondence went on to 1930. Cf. interview with Prior Dominic, Manchester, Aug. 25, 1954. The dialog Mass began among the monks on March 8, 1927, and shortly thereafter among the students. Casimir Mulloy, O.S.B., of St. Anselm's Abbey attended the liturgical summer school at St. John's in 1929, and later Pius X School. In the mid-thirties Christopher Hagen, O.S.B., studied liturgy at Maria Laach. Today St. Anselm's Abbey has one of the finest monastic liturgical observances.

48 Cummins to Michel, Keuterville, Idaho, Oct. 24, 1926; cf. esp., Jan. 19, June 16, and Dec. 29; Conception, Aug. 29, Sept. 27, 1926, and Apr. 7, 1927; Michel to Cummins, Collegeville, Oct. 20, 1926, Sept. 13, 1927, Jan. 17 and 24, 1928, copies.

49 Of his days at St. John's Scholz wrote, "Father Virgil and I went out on a walk to discuss the liturgical movement twice a week. Every other Sunday Fathers Virgil, Basil, Cuthbert, Oliver and I had a sort of seminar. Father Virgil did most of the work. He would type out things for discussion and have many sources for reference to elaborate on the subject. He and Father Basil of course did not always agree. I always admired Father Virgil for the capacity he had for work. . . . When he was working on the religion textbook series he timed himself so many pages each

day. If he did not get the amount finished during the day, he would stay up at night and was under constant tension. I have never seen any monk observe poverty as he did. . . . After leaving St. John's we often met at O'Fallon. . . . We would be up to the early hours of morning talking over matters liturgical. . . . I am sorry that three years ago I destroyed my correspondence with Father Virgil. In these letters he constantly encouraged the efforts we were making at Conception" (to writer, Weston, June 16, 1954).

[50] Michel to Mother Ellerker, Collegeville, Sept. 1, 1927, copy.

[51] *Altar and Home*, VI (1939) n.p.g. Actually Raymund Meyerpeter, O.S.B., started this periodical, first edited by Henry Huber, O.S.B., named by Bonaventure Hirner, O.S.B., and made exclusively liturgical by Bede Scholz, O.S.B.

[52] Britt to Michel, Lacey, Mar. 31, 1930. Britt's *Dictionary of the Psalter* (New York: Benziger, 1928) and *Hymns of the Breviary and Missal* (New York: Benziger, 1922, 1924, 1948) are standard references.

[53] Interview with Abbot Patrick, Newark, June 19, 1954.

[54] Michel to Bradley, Collegeville, Jan. 23, 1930, copy. Among the many Bradley interested in the liturgy was Monsignor William Griffin of St. Michael's parish in Jersey City. Later as bishop of Trenton, Griffin made efforts to interest his clergy in the liturgy, among other ways, by ordering the introduction of the *Leaflet Missal* into all parishes (cf. John Aschemeier, "The Trenton Plan," *OF*, XXI [1946], 32–35; XXII [1948], 271–274).

[55] Bradley to Michel, Newark, Dec. 5, 1929.

[56] Michel to Bradley, Collegeville, Apr. 13, 1927, copy.

[57] *Ibid.* Bradley's answer: "Your letter . . . was read with care. I want to thank you sincerely for the frankness with which you express your opinion. I am not a bit hurt over the refusal to go on with the work of publishing the Conferences. You are doing only what you should do, and I find no fault with your action. May I ask you, however, to respect the confidence I have reposed in you. I see His will in everything that God permits. What He will do in the future only He knows. I shall leave matters entirely in His hands. . . . I know you are a busy man. . . . I regret having put you to so much useless trouble with the Conferences" (Newark, Apr. 16, 1927).

[58] The Conferences were edited and published under the title *Greater Perfection* by Sister Miriam's brother, the Reverend Charles C. Demjanovich in 1928, and have gone through three printings. The statement to which Michel objected occurs on page 63. Sister Miriam died at the age of twenty-six on May 8, 1927. Bradley died on December 19, 1945, believing to the last in her heroic sanctity. Theodore Maynard's *The Better Part* (New York: Macmillan, 1952) is the story of her life; Maynard claims (p. 199) that she read Michel's writings but offers no evidence.

[59] In 1926 he gave summer lecture-courses at Pius X; 1927 at St. Benedict's Convent, St. Joseph, Minn.; 1928 at St. Cloud Music Institute; 1929 at St. John's Liturgical Summer School and Marywood, Grand Rapids, Mich.

[60] Apostolate, *OF*, III (1929), 317.

[61] New York, Feb. 7, 1928.

[62] From one of many interviews at Marywood and Washington, generously granted by Sister Jane Marie. Sister Estelle, as a lay grade school teacher, was so appalled by the children's ignorance of their faith that she resolved to dedicate her life as a nun to their instruction.

[63] These were the work of eleven Sisters of Marywood and eight monks working under the direction of Michel and Busch at the liturgical summer school of 1929, when the Liturgical Press published them. Later Sister Estelle wrote to Michel, "Truly God must have given you a special light and a holy daring when you consented to sponsor an enterprise so vaguely described and by people unprepared and unlearned in the very thing we were proposing" (Sister Estelle to Michel, Marywood, n.d.). Typical of many nuns writing to Michel: "I . . . knew nothing of the beauty and sublimity of the Mass in its liturgical interpretation. Although the Mass was first, I considered it merely one of many devotions of the Church. All this time I felt the lack of the unifying bond and my religious life unsatisfactorily divided between devotions and practices. About a year ago now I first heard of the liturgy in its correct sense and at the same time heard of *Orate Fratres*. Father, I know you will realize from what I have told you what this new light has meant to me. . . . At last after all these years the craving of my heart is being satisfied. If God wills and obedience permits, I shall devote my energies in this cause. My work of assisting and supervising the elementary teachers gives me many opportunities to share the joys which the liturgy brings to others. . . . How have you succeeded in so completely effacing self from your actions, Father?" (Marywood, Nov. 1, 1929).

[64] Collegeville, Dec. 21, 1929, copy. Sister Jane Marie recalls that Michel gave thirteen one-hour lectures in five days to the Dominican Sisters gathered at Marywood from the missions.

[65] Circular letter found in the Michel Papers.

[66] Correspondence shows him advising teachers of religion at the following colleges: St. Mary's College, Notre Dame; Rosary College, River Forest; College of St. Catherine, St. Paul; Sacred Heart College, Grand Rapids; Manhattanville College, New York; Sisters' College, Washington.

[67] Chaplain at Monroe since 1921, Father Walter Marron needed no liturgical movement to make him realize that the liturgy is the exercise of the priesthood of Christ; he functioned accordingly; in 1923-24 he began a course, perhaps the first of its kind in the country, on the liturgy in the best sense of the word, for both collegians and Sisters.

[68] Busch in 1928 suggested a plan for high school religious education based on the liturgy which was worked out and used in all the high schools of the community for a number of years. "But it was really Father Busch's letter and all the interest he and Father Virgil continued to show in us that encouraged Mother Domitilla to make the teaching of the liturgy a community apostolate" (Sister Mary Judith to the writer, Detroit, May 14, 1955). Father Power gave six lectures on the liturgy at Monroe in the summer of 1928,

[69] Detroit, June 8, 1930.

[70] Monroe, July 10, 1927.

[71] Collegeville, Nov. 20, 1927, copy. On Marygrove, cf. "Aux Etats-Unis," *Bulletin Paroissial Liturgique,* XIV (1932), pp. 41–42. Apostolate, *OF,* I (1927), 348–352; III (1928), 62; IV (1929), 38–39; XV (1941), 332–333. Marygrove *Watch Tower,* Apr. 12, 1927. Many letters between Michel, Busch, Derry, Power, and Sister Mary Judith, 1927–1930.

[72] Sister M. Florian Reichert, S.S.J., to the writer, Rochester, N.Y., May 11, 1955.

[73] Documentation withheld.

[74] Joseph Dowling, "The Liturgical Revival — Whither?" *Homiletic And Pastoral Review,* XXXIX (1938), 140–143.

[75] *Acolyte,* Mar. 24, 1928. Italics, Michel's. Somewhat later Stegmann and Power followed with a series of articles on phases of liturgical life.

[76] Damian Baker, O.S.B., Washington, Sept. 6, 1927. However, Father Edwin V. O'Hara wrote to Michel, "I am very grateful to you for the study club outlines and the pamphlets. . . . I am teaching a class in Parish Sociology at the Catholic University, in which we shall be discussing the liturgical movement. . . . Shall get the students acquainted with your literature" (Washington, Feb. 25, 1930).

[77] Michel answered, "It is too bad you could not go on with the canvassing, but that can't be helped and we must be resigned" (Collegeville, Jan. 24, 1930, copy). Michel was in contact with seminarians at the following seminaries: St. Paul, St. Francis, St. Vincent, Kenrick, St. Louis University (scholastics), St. Joseph, (Dunwoodie, New York), Notre Dame (New Orleans), etc.

[78] Michel to Henry Gebhard, Collegeville, Nov. 20, 1927, copy. For dissertations, cf. Apostolate, *OF,* II (1928), 351–352; III (1929), 93. "I have been tempted a number of times to write a full account of our children's Mass here in the parish church. . . . We are succeeding in making the Mass intensely real to our children" (Johnson to Michel, Washington, Nov. 26, 1927).

[79] Justin McGrath to Michel, Washington, Sept. 8, 1928; Michel to McGrath, Collegeville, Sept. 12, 1928, copy. Apostolate, *OF,* IV (1930), 277. For a time the *Ordo* was prepared by Bussard.

[80] In letters to the Wanderer Printing Co. (to A. Matt, Collegeville, Mar. 2, 1928, and May 17, 1929, copies) Michel asked for quotations. "As for the leaflets, I do not think the plan is worth trying" (Power to Michel, Springfield, Apr. 9, 1928); cf. Apostolate, *OF,* II (1928), 159, 252–253. In the 1925–30 period there were a number of projects that did not materialize, among them a Lenten missal and some kind of breviary for the laity. Thinking current missals could be improved, Power and Michel had also planned an all-English Sunday missal for American Catholics.

[81] Jennings, Bussard, and Father Louis Gales launched the *Catholic Digest* in 1936. Besides articles for *Orate Fratres,* Bussard also contributed to the Popular Liturgical Library. Bussard has done much to bring an understanding of the Mass to the man on the street with his many articles on the holy Sacrifice in syndicated columns in Catholic papers.

[82] Cf. many letters, Bussard to Michel, St. Paul, n.d. "Your very welcome letter was received. . . . We are glad to receive the advertising you spoke of. . . . About the AGENCY, we shall be glad to have you act for us. . . . The first chance I get I will run up to see you, and in a few minutes we can do more than in 20 pages of correspondence. We sincerely thank you for your kindness, and hope that we may in some way be able to repay you" (Jennings to Michel, Minneapolis, Nov. 20, 1929).

[83] "The *Leaflet Missal* which you have so capably sponsored has certainly done more than any other individual publication to further the Liturgical Movement in this country" (Louis Kenedy to Bussard, New York, Oct. 18, 1939). On November 7, 1929, Bussard wrote to Michel from St. Paul concerning the future *Leaflet Missal*, "I lost hours of sleep. . . . I hope to heaven it doesn't flop. . . . If that ever goes over — sure a great thing — I almost get excited about it." Four years later on February 13, 1934, Bussard, then a student at the Catholic University told Michel, "Things have been happening thick and fast. When I look back on the last four years, I often wonder how it all came about. Even the people at the Catholic University are talking about the liturgy. I took Johnson's Seminar on the subject recently, and used your fine articles in the *Ecclesiastical Review* on the juridic concept of the Church with great effectiveness. That is really a remarkable piece of work. Everyone seemed to be impressed, and there was no irritation at all. Then Johnson asked me to do the same thing at Teachers' College. . . . Then the Sulpician [Louis Arand] in charge of Caldwell Hall asked me to give a conference to the priests there on the leaflet missal!"

[84] Anselm Stolz, O.S.B., to Deutsch, Rome, Dec. 21, 1938.

[85] Collegeville, Apr. 10, 1930, copy.

[86] Michel to Jerome Wisniewski, O.S.B., Collegeville, Jan. 28, 1930, copy.

[87] Preuss to Michel, St. Louis, Apr. 6, and July 2, 1927.

[88] J. P. Donovan, C.M., "Friends of Brownson," *Acolyte,* Jan. 15, 1927; cf. also "Why a Brownson Revival" by the same author, *ibid.,* Mar. 12, 1927.

[89] "What is Catholic Opinion?" *Atlantic Monthly,* CLI (1928), 396–397; cf. Apostolate, *OF,* II (1928), 187. Articles mentioned in this paragraph can be found in the bibliography.

[90] Stegmann, "As We Knew Him," *OF,* XIII (1939), 100.

[91] Actually no one was prepared to assume the editorship of *Orate Fratres* after Michel's breakdown : Kreuter generously volunteered and expended much effort in keeping it going. He had acquired an interest in the liturgical movement from reading European German liturgical literature and from conversations with Michel. Kreuter believed that some of the first promoters of the liturgical apostolate had neglected the ascetical aspects of the spiritual life. According to Michel's correspondence, there were a number of complaints registered by associate editors and others about Kreuter's editorial policies. In 1929 Kreuter founded at St. John's Abbey *Sponsa Regis,* the first spiritual review for American sisterhoods, in fact, the first such monthly in the English-speaking world. It had been

founded to promote the spiritual life of the Sisters, with special emphasis on asceticism. The liturgical content of *Sponsa Regis* was very thin. Only when Paschal Botz, O.S.B., took over the periodical in 1946 was there a growing and balancing emphasis on the liturgy. For an evaluation of Kreuter's work, cf. Barry, *Worship and Work*, pp. 276–281.

[92] Wilfred Parsons, "The Catholic Year in the U.S.," XXXVIII (1927), 294.

[93] *The Catholic Church and Current Literature* (New York: Macmillan, 1930), p. 99.

[94] Stegmann, as co-editor of the Christ-Life Series, Busch and Hellriegel also contributed generous advice to Sisters Jane Marie and Estelle during Michel's convalescence.

[95] Michel to Deutsch, Cass Lake, Nov. 28, 1930; White Earth, July 1, 1933; Ball Club, June 18, 1934.

[96] Justin Luetmer, O.S.B., to writer, Mahnomen, Minn., Jan. 27, 1953. "I wanted to ask you if you could put someone else in charge of White Earth and give me the chance to take care of my eyes that we both thought I would get when I was going to White Earth" (Michel to Deutsch, Moorhead, Minn., April 14, 1932). But lest "someone else be overburdened," he offered later to stay. "I have been overwhelmed so that both Friday and yesterday I did not get my rosaries said until I should have been in bed" (*ibid.*, Feb. 7, 1932).

[97] Luetmer to writer, Mahnomen, Jan. 27, 1953. An Indian missionary asked him to give a mission some years later: "I am sure you would be the one to move many of the Indians. . . . Your past experiences here assure me of that. . . . For success the mission will have to touch the Indians the way you know how. The crowds you would draw to various places is our proof" (Denis Parnell, O.S.B., to Michel, Ball Club, Minn., Mar. 15, 1937).

[98] Interview with Benno Watrin, O.S.B., Collegeville, Sept. 20, 1952.

[99] "Chippewa Congress of Minnesota," *Indian Sentinel*, XII (1933), 174.

[100] Luetmer to writer, Mahnomen, Jan. 27, 1953.

[101] The writer heard Abbot Alcuin mention this in a eulogy to the students at the time of Michel's death.

[102] Michel to Deutsch, Cass Lake, Aug. 31, 1933.

[103] Collegeville, Sept. 4, 1933.

[104] Ball Club, June 14, 1934.

CHAPTER 7

LITURGY AND CATHOLIC LIFE

DOM VIRGIL MICHEL started the school year at St. John's Abbey as dean of the college in September, 1933. After another stint with the Indians that fall for reasons of health, he returned permanently in December, and once he had swung into action, there was to be no relaxing until the Lord called him on November 26, 1938. Beginning in 1936, he taught a unique and stimulating seminar inspired by the conditions of the times, "Catholic Backgrounds and Current Social Theory." Except for this, the administration of the college, and editing *Orate Fratres*, Abbot Alcuin relieved his subject of other duties in order that, as he said later, Dom Virgil "might devote himself to the interests of the Church in a wider field, in view of the fact that God had given him special gifts." [1]

This wider field included editing the Christ-Life Series, lecturing and writing, giving retreats and engaging in the numerous projects and movements with which he became associated. Once again he took up the apostolate of writing letters. Judging the liturgical movement to have matured sufficiently, in 1935 Michel reorganized the staff of *Orate Fratres* and reshaped its policy along more social lines. [2] The organ of the liturgical apostolate then became charged as never before with the living social implications and values of the liturgy. In the fall of 1933 Father Godfrey Diekmann, O.S.B., had returned from his studies in Europe to help in the editing of *Orate Fratres*, and with his able assistance as managing editor Michel was even more

176

free to engage in the social apostolate. Convinced about the needs of Catholic education, he now continued his predecessor's efforts and achieved in April, 1938, the accreditation of the college by the University of Minnesota.

A man's thought can only be understood against the background of his times. But to describe adequately the social conditions of the 1930's is a vast and difficult task. Since that time there has evolved in the United States what amounts to a social and economic revolution due to the depression, the social legislation [3] of the New and Fair Deals, a world war, and the tremendous boom in production — no less a revolution because it was gradual and quiet. In any case, the Indian missionary returned to academic life in a very troubled world. History's worst depression was heavy upon the land. In the years 1930–32 alone 5,000 commercial banks, about twenty percent of all banks in the United States, had failed.[4] The organized labor movement, with a meager 3,000,000 members in 1933, was weak and riddled with active communists.[5] Soup kitchens and breadlines dotted city streets, as the number of the unemployed reached 15,000,000 by March, 1933; and there continued to be some 10,000,000 unemployed through most of the decade. At one time about one-fourth of the nation's families were on relief. In the midst of plentiful resources there was a hunger march upon Washington. Beginning its noble work of teaching the social doctrine of the Church to the working man in May, 1933, the *Catholic Worker* in its first editorial addressed itself to "those who are sitting on benches, huddling in shelters, walking the streets." After droughts, dust bowls formed, and farmers were leaving the land to swell the city slums. In 1933 the birth rate dropped to an all-time low. The moral standard of the movies had fallen to a point where the American hierarchy formed, in 1934, the Legion of Decency. Father Charles E. Coughlin's *Social Justice* appeared, the Christian Front was born, the Nazi Bundists gathered new members at rallies, the technocrats flourished, and Huey Long gained national attention. Civilization seemed in danger of collapse, as extremes of Right and Left fought for a hearing. "The whole economic life has become hard, merciless, and sinister," Pius XI had written in *Quadragesimo anno* in 1931. If conditions in the United States were ripe for communism, they were also ripe for social and economic reform. Yet, in 1933 there was practically no organized lay apostolate among American Catholics; nor were there social action groups such as exist today.

On the international scene Hitler took over Germany in 1933;

Mussolini invaded Ethiopia in 1935; Japan walked out of the League of Nations; the Spanish Civil War broke out in 1936. Economic liberalism had borne its fruit and totalitarian systems were having their day. A new era had dawned, a time of world-wide social unrest; and pessimism of every kind flourished. As is always the case in a time of acute social distress, there were hundreds of cure-alls. Facile, even dangerous, solutions were proposed. No wonder Pius XI in his encyclical *Mit brennender Sorge* of 1937, spoke of "a world sick unto death." In the chapters that follow the reader should keep this background in mind.

Ever since Leo XIII, the popes had pointed to the handwriting on the wall and had enunciated the Catholic social principles by which to overhaul liberalistic capitalism and by which to remedy the abuses of industrial society. But until the depression set in and *Quadragesimo anno* made its appearance in 1931, comparatively few [6] were aware of the program Leo XIII had outlined in *Rerum novarum* in 1891. True, there were the work of the German Catholic Central Verein,[7] the pioneering of Monsignor William J. Kerby [8] in the field of organized Catholic charities, the toil and activities of the "labor" priest Father Peter E. Dietz [9] in the first quarter of the twentieth century, and the writings of Monsignor John A. Ryan, starting with his *A Living Wage* in 1906. In 1919 the American hierarchy issued the epochal *Bishops' Program of Social Reconstruction*, and in the following year had established the Social Action Department in the National Catholic Welfare Conference. But despite these efforts to check the evils of laissez-faire capitalism, as Ryan observed in speaking of the 1920's, "For more than a decade, social thinking and social action were chilled and stifled in an atmosphere of pseudo-prosperity and thinly disguised materialism." [10] How Catholic social philosophy and the encyclicals applied to the whole scene of American life had yet to be shown. The American Catholic social conscience had to be aroused by what Father Paul Hanly Furfey chose to call "the new social Catholicism," to which he contributed in no small measure.[11] "Who will come with some hopeful doctrine of reform out from under the surface of decent reticence and restraint now covering the misery and needless suffering of millions . . . ?" inquired Michael Williams, editor of *Commonweal*, in 1930. And he added, "If Christian leaders do not appear with such a hopeful and reasonable doctrine, it is certain that wide and eager will be the hearing given to the apostles of Bolshevism or to the preachers of less logical but equally erroneous nostrums of social betterment." [12]

Among those who rose to meet the challenge in the depression thirties was Dom Virgil Michel, now deeply steeped in the liturgy, the doctrine of the Mystical Body of Christ, and fully armed with the principles of a sound Catholic social philosophy. Some, exhibiting more good will than perspicacity, thought of the social problem as a purely economic one and of its solution, therefore, as a purely economic solution. They tended to identify the social question with the wage question or blamed the money system, while Dom Virgil went to the roots of the problem and laid bare underlying causes — godless individualism, hidden paganism, a subtle bourgeois spirit, rank materialism, and their supporting ideologies.

He made it clear that the social question was not only an economic one to be resolved merely by the application of social ethics and legislation. He insisted that social reconstruction could be achieved only by restoring an organic structure to society. Taking his stand on the papal encyclicals, Thomistic social philosophy, the data of social science, and the ideology of the liturgical movement, he made it even clearer that social chaos *about* us is often only the reflection of spiritual chaos *within* us; that unless modern man recovered human spiritual values, there would be no lasting Christian social reconstruction — the first requisite being an inner spiritual awakening and reconstruction which begins with the individual. And precisely here the liturgy would make an indispensable contribution, for one works in vain to change society unless he also changes hearts, souls, persons first. Spurred on by an apostolic vision of society and living individually and communally a renewed spiritual life, Christians could hope gradually to reform their social institutions. In this way liturgical life could regenerate all of Christian society and, through it, eventually all of human society. The liturgical movement, with its core-idea of the Mystical Body, the social encyclicals, and a sound social philosophy must point the way, first, to a spiritual rejuvenation and second, to a sound, practical program of social action.

With the organized liturgical apostolate of the 1920's the Catholic social movement in the United States was bound soon to take on a new dimension. No longer would it then be concerned only with ethico-economic problems of industrial life and forms of organized charity. As an increasing number of Catholics realized that they not only belonged to the Church but *were* the Church; as the truth struck home that they were "members one of another" living through the liturgy one common supernatural life in, with, and for Christ; as Catholics came to realize their mutual responsibility for the spiritual growth of the Mystical Body in society, it was inevitable that the resultant spirituality would flower into a deepened vision of Christian society and the Christian social action to effect such a society.

As the public exercise of the virtue of religion, the liturgy is eminently social. "One could very well say," Michel maintained, "that the liturgy is as social as man is." And if the comparison lacks point, he went on, it is because four centuries of extreme individualism in political, economic, social, and religious life "are our inheritance, and we have forgotten almost entirely how thoroughly social man is in ultimate nature and being." And that is why, too, so fundamental and all-embracing an aspect of the liturgy as its social character had also been overlooked. Yet, as Michel noted, the social aspects of the liturgy are but counterparts of the natural life of social man. He then continued:

The supernatural builds on and elevates nature. Today the natural social bonds have been disrupted. . . . It is not too much to say that the revival of true social human life will be achieved only under the inspiration of the liturgical life, since the specific divine purpose of the latter is to transform human nature after the mind of Christ and inspire it unto a life replete like His with love of God and man.[13]

Because very little had been written on socio-liturgical subjects,[14] Dom Virgil in the 1930's traced the social implications of the liturgy for an integral and revitalized Catholic living. Here he did his most original thinking and made his specific contribution to American Catholic social thought and life. And in explaining these values, implications, and consequences, he was ahead of the proponents of the liturgical apostolate in Europe, who still occupied themselves mainly with the dogmatic, archeological, and historical aspects of the liturgy. As H. A. Reinhold has observed:

We had no Virgil Michel in Germany. The close inter-connection of the liturgical revival with social reform. . . was never expressed in that forceful way in which you see it in the writings of the late Dom Virgil and *Orate Fratres*. . . . Maria Laach, Guardini, Pinsk and Klosterneuburg only occasionally pointed out the necessary social consequences of a true liturgical revival among our Catholic people. . . . America is in an enviable position. . . . While in Germany the leaders of the liturgical and the social revival, both strong and powerful movements, never really met and sometimes antagonized and criticized each other — here you have a close cooperation of the two, a unity of both, right from the start."[15]

This and the next two chapters will treat Michel's socio-liturgical writings, while a later chapter will deal with his purely social and philosophical thinking.

The doctrine of the Mystical Body of Christ framed all of Michel's socio-liturgical thought. Its supernatural reality is a focal and all-pervading concept of the Christian life, and as he stated in 1929, grasping that reality results in an experience "akin to that of conversion," [16] so rich in meaning and instructive guidance is it for all phases of man's natural and supernatural life. One's status as a Catholic, all worship and work, all human and Christian life in the world, should be thought of in terms of the Christian's organic union with Christ, and with one another in Christ, the divine Mediator and Exemplar. In the supernatural community of the Mystical Christ, therefore, Father Michel found the pattern and inspiration for all natural and supernatural social living, for the solution of the knotty and ageless problem of the relation between the individual and the community, for the lay apostolate and Catholic Action, in short, for all Christian activity.

In re-establishing relations with humanity through Christ, God did not do violence to human nature as He had created it. Rather, He accommodated Himself to human ways, to the needs and properties of man's nature. Far from being contrary to the basic make-up of human nature, the Mystical Body is in fullest harmony with it. Because in the Christian dispensation the natural and the supernatural are inseparably linked, Michel concluded that the "supernatural organization of men into the fellowship of the Mystical Body is also for human life here below the best model and guide for all social organization of men. Man cannot improve on God." [17]

Since grace supposes nature and since the supernatural life of grace is built on the natural life of man on earth, the supernatural organism of the Mystical Body must find its counterpart in the organic life and forms of natural society. Obviously, the apostolic Christian must be active on both the natural and supernatural levels. The Catholic needs to learn to cooperate with his fellows in the Mystical Body of Christ, and he will then possess a model of such cooperation in all other societies and groups to which he belongs. These thoughts run like a core through many of Michel's socio-liturgical writings, especially through his *The Christian in the World*, an individual and social ethics based on the Mystical Body. Therein he stated:

When we ask ourselves what should the right structure of any human society be, or how should the individual be related to any society of men, we can always point to the Mystical Body and say: There is the model that we should try to follow in all our human relations; for God constructed it on the basis of what is best in and for our natures.[18]

Thus, he thought, one can profitably think of the diocese, the parish, even the family or religious community, as the Mystical Body in miniature, to say nothing of other human societies and groups for which it may serve as a divine model of human fellowship. Especially is this true of the natural civil society called the state, which should be an organic network of relatively autonomous and functional groups composed of free and responsible persons. "It takes but a momentary glance," Father Michel explained in 1936, "to see that both the totalitarian state and the amorphous mass-rabble aggregate that individualism has made of democracy are quite out of harmony with the Christian concept as reflected in the Mystical Body of Christ." [19] He also liked to remind social thinkers and reformers that no one less than Pius XI had said a number of times in his encyclical, *Quadragesimo anno*, that in the Mystical Body they had at once the model and inspiration for Christian social reconstruction, even in matters economic, for the Pope had stated:

If then the members of the social body be thus reformed, and if the true directive principle of social and economic activity be thus re-established, it will be possible to say, in a sense, of this body what the Apostle said of the Mystical Body of Christ: "The whole body being compacted and fitly joined together, . . ." [20]

Michel's thought was that lucid understanding of the Mystical Body was helpful to develop a proper conception of a corporatively organized economic order as was called for by Pius XI. The supernatural community of Christ's Body on earth, then, as in earlier Christian centuries, must become once more the God-given model in rebuilding an atomized economic and social life according to current conditions of time and place.

Centuries of individualism have robbed Christians of their corporate mentality, their sense of community and oneness in Christ, just as they have destroyed also the organic structure of society on the natural level. Yet the solidarity of all men in Christ goes to the very heart of Catholic Christianity. Even before baptism all men are one before God, at least by destiny; thus they are all children of a common Father by one creation, and they are all by destiny supernatural children of God by one and the same redemption. And baptism, Dom

Virgil explained, makes them all members of Christ in the sublime union which is life in the Body of Christ.[21]

This fellowship every member of Christ must live out in all his conduct. While each one has his own personal responsibilities, he is never an isolated individual but always a member of Christ. In Christ he is united with his fellows, and thus becomes part of a greater whole, from which he may not separate himself without the penalty of spiritual suicide. A Catholic's every action is already a social action by virtue of his membership in the Body of Christ, "which grows or diminishes through his actions." [22] For the Church is an organic community of life, not a mere juxtaposition of members, an unorganized heap of individuals with no inner relation to one another and to the organic whole. In fact, such is the organic unity in the Mystical Body that each member is responsible, according to his circumstances and position in the Body, for the welfare of the whole Church of Christ.

The magnitude of this social responsibility would overwhelm the Christian, Michel admitted, were it not for the fact that it is actually Christ who works in him. Of the individual is required good will and effective effort.[23] Consequently, whatever good anyone does, is accomplished only through Christ and through membership in Christ; therefore, it belongs to Christ. In this way is formed the common treasury of merits and life, that is, the combined merits of Christ, the saints, and all members of Christ. Out of this treasury, held in common and shared in by all, does the Church dispense to each according to his needs and deserts. Here race, color, and other secondary factors do not matter, as they should not in the natural order. It remains to say that each member has the obligation according to his circumstances to come to the aid of needy fellow members and thus to maintain or increase the common life of the entire Body.

All of this has its counterpart in the natural order. In a just and organic social order, the social and economic structure of society would "reflect in material things the Christian solidarity and fellowship that is realized in regard to supernatural goods." In this way Michel explained the virtue of social justice, which in the natural order bids each member to contribute to the common good what is owing to it on the part of each, according to his abilities and the needs of the group or larger society.

The basis of this obligation of social justice is man's inescapably social nature. For his physical, moral, intellectual, and spiritual development every person is dependent on others. Whatever he achieves is in some way due to the work and accomplishments of those who have gone before him or who help him now, proximately or remotely; in short, he is always dependent on a social heritage into which he has been born.

This has its counterpart, or rather sublime model, in the Mystical Body of Christ and in the common treasury of the communion of saints, i.e., the merits of Christ and the saints and all the members of Christ. To each member of Christ the Church bestows what is needed and deserved, and the member of Christ is ever dependent on the accumulated merits gathered by the Church through the ages. And just as in the natural society each member should contribute to sustain and increase the social heritage, so too in the supernatural order each Christian is obliged to contribute to the welfare of the whole Body to which he belongs.

Thus, social justice plays an important role in governing the relations of the individual to the various groups — home, civic, national — of which he is a member. He bears responsibility for the common good of each group, just as does the individual member of Christ to the general life of the Mystical Body. For this reason Father Virgil held that the duties of the lay apostle in the Church are "specifically duties of social justice." Finally, just as the member of Christ shares in the common treasury of supernatural merits gathered through the centuries and must do his share to sustain and add to it, so the member of the society of mankind in the natural order shares in the social heritage constructed through the ages, and he must likewise do his part to maintain and contribute to the common treasury of civilization according to his abilities.[24]

However, if each member is responsible in some way for the well-being of the whole social organism, whether natural or supernatural, the latter is similarly responsible in some way for the welfare of each member. This can be clearly seen, for instance, in the case of poverty or for that matter in any other social abuse, which makes living the life of Christ difficult or impossible. To practice virtue, to develop the Christ-life, to do one's part in the Mystical Body, man, being a physical-spiritual organism, needs a certain amount of material goods. To be deprived of them, to have to worry unduly about such a condition, to be forced to exhaust oneself in the attempt to get the necessities of life prevents a man from giving adequate effort to the development of the Christ-life. Because of the mutuality of supernatural life in

Christ, all suffer. Such a condition, Michel showed, is both immoral and unchristian — a condition for which the whole fellowship is responsible and which it must strive to remedy, at least to the extent of making it possible for all members to secure what the needs of human nature and membership in Christ demand. That the early Christian communities had a keen realization that they must give to each according to his needs is indicated in the Acts of the Apostles: "And all who believed were together and held all things in common, and would sell their possessions and goods and distribute them among all according as anyone had need." [25] Mutual assistance was for them a reflection of the spiritual unity of the Mystical Body of Christ of which they were members. And their daily life of mutual charity was, in turn, an echo of their active and intelligent participation in the Sacrifice of the altar, at which they dedicated themselves and all their goods to God, and to the service of God in their fellow men.

From the Christian viewpoint one can see what a high dignity material goods have when used directly in the service of God and indirectly in the service of men in God. Yet, instead of being the instruments for living a truly human and so for Christians a fuller life in Christ, material riches in modern times, Michel asserted, have in general come to be looked upon "as so many instruments of personal pleasure and aggrandizement." This attitude was due to the prevailing materialistic and naturalistic philosophy. For the same reason had the obligation of the natural society of the state for the welfare of each person and all groups often gone unobserved. Therefore, until the social framework of natural society takes its direction and inspiration from the supernatural model of the Mystical Body, Father Virgil warned, the society of men in the world "can hardly avoid becoming increasingly unchristian." [26]

In yet another way, Michel indicated, the supernatural community is a divine pattern for all natural living, individual and social. The history of modern times began with the revolt against the social aspects of religious life in favor of stark individualism. From the sphere of religion this attitude eventually seeped into economic, political, and social life as well. This has pointed up the great problem in modern times of the relation between the individual and the community, the whole problem of personality. An unnatural and unchristian individualism overlooks or denies the fact that man is dependent on his fellows for his full development, in other words, that man is social to the core of his being, and is dependent on others for the development of the total complex of his personality.[27] Totalitarianism is the modern reaction to excessive emphasis on the individual, and, Michel believed, one of the signs of the end of the modern period of history. But while totalitarianism upholds the universal fellowship of all men, it threatens to eliminate all human personality. In the liturgy of the Mystical Body, Michel showed, the individual and social elements of man's nature find their harmonious solution, that is to say, the golden mean between an unsocial individualism and an anti-individual or anti-personal collectivism. The union of all members does not violate the autonomy of each person. While divine life flows from the Head into each member, yet it is lived by each person "separately and conjointly" with fellow members. In this way nature and supernature are fused into one organism, energized by one common life, lived by free and responsible persons in communion and cooperation with other members in Christ. As Dom Virgil explained:

There is only one answer I know of to the problem of the balanced harmony between the individual and the social: *The Mystical Body of Christ*. There the individual retains his full responsibility, the fullest possibility of greater realization of his dignity as a member of Christ; yet he is ever a member in the fellowship of Christ, knit closely with his fellow members into a compact body by the indwelling Spirit of Christ: *There* is the pattern of all social life lived by individuals.[28]

Only through cooperation and association with others, it has been pointed out, can man develop his best self, physically, morally, intellectually, and spiritually. Again the liturgy of the Mystical Body is the model for this association and cooperation. By active participation in the Church's worship of God, the person is brought into the highest cooperation in this world: cooperation with Christ in intimate association with all the members of Christ. The liturgy, imbued as it is with Christ's love for all men, holds before man the highest ideals, roots him with his fellows in life eternal, teaches him the proper relation between human and divine, natural and supernatural, material and spiritual. In the liturgy it can be seen how all of material creation serves and praises God in serving the human personality, raised into the life divine by Christ's own action.

Above all, the liturgy constantly stresses the higher aims of life: the free and personal subordination of one's life to the legitimate demands of the community; the daily dying of the old self of passion and sin and the consequent joyous rising with Christ. If in the liturgy all the material and human elements in man are properly ordered and subordinated, yet they are never suppressed. Due allowance is always made for diversities and differences. In fact, in the liturgy the Church shows such respect for the individuality and dignity of the free human being that she will allow an apparent decline rather than to use violence in forcing one human will. If force is often man's only answer to every problem, Michel said, that is not God's way.

In a depersonalized society the Church daily pays honor to man's highest prerogative — self-determination — by ceaselessly inviting the minds and wills of her children to active participation. Indeed, she is the greatest respecter of human freedom, and as such she teaches the world daily the lesson that the human person is of highest value in all creation. This is a most important lesson to learn, Dom Virgil said, in an age of collectivism, technology, mass-communication, and bureaucratic government. All of these tend to swallow up the human being, or at least to lessen his self-direction. In this connection he remarked:

Far from depreciating or suppressing the values of individuality and personality, the Mystical Body of Christ gives these their best possible realization. The responsibility that each member has, not only for his own self, but also for the good of the whole Body, is the highest personal responsibility that the individual man can be privileged to share; it is implicitly the highest possible acknowledgment of the true dignity and value of the human person.[29]

Having learned from the liturgy and the Mystical Body the harmonious relation of responsible persons and their free cooperation in the common life of the supernatural fellowship, lay apostles, Father Virgil declared, "must apply these Christian concepts to all the forms of our social life, the family, the community, the state, and thus build up anew a Christian social order of life."[30]

But without the liturgy, the source of the true Christian spirit, this ideal will never be realized. For history shows and daily human experience confirms, Father Virgil maintained, that man or society, left to mere natural means, swings from extreme to extreme. The middle way can only be achieved with the help of the supernatural, "without which either the individual bursts all bounds of restraint, or society crushes out his individuality."[31] No matter how the moulding of the best personality is viewed, Dom Virgil insisted, "the liturgy furnishes both the inspiration, the guiding idea, and at the same time the necessary grace for its realization in life."[32]

The welfare of the whole Church is dependent on well-developed and responsible persons as members. In fact, the divine mission of the Church is precisely to raise the individual personality to its highest supernatural perfection, as it is the mission of the state to make possible the best natural personal development. To the extent that the Church succeeds or fails, she waxes or wanes. Neither the whole Mystical Body, nor an individual member, can develop to the detriment of the other, but only to the advantage of each, for "the life and development of the Church at any time depends on the full-fledged Christianity of her individual members. What they become or are, that the Church becomes or is." [33] Obviously, this holds true for the relation between the individual and any community or group to which he belongs. So closely related is the welfare of individual and community that they stand or fall together.

With this, one comes to a most important consideration: the essential role of each person in the Church, the whole question of the laity's role in the Mystical Body, the lay apostolate, and Catholic Action. About these Michel had, indeed, very much to say.[34] All of his liturgical work and writings can be said to have had one aim: To make every Catholic keenly aware that he must be an apostle in the world *by the very fact that he is a Christian* and a member of the Mystical Body of Christ. If he understands the liturgy and its central idea, the Mystical Body of Christ, this fact will become evident to him; and if he is a man of good will, he will be an apostle also, for then he will see that, in Michel's words, "the whole cause of God here on earth is made to depend in some degree on the responsible action of each member of Christ," [35] by virtue of the organic activity that is the life of the Church. Thus Pius XII in his encyclical, *Mystici Corporis*, stated that God did not will to impart His graces to man directly but through "a visible Church made up of men, so that through her all [laity not excluded] might cooperate with Him in dispensing the graces of redemption." A Catholic laity, actively participating in the liturgy, witnessing to the truth of Christ, and living His life in the world was always Michel's answer to the problem of secularism.

In Chapter six it was pointed out that as early as the 1920's Dom Virgil was convinced that if all things were to be restored in Christ, the laity would have to rediscover and live once more their proper role in the Church. The same chapter records the efforts he made at that time to awaken the laity to their responsibilities.

"The whole status of the Christian as a living member of Christ can be expressed functionally," Father Michel stated, "as active participation in the life of Christ," as lived by the Church, "both in her inner worship of God through the liturgy and in her external mission of fostering the growth and the spread of the Christ-life in the world." [36] In other words, every Christian is another Christ, and so the life of every Christian, as the extension of the Incarnation, must become the extension of the Church or of Christ's life and activity in the world. But this activity of the Christian must be inspired by the very conception of the position he holds in the Mystical Body; it must be rooted in the Christ-life, that is, the sacramental life of that Body attained through active participation.[37] For men fashion their spiritual life and religious outlook according to their conception of the Church and their role in it.

Christ conceived His whole mission in the world — a mission which the Church now continues and which every member is obliged to promote — in terms of life. As He said, "I came that they may have life, and have it more abundantly." [38] As stated earlier, man is not only physically a living being, but also intellectually and spiritually. Life, above all spiritual life, must display itself in activity or die. Consequently, membership in Christ, which is at once participation in the divine life, must likewise express itself in spiritual activity or perish. Furthermore, precisely because life craves expression, "mere inaction on the part of the Christian is a refusal to let the life of Christ in him function and bear fruit." [39] That is why the Christian must live his Christ-life and be active first in his parish church and then also in the apostolate in the world. In regard to both Dom Virgil observed in 1937, "We are the inheritors of a widespread attitude of lay quietude and lay passivity." This quietude and passivity "ingrained for centuries in our blood," is due to a "subjective individualism" in the spiritual lives of Catholics. It is due, moreover, to a failure to understand the true life and nature of the Church, the liturgical or sacramental life, especially the sacraments of baptism, confirmation, and the Eucharist, as well as to a failure to realize that Christ continues through the members of His Mystical Body His redemptive work in the world, once accomplished in His physical body.[40]

For the early Christians the realization of living membership in the Mystical Body of Christ was in Michel's words "*the* inspirational idea of Catholic life as it should be." [41] They were active members of Christ in the first place in the common celebration of the Eucharist, the Sacrifice of the Mystical Body. To the altar they brought the fruits of their labor, their gifts used in the Sacrifice and for the poor. In the gifts they saw themselves, offered and dedicated directly to the service of God and indirectly to the service of God in neighbor. For that reason, in Michel's words, "their everyday careers were but a further unfolding of what they did in their eucharistic gatherings." [42] Always conscious of their living unity in Christ, they stood around the altar, actively participated in the action of the Mass, together chanted the responses, while each prayed for all and all for each. In union with the celebrating priest they offered the Sacrifice with the priest and then completed the common offering by joining him invariably in the reception of the sacramental Christ, by whose divine energies they continued the sacrificial consecration of their lives to God and neighbor in their daily life and work. For the giving of self to Christ at Mass, Michel pointed out, will always be sham unless it includes the pledge of serving neighbor in God.

Contrast this, Dom Virgil asserted, with the inactivity and passivity of modern Catholics at the holy Sacrifice. In 1928 Pius XI had regretted in *Divini cultus* the "merely detached and silent spectators" at Mass. Very many Catholics, Michel said frankly in 1937, do not know what the Mass is all about, being conscious only of the minimum requirements set down by the Church; and the observance of these minimum requirements of a legal and juridic nature becomes the whole of their service to God. Rather than being active during liturgical functions, he remarked, they dream "vaguely of what they can do in an active manner once their passive religious duty has been performed." Because this takes place at the very source of Christian spirit and the Christ-life, Father Virgil asked:

Is there any wonder that the life of so many Christians is made up of a minimum of passive submission to rules and formulas in matters religious, and a maximum of activities outside the church in matters secular? In other words, the Christian becomes active in life in proportion as he is removed from the altar, which is just the opposite of what should be taking place, of what is demanded by the true Christian spirit. If we seek for an answer to the question of why Christians have functioned so little as lay apostles in the world in our centuries, we have it here. The entire life of the true Christian . . . must be a reflection and a further expression of his life at the altar of God, at the true source of the Christian spirit. If he is predominantly a passive Christian there, can we expect him to be an active Christian in his daily life out in the world? [43]

The same apathetic people whose vocation as Christians calls for their being apostles fail to understand, appreciate, and live the significance of the sacramental character as "participation in the priesthood of Christ." In Dom Virgil's judgment baptism, the initiation into the Christ-life, had too often been viewed chiefly as something negative, as something ending the state of separation from God by the washing away of original sin. Hence it followed that the Christian's duty was chiefly the negative one of not doing anything to mar the new relation to God, of merely avoiding mortal sin. Where positive action was engaged in, such as attendance at the Eucharistic Sacrifice, it was all too often merely to avoid a break with God. In other words, the whole life of the Christian, baptized into Christ, was passively and negatively conceived. This, according to Michel, is anything but the mind of Christ and the Church as expressed in her liturgy.

Baptism is much more than the forgiveness of sin, or the performance of a certain rite that bestows a title to a future eternal life after the fulfillment of a certain number of precepts. Instead, baptism must again come to mean for every man who glories in the name of Catholic the engrafting of a human branch into the living vine that is Christ, the taking on of a living membership in the living organism of the Mystical Body. Rather than a passive submission to ritual demands, Michel insisted, baptism must again mean for Catholics an embracing of a new status. This status includes a new and higher, supernatural life, entrance into the Mystical Body, in which being Christian will always mean daily to live consciously in and for Christ, in short, as the baptismal rite itself says, to "have part with Christ." After baptism the same Holy Spirit who lives and works in the Pope, lives and works in the lowliest Catholic day laborer, binding all hierarchically into one living organism that must become active in worship and apostolate. How shortsighted and inadequate, then, to view initiation into the Christ-life as a mere past event with no bearing on the present, when it is the real beginning of the eternal life of heaven in the soul, when it effects therein a living reality that must daily grow as the divine seed of Christian life and of all holiness.

Catholic laymen must always be conscious of sharing in the priesthood of Christ through the baptismal character and of having the right, duty, and privilege of participating actively in the worship of the Mystical Body as well as of receiving the other sacraments. So, too, they must effectively realize that confirmation completes their living membership in the Church and participation in the priesthood of

Christ. An individual Catholic layman attains his own full life in Christ only by promoting the life of the whole Mystical Body.[44]

The laity are anything but "a spiritual proletariat" with no intelligent role to play in the Church's life and work and with no responsibility to exercise, as Michel said, "except that of a passive obedience like the chess pawn," waiting "to be moved to the right or the left." [45] Confirmation, Dom Virgil constantly insisted, makes every Christian responsible for the social environment in which the Church operates. The apostolic layman must not be aloof from the world. Rather, he must carry and apply not only Catholic social principles but also the healing and sanctifying presence and power of Christ into the marketplace — into the whole temporal order. In the temporal order the lay apostle of Christ realizes his indispensable vocation of diffusing the principles, truth, and grace of Christ as an effective leaven to set things aright in the natural order for the building up of the supernatural kingdom of God. Where the lay apostle is, there is Christ already at work. According to Father Virgil, public life in general has become secular and even pagan precisely because priests have failed to arouse the laity to their responsibilities. How unchristian modern Catholics have become, he used to say, not to realize that the sacramental graces are given to them by God not just for themselves but bind them to convert their neighbor and to christianize their environment. Writing for the readers of *Orate Fratres* about the characters of baptism and confirmation and about Catholic Action in its various forms in 1929, he stated, "What a wide vista of possibilities in this regard has remained unrealized in our lives!" [46]

The words of the baptismal ceremony about having "part with Christ" can only mean that the Christian engages in the apostolate by having part with the whole and undivided Christ as Teacher, King, and Priest. The true Christian can never divorce himself from any of these aspects of Christ without to that extent departing from the whole Christ:

> As Christ is ever the Way, the Truth, and the Life — King and Teacher and Priest — so must every member of his as an "other Christ" be in some degree king and teacher and priest unto himself and unto others. Can he otherwise really be said "to have part with Christ?" [47]

He exercises the sanctifying and priestly powers received in baptism and confirmation first of all by active participation as co-offerer and co-victim with Christ at Mass and by receiving the other sacraments.

He exercises this power toward others mainly by the compelling beauty of his example and holiness. Likewise does he exercise his power of teacher and king toward himself by continually studying the truths of Christ, by guiding himself accordingly, by more intelligently participating in the liturgy so that his mind and heart are daily moulded after the mind and heart of Christ. Toward others he carries out the office of king and teacher by guiding and instructing with his word and example — especially by properly directing and teaching his family, dependents, and associates. Michel could think of no time and no place when the total Christian cannot be a lighthouse for the Way and the Truth and the Life that is Christ.

Thus the Christian is invested with power and responsibility to share in the work of the Church. Dom Virgil remarked:

What a striking contrast there is between this exalted dignity and privilege of the true member of Christ and the passive attitude and apathy so frequent in our day! How much inspiration is found in understanding rightly that baptism is something that we must ever after its reception strive to act out more fully, the continuous understanding of whose meaning should be accompanied by a continuous will influencing our lives. Likewise in regard to confirmation, the sacrament of official lay apostleship. It should not only be an outstanding historical event in our lives (sometimes it is not even that), but a transition point, whose influence becomes stronger and stronger in our later lives. Only thus can we properly do battle, as is the office of consecrated soldiers and apostles of Christ, against the many enemies that today oppose the cause of Christ, and help to prevent the inroads of the new paganism into the very ranks of the fellowship of Christ.[48]

In an effort to convince his contemporaries, Father Virgil again and again quoted Pius XI on the nature and need of Catholic Action and its indispensable basis, the liturgy. Here is one example:

The apostolate is one of the duties inherent in Christian life. If one considers well, it will be seen that the very sacraments of baptism and confirmation impose — among other obligations — this apostolate of Catholic Action, which is spiritual help to our neighbor. Through confirmation we become soldiers of Christ. The soldier should labor and fight not so much for himself as for others. Baptism, in a manner less evident to profane eyes, imposes the duty of apostolate since through it we become members of the Church, or of the Mystical Body of Christ; and among the members of this Body — as of any living organism — there must be solidarity of interests and reciprocal communication of life. One member must therefore help the other; no one may remain inactive and as each receives he must also give.[49]

Obviously, the loss of the liturgical spirit entailed the loss of its handmaid, the lay apostolate. That is why Dom Virgil, from the first days of the liturgical movement, predicted that once the liturgy was fully understood and lived, an active Catholic laity would inevitably develop. For the same reason, he maintained, the papal calls to Catholic Action received such a belated response in the United States. When they were finally heeded, Dom Virgil said, they "fell upon ears as something quite new and hitherto unheard of." Hence, too, it often happened that zealous members of the laity who saw their role and wished to do their part were, he said, "frowned upon by others or looked at askance," even at times "discouraged by those who because of official position should have encouraged and blessed them for their good will and their spirit of self-sacrifice."[50] For such priests Michel quoted Pius XI: "Nothing is in fact more traditional than that the pastors of the Church . . . be assisted with eagerness by the lay folk, who by their very condition can perform such things as the sacred ministers, however much they desire, cannot do."[51]

It was no mere coincidence, Father Michel often said, that the restoration of the liturgy by St. Pius X should be followed by 500 pages of pleas for Catholic Action written by Pius XI. Unless one understands the Church as the Mystical Body carrying on the mission of Christ through the apostolic life of every member, and unless one grasps the true significance of the liturgical — that is, sacramental — life, it is difficult, Dom Virgil believed, to see the true status and role of the laity in the Church. Finally, for clergymen who saw the spectre of a revived lay trusteeism, or even anti-clericalism, in an active laity, Michel warned that there was actually much more danger of anti-clericalism if they were not given their rightful place as active apostles of Christ.[52]

Novel as Catholic Action seemed to be, the papal summons was given a sudden and widespread response in the United States. However, as Michel observed, it was a response of enthusiasm unguided by proper understanding, since the traditional sense of the true Christian spirit had been lost by so many of the faithful. "It became almost a fashion," Dom Virgil recalled in 1936, "to label any favorite activity of any Catholic individual or group as Catholic Action. The phrase became a byword to conjure with, a label that seemed to lend dignity and official approval to whatever activities one carried on." [53] For this reason the American hierarchy, assembled in Washington in November, 1935, had to restate and explain Pius XI's definition of Catholic Action — "the participation of the laity in the apostolate of the hierarchy" — and also to distinguish officially mandated Catholic Action from Catholic activity.[54] Since Catholic Action is participation by the faithful in the hierarchical apostolate, it obviously cannot exist without the guidance and direction of the bishops. Now the liturgy is the exercise of the priesthood of Christ; the priesthood of Christ was passed down to the apostles and through their successors, and is shared in by the faithful only through the liturgical ministry of the ordained priesthood, Michel explained. Likewise, the faithful exercise their official apostleship, rooted in the sacramental characters of baptism and confirmation, only in proper relation to the hierarchy of the Church. Hence the Christian's official position finds its explanation and basis in the liturgy of the Mystical Body, from which also must come the inspiration to engage in Catholic Action and in the Catholic activity of the wider apostolate.

Father Virgil found it necessary on many occasions to emphasize that officially organized Catholic Action does not at all exhaust the duties and possibilities of lay apostleship. Realizing his active membership in the Mystical Body, filled with the Spirit of Christ and formed by the liturgy, the lay apostle will engage in Catholic activities far beyond what mandated Catholic Action demands. For he is at all times and places a consecrated apostle of Christ, both in his individual and social life. As a matter of fact, such Catholic endeavors on a wider scale should be the natural result of Catholic Action, "just as both are the logical development of the liturgical life and the Christian spirit." [55]

Nor is this wider apostolate of the confirmed member of Christ unrelated to Catholic Action, to the hierarchical action of the Church and to her liturgy, because its efficacy is always dependent on the intimate union of the lay apostle with the Church as the Mystical Christ. "As the river can never rise above its source," Dom Virgil observed in 1929, "so the spiritual results of the lay apostolate as such cannot rise above the spiritual level of the lay apostles." [56] Rooted as it must be in a thoroughly Catholic spirituality, the apostolate will always be the overflow of the apostle's holiness, of his life in Christ, or better, of Christ's life in him. Thus Catholic Action is Christ acting in His incorporated members. In Michel's words:

The parallel commonly drawn between man's "religious" and "profane" life as if the two were mutually independent and even exclusive has no foundation in fact. A baptized member of Christ is not a dual personality, one natural and the other supernatural; rather his human nature is supernaturalized, so that whatever he does, . . . he must do all in Christ Jesus. Since, therefore, man's whole BEING is Christianized, all his actions should be Christ-like. Being governs operation. Hence our insistence on the essential relation between liturgy, the primary source of the Christ-life, and Catholic Action, the external operation of the Spirit of Christ within us.[57]

Precisely because he is another Christ in the Mystical Body, the lay apostle must see the whole world and his relations with it as the Church or Christ sees them. But that again brings him back to the liturgy, which is the visible embodiment of the mind and life of Christ.

Above all, an active sharing in the holy Sacrifice is important here. All apostolic activity, to be truly effective, must be the result of the offering of self with Christ to God in the corporate worship of the Mystical Body. From this viewpoint, Catholic Action is a prolonged worship, according to Dom Virgil's mind, for it is the continuation in the workaday world of the sacrificial dedication to God and God-in-fellow-men pledged at the altar. The offering that the layman makes here he lives out and completes in his life in the world. By active participation in Christ's own Sacrifice, the apostolic layman acquires, therefore, Christ's own spirit of sacrifice and victimhood; the life he acquires here he must spend in serving Christ in neighbor. From the liturgical services the apostle of Christ imbibes the needed perseverance and courage, the spiritual strength and the apostolic spirit, and the Christian vision to implement the mind of Christ in a Christless world. Hence Dom Virgil in 1929 spoke of

the inseparability of the liturgical life and Catholic Action. . . . Catholic Action is but the further development of the liturgical life. . . . Not only are the liturgical life and Catholic Action inseparable, but the two go to the very heart of the Christian dispensation. . . .

The true significance of the liturgical movement, therefore, lies just in this: that it tries to lead men back to the "primary and indispensable source of the true Christian spirit"; it tries to restore that of which Catholic Action is the further flowering and fruitage.[58]

In treating the relation between the liturgy and the lay apostolate, one can already see the broad outlines of Virgil Michel's approach to Christian social reconstruction and reform. The concern here, of course, is with Catholic social action, which Archbishop Karl J. Alter has defined as

a special form of the broader function of Catholic Action . . . in the socio-economic field. It concerns itself not so much with the life of the individual but rather with the life of society. It is interested in the problems of social organization and social institutions. It seeks to imprint Christian principles on the whole social fabric, but it is particularly interested in social legislation, social policy, and social systems.

Catholic Social Action is designed to give practical expression to the virtues of social justice and social charity.[59]

Since the supernatural community of the Mystical Body is built upon a sound and natural organic society, the Church is understandably concerned with having her spirit permeate the fabric and institutions of man's natural social organization, so as to make more effective the work of grace. Keeping in mind that all men are actual or potential members of the Mystical Body of Christ, Dom Virgil believed that all Catholic social action had as its ultimate purpose to remove or to ameliorate those social conditions which make living one's life in that Body difficult or even impossible, and to promote all those conditions which enhance or favor the development of that life. Rather than believe like some that the world conditions of the 1930's were a mere passing phase of a cyclical depression, he wrote in 1935, "Our world crisis is definitely a radical one; it is morally and spiritually basic and fundamental; it is anything but superficial." [60]

In the face of this conviction, what was the task at hand? It was not at all different from that of the early Christians, who lived in somewhat similar circumstances, and who, by an intense living of the liturgical life that flowed over into practical action for the cause of Christ, converted the pagans. By building up a Christian culture, they effected the greatest transformation of all time. Like the Christians of old, twentieth century Catholics must become an active and effective leaven in a pluralistic society. In the liturgy they will find the inspiration and basis of Christian social regeneration for an ever wider social growth in Christ. For those liturgists who had trouble seeing beyond the sanctuary of the parish into the sanctuary of God's world, Dom Virgil emphasized, "No person has really entered into the heart of the liturgical spirit if he has not been seized also with a veritable passion for the re-establishment of social justice in its wide ramifications." [61] He never failed to insist that "the liturgical movement, under pain of remaining sterile, needs to flower out into an ever-increasing Christian cooperation in all the things of life." [62]

But basic and indispensable as the liturgical life is for Catholic social action and reform, it by no means constitutes the whole program, as some liturgical literature seemed to suggest. One must also know the encyclicals, and not only those dealing primarily with social and economic problems, but also those touching more specifically the spiritual life.[63] This knowledge, in turn, will demand some grasp of the social sciences to enable one to apply intelligently the broad philosophical and theological directives of papal teaching. Nor is even this enough. One must also understand the kind of world one is living in with all its false philosophy and ideology. Otherwise in attempts at reconstruction, there is danger of being concerned with mere effects rather than with underlying causes. Finally, all must, as Michel expressed it,

> put forth the utmost endeavors also in the practical as well as the theoretical work of direct reconstruction of the social order — and this, as we have seen, by straightening out many of our ideas and concepts, e.g., on labor, property, and then by putting them into practice both individually and socially.[64]

What he advocated and attempted by way of changing institutions and his activities in this regard will be taken up later. Here the concern is with his insistence on the indispensability of the spiritual element in social reform, in other words, with the role of the liturgy. But before this role is discussed, it will be well to summarize Father Virgil's frequent analyses of the philosophical and moral climate of his time.

"Nowadays, as more than once in the history of the Church," Pius XI remarked in 1931, "we are confronted with a world which in large measure has almost fallen back into paganism." [65] In Michel's judgment too many Catholics were unaware of this fact. On more than one occasion, therefore, he detailed for his contemporaries the philosophical and religious errors of the past and present. Only by knowing these errors could one understand the modern crisis and the pagan viewpoints that make up the typically modern mentality toward life. Only when Catholics knew what they were up against could they, with the Mystical Body as supernatural model of natural social life, start reconstructing society by the gradual restoration of functional groups, built up, as Pius XI had said in the same encyclical, "from just natural principles."

First of all, there was a this-worldliness resulting from modern man's denial of another world, thus limiting his hopes and beliefs to this earthly existence. To Michel this situation developed because the past four centuries had witnessed a decreasing influence of Christian religion in the lives of many. In the eighteenth century a large-scale denial of the divinity of Christ was prevalent. The deism of the time still acknowledged a God in a far-off heaven; He was, however, not the loving Father of mankind but a God who at best toyed with, mocked at, or else entirely ignored the fortunes and foibles of men. In this manner men lost their concept of God's Providence. Quite logically, this loss led in the nineteenth century to a wholesale denial of God's divinity and an open espousal of atheism, while in the present century one comes full circle to whole nations — Russia, Nazi Germany, and Mexico in Michel's time — making use of every subtle force for the universal spread of atheism and the extinction of the Christian religion.

While not everyone fell vicitim to this vicious thought-climate, the prevalent philosophy of the times, Michel maintained, was that of pure naturalism, over against Christianity's supernaturalism. "It is in harmony with this view," he stated, "that our day has engaged so extensively in the cult of the body. The phenomenon of nudism can be a matter of surprise only for those who have been living in total seclusion from the world." [66] That this religion of naturalism should have resulted in the exaltation of sex was also quite consistent. He asserted in 1936:

> We are witnessing today the cultivation of sex for its own sake, which is in reality nothing but the glorification of sexuality. Why not, if there is no after-life, no spiritual element in us, if all that counts is the highest pleasure we can snatch out of the present? [67]

That this whole attitude of life, this frank espousal of epicureanism and hedonism, had bred extreme egoism and individual selfishness should be evident. In such circumstances, Michel iterated, life tends to become a bitter struggle of each against all, instead of a peaceful and brotherly cooperation on all levels of human endeavor, as would be the case in a truly Christian society. After all, if the life of man is to be that of the animal, then his rule of life must also become that of the jungle: a free-for-all struggle or a mad "gamble and scramble in which the best men will win; or rather those who win are considered the best." [68] This principle of action applied no less to nations. Over against the exaggerated and unnatural individualism of past centuries, Michel said in 1936, the reaction towards totalitarianism was strong. In this the Christian could not rejoice, first of all, because it was a reaction that sponsored the same materialistic philosophy of life as did individualsm; moreover, it was entirely this-worldly and anti-religious. Again, totalitarianism was a denial of a basic Christian principle in regard to man, namely, that he is a human person innately endowed by God with inalienable rights. At the impasse to which society had come, the only solution lay in the domain of a sound social philosophy and in a return to the traditional Christian spirituality as enshrined in the liturgy of the Mystical Body.

The trend toward religious individualism, given impetus by the Renaissance and its naturalistic humanism, was heightened by the religious developments of the late Middle Ages. Later, at the time of the Protestant Revolt, whole groups broke with Christian tradition and particularly with its teaching of corporate life in Christ and of the visible mediatorship, that is to say, with the liturgy of the Church. Each one's conscience, the reformers held, is his own highest law in matters of religion; each one is his own interpreter of Scripture; Christianity for such soon became entirely an individual and private affair, a matter between a soul and its God, so that the Christian fellowship came to mean no more than an extrinsic collectivity of isolated or self-sufficient individuals. With the introduction of this subjective individualism into religion, the social religious bonds were cut asunder and a corporate religious mentality was lost. Furthermore, with the entrance of this extreme individualism into the Christian tradition, a strong impetus was given to the secularization of life.

With the passage of time there ensued the decline of religion, particularly among the adherents of the many and fast-dividing Protestant sects. Mention has already been made of the gradual transition to deism, next to naturalism and rationalism, and finally to the wholesale preaching of atheism through the "scientific," evolutionary theories of the nineteenth century. Thus paganism returned with a vengeance. However, if religion in religious individualism declined, individualism itself in no way waned but grew stronger, if anything. In this way eventuated the so-called liberalism of the self-styled enlightenment. This liberalism rejected all authority and tradition, and, above all, all fixed moral laws and supernatural authority. Each man, then, became a law unto himself. With relentless logic this unchristian liberalism diffused itself into social, political, and economic life. "The first third of the twentieth century," Dom Virgil observed, "has witnessed the full outcome of this philosophy of individualism." [69]

Liberalism, applied to the theory of the state, brought, instead of the Christian democracy outlined by Aquinas and others, the democracy of the eighteenth century, which not only rejected God but even set human reason on a throne in Paris and, in the spirit of the age, in the living form of a lewd woman. Thus the arbitrary will of man became the supreme law of the land: *Vox populi, vox Dei*; the people, not God, were to guide the world and its destiny. This dethronement of God by man was a fundamental perversion of right order in God's world. The consequences could not but be dire. Hence the progression from disorder to an ever increasing chaos, and "until a few years ago we boasted of it as progress!" [70] The rise of all sorts of "isms," ranging from the totalitarian state of fascism to the tyranny of bolshevism was but the reaction to the blatant injustices of economic and political individualism, stemming, in turn, from a loss of belief in God.

But liberalism, or pagan individualism, had perhaps caused its greatest havoc in economic life, where it gave birth to dog-eat-dog competition with no regulatory governmental interference, since "business is business." Just as in politics, "it is all part of the game." The good of all, Adam Smith had said, is best attained if each looks out only for his own interest to the disregard of all others. This is the doctrine of enlightened self-interest. The doctrine of utilitarianism, the greatest good for the greatest number, was hardly a better guide. And because no supernatural life was admitted, instead of serving man's needs and personality and so his spiritual life, what alone counted was economic values and material comforts, to be sought with no holds barred. In this way the economic element in human life was over-emphasized beyond all proportion, while the final advent of the millenium was confidently awaited. In such a moral climate eventuated the immense maldistribution of wealth and the economic slavery of many in depression days. "Economics was like all else (war, e.g., and love) divorced from ethics," Dom Virgil commented, "since moral principles were at their worst a relic of bygone traditional superstitions, or at their best, a matter for each individual to decide for himself." [71]

That, in broad outline, was Michel's analysis of the general trends in the mid-1930's, of "the overwhelmingly pagan nature of the world" in which the Christian must work out his eternal salvation. He never failed to add that many Catholics had imbibed in varying degrees such unchristian viewpoints. For those who saw their age for what it was, and who retained an undiluted Catholicity, he wrote:

Have we Christians lived up to it as we should? *As we should,* I say. For it is not enough to live up to these sublime truths in the secrecy of our hearts or our home hearths. It is not even enough to live up to them openly and in public. As apostles of Christ we must also on all proper occasions preach these truths by word of mouth as well as by example, and do our part to mould public life after their pattern, that is, after the pattern of Christ.[72]

Because of the naturalistic, pagan character of modern life, Michel never failed to insist on the absolute need for a general spiritual revival to accompany any efforts at Christian social regeneration. For that reason he was so convinced that the liturgical movement was the primary apostolate. Rightly understood, only this could make other movements truly effective. As early as 1901 Pope Leo XIII had observed:

It is the opinion of some, which is caught up by the masses, that the social question, as they call it, is exclusively economic. The precise opposite is the truth. It is first of all moral and religious, and for that reason its solution is to be expected mainly from the moral law and the pronouncements of religion.[73]

Such papal statements could, of course, be multiplied many times. To cite one more: Pius XI, after analyzing socio-economic life in his *Quadragesimo anno,* stated "Two things are most necessary: reform of institutions and reform of morals," and then later added:

Indeed, if we examine matters diligently and thoroughly, we shall see clearly that this longed-for social reconstruction must be *preceded* [*praecedat oportere*] by a renewal of the Christian spirit, from which so many persons far and wide, devoted entirely to business, have unfortunately departed. Else all endeavors will be vain, . . .[74]

In effect the Pontiff said: Institutions are reformed in vain unless there be "a Christian reform of morals," and the latter is impossible without the "renewal of the Christian spirit."

Now the liturgy, in the words of Pius X, *is* "the primary and indispensable source" of "the true Christian spirit"; not only that, it is also the primary source of grace; therefore, it can alone furnish the requisite spiritual means for the rechristianization of social institutions and the life of society. In the final analysis, Michel believed, the spirit behind the social structures, patterns, and habits called institutions — that is to say, the ideals, ideas, and attitudes — determines the moral climate of everyday society and generates the atmosphere which men daily breathe and by which they continually shape their lives. Fail to change this, and all change of social conditions will be, in Dom Virgil's words, "an artificial gesture destined to fade away." [75] As J. Messner has written:

Indeed, ultimately it is the spirit that gives a social system its life, makes it work, and inspires its achievements. Experience has shown that even the best institutions fail if the corresponding spirit is lacking in the members of society. [76]

The liturgy of the Church is the "traditional embodiment of the Christian philosophy of life," Father Virgil said, and then explained:

Everything in the life of man depends on the ultimate outlook upon life, on the ultimate meaning and value set upon life. The liturgy . . . sets supreme value on human life by properly aligning it with the source of all life. And it is at once the embodiment of the teaching of Christ and the continued realization of his mission. [77]

No one would disagree that the ultimate purpose of Catholic social action is to christianize society. To believe, to say, to imply, to make remedial recommendations as though the liturgy had no role to play in effecting a Christian society is to support the absurdity that one can have a Christian social order without Christ's redeeming work as continued in the liturgy. Yet, it is precisely this mistake that those make, Michel pointed out, who think of a Catholic social movement only in terms of ethics and moral theology applied to economic life. Also, praying and living with the Church through her official life and worship constitute at once a preparation for the acceptance and practice of the social ideal outlined in the encyclicals. These, like the liturgy, are another expression of the mind of the Church for modern Catholics.

Reference has been made to the remark of the Archbishop of Cincinnati that social action has to do with the practical realization of social charity and social justice. As Father Virgil often remarked, the Eucharist is the very source of social charity, and the realization of one's membership in Christ's Mystical Body, the very inspiration of social justice. The effect of the Eucharist is the unity of the Mystical Body, i.e., the ever greater union of members with Christ and with one another in Christ. This is God's way of forming the Christian community from within and of forging a Christian social consciousness in each member. In the most intimate possible personal union with God in sacramental Communion is effected the highest supernatural realization of human personality as of the community of human persons. In Father Virgil's many writings on the Eucharist appears this passage:

The eucharistic spirit of a sacrificial victimhood with and in Christ must pervade our everyday life increasingly. . . . In fact, our life must be a continuous offering of self to God as inspired by the Eucharist. . . . Frequent communion, as the full participation in the sacrifice, is thus Christ's essential way of effecting in men the death of disruptive selfishness and individualism and of effecting in them the union of supernatural charity, both of which are essential here on earth for the formation of the social order after the heart of Christ.[78]

Christian social reconstruction, he said, is of heroic proportions. It demands "martyr-spirits." To attempt a program of Catholic social action without rooting it in or linking it to the Mass or Eucharist in some way is to commit the supreme folly of excluding the means whereby the world was redeemed and needs daily to be renewed.

Social work and the humanitarian ideal were held up in Michel's time as "the new religion." Unless social workers see Christ in their clients, they serve themselves, "for a service of neighbor not based on love of God logically becomes a service of self, being based on pride and self-love. Such a service, being fundamentally unchristian, is compatible with all that is pagan in civilization." [79] All men, because of their social nature and high interdependence, no matter in what they are engaged, are called to serve fellow men. For the Christian, this can always be a service of God. As Michel said:

The ordinary occupation of daily life thus can become part and parcel of the divine service the Christian renders to God through the Church; he can at all times both work and pray, he need never abandon the divine conversation which he experiences at its best in the sacrament of the Eucharist in intimate contact with the altar of Christ.[80]

In this way the liturgy teaches and inspires the God-given way of realizing the ideal of humanitarianism, the failure of which in the modern world was derived from the mistaken notion "that it could divorce the service of man from that of God and yet retain the former in its full idealism." [81]

Finally, who should better see the implications of social justice, "one of the most important outward manifestations of the Christian spirit," than he for whom the Mystical Body is an ever-present reality and who realizes that he fulfills the law of Christ precisely to the extent that he carries another's burden, since all are members one of another? A grasp of the doctrine of the Mystical Body makes racial prejudice and economic injustice, for instance, monstrosities for sincere men. True, as Dom Virgil reminded his confrere, Martin Schirber, O.S.B.:

The liturgy does not offer a detailed scheme of economic reconstruction, or anything of the kind. But it does give us a proper concept and understanding of what society is like, through its model, the Mystical Body. And it puts this concept into action in its worship and wants us to live it out in everyday life. The liturgy furnishes an admirable basis for education along social lines.[82]

Certainly few, if any, prominent American Catholic social thinkers or reformers had been so naive as to consider the social question and its solution as purely economic. But, according to Michel, from what some advocated or failed to advocate, one could easily get that impression. First, there were those who, by a constant and almost exclusive emphasis on the economic side of social reform, seemingly put all their hope in social legislation and the application of social ethics and moral theology. Thus, for instance, some harped on Pius XI's insistence on the need of reforming social institutions and said little or nothing on the Christian reform of morals and the essential preceding renewal of the Christian spirit.[83]

The passing of social legislation and the application of social ethics, in Michel's view, was indeed necessary and yet at best only part of the task. However, men can legislate and apply ethics until doomsday without much permanent effect, he said, unless and until by Christian ideals and spiritual means they dispose and motivate persons from *within* to obey freely and to want to do what social justice and charity demand. As early as 1921 he deplored what he termed "the mania for legislating ourselves out of all human ills."

Ultimately to change society one must change men. And if so, was it not high time for Catholics to learn — if not from common sense or daily experience then at least from papal documents — that this was not to be hoped for without God's grace and the general inspiration of the liturgy as the best expression of genuine religion? In his encyclical on the Eucharist in 1902, Leo XIII, referring to the social question which he said was characterized by "arrogance, asperity, fraud among the more powerful, and misery, envy, and the spirit of revolt among the poor," insisted that "one vainly seeks a remedy for those evils in legislation, in the threat of penalties, or in the devices of human prudence." [84] In the previous year the same Pope observed, "Trial and experience have made it clear that many a workingman lives poorly and miserably in spite of shorter hours and higher wages because of his immoral life and lack of religious discipline." [85]

Secondly, Michel pointed out the inconsistency of deprecating individualism in economic and political life but of never even adverting to selfish individualism in the spiritual life, where it pervades, vitiates, and distorts man's whole outlook. Because man is a unitary being having in his nature individual and social elements, his integral spiritual life must combine individual and social elements. Otherwise the twin tragedies of modern times are inevitable: the double standard and the divorce between religion and life.

This phenomenon was reflected in the 1930's, Michel maintained, in the lives of Catholics who suddenly became aware of a social question and of individualism in the atomized economic and social order, that is, when it touched their pocketbooks, but who remained blissfully unaware of individualism and selfishness in their own spiritual attitudes and prayer-life. Deprecating the one-sided emphasis on private prayer to the neglect of the social or community prayer of the liturgy, Busch remarked in the *Wanderer* for January 30, 1936: "If we cultivate only private prayer, it tends to deteriorate in quality. It becomes self-centered and selfish. . . . We introduce the spirit of private profit-making into our prayer and develop a kind of spiritual greed for the profits of novenas and indulgences." Hence Michel's many pleas like this one: "We must slough off our unchristian individualism and become social-minded, above all in our spiritual life.[86] Speaking of the community Sacrifice of the Mystical Body, Michel stated:

One cannot steep oneself in the true meaning of the Mass as corporate worship to be participated in by all and enact the dedication of oneself to God with Christ in the sacrificial prayer of the Mass, and yet remain a cold-blooded individualist in one's life outside the precincts of the altar. Similarly, one cannot become social-minded in regard to the large economic problems of our day — unless one's interest is purely academic or "scientific" — without adverting to the fact that such social-mindedness has its proper place also in the religious life of the Christian. The two go hand in hand. It is impossible to remain individualistic in prayer and sincerely social in daily life, or to remain individualistic in daily life and become sincerely social in prayer. The Mass properly understood must be the inspiration of all one's daily life; the whole of this life must be centered in and flow out from the daily Sacrifice of the altar.[87]

Thirdly, in the necessary efforts to make changes in the institutional order to remedy economic and social abuses, the fact must not be overlooked that the naturalistic and materialistic spirit of our culture is also an obstacle to the work of grace or the acceptance of the Gospel.[88]

Hence Michel's frequent efforts to call the attention of his contemporaries to the prevalence of pagan thought and attitudes. This secular environment, however, is only one more reason why the liturgical spirit, that is to say, the spirit of the Church, must replace the this-worldly and godless social attitudes that poison hearts, minds, and souls. Above all, he insisted, if Catholics set about curing their spiritual disorders by becoming thoroughly and integrally Christian, then their other problems will also become more manageable, or at least they will see them in clearer perspective and better understand what really needs changing in the social habits of society known as social institutions. Then also will there be less danger of assuming that a mere raising of the standard of living, a better distribution of wealth, and the like will automatically guarantee a Christian life and society. This is no small danger, he thought, for those who complacently live in a society in which the divorce between ethics and economics is taken for granted and who, because they tend to underestimate the spiritual bankruptcy of modern times, fail to see that the modern crisis is, as in all times, "a basic clash between Christ and anti-Christ."

Today it is sometimes said that the job of the layman is to apply Catholic social principles to life in the secular order. While that is true, it does not state the whole truth. Michel would find the statement inadequate. For Christianity is infinitely more than a doctrine, a set of truths, or a code of ethics. So, too, Catholic social action is infinitely more than the application of social doctrine, ethics, or moral theology to a secularized social fabric, tacked on, as it were, from the outside. Catholicism is human life supernaturalized in Christ. Christian life then becomes life lived every moment of the day in and for Christ, who incorporates mankind into Himself, active through His living members and supernaturalizing *all* their life and activities

— social and economic life included. Catholic laymen, then, must bring to bear on the temporal order not only religious truths, Catholic social principles, or social ethics, but also the redemptive powers of Christ. For Christ brought into the world not only a body of truth but the supernatural life of grace. Society is always dependent on the Church, the channel of divine Life to mankind, not just for a moral code but for the supernaturalizing effects, powers, and graces of the redemption operating in Christ's own living and active members. Only in this way can laymen be dedicated apostles of the Mystical Body. Such laymen will understand the implications of Pius XII's statement in *Mystici Corporis,* "Christ has need of His members."

To Dom Virgil's mind, St. Paul's words: "I live, now not I, but Christ lives in me," can only mean "that Christ is acting and doing in my person."[89] Surely, Christ does not cease "acting and doing" when the laborer, for instance, participates as he should in his union. For if Christ abides in us and we in Him, Michel explained, then in this "union-of-being" Christ's life becomes our life and His action our action. In a word, Catholic social action must begin from *within,* that is, it must be rooted in the life of the members of the Church. In that sense Catholic social action begins with the individual. And as will be pointed out in another place, a Catholic social movement can then become a groundswell.

As a matter of fact, the social question rooted in original sin presents an ontological problem and, therefore, demands an ontological approach and remedy. In *Quadragesimo anno* Pius XI gave among the causes for moral chaos in social and economic life "the disorderly affection of the soul, a sad consequence of original sin" and "sordid selfishness, which is the disgrace and the great crime of the present age." Hence Michel's frequent quotation: "Not paper programs, not highsounding, unfulfilled resolutions once renewed the world, but new and living men born out of the depths of Christianity."[90] Individual actions presuppose individual piety and sanctity; social action likewise presupposes a social piety and sanctification. The latter is provided for by active and intelligent participation in the corporate worship of the Mystical Body; the former should in general find its inspiration in the same place, Michel maintained. As Pius XI remarked, "In the final analysis all permanent Catholic social reform begins in the sanctuary."[91] Without the liturgy, without the redeeming power of Christ, there is much danger, Virgil Michel believed, that Catholic social action will often end in a rootless activism in which the human, not the divine, predominates. As he showed:

The germ, the mainspring of all Catholic life is divine grace. There is no flourishing of Catholic life except it come from God; it takes place only through the operation of the Holy Ghost, through the fructifying of grace and the gifts of the Spirit of Christ.[92]

To mediate God's life to men so as to make possible a truly Catholic social living — that is the essential function of the liturgy in a social movement which calls itself Catholic. In Dom Virgil's opinion, to separate the social from the liturgical apostolate is to have no apostolate at all.

To recapitulate, all that was said about the relation between the liturgy and Catholic Action applies likewise to the wider Catholic social action. The liturgy teaches that all men are brothers under a common father, actually or potentially members of Christ's Mystical Body; therefore, a brotherly cooperation and an active charity, not a selfish competition, should characterize all human and social relations. Each man is his brother's keeper. The liturgy presents in the supernatural community of the Mystical Body the divine and God-given model of all human society. The official worship of the Church instills the needed spiritual awareness, a Christian sense of values and philosophy of life necessary to see and judge what is wrong with an unchristian world and what a Christian social order should be. The liturgy imparts a refreshing, sacramental view of the world. The corporate action of the Church teaches, furthermore, that the goods of the world are meant by God for all mankind; that redeemed man is creation's priest; that in properly serving man and the needs of all men, creation is redeemed, realizes its purpose and dignity, serves and praises God through man's worship. The prayer-and-grace-life of the Church also teaches the follower of Christ to let the Christian spirit permeate his whole life with all its activities, and to make his whole life one continuous act of worship of God. Again, the liturgy of the Church lifts the Christian out of the narrow confines of self. It broadens his spiritual horizons, deepens his Christian vision, forms his very mind and will after the mind and will of Christ. The result is that he sees the world as Christ sees it — Christ, of whom he is a living member and apostle, in whom he lives and whose redeeming work he must continue daily. The liturgy brings home to the

Christian again and again that spiritual inactivity, in church as in the apostolate, is a veritable abomination before God and a contradiction of the Christian vocation, personally responsible as every Christian is for the welfare of the whole. Hence the liturgy generates a social and corporate mentality and piety rooted in Christ, while imparting Christ's own sympathy for all men. From the liturgy of the Mystical Body it is clear that individualism in all areas and levels of human life, not the least in man's spiritual life, is in the words of Emmanuel Cardinal Suhard "a type of a lie"; that all authority is service of the brethren and that obedience to authority is noble. Finally, the liturgy instills the inspirational truth that every Christian is another Christ and so in his own way another mediator, a living temple of the Holy Spirit, a bearer of God to mankind, and a lighthouse for Christ to all men. These, Michel maintained, are some of the lessons that the liturgy teaches. All are necessary for integral Christian living and social regeneration. The most important lesson, however, has yet to be mentioned: the liturgy imparts from God's own divine charity all the graces needed to live out the lessons it inculcates. In a widely quoted syllogism Father Virgil once summarized his concept of the liturgy's role in Christian life and social reconstruction:

Pius X tells us that the liturgy is the indispensable source of the true Christian spirit; Pius XI says that the true Christian spirit is indispensable for social regeneration. Hence the conclusion: The liturgy is the indispensable basis of Christian social regeneration.[93]

NOTES TO CHAPTER 7

[1] Deutsch to Serge Bolshakoff, Collegeville, n.d., copy.

[2] For Michel's plans, cf. "Nine Years After," *OF*, X (1935), 2–7; "The Liturgical Movement and the Future," *America*, LIV (1935), 6–7. "The time has now come when it appears imperative to widen the scope of our Review by showing how the liturgical spirit can and must be made to bear on our present-day culture and civilization, so as to effect the true reconstruction of society in the spirit of Christ and His Church" (Apostolate, *OF*, IX [1935], 562).

[3] For a summary of social legislation for the years 1935–52, cf. Richard M. McKeon, S.J., "New Capitalism VS Old," *Social Order*, III (1953), 99–102; for the 1930's, cf. Patrick Gearty, *Economic Thought of Monsignor John A. Ryan* (Washington: Catholic University of America Press, 1953), pp. 263–264.

[4] Lester V. Chandler, *Economics of Money and Banking* (New York: Harper, 1953), p. 145.

[5] Charles Owen Rice wrote that the communists once "controlled a million actual or potential members" in the CIO (cf. "Philip Murray, Great Leader," NCWC *Social Action Notes for Priests,* Nov., 1952, p. 5). For a good picture of the conditions in the 1930's and the communist threat at that time, cf. James O'Gara, "Communism in the Thirties," *Commonweal,* LXII (1955), 424–427.

[6] Cf. LaFarge, *op. cit.,* pp. 241–252. In the nineteenth century the American Church was largely preoccupied with bringing pastoral care to the swarming immigrants, with winning an acceptance of the Church in American society and with meeting attacks of the Know-Nothing variety. Labor won a victory in 1887, when James Cardinal Gibbons' pleadings in Rome saved the Knights of Labor from being condemned by the Holy Office.

[7] Cf. Sister Mary Liguori Brophy, B.V.M., *The Social Thought of the German Roman Catholic Central Verein* (Washington: Catholic University of America Press, 1941). In the work of the Verein, the name of Frederick Kenkel, from 1909 to 1951 Director of the Central Verein and editor of *Central-Blatt and Social Justice,* looms large. Other significant

names in the American Catholic social movement are those of priests like Yorke, McGowan, Husslein, Haas, Maguire, LaFarge, and Muntsch.

[8] Cf. John A. Ryan, "Monsignor Kerby: Progressive Leader," *Review of Catholic Charities,* XX (1936), 228–229. The first National Conference of Catholic Charities was held in 1910; the *Review* was founded in 1917.

[9] Cf. Mary Harrita Fox, *Peter E. Dietz Labor Priest* (Notre Dame: University of Notre Dame Press, 1953).

[10] *Social Doctrine in Action* (New York: Harper, 1941), p. 149. For Ryan's contribution, cf. Gearty, *op. cit.*

[11] Cf. Furfey, "The New Social Catholicism," *Christian Front,* I (1936), 181–184.

[12] "Under the Surface," *Commonweal,* XI (1930), 646.

[13] "Social Aspects of the Liturgy," *Catholic Action,* XVI (1934), 11, 9.

[14] Thus Michel wrote to a confrere at the Catholic University of America, "I think you should grab the chance at once to write your M.A. thesis on liturgy and sociology, provided Father Furfey understands that there is practically nothing done on the subject. . . . The subject has hardly been treated" (to Martin Schirber, Collegeville, Nov. 27, 1935).

[15] "Liturgy, True Remedy," *Social Forum,* December, 1938.

[16] Cf. Apostolate, *OF,* III (1929), 187–188.

[17] "Natural and Supernatural Society," *OF,* X (1936), 244; for the next few pages, cf. a series of five articles with this title in volume ten of *Orate Fratres,* pp. 243–247, 293–296, 338–342, 394–398, 434–438. Here Michel, in presenting the Mystical Body as a model for man's social life on earth, quoted St. Thomas, *(ibid.,* p. 243), who gave the sacramental principle its widest extension in saying, "The spiritual life is conformed to the corporeal life by the fact that corporeal things bear the likeness of the spiritual" *(Summa Theologica,* III, q. 3, a. 1), and again, "For God provides for all according to the capacity of their nature" *(ibid.,* I, q. 1, a. 9).

[18] *The Christian in the World,* pp. 76–77. Said Pius XII: "The effort to draw a clear line of distinction between religion and life, between the supernatural and the natural . . . as though they had no relation with each other . . . is completely alien to Catholic thought and is openly anti-Christian" ("All'alba della storia," *AAS,* XXIX [1947], pp. 60–61). Joseph P. Fitzpatrick, S.J., suggested recently starting with what Michel considered the copy rather than the model of human social organization: "And if God chose to establish a community as the necessary means for salvation, certainly the more we can know about the nature of community the better we will understand the reality of the Church's life" ("Catholics and the Scientific Knowledge of Society," *American Catholic Sociological Review,* XV [1954], 1). For an empirical sociologist such a procedure is certainly legitimate.

[19] "Natural and Supernatural Society," p. 246; cf. Michel's comparison of the relations between members and Mystical Body to the proper relations of citizens to the state in *The Christian in the World,* p. 142.

[20] "Quadragesimo anno," *AAS,* XXIII (1931), 207. Somewhat later Pius XI said that there will be no "sound and true order" in economic and social life "unless all men's activities harmoniously unite to imitate and, as

far as is humanly possible, attain the marvelous unity of the divine plan."
Cf. "Natural and Supernatural Society," *OF*, X (1936), 246.

[21] Cf. Michel, "Are We One in Christ?" *Ecclesiastical Review*, LXXXI
(1934), 395–401.

[22] *The Christian in the World*, p. 78.

[23] "Natural and Supernatural Society," p. 295. There is no semi-pelagianism in the liturgy: God works in Christians both the will and the performance; Christ is more in them than they in Him, since He lives His life in them.

[24] *The Christian in the World*, p. 73; cf. also, Michel, *Christian Social Reconstruction* (Milwaukee: Bruce, 1937), pp. 8–13 and 126–132, where Michel explains the nature of social justice; cf. "Natural and Supernatural Society," pp. 434–438.

[25] Acts 2:44–45; cf. also 4:32; in the depths of the depression there was frequent mention of the so-called "communism of primitive Christianity"; cf. Michel's refutation, "Natural and Supernatural Society," pp. 394–398; "Liturgy and Catholic Life," pp. 144–160.

[26] "Natural and Supernatural Society," p. 436.

[27] Because of the destructive individualism in his time, Michel explained man's social nature and "immense" interdependence again and again; cf., e.g., his thorough treatment of this in *The Christian in the World*, pp. 61–83.

[28] "Natural and Supernatural Society," pp. 244–245.

[29] "Natural and Supernatural Society," pp. 434–435; cf. pp. 161–177; "Personality and the Liturgy," *OF*, XIII (1939), 156–159; *The Christian in the World*, pp. 49–78, *passim*.

[30] "Scope of the Liturgical Movement," *OF*, X (1936), 489. "The relation between persons and fellowship must depend, not primarily on any kind of machinery of force, but on a framework of accepted ideas, of ideals that are alive with the true Christian conception of the dignity of personality together with the need of fellowship. It is only by means of social institutions built up primarily on the free acceptance of ideas and viewpoints, that the necessary cooperative adjustment between persons and social bodies can find its solution. Without such a framework of institutionalized vital ideals, no structure or society can be anything but artificial and deadening. Every social form lives only by inspiration of the freely accepted ideas that underlie it. And so any Christian social framework, either in the political or in the economic domain, must be the natural outgrowth of the free acceptance and influence of Christian ideas; and these ideas are found at their best in the supernatural society of the Mystical Body, in which under divine guidance the proper balance is struck between the demands of the individual personality and man's essential need of fellowship" ("Liturgy and Catholic Life," pp. 172–173).

[31] *Ibid.*, p .173.

[32] *Ibid.*, p. 176.

[33] *Ibid.*, p. 174.

[34] Cf. bibliography, Editor's Corner and Apostolate sections in *Orate*

Fratres, I–V and X–XIII; "Liturgy and Catholic Life"; *The Christian in the World* and *Our Life in Christ*.

35 *The Christian in the World*, p. 77.

36 "Liturgy and Catholic Life," p. 66.

37 "The True Christian Spirit," *Ecclesiastical Review*, LXXXII (1930), 139.

38 Jn. 10:10; *ibid*., 6:58; 1 Jn. 5:12. Christ is not only a model for Christians but their life as well.

39 *The Christian in the World*, p. 10. "God has chosen to make the increase of divine life among men here on earth conditioned upon the expenditure of human effort and good will. . . . In the same way, of what avail are the graces of God poured into our souls, if we are overcome with apathy. . . . Our graces are wasted talents unless we are willing to put forth full effort, since it is only through our endeavor that these graces are put to use. Need one stress further in this regard, that our efforts must be directed in God's way rather than in our own ? . . . What efficacy can our sacramental communion achieve, when our entire effort in our thanksgiving and elsewhere in life is individualistic and self-centered, whereas the graces of the Eucharist are above all given for a flourishing of the social virtue of divine charity in our hearts, for growth in all of us of the life of the Mystical Body ?" ("Liturgy and Catholic Life," pp. 258–259).

40 "Liturgy and Catholic Life," pp. 66–67.

41 "The True Christian Spirit," *Ecclesiastical Review*, LXXXII (1930), 131–132; italics, Michel's; cf. Apostolate, *OF*, III (1929), 187–188.

42 Michel, "The Layman in the Church," *Commonweal*, XII (1930), 124; cf. also "Liturgy and Catholic Life," pp. 66–68; Michel, *The Mystical Body and Social Justice* (Collegeville: St. John's Abbey, 1938), pp. 5–16.

43 "Liturgy and Catholic Life," p. 68.

44 "His responsibility for the growth of the Christ-life is always twofold, for growth in himself and for growth in the entire body. As soon as he shirks either one of these responsibilities he is also neglecting the other. . . . In the twentieth century, more than ever before, a supremely important factor for the cause of Christ is the Christian in the world" (*The Christian in the World*, pp. 11–12). "It is for the soldiers of the ranks to battle for Christ and to lead the willing to the priests. . ." ("Confirmation: Call to Battle," OF, II [1928], 238).

45 Cf. *Ibid*., pp. 76–78, and "The Layman in the Church," *Commonweal*, XII (1930), 123–125. On February 28, 1954, Pius XII, speaking of the importance of the lay apostolate, told the Roman pastors: "Be exacting in pointing out their goals to them and be constant in encouraging them towards their realizations. As is clear, they will not have to give orders, but neither may they be reduced to merely carrying out orders. Therefore, leave them sufficient scope for developing a spirit of eager and fruitful initiative; this will also make them happier, more alert, and ready to collaborate with you" ("Ci sarebbe riuscito," *AAS*, XLVI [1954], 103).

46 "On Pentecost," *OF*, III (1929), 197. Theodore Hesburgh, C.S.C., in his *Theology of Catholic Action* (Notre Dame: Ave Maria Press), wrote in 1946: "The sacramental characters have been assigned by the few who

have ventured into this field as the key to any understanding of the lay-man's part in Christ's redemptive work through the apostolate. . . . F. Connell, one of the very few who has mentioned the subject in English, does better by including the character of baptism in his view" (p. 42), and Hesburgh then refers to Connell's, "Theology in Catholic Colleges as an Aid to the Lay Apostolate," in *Man and Modern Secularism* (New York: Catholic Alumni Association, 1940). The function of the sacramental characters and membership in the Mystical Body as the basis of the lay apostolate were emphasized by the promoters of the liturgical apostolate in the United State almost from its inception in 1926, as an examination of the first ten volumes of *Orate Fratres* will show; cf. footnote 48 for some reference to Michel's part in this.

⁴⁷ "Liturgy and Catholic Life," p. 78.

⁴⁸ "Liturgy and Catholic Life," p. 71, also pp. 66–81. On baptism and confirmation, cf. *Our Life and Christ*, pp. 117–140, *passim; The Christian in the World*, pp. 1–34, *passim.* "Baptismal Consciousness," *OF, I* (1927), 303–313; "Announcing Baptisms," *OF, II* (1928), 404–407; "Confirmation: Our Apathy," *OF, II* (1928), 167–171; "Confirmation: Its Divine Powers," *OF, II* (1928), 197–204; "Confirmation: Call to Battle," *OF, II* (1928), 234–238; "The True Christian Spirit," *Ecclesiastical Review,* LXXXII (1930), 128–142 — cf. bibliography.

⁴⁹ "Ex officiosis litteris," *AAS,* XXVI (1934), 629.

⁵⁰ "Liturgy and Catholic Life," p. 72. There is much evidence of this in the letters of laymen writing to Michel in the 1920's and 1930's.

⁵¹ A. M. Cavagna, *Pio XI e l' Azione Cattolica* (Rome: Via Dei Cestari, 1929), p. 36, as quoted by Michel in "Liturgy and Catholic Life," p. 75. Pius X had already said, "In this arduous work of restoring all mankind to Christ, priests must have the help of laymen" ("E supremi apostolatus," *ASS,* XXXVI [1903], 183).

⁵² Cf. "Will Anti-Clericalism Increase in the United States?" *Ecclesias-tical Review,* LXXXVI (1937), 287–288.

⁵³ "Liturgy and Catholic Life," p. 73.

⁵⁴ For hierarchy's statement on this, cf. Raphael M. Huber (ed.), *Our Bishops Speak* (Milwaukee: Bruce, 1952), pp. 211–212; statement quoted by Michel in "Liturgy and Catholic Life," p. 73.

⁵⁵ "Liturgy and Catholic Life," p. 77; cf. also pp. 66–81.

⁵⁶ "Significance of the Liturgical Movement," *NCWC Bulletin,* X (1929), p. 8.

⁵⁷ Apostolate, *OF,* XII (1938), 419; cf. Apostolate, *OF,* XIII (1938), p. 52.

⁵⁸ "Significance of the Liturgical Movement," *NCWC Bulletin,* X (1929), pp. 8, 26.

⁵⁹ Introduction to John F. Cronin, S.S., *Catholic Social Action* (Mil-waukee: Bruce, 1948), pp. vii–viii.

⁶⁰ "What Can Be Done?" *OF,* X (1935), 306.

⁶¹ "Social Justice," *OF,* XI (1938), p. 132. "The Liturgical Movement and the Future," *America,* LIV (1935), p. 677.

⁶² "The Cooperative Movement and the Liturgical Movement," in

Catholic Rural Life Objectives (St. Paul: National Catholic Rural Conference, n.d.), p. 13.

[63] Perhaps no social thinker has emphasized this more than Father Furfey in his writings.

[64] *Christian Social Reconstruction* (Milwaukee: Bruce, 1937), p. 110.

[65] "Quadragesimo anno," *AAS*, XXIII (1931), 225.

[66] "The Unchristian Character of Modern Life," unpublished manuscript, p. 3. For the next few pages and for Michel's analysis of his times, cf., e.g., "Liturgy and Catholic Life," pp. 1-16, *passim*; *The Christian in the World*, pp. 19-36 and 197-233.

[67] "The Unchristian Character," p. 3.

[68] "Liturgy and Catholic Life," p. 10.

[69] *The Christian in the World*, p. 23.

[70] "The Unchristian Character," p. 6.

[71] *Ibid.*, p. 6.

[72] *Ibid.*, p. 8. Italics, Michel's.

[73] "Graves de communi," *ASS*, XXXIII (1901), 389.

[74] "Quadragesimo anno," *AAS*, XXIII (1931), 181, 202, 209, 218. Italics added. Cf. Michel, "A Layman's Lament," *OF*, XII (1937), 80-84.

[75] *Christian Social Reconstruction*, p. 111.

[76] *Social Ethics*, trans. F. F. Doherty (St. Louis: Herder, 1949), 265.

[77] "Liturgy and Catholic Life," p. 251.

[78] "Liturgy and Catholic Life," p. 143.

[79] *The Liturgical Movement*, pp. 20-21.

[80] Michel as quoted by Lydwine Van Kersbergen, *The Normal School of Sanctity for the Laity* (Loveland: Grailville, 1949), p. 37.

[81] "Liturgy and Catholic Life," pp. 251-252.

[82] Michel to Martin Schirber, O.S.B., Collegeville, Nov. 27, 1935.

[83] Thus, from John F. Cronin, S.S., *Catholic Social Action* (Milwaukee: Bruce, 1948), and *Catholic Social Principles* (Milwaukee: Bruce, 1950) one could easily gather the impression that Catholic social action and a Catholic social movement consist only in knowing and applying moral theology, Catholic social principles, and ethics along with mastering "essential economic and social facts." In 247 pages of the former book, the Mass and sacraments are not mentioned and the doctrine of the Mystical Body but once or twice, in connection with Jocism, despite Pius XI's repeated insistence on the doctrine, for instance, in *Quadragesimo anno;* in both books Cronin, like others, narrowly identifies "the renewal of the Christian spirit," which Pius XI insisted must precede (or, in the practical order at least, accompany) change in institutions and morals, with mere moral reform. Michel would certainly have considered this shortsighted while at the same time acknowledging Cronin's excellent contribution to American Catholic social action, of which the reader needs no reminder. "All social action in other words must be under the inspiration of this same Christian spirit that is to produce a reform also in our morals: that brings us back to the liturgy" (Michel, "Liturgy and Catholic Life," p. 133). — Despite his admiration of the pioneer work of the great John A. Ryan, Michel confided to intimates his belief that Ryan relied too much on

legislation and the state, and tended to be too purely "economic" and "statist" in his approach to the social problem, that there was nothing cultural about his program, and too little insistence on the absolute need of the spiritual in social reform and on the need for a general spiritual revival for a complete program of Christian social regeneration (Michel to Martin Schirber, O.S.B., Collegeville, Feb. 11, 1936, copy). Kenkel confided similar misgivings about Ryan's program (to Michel, St. Louis, Feb. 6, 1937). Both Kenkel and Michel, however, would have been more effective as social reformers had they had the grasp of economics that was the pioneering Ryan's, without whose specialized work there would hardly have been a social movement in the 1930's and 1940's. Ryan and McGowan had agreed to have the NCWC publish the lectures given at the Social Institute at St. John's (cf. Chapter XI) if Michel would get them ready in time (Michel to Deutsch, July 29, 1936). Besides, Ryan wrote a nationally syndicated letter in 1930 promoting the newly founded Leaflet Missal. In Michel's comment on the first National Catholic Social Action Conference, held at Milwaukee, May 1–4, 1938, and sponsored by the Social Action Department of the NCWC, the School of Social Science of the Catholic University of America, and the Catholic Conference on Industrial Problems, the theme of which was "A Christian Social Order and the Church," there is an implied criticism of the Social Action Department and others: "Too often the activities of well-meaning Catholic social apostles have concerned themselves quite exclusively, not even with the whole economic side of social reconstruction, but only with one aspect of the entire economic problem, namely, the narrowly industrial aspect as reduced primarily to the one question of adjustment of wage relations between employer and employee. How such a narrowing down of the concept of Christian social reconstruction may do harm rather than good is self-evident. The present conference is much wider and therefore much more profound in its outlook. It is for that reason that we are doubly urgent in asking all liturgical apostles to attend who can possibly do so, and in attending to do their part towards bringing the fundamental truths of the Christian spiritual revival to bear upon all matters of theory and practice that come under discussion" (Apostolate, OF, XII [1938], 273–274). — Michel also had a gentle complaint about the National Conference of Catholic Charities neglecting the divine source of all charity: "The writer had the good fortune to read a paper on the social encyclicals at the National Conference of Catholic Charities of the past summer. Afterwards a young seminarian accosted him in the corridor with the question of why the NCCC gave no place to the liturgy of the Church on its program of agenda; surely, the liturgy was the mainspring and the guiding light of all true Christian charity. It certainly is that, my dear young man, but you can answer your very pertinent *Why* yourself if you remember that God works ever through human means, and for that reason alone the cause of Christ here on earth often takes much time to grow and spread" ("Liturgy and the Changing World," OF, XII [1937], 2–3).

[84] "Mirae caritatis," ASS, XXXIV (1902), 647–648. The Pope suggested as a solution the Eucharist as the source of social charity.

[85] "Graves de communi," *ASS*, XXXIII (1901), 389. For this section, cf. "Liturgy and Catholic Life," pp. 129–143, 178–206.

[86] "Timely Tracts," *OF*, X (1936), 267.

[87] "Our Social Environment," *OF*, XII (1938), 318. "As long as the Christian is in the habit of viewing his religious life from the subjectivistic and individualist standpoint, he will be able to live his daily life in terms of the prevalent individualism and subjectivism without any qualms of conscience" ("Liturgy and Catholic Life," p. 136).

[88] Cf. "Liturgy and Catholic Life," p. 129. It is interesting to note that Bouyer, *op. cit.*, p. 260, years later, makes the same point.

[89] *The Mystical Body and Social Justice*, p. 14. Cf. the pertinent remarks of Messner, *op. cit.*, 262–278, and Busch, "Liturgy a School of Catholic Action," *OF*, VII (1932), 6–12.

[90] George Bichlmair, S.J., *Urchristentum und die katholische Kirche* (Innsbruck: Verlagsanstalt Tyrolia, 1925), as quoted by Michel, e.g., in *Liturgy and the Layman*, p. 23.

[91] "Mit brennender Sorge," *AAS*, XXIX (1937), 154.

[92] "Catholic Leadership and the College," *OF*, X (1935), 22.

[93] "The Basis of Social Regeneration," *OF*, IX (1935), 545.

CHAPTER 8

LITURGY AND
RELIGIOUS EDUCATION

FATHER VIRGIL MICHEL expended much energy in furthering the movement for a more vital and effective religious education in the United States.[1] Fundamentally, the real task of a liturgical
movement is an educational one. A study of the origins and development of the liturgical renaissance in any country will show that
everywhere the obstacles are the same: ignorance of the people, lack
of liturgical literature and properly trained teachers, and, not infrequently, clerical indifference or opposition. Even if Michel had not
been intensely interested in religious instruction before becoming
involved in the promotion of the liturgical apostolate, he would have
had no choice in the matter. According to his own word many times
repeated, the greatest hindrance to the liturgical revival in this country was ignorance and misunderstanding as to its nature and aims,
perhaps best stated as mis-education. Hence the need for a serious
and intensive process of liturgical instruction, truly a gigantic work
in view of the need to go against the inertia of centuries. And this
education was best begun, he said, at the bottom, i.e., with the young
whose impressionable minds are still open and unformed, and whose
thoughtways, therefore, are not set against acquiring a liturgical spirit,
sense, or outlook — the spirit, sense, or outlook of the Church and
of an integral Catholicism.

Chapter six told of Michel's effort in the 1920's to interest various sisterhoods, seminarians, and others in the liturgical revival. The same chapter spoke of the Dominican Sisters of Marywood and Michel's ambitious plan to collaborate in producing a graded series of liturgical textbooks in religion: one volume for each grade, each year of high school and college.[2] These texts were meant to form a generation of liturgically trained and apostolic Catholics who, from the first day in grammar school to the last day in college, would be exposed to, and eventually permeated by, the ideology and ideals of the liturgical apostolate. So trained, such Catholics would make the Mass the source of their piety, know and experience the vital role of the sacraments and sacramentals in daily living, have some knowledge and appreciation of the Church's prayer life, and gain a familiarity with the missal so as to follow the liturgical year as a spiritual guide-book by which to walk continually with Christ. This was Michel's aim in guiding the composition of these texts. However, he died before that ideal could be fully realized.

It is elementary to say that every time the Church performs the liturgy she also instructs. To many Catholics it may come as a surprise to learn that for many centuries the traditional liturgy and the Scriptures were almost the exclusive method and means[3] of religious instruction. The liturgy was once "the theology of the people." As such, the liturgy was not only the instrument of the world's conversion but also the inspiration for the upbuilding of a Christian culture. The same persons may be even more surprised to learn that Martin Luther, who rejected the liturgy precisely as the continued, visible, living mediatorship of Christ, inaugurated or pop-ularized the catechism, made up of short questions and answers. He insisted on slavish memorization and on the mechanical application of this method in religious instruction.[4] Thus, one aspect of Luther's method was its complete divorce from the liturgy. "That Catholic instructors," Dom Michel observed,

should imitate Luther also in the total divorce of their catechetical instruction from the Church's liturgy is an enormity in the face of the traditional purpose of the liturgy and of the traditional place it has always held in the religious instruction of the faithful.[5]

What, then, is the role or method of the liturgy in religious education? That question cannot be answered without considering the purpose of religion itself. This purpose must guide both content and method of education. The essence of religion is worship or cult, the assimilation of man to God through worship with Christ. Or stated in another way, it is to glorify God individually and socially through the individual and social sanctification of man in union with Christ. Obviously, while the liturgy as the worship of God is an end in itself, it nevertheless includes all the aims and purposes of religion.[6] Therefore, all religious instruction must prepare for, and lead to, the sanctifying powers of the liturgical worship of the Church, the sacramental continuation of Christ the Teacher, King, and Priest.

Religious education must embrace the whole person, individual and social. It must prepare the student for Christian living in today's world. As such it must be as extensive as education itself. Furthermore, as Dom Virgil wrote in 1924, religion "must be possessed by the whole man and must therefore be rooted in and find a response in everything that makes up human nature." [7] The Church has always endeavored to activate and cultivate, to educate and train the total man by orienting his whole life entirely to God. She has done this by using methods and materials adapted to man's nature, as is best evidenced in the liturgy. In the sacramental principle God adapted Himself to man's ways and needs. God knows man best. In the liturgy He provided for the whole human being with all his faculties. For this reason Christ took on a visible human nature and instituted a visible organism to continue His work and mission by visible sacraments and sacrifice.

Years before television and other mass-communications media had their full impact, in 1925 to be exact, Virgil Michel observed that the sensory aspect of modern life had been intensified by the vast changes of material civilization; that for anything, and religion not the least, to be of absorbing interest to the man in the street, an appeal had to be made to the whole person, much more so than formerly. If a coldly intellectual, catechism grasp of religion or an uninstructed faith sufficed somehow in a simple and less material past (and it was doubtful, he said, that they ever did), these would no longer hold Catholics to their spiritual duties in a more complicated present or future civilization appealing to modern man's mind and loyalties by saturating his five senses. Therefore, in an increasingly sensistic culture, he argued, the truths of the faith "must be taught . . . in . . . their living appeal to the whole man." [8] More and more, in an age of the concrete, in a materialistic culture, the spiritual and the abstract and the invisible could be effectively taught only through the material and the concrete and the visible.

For this essential task, Michel maintained, the liturgy qualified eminently: a sacrament is an outward sign of inward truth and grace; in fact, all of the liturgy is sacramental in the wide sense. That is to say, all the externals that the Church employs have an inner spiritual meaning and function. They are used precisely to convey to or to keep before the worshipper, by appealing to his senses, emotions, and heart, these inner spiritual truths, to say nothing of the graces poured into the soul by the efficacy of sacramental signs. Consequently, all the homely exterior elements used in the liturgy — fabric and sound, water and wine, ashes and salt, gestures, and postures — are so many concrete signs, visual aids, he said, to bring the supernatural truths of the Christ-life to the soul in accordance with man's natural apti- tudes. In the liturgy, Dom Virgil stated in 1927, the supernatural truths of the faith are

expressed in palpable terms, the invisible in visible signs, the divine in human forms, always in imitation, nay in continuation, of Christ Himself, God-man, the Word made flesh. The liturgy teaches the mind through the senses, the heart through the emotions, the individual by aid of the social, the human through the divine. It answers the whole man, body and soul, heart and mind — and is the one complete and genuine form of the holy grail so earnestly sought today: religious experience.[9]

According to Michel, the Church is no less an educational psychol- ogist and sociologist than Christ was. She *is* Christ. Just as the Church did not need modern education or the sociology of groups to teach her the values of visual aids and of corporate, collective action, so she did not need modern educators and sociologists to assure her that learning by doing and instructing by experience and group activity have their proper place in the natural-supernatural life of man. The life of grace is always built on natural life. As mere abstract or formal instruction is inadequate in the latter, it is also insufficient for the former. For this reason the liturgy, Michel insisted, continually de- mands active participation by the whole person as a member of a whole praying community. This participation will be the greater as the liturgy is better understood. Hence the audible words, the visible gestures and actions, the music and singing, and all else are intended to arouse the person to achieve the best assimilation of the supernatural truths being taught and enacted.[10] All of this is, of course, enhanced by the social nature of the liturgy, which makes use of the best possibilities of group psychology and sociology by inviting the active and collective participation of all as a visible expression of their living unity in Christ.[11]

Nor does this exhaust the sound educational psychology of the Church's liturgical life. The principle of repeating key ideas and keynote statements, e.g., introit and responsories; the constant emphasis on the double aspect of the spiritual life, the negative and positive: the dying to self in order to rise with Christ and to live for God, or again, the avoidance of sin over against the higher and positive ideal of pure love of God proven in service of Him in neighbor; the continuous exhortation to progressive development and growth in Christ which is only a continuation of the baptismal plea to advance "in perfection from day to day"; the beautiful variety of daily and seasonal cycles of prayer in place of the drably sentimental, man-made prayers of individualistic and negative Catholics: in all these ways and in many more, Dom Virgil explained, does the liturgy provide for an integral growth of the whole person in Christ. With this in mind the Church each year relives in the liturgy the life of Christ, applying the fruits of His redemption through dramatization of the life of our Lord as the source and model of all holiness.

One of Virgil Michel's chief criticisms of much religious instruction in his day was the almost total separation of classroom instruction and knowledge from what he termed "the actual worship by which the Christian gives living expression to the truths of Christ in his own life and thereby makes them into vital bonds relating him properly to God."[12] In the previous chapter it was shown that Christ is always undividedly the Truth, the Way, and the Life, and that the Christian as another Christ must therefore participate in all three of these aspects of Christ. His must first be the inner life of worship in church and then as a confirmed apostle of Christ in the world. Neglect one aspect, and you have neither the whole Christ nor the perfect Christian; let the teacher overlook or underemphasize one, and he has given a distorted view of the Christ-life. More simply, the three aspects of Christ embrace doctrine or dogma, morals or ethics, and worship or liturgy. These three elements compose the whole of religion and deal respectively with truths of the mind, rules of conduct, and spiritual contact with God. The integral life of the Christian must give expression to all three of these in their proper interrelation and emphasis. Only that religious instruction is truly Christian that contains these three elements and attempts to effect integral Christian living.

The fact that current methods of religious instruction had failed to include or to emphasize properly these three elements of the Christlife, Michel insisted, was "one of the strongest indictments that can be made against that instruction."[13] And the results? Apart from being frequently ineffective, classes in religion have often been "notoriously the least interesting" for students. The reason for this, Michel asserted, was not only the assumption that anyone could teach the subject. The chief reason was that instructors appealed in an abstract and formal manner and almost exclusively to the intellect or even merely to the memory. Intellectual growth does not necessarily guarantee spiritual growth. Religious instruction that cultivates only the intellect is "narrowly one-sided" and prepares only "one phase of human nature." Yet religion must grip and form the whole man, develop and turn all his tendencies to God. Especially is this necessary in modern times, Father Virgil stated in 1924, "when the child is surrounded by the means of satisfying these tendencies in an endless variety of ways." Man is not just an intellect: he is made up of body and soul, is possessed of mind and will, senses and emotions; he needs and craves religious experience, and this entails his whole being. Christian dogma teaches that character is formed and the soul perfected by acts of the will rather than by acts of the mind, although the latter are by no means excluded. And when one speaks of acts of the will forming a supernatural character, one is already in the realm of grace, the ordinary channel of which is the liturgy. Merely to learn Christian doctrine intellectually, for a person who has already implicitly accepted all that the Church teaches, Dom Virgil warned in 1924, "may bear no fruit whatsoever." Religious education must produce not only religious knowledge but also religious living and spiritual growth. "Today," he continued, "more than ever is it necessary to go beyond mere doctrinal instruction of the mind, to relate religion with all phases of human nature, with all of life."[14]

Here, too, there was only one remedy for Michel: a return to the traditional Christian method of the liturgy, to the Church's own way as model and inspiration, at least, as he put it, "to the extent of knitting up the teaching of doctrine immediately with the official liturgical worship."[15] If anyone thought that this would be neglecting the dogmatic or doctrinal aspect of religion, he had indeed an inadequate concept of the liturgy. In the words of the author whom Michel translated:

> It is evident that in the liturgical texts dogma is not presented under the form of theses and canons. . . . But the liturgy assimilates dogma, adapts the latter to its nature, and expresses it in formulas, rites, and symbols. . . . The liturgy is theology, not scientifically expounded, but applied to the art of glorifying God and sanctifying souls. . . . The liturgy gives testimony of dogma, . . . it popularizes dogma by introducing it into the mind, the heart, and the soul of the faithful with consummate pedagogical skill.[16]

In other words, the liturgy is dogma confessed, experienced, chanted, felt, prayed, acted, and lived out in the official worship of the Mystical Body. Father Virgil believed that no liturgist had ever dared to state so boldly the dogmatic or instructive values of active participation in the liturgy as did Pius XI:

> Early initiation of the people into the realities of faith, whereby they are lifted up to an interiorly joyous life, is more effectively achieved through the annual celebration of the sacred mysteries than through even the solemn statements of the teaching Church. These latter, for the most part, are suited to relatively few men of superior culture; they are uttered but once, and the impression they make is chiefly on the mind. But liturgical celebrations interest and instruct all the faithful; their annual recurrence makes their effect lasting; and they exert an influence on both mind and sentiment, in fact, on the whole man. Man is made up of body and soul; he must, therefore, be stirred and stimulated by the external solemnization of feastdays, to the end that he may more fully absorb divine doctrine through the variety and beauty of sacred rites, and have doctrine become in him strength and energy that will serve his progress in the spiritual life.[17]

The question, then, of whether religious instruction should be basically dogmatic or liturgical made no sense to Michel. All liturgical instruction is basically dogmatic; there is no understanding of the liturgy, he said, without understanding the dogmatic truths underlying it, quite apart from living these truths in liturgical worship. But while undogmatic liturgy is an "anomaly," dogma can be taught as religious instruction apart from its proper setting in the liturgy. In fact, Michel commented, "it has been done only too long and well." [18] Consequently, teachers of religion have the choice of teaching Christian dogma as lived and prayed by the Church and as influencing the whole life of the Christian or abstract dogma unrelated to worship and life. And what are the consequences of the latter?

First, a coldly intellectual grasp of a "dry catalog of dogma" without its life-giving inspiration. Hence, too, the impression frequently given that everything about the faith is "dull and dry," even impractical, related neither to the practice of religion in church nor to actual life in the world. A second consequence was a passive, mechanical, and unintelligent attendance at liturgical worship. A few thoughtful observations of worshippers at Sunday Mass make the latter abundantly clear, Father Virgil noted, and should be sufficient proof that doctrinal teaching must be linked with the liturgy. A third consequence was that Catholics evidenced no living faith, no wholehearted practice of truths taught, no apostolic spirit. Another frequent result was failure to practice the faith once the student was removed from external conditions of social pressure or coercion of home or school. People of the modern age are becoming ever more critical, he warned; they do not easily practice what they do not understand.

Religion had become for many "a mere formalism that is easily shaken off." This, along with pre-school parental neglect and later parental failure to second the efforts of the school, explained in part the leakage from the Church which to Michel's mind had been "nothing less than enormous for generations." How long, he used to ask, can one expect Catholics whose faith is already weakened by a pagan culture to continue to go to church when the Mass is not an intense, living, and uplifting experience and no rededication of self and life to God through Christ? They have no part in the worship because they hardly know what is going on. Thus Michel wrote in 1937:

The neglect of the liturgy and the absence of liturgical inspiration in our teaching of religion may account for many of the characteristics that we find extant today in our Catholic life in its relation to the world about us: the lack of inner vitality of the faith that is in us, the absence of apostolic ardor, the lamentable confusion that mistakes regimentation and external *conformism* for the flourishing of spiritual life, and the spiritual inferiority complex which makes many Catholics hide their light under a basket only too often unto its own extinction.[19]

Dom Virgil believed that not a few teachers of religion committed the Socratic error of confusing knowledge with virtue by instilling chiefly abstract knowledge of doctrine, and this often of a negative and polemical nature. To him this was not far removed from the humanitarian error of identifying sin with ignorance. "A minimum of religious knowledge knit up with practice," Michel reminded instructors of religion in 1926, "may be far more effective than a maximum of instruction separated from practice." [20]

To know, to love, and to serve God in this life and to be happy with Him eternally — that is one of the first answers in the catechism. Essential and fundamental as religious knowledge is, yet without love and service of God it is of no avail. The scope of religious education must always be defined by its purpose, which can only be Christ's own purpose for coming into the world, namely, so that men might "have life and have it more abundantly." For this purpose Christ instituted His Church and now continues to be active in the liturgy. The latter is Christ's own way of fulfilling His mission, and therefore also His means of continually revealing to mankind the Glad Tidings of God for a joyous Christian living. Now, the purpose of bestowing these truths, whether in their knowledge or in their teaching, Dom Virgil said, can be no other than to glorify God and to sanctify men. Consequently, if efforts at religious instruction are to have the purposes of Christ, doctrine must lead to worship and grace as Dom Virgil remarked:

The truths of Christ, then, must ever be taught in their relation to love and service of God. Christian doctrine must be taught in its direct relation to Christian life. That means first of all the liturgical life of the Church in her worship, and then also the daily life of the Christian in the world. Unless the connection is properly made, the religious instruction will be greatly ineffective in producing true Christians; it will not be able to prevent the anomalous phenomenon of men who are Christian for an hour on Sundays and quite secular individualists all the rest of the week, or at all events negative Christians.[21]

All religious instruction, all teaching of dogma and morals, should be oriented in some way to the liturgy. It ought to prepare for active participation under the penalty of otherwise remaining more or less sterile, intellectualistic, removed from true Christian life. For only in the liturgy can the inspiration and grace be found to live out the relation between doctrine and morals. The liturgy, Michel showed, is Christ's own way of bringing the truths of revelation to bear on the actions of our daily life.[22] It is in the very nature of the Church and the liturgy to apply the truths of Christ to the daily routine. The Church is not only the authoritative interpreter and minister of the intellectual content of the Word, but also of its positive working in the lives of her children. In the Mass, for example, Christ speaks and instructs through epistles and gospels; in collect, secret, and postcommunion she urges and shows how to apply and live the truths taught. Michel gave numerous examples from all parts of the liturgy.

We have, he pointed out, taught the truths of Christ our teacher, the rules of Christ our guide; but in failing to teach the liturgy, which relates the truths and rules to the channels of grace, we have neglected to teach Christ our Life.[23] And this has been done even though "Christian education is not so much information apart from Christ as formation of Christ through Christ." [24] The Mass, the sacraments, and the sacramentals constitute the school of Christian formation. To active and intelligent participation therein all else must contribute if there are to be informed and formed Christians. Even the efforts of students and teacher must be, as it were, "immersed in the channels of grace, in the Sacrifice of the altar, the sacraments and the prayer-life of the Church." [25] And might it not be Satan's favorite temptation, Michel asked, to separate all human efforts at religious instruction and growth from the very sources of that growth?

It lies in the very nature of the liturgy to effect, through the active participation by mind and will, a carry-over into life both now and later. There is, however, another phase to carry-over which Dom Virgil emphasized in and out of season: The teacher must not only know the needs of the students but also the culture and environment in which they are living. If this is less important in primary religious education, it becomes absolutely essential in the last years of high school and in college. Here the teacher must dislodge as far as possible the notions of individualism, naturalism, and materialism imbibed from a pagan culture and even in the secularized home. Failure to do so is to teach religion divorced from life and to insure the production of "hothouse plants" unprepared for life's battles. "Every subject," Father Michel wrote in 1923, "should be brought in touch with life and views of life in every classroom or lecture hall. . . . All educational activities are . . . only the beginnings that must be continued throughout life." [26] But this, he insisted, is *par excellence* true of religious education. Since religion consists in living "the truths of God as far as possible," the instructor must also teach how to live these truths, and this he can not possibly do without knowing the kind of world into which he sends his students. In the classroom the teacher *and* the student must confront themselves with conditions in the world and then *together* work out the living Christian solution. How can I make classroom truths the basis of practical action here and now and later in *this* kind of world? — that is the question which must constantly be in the mind of both the student and the instructor. In the final analysis, the test of all effective religious instruction will be apostolic Christian living.

By way of summary, what does the claim mean that the liturgy must be made basic in religious instruction? Michel answered in this way:

It means just this (and perhaps much more): that we must teach the truths of our religion in their practical relation to that living religion, to the actual living out of these truths in the Church both by the Church as a whole and by each member as an active participant. It means that the truths in their interrelation of dogma and worship must also be taught in their mutual relation to the everyday life of the Christian, which must ever be but an extension of the sacrificial dedication of himself to God at the altar. It means that the truths must be taught with all the interrelations they have in the living liturgy itself, psychological, emotional, intellectual, volitional, natural and supernatural.[27]

Heated discussion concerning content and method of religious instruction, teacher-training, and like problems in his time often left Father Virgil with the impression that for the participants the whole problem was one of achieving divine results by merely human means. Yet all religious education has a supernatural purpose and aims to achieve spiritual and supernatural effects. Anything Christian about us, Michel observed, is wrought by God. "In the abundance of our efforts," he remarked, "we have indeed planted and watered, but we have almost forgotten the most important of all, that God alone can give the increase." [28] And He does this primarily through the liturgy. Actually, the teacher of religion prepares the student for, and leads him to, the action of the divine Pedagogue, present and active in the Mass and the sacraments. If Pius XI, speaking of Christian education in general, explained that its "true and immediate end . . . is to cooperate with divine grace in forming the true and perfect Christian, that is, to form Christ Himself in those regenerated by baptism," [29] then it is all the more true that teachers of religion at best but "cooperate with divine grace."

Michel's thesis that all teaching of creed and code must be oriented to cult finds striking confirmation in a statement by Pius XII in *Mediator Dei*, "When the Church teaches us our Catholic faith and exhorts us to obey the commandments of Christ, she is paving a way for her priestly, sanctifying action in its highest sense." [30] No wonder Dom Virgil wrote that "it is almost criminal to neglect the liturgy in religious instruction."[31] And this neglect, in his view, amounted to teaching a "Protestant conception and delimitation of Christianity." This was done at times even in Catholic pulpits.[32] Hence the failure to convey the inspirational content of the faith. For instructors of religion to teach primarily creed and code, to neglect or to fail to prepare for active participation in the primary source of genuine religious experience and spiritual growth, was — for Michel — to make the same mistake that Catholic social reformers made when they aimed to build a Christian social order primarily by social ethics, moral theology, and governmental legislation, while naïvely overlooking Christ's own means of social sanctification.

It should be evident why Michel would hardly have had patience with the dispute which arose after his death as to whether one should teach technical theology or religion as related directly to actual life. In this regard, suffice it to repeat here Father Virgil's insistence that the whole task consisted in teaching "doctrine, living worship, and worshipful living" — creed, code, and cult as a "genuine living totality with no abstract isolations," as a truly living whole eliciting a response from the whole man in worship and life. Only then will Christ be for his abiding and active member the Way, the Truth, and the Life as King, Teacher, and Priest. By all means must religious education be based on doctrine or theology. Michel insisted repeatedly: to love one must know. Therefore, as early as 1925 he pleaded that "the truths of faith, the grand teaching of our religion, must be emphasized with rigorous thoroughness and exactitude."[33] But he hastened to add that this was only the beginning, the basis, the foundation of religious life. And as for teaching religious truth in terms of life-problems: of course, religious instruction had to be immediately related to life — otherwise, he asked, why teach?

It is worth repeating Michel's insistence that dogmas must be not only known but also experienced and lived out in active worship that engages the integral man, and through the grace there acquired find continued expression in the love of God and neighbor in everyday life. Father Virgil frequently stated that, while the liturgy is by no means the whole of religious instruction, little has been accomplished if students have not been initiated into a meaningful understanding and vital appreciation of the Mass and the sacramental life. This was Michel's profound conviction: if every student could be taught the liturgical life of the Mystical Body of Christ and his active share in it with all its implications for daily living, then he would have in the liturgy a lifelong teacher accompanying him as a kind of adult educator; in various life-situations truth, inspiration, and grace would be imparted as needed. And the teacher would be none other than the Holy Ghost, the Spirit of Christ, working through the liturgy, by the spirit of which, in turn, the Church always aims to imbue all of human existence. Father Virgil frequently expressed the conviction that the time had come for religious educators to change their whole attitude and approach to religious instruction.

In line with this conviction, Father Virgil wrote a number of times about teacher preparation and the role of the instructor. Space allows only a brief discussion. One can summarize much of what he said about the role of the teacher with the modern adage, "What you are speaks so loud I cannot hear what you say." Briefly, not only must the teacher know his subject-matter thoroughly, use the best pedagogical methods and skills, be acquainted with human psychology and needs at the various ages, and understand the prevalent environment and culture, but above all, he must *live* what he teaches.[34] Death to self, a profound and joyous living of the Christ-life — that is the essential lesson that must be caught from, if not taught by, one who must be seen by the student as a co-victim with Christ and as a happy messenger of Good Tidings from God. The teacher of religion, unless he lives thoroughly what he professes to teach, implicitly denies what he would have his students carry over into their lives. It is hardly surprising, then, that Michel, when asked by the editor of the *Journal of Religious Instruction* what he considered adequate knowledge to teach the Mass, should have answered that "no amount of mere knowledge"[35] was enough, that to live the Mass in and out of church was "the most important element in a teacher's preparation."

What Michel then set down in two articles as adequate knowledge for teaching the Mass is enough to make any teacher hesitate and religious superiors think twice before appointing instructors for what ought to be the core of every Catholic curriculum. The question regarding sufficient preparation to teach the Mass had been asked by the editor because, she said, "over and over again I come in contact with elementary school teachers who do not have the basic knowledge essential for teaching. If they did, their practice would be entirely different."[36] To teach the Mass properly to the upper grades or to high school students, Dom Virgil believed, the teacher should have a well-rounded, liberal arts college training. "I do not mean," he said, "the motley secularized mosaic of a course that even some of our

Catholic colleges offer, but really a Catholic college education, one that has mastered knowledge and views of life in terms of a living Catholic philosophy." Why? Because "the Mass is not an isolated fact or factor in our lives or in the world, but should be intimately related to everything a Catholic says and does and thinks." Any teacher who ignores this truth

might very possibly teach much concentrated and correct knowledge about the Mass in a very specialized manner and yet miss the whole purpose of the Mass' existence and therefore of any teaching of the Mass.[37]

And to miss the whole purpose of the heart of Christianity is tragic, he said, because

what happens in concentrated form in the Mass when it is intelligently and wholeheartedly participated in must unfold itself in detail through all the moments of our life between Mass and Mass, regardless of whether we can attend the Sacrifice daily or only on Sundays. The Mass is at once cult, creed, and code — worship, dogma, and life — and no teaching of it that does not embrace it in its totality is in any sense adequate.[38]

Therefore, he would oblige the instructor to teach the Mass as containing all the mysteries of Christ; as the praying of the doctrinal truths of revelation; as "the central prayer-action" of the Mystical Body. This implied that each member join with all other members and with Christ in consciously giving himself to God in the collective offering and in receiving the sacrificial Christ in the Eucharist. The Holy Eucharist must be understood and taught in its proper interrelations and with emphasis on Real Presence, sacrifice, and sacrament. The Mass must be taught according to its nature. "To teach only the externals of the Mass or the liturgy would be 'bosh,' and, by implication at least, false Catholic doctrine," Dom Virgil stressed. Externals, in fact, are to be taught only to clarify the internal, spiritual, doctrinal nature of the holy Sacrifice. Needless to say, the pedagogue must have sufficient knowledge of the New and Old Testament. Again, the instructor must understand and teach grace, not just as a state of soul, as a "thing," or as a ticket to heaven which one must keep frantically clutched in his hands until that last moment, but rather as *life par excellence*, as living and abiding in Christ here and now, indeed, as the very beginning of heaven. Furthermore, the teacher must be able to relate the Mass properly to the whole of Catholic dogma and teaching. He must be able to show that the Eucharist is the font and center of all the sacraments. He must relate the Mass to the concept of the Mystical Body, to all truths and mysteries of Christ's redemption as unfolded and lived in the liturgical year, to the whole liturgy. In Dom Virgil's words:

The Mass is, in fact, all of these in concentrated form and any "knowledge of the Mass" that does not understand the Sacrifice as the concentrated embodiment of the whole scheme of our redemption as well as of the whole of Christian truth and life is an abstract, and most likely, a distorted kind of thing.[39]

To assure the application of this doctrine by students to present and future life, the instructor must teach always in terms of immediate participation in the Mass; otherwise the students will be learning without doing and doing without learning — and in the end, perhaps, neither learning nor doing. In other words, if the truths and spirit of the Mass are to suffuse daily living, the Mass must first be meaningfully lived and experienced at the altar in church. If, then, the learner intelligently shares in the Sacrifice according to his capacity, carryover will be assured, especially if the teacher has related the "inspirational projection" of the Sacrifice of Christ to daily student living, while obviously living the Mass himself. Dom Virgil observed:

The above requirements are not even what the teacher of the Mass should know by reason of his specializing in the Mass. They are what every intelligent layman should know as a matter of course; and they are also, I hope, what every graduate of a Catholic high school and college will know *ipso facto* in the next generation.[40]

Ultimately a proper religious formation must begin, after proper home training, with the first days of school and by a progressive development carry through to the end of formal religious education. By that time the student should be sufficiently motivated to inquire into the faith on his own for the practical realization of a living *fides quaerens intellectum*.[41] To have given Michel's philosophy of religious education is to have stated what one may find in his texts. But before turning to these, it may be well to consider briefly why he virtually declared war on the almost exclusive use of the short question-answer, memorize-then-explain, or "rattle-off" system of catechism teaching so much in vogue in his day. To his mind this parrot system was educationally unsound and psychologically wholly inadequate; it called for a memorization of "cut and dried answers" without much, if any, understanding and carry-over into worship and daily human existence. It was devoid of Biblical and liturgical, and therefore, of inspirational elements. It was the product of a rationalizing age, of a polemical and watered-down Catholicism; it was based on what he called "the heathen principle that knowledge is *per se* virtue." The uninspirational and limited content and the stultifying rote memory method of the past, Michel asserted, explained why the Mass "has often been understood least of all by Catholic school graduates" and why the lives of

intelligent and educated Catholics have been spiritually divided into two air-tight compartments, one that of their faith, which is lived at intervals during the week, and the other that of their secular knowledge and their business, which occupies most of their time and energy.[42]

Of course, Michel had in mind the exclusive use of the question-answer method. Certainly, such a method can be intelligently and prudently used together with other methods, and when so employed, is a legitimate procedure, as he readily admitted. Much the same can be said for memorization when skillfully handled. But as used in his day, the catechism and its equivalents, as synopses of pure theory divorced from practice or as a minimal, basic theological treatise, were at best, perhaps, books suitable for an imaginative and alert teacher, he said, for the theologian who could and would supply their many deficiencies. But to hand such texts to children as the sole means of their instruction and training was pedagogically unwise and, according to Dom Virgil, even cruel. Such books engendered no religious enthusiasm; at best they fostered only a passive Catholicism, certainly not a liturgical or apostolic mentality. No other subject, he pleaded, was taught by the "rattle-off" system — why religion?

In 1953 Pius XII warned, "Beware of being satisfied . . . with questions learned by heart without any understanding of their meaning."

The eight volumes of the Christ-Life Series for the elementary grades were meant to remedy this condition by the presentation of an integral Catholicism. The Series was a comprehensive synthesis and integration of doctrine (catechism), Scripture (Bible history), liturgy, art, and music. The authors aimed to present the truths of faith not merely as abstractions or formulas merely to be learned and committed to memory, but as living realities influencing all phases of human life. If other texts had embodied parts of the liturgy as auxiliary aids, the Christ-Life Series was an avowed attempt to build a primary school religion curriculum based on, and inspired by, the liturgy, but without neglecting doctrine. Attractively presented, this Series embodied the latest findings of child psychology and modern educational methods and techniques.

In his *L' Année liturgique* Guéranger stated that in the course of the liturgical year the Church presents for the contemplation of the faithful the whole of Christian doctrine. "For the people there is no closer definition of truth than a feast," Pius XI had said in *Quas primas*. A unique feature of the Christ-Life Series, therefore, was the correlation of doctrine, Bible history, and the feasts of the liturgical year. The traditional narrative, descriptive or Scriptural method was employed, calculated to elicit and preserve, by projects and activities,[43] the natural creativity of children. This Series tried to appeal to the child's heart, mind, and will — in other words, to bring a response as much as possible by self-activity from the whole person. For religious instruction must effect self-reliance, Father Michel explained, not a mechanical dependence on rote memory or book. Therefore, rather than memorizing pat answers to pat questions with little or no comprehension, the authors aimed to arouse and activate the child-mind to give an active response to Christian truths. These truths were presented in a continuing restatement and progressive development of doctrine, by expanding concentric circles as it were, with an inner relation of growth from the first book onward, always, of course, according to the physical and mental capacity of the growing child. The Mass, the sacraments, the sacramentals, and the liturgical year, together with the history of the redemption, were outlined for the children in an effort to elicit as much as possible conscious participation in the sacred liturgy, "wherein Christ Himself teaches and sanctifies them." As Michel stated almost ten years before the Series appeared:

If any success is had in teaching the young to live something of the interior life that is for us the Life of Christ, which means first of all an intelligent participation at times of the whole man in the functions of the Church of Christ, the problem of religious education of the respective children is, in its essence, solved.[44]

In 1924 he wrote that "religious life must from the beginning be developed in all its aspects, in all its appeal to the different capacities of human nature." [45] To develop the emotional life and the aesthetic sense of the child, pictures, illustrations, and liturgical symbolism were abundantly inserted. After showing how, in religious education especially, the invisible is best taught through the concrete, Michel observed in 1928:

Think now, to what pains the catechist must go to illustrate the mysteries of our holy faith in such a manner that the child-mind can sufficiently grasp them, and then reflect on the treasury of picturesque symbolism in the liturgy, which is the plastic presentation of all dogma, our faith in word and deed! Would not our catechism lessons become a living and vital everyday experience, if they were built up on the daily or familiar liturgical acts, if the supernatural truths were taught as caught from the prayers and rites of the Church? . . . We must therefore begin with the young, yet unspoiled by the glamor of the world, and fill their impressionable minds with the beauty of divine worship by pinning the expanding threads of their faith on the attractive symbolism of the liturgy.[46]

The more than 250 letters that these eight volumes occasioned indicate to what lengths Michel went as *censor artium* to make them as perfect rubrically, liturgically, and artistically as possible. In this regard, he thought, other texts had seriously offended. This is a good example of his constitutional dissatisfaction with anything but the best. If, as some insist, we are still in pioneer days as far as creating a living sacred art is concerned, it becomes evident why he experienced so much difficulty in finding artists to illustrate liturgical ideas and to execute symbolism. Long negotiations with artists of Maria Laach had fallen through. When artists were finally found, Michel directed the art work, drawing some sketches himself.[47] His role in the production of the whole Series was to shape and guide their plan; with the Dominican Sisters he wrote the outlines. While the Sisters wrote the texts, Michel edited the Series.[48]

Virgil Michel was well aware that the Christ-Life Series was in many ways a complete departure from the content and methods of the prevailing religious education of the day. "If we can work out the ideas as we have them planned," he wrote to Benziger in 1930, "the work should almost be epoch-making in religious instruction in this country."[49] Michel believed that one who had mastered the Series at the hands of competent teachers would have a grasp of Christian doctrine, liturgy, an integrated history of God's dealings with mankind, and some appreciation of Christian art and symbolism. He would be trained for a lifetime of active participation in the truths and mysteries of the redemption as unfolded and lived in the Church's liturgical life.

After having been completely rewritten and rearranged at least four times, the Series appeared in 1934-35. The texts demanded instructors who had a sympathetic grasp of the liturgy and the Bible. Seemingly such teachers were very few at that time. In a private conversation with Father William Busch, the latter remarked to the writer that the Series came twenty years too soon. It was variously received. A frequent complaint by Sisters was that it was too difficult to teach. The University of Michigan's Bureau of Educational Reference and Research, in evaluating the methodology of the Series, pronounced it sound, and stated that the content of the Series was written in an interesting form calculated to induce meaningful experience in religious training. It judged the material in the first book, however, too abstractly presented, and many sentences too long.[50] In a review of the first four books, Mother Bolton, R.C., stated that "they would be very useful as religion-appreciation readers, but it is doubtful if they would ever produce an active, vigorous mental attitude toward doctrine." On the other hand, Father Ellard called the Series "magnificent" in his review of the last four books.[51] By April, 1937, only 41,515 of the 159,490 copies printed had been sold, and the total sales could not have exceeded 100,000 books.

Although they certainly did not win the attention they deserved, they were no failure. A beginning had been made. The Series set a pattern for others to follow and brought liturgical ideas and ideals into many a home, school, and study club. They are still being used. Father H. A. Reinhold was perhaps not far wrong when he observed that "Dom Virgil would have earned the lasting gratitude of the Church in the United States had he done nothing else but plan and edit the Christ-Life Series in Religion."[52] So important did Michel consider the mission of the Series that he had resolved to spend parts of his future summers teaching its methodology and the liturgy in various Sisters' institutes throughout the country; this program he had actually inaugurated in the summer before he died.

The Christian Religion Series for high school and general reading was planned as a further development of the grade school Series. Michel only lived long enough to help in outlining the first two volumes, the first of which appeared in his lifetime. The plan called for emphasizing in the last books an integral social Catholicism as the apostolic Christian must live it in the modern world.

As for Michel's college texts, *Our Life in Christ* (1934) was a doctrinal survey of Christian theology as a preparation for active participation in the liturgy of the Mystical Body. This volume is Michel's best purely theological work. *The Christian in the World* (1937) was a treatise on individual and social ethics based on the theology of the Mystical Body as explained in *Our Life in Christ*. Both volumes represent Michel's efforts to work out a suitable lay theology based on the layman's position in the Church and in the world. They were meant to generate an integral Christian living and social consciousness as a necessary step to building a Christian culture. This thought will find further development in the next chapter.

Dom Virgil did not write much which dealt specifically with the content of the curriculum at the various levels; one has to infer his ideas as to content from his books. In *The Christian in the World* he traced the role of the apostolic Catholic as a member of the family, the parish, the Mystical Body, the State, the political, social, and economic world. The reader was never left in doubt as to the kind of world in which he was living nor as to his obligations as a member and apostle of Christ armed with the truth in a secularized world. As a synthesis of theology, liturgy, art, social philosophy, and encyclicals, *The Christian in the World* easily ranks with the best of Michel's writings, even though, like many of his writings, it lacked warmth. He died before working out in definitive form these college texts, the first editions of which were lithoprinted.

Much more could be said of Michel's views on religious education. The reader can find them in more than twenty-five articles, numerous editorials in *Orate Fratres*, in his texts, and in the manuals by the authors of the Christ-Life Series. One feels constrained to say that he blazed trails in the 1920's and 1930's that some religious educators are still groping for today.[53] Perhaps it should be added that Gustave Weigel, S.J., confessed recently that in the 1930's many of the Jesuit colleges were still using books with an apologetic orientation, while other colleges were giving a fuller development of the catechism.[54] There can be no doubt that Virgil Michel and his collaborators pioneered instruction in religion based on the liturgy and were responsible, at least in part, for the introduction of the liturgical emphasis in religious education in America. Wrote the former editor of the *Journal of Religious Instruction*:

I would say that all of us in the field of religious education have learned much . . . from Father Michel. . . . We are all much indebted to him for correlating doctrine with the liturgical year, and for helping us to recognize the social implications in the liturgy and our participation in it. In a short lifetime, his contributions were many, far reaching, long lasting.[55]

For his work in religious education Michel was invited to membership on the advisory board of the above named journal.[56]

Related to religious education are Michel's ideas concerning the revival of theology and Scripture, of an effective apologetics and Christian leadership. In his articles on religious education he again and again came back to the importance of better understanding the written Word of God since the liturgy embodies so much of it. Precisely because liturgical worship was dogma confessed and prayed, the liturgical movement, he believed, could not but result in a renewed interest in the basic truths of the Christian dispensation as foreshadowed in the Old Testament and contained in the New.

So much of theological teaching, he maintained in 1936, was still affected by individualism and rationalism, i.e., by what he called "the penchant for extreme analysis without a corresponding synthesis." Rather than being a living science, much of what was embodied in theology as taught in seminaries still reflected an opposition to a now largely ineffectual Protestantism and the general turmoil of post-Reformation days. In a word, the theological conception of Catholicism was not presented as the inspirational, integral, living whole that it is.[57] And the ineffective compartmentalized lives of Catholics proved it in the very way they had often absorbed moral rules divorced from their dogmatic bases and in the way ascetical practices were separated from true liturgical sources and inspiration. How else explain, Dom Virgil pointedly asked, why so many priests are so often so satisfied with a passive Catholicism in their flocks? [58]

In Michel's day there was much discussion about the need of a new apologetics. This was another of Michel's lifelong interests. "Not the least task of the apostle of Catholic Action today is to make Christianity understood by those who now reject or attack it," he stated in 1936. But of what value is the liturgy in apologetics?

First of all, every consecrated lay apostle of the Church must be a Christian apologist at all times and in all places. So much follows from the fact of his conscious participation in the life of Christ as Teacher, King, and Priest. Because of the attacks by rationalists of the eighteenth century as well as by their predecessors and successors, Catholic apologists had expended, Michel said, much labor to meet these attacks. A predominantly rationalizing apologetics was thus forced upon Catholics. He believed, however, that one could question whether such efforts bore much fruit, or at least, whether they were still effective in changed times.

He recalled how Orestes Brownson had insisted that the Scholastic presentation of truths was more suited to confirm the believer than to win the unbeliever; how St. Thomas had said in the *Summa Contra Gentiles* that certain revealed truths of faith could indeed be known by natural reason while others were entirely inaccessible to it; and furthermore, how the Angelic Doctor had warned that much harm was often done by advancing inadequate proofs or reasons in defending the faith. According to Michel, we have inherited a post-Reformation mentality of defending the indefensible, often irrationally and even uncharitably, to which he added, "while our lives only too often contradict the truths we tried to preach." [59] In any case, it was not so much the abstract truths of Catholicism that were keeping non-Catholics out of the Church, Dom Virgil pointed out, as the frequent failure of these truths to find expression in the lives of Catholics.

Dom Virgil was a successful broadcaster of Catholic ideas. As will be pointed out, he enjoyed a considerable influence among non-Catholics. If Michel took his own advice, these words might be part of the reason:

How much energy do not apologists waste by trying at once to convince the other man that he is wrong and the apologist is right? Christian apologetics must rather proceed today by a simple straightforward exposition of truth, and in accordance with present pagan conditions this means first of all an explanation of the essential elements (creed, code, and cult) that make up religion. Unless that is done successfully and some desire aroused, all further effort is useless.[60]

While reasoning has its proper place in the defense of the faith, and while old truths must be clothed in attractive twentieth-century dress, nonetheless, "the best defense of faith as well as its best offensive is that same faith lived wholeheartedly." And in his opinion, precisely this total Christian living had been lacking in general apologetics as well as in the lives of Catholics. He continued:

In consequence, we have Catholic homes that show not the slightest sign of Catholic faith. . . . Catholic families that read only the same literature as their non-Catholic friends; and Catholics that endeavor above all to show their non-Catholic friends that they are no different from them. . . . To these negative Catholics must be added those who are positively un-Catholic in much of their daily lives. . . . A strong argument could be built up for the view that never before could such persons (sincere non-Catholics) see more professed Catholics whose lives contradict their faith, whose religion seems to be mere formalism if not pharisaical hypocrisy, whose actions belie the service they render to God in their prayers, whose faith is to all appearances concealed beneath an active espousal of pure secularism in their daily lives. It takes little contact with prospective converts to learn that one of the biggest stones of scandal is furnished them by the lives led by so many apparently sincere Catholics. Nor may we object to this reaction on their part, since our Lord himself has given us the rule we must go by: "By their fruits . . ." [61]

Catholics of this type, when questioned about the Mass and the sacramental life by sincerely inquiring Protestants, confirmed the latter's worst suspicions, he added.

"He who is not with me is against me," the Savior had said. Too many Catholics, according to Father Virgil, understood this to mean: "He who is not against me is with me." Instead of blaming the Protestants, let them, he insisted, "slough off the false skin of self-complacency"; let Catholics steep themselves in the liturgy to become assimilated to Christ, the Truth, Way, and Life. Then will their lives be everywhere an epiphany of God, while Christ is proclaimed by every thought, word, and action. Such Christian living, Michel commented, constitutes "an apologetics that cannot be answered." To intellectual reasons one can always make a reply, "but not to a wholehearted and sincere Christian life." If the unwilling reject it, they cannot gainsay it; meanwhile to all sincere men will it appeal, just as it "will draw them into a desire for God, and thus pave the way for that divine grace which alone can produce faith." Indeed, a life steeped in God through the liturgy will wring from the reluctant mouth of the modern pagan as from the pagan of old, "They must be Christians, for see how they love one another." And that, Virgil Michel reminded his contemporaries, was the kind of apologetics that the liturgy teaches, a truly Christian apologetics that unifies teaching, practice, truth, and life, that once renewed the world. [62]

This leads to another point often discussed by Catholic educators in Michel's time, namely, the general failure of Catholic colleges to produce graduates exerting a vigorous Catholic leadership in public life. Such failure Michel once attempted to explain theologically or liturgically. The point at issue was really only one facet of a larger question which haunted him all his life, namely, why is Catholic life often so ineffectual, so unapostolic, so uninfluential, compared to what is realizable with the infinite generosity of God's grace?

In this connection he maintained that

Where there is no leadership in a society of men, there is no real growth; and consequently there is no life. It is only where Catholics zealously "push on" in every aspect of life under the inspiration of their faith that we have at once true leadership among the rank and file and true growth of life in the corporate body.[63]

If the early Christians by their public influence and conversion of the world were a demonstration of this, it was because God's grace, the mainspring of all flourishing Catholic life, was fully operative in them. Why then, Father Michel asked, had the graces of God, His abundant gifts, and the Holy Ghost been less operative in Catholic graduates who had been specifically trained for outstanding Catholic leadership? Surely, they had been given more than a secular cultural education, Michel argued, and they went frequently to the sacraments even when out of school; so divine aid was not lacking. How, then, explain the fact that these same persons had not been more effective in public life?

Dom Virgil believed there are chiefly two reasons why the grace of the sacraments does not operate in human life, namely, bad will and a "wrong mental attitude, a false view of what is required or wanted, a wrong psychological 'slant' on the demands of Catholic life or even on the nature of Catholic life." [64] No one should want to say, as being completely unfair and mistaken, said Michel, that Catholic colleges produced or cultivated in their students bad will or lack of the will to cooperate with grace. Hence it must be the second reason: the wrong attitude or false view of the demands and nature of Catholic living. Where this latter obtained, Dom Virgil stated,

the best efforts of the best good will are greatly spent in vain, since they are directed along lines that differ from those along which grace is meant to operate. It is my humble thesis that this has been frequently true of Catholic life, that Catholic education has not fostered bad will — God forbid! — but that it has only too often instilled wrong psychological attitudes, or else has not succeeded in dislodging the common attitudes of our day which by their very nature hinder grace from getting a proper chance to develop. This view is on the face of things anything but bizarre, since our very atmosphere is pagan and unchristian.[65]

What, then, were these wrong attitudes? The first was the false approach to the problem of worldliness. The conditions of modern times had again brought to the fore the old antithesis between this and the next world, or between this-worldliness and other-worldliness. If the modern man solved this antithesis by denying the existence of another life and so unashamedly lived only for this world, many Christians had also accepted this antithesis, even if, like the monks of the Thebaid, they had not yet escaped into the desert, or like the Manichaeans, had not accepted it wholly. Father Virgil's point was that something of this false viewpoint, this lack of a sacramental view of life, has entered into the Catholic teaching and conception of the spiritual life. In the training of the young the impression was often given that the world is wholly evil, that all contact entails compromise and spiritual contamination. But who, he asked, can avoid contacting the world? In any case, with such a viewpoint the college graduate becomes a divided kingdom upon taking his place in the world: "He is faithful to God in the larger things," Dom Virgil explained,

but thinks it inevitable to be faithful to the world at least in smaller things. He feels it necessary either to reject the view that the world is all bad and he then finds something of his early foundations shaken, or else he thinks he must compromise and so cannot be wholehearted about anything.[66]

The true Christian attitude, of course, springs from the realization that the world is good because God made it; that even if it suffers from the curse of man's original sin, it has also been redeemed, and "can be lifted up into the service of God." The layman, as another Christ, is the connecting link, a mediator in his own right between God and world, one whose role impels him to master the world precisely in order to use it for the glory of God and so offer it back to its Creator. Consequently, the sincere Christian "will not run away and hide," but rather "face and transform [the world] unto Christ." In fact, contact with the world should be avoided only in those rare cases where, utterly corrupt, it cannot be sanctified. In all other cases the apostolic layman must spread to his environment, as it were, the sanctifying life that flows through him from Christ.

The second attitude inimical to the proper working of God's grace was the layman's false conception of his role in the Church. He erroneously considered his role to be a passive one — "to receive and to obey and to keep out of the way" — whereas by virtue of baptism, confirmation, and membership in Christ his position demands of him to share actively in the sacramental worship of the Mystical Body and then to continue to act and *to do,* to labor and to share in the apostolic mission of the hierarchy in the world, or in Michel's words, "to sanctify, teach, and govern, by example and word of mouth and action." And, of course, the passive "dumb spectator" attitude at Mass was transferred to the rest of his life. But enough of this, except to add Dom Virgil's frequent plea for teaching and preaching an apostolic Catholicism, for allowing a reasonable and guided initiative to students in school. How else can leadership be formed? In 1937, when the National Catholic Youth Council was established, he stated that in home, parish, and school

for too long a time we have taken the stand that our youth are to be little more than blind followers of us older and wiser members of Christ. And so we have preached obedience and submission day in and day out to them until we unconsciously held forth only the ideal of a passive Christianity. Everywhere our youth were supposed to be seen (in meek submission) and not to be heard. . . . It is up to us to unteach the attitude of a mere passive following.[67]

Then the stifling and pervasive spirit of individualism in the religious life of so many also posed difficulties. It is the "I-and-God" attitude of many at Mass, sacraments, and prayer, in their whole spiritual life, to the practical exclusion of all others. Yet the Christ-life given to the collegian "was never intended to remain confided to himself alone" since it is "essentially corporate in nature" and must be lived corporately, Dom Virgil said in 1935. Pius XII wrote in 1943: "In the Church the individual members do not live for themselves alone, but also help their fellows, and all work in mutual collaboration for the common comfort and the more perfect building up of the whole body." [68] Let the college graduate or any Christian have all the good will in the world; yet, if he cooperates with the Holy Ghost or grace in an individualistic way, not realizing that the Indwelling is social in nature and that all grace is given for a social supernatural life in the holy fellowship of Christ, such a person could not cooperate with grace "fully and adequately"; hence the Christ-life would not flourish fully either. As Michel put the question: How many students left college with a living realization that, in failing to develop their most perfect selves naturally and supernaturally, they were also failing in a social obligation by virtue of their membership in Christ?

Finally, many students had a worldly conception of true Christian leadership. Often "leadership" meant staying in the lead by "dash," "dominance of personality," "showmanship," or the other trappings for which the world has large eyes. While genuine Christian leadership is indeed rooted in the highest development of all the traits of Christian personality, yet Christian leadership is "essentially one of service." The greatest Leader of all had said that anyone who wishes to be great must become the humble, unnoticed servant of all, "even as the Son of Man has not come to be served but to serve, and to give his life as a ransom for many." This, incidentally, was one of Michel's favorite sermon quotations. This paragraph written by Michel for Catholic college graduates was his description of genuine Christian leadership:

Christian leadership takes place first of all by means of the impressive beauty of personality shining through an unostentatious but perfect living of the Christ-life. It has all the courage and the drive of the world when occasion demands. But it is based first of all on the unobtrusive performance of good wherever possible, of all the spiritual and corporal works of mercy, whenever occasion demands or permits, and regardless of whether the actions are seen and applauded by men or not. The strength of God developed in the faithful pursuit of such hidden service will never fail when a more public appearance is demanded. It will not have the ephemeral dash of the modern go-getter, or the pep-man, but the intrepid courage that is rooted in divine truth; it will not revel in self-glorification, but ever be truly humble. Unless it be humble it cannot be entirely of Christ or be fully seconded by His grace.[69]

Such were some of the mistaken attitudes and misconceptions which, as Michel believed in 1935, explained in part why there was so much apathy and ineffectiveness among Catholics in society, so little Catholic leadership, above all among Catholic college students. And they may explain in part, too, why Edward Marciniak was constrained to say as late as 1953 that "with few notable exceptions, Catholic colleges do little to furnish leadership for social reform." [70]

Michel's analysis also brings into clear light the focal importance of liturgical education. How can the Catholic cooperate with Christ in the liturgy with the correct attitudes unless he *knows* according to his capacity the true nature and aims of that liturgy and his active part in it? The organizer of the liturgical movement never finished insisting that, because the Catholic must cooperate *in God's way and not in his own*, the loss of grace or its ineffectiveness is "immeasurable." It is not enough merely to count heads at the Communion table: one must not only induce the faithful to receive our Lord often but to do so with the right mind and will. Perhaps now one is in a position to see through Michel's eyes some of the immense tragedy in the lives of millions of American Catholics who, in attending Mass, still cultivate their own private devotions in their own way and with no thought of the Sacred Action at the altar, and thus withhold unwittingly their full cooperation with divine grace at its very source. Here the primacy of the liturgy can be seen: In presenting to her faithful her thoughts and prayers in the liturgy, the Church means to form the right mind and mould a docile will for cooperation in God's own way at the very font of grace. Anything less than this cooperation leads to a subtle and thinly-veiled semi-pelagianism. With reason did Pius XII insist in *Mediator Dei* on "the tireless collaboration of man, who must not render vain the gift of God." And what is secularism, Michel asked, if not the failure to be of one mind and action with the Church at all times? As for the college graduate: Let him study his field or profession well — master it; let him enter God's world as an apostle of Christ and strive daily to win that field or profession and environment for Him; let him make his everyday life "but a further unfolding" of what he does in a concentrated way at each Sunday Mass (or, where possible, at Mass each day); let him live only for God and God in the brethren — that was Michel's advice for the collegian, who, like every other Christian, must reproduce in Himself the life of Christ.

It is safe to say that everyone who has written a textbook in religion has surely had as his larger intention to curb the devil. In a widely quoted article Michel once told of what he would do if he were Satan. The following excerpt may therefore serve as a summary, negatively stated, to this chapter. Having donned the satanic mantle, Dom Virgil wrote in part:

WERE I SATAN, I should use my utmost cunning, not in attacking the letter of the law of Christ but rather its spirit. Thus in an age of individualism and materialism, I would trump up the note of individualism in the religious life of the members of Christ, and attempt to give them excessive concern over the material goods of the earth. . . . I would not try to change true religious zeal immediately to apathy, but rather direct it into formalistic channels . . . would not expect to abolish religious instruction among Catholics as a whole, but I should try to change all such instruction, even theological teaching, into a matter of coldly intellectual formulation and apprehension; and likewise to change the conception of Christian life into a literal performance of so-and-so many obligations that satisfy individuals with a faithful adherence to minimum essential requirements and get them to feel great satisfaction with this as their adequate Christian observance.

Where a strong desire for more devotional life is irrepressible, I should direct efforts to a multiplication of extra-liturgical functions, with great display of pomp and with much emotional satisfaction. Above all I should try to keep this religious hunger from centering in the Mass itself or from anything like intelligent participation in the essential sacramental or liturgical life of the Church. Where the latter is unavoidable I should try to make their attendance mere occasions for the satisfaction of subjective religious emotions . . . insinuate a great self-complacency with conditions as they are, for instance, the proud thought that never was the inner spiritual life of Catholics more flourishing and more truly Christian than today. With this could easily be coupled the belief that all untoward happenings in the world are solely the fault of those outside the fold.

Under the guise of friendliness, I should try to induce Catholics to hide their religion before their non-Catholic friends so as not to embarrass the latter, and even where questioned about their religion to have them turn the conversation from a discussion of religion to other and neutral topics.

Among the chosen of Christ's flock, pastors and religious, etc., I would work with utmost subtlety at a seemingly minor matter, that of Christian charity, by arousing petty jealousies among members of religious communities or among the diocesan clergy, between different orders, between diocesan and religious clergy, etc., knowing well that wholehearted charity is of the intimate life of Christ, and that where it is lacking in His members there His cause loses immeasurably. In this regard I should also watch eagerly for the rarer cases where under the guise of zeal for Christ or for social justice I could sow seeds of class hatred.[71]

NOTES TO CHAPTER 8

[1] As articles in the earliest German and English Catholic magazines show, such efforts were as extensive as Catholicism. It is arbitrary to assign dates to the origins of a movement. A few names, dates, and titles of books will suffice. An important early date for English language religion study is 1885, when the Baltimore Catechism was published. (Revisions appeared in 1941.) Thereafter various graded texts based on it were published, notably Peter C. Yorke's *Textbooks of Religion for Parochial and Sunday Schools* in 1898, many times revised. Although having its roots in the nineteenth century, the catechetical "movement" received official sanction in 1905 with Pius X's encyclical, *Acerbo nimis*. The work of Thomas Edward Shields in the first and second decades of this century was the first effort to get away from excessive memorization and to apply the findings of modern psychology to religious education. But his pioneer work came to a standstill with his premature death in 1921. According to documented claims the first vacation schools were held under the inspiration of Edwin V. O'Hara in 1921; perhaps one can now refer to this period in terms of the beginnings of a catechetical movement in the United States; Rudolph Bandas taught the first seminary course in catechetics at St. Paul in 1926; in 1934 the center for the Confraternity of Christian Doctrine was founded in the National Catholic Welfare Conference; the real impetus, however, came in 1935, when a decree by the Sacred Congregation of the Council, *Provido sane consilio*, commanded every bishop to establish the Confraternity in every parish and to give a report every five years. Cf. William S. Stone, *The History of the Confraternity of Christian Doctrine*, unpublished master's thesis, Catholic University of America, 1948, and the symposium, *The Confraternity Comes of Age* (Paterson: St. Anthony Guild Press, 1956). *The Journal of Religious Instruction* (since 1947 the *Catholic Educator*) began in 1930. In the late nineteenth century texts for college slowly veered away from the catechetical form and style but were characterized by a polemical approach to theology and a negative approach in moral instruction. Such texts persisted until the more positive doctrinal and cultural approach of John M. Cooper, apparently the real innovator, whose four volumes, *Religion Outlines for College* (Washington: Catholic Education Press, 1924–30), then dominated the

field. For a brief historical sketch of religious education as to content and methodology, cf., Roland Simonitsch, C.S.V., "Problems for Religious Education," *Bulletin of the Educational Conference of the Priests of Holy Cross*, XX (1952), 53–68. Michel's first article on religious education appeared in 1923.

[2] The first fruit of their efforts had been to supplement the catechism with five liturgical laboratory manuals, *With Mother Church*, published in 1929. Out of this grew the eight volumes of the *Christ-Life Series in Religion* (New York: Macmillan, 1934–35) for the grades, along with two manuals for teachers; the *Christian Religion Series* (Milwaukee: Bruce) for high school, of which only the first volume appeared before Michel's death; of the college series, *Our Life in Christ* first appeared in 1934 and *The Christian in the World*, in 1937.

[3] For an enlightening statement of how the liturgy in religious instruction was lost, cf. Michael A. Mathis, C.S.C., *Bulletin of the Educational Conference of the Priests of the Holy Cross*, XX (1952), 69–89; cf. also Dawson, "Education and the Crisis of Christian Culture," *Lumen Vitae* V (1950), 171–186.

[4] Cf. the amazing statements of Luther in Joseph V. Tahon, *The First Instruction of Children and Beginners*, trans. E.V.B.M. (London: Sheed & Ward, n.d.), pp. 67–68, as quoted by Michel, "Liturgy and Catholic Life," p. 100. Indeed, longer questions and answers had been in use for centuries before Luther. J. Brodrick, S.J., *Saint Peter Canisius, S.J.*, 1521–97 (London: Sheed & Ward, 1935), pp. 222–223, strongly rejects Tahon's general thesis because (in the opinion of the present writer) he completely misunderstood it, namely, the imitation of Luther's imposition of abstract concepts on child-minds; cf. Tahon, pp. 42–93.

[5] "Liturgy and Catholic Life," p. 101; for the next few pages, cf. pp. 99–114.

[6] Cf. Romano Guardini, *The Church and the Catholic and the Spirit of the Liturgy*, trans. Ada Lane (New York: Sheed & Ward, 1953), 76–78.

[7] "A High School Course in Religion," *Catholic Educational Review*, XXII (1924), 410.

[8] "A Religious Need of the Day," *Catholic Educational Review*, XXIII (1925), 454. Cf. "Are We Educating Moral Parasites?" *ibid.*, XXV (1927), 147–155.

[9] "The Liturgical Apostolate," *Catholic Educational Review*, XXV (1927), 5–6.

[10] Here seems verified what Shields considered "a fundamental educative principle: the presence in consciousness of appropriate feeling is indispensable to mental assimilation" (*Philosophy of Education* [Washington: Catholic Education Press, 1917], p. 309).

[11] "What possibilities of good are not left untried in the inertia of our individualism! Even the perversions of collective action in the mob demonstrations of our age give us some hint of the power for good now left unused by us, but ever known to the traditions of the Church and so

ardently desired by her" (Michel, "Sanctity and Dignity," *OF*, IV [1930], 661).

[12] "Liturgy and Catholic Life," p. 105. "Certainly the divorce between doctrine or dogma and the liturgy has been almost complete in many instances" (*idem*).

[13] *Ibid.*, p. 106.

[14] "A High School Course in Religion," *Catholic Educational Review*, XXII (1924), 414–415. "The dogmatic tenets of our religion may be as dead matter in the mind unless they are so many bonds uniting the soul more closely to God, unless they are so many watchwords calling forth the virtue of religion to activity" (*idem*).

[15] "Liturgy and Catholic Life," p. 106.

[16] Beauduin-Michel, *Liturgy the Life of the Church* (Collegeville: Liturgical Press, 1929), pp. 104–106. "Dogma is to the liturgy what thought is to the orator, what the ideal is to the artist" (*Manual II* to the Christ-Life Series [New York: Macmillan, 1935], p. 48).

[17] "Quas primas," *AAS*, XVII (1925), 603. "Had anyone else than a Pope said this, what a storm of abusive protests and denunciations, blindly emotional, would the statement have evoked" (Michel, "Faith Without Understanding," *OF*, X [1936], 415).

[18] "Liturgy and Catholic Life," p. 107. Active participation in the liturgy is "a living absorption of the truths of God: an ever deepening understanding of them according to each one's capacity, and an actual shaping of daily life in accordance with the truths absorbed" (Apostolate, *OF*, II [1928], 91).

[19] "Liturgical Religious Education," *OF*, XI (1937), 269.

[20] "The Problem of Religious Education," *Fortnightly Review*, XXXIII (1926), 262. "Mere intellectual possession of truth may be upset by the sophistries of the atheistic, but even the very simple soul that has some experience of the great truths and mysteries of our religion will prove impregnable against higher intellectual attacks" ("A Religious Need of the Day," *Catholic Educational Review*, XXV [1925], p. 455).

[21] "Liturgy and Catholic Life," p. 109.

[22] *Ibid.*, p. 218–220.

[23] "Religious Instruction Again," *OF*, XI (1937), 321–322; cf. "Religious Education," *ibid.*, pp. 218–220.

[24] "Liturgical Religious Education," *OF*, XI (1937), 269.

[25] "Liturgy and Catholic Life," p. 112.

[26] "Religion For Credit," *Catholic Educational Review*, XXI (1923), 467, 469.

[27] "Liturgical Religious Education," *OF*, XI (1937), 267.

[28] "Liturgy and Catholic Life," p. 111.

[29] "Divini illius magistri," *AAS*, XXII (1930), 83.

[30] "Mediator Dei," *AAS*, XXXIX (1947), 536.

[31] "Liturgy and Catholic Life," p. 111.

[32] Cf. "Religious Education," *OF*, XI (1937), 218–220, for Michel's example of a sermon he heard.

[33] "A Religious Need of the Day," *Catholic Educational Review*, XXV (1925), 454.

[34] Speaking of teaching religion convincingly, Michel wrote: "Need one mention in our day that teaching is not convincing unless it arises out of conviction, and that there is no more sensitive gauge of the existence of this intangible element in the teacher than the sophisticated pupil of the present?" ("Adequate Knowledge for Teaching the Mass," *Journal of Religious Instruction*, VIII [1938], 597).

[35] *Ibid.*, p. 595. "Knowledge of the Mass may never be inculcated on the principle of knowledge for knowledge's sake. Especially in regard to the things of God that principle is a perversion of the divine order according to which we are to know in order to love, and to love in order to serve" (*idem*, p. 596).

[36] Ellamay Horan to Michel, Chicago, Dec. 14, 1937. In a study of exams given to primary school children in 1935 in nine Eastern dioceses, Bussard found that out of 167 questions on the Mass and Eucharist, only two dealt with the internal, sacrificial nature of the Mass — the rest with externals, chiefly vessels and vestments ("The Sacrifice of the Mass," *Catholic Educational Review*, XXXIII [1935], 26–29).

[37] "Knowledge Requirement for Teaching the Mass," *Journal of Religious Instruction*, VIII (1938), 765.

[38] "Adequate Knowledge For Teaching The Mass," *Journal of Religious Instruction*, VIII (1938), 596. Cf. "A New Parish Building Up," *OF*, XII (1938), 507–510, for how Michel would teach the Mass to a parish.

[39] "Knowledge Requirement For Teaching The Mass," *Journal of Religious Instruction*, VIII (1938), 767.

[40] *Ibid.*, p. 770. Michel was aware that his requirements for teaching the Mass would "seem strange to those who have been living in the narrow tradition of the past before the present Catholic revival came upon us. . . . If the above requirements do seem gigantic for the moment to present teachers of the Mass, the reason is that they have been brought up at the end of a closing period of history and of Christianity, when the last stand for the old and inadequate methods and approaches was being made" (*idem*, pp. 769–770).

[41] Cf. "Faith Without Understanding," *OF*, X (1936), 413–415. "The course in religion must be to after-life what an apprenticeship in any trade is to the actual profession later on" ("A High School Course in Religion," *Catholic Educational Review*, XXII [1924], 485).

[42] "Faith Without Understanding," *OF*, X (1936), 415. Michel, of course, was inveighing against the Baltimore Catechism of 1885 (revised only in 1941) and its derivatives. How negatively and inadequately the former treats baptism for instance, cf. Reinhold, "A Word for the Fuller Parish Liturgy," *Ecclesiastical Review*, CIII (1940), 173–178. The reader should bear in mind that religious instruction has improved very much since Michel's day.

[43] Cf. accompanying *Manual I* and *Manual II, passim*, for excellent sug-

gestions of activities. "Religion must be taught for what it actually is —
an activity not merely of the teacher but especially of the pupil" ("A High
School Course in Religion," *Catholic Educational Review*, XXII [1924],
472).

[44] "A Religious Need of the Day," *Catholic Educational Review*, XXIII
(1925), 454–455.

[45] "A High School Course in Religion," *Catholic Educational Review*,
XXII (1924), 415.

[46] Apostolate, *OF*, II (1928), 157–158. "It is the essence of the liturgy to
give living expression to all the fundamental truths of our religion by
means of a symbolism that is tangible to the senses, certainly fully as
tangible as any of the new devices of modern life are. The liturgy expresses
the sublimest truths of God in a wealth of external symbolism; it presents
these truths in their living, throbbing aspects. In doing so, it runs through
the entire gamut of the sentiments that the human heart should direct
towards God, and in recurring cycles offers for contemplation all the
things that God has done for man, the complete series of bonds that unite
man to God" ("A Religious Need of the Day," *Catholic Educational
Review*, XXIII [1925], 453–454).

[47] Pleading for artists of Maria Laach to illustrate the last two books,
Michel stated, "No other artists could illustrate the matter of these books
adequately" (to Albert Hammenstede, O.S.B., Collegeville, Dec. 7, 1934,
copy). "Is the field of competent art illustration really so poor in lusty
artists?" (Michel to Agnes Barry, Collegeville, Jan. 30, 1935, copy). "Perhaps with her [Hildreth Meiere's] arrival we shall have found that apparently rare person, a competent artist with a good knowledge of Catholic
liturgy" (Barry to Michel, New York, Feb. 7, 1935).

[48] Sister Estelle, one of the co-authors and a student trained under
Shields, had been the talented author of children's books, the *Marywood
Readers,* and of *Curricular Studies* — both published by Macmillan in the
1920's. The remarkable adaptation of liturgical ideas to the minds of
children was largely her work and that of Sister Jane Marie, although
Dom Virgil was himself no little interested in the educational psychology
of children. His lecture-notes show that he studied the Montessori Method.

[49] Collegeville, Jan. 7, 1930, copy; cf. Apostolate, *OF*, III (1929), 249.

[50] Clifford Woody to Sister Jane Marie, O.P., Ann Arbor, n.d. "As I
have gone through volume after volume of this Series, I am of the opinion
that they serve admirably the needs for which the books were constructed,
namely, as a basis for religious instruction in the parochial schools. In
general, I think the psychology employed is excellent" (*idem*).

[51] For Bolton and Ellard's reviews; cf. "Our Experts Disagree," *America*, LV (1936), 211.

[52] "The Catholic Faith Catechism," *OF*, XV (1941), 315. The authors
of the *Christ-Life Series* certainly anticipated a good deal of what Josef
Jungmann, S.J., had to say in his *Katechetik* (Vienna: Herder, 1953): cf.
John Hofinger, S.J., "Catechetics and Liturgy," "Teaching Good News,"
"The Grade School Child," *Worship*, XXIX (1955), 89–95, 126–135,
461–468. Cf. Busch, "The Christ-Life Series," *OF*, VIII (1935), 216–221,

253–260, 302–309, for the best description of these texts. Busch taught liturgy at the St. Paul Diocesan Teachers' College from September, 1927, to June, 1939.

[53] Cf. Simonitsch, *op. cit.*, pp. 56–68.

[54] Address to Association of Teachers of College and University Religion — Washington-Baltimore Region, Notre Dame College of Maryland, Nov. 1, 1955, p. 1. In two now famous articles, "Towards a Theology for the Layman," *Theological Studies*, V (1944), 43–75, 340–376, John Courtney Murray, S.J., outlined in a much more complete and scholarly way what Michel called for and tried to do in the previous decade; cf. Michel's bibliography, *Our Life in Christ*, and especially, *The Christian in the World*. Cooper's pioneer work should be noted.

[55] Ellamay Horan to the writer, El Paso, Feb. 15, 1955. Cf. *Ou en est l' enseignement religieux?* (Paris: Casterman, 1937), 325; Albert Leonard, S.J., "Textbooks in the United States," *Lumen Vitae*, VI (1951), 532; London *Tablet,* June 14, 1952. The late Monsignor William Russell, who discussed religious education with Michel in the 1920's, wrote to the present writer about the Christ-Life Series, "As source material for authors who want to give the liturgy its place in grade or high school, his Series ranks high. He was the theorist, not the practical applyer. No one should write either grade or high school texts without studying his theory" (Rochester, Dec. 26, 1952). Mention should also be made of Ellard's *Christian Life and Worship* (Milwaukee: Bruce, 1933); revised several times, this book did more to bring the liturgy to college religious instruction than any other.

[56] T. V. Corcoran, C.M., to Michel, Chicago, Oct. 2, 1935. Having declined, Michel suggested confrere Roger Schoenbechler, who took the position.

[57] In 1940 the Jesuit theologian, John Courtney Murray, made the same observation of seminary theology in no uncertain terms, cf. "Necessary Adjustment to Overcome Practical Difficulties," in *Man and Modern Secularism*, pp. 152–157.

[58] Cf. "Liturgy and Catholic Life," pp. 32–33, *passim*: "The Scope of the Liturgical Movement," *OF*, X (1936), 488–490. Michel privately spoke of the need of revamping the tradition-laden seminary curriculum to train priests in the liturgy and for social action. He had the highest regard for the work of Monsignor Reynold Hillenbrand, rector (1936–1944) of St. Mary of the Lake Seminary, Mundelein, Illinois (Cf. interview with Mary Moriarity, New York, Dec. 29, 1952). On November 20, 1938, Hillenbrand wrote to Michel, "I have always been an admirer of the writing you have done, plus all the other work which rests in your hands. Would that I could fathom the secret. . . . Sometime I shall come to St. John's. I shall make sure beforehand that you will be at home." After a lecture-tour, on December 22, 1936, Maurice Lavanoux wrote to Michel from New York: "The lecture at St. Mary of the Lake, Mundelein, was very successful. The new rector, Rev. Reynold Hillenbrand, is a fine fellow — about 35 or 40 — and anxious to do things. If we could have young and aggressive rectors in seminaries and deans of the same calibre

in our colleges, much more could be done than is now possible, although I felt a change in that direction, for the better."

[59] "Liturgy and Catholic Life," p. 32; cf. "Examining Our Conscience," OF, X (1936), 367–369.

[60] "Preface to Religion," OF, X (1936), 209.

[61] "Liturgy and Catholic Life," pp. 80–81. Michel read and highly esteemed the theological work of Vincent Contenson, Theologia Mentis et Cordis, which was an attempt to combine speculative with spiritual theology and which was a kind of forerunner of what is today known as kerygmatic theology.

[62] "Liturgy and Catholic Life," pp. 80–81.

[63] "Catholic Leadership and the College," OF, X (1935), 22. Cf. Michel, "A New Manual of the History of Philosophy," Fortnightly Review, XXXIV (1927), 412.

[64] "Catholic Leadership and the College," OF, X (1935), 23.

[65] Ibid.

[66] Ibid., p. 24.

[67] "A Youth Sunday," OF, XI (1937), 412–413; cf. "Adolescence In The Parish Family," OF, II (1928), 123–126.

[68] "Mystici Corporis," AAS, XXXV (1943), 200. "Were we fully conscious of this social nature of our life in Christ, what a host of petty jealousies, envies, hatreds, machinations of all kinds — such as are a scandal to the saints and to the heathen as well — would cease to be and at the same time would cease to hinder the flourishing of the grace that was given so abundantly!" ("Catholic Leadership and the College," p. 26).

[69] Ibid., p. 27.

[70] "Catholics and Social Reform," Commonweal, LVIII (1953), 560.

[71] "If I Were Satan," OF, XII (1937), 77–78.

CHAPTER 9

LITURGY AND CULTURE

AMID his multiple tasks of research, writing, lecturing, and traveling, a continuous cross-fertilization of ideas was going on in the mind
of Father Virgil Michel. There was also progression in his thinking.
That progression led in the last years of his life to the profound conviction that the essential task facing American Catholics, and the
liturgical apostolate in particular, was the building up of a Catholic
culture under the inspiration of the liturgy totally lived. This was the
final development of his socio-liturgical thought. Since the early
1920's he had warned that a corroding secularism was on the march.
In 1926, in the foreword to *Orate Fratres*, he had written that "many
and varied interests meet in the liturgy. The latter is a great mine
of the widest cultural life." Now, in the chaotic days of the depression
thirties and, as he said, "at the end of an era in the history of the
world," it became what he termed his "overwhelming conviction"
that the liturgy

       is the one true basis of Christian culture and civiliza-
tion. The liturgy, understood and lived after the mind of Christ and
His Church — therefore lived both individually and socially — cannot but flower out into a genuine Christian culture that embraces
every aspect of human life and experience. This is a most important
truth for our day, when the Holy Father calls for a Christian reconstruction of the social order, when we are living in a world torn by
a struggle of cultures, and when we are a minority group in a pagan,

materialistic, and naturalistic culture and civilization, much as were the early Christians, but without possessing their solidarity and their perfect charity, and apparently without their wholehearted devotion and zeal for the things of Christ. . . . Our task is similar to that of the early Christians, and our implements and tools are identical with theirs.[1]

So convinced was he of the need for a revival of Catholic culture in a morally bankrupt civilization that he stated, "Unless there is a Christian cultural revival, Christian dominion of the world will yield more and more to the neo-pagan, mayhap even till but a small band of faithful remains to go through the fructifying experience of another catacomb existence."[2] A week of observations and discussions in Mexico in 1935 only strengthened his conviction that a Christian culture can be a bulwark for the Faith, and that in the United States such a sense of Catholic tradition and culture in daily life was lacking, in view of historical antecedents and for other reasons.

With the distinct aim of promoting a revival of Christian culture, Dom Virgil in the 1930's made a thorough study of what a Catholic culture might be, while he continued to guide the liturgical apostolate and edit *Orate Fratres*. The latter then became an organ for the furtherance of a Christian cultural revival.[3]

In forming a concept of Catholic culture he had to know first of all the nature of culture as such. In 1935, upon investigating standard sources, Michel met one of the surprises of his life. He stated that he was "dumbfounded" to find nothing by Catholics suitable or in any way adequate for his purpose. The *Catholic Encyclopedia*, for instance, had no article on culture. Finally he wrote to Frederick Kenkel, his friend who headed the Central Verein, for a book or treatise giving a "fundamental exposition or a philosophical analysis of the thing we call culture." Kenkel answered, "I cannot at the present moment remember a book or brochure on culture which would meet your requirements. It is a most difficult term to define, and used rather indiscriminately, very much as Social Justice is." Michel had also asked Kenkel to collaborate with him in writing a book on Catholic culture.[4] That book, by the way, still remains to be written. Nothing by an American Catholic, it seems, approaches such a work more than Michel's own unpublished manuscript, "Liturgy and Catholic Life," which he wrote as a sequel to his *Liturgy of the Church* and which the Macmillan Company rejected in 1938. Concerning the manuscripts for this two volume work, Michel wrote to the publisher, "The first of these books unfolds the basic ideas of the liturgy and the liturgical movement out of the texts of the liturgy itself. The second applies the resultant ideas to all aspects of Catholic cultural life. So far, there is practically nothing out like them in English."[5] That Father Virgil should so early have hit upon the anthropological concept of culture as an integral, comprehensive, organized whole or as a total way of life and then worked out an analysis of Catholic culture is one more indication of his alert mind.[6]

This extremely difficult but rich concept of culture has many ramifications. After seven pages of a closely reasoned analysis of this concept, Father Virgil stated:

Human culture would have reference first of all to man himself, to his own abilities of understanding and will, of knowledge and creation, and then to his own entire environment insofar as this is intimately connected with human life. The whole field of human culture in its widest sense embraces all the activities and abilities of man, all the aspirations and inspirations of his nature, the entire field of human existence. It includes the mental or intellectual realm as well as the material, and the individual as well as the social aspects of life. From this standpoint culture has been defined as "that complex whole which includes knowledge, belief, art, morals, law, custom, and any other capabilities and habits acquired by man as a member of society." . . . All culture has to do with a set of ideas or ideals inspiring men to action; it includes the manipulation of nature, and the use of the material elements of life in relation to these ideas and ideals. Hence the judgment passed on any culture will naturally depend on the ideals of life held by the one who passes the judgment.[7]

Because human nature and life are so complex, a culture may be studied from various levels or aspects: the material, the sensory-emotional, the social, the purely intellectual, the moral, the religious — all integral elements of human nature. To overemphasize any one, therefore, is to neglect another. This easily leads to a cult. Hence the cult of the body, the cult of nationalism, the worship of mammon. Even though a culture may be dealt with descriptively, in the final analysis, Dom Virgil maintained, the question of culture is a normative one, since the very concept ultimately implies improvement of person or environment in terms of a norm or an ideal. To say that there are no ideals or values striven after in a culture is to assert that life is only "a meaningless accident of blind forces," or that the search for values is likewise meaningless. What those values, norms, and ideals are will depend on one's notion of human nature, of the purpose of human life, of the place man occupies in the whole scheme of existence. A true culture is as all-inclusive as the nature of man. Hence it embodies the material, intellectual, spiritual, religious, and esthetic domains. It is a social phenomenon; it must be unified, integral, all-embracing — presenting a unified pattern and general harmony characterized by integration and subordination on the basis of a scale of values derived from a common philosophy of life. A culture is anything but inflexible. It is characterized by the possibility of constant improvement and entails social cooperation, the latter because men are highly interdependent; they depend on others for the very means to develop themselves. Culture presupposes human society, and every society has a definite culture. "In every way, then," Michel wrote,

> man's own nature must furnish the cue to the proper development of culture. . . . True human culture must have all the spontaneity and rich variety of human nature and of different national temperaments, else the possibilities latent in the same human nature are not being developed. Any attempt to hamper freedom of development in this regard, and to standardize cultural development according to a set pattern in imitation of our standardization of material products is to mechanize life, and the mechanization of life is ever the first step towards its extinction. Here we have one of the strongest indictments that can be passed on our highly mechanized bourgeois civilization and culture.[8]

A truly flourishing and living culture demands, Michel said, four things: 1) cooperation — rugged individualism rules this out; 2) freedom of the creative human spirit — totalitarianism kills this; 3) coordination of the material and the spiritual since man is a natural-supernatural, material-spiritual being — the one-sided, this-worldly pursuit of the material tends to snuff out human and spiritual values; 4) balance of all integral human elements — our sensuous culture glorifying emotion, passion, and the senses is a constant invitation for man to abdicate his reason and thus surrender his humanity as well as his soul. When Michel measured the culture of his time in terms of these demands, he found, indeed, much to criticize even on the purely natural level.[9]

Evidently a culture is always the product of a basic philosophy of life, whose spirit embraces and impregnates every aspect of human living and environment. A pagan, individualistic, and naturalistic culture will always be the reflection of the way people think, of the ideals they cherish, of the aims they pursue in dealing with their environment. Examine, Father Michel suggested, the cinema, the press, advertising, modern literature, the ordinary ways and means of recreation — then you will know the ideas and ideals, the norms and values by which most people guide their daily life. And if the Catholic reflects long enough on this, he will even see the enormous tragedy that has resulted from his keeping his religion to himself or within the walls of his church, in any case apart from his environment and culture. Here Christopher Dawson's thought was certainly Michel's also:

But while the Church is the bearer of life to humanity, it depends on the individual members of the Church whether they will be merely the passive recipients of this gift or whether they will be the agents of its diffusion in the world. All the tragedies of Christendom arise from the failure of individual Catholics to rise to their opportunities and to permeate their life and their social and intellectual culture by their faith. Wherever Catholics cease to be active, when they rest in a passive acquiescence in what they have received, Catholicism tends to lose contact with contemporary culture and the world drifts away from the Church.[10]

Consequently, if the secular and sensate culture is to be changed, that can only be done by substituting an informing Christian spirit stemming from a Christian philosophy of life and rooted in a wholeheartedly Christian life. But this Christian life must be lived in conscious and active contact with the environment. Instead of a materialistic, worldly spirit, a Christian spirit will then transform all human conduct and leave its impress on the human product that is culture, which in the past had too often been formed by practical pagans due to the default of lukewarm Christians. A Christian culture, therefore, will also embrace spiritual, moral, esthetic, intellectual, and material values in a properly integrated and hierarchically ordered whole. Such a culture will, furthermore, influence religious and moral, political and economic, artistic and literary life, just as it will bend all the products of human activity and making into serving man, creation's priest and mediator, so that man can better serve God. And if the culture is truly living, it will express its ideals in all the ways mentioned. By and large, the social and cultural environment, Michel insisted, will always be a kind of mirror in which Christians can see to what extent they are living the Christ-life sincerely. We work in vain, he repeatedly reminded his coreligionists, to christianize man if we fail to christianize the social conditions in which he meets a constant denial of what we try to instill.

This thought leads to the social and cultural environment of Michel's time and his conception of the Catholic's role in it. This may be briefly stated, as sufficient attention has already been given to Michel's analysis of his age. The reader should also recall here what was said about the liturgy in its relation to Catholic social action, Catholic Action, and the laity's role in the Church.

With the great apostasy of the Protestant Revolt, the Church was rejected in public life, and the subsequent anti-Christian trend culminated in a dominant cultural attitude of secularism, materialism, and naturalism. "We have as a whole," Michel ventured to say in 1935,

little or no understanding of what Christian culture really is, and have also lost much of the instinct of what it should be, since we have been living through centuries of a declining Christian sense and a growing pagan atmosphere of life.[11]

Modern culture measures social status by accumulated wealth and aims at material prosperity without ethical considerations. It repudiates the spiritual and the supernatural and considers religion a myth. It glorifies impulse, passion, and sex while laughing reason, permanent truths, and eternal principles out of court. Could there be surprise, he asked, that a culture with these predominant trends should be "at the opposite pole of any genuine Catholic culture?"[12] Hence unjust, inhuman, economic and social conditions.

Of course, elements of Christian culture have persisted to modern times. Nor is every element of contemporary civilization "bad or unchristian." Rather it is the dominating spirit that is so. To long nostalgically for any literal return to some past Christian age is folly. In the turbulent 1930's it was not infrequently suggested that sincere Catholics should isolate themselves from the wicked world so as to be able to live a truly Christian life and thus to give more effective witness to the truth to a Christless world. On the contrary, Father Virgil believed that "one of the greatest needs of our day is wholehearted Christians who remain in the world, but not of the world, doing good for Christ wherever possible."[13] To run away from the neo-pagan world is admission of defeat, cowardice, and betrayal of Christian duty. This would amount to abandoning the world to anti-Christ, failing to heed the papal pleas for Catholic Action, forgetting that confirmation makes each Catholic personally responsible for the environment in which the Church carries out her mission. Nor is it sufficient, he thought, to be negatively wholehearted in keeping oneself unstained from the worldliness of an unchristian civilization. "The Christian," Dom Virgil contended in 1937,

can be a wholehearted apostle of Christ only if he also works positively at christianizing his pagan environment and at the ever greater spread and growth of the kingdom of God here on earth. The call to Catholic Action in our century is a God-given indication that no Christian life is adequate unless it strives wholeheartedly to exercise this apostleship.[14]

The work at hand, then, in Michel's mind was to imbue the culture and civilization with a renewed Christian spirit, "the age-old inspiring and unifying spirit of Christian love." Right here the Catholic task begins.

However, if the Christian is to fulfill his vocation of being another Christ and of living to restore all things to Christ, he must understand the cultural environment in which he is living. Above all must he realize that a culture, since it is the result of human thinking and willing, acting, and association together, can, like men, be for or against Christ — and modern culture according to Dom Virgil was decidedly against Him. Therefore, Christians must not only become apostle-conscious, he exhorted, but also *culture-conscious*. This the average Catholic had not been. In fact, most Catholics have lived their religion "very privately"; they had contributed to "a culture and lived in a culture foreign to the true Christian spirit"; worse than that, very many had taken it almost for granted as a normal state of affairs. And if Catholics have in this life no lasting city but actually feel at home in an "ubiquitous pagan atmosphere," then it is not too much to say, he thought, that in many ways not a few have been contaminated, have consciously or unconsciously compromised often, have contributed to the reasons why the Church has been ineffective and exerted so little public influence on the temporal order. How can the Church exert such an influence except through the individual Catholic layman at the scene of action where the spiritual and the temporal meet and must be, as it were, bound together? As Michel wrote in 1935, the Christian living the liturgical life must daily strive to effect "the penetration of all human contacts and activities with the spirit of Christ." [15] Only in this way can there be gradually restored what Dawson in 1948 called "the liturgical character of popular culture," [16] destroyed by the Protestant Revolt. Speaking of participation in the priestly and sanctifying action of the liturgy in 1947, Pius XII remarked:

> Not only through her ministers, but with the help of the faithful individually, who have imbibed in this fashion the spirit of Christ, the Church endeavors to permeate with this same spirit, the life and labors of men, their private and family life, their social, even economic and political life — that all who are God's children may reach more readily the end He has proposed for them. . . . The most pressing duty of Christians is to live the liturgical life, and increase and cherish its supernatural spirit.[17]

As a matter of fact, so intertwined with his culture is the Catholic's life that he either christianizes the pagan environment surrounding him by instilling into it his Christian spirit, or else the pagan environment will paganize him, at least to some degree. Here, too, there is no middle way. Dom Virgil observed:

> Only too long have sincere Christians looked upon their spiritual life as something shut up entirely within themselves and have tried to harden themselves against the evil influence of the world even while leaving that same world to itself. We must be with Christ or against Him; we must either affect the world in which we live or else the world will affect us."[18]

In this connection, increasingly more is heard these days about a "lay spirituality." Insofar as the latter is the spirituality of the Church rightly understood in terms of the layman, most of Michel's liturgical writings dealt with it. But he made a more specific reference to it as early as 1936. Different ages and times, he said, call forth different types or ideals of sanctity. Thus there was the martyr-saint in early Christianity; in the Middle Ages more than one person abandoned the world to seek holiness. The ideal of the present and that of the immediate future, Michel remarked, will be one in which the saintly life will be lived, not in fleeing the world but in showing the world how the daily routine and concerns of life — the whole natural order — can be raised into the supernatural and so sanctified. Then he added:

> Certainly this type of sanctity is most sorely needed in our day. It could very properly be called the liturgical type, since the liturgy is the indispensable source of the Christian spirit for all men, and since its inspiration reaches so completely into all the angles and aspects of daily life in the world.[19]

In that world modern secularism has driven a wedge between worship and work, between religion and life, between the inner life of the spirit and the outer life of daily affairs. Many Catholics, Father Michel affirmed, have unwittingly accepted this unchristian dichotomy as normal. Hence their compartmentalized thinking and indifference to unchristian social conditions. Even priests fail to understand at times, he thought, that a correct and active worship by people in church would also necessarily awaken them to live more actively apostolic lives outside of church, in the workaday world where their worship should continue in the work they perform. After all, the whole life of the Christian should be a continuous living out of the Christ-life, one unceasing act of worship. In the liturgical worship at Mass, for example, the Catholic only lives the Christ-life more intensely, while participation in the mysteries of Christ moulds heart and mind for the whole life of the Catholic.[20] "The Christian cannot enter actively into the liturgical worship of the Church," Michel emphasized,

> without receiving therefrom the inspiration to extend the expression of his love and service of God and neighbor also into the daily actions of his life; for anything but such an effect of one's participation in the liturgy, would brand that participation as merely external and insincere instead of being the wholehearted communion with God and the members of Christ that it should be.[21]

Unwitting acceptance of the divorce between worship and work may explain, he believed, why even religion has been taught too often as a separate specialism with no more application and carry-over into worship and daily living than "Latin declensions or geometry." Furthermore, a false concept of worship, or no concept at all, along with the consequent failure to participate actively, may account for the fact, Father Virgil asserted, that many of the faithful lack a Catholic mind, a Christian spirit which should pervade their whole lives and through their lives actively infect their homes and environment. Again, this lack of a *sensus catholicus,* this inability to think with the Church concerning all elements and phases of life, individual and social, natural and supernatural, may explain the peculiar phenomenon of modern times: the pursuit by good Catholics of unchristian aims or the seeking after Christian goals in an unchristian way by apparently sincere Catholics. That the materialistic spirit of a secularized civilization influences much of the lives of such Catholics needs, Father Virgil said, no commentary. One of the greatest anthropologists speaks of "the enormous influence of culture on the behavior and activity of individual men and of men in groups," and he goes on to comment on "the strength and fulness with which the culture holds us all." [22] Father Virgil was keenly aware of this all-embracing grasp of culture. And he worked hard to awaken American Catholics to that fact and to arouse them to commence in a positive way the formation of a Catholic culture.

From the foregoing it should be obvious why he conceived the scope of the liturgical apostolate so broadly. Apostles of the liturgy must see that renewal of the Christian spirit embraces the whole of culture and civilization, all of human life and environment, "under the pain of rendering the spiritual life unproductive." The Christian renewal must not only take place in individual souls; that would not be progressing much beyond modern individualism. So too, to think of this restoration in Christ apart from daily human attitudes and contacts and work, he explained in 1935,

would still operate in the spirit of present-day secularism which long ago commenced the destructive divorce between religion and life. . . . All zealous workers in the liturgical movement must visualize their task with the all-embracing sympathy and the inclusiveness that was Christ's — else their efforts will be greatly frustrated or entirely doomed to failure. What would have happened if the early Christians, one and all, had gone literally to the Thebaid? What, if they had done so figuratively by keeping their religion strictly to themselves, if they had kept it out of all contact with the cultural environment in which they found themselves, had kept it confined within the walls of the churches in which they worshipped? [23]

Moreover, Christ had said that He would draw all things — not just all men — to Himself. The father of the modern liturgical movement had called for the forming of Christ in all, for the restoring of *all things* in Christ, just as he had pleaded "that the true Christian spirit may flourish again *in every way* and be preserved by *all* the faithful." Finally, in Dom Virgil's words, "just as the liturgical spirit is the inspirational font or core of Catholic Action, so it is also the source of any genuine Christian culture." [24]

In regard to culture the Church is truly catholic. She despises no part of creation and welcomes all true human progress; nothing human is foreign to her. Committed to no particular culture, she is supra-cultural and supra-national as she is super-natural. Precisely because the Church is a living organism overflowing with the life and spirit of Christ, she assimilates whatever she finds of true value;

from every culture she draws its unique contribution and so adds to her total being. To realize her life fully, her spirit must pervade the whole culture since the latter is always an integral whole.[25] Also, the higher the true development of a culture, the better medium does the Church have to express her spirit — and no amount of culture will ever "exhaust the expression of the spirit of Christ in her." A truly Catholic culture, Father Virgil explained,

would include the sound concepts and traditions of all times, the best developments of human progress of all ages, and that in all fields of human interest and endeavor, theological, philosophical, historical, social, political, economic, literary, artistic, ethical. It would be truly Catholic in its scope and thus realize the ardent desire of Pius X that the true Christian spirit flourish again in every manner and that Christ be formed in all.[26]

Such a Christian culture the Church strives to fashion through the continued realization of the redemption that is the liturgy. Through the Mass and sacraments she endeavors to color, refresh, and integrate the whole of man's life, and in her prayers she sanctifies every hour. Through the sacramentals the Church accompanies the Christian in life, forms a suitable environment, frees material creation from the curse of Satan that it may praise God freely. She blesses space and time, persons and things, and lest anything be overlooked, she has a blessing *Ad omnia*. Thus the Church breathes the spirit of Christ into all the details of modern life. For she wants her living members to "know no life outside the pale of her influence"; they must "vibrate to the slightest of her inspirations" while she pursues through each and all her mission of "drawing all creation into the life and love of Christ." [27]

Culture is, then, a supra-individual or social reality. Its best development calls for harmonious association and cooperation among men. Now the liturgy furnishes the Christian with the divinely established model of all human cooperation; more than that, it effects in him Christ's own all-embracing sympathy "for all men, for all things human, for all that is good in God's world." [28] The liturgy, properly understood, helps man to see the material things of the world as so many signs and instruments of the spirit. In this way will the resultant Christian culture align "all the elements of life with Christ even as does the liturgy in a concentrated manner." Thus, too, will be formed the truly cultured man, cultured in heart and soul, in intellect and manners, in all the integral elements of his being. His external environment will be the symbolic expression of his cherished higher ideals, even as the ugliness of the mechanical artificiality of so much of contemporary culture is the sign of a vapid paganism or of the deadening, legalistic observance of religion. Material creation will in this fashion serve man in his Christ-life, the living mediator between Creator and creation. Thus can a Christian culture be gradually formed that is at once the "unified embrace of all aspects of life in their proper relation to the divine." [29] Even recreation would then reflect this proper relation to God and become a truly cultural force.

Because the Christian family is the basic unit of society in and through which Christian culture is formed, preserved, and transmitted, it is not surprising that Father Virgil should have spoken and written frequently on the role of the Christian woman and the family in the apostolate of the Church. Similarly, beginning in 1927, he had much to say about the nature, formation, and function of the living parish, which is a family of families.

In 1928, sixteen years before Pius XII discussed *Woman's Duties in Social and Political Life,* Dom Virgil outlined for the National Catholic Women's Union the place of woman in modern life.[30] He often returned to the subject thereafter, especially in speaking to Catholic colleges for women. American Catholic social writers had almost entirely overlooked [31] the problem of feminism.

The proponents of the feminist movement, he insisted, were not the first champions of woman's rights, freedom, and higher status. Only ignorance of Christian tradition could allow so false and facile an assumption. It was precisely Christianity that had rescued woman from the more or less qualified slavery and subjection to men in pagan Greece and Rome. The fact of Christ's coming through the instrumentality of a woman and Mary's role in the work of redemption already indicate woman's true position and dignity in Christian society. Among those helping the Redeemer in His ministry on earth were women, who also helped the apostles in the spread of the Gospel. Thus St. Paul ordered Philemon, "Help those women who have labored with me in the Gospel. . . ." [32] So too the Church in more Christian times had always sponsored the education of women and held out feminine vocations besides the glorious one of motherhood. In the face of pagan degradation of womanhood, Michel showed, the Church Fathers extolled the ideal of virginity. Not only did the Church insist on women's fundamental equality with men before God but also held both equally responsible for the observance of the same commandments.

Again, deaconesses helped in the administration of baptism, instructed souls in times of persecution, and prepared them for the reception of the sacraments; generously they practiced the corporal and spiritual works of mercy in public. In the canon of the Mass appeared the names of women-martyrs along with those of men. Women, like men, actively participated in the Church's worship and the lay apostolate since they shared as members of the Savior's Body in the same priesthood.

Then there were the double monasteries for men and women, sometimes even ruled by a woman. Somewhat later, in the guilds, especially those of a religious and charitable purpose, women enjoyed an equal status. In the Christian centuries holy and learned women were the sought advisers of bishops, kings, and popes, and, as Father Virgil observed, spoke "to the latter with a frankness that astounds us today." [33]

From the earliest Christian times, therefore, married and unmarried Catholic women enjoyed a christianizing influence not only in the home but also in public life. While the home, the family, the training of the young are her primary responsibility, woman's professional work outside the home is not contrary to the orders of nature and grace — provided that such work fits her unique gifts and psychology. According to Father Virgil, "Women are born to be in their own way apostles, not only examples, of Christian ideals and life." [34] As such they aid in wiping out the unchristian distinctions between men and women handed down by a pagan culture.

A radical change came with the Protestant Revolt. In many parts of Europe convents were closed, and soon virginity was no longer valued. Naturally the respected calling of women as nuns, educators, and social workers was lost. Schools for the education and training of young girls were closed. Much of Catholic institutional welfare was abandoned or secularized. When the guilds were dissolved, women were again practically confined to the four walls of the home without education and without opportunity for positive service to fellow men in the wider society. With the Industrial Revolution they entered the dingy factories only to become more unfeminine and depersonalized.

However, as Father Virgil was at pains to prove, the fate of any civilization and culture rests with its women. If the paganism of old had refused to look upon woman as a human person and considered her a mere thing and instrument to be used according to man's pleasure, modern unchristian feminism views her as an isolated individual, "an all-sufficient center of self-interest," or else as a cog in a totalitarian social collectivism. Yet only through the proper recognition of her unique temperament and endowments can her personality grow and develop. Having different abilities, men and women have different functions and tasks. They complement each other.

The feminist movement lost for woman what Christianity had gained for her. The movement is guided, he said, by the prevailing philosophy which is one of selfish individualism and material pleasure. If, then, the feminist enters the public professions, which her Christian forebears had engaged in with benefits to society,

it is acknowledgedly to get more out of life for herself, and not to do more real good in the world. The latter goal means self-denial and self-sacrifice, and nothing is farther from the spirit of modern feminism. That is why divorce is so rampant, and why personal pleasure, or glorified passion, supersedes the high ideals of the welfare of children, the sanctity of married life, and even justice itself, social justice above all. The women of today cultivate the appeals that address themselves to the lower nature of man, or again women seek their position of power and independence by becoming most like men, that is distinctly unfeminine.[35]

On the contrary, Father Virgil would have every Catholic woman know that there is something in her soul divinely called to lead man on to purity and refinement of soul, to light up for him the path that leads to God. Unless her nature is artificially distorted or repressed, she thirsts for the spiritual in a degree far above that of the average man. Woman is much more capable, he maintained, of cultivating the human virtues and of raising them to the supernatural realm. If men have made most of the intellectual advances, nonetheless it was always woman as the inspirer of man who kindled and preserved the spiritual in the hearts of men. In 1929 Michel stated:

The Christian woman is as it were a natural sacrament in the world, an external sign of inner grace radiating goodness everywhere. She is a power for good in the world to which only the most debased men will fail to respond, and whose active influence the world never needed more sorely than today.[36]

Actually, there are two possibilities for woman in regard to man: either she plunges him deeper into hell than man would descend by himself, or else leads him farther up into heaven than man would ascend by himself. If man's weapon of domination in a pagan civilization was brute force, woman's in a Christian culture is the strong one of spiritual influence. By temperament, inclination, and ability, she is in many ways better fitted for God's battles and the cause of the Church, Father Virgil explained, and that is why wherever the Church has triumphed, woman has played a major role. And that is precisely why, as he told the Minnesota Council of Catholic Women in 1936, "The worst that can happen to a civilization is that its women descend to the moral depths of the unchristian men of the age. We are at that stage today." [37]

The remedy? Father Virgil suggested in 1928 that women, after properly fulfilling their first responsibility of safeguarding the home and family, step "out more actively into the affairs of the world" because "the world needed them more than ever." [38] Compare this with Pius XII's words spoken in 1945: "Your day is here, Catholic women and girls. Public life needs you. To each of you might be said: Your destiny is at stake." [39]

In another connection Father Virgil stated in 1936 that woman's influence must penetrate "far beyond the confines of the home into all the professions that woman is naturally fitted for. . . ." [40] In entering these professions to care for the wounds of mankind and of Christ's own Body, she is only fulfilling her traditional Christian role, he insisted. Unless she pursues her God-given role of civilizing and christianizing man, no Christian culture can be maintained, much less built up, conserved, and transmitted from the sanctuary of the home. Needless to say, to do this she must, like her Christian predecessors of old, drink deep of the life and spirit of the liturgy by which alone she can become a genuine apostle of Christ and the natural instrument for the spread of God's kingdom on earth.

Obviously, woman's greatest possibilities lie in the home. The family, as the first community and school of Christian virtue and of social life, is the nursery of society. Michel concurred with the historian Kurth's idea that Europe was once won for Christ largely by women who in the home converted their husbands and instructed their children. In the home woman lays the whole natural substructure for the supernatural life.[41] From her queenly position in the family circle she is indeed "a gardener of God doing a veritably priestly work." Here she cultivates the seeds of divine faith, hope, and charity and the gifts of the Holy Spirit implanted in her offspring by baptism. Only through her tender solicitude will these seeds come to flower and fruit. As Father Virgil pointed out, "The entire work of rechristianization, as embodied in the scope of the liturgical movement . . . must find its first beginnings in the Christian home under the inspiration of the mother." [42] He clarified in detail how she could do this through the use of the sacramentals for hearth and home and by liturgical customs and practices. In this way the liturgical life could unite the community of parents and children, the spiritual family of the parish, and the wider family of God which is the Mystical Body of Christ.[43]

Thus the home could be, as it were, "an extension of the house of God," and the family the Mystical Body's spiritual miniature. Active sharing in the common religious life of the home could be the preparation for or continuation of corporate worship in the parish church. In such a family each significant feast would find its echo. Such Christian homes would be citadels of Christian culture radiating light into their neighborhoods, and a kind of sanctuary of God in which future priests, lay apostles, and saints would be nurtured. Speaking of the mother as God's gardener in such a family circle, Michel noted:

The entire atmosphere of the home as well as of the life that radiates from the home is her work, so that she must be interested in social and civic questions, help in the Catholic Action of her parish and in its other activities, enhance the general cultural atmosphere of her home, and thus in every way perform the sacerdotal task of informing all the aspects and instruments of life with the true spirit of Christ.[44]

Even her marriage is a reflection of and participation in the union of Christ and His Church. Strong faith assures parents that through the instrumentality of their wedlock God begets children. Only through motherhood can Christian marriage play its high role in God's plan for the creation and redemption of mankind. Dom Virgil noted:

The purpose of a Christian marriage is by no means properly expressed in procreation and education of children, unless the phrase is interpreted, as it really should be, in terms of the supernatural purposes of life. Then the purpose of marriage and motherhood is seen to be a true cooperation in the very work of God and Christ here on earth.[45]

To produce Christians, to augment the number of the elect, to be the mother of saints — such is the true and glorious function of woman. Her life thus becomes an extension of the Incarnation. Sacrifice is the key to successful family living, he suggested, sacrifice learned from Christ and often renewed at Mass. And such sacrifice will, in turn, inspire "sacrifice of woman for man, of man for woman, of both for the society of men, for the Church, for God." [46] With sacrificial living assured in the home, woman will not fail in her great mission in public life. For then, as Michel expounded:

The Christian wife will inspire the husband, the daughter the father, the sister the brother — the woman worker in the world those with whom she deals, especially the social worker, the nurse, the religious Sister, the teacher, the woman lawyer, or doctor.[47]

Thus in home, parish, and society at large woman is always the natural instrument of God. In this light, too, can the full proportions of her failure at home and beyond be seen in modern times as well as the tragedies for society resultant upon the continued growth of feminism. Clearly, the feminist movement, he said, is one more expression of the unchristian philosophy that pervades the culture of modern times. Yet such a culture can only be redeemed for Christ through the apostolic life and work of apostolic Christian women, "the natural moulders of the hearts of man." For history proves that the rise and fall of the status of woman affords an index to the rise and fall of Christian culture.

Only this much can be said here about Father Virgil's extensive treatment of womanhood, marriage, family, and their relations to a Christian cultural revival. One must be even briefer in referring to his many writings on the living parish.

Echoing Pius XI's dictum of 1928 that the pastoral theology of a former day is no longer sufficient, Dom Virgil remarked that it was necessary to rethink the whole question of the care of souls and parochial methods. That is why he had begun discussion of parochial work as the second project in the Apostolate section, in the second volume of *Orate Fratres*. However, the utmost patience and prudence were needed. An older generation of priests, he observed, "had their ironclad 'traditions', from which it is hard to set oneself free." Yet a beginning had to be made, if a new generation of priests was to associate with themselves more actively a trusted laity in worship and apostolate.

What the individual family is to the social community that the parish family is to the whole Church. The pastor is the spiritual father of the supernatural parish family. His most important society is the parish society, itself, and the liturgy is the pastoral work *par excellence*. Only to the extent that these are first revitalized can all other parish societies properly fulfill their purpose, namely, to build up the parochial spiritual community, miniature of the Mystical Body of Christ.

Even when thinking of the parish Michel could not but concern himself with the Christian's whole way of life, natural and supernatural, individual and social. The parish should be the center of the spiritual, cultural, social, educational, and even recreational life, as far as possible. In his words:

Insofar as the spiritual life of the Christian is not something that can be lived in a separate compartment in isolation from his other, worldly activities, the scope of the parish also includes other aspects of human life. Even in the earliest Christian days we see the general concern of all for the relief of the poor and the needy widows and orphans, and in the ages of Christian faith we see added to this also other social functions, not least also of healthy recreation and amusements (e.g., the miracle plays and mystery plays of the middle ages). Thus the term *parish life* includes not only the personal religious life of the members of the parish, but also their *social religious life,* and beyond this the other *activities that help to foster spiritual and corporal works of mercy.* . . . They [member families] must not only be aware of each other as spiritually interrelated, but their common membership in the Body of Christ must be the basis of an active love and cooperation between them in all the activities that make up the entire parish life. The people must respect and help Christ as operating in the priest, and the priest must at all times serve Christ in his flock.[48]

In this way the external social conditions of the parish community can be again closely knit in with its liturgical life. In fact, the social environment would be the reflection of such corporate parish life. In such an ideal parish there would be no distinction of race, color, or class, just as there would be no passivity in worship or apostolate, no mere observance of minimum essentials, no divorce between social and liturgical life.

At the hearth of the parish family — the altar — the active participation begun in the external expression of corporate spiritual life in the home should find its further cultivation and development. Similarly, the social virtues which are practiced in the home and begin to flower there must be fully exercised in the wider parish community. As in the natural family, so in the supernatural family of the parish, each member must contribute to the welfare of the whole as much and as soon as he is able. In the parish community the members have the first obligation to practice the virtues of social justice and charity, already nurtured and cultivated in the community of parents and children in the home. The parish is likewise the first center of official Catholic Action. Intensification of inner parish life is thus a preparation for the wider apostolate. In the parochial liturgical life apostolic Christians can find all the spiritual means to relate the whole context of life to God. And when this is done by many, a Christian environment and culture — always the fruit of corporate Christian living rooted in Christ — will begin to do for the modern world, Michel thought, what the Catholic culture of Christian communities did in the early centuries of the Church.

Certainly part of a Christian cultural revival will be the revival of the arts. In fact, art is always the finest expression of a culture — it's precipitate, as it were.

Mention has already been made of Michel's contacts with artists and with the Liturgical Arts Society. His efforts in the pioneer period of the 1920's to promote a revival of the sacred arts through *Orate Fratres* and in other ways have also been related. From the first days of the organized liturgical movement in 1926, he observed that a genuine liturgical revival will certainly bring also an artistic revival. That was hardly a profound observation. For just as the sacred drama of the liturgy is a synthesis of theology and Scripture, so it is the integration or synthesis of all the arts in the worship of God: Sacred literature, architecture, sculpture, metalcraft, painting, music, poetry. But while the Church employs all lower creation as well as the highest achievements of human art in giving glory to the God of all truth, goodness, and beauty, the liturgy in its very nature is the supreme expression of living art. Just as one cannot fully understand and sincerely live the liturgy and still remain individualistic in his general mentality, Father Michel believed, so too, to understand the liturgy is also to become concerned with its externals. In other words, to know, to love, to live the liturgical life is to become interested in the arts. A renewed and sympathetic understanding of the liturgy, therefore, necessarily leads to a revival of sacred art.[49]

So closely is art tied in with religion, Michel contended, that it will always go the way of religion. Furthermore, the art of any age reflects its temper, tastes, values. That is why, he said, the art of his day in general bore the marks of mechanical externality, of empty naturalism, of mawkish sentimentalism, of modern pessimism; it was individualistic, subjective, esoteric; it was anything but vital. In the midst of the depression, he wrote:

> Mechanical efficiency has supplanted the spontaneities of nature to such an extent that whole masses of people

know nothing of the beauties of life in the open fields. . . . With the desertion of man's natural love and reverence for nature, the inspiration of the latter for beauty wanes, and never before has there been such a cult of the drab and the ugly and the commonplace. Artistry and craftsmanship have all but disappeared as matter of popular appreciation or of social inspiration and enjoyment.[50]

Works of art, moreover, speak of what men worship, and objects of worship can be material or spiritual. The undeniably sad condition of Christian art, especially of ecclesiastical art, is but one more example, he noted, of the inroads into Christian life that the pagan temper of the times had made. And certainly the esthetic education and appreciation of American Catholics left much to be desired. Here also the liturgical movement could play an important part in restoring art to its rightful place in human life, above all in the spiritual life.

In 1934 Dom Michel told a meeting of the Liturgical Arts Society in New York City:

In the field of art, too, new inspiration is needed. After the gothic art of medieval faith, we have had little more than the classical renaissance with its rather too unjoyous dignity and baroque with its playfulness gone wild, ending often in uncontrolled frivolity. After that there has been almost nothing beyond an attempt to recapture a past that no longer lives today.[51]

How the liturgical spirit, that is, the spirit of Christ as the fruit of active participation, could engender a living Catholic art will be stated after a brief summary of Michel's philosophy of esthetics. But perhaps it should first be remarked that Dom Virgil was no artist, as that term is commonly accepted. His artistic tastes are not beyond criticism. Thus, he said more for than against the cold, almost geometric rigidity of Beuronese art. His was an intellectual appreciation of art. He wrote about the latter from the standpoint of the philosopher and of the liturgist. As such, his remarks in reference to the concrete were casual, tentative, provocative.

Michel's theory of esthetics may be said to center in the sacramental principle, which he called "the supreme principle of art, that of revealing inner mind and spirit through external tangible signs." [52] It is of the nature of art to bring us into contact with the unseen, the mysterious, the spiritual through use of the material. All art is idea in material garb, or idea and spirit and meaning shining through the external media used for their expression.

The whole of material creation with all its elements is embodiment of idea, the reflection of God's mind, of His truth, goodness, and beauty. If this is the widest extension of the sacramental principle, its highest realization is found in Christ, in whom divinity manifested itself in visible human form. Apart from being the highest manifestation of the sacramental principle, our Lord while on earth also used the sacramental principle by employing material things or visible gestures to perform the miracles that His divinity could alone effect. The sacraments as the actions of Christ are outward signs of inward grace. They contain what they signify. In his homily for the feast of the Ascension, Pope Leo the Great stated, "The visible presence of our Redeemer in the flesh was changed for an invisible presence in the sacraments." In a beautiful phrase of *Mediator Dei*, Pius XII said, "Christ acts each day to save us, in the sacraments and in His holy Sacrifice." Similarly the Mystical Body is the sacramental continuation of Christ. Here again the invisible being and life of our Lord are hidden beneath the visible hierarchy and fellowship of His members, while the divine powers of Christ are exercised through certain visible actions of Christ's priesthood.[53] The sacramental principle, therefore, pervades the whole being of Christ, of the Church, of the liturgy, which gives this principle a universal application. According to Dom Virgil, in the eyes of the liturgy

all the world is a symbol of God, all creation sings forth the beauty of its Creator. Everywhere does it see in the things of time the symbol of eternity, and in nature the symbol of the supernatural. It makes use of all the objects of nature and of all the creations of human skill for the better expression of the ineffable sentiments of the divine, for revealing as far as humanly possible, the truth and the beauty of the life of God. . . . It constantly holds forth Christ, the supreme symbol as the most perfect realization of the sacramental principle, the living God as active under the external visible form of man. By further application of the sacramental principle the divine action of Christ is extended throughout time; it transforms man into a symbol of the divine, through whom the sacramental principle is expressed in his personal life of fidelity to Christ and extended into all his environment, upon which he must put the universal stamp of Christ.[54]

Keeping this in mind, one may ask, What is the nature and purpose of liturgical art? And how does it differ, if at all, from sacred art in general? Briefly stated, since the liturgy is the external embodiment of interior soul and divine spirit and, in the sacramental mysteries, the actual depository of the divine action, art finds in the liturgy its most natural sphere. But even considered from the human standpoint, the

liturgy is a great work of art. The whole liturgy, like its every ceremony, is an integral unit exhibiting the selectiveness of art in view of
achieving a given end. It takes on the character of profound art not
just by its externals but in the special way that these embody or express
or call forth the full depth of human sentiment and aspiration; for in
the liturgy the Source of all truth, goodness, and beauty is sought, and
this is man's most profound quest. If the liturgy is full of God's love
for man, it also enshrines man's deepest thoughts and feelings toward
the Creator. In the liturgy nature is not suppressed or distorted; nor
is it given an artificial interpretation; the symbols employed reflect the
God-given and natural purpose of the materials used. And these
materials are given their most beautiful and meaningful forms in the
worship of God.

In many other ways the liturgy of the Church embodies in the
highest degree characteristics common to all true art. It has organic
structure, progressive development organized around a focal idea or
ideal, integration of gesture, postures, words, music, color — all selected and blended to produce a unified effect. If sincerity and honesty
are required of the worshipper's inner participation, the liturgy demands no less in the choice of materials, down to the least item.
Precisely because the liturgy is the "supreme expression of the spirit
of art," Dom Virgil showed, "nothing is farther from the mind of the
liturgy than haphazard action, cheap or gaudy display, falsity or sham
of any kind." [55] Modern secular art, feeding as it must on a spiritually
bankrupt civilization, is often depressively pessimistic. Not so liturgical art which, like the liturgy, is always eminently optimistic; it
always reflects the joyous victory of the glorified Christ, even while it
teaches mortification and death to self, for example, during Lent.
Furthermore, liturgical art is as social as the liturgy; it is not the
esoteric preserve or snobbish hobby of a select few, but the property
of all members of Christ; it is catholic, universal in its appeal, communal in its appreciation. "Who knows," Michel asked, "but that
the liturgical revival, in regaining this character for its art, may not
also be the inspiration for a return to a more social art in general, and
so help overcome the abundant futilities and great emptiness of so
much of our subjectivistic and individualistic art." [56]

Again, he commented:

Art is eminently the product of love, of
devotion to an ideal, to a cause that reckons neither its failures nor its
sacrifices. The mainspring of liturgical participation likewise is love.
In it, too, the divine ideal is reached by sacrifice and self-denial,

through a persevering courage inspired by the love that never falters. Art and liturgy are truly kin, as are nature and supernature. And their meeting place is in the performance of the liturgical worship, where art is elevated to the highest dignity, just as all nature there reaches its true destiny of being wedded to the supernatural.[57]

However, not every kind of art or artistic inspiration makes for a happy marriage between liturgy and art. About this Dom Virgil was most emphatic. Always must art serve the liturgy as tool and means; never must the liturgy be adjusted to the whims and ways or even to the unguided inspirations of individual artists. Music and singing, for instance, must glorify God — not the organist or choirmaster. Nor is all religious or sacred art necessarily liturgical. Organic, not accidental or artificial, is the union between art and the liturgy.[58] For art to be truly liturgical, then, it must be an integral, organic, but subordinate element of the liturgy, and furthermore, it must be entirely inspired by the ideas and ideals of the liturgy. In this connection Michel remarked that

in many instances, the "artistic" features of our churches are determined not by the traditional wisdom of the liturgy, but by the individualistic quirks of pious donors, who litter the church walls, or even the altar itself, with ornaments and statues of all sorts, entirely unrelated to the aims and spirit of liturgical worship.[59]

To include here Michel's lengthy discussion of liturgical music [60] — the highest and most spiritual of the liturgical arts — and liturgical symbolism [61] would take the reader too far afield.

Michel's belief that a maturation of the liturgical apostolate would also effect a renewed interest and appreciation of the sacred literature of the Scriptures has already been recorded.

But Father Virgil's most important observations about the liturgy and art remain to be stated. Liturgical art must be understood in two ways: liturgical art by inspiration and purpose, and liturgical art in action. All art is the external or sensible manifestation of what is essentially suprasensible. Now the art symbols of the liturgy indicate an inner spiritual reality; but the sacramental signs of the liturgy actually effect what they signify. The liturgy at its best may, therefore, be called, Virgil Michel stressed,

the supreme living art, in which both the human and the divine are operative together, in which the divine is present in human form and takes on increasing stature in the person who lives and acts in it as a true member of Christ. What is thus presented by analogy in all the art-forms that are in the service of the liturgy becomes supreme realization in the liturgical enactment itself. And both the priest and faithful who participate actively in the liturgical mystery, thus become supreme living artists in proportion to the perfection with which their external words, gestures and postures reveal and enact the inner divine reality that is the essential nature of liturgical worship.[62]

The liturgy in action, then, is living art of the highest possible kind.

So much having been said, the role of the arts in the liturgy can be briefly stated. Since liturgical art serves the liturgy, it has the same purpose as the liturgy, namely, the glorification of God and the sanctification of man. Negatively, it must in no way call attention to itself and so distract the faithful from the divine saving action that is transpiring before them and in which they ought to be personally and actively involved. Positively, it must make liturgical worship more intelligible to all the faithful, inspire, urge, prepare them for, and facilitate their active and collective participation as well as give them the right attitude toward the church as the House of God. A properly adorned church lifts Christians above themselves and their daily routine to God, not by a "momentary hypnotism of atmosphere," but by speaking to them positively and concretely of the great truths underlying their worship, such as the living mediatorship of Christ, the living unity of all in the Mystical Body, and their active union with the priest at the altar. If Catholics cannot always live in a cultural atmosphere in which they feel environed by the faith, Father Virgil said, at least they should vitally experience this in their contact with God in church. And if so, the church will be for the faithful the threshold of heaven, and their active worship and communion with God the means to christianize the world so as to make it a reflection of heaven and a fitting environment for the children of God. "All liturgical art," Michel summarized, "has in its own way the same noble purpose as the Church's chant, or as the Mass of the Catechumens in relation to the august Sacrifice of the altar." [63] To which one may add the recent words of Pius XII: "Souls ennobled, elevated, and prepared by art, are thus better disposed to receive the religious truths and the grace of Jesus Christ." [64]

Because art as the handmaid of the liturgy performs a mediatorial service, the liturgical artist engages in a sacerdotal function. Since his artistic creations must serve the purpose of the liturgy, the artist mediates by preparing the worshippers for Christ's operation in the Sacred Action. This the artist does not so much by "conscious design"; rather the hieratic quality of his art results from "a spontaneous inspiration out of the depths of the artist." Therefore, even more than the ordinary Christian, he must live and produce for God. Indeed, his art must glorify God — not himself — and lead others to Christ. However, all art is self-revelation at least to some degree. It is a kind of confession. The artist cannot but put his personality into his work, if he is to remain an artist; even liturgical art, then, will reflect the artist. But just because his work must glorify God, Dom Virgil explained, but will nevertheless reflect his personality, the liturgical artist must be

genuinely another Christ in the innermost depths of his heart. He must live the liturgy at the altar as well as in his daily life; in his every thought and action he must exercise the priesthood of Christ he shares in through the sacraments of baptism and confirmation. Only then will he live and breathe Christ; only then will his art perform the priestly function that is its high privilege.[65]

Pius XII might have meant this when he advised artists in *Mediator Dei*, "Let them be capable and willing to draw their inspiration from religion to express what is suitable and more in keeping with the requirements of worship." [66]

Virgil Michel attempted to pursue the implications of the liturgical spirit to its widest extent in all Catholic activity, not the least in the arts. While in Europe he had noted the relation of the liturgy to Catholic architecture. Speaking to a group of architects in St. Paul, in April, 1927, on the way in which a renewed interest in the liturgy could and would influence church building, he remarked that, due to the limitations of pioneer conditions beyond the control and, therefore, blame of anyone, it happened that "this youthful country was strewn with churches which are products of the art of construction, but not of the higher art of architecture." [67] But pioneer conditions would pass. Meanwhile church architecture had an important social mission to which the then fledgling American liturgical movement — not yet a year old — could contribute. What is interesting and, perhaps, significant about this thirty-four page address is that he should have thought through this problem so early. When it was published in part nine years later in *Liturgical Arts*, some thought the ideas new.[68]

In artistic circles, too, he was ever interested in stirring up fruitful discussion amidst what he considered was too great satisfaction with the *status quo*. After paragraphs on Catholic architecture and art here and there throughout his liturgical writings, he returned to the pages of *Liturgical Arts* ten years later, in 1937, to insist that "it is really high time for us to begin disputing [about art], despite any adage to the contrary." [69]

Like all art, Michel affirmed, the architecture of any building must be inspired by a central unifying idea that amounts to an ideal. This is never more so than in the building of a church, which — as a sermon in stone — must preach the ideals and truths of Catholic faith and life somewhat as these are taught from the pulpit. In the ages of faith this was done through the wordless language of Christian symbolism, "which expressed in a variety of outward forms the truths that the faithful should absorb in their worship, on which their worship was based, and according to which their lives were to be directed." [70] In this way the churches became the living embodiments of the spiritual ideals of Catholic life. Even the church building itself reminded the faithful that they were living members of the Mystical Body: "O God, who from living and chosen stones does prepare an eternal habitation for Thy Majesty," the Church prays in the Postcommunion for the Dedication of a church. Thus the church edifice was the emblem of God's kingdom on earth, of all the faithful united in Christ, of the Mystical Body, of the heavenly Jerusalem. Hence, that a Catholic church was a unique building with a supernatural purpose and, therefore, must also embody a unique spirit, all, Michel said, should concede.

But what is the fundamental guiding principle, the central idea or ideal behind the external form of the House of God? "It seems to me," Michel told the architects, "that it is to be found in a realization of the spiritual significance of the liturgy." If the mission of art is to be found in the pursuit of perfection, then Catholic churches, as works of artistic construction, "must pursue religious perfection as expressed in the Catholic ideals of worship." In other words, in the liturgy will be found the characteristics that distinguish Catholic worship from all other worship, and, therefore, by these must the Catholic art of church building be guided. While architects must always avail themselves of the experience of past ages and retain the best that sound tradition has to offer, nevertheless, it will not do, he warned them, merely to copy slavishly past forms of church architecture and to overlook what gave these forms soul in their time. After all, as long as men are free, legitimately use their imagination, and think, he emphasized, the creativity of the human spirit will not allow intelligent men to believe that art has exhausted all its possibilities, "for all art must be buoyant and living." [71]

The focal point of Catholic worship is the altar, on which the Mystical Body, at the hands of the priest, offers the Sacrifice of Christ, the unifying bond of all Catholic life and worship. In the Mass, in which the whole liturgy is centered and from which it radiates, the whole Christian community collectively participates in a concrete realization of its fellowship in Christ. These all-important truths, Michel maintained, the nascent liturgical apostolate would have to make increasingly clear in coming years. He gave reasons. He showed how active participation of the community had once been a reality; how the liturgy repeatedly calls for it, and how this participation and general liturgical awareness, once again recovered, should have a bearing on future Catholic architecture. He told his St. Paul audience in 1927:

For historians it is making but a trite point to say that Catholic beliefs have not had the concrete influence on the culture and civilization, the thought and art and life, of past centuries that should be expected of so intensive a living religion. If this is true, one of the reasons undoubtedly is that in the mind of the individual Catholic his beliefs, accepted and understood in a general way, have not always possessed that sharper detail, which would have made of their contact with the world *ipso facto* a means of stronger influence on the culture of the day. We are in a questioning age, and in an age that is looking increasingly to its religious convictions for the solutions that hopes based upon a material progress have not furnished.[72]

A better understanding and living of the Mass would make the difference, and it is the centrality of the holy Sacrifice in the church and in Catholic life which, likewise, must direct the architect in planning his edifice. Here, then, in the meaning of the altar the architect had the underlying motive and guiding principle for the art of church building. And since the liturgical movement was above all concerned with furthering active and collective participation at the altar and bringing to bear on the life and culture of the times the essential spirit there imbibed, it could in the coming years clarify for the architect the true Catholic spirit in church architecture as well as Christian art in general. And he went on to say that, if a church is primarily an integral setting for the celebration of the liturgy, then — besides being masters of the natural laws of sound architecture — the architects could hardly know too much about the Church's official worship.

By reason of its consecration the whole church is a sacramental and so an integral part of the liturgy; since the sacramental principle is of the very essence of the liturgy, the outward expression of the latter should as much as possible give evidence of its internal mind. Therefore, because the Mass is central in Catholic worship, the altar — as the unifying factor of the church — should be most prominently elevated and near to the people so that all can more easily see and hear and intelligently share in the Sacred Action. "The altar should be to the church," Father Virgil submitted, "what the Mass is to the worship." No pillars should obstruct it from view, nor should the three altars be on an even line; in fact, there is no need of three altars, "probably a relic of the days when altars were bought in catalogue fashion." The side aisles might be narrowed to make a larger central space; the choir chancel could be less deep or even entirely removed. If it were, the choir could be placed behind the altar and screened from view. The architect might try to place an external element in the design, e.g., a tower — if there must be such — directly over the main altar. Baptism is initiation into Christ and His Church. Quite fittingly, therefore, is the baptismal font placed at the entrance. Because a church is "no mere sheltered meeting-place for common prayer of some kind," he explained the traditional Christian symbolism of a church.[73]

Above all, the whole church must be built to become a consecrated structure and place that bespeaks man's homage and gratitude to God, but it is also "a place that speaks to the people of God — not of God as being far away in the heavens, but as present in the mysteries of the altar; and it must, as it were, naturally invite" the people to active and intelligent participation while cultivating their sense of unity and community. In constructing a church, rubrical and liturgical correctness and artistic perfection are not enough. If the church is not to be a "cultural monstrosity," the church must also harmonize with its surroundings. Nor is that enough. If the church edifice is to breathe forth a living inspiration for God's worshipping family to participate actively in the Christ-life in and out of church, it must be the fruit of efforts by "persons who possess this Christ-life in a vital way, not merely intellectually, nor merely in its external forms." *Omne vivum a vivo*: life comes only from life — never from mechanical rules — regardless of how well they are "studied and applied." Consequently, pastor, artist, and builder must not only understand the liturgy but live it intimately, "even in their innermost and private moments." He added:

As long as we do not drink deep at this font,

we are not working fully with God. And even if our efforts are then directed to the building of a church for the service of God, the words of the Psalmist will still be true of us: "Unless the Lord build the house, they labor in vain who build it." [74]

In building churches there is, indeed, he admitted, much room for opinion and disagreement, but there is nothing that makes for mutual understanding and cooperation so much as the liturgy properly lived, since its Christian spirit is "the very unifying basis of all Christian cultural work."

This brought Michel to an interesting moral problem in connection with the responsibility of the proper spending of entrusted parochial funds. Obviously, it was not for pastors to follow out personal whims to erect monuments to themselves; their sacred duty was to raise for the faithful churches which embody the purposes for which churches exist, namely, the glorification of God and the sanctification of man. But again this is likewise the purpose of the liturgy, and so he was quick to add that the fulfillment of moral obligation in this case calls for "an interpretation of the religious or the spiritual that is derived from the liturgical worship of the Church when this is rightly understood and appreciated." In other words, the liturgy works in souls not only through the *ex opere operato* efficacy of the sacraments, but also "in the more human way of informing the mind and inspiring the will." Liturgical worship is more than rubrics correctly observed. The liturgy is a way of life, a source of Christ's spirit, the embodiment of the continuing divine, saving action of Christ and the God-given source of inspiration for a total Christian life and culture. If a church does not provide all of this for the people, that is to say, all that the liturgy embodies, then the parishioners are not getting their money's worth — especially since it costs no more to erect the kind of church the rubrics, the canons of art, and the true nature and purpose of the liturgy demand.[75]

After stating in 1927 how he envisioned in an uncertain future the influence of the liturgical movement on Catholic architecture, Dom Virgil concluded:

Whether future Catholic architecture will take on the structural details indicated by attempts like the above is at present problematical. But two things are certain. The Catholic world is in the first beginnings of a spiritual renaissance that will go on developing far beyond our own time, if it remains true to itself. If it remains true to itself, there will inevitably come a reflourishing of Catholic art second to none in the past, that will vindicate the title of the Church as the mother of all arts. And the spirit underlying this renaissance of life and art will be the age-old spirit of the Christian social fellowship of men united in Christ — not an abstract, academic fellowship merely, but an active, living one, as exemplified in the collective participation in the official and unofficial forms of worship.

Such a spirit cannot but be an inspiration for all of life, embracing as it does heart and soul, body and mind, feeling and intelligence. In it the coming architecture will find not only the inspiration of its basic, central idea, but at once the guiding spirit of all the rules of art. . . . In the spirit of Catholic worship, the new architecture will therefore find the inspiration for that optimism based on the virtues of faith, hope, and charity, but not an optimism based upon mere atmosphere.

Finally, . . . by ever preaching and sowing in men's hearts the seed of the unifying bond that ties them all to God and to each other in an intimate social fellowship, this art of arts [the liturgy] will transmit the solid values of traditional civilization, and dispense for the present and the future that healing balm that was never more needed, the solid foundation of social peace and weal. Thus church architecture will, on the one hand, perform the apostolic mission it assumes by its union with religion, and on the other fulfill most perfectly the cultural mission it has in common with all art, that of being at once the conserver of the best values of the past, the inspirer of the present, and the prophet of a bright future.[76]

While there are still church architects and artists whose ignorance of the liturgy is apparent in their work, nonetheless, it is not, perhaps, too much to say that Catholic church building has taken a development in the direction Michel foresaw in 1927. That the liturgical movement had influenced church building and the ecclesiastical arts was the frank admission of Charles D. Maginnis in 1941, who wrote in the tenth anniversary issue of *Liturgical Arts*, "A decade ago the liturgical movement had notably aroused the interest and sympathy of many of the hierarchy and priesthood of this country, so that more and more obviously its implications became a challenge to the thoughtful concern of those creatively identified with ecclesiastical art." He went on to say that "it has been the stirring of the liturgical idea in the mind of the architect which has brought the most notable consequences. . . . The new deference is unmistakable." [77]

According to Michel, every member of Christ can contribute in his own way to the revival of a Catholic tradition of art. Even in the natural order every man is an artist. God has made every human being unique. Hence every man has a unique and distinct insight into reality. Each person can discover, reflect, and reveal in his own way something of God's truth, goodness, and beauty. Thus every Christian is also an artist in the way he lives out the Christ-life. As a living member of the Body of Christ, he is "the visible embodiment of the invisible Christ-life." If Christ's every action and word, all His doing and making — His whole life — were visible manifestations of God, so must all the actions and words of the Christian, all his making and doing — his whole life — be a visible manifestation of Christ living in him. Dom Virgil put this in words which defy paraphrase:

Next to Christ, among living beings, the highest expression of this sacramental principle is the member of Christ, who as "another Christ" must give ever greater realization to this principle in the world. In this way all the life of man, and all his actions and contacts, become a living enactment of sacred art, in which the beauty of the truth of Christ is made to shine forth in everything that man does and produces.[78]

For this the liturgy is not only the inspiration but at once the model and guide. As a part of the Church, the Christian must do as the Church does in regard to material goods. In the way the liturgy of the Church makes honest use of material things according to their true nature, in the way it reverences and devotes them entirely to God, in the manner it employs them as a means to build up the Christ-life, so must the Christian use them in his daily life to sustain his natural and supernatural life. For matter was created to glorify God by serving man; nor does it play its proper role in man's life unless it bears the spiritual qualities of man's mind or those he sees reflected in the universe mirroring its Creator. God is the supreme goodness, truth, and beauty. With these has He stamped His material creation. Man must not destroy God's truth, goodness, and beauty in things. On the contrary, he must reverence these qualities and by his creative work make them shine forth. Then his works will be the images of these qualities in his soul and, at the same time, indirectly reflect the attributes of God. Because man must ever imitate as far as possible the Divine Artist of the universe, it is well that the Christian always remember, Michel said, that "there is no make-believe, no pretense, no wood painted to look like marble, no 'fake-materials' in God's ordering of things." Then he commented:

This genuineness, truth and order man must express in all he does and in all he makes, in all his art, if he is to live and act as a true image of God and a member of

Christ. That is the true realm and meaning of art, the idea of which is so perverted in our day. The art that tries to disguise the genuine nature and purpose of things is but a sham art, the art of disguise, which reflects the arch-liar, Satan, who first practiced the art of deception in Paradise. True art is ever honest and genuine; it is a reflection of the truth of God Himself in things, and it aims above all at revealing genuine truth.[79]

In other words, art must always be linked in some way to the purpose of man's existence.[80] But what is the true purpose of art in human life? The means, Father Virgil answered, by which to fulfill for man in the best possible way the over-all purpose of material things: serving man's needs and higher life and raising him up closer to God.

Why did a practical man of action like Michel expend so much effort to further the arts? Surely he had other things to do. But as St. Pius X, the parish priest in the Chair of Peter, said: "Among the cares of the pastoral office, not only of the supreme chair . . . but of every local church, a leading one is without question that of maintaining and promoting the decorum and beauty of the House of God." [81]

It may be of value to speculate why the liturgical movement was once identified with estheticism in the minds of some, all the more so in view of papal documents in its favor. Was it, perhaps, because priests have generally lacked the esthetic education and training that long-standing and recent papal statements have indicated they ought to have? [82] Or was it because they failed to grasp the fruitful concepts of Christ present and active in the sacramental liturgy, of the liturgy as continuing the redemption through space and time, of the liturgy as the ordinary means established by God whereby man can have direct and active contact with divinity? For once these fundamental concepts are mastered, then, as Father Virgil stated, no element of the liturgy is unimportant, "not even the slightest word or gesture." Through the externals of the liturgy the truth and life of God is mediated to human beings according to their nature. The externals of the liturgy are the shell, the spiritual and the divine, the kernel. But, as he insisted, these must never be separated.

The liturgy provides for natural as well as supernatural needs. Thus the Creator, Father Virgil indicated, provided for man's need of esthetic experience in the various forms of worship, particularly in corporate worship at Mass. At Mass this esthetic experience should be a part of that all-important but difficult to describe essential, religious experience. American Catholics do not fully appreciate this important truth, he said, and as a result — not actively sharing in the true and Christian means of genuine esthetic and religious experience — they have often become involved in myriads of worldly or even pagan experiences and amusements as substitutes to satisfy a normal craving of human nature for the beautiful, the dramatic, the mysterious, the meaningful. In this connection, Harry E. Barnes has written:

Another function of religion in the past which has received much support relates to its esthetic services. It is held that the ritual, pageantry, and liturgy of the church provide a creatively economical and highly valuable esthetic service to the community. . . . While there was much to be said in support of this view in regard to the service of the church in earlier periods, this function may be, and indeed is, conceived more adequately by various secular enterprises, such as the opera, the theatres. . . .[83]

More than thirty years ago[84] Virgil Michel warned of, and made efforts to arrest, a situation which Barnes has since observed as a sociological fact. Nor did Father Busch speak idle words when, commenting on the need of the Legion of Decency in 1935, he said:

We would not be where we are in this movie matter, we Catholics, if we had been well schooled in the liturgy, in the chorus of divine praise, in the enjoyment of divine life, in the drama of our public worship. . . . There is this difficulty in my present argument, that those who really know what the liturgy is do not need to hear what I am saying, while those whom I would like to persuade may, from their inexperience of the liturgy, not understand what I mean.[85]

As Busch indicated, there was a time when Christians found even their recreation in the shadows of the church.

Those who do not care to accept the artist's word for it may want to believe the philosophers: without esthetic experiences, without art, signs, and symbols man cannot live, as unscrupulous advertisers only too well know. And as Michel observed, since human beings need art, signs, and symbols, it is only a question of which they choose to live by: those inspired by the world or those inspired by the Church, "whose liturgy and art," Pius XI said in his encyclical on the *Christian Education of Youth*, "have an immense educational value." Catholics have often been misled by the symbols of Hollywood or by the inanities of modern advertising, often even morally offensive. To Dom

Virgil it was strange that Catholics spontaneously register their approval at athletic stadia and in theatres, frequently advocate learning by doing and experience in the classroom, and then are complacently satisfied with silence in the praise of God in church. Why is it, he frequently asked, that American Catholics, who glory in the word "progress," become mentally paralyzed when it comes to dramatizing the things of the spirit as the Church bids? "Why should we not be able," he queried in 1930, "with our perfect technic for 'putting things across,' to succeed with something that in its inherent nature is so full of possibilities of appeal?" [86]

Very many Catholics go to Mass, Michel observed, more conscious of paying a debt, of fulfilling an obligation, of avoiding a sin than of participating in a mystery, of acting with Christ, of having active contact with divinity in the greatest drama in this world. By and large, for the same Catholics, advent was like lent and both were like the rest of the year, except for a few accidentals and externals. If through active and corporate participation these could catch and live the spirit of the liturgical seasons and experience the joys of the various feasts; if their worship were an experience in which the whole person intellectually, emotionally, and physically shared, the empty blandishments of the world, Dom Virgil believed, would not have the same lure.

To summarize, Virgil Michel's writings bearing on culture and the arts once more indicate with what a broad sweep he conceived the liturgical apostolate. The liturgy, he noted, "is the highest cultural achievement of Christianity"; and either a genuine liturgical revival will flower out into a genuine Catholic culture, the great need of the time — or a paganized culture will snuff out any Christian spirit that attempts to live by itself. A fundamental and all-pervading renewal of the whole Christian life in all its natural and supernatural, individual and social, aspects — that is the scope and task of the liturgical apostolate. If the latter aims at less, it is doomed to failure, for there can be no "true renewal in Christ that does not embrace every aspect and activity of human life."

Today American Catholics have apostolic and liturgically-minded movements like the Young Christian Students, the Young Christian Workers, and especially the Christian Family Movement, which are concerning themselves with "changing the environment." Dom Virgil anticipated these by several years.[87] Recently some have boldly asked the question: Have any effective apostolic lay movements survived which have not attached themselves to the liturgy in some way?

For law cannot give life. As long as a deadening legalistic attitude and moralistic practice prevailed in religious life; as long as the liturgy meant an outmoded apparatus of rigid and sterile rites to be submitted to, there would be no revival of a living Catholic culture and of a healthy sacred art. The creative spirit would be stifled and the imagination frustrated — or they would find expression in secular activities and pursuits. This was Michel's frequent assertion. And as a contemporary art critic has stated, "Modern man does not have enough faith in invisible realities to depict their visible counterparts." [88]

The revival of Christian art, especially of liturgical art, would be the natural fruit of a sound liturgical revival. "Take great care to enlighten and direct the minds and hearts of the artists," Pius XII urged in *Mediator Dei* in 1947. This Dom Virgil had been doing since 1926.[89] Through the Christ-Life Series he attempted to bring an awareness — as well as a cure — of the art-problem into the schools. Although, as Father LaFarge told the Liturgical Week at Boston in 1948, the art situation is "very unsatisfactory, to say the least," the noted Jesuit would be the first to admit that some progress has been made since the founding of *Liturgical Arts* in 1931 and the *Christian Social Art Quarterly* in 1937 — progress, by the way, to which Father LaFarge has contributed much. Recall from chapter six Michel's efforts in the 1920's to promote an artistic revival and add that to what was said in this chapter, and evidence is at hand that here, too, insofar as there is a revival, Michel was a forerunner.

Lack of time did not permit him to accept the invitation to act as associate editor of liturgical arts for *Church Property Administration,* when it began in 1936.[90]

Interpreting the signs of the times in 1935, he wrote, "In parts of the earth's surface we are even now witnessing the attempted rise of a culture that is impersonally collectivistic but otherwise at least as materialistic and naturalistic as its moribund predecessor." [91] Today these words are better understood then they were in 1935. That the great need of the age is a living Catholic culture that confirms his faith at every turn, no thinking Catholic will deny. That such a culture can only be built up through the inspiration of liturgical life and spirit, some would hesitate to say. But for these Dom Virgil would undoubtedly pose two questions: In what other way? By what other spirit?

NOTES TO CHAPTER 9

[1] "Nine Years After," *OF*, X (1935), 5–6.

[2] *Ibid.*, 6.

[3] In resuming the editorship of *Orate Fratres* in 1935, and in reorganizing the staff, Michel explained, "We shall include more articles dealing with all phases of human activity, art, literature, social theory, etc., in their relation to the true Christian spirit. . . . We shall concentrate above all on the liturgical spirit, but we shall view it also as the only true inspiration for every field of higher human speculation and endeavor, for a Christian ideology that can cope successfully with the ideologies of anti-Christian or unchristian bias that are sponsored so universally today, and fill our literature and art, our whole life, to overflowing" (*ibid.*, p. 7). Michel's liturgical writings — from their beginning in 1925 — are filled with many references to a Catholic culture; but in the last five years of his life the need and nature of a Christian culture as expressed in his writings became very explicit (cf. bibliography).

[4] Kenkel to Michel, St. Louis, June 20, 1935; cf. "The Liturgical Movement and the Future," *America*, LIV (1935), 6–7. Kenkel tentatively agreed to collaborate with Michel but neither found the time for writing the book; Michel collected materials for the book to the end.

[5] To P. A. Knowlton, Collegeville, Sept. 30, 1936, copy. *Cultural Anthropology* (Milwaukee: Bruce, 1934), was the first book by an American Catholic. The Catholic Anthropological Conference was founded in 1926.

[6] "I have been entrusted with the difficult task of speaking about culture. But there is nothing in the world more elusive. One cannot analyze it, for its components are infinite. One cannot describe it, for it is protean in shape. An attempt to encompass its meaning in words is like trying to seize the air in the hand, when one finds that it is everywhere except within one's grasp" (A. Lowell, *At War with Academic Traditions in America* [Cambridge: Cambridge University Press, 1934], p. 115). A. L. Kroeber writes that the first definition of culture in its anthropological sense appearing in English dictionaries was in the late 1920's (*Nature of Culture* [Chicago: University of Chicago Press, 1952], p. 119); cf. pp. 118–135 for an excellent analysis of the concept. For an interesting history, the gradual evolution, and late formulation of the concept, cf. A. L. Kroe-

ber and C. Kluckhohn, *Culture: A Critical Review of Concepts and Definitions,* Papers of the Peabody Museum of American Archaeology and Ethnology, Harvard University, XLVII (1952), (1), 9–37, 180–184, *passim.* For an analysis of the relation between religion and culture as seen by Dawson, who is an historian of culture, cf. Daniel A. O'Connor, C.S.V., *The Relation between Religion and Culture* (Montreal: Librairée Saint-Viateur, 1952). Lately Dawson has emphasized the centrality of the liturgy in restoring a Christian culture, cf. *Understanding Europe* (New York: Sheed and Ward, 1952), 241–255, and "Problems of Christion Culture," *Commonweal,* LXII (1955), 34–36.

[7] "Liturgy and Catholic Life," pp. 193–194; Michel quoted the classic definition of Edward B. Tylor.

[8] *Ibid.,* p. 198–199.

[9] Cf. "Liturgy and Catholic Life," pp. 193–206.

[10] *Religion and the Modern State* (New York: Sheed and Ward, 1935), p. 150.

[11] "The Liturgical Movement and the Future," *America,* LIV (1935), 6.

[12] "Liturgy and Catholic Life, p. 200; cf. *The Christian in the World,* pp. 15–34, 197–233.

[13] *The Christian in the World,* p. 29.

[14] *Ibid.,* p. 30.

[15] "Nine Years After," *OF,* X (1935), 6; cf. "Liturgy and Catholic Life," pp. 135–138, 191–192.

[16] "Education and the Crisis of Christian Culture," *Lumen Vitae,* I (1946), 209. "All true religious education leads up to the contemplation of divine mysteries, and where this is lacking, the whole culture becomes weakened and divided. It may be objected that this is the sphere of worship and not of education, but it is impossible to separate the two, since it was largely in the sphere of worship that the Christian tradition of education and culture arose and developed" (*idem,* pp. 208–209).

[17] "Mediator Dei," *AAS,* XXXIX (1947), 536, 591.

[18] "Liturgy and Catholic Life," p. 136.

[19] *Ibid.,* p. 239.

[20] Always eager to show the practicality of the liturgy in daily living, Michel throughout his writings quotes excerpts from all parts of the liturgy to prove this: cf., e.g., *The Christian in the World,* pp. 103–105.

[21] "Liturgy and Catholic Life," p. 22; "For the liturgical spirit is essentially one of an inner soul radiating forth into its external environment; the liturgical life, both at worship and outside, must needs be a harmonious life of exteriorized interior spirit" (*ibid.,* p. 135).

[22] Kroeber, *The Nature of Culture,* pp., 24, 28; "Values," like all sociocultural manifestations, are largely superpersonal. That is, far more of any individual's values are instilled into him from outside, directly or indirectly from his society, then he produces within and by himself" (*idem,* p. 28).

[23] "The Liturgical Movement and the Future," *America,* LIV (1925), 7.

[24] *Ibid.*

[25] It would be more correct to say that a culture *tends* to integration; no culture is ever fully integrated since, in the parlance of anthropologists, it is a dynamic, living, evolving continuum. Note how Michel's ideas on the Church and culture agree with what Pius XII told the International Congress of Historical Sciences in 1955: "Vous avez voulu," *AAS*, XLVII (1955), 681.

[26] "Liturgy and Catholic Life," p. 202.

[27] Cf. *ibid.*, p. 202, and *Our Life in Christ*, pp. 188–189.

[28] "Liturgy and Catholic Life," p. 203.

[29] "Unless the Lord Build the House . . ." *Liturgical Arts*, VI (1936), 66.

[30] "Questa grande vostra adunata," *AAS*, XXXVII (1945), 284–295. Michel, "The Liturgical Movement and the Catholic Woman," in Catholic Central Verein of America: *Annual Report* (1929), pp. 57–62; "Liturgy and Catholic Life," pp. 82–98; "The Liturgy and Catholic Women," *OF*, III (1929), 270–276.

[31] Cf. William B. Faherty, S.J., *The Destiny of Modern Woman* (Westminster: Newman, 1950), p. xiv. Faherty gives pertinent papal documents. With Leo XIII the popes began to urge Catholic women into the field of social reform, but they were almost entirely unheeded (p. xv).

[32] Phil. 4:3.

[33] "Liturgy and Catholic Life," p. 85.

[34] "The Liturgical Movement and the Catholic Woman," p. 58.

[35] "Liturgy and Catholic Life," p. 95.

[36] "The Liturgy and Catholic Woman," *OF*, III (1929), 274. "Nothing can withstand the patient perseverence of Christian virtue [of women]. And it is a plain matter of fact that the average man is quite helpless over against it. None can gainsay the influence and power of the woman who is a model of interior perfection. The latter is the supernatural elevation and intensification of the natural refinement and sanctity of woman, over against which the greater coarseness and brute strength of man avails little" ("Liturgy and Catholic Life," p. 96).

[37] "Synopsis of Address of Virgil Michel to Minnesota Council of Catholic Women," (in Michel Papers), p. 2.

[38] "The Liturgical Movement and the Catholic Woman," p. 59.

[39] "Questa grande vostra adunata," *AAS*, XXXVII (1945), 288.

[40] "Liturgy and Catholic Life," p. 96. However, he failed to delineate exactly what those professions were.

[41] Michel had pronounced views on the education of children by parents and the proper use of authority, e.g., "The parents must teach their children how to think and to will properly. The parents in a secondary way create the minds of their children — not out of nothing which was done by God. But they help to mold the mind and soul created by God from being something inactive to being a source of personal thought and action and decision. In earliest childhood, the minds of the children function with those of the parents; that is, the children say the words the parents say, think their thoughts as far as possible, and feel the joys or

sorrows of the parents. This is the most important time of the children's growth of soul, the most malleable period. . . . Whatever the parents neglect in this regard will to some extent remain neglected for life" (*The Christian in the World*, p. 120). Like education, authority is to be used to develop persons: "This means that as soon as children arrive at the use of reason they must be taught to act and to choose for themselves. The method of exercising *parental authority* must then change *from that of external compulsion to that of inner persuasion and reasoning*. This may take more time and patience on the part of the parents, but it is alone fitting the nature of reasoning man; any other policy, as a policy, is miseducation" (*idem*); italics, Michel's.

[42] "Liturgy and Catholic Life," p. 92.

[43] Cf. *Our Life in Christ*, pp. 170–192, esp. 183–186; *The Liturgy of the Church*, pp. 263–267; *The Christian in the World*, pp. 112–139; cf. also articles in the bibliography. How these ideas on the liturgy and the family and home have caught on is evidenced by the literature on that subject in late years.

[44] "Liturgy and Catholic Life," p. 97.

[45] *Ibid.*, p. 91. "Birth Control," in *Social Concepts and Problems* (Collegeville: St. John's Abbey, 1936), pp. 114–120, is Michel's best philosophical analysis of that problem.

[46] "The Liturgical Movement and the Catholic Woman," p. 61.

[47] *Ibid.*, p. 62.

[48] *The Christian in the World*, p. 133; italics, Michel's. Cf. articles on parish in Michel's bibliography, and Apostolate, *OF*, II–IV; IX–XIII, *passim*.

[49] This seems confirmed by the frequently observed fact that those not interested in the liturgy are often not interested in — seem not even aware of — the art-problem; hence the sham and shabbiness in so many churches.

[50] "Liturgy and Catholic Life," p. 188; cf. Furfey's pertinent remarks, *Fire on the Earth* (New York: Macmillan, 1937), pp. 151–153. "Seek God here below in nature and in man, but above all within yourselves" (Pius XII, in an address to Italian artists: *The Function of Art* [Washington: NCWC, 1952], p. 5).

[51] "The Philosophical and Theological Bases of the Liturgical Movement," p. 34.

[53] "Liturgy and Catholic Life," p. 212. By the word *sacramental* the reader should here understand the use of external, material, visible things as signs or manifestations of deeper, hidden, spiritual realities or truths.

[53] Cf. *Our Life in Christ*, pp. 76–79.

[54] "Liturgy and Catholic Life," p. 211.

[55] "Liturgy and Catholic Life," p. 212. "If in single instances we cannot fully account for the presence of a detail here and there, this is due to the fact that the liturgy is in no way the product of mathematical precalculation; it is too human for that, too living and in its growth too spontaneous" (*The Liturgy of the Church*, p. 317).

[56] "Liturgy and Catholic Life," pp. 214–215.

[57] *The Liturgy of the Church*, p. 318. "The liturgy . . . is not only the depository of the best religious sentiments of the entire span of the world's existence, but also the depository of some of the best accomplishments of the artistic powers of man or else the inspiration of them. Around the traditional worship of the Church have been gathered some of the best products of artistic genius in painting and sculpture, architecture, poetry and music" (*idem*, pp. 316–317).

[58] "That can ever be truly so only when the smaller merges in the greater, when the lesser in dignity is properly aligned with that which is more sublime in its being and end. . . . Art in general is wider in scope than liturgical art and includes the latter; but when the liturgy gives its name to art, the latter must live the life of the liturgy" (*ibid.*, p. 319). Not everyone would agree with Michel's distinction between sacred and liturgical art.

[59] "Liturgy and Catholic Life," p. 214.

[60] "In the Church music enters into the very fibre and action of the liturgy, while in comparison with it, other art only enhances the liturgical environment" (*The Liturgy of the Church*, p. 320); Pius XII said exactly this eighteen years later in his encyclical, *De musicae sacrae disciplina*, of December 25, 1955. For Michel on chant, cf. *The Liturgy of the Church*, pp. 316–319, *passim*, articles in bibliography, and chapter four.

[61] Cf. e.g. *ibid.*, pp. 73–79, *passim;* unpublished manuscript, "The Catholic Spirit in Architecture," pp. 7–15; "Religion in Pictures," *OF*, *IV* (1930), 223–226; "Advertising Our Wares," *OF IV* (1930), 122–126.

[62] "Liturgy and Catholic Life," p. 221; cf. Apostolate, *OF*, II (1928), 221–222, X (1936), 272–273; *The Liturgy of the Church*, pp. 316–320.

[63] "Liturgy and Catholic Life," p. 215.

[64] *The Function of Art* (Washington: NCWC, 1952), p. 5.

[65] Michel reviewing R. Hoornaert's *The Breviary and the Laity* in *Liturgical Arts*, V (1936), 153; cf. "Liturgy and Catholic Life," pp. 207–222.

[66] "Mediator Dei," *AAS*, XXXIX (1947), 591. "Thus, the more the artist lives religion, the better prepared he will be to speak the language of art, to understand its harmonies, to communicate its emotions" (Pius XII, *The Function of Art*, p. 4).

[67] "The Catholic Spirit in Architecture," p. 2.

[68] For Charles D. Maginnis' practical work in this direction, cf. the whole of number four, XXIII (1955), *Liturgical Arts*. Cf. also Sister Helene, O.P., "American Catholics and Art Since 1900," in Ward (ed.), *op. cit.*, pp. 230–240. The first book on possible modifications in church structure as inspired by the ideology of the liturgical movement seems to have been I. van Acken, *Christozentrische Kirchenkunst* (2d. ed.; Gladbeck i.w. Verlag von A. Theben, 1923); about 1925 the first churches in Europe gave evidence of such modifications, and there has been a gradual evolution since — but somewhat later in the United States. Out of this ferment in Europe came the first liturgical art periodical, *L'artisan liturgique* in 1927 (now *L'art d'église*), and *L'art sacré* in 1935; the

American *Liturgical Arts* first appeared in 1931, after discussions which began in 1928; cf. Lavanoux, "Prolegomena," *Liturgical Arts,* XXII (1953), 1–3, where he says, "We are at the threshold of an immensely interesting and important period in art and architecture, but the way is still clouded."

⁶⁹ "Unless the Lord Build the House . . ." *Liturgical Arts,* VI (1937), 65. Maritain had been asked to write this article, which was to merge "the two ideas of the 'wider reaches of the liturgical movement' with a consideration of its 'practical aspects'. What we are particularly interested in at the present time is to show that the movement is not merely an 'arty' one, but that a sensible and logical consideration of the liturgy qualifies building problems and this, in turn, reacts on the congregation in terms of funds which, in turn, react on the pastor in terms of annoying references to money, etc., etc.; in other words, building for the Church should take into consideration the liturgical requirements, the budget and competent professional advice. All these combined have a definite apologetic value. Harry Binsse is always after me because I stress common sense and logic in all these matters and he tells me that many — priests and laymen — do not work according to common sense. I leave it to you to combine all these elements" (Lavanoux to Michel, New York, July 31, 1937). Michel's writings on church architecture agree well, except for a few items, with the recommendations for church building issued by the German hierarchy, cf. Theodor Klauser, "Directives for the Building of a Church," *OF,* XXIV (1949), 9–18. Archbishop Joseph E. Ritter's "Toward a Living Climate of Religious Art," *Liturgical Arts,* XXIII (1954), 3–4, Lavanoux writes (*ibid.* p. 1), "is certainly the first forceful and positive statement in these matters by an American prelate." Michel was somewhat critical of Gothic: While he admitted it was "an advance as art" and "indeed religious and inspirational," yet it exhibited a tendency towards "an individualizing art" and as such was "a setback as ideal Catholic church art." "For some persons it must come as a shock to hear a word said against Gothic, but the world seems bound to go on. And should there be Gothic today, it must at all events be a Gothic of our own" ("The Catholic Spirit in Architecture," pp. 27–30).

⁷⁰ *Ibid.,* p. 8.

⁷¹ *Ibid.,* pp. 5–7.

⁷² *Ibid.,* pp. 14–15. Recalling that there were 3,000 clergymen present for a Catholic building convention in Chicago while at the same time the Boston Liturgical Week of 1948 attracted 300 priests, the late Msgr. William H. Russell remarked, "Perhaps with some justification one might write about secularism or materialism within the Church" ("Where Are the Nine?" *OF,* XXIII [1949], 97).

⁷³ "The Catholic Spirit in Architecture," pp. 7–15, 25–27, 30–32; cf. "Architecture and the Liturgy," *Liturgical Arts,* V (1936), pp. 15–17.

⁷⁴ "Unless the Lord Build the House . . ." *Liturgical Arts,* VI (1937), 67–68. "No degree of perfect craftsmanship as such can produce inspiring or attractive art; the craftsman must also be an artist for that. And no

amount of artistry as such can produce a work that is hieratic or priestly in its functioning. Such a work can come only from living priests, or other Christs, or members of the Mystical Body" *(idem)*.

⁷⁵ *Ibid.,* pp. 66–68. In the Michel-Lavanoux correspondence there is frequent mention that, in the remodeling of churches, etc., pastors had first to spend considerable money to "undo" what a predecessor had unwisely built and how the national total of this kind of spending must be enormous. Hence Michel's concern over the involved moral problem.

⁷⁶ "The Catholic Spirit in Architecture," pp. 32–34. It is interesting to compare Michel's ideas on church building and art with an instruction issued by the Holy Office on June 30, 1952: "Sacred architecture, although it may adopt new styles, cannot in any way be equated with profane building, but must always perform its own office, which regards the house of God and the house of prayer. In addition, in building churches care should be had of the convenience of the faithful, so that they can take part in the divine offices with a better view and better attention; let new churches be resplendent also for the simple beauty of their lines, abhorring all deceitful adornment; but still everything that savors of a neglect of art or of a want of pains should be avoided" ("Sacrae artis," *AAS*, XLIV [1952], 544).

⁷⁷ "A Survey and a Hope," *Liturgical Arts,* X (1941), 3.

⁷⁸ "Liturgy and Catholic Life," p. 212.

⁷⁹ *The Christian in the World,* p. 104.

⁸⁰ "Art and the Christ-Life" *Catholic Art Quarterly,* V (1941), 2–5. "True objects of art are serviceable genuinely so. . . . It is a characteristic of our modern unchristian mind to think of objects of art as interesting curios that have no further place in human life than that of exciting an interest unconnected with life, just as it is a characteristic to use human abilities to disguise the true nature of things by means of human 'art' " *(The Christian in the World,* p. 104). Art, he said, must be also "practical"; if not, it will become "dilettantism or aestheticism"; if craftsmanship is not also artistic, it will be merely practical and then so often "cheap and ugly"; if art is to be wedded to life, it must be practical, and the practical "must in turn strive to be beautiful" ("Liturgy and Catholic Life," pp. 208–209).

⁸¹ "Tra le sollecitudini," *ASS*, XXXVI (1903), 329–330.

⁸² E.g. "Finally, care should be taken that aspirants to sacred orders in schools of philosophy and theology be educated in sacred art and formed to its appreciation, in a way adapted to the ability and age of each one, by masters who reverence what our ancestors cherished and established and comply with the prescriptions of the Holy See" ("Sacrae artis," *op. cit.,* pp. 545–546). In 1903 Pius X, after saying that besides teaching theology, liturgy, and canon law, "the principles and laws of sacred music" must also be taught, added: "And means should be sought to complete this teaching with some special instruction on the esthetics of sacred art, so that clerics may not leave the seminary in ignorance of the right ideas on this subject, ideas which are a necessary part of full ecclesiastical culture" ("Tra le sollecitudini," *op. cit.,* p. 338). In 1952 the Holy Office instructed the Catholic bishops of the world in this manner.

[83] *Social Institutions* (New York: Prentice-Hall, 1942), p. 705; cf. W. Lloyd Warner, *Democracy in Jonesville* (New York: Harper, 1949), p. 289, Aldous Huxley, *Text and Pretexts* (New York: Harper, 1933), p. 1, and *Ends and Means* (New York: Harper, 1937), 265–266.

[84] Cf. "A Religious Need of the Day," *Catholic Educational Review,* XXIII (1925), 453–456.

[85] "The Legion of Decency," *OF,* IX (1935), 303, 305.

[86] "Advertising Our Wares," *OF, IV* (1930), 124; cf. "Religion in Pictures," *OF, IV* (1930), 223–226; "Sanctity and Dignity," *OF, IV* (1930), 265–269.

[87] The Young Christian Students were founded in 1940, the Christian Family Movement, in 1946, cf. Vincent J. Giese, "Chaplain to the Working Apostolate," *Today,* X (1954), 3–5.

[88] Pie Régamey, O.P., "Modern Man and the Religious Arts," in *Towards A Living Tradition* (St. Louis: Pio Decimo Press, 1953), p. 81.

[89] Michel's correspondence shows him in contact with artists to the end; thus he wrote shortly before his death to the present head of the art department at the Catholic University who had asked for help, "Unfortunately there is little precedent to go by since art must be a living thing. I would advise nothing else but what you are doing now — steeping yourself more and more in the spirit of the liturgy and letting that spirit work itself out in your art creations" (Michel to Clare Fontanini, Collegeville, Nov. 14, 1938).

[90] H. A. Frommelt to Michel, Milwaukee, May 30, 1936, Michel to Frommelt, Collegeville, June 3, 1936, copy. Instead, Michel's confrere, Gilbert Winkelmann, assumed this position.

[91] "The Liturgical Movement and the Future," *America,* LIV (1935), 6.

CHAPTER 10

SOCIAL AND
PHILOSOPHICAL THOUGHT

ONE COULD write a small volume on Father Virgil Michel's social and philosophical thought. This is an area of activity quite different from what has been treated so far. But this chapter will include only highlights and bare summaries, while emphasizing in his contribution what may be of value today. The chief aim of this work has been to deal with Father Virgil's liturgical and socio-liturgical thought and work. Besides, much that he had to say in the roaring 1920's and troublesome 1930's has now entered into the accepted stream of American Catholic thought.

Because change is of the essence of economic life, it is important for the reader continually to remember that Michel's social writings fell largely in the depression period and before the social legislation of the 1930's was passed or became effective. The progress of the Catholic social movement in the United States has been such that it is somewhat difficult to imagine the conditions of those times. But it is sobering, if not shocking, to recall that as late as 1937 — the year before Michel died — the Supreme Court weighed the constitutionality of the Wagner Act, the Social Security Act, and state minimum wage laws. And to cast Michel's life and work into proper perspective, it may be worth mentioning that Dom Virgil died before the first meeting of the American Catholic Sociological Society in December of 1938; in the following year the Jesuits organized their Institute of Social Order. This study is not concerned with the social and Scholastic movements beyond 1938, except for purposes of clarification.

Dom Virgil's many commentaries on those confused and fermenting times present a good picture of the great depression. However, he was concerned above all with underlying causes of social ills and not just their effects; with long-range programs, with basic principles, and fundamental concepts rather than with their immediate application to concrete situations. He had little formal training in economics or the social sciences, as he had almost none in the natural sciences. Although he considered economics extremely important and studied it as he found time in his last years, reading particularly the writings of John Maynard Keynes, Father Michel's approach to social and economic problems was largely philosophical. The prevalent unjust social conditions, he believed, were not merely the results of a cyclical depression but "the logical result of the general philosophy of life that guided human affairs for some centuries."[1] To lay bare the inadequacy of a philosophy compounded of an unchristian individualism and a complacent bourgeois spirit — secularism it is called today — that was his self-chosen task. And he chose it because he was convinced that the irresponsibility of laissez-faire capitalism, the breakdown of the family, the atomization and depersonalization of modern society, and the prevalent materialism were but the logical results of a false philosophy. Unless this were exposed and corrected, the mere concentration on the removal of particular surface evils could not result in sound social reconstruction.

Nor was it merely a question of a vicious and pervasive *philosophy* of life: "The march of history," Michel said, "has for centuries been progressively under the inspiration of a denial of the Church of Christ, then of Christ, and finally of God."[2] The crisis in society was but the full and final development of this trend away from God; in fact, it was the bitter fruit of a new paganism worse than the ancient because of its rejection of the Christian dispensation. He felt it his duty then, to uncover and to attack the godlessness in economic, political, and social life, and this in terms of a living Thomism, of the encyclicals, and especially of *Quadragesimo anno*, of an integral and dynamic social Catholicism. Concerning the latter enough has already been said in previous chapters. The last pages of this chapter will survey his philosophical thinking and contribution.

Dom Virgil's social thought is found partly in *The Christian in the World* and in *Christian Social Reconstruction*, a popular commentary on *Quadragesimo anno* written, as he said, because of "the surprisingly meager basic literature extant on *Quadragesimo anno* even five years after its official promulgation." He contributed a set of nine pamphlets on the social question. In these he gave an exposition of fundamental philosophical concepts dealing with social reconstruction in a popular way. Two other pamphlets dealt with ownership and modern individualism respectively. His most creative effort was a brochure of seventy-eight pages, *St. Thomas and Today*, a brief and unified survey of basic principles on the economic views of Aquinas, related to social disorders of modern society. Finally, he wrote more than fifty articles — not to mention book reviews and editorials — on a variety of social subjects scattered through many periodicals but chiefly in the *Wanderer, Orate Fratres, Commonweal,* and the *Christian Front*.[3] The best of some twenty philosophical articles of varying lengths appeared mainly in *New Scholasticism, Ethics,* and the *Philosophical Review*.

It is important to remember that Michel's social writings appeared at a time when the Catholic press was extremely conservative, when the social encyclicals were little known and less understood, and when, comparatively speaking, Catholic schools were doing little by way of teaching Catholic social principles.[4] It should be added that Father Virgil wrote chiefly for the clergy, for a group of liberal-minded laity, and for leaders, both Catholic and non-Catholic. While these writings entailed much study and research on his part, they made no pretence of being scholarly treatises. In an age of confusion and complacency he was principally interested in stirring up discussion that would lead to sound, effective action and long-range social programs. To his fingertips he was alive with practical plans and action. In an age of transition he sifted and saved what was good in many suggested plans and programs. Instead of repeating the clichés of the day, his social writings in large part concern themselves with clarifying key concepts like "capitalism," "person," "human rights," "state," "labor," "property," "common good," "social justice."[5] Essential for social regeneration, said Pius XI, are the reform of institutions and the correction of morals. Carefully distinguishing between the natural and the supernatural and yet insisting that it is necessary to work on both levels for social regeneration, Michel often showed how *Quadragesimo anno* was "packed with solid philosophical thought" which must be intensively studied and prudently applied.

Pius XI had himself spoken in the same encyclical of "the social order, to the restoring of which according to the principles of *sound philosophy* and its perfecting according to the sublime principles of the Gospel law our predecessor Leo XIII devoted his every care and thought" — a passage, Michel said, which the current English translations garbled entirely by confusing the principles of philosophy with those of the Gospel.[6] To say more here would be to anticipate the discussion of Michel's concept of social reform.

Virgil Michel was a modern monk intensely interested in the social climate of his time. "The period of mental, ideal readjustments is yet only beginning," he observed after World War I in 1921, and then added, "Whatever the tendencies, . . . the Catholic thinker obviously cannot ignore them. He must keep abreast of the stream of time, even if he does not swim with every one of its currents." Speaking of the symptoms of the times, he continued, "The latter we must examine to their very roots."[7] Shortly before his death in 1938 he wrote, "All social movements are the embodiments of ideas sown in previous generations."[8] Between these two dates Michel conceived it his role to analyze for his contemporaries the temper of a world changing, as he remarked in 1938, "at a breakneck speed" due to the advancements of science and technology;[9] but more than that, to sow the seeds, wherever possible, for a better world in the future.

For Michel the chosen way to begin was always to engage in basic study of past and present masters and to do some fundamental thinking with a view to present conditions. "If our present social system is in question," he wrote in 1935, "then its fundamental concepts are also in question, for they have been the theoretical guiding stars of the system in its growth and operations."[10] The economic system of historic capitalism presupposed many basic concepts and assumptions. In the depressive 1930's the wholesale, uncritical condemnation of capitalism was a favorite indoor sport. As did others of his time, Father Virgil gave much attention in his writings to the origin, nature, historical evolution, benefits, and evils of laissez-faire capitalism. Realizing the difficulty of defining the latter, he was often at pains to show that it was not to be identified with ownership of productive property, as the socialists had tagged it for their own ends, nor was it to be identified with technological mass production. All the admitted benefits of the capitalistic economic system, he insisted, can and must be preserved in a new Christian social order. Frequently, therefore, he found it necessary during the depression to state the many advantages that the *economic* system of capitalism had conferred on civilization. But he also hastened to add that "present-day capitalism cannot be well understood except in its historical setting, and in conjunction with the ideas and ideals of life, both philosophical and economic, under which it grew to what it is today." [11]

Every economic system operates within the context of a general philosophy of life held consciously or unconsciously. Capitalism as an economic system, therefore, had to be rigidly distinguished from the dominant false philosophy of life in modern civilization. As an economic system he defined it as "a system that invests money for the sake of gain or profit." But the capitalism which Michel condemned was the oppressive, mismanaged system that grew out of the unchristian philosophy of individualistic liberalism, with its false concepts of man, of society, of economic life, of the purpose of material goods and human life, of the universe itself. This liberal capitalism proclaimed the ethical autonomy of man and the autonomy of economic life. It also regarded enlightened self-interest as the promoter of the common good, the inevitable natural laws of economic and unlimited competition as the ruling principles of economic life. Such doctrines, Father Virgil insisted, led to the complete divorce of economic life from ethical considerations, as well as to the separation of the right of ownership from social duty. Accordingly, to the ruthless making of profits all else was subjected, even man himself, who should be the center of the economy. Hence destruction of the necessary organic forms of society, leaving only the state and helpless individuals, the maldistribution of wealth, despotic economic domination by the few, class struggle, loss of true freedom and human dignity. In eloquent language Michel showed how such a greedy and irresponsible capitalistic spirit had pervaded the whole of modern culture, life, and thought. Hence his frequent plea that before condemning the exploiting idle rich, Catholics ought first make sure they were not secretly envying them. [12]

For the sake of clarity it should be stated that the American economy has undergone many changes in the last twenty years. Although social evils remain to be remedied, we no longer have the exploitative system prevailing as in the 1930's; we have now a mixed economy, as economists say, or better, a free enterprise economy with institutional controls.

In the 1930's there was much discussion and confusion, even among economists, over the money system and over the extent to which it

was responsible for the social ills of the depression. Afraid of no
labor, Michel spent two winters studying current monetary systems
and theories as well as the role of money through the centuries. One
of his booklets on the social question was entitled, "Money and the
Common Good," a subject to which he frequently returned in his
socio-economic writings. While these writings indicate that he knew
much about the nature and function of money, the economist of
today would detect errors in his writings. Surely here Dom Virgil got
himself in deeper than he knew. For instance, it was at least mislead-
ing to say, despite his qualifications, that "money, which should be
the lifeblood of the community, the public utility *par excellence,* has
for decades, to say the least, been a commodity of private traffic
manipulated for private gain." [13] In some instances where he blamed
the monetary system he should have found fault with the inadequate
and unwise monetary and fiscal policies of the government. However, it must also be said that he advocated some of the correc-
tive policies that were adopted later. In his *Money and the Common Good* he hedged whenever he was on the verge of saying
something significant, indicating a lack of complete understanding
of the field. On the other hand, there were no blind denunciations of
bankers, the popular sport of many in the 1930's.[14] He thought it
important to point out that the money system was a "man-made institution set up by fallible human creatures," and not "an automatic
machinery which operates according to rigid natural laws" and therefore not to be re-adjusted, "as much propaganda had instilled into the
minds of many." He did not fall victim to the widely held myth that
bankers irresponsibly create money at will by a mere stroke of the
pen. Nor could he agree with those who advocated that the whole
money system should be put entirely into the hands of the government. However, he did say that the government must re-align the
availability of credit, especially for the needy and, of course, always
for the common good. But as far as making necessary changes in
the monetary system was concerned, Michel gave his usual warning
of caution for all social changes: "Go slowly, and watch your step."
Further elaboration of his monetary views is not necessary. What
may be worthy of note here is not what Father Michel had to say
about money but that he should have expended so much effort to
understand an exceedingly complicated subject.[15]

When speaking and writing on the institutions of private ownership and property Michel was on more familiar ground. One of

the underlying principles that had aided in the development of the characteristics of laissez-faire capitalism, he maintained, was the unquestioned "supremacy of the right of ownership over all other rights of man." Today it may be difficult to imagine such a prevailing situation, but as Father Virgil pointed out in 1936, "until our own day the man who challenged this undisputed and absolute right of ownership was looked upon as an exception and as a crank." [16] To his confreres he confided that if an understanding of St. Thomas' teaching on ownership could be brought to American Catholics and all men of good will, a notable change in socio-economic conditions would result. Hence he wrote much on the subject, always with a view to prevailing conditions.[17] To both Catholic and secular journals he brought St. Thomas' teaching on property, on the individual and social character of labor, of ownership and wealth, of all economic life as well as of the vital relations between the human person and property. Through the centuries he traced the loss of social duty and responsibility attached to ownership of wealth. He proved that the Church Fathers had "almost violently" insisted upon such responsibility. Moreover, he objected to what he considered pagan definitions of property and allied concepts in reputable economics texts because they failed to take into account the human dimension. Finally, without the free disposal of a sufficiency of material goods, he insisted, man is not free to develop the invaluable inner kingdom of his personality. Loss of ownership spells loss of liberty. Political freedom without economic security is illusory, and because a Christian society cannot function properly without the maximum respect for human personality, "true liberty is indispensable to it." Then Michel continued:

And since liberty is impossible without ownership of some kind and degree, distribution of ownership is indispensable for a Christian reconstruction of society. This means, in fact, the widest possible distribution of at least a minimum of ownership among all men. Without that we cannot escape, on the one hand, the slavery of economic helplessness, or, on the other, the threatened legal slavery of the totalitarian state.[18]

It is easy to see why Dom Virgil was drawn to the distributist ideas of G. K. Chesterton and Hilaire Belloc and tried to implement them in American society chiefly by way of a wider distribution of property. By the 1930's the previously wielded despotic economic power of a few men had raised the right of private property above human rights and spiritual values so that the "fundamental right to live, to work, to develop personality" had become in many instances a mockery. And the mass of helpless and depersonalized men had acquiesced, because they were bewildered and did not understand the issues involved.

But if liberalistic capitalism was vitiated by a false philosophy, the labor movement — "distinctly a product of modern capitalism" — was not untainted. "There are no greater economic individualists," Father Michel asserted, "than some labor union leaders or organizers." [19] In many ways the labor movement was motivated by the same spirit of ruthless acquisition of power as were some unscrupulous employers. And why not, since unionism was but "labor's belated answer to the unspoken but most definite challenge of capitalism," a challenge rising out of the class struggle inherent in materialistic capitalism? Both must look to new ideals of life, away from the unchristian aims of a morally bankrupt, liberalistic society. "The first requisite for this is the consciousness that capitalism as we have had it is dying and should die," [20] he said in 1938. Then also there must be a growing consciousness on the part of labor (as well as employers) of the principles of a Christian reconstruction of the social order, followed or accompanied by the necessary social action to remove social injustices and abuses.

In this social action for reconstruction, Father Virgil explained, every Catholic laborer and social apostle should engage. Labor would have to work out gradually a long-range, practical program and set of ideals to effect a Christian social order. Among the suggestions for such a program he mentioned a degree of participation in management, ownership, and profits; cooperation; a credit system operated for the common good; and restraint or abolition of irresponsible absentee ownership. Again, labor's cause would be much strengthened if it linked itself to various movements with allied ideals and interests. What these were will be stated presently. If the labor movement concerned itself with social justice and the common good, in other words, with the welfare of all segments of society and not only with its own in imitation of individualistic capitalism, he did not hesitate to say that the labor movement could well become "the most vital and important movement of the day in our country." [21]

Father Virgil once briefly outlined the criteria by which any economic system must be judged:

1) How does the system fulfill the general purpose of material goods in regard to mankind? Does it

help to make these goods subserve the needs of men? How efficient is it in attaining the distribution of the necessary goods to all men?

2) What is the relation of the system to family stability and moral virtues on which rests the stability of the family and of social life in general? Does it promote the social relations of men, and foster the spirit of solidarity among human beings?

3) How does it safeguard the individual rights of man: the right to live, to work, to determine one's means of livelihood, to exercise free choice in the development of one's abilities and personality, to obey the moral law, to worship according to one's conscience, to be a respectable member in the society of men, etc., etc.?

These three classes of values go to make up the full life of man here on earth. The first regards the necessary means for the development of the other two, and the last two embrace all that is of value to man here below as an individual and as a social being. An economic system must stand or fall by its attitude on the true values of human existence and by its being a successful means for the attainment of these by all.[22]

Measured by this standard Michel found modern capitalism seriously wanting. If the purely economic system must be salvaged, its inherent philosophy must certainly be abandoned. Thus he wrote in 1936:

> Can we conserve all the evident advantages and benefits of the capitalistic system and yet retain also all the best human values that are the heritage of Christianity? For instance, in order to realize the possibility of plenty, must we give up the basic rights of which we have been so increasingly conscious in the past centuries? That is the important question, and it becomes a portentous one for us, because the current historical answers in terms of bolshevism and fascism all say we must.[23]

But precisely because individualistic capitalism was doomed, it was absolutely necessary for Christians and all men of good will to look forward with a positive program, and not backward. They must be "pro-something" and not just "anti-communism" or anything else. But pro-what? Michel asked and then answered by asking a further question:

> Who can look into the future and determine the right technical structure of a Christian order? Certainly, the Pope refused to do that in *Quadragesimo anno*. He pointed out fundamental principles of Christian social reconstruction and leaves the rest to time and to us.[24]

In other words, there was no simple solution to a many-sided problem. Certainly Catholics must begin from the rock-bottom of sound Christian philosophy. To know by what they were confronted, to know the problems, there must be careful studies yielding factual analyses. Once the socio-economic facts are known, there must be the fullest clarification of the fundamental philosophical concepts and principles involved. Nor was that enough. There must be a continuous study of the phenomena of modern civilization. Then, under the guidance of fundamental principles and the broad directives of the social encyclicals, modern men, he said, will be in a position to rethink fruitfully their lives, their culture, their social system, and so come to some kind of agreement as to practical programs of action. Suffice it to say here that if Michel had little patience with panaceas, he had even less patience with the mentality which freezes persons into inaction because they fear that some day, somehow, somewhere, something will go awry. In a word, he recommended a courageous though prudent readiness to experiment.

Meanwhile there were four movements which, while they did not constitute an all-embracing Christian program, nevertheless were in line with Christian ideals. According to Father Michel, every apostolic Christian worthy of the name should support at least one of them. They were: 1) the corporative order, 2) the personalist movement, 3) the cooperative movement, and 4) the distributist-agrarian movement. The active unionist should also, like the apostolic Christian, give his attention and support to at least one of these movements. The next chapter will touch upon the cooperative and distributist-agrarian efforts.

Before taking up Michel's ideas concerning the corporative order and personalism, it is well to emphasize his own statement in regard to social regeneration:

It is characteristic of the mentality of today that the moment we speak of social regeneration we also look for a definite worked-out scheme or plan. We are in the blueprint age of mechanical organization. Contrary to what some may think, there is not extant anywhere a completely worked-out scheme, much less the true scheme or plan, of a corporately organized society. Least of all does *Quadragesimo anno* pretend to furnish such a plan. The encyclical concerns itself with underlying principles and especially with the moral aspects of society and of social regeneration.[25]

What, then, are the remedies for the reconstruction of an atomic society in which the individual person in many instances tends to lose his identity because he is only one of a heap of helpless, unrelated individuals? Michel's ideas center around two basic and related concepts: the corporative order as outlined by Pius XI in *Quadragesimo anno* and the social philosophy of personalism. Father Virgil wrote considerably on the corporative order at a time when comparatively little had appeared in English on the subject.[26] Nor did he restrict the concept of the corporative order to management and labor in industry as is predominantly done today. A decade later a committee of seven members of the American Catholic Sociological Society, after a study of two years, decided to use the term industry council plan or idea.[27] As for personalism, which runs like a core through all his social writings, one of Michel's students, Emerson Hynes, wrote that no one did more than he to make it known in the United States.[28] At any rate, in 1936 Michel began a correspondence with the great French personalist, Emmanuel Mounier, and in 1938 translated with the help of a confrere, Father Gerald McMahon, the French thinker's *A Personalist Manifesto*,[29] and wrote an introduction to it. Mounier and Michel agreed to collaborate in making known the role of the philosophy of personalism in social reconstruction. Michel liked Mounier's dictum that the great task was to introduce Christianity into Christendom.

One can only give a summary of Michel's treatment of the corporative order; even this is exceedingly difficult since his writings are already so condensed. First of all, he showed that the corporative order was not to be identified with the corporate state or with totalitarianism, as was commonly believed. In fact, a society organized on the basis of vocational or occupational groups accorded with the best democratic and Christian traditions. For society is not an atomized horde of competing individuals preying upon one another; it is an organic fellowship.

To clarify the concept of the corporative order Michel usually began with a philosophical explanation of the organic nature of society, of the essential and reciprocal relationship between the individual and society. In a word, he commenced with man's basically social nature. Then he applied these ideas to current socio-economic conditions. Because man is social by nature, he can develop himself physically, intellectually, and spiritually only by constant contact and interaction with his fellows. The welfare of man and of society, the individual and the common good, are intimately interlinked and inseparable, but not identified. The one presupposes and is dependent upon the other. Here is a fundamental principle of all right social order. And this principle of mutual interrelation between individual and society applies not only to the larger society of mankind or to the all-inclusive society of the state, but also to all the other various forms of social living—the family, small political units, cultural groups, economic associations, and so on. In connection with this Father Virgil stated:

This social nature of man and of all of his spheres of activity holds for everything which man has to do. Thus human work of every kind becomes a duty of social solidarity, also a social service and not merely a means of individual enrichment, least of all such a means at the expense of other members of society.[30]

In a similar way he explained the individual and social aspect of property ownership. If society is an organic structure, then each person must work also for the good of all. And Michel always insisted that this is as true of natural society as of the supernatural society of the Mystical Body.

Now the fundamental principle of corporatism, which aims to eliminate the excessive duties and functions of the state, has as its goal to make men capable again by union with one another of doing as much as possible for themselves, independently of any state action apart from that of protecting them in their inherent individual and social rights. Thus the state would function as the promoter of freely organized, relatively autonomous, socio-economic groups or families; and in such groups every individual person would have a functional place and, as a result, meaningful and emotionally significant relationships. For the industrial worker to have something to say, e.g., about his working conditions or his job is of "immense psychological value."

To clarify the role of the state, he further commented that the natural and necessary forms of social life and intercourse antedate the formation of the state, and not vice versa. The true basis of the corporative order, therefore, was neither a political set-up nor a special kind of economic structure. These would depend on the living traditions of the respective country and on the peculiar genius and temperament of its people. Dom Virgil insisted:

If we start with the formation of a particular political set-up, or a particular economic structure, which is legislated into existence, we are trying to reform society from the top down. Such a reform will hardly have the spontaneity of life, and it will moreover have to be instituted through the mighty arm of the state. . . . This is quite contrary to a basic principle of corporativism.[31]

The obvious lesson was that a social movement and social reconstruction must come from the bottom up and not from the top down. But this would again require that all rid themselves of the unchristian individualism born of false liberalism and acquire correct ethical and social conceptions of true social organization and of human life. Finally, the center of initiative and of self-determination had to remain to a maximum extent with individual persons and families as well as with the organic units above these, so that the larger organic groups and the state above them would have only that to do which the smaller groups could not themselves perform. In the 1930's Michel believed it exceedingly difficult for any government to reconstruct industrial and economic life from the top down without the danger of becoming totalitarian. Of course, he did not deny the necessity of basic social legislation in the spirit of *Quadragesimo anno*. But he also observed in 1938 that he saw "no real or permanent remedy for social ills in an increased passing of laws." Therefore the real and permanent remedies lay elsewhere.

Nor did Michel underestimate the job at hand in building a corporative society. He observed in 1938:

No one today can give a detailed blueprint of the corporative order, for the reason that such an order is one of living men and not of mechanical appliances and is moreover still very much in the making if not really existing rather in the embryo form of very general ideas and principles.[32]

Needed was an endless process of social education and propaganda. Again he stated in reference to social regeneration:

This is a long-range action, of course, because it takes some time before men who are used to one way of looking at things begin to understand basic ideas of another kind, and then digest them into their system of life, and especially before so many members of a society are thus "regenerated" as to influence the public life of the entire society.[33]

And because changing social institutions would not suffice if the general ideas dominating society were not sound, everyone aware of the true situation and its needs must spread the correct ideas in both theoretical and practical ways. He said:

In a practical way we must

make known everywhere the different schemes being tried out in different places. They are the practical examples of what the ideals stand for. And they are at least the first step towards forming social and economic units in which all the members work together instead of pulling apart. What is more, they are a beginning at reconstruction that is both Christian and democratic, and that starts from bottom up, that starts with the people themselves. It is from these smaller units that the larger social units can later be formed in the light of what our experiences will teach us.[34]

Among the "different schemes" of which Michel spoke and wrote were the programs of sound labor unions and of enlightened employers, the various cooperatives, the distributist-agrarian efforts, and the National Catholic Rural Life Movement. In general, he aimed to expose social abuses and wrong ideas and then to clarify the nature and function of the good society and each person's role in it. He frequently regretted in the 1930's that even men of good will often knew of no other way than that of individualistic capitalism or of communism and fascism. "Basic is the re-capture of the ideology of the corporative order," he said, perhaps too simply, "and if that is revitalized in men, all the rest will take care of itself." [35]

Without this revitalized ideology there can be no effective economic democracy. But Michel was even more certain that the recovering, fostering, and preserving of human and spiritual values amidst big government, big business, big labor, and a rapidly developing technology was the great task of present and future. Addressing a symposium at the University of Notre Dame on November 5, 1938, he remarked that "the sin of modern civilization is that it has failed to recognize the inner sanctuary of the human person and has failed entirely to accord it its proper reverence and respect." [36] If space allowed, it would be interesting to show to what extent Father Virgil, while by no means a social scientist, anticipated some of the findings of industrial sociologists as well as many of the remarks and observations of Pius XII in his Christmas messages of 1952 and 1953 on personalism and the harmful effects of a misused technology upon the human personality.[37]

Today much is being said of the impersonality of modern life, of the "fractional man," of the "lonely individual," of the "other-directed person," of the loss of the sense of community, and the like — all purportedly the results of the mechanization of life in a technical civilization. Such thoughts were expressed frequently in Michel's writings. Thus he depicted what he considered the depersonalizing capitalistic civilization had done to the human person:

All who can see with the eyes of the spirit cannot but be horrified at the corruption underneath. The greatest of the evils is perhaps the depersonalization of man, the reduction of man to a mere cog in a machine. . . . The greatest evil of bourgeois capitalism is the harm it has done to man himself, to the rational animal made after the image of God and called to the spiritual vocation of childhood of God and brotherhood with Christ, and destined to be master both of himself and of the earth.[38]

If such words seem extreme for a time of many sitdown strikes when nearly twelve million men were unemployed, one need only recall the recent warnings by Pius XII concerning the dangerous influences of "the technological spirit" upon the human personality.

Most of his contemporaries, Dom Virgil maintained in 1938, were aware of the menace of communism and fascism to human civilization but very many overlooked the insidious menace that modern capitalism posed to all spiritual values. All forms of political and economic organization — be they capitalist, fascist, national-socialist, or communist — have consciously or unconsciously sacrificed the sacred dignity of the person, and with it the human and spiritual values that alone can make up the true soul of a healthy society. Extremes breed extremes. And the extremes of individualism and collectivism meet precisely "in the extinction of the spiritual person." No mere juggling of the economy or paternalistic statism could solve this problem. Actually, communism and fascism, Michel declared, were but the logical outcomes of an unchristian liberalism which had once fathered the now dying individualistic capitalism and had glorified atheism and material aggrandizement. Thus, out of the philosophy of liberalism had emerged by way of reaction the state capitalism of Russia.

At a time when the Nazi Bundist rallies were comparatively large and the communists very active in labor circles and elsewhere, a distinct feature of Michel's social writings was his lucid exposition of the Christian middle way between a false individualism and a crushing collectivism. Furthermore, he vigorously held to the distinction between the individual on the one hand, and the spiritual and social person on the other.[39] Meanwhile, to all thoughtful men it should be obvious that the predominant ideas and ideals of past and present were now wholly inadequate. In his introduction to *A Personalist Manifesto* Father Virgil emphasized:

We are definitely at the end of an era of human history. One of its characteristics is — or is this a universal mark of such times? — that an alarmingly large number of both the secular and spiritual leaders of today still seem blissfully unaware of the fact of its vast significance.[40]

What was needed was a fundamental reconstruction, not merely a restoration. And that reconstruction must come by way of personalism.

To define the philosophy of personalism is not easy. But to describe it is to touch the heart of Michel's approach and ideas concerning social regeneration. First of all, personalism is nothing new; it is as old as Christianity; but amidst a welter of philosophies it had become obscure. Personalism may be loosely defined as a philosophy which aims to provide for the preservation and development of the human personality in all economic, political, and social organization and policy. Since the free human person is the most valuable being in all creation, personalism insists on the primacy of men over material things and on the autonomy of natural societies. It accepts as realities the technological instruments of modern economic life; but it would humanize them. Because the modern crisis is fundamentally spiritual and has its roots in economic, political, and social institutions, personalists recognize that all efforts at reform will ultimately come to naught unless they eradicate the false philosophy that inheres in those social institutions. These institutions they try to bring under human control, but always by efforts and programs that accord with the true nature of the spiritual person. In short, personalists reject all attempts to enslave the human spirit in any way, to make the human being a means rather than an end. While personalism is ready to accept the wisdom of the past, it refuses to be mechanically controlled by the past. It has no time for the simple answer or the pat solution. It rejects definitive social blueprints.

Obviously, personalism is not a rigid system; rather it is a flexible body of living ideas, a creative outlook. In every possible way personalists strive to accord the human person his highest prerogative, self-determination, and to provide opportunities for self-development in a free society, in a civilization that is social and communitarian rather than competitive and individualistic. "We can safeguard the freedom and spirituality of man," Michel insisted, "only by making man the starting point and goal of all endeavor at building a better social framework of existence." [41] How? Personalists answer: by serious study and research, by discussion and education, by rationality and persuasion, by the spreading of fundamental concepts and basic principles. Such a procedure, they hope, will lead to intelligent action and prudent experimentation by aroused persons who reject what Mounier called "the established disorder." For personalism begins, the French thinker said, "by arousing each person to a state of disquietude." [42] The sincere personalist abhors unthinking conformity and spiritual mediocrity. For each person is unique, never a sample of the mass. Therefore, in a personalist society the economy, social institutions, technology, science, and all else will serve the human person as the center and end of society. In this way will the philosophy of personalism aid in the essential task of cultivating and preserving human, cultural, and spiritual values.

Precisely because personalism is flexible and forward-looking, it can absorb new ideas — the fruit of study, common experience, and combined efforts. In a fast-changing world no one should be apodictic in suggesting final solutions. And the solutions that personalists offered were for that very reason largely experimental and tentative. In the 1930's some persons offered panaceas for the ills of the age. While Michel considered the widespread distribution of property, a sound labor movement, decentralization, and cooperatives to be basic and essential for social reform, he refused to put his hope and efforts for a better world in any single plan or program, not even in a program stressing a society of organized occupational groups. As one of Michel's disciples has observed:

Personalism had a special attraction for Virgil Michel, for it embodied his concept of reconstruction: a broad form in which every good practical plan and movement would find a place. The particular plans could grow within the protective wall of the general principles of personalism. They would not be imposed schemes bureaucratically run. [43]

But there was yet another reason why personalism appealed to him. Dom Virgil always looked for common ground between various groups — religious or non-religious — and men of ideals everywhere; and he was convinced that a sound social movement must seek support from all men of good will, as Pius XI had also observed in *Quadragesimo anno.* Thus all men of ideals, even though of various faiths, could accept as a basis of agreement the supreme value of the human person and spiritual values in human life regardless of how they interpreted other aspects of the spiritual life. Dom Virgil believed that the world had reached a time when all those who believed in man's spirituality must stand together rather than dispute with one another in the face of a threatening fascist or communist collectivism. Hence, many of his social writings were also meant for non-Catholics. In this light, too, must be understood Michel's cooperation with men of other faiths. In what that cooperation consisted later pages will record.

Dom Virgil frequently deplored the narrow, sectarian mentality found among certain Catholics toward their non-Catholic brethren. Such a mentality says that "all is fine in our camp while all is foul in yours." He made sincere efforts to bring Catholics and their non-Catholic compatriots into a more sympathetic understanding. In the 1930's the Church had been woefully misrepresented in liberal journals as being fascist and reactionary or worse, and accused of having no social program for changing times. Thus some even held that the Church was the accomplice of social injustice and capitalist oppression. After letters of protest and explanation to the editors of such journals, Michel in the summer of 1938 submitted a thirty-four page manuscript to the *Atlantic Monthly*, convincingly showing how and why such accusations were "grossly false." [44] But if Michel's defense was strong, the manuscript contained no consolation for complacent Catholics, and it is to this phase that attention will chiefly be given here.

Dom Virgil frankly admitted that there were "many Catholics, too many, who are Catholic only in name and not in spirit or in life, and often not even in knowledge of what the Church stands for." After explaining the true nature of the Church, he pleaded that she be not judged by these men. Nor could Catholics object in general, he said, to his own charge that many were Catholic in name only; even Pius XI himself had made it plain in his encyclical *On Atheistic Communism* that "even in Catholic countries there are still too many who are Catholics hardly more than in name." Michel quoted even stronger papal statements and similar ones by a few well known Catholics. Apart from the obvious insincerity of self-styled intellectuals and the failure of others to make adequate investigation, Michel believed that at least one reason why non-Catholics so often misunderstood the Church was that his co-religionists frequently chose to be aloof in an unchristian way and also failed to be "sympathetically articulate" about the faith. Nor could he agree with those Catholics who advocated monolithic Catholic thinking beyond matters strictly of faith and morals so as to present a "united front." Self-criticism, he said, is "one of the signs of true vitality." He indicated that Pius XI, as well as some bishops and a few prominent Catholic laymen, had given eminent example of such self-criticism. When Professor Louis Mercier of Harvard University told him that there was altogether too much mutual criticism among Catholics, Michel observed that "the alternative would be a common agreement that simply does not exist, a false front of 'all's well,' " and so he replied that there "was not even enough self-criticism." [45] Finally, he regretted the "black-or-white" thinking among Catholics, although he pointed out that this was by no means a Catholic monopoly.

One example he gave in the 1930's of such thinking was the uncritical attitude of many Catholics on the Spanish Question: Franco was a Catholic, and so he could not possibly do any wrong; the opposite side must be 100 per cent at fault — no distinctions whatever need be made.[46] Father Virgil explained:

Some went so far as to speak of a Holy War, and in a most uncatholic way identified the eternal interests of the Church with a particular set of conditions and circumstances of which they knew very little. The sin of violently emotional thinking on the question was a universal one in the world; Catholics were not exempt from it, neither pro-Franco nor anti-Franco Catholics, though I believe the former, being greater in number, also did the greater sinning.[47]

In regard to the relations between Church and state, Michel believed that in modern pluralistic society, the only reasonable and practicable solution seemed to be separation with cooperation. But on this delicate issue Father Virgil must speak for himself:

This must mean for Catholics . . . a clearer theoretical distinction between the spiritual and the secular spheres of human life and less practical confusion between the two domains. It means the absence of any official interference by the secular in the spiritual or by the spiritual in the secular. The influence of spiritual ideals in the different forms of public life must come through the personal action of citizens thoroughly imbued with the true Christian spirit of justice and charity.

It must mean also a clearer distinction between the eternal and the changing in Christian life — the permanence of the eternal values and verities amidst the constantly changing conditions of life here on earth. It means a better realization of the fatal consequences of confusing or identifying the two — the spiritual suicide of a modernism that reduces the eternal to the ephemeral, and the equally mortal suicide of a strait-laced formalism that identifies the eternal with a particular set of temporal structures, an identification that has more than once killed the spirit by adherence to a dead letter and that has more than once brought upon Catholics veritable historical cataclysms.[48]

What the Church needed was freedom; and because the supernatural order presupposed the natural order, the state could do the Church a great service if, remaining in its own domain, it cooperated in preparing a sound social order by intelligent legislation based on the natural law and right reason. In this regard, the state had, indeed, a long way to go.

Such viewpoints or the evolution of such an outlook and the needed spiritual re-awakening, Father Virgil admitted in 1938, will "cause many aches and pains." And he might have added: misunderstanding, unkind exchanges, and even emotional outbursts, as witness the subsequent Church-state controversy among Catholics in the United States. Welcoming a "renewed type of Christian outlook and spirit" among awakened young Catholics who were in turn distrusted by "a certain type of nineteenth century formalistic and self-complacent Catholic," he concluded his study by stating:

There are the old (in spirit) who are greatly perturbed, and the young who feel all the zest of liberation and of new life. Many of the old are quite bourgeois in their attitudes and inclined to identify these with Christianity. They are more than perturbed by anti-capitalist statements of their fellow Catholics. But the young as a whole accept such statements with a sigh of relief — as if at last it were going to be more possible to live a wholehearted Christian life! [49]

The activity of communists in the United States in the 1930's is now well known. During the year 1936–37 a campaign was waged from American Catholic pulpits against communism. Dom Virgil judged it a "definite flop," because "too often it took on at least the semblance of preaching hatred — which is anti-Christian" — and because it remained negative in its approach, being "merely anti-something or other" rather than vigorously "pro." Communism, he reminded his fellow Catholics, was not to be fought merely by counter-propaganda nor "by emotional denunciation." [50] Much harder, of course, was the task of positive Christian social reconstruction. The way to fight communism in the C.I.O. was not by condemning the C.I.O., as a large part of the Catholic press was doing, Michel observed, but by bringing papal social doctrine to the many Catholic workers in the newly formed labor organization. Not only did he aim to expose the ominous "spectre of Communism"; he also tried to show how genuine Christians might meet the challenge — especially after some had suggested a "holy war" or a "concerted crusade" against atheistic Marxism.

He was all for such a war or crusade, but only if it was to be fought in a Christian way and with spiritual weapons, forged out of the liturgy and the Church's social teachings. He proceeded to outline the "ideal Christian warfare." First of all, every Catholic must again fully realize that he is always a soldier of Christ and so must ceaselessly engage in the battle against the enemies of Christ. But the Christian's supreme weapon is always the supernatural virtue of charity, shown even to undoubted enemies like the communists. Another basic point: Christian warfare always starts at home, i.e., by personal sanctification through prayer and self-denial. Next, by the constant use of pulpit and other means these fundamental doctrines could be taught: the universal brotherhood of all men, the Mystical Body, the supreme role of love in that Body, social justice with all its ramifications — and not least, the doctrine that the material goods of the world have the divine purpose of caring for the needs of all men. Once these principles are grasped fully, then Catholics will also understand the social duty attached to ownership of wealth, superfluous wealth above all. They might even be convinced that in this regard they have been "very negligent" in the past. Obviously, an understanding of the little known social encyclicals, *Quadragesimo anno* in particular, would be most helpful. Again, if Catholics used, of their possessions, only what was needed for their decent Christian living, the rest could be employed in practicing the corporal works of mercy. And since some were asking for an all-out attack upon communism, perhaps even the superfluous space of "all residences and halls belonging to the Church" could be used in providing for the shelterless. Thus all priests and religious could gain the invaluable experience of personal contact with the extreme poverty of God's poorest in a time of extreme need. Third order groups of religious communities could be the "special regiments" fighting as if the whole victory "depended next to God on themselves alone." Naturally the daily Christian warfare must begin as often as possible with each soldier's full participation in the Sacrifice of Christ. Father Michel explained:

There, at the altar, they would dedicate themselves wholly, and especially also their entire material goods, to God and to the cause of God alone: that is, to the service of God, with a particular emphasis on serving God throughout the day in doing good to all men to the fullest extent of their means.[51]

But there was another kind of war, not so holy, with which Michel occupied himself. Since World War I the morality of war and pacifism had been debated with increasing vehemence. In the 1930's discussion became, in Michel's words, "violent and widespread." The result was a strong peace movement, especially after the communists posed as the only promoters of peace.

Briefly, Dom Virgil was certainly not a doctrinaire pacifist. At the same time he expressed his dissatisfaction with the simple acceptance in practice of each and every war by Catholics. He had no patience with the statement that a Catholic cannot be a conscientious objector. His writings on the morality of war are best summarized by his own quotation from Michael Cardinal Faulhaber:

We live in a period of transition; and just as in other questions, so, too, in the question of war and peace, a change of heart will be effected. . . . Even the teaching of moral theology in regard to war will speak a new language. It will remain true to its old principles, but in regard to the question of the permissibility of war, it will take account of new facts.[52]

In connection with the morality of war, one can do little more here than mention Michel's prophetic comments on the absolute need for, obstacles to, and possibilities of, some kind of organized international society.[53] The white man's real burden, the burden of the "Christian" western world, he warned, was to bring economic cooperation, a sound philosophy of human values, as well as the Christian spirit and message to suffering "backward" peoples. In 1938 he observed, "All the different parts and peoples of the world are interrelated in their ordinary lives as never before. . . . It is more imperative than ever for the lay apostle of today to study the problem of international society." Again: "The question of internationalism must be kept alive, or else we may all perish in the ensuing chaos." Speaking of the recognition of the natural moral law as the only hope for a sound international community, Father Virgil noted ominously, and perhaps, prophetically: "If this is a matter for despair and not for hope, it cannot be helped. We must see the situation as it is." [54]

It seems a safe generalization to say that there was hardly a question of current discussion in his time on which Michel did not make some comment. To Mounier he wrote that a good part of the task of social regeneration was to awaken Catholics and all men of good will to the true conditions and then "to disturb" them into realistic social action. For Michel, alive to his times and its defects, this often amounted to calling attention to problems and situations on the social scene that were being overlooked by many. These words, written in 1936, constitute one example:

The injustices suffered by sharecroppers, the gross discriminations against negroes (even at times within the walls of Catholic churches), economic oppressions of all sorts, crying court injustices, violent vigilante antics . . . go on with hardly a prominent Catholic voice raised in protest. How the Church fathers of old would have made the welkin ring with righteous indignation of the Lord! [55]

Many and strong were his pleas in *Orate Fratres* and elsewhere for study and application of the social encyclicals. His insistence takes on significance if one remembers that in Michel's lifetime there was no comprehensive collection of encyclicals, or bibliographical data about them, in any language. As late as 1938 he had cause to complain that Pius XI's *Quadragesimo anno* had been "to a great extent a voice crying in the wilderness," and that even among the Pope's "trusted followers there had been an unintelligible apathy shown to his guidance." [56]

Boldly and yet prudently Michel described in the *Ecclesiastical Review* what seemed to him growing signs and causes of an incipient anti-clericalism.[57]

An analysis of Virgil Michel's social thought should include a critique of his nine booklets in the social question series. Concerning this series, a few remarks will suffice. To give their titles is to state their content: *Human Rights, Ownership, Labor and Industry, Nature of Capitalism, Critique of Capitalism, Ideals of Reconstruction, Money and the Common Good, The Theory of the State*, and *Reconstruction Schemes*. It may be worth noting that the latter pamphlet was Michel's critique of the solutions and cure-alls proposed in the 1930's. Nor was he content with pointing out deficiencies in the capitalist civilization of depression days. He was also positive in his attitude and efforts. Yet, as already noted, the suggested remedies were tentative and

experimental. Hence he spoke of "ideals" and "schemes" of reconstruction. He frankly admitted that much in modern civilization
perplexed him. But that was only reason for more study — then
attempts at intelligent action. Besides, only a cautious experimentation, and future events in some cases, could lend further lights. Thus,
e.g., he stated, speaking of the distributist ideals:

Whether such decen-
tralization [of economic power and ownership] is possible, without
losing the advantages of centralized organization on the large scale
such as we now have it in the economic field, is a question for the
future to solve.[58]

And again: What is really possible under the ideals of Christian
solidarity in our modern technological economy no one can know until experience makes the trial. Yet again a real trial cannot be made
until the ideals of Christian solidarity have again been more generally
accepted by men. That is why the basic work in the reconstruction
of society must be the rebirth in mankind of Christian ideals.[59]

One striking characteristic of Michel's approach to social ills was
his broad vision linked with attempts to get to the bottom of things.
In this regard Mortimer J. Adler, writing in *Orate Fratres* for January
22, 1939, observed "that the reason why Father Virgil was one of the
clearest voices to interpret the message of the great encyclicals was
due to the breadth of his understanding, cultivated by reading Marx
as well as St. Thomas." In the 1930's some Catholics were saying that
men need only become totally Christian again, as if there were nothing wrong with the socio-economic order and as if this was not in
need of being set aright by "total" Christians; others, that the money
system must be revamped; still others, that the economic system must
be overhauled — then all would be well. But all of these, Michel
insisted, were partial answers. Reality was of one piece, all must be
restored to Christ and so related to God. The natural and the supernatural were intimately interrelated; they were the distinct and
integral parts of one whole. Michel saw clearly how the natural order
— economic, political, social — impinged upon the supernatural life of
men. A sound Christian social movement had to proceed, therefore,
on the natural and supernatural levels. Or as Pius XI said, needed
was a change of soul *and* of institutions.

Dom Virgil's integral approach may be summarized in these
words: We need social science to present an analysis of the current
socio-economic order; social philosophy to analyze the currents of our

time and to interpret realistically the results of empirical science in terms of a sound philosophy of human life in the good society; and finally, the liturgy to bring to bear on the social order Christ's redemptive powers through enlightened and apostolic Christians active in the world. Consequently, knowing and living the liturgy was obviously not enough. Spiritual reform was only part of the needed total program; and even a pervasive and lasting spiritual rejuvenation would be impossible without effecting at the same time a just and charitable framework of society by intelligently grappling with economic and social problems in the natural order.

However, no one man ever embodies the social ideal in its entirety. Before evaluating Michel's social thought, it should be stated that he was not formally trained in the social sciences as such, even if he saw their value. He concerned himself with economic, social, and political affairs — and then largely from a philosophical point of view — only in so far as they touched upon the apostolate. The latter remained his special interest. His writings embody no all-inclusive synthesis, no striking and original theories, no empirical studies and experiments. Apart from their constituting a sound social philosophy perennially true, his social writings are of little special interest today, except perhaps as keen insights into, and descriptions of, his time, or, in retrospect, a sharp analysis of the shape of things to come. The concept of a strictly empirical sociology had not become explicit in Catholic circles of his day.[60] And even if it had, he would not have engaged in it beyond using its findings as he used, e.g., available empirical data in *Christian Social Reconstruction*. Because his grasp of theoretical economics was insufficient, he at times overlooked economic realities. This is always a danger for philosophers intensely interested in social reforms.

While Father Virgil correctly outlined the role of the state, the concept of the government as a balancing factor in the economy such as it is today, seems to have escaped him. He perhaps also underestimated somewhat the recovery powers of the capitalist economic system whose modification he called for. Interested in voluntary programs of social reform at a time when not a few were ready to sell their political freedom for economic security, he said almost nothing specifically about the social legislation he generally advocated. It could be that he left this task to such contemporary stalwarts as Monsignors John A. Ryan and Francis J. Haas. Despite Michel's efforts to seek solutions to existing problems resourcefully, his commentaries on social subjects at times seem coldly theoretical and academic. Is this because he attempted to expound fundamental concepts and principles? An editor and collaborator with Michel told the writer that he once heard Michel give a brilliant lecture on social justice. Later, when he thought of how to apply Dom Michel's message to existing conditions, he was quite at a loss. But one must also take into consideration Father Virgil's avowed purpose: to propagate the right social ideas and inspirational ideals; unless these prevail throughout society, practical and institutional changes will "be little more than passing events." Social movements, he often stressed, are the outgrowth of ideas sown in the past. Shortly before his death he defended this view when he said:

Is it worthwhile to do battle, as this article has done, in the realm of ideals? The task could be extended endlessly, while the general propounding of these abstract ideas might seem hollow and futile to many. History disproves this latter contention, however, and subsequently history will no doubt confirm the past. Any proposed social changes that are not based on commonly accepted ideas are bound to collapse. And any changes wrought under the impetus of ideas that are humanly and ethically unsound will end in ruin and chaos. However, when studied in the light of antecedents, the successes of future generations — whatever they may be — will be found to be the fruits of abstract ideas propagated in the past.[61]

Since what Father Virgil had in mind here is in large part the task of social philosophy, a brief analysis of his more strictly philosophical thought is pertinent. The reader will recall that Michel returned from Europe in 1925 with plans and outlines for a series of five textbooks in philosophy. If he had not become involved in the liturgical apostolate, he might have made some lasting contribution to philosophical thought. Even so, his writings in this field are not insignificant, and in view of his other work, certainly considerable. Once convinced that liturgical work was providentially to be his lot, he used to refer to philosophy as "my pet hobby." But it was always more than that. His writings and correspondence show a thorough familiarity with contemporary philosophical literature as well as with St. Thomas. And there were few things he enjoyed more than to engage in philosophical discussions with thinkers — Catholic and non-Catholic — wherever he met them, and especially with philosophers from the University of Minnesota who came to Collegeville to discuss modern thought. His letters also show a continuous correspondence with philosophers, in his last years, largely with non-Catholic scholars.

Urged on by philosopher-friends of the American Philosophical Association, he volunteered to address that body in 1936 on the topic, "Philosophy at the End of an Era," a speech already written. "I presume there will be no objection to having a Catholic priest appear on the program," he wrote to Professor Charner Perry of the Social Science Research Council, "although I dare say it will be rather a novelty, if nothing else." [62] The address, if given, was never published. As to its content, something will be said later.

In the 1940's Emmanuel Cardinal Suhard echoed one of Michel's deepest convictions when he stated, "The first apostolate, at the crossroads where we stand, is the apostolate of thought." [63] Twice — in 1921 with his "Mission of Catholic Thought" [64] and again in 1937 with his "Towards a Vital Philosophy" [65] — Dom Virgil explicitly outlined the role of Scholastic philosophy and of Catholic philosophers and intellectuals in the changing, chaotic world. Past pages have pointed out the enormous influence of the thought-climate of any culture on the behavior of individual persons. All the more is this true in a society already suffering from a general intellectual confusion. As Dom Virgil observed in 1921, "The tendencies of any age form, as it were, the colored glass through which most of its people view the different problems of the day; and they will be met with at every turn of the devious course that life pursues." Later in the same article he added that Catholic philosophers could not afford, therefore, to "ignore the different systems of thought permeating the contemporary world." [66] This was even more true, Michel said, because for some four centuries Catholic thought had been leading "a sort of catacomb existence." The fact was that Catholic thinking in those centuries and in his own time enjoyed comparatively little influence in the cultural life of civilized nations. Add to this the confusion and moral bankruptcy of contemporary philosophy, of ethics above all, as evidenced in American secular philosophical books and journals, and it became clear that Catholic thought had an important mission.

What, then, is the task of Catholic philosophers in a secular culture? What would be a vital philosophy? These related questions will be taken up in turn.

After summarizing current philosophical errors, Dom Virgil emphasized the necessity of arming the student with the principles and fundamentals of a sound philosophy, but always with an eye to contemporary false views and theories. Because the Catholic philosopher, guided by faith and sound tradition, knows some ultimate answers, there is danger of his believing it unnecessary to concern himself with opposing thought systems. That was why a Catholic instructor, lacking a healthy skepticism, often easily dismissed such systems by labeling them as "pantheistic," "idealistic," "hedonist," "materialist," etc. This was the easy way out — actually, the self-complacent way. No wonder Catholic thought had brought little influence to bear on other philosophical systems. Meanwhile, exponents of modern secularist thought disregarded Scholastic philosophy, which to them seemed tradition-laden, ineffective, authoritarian, and obsolete. Yet, if the thought of the Schoolmen led to truth and represented something truly vital in society, then it must be presented so as to reach as many minds as possible; moreover, it must win its due recognition amidst the differing and changing patterns of thought.

For these and other reasons Virgil Michel maintained in 1921 that Catholic philosophers "must study the symptoms of the day, the tendencies that are injurious not only to Catholicity, but to all the world of its fellow men." Obviously they can aid in removing modern maladies only if they search seriously into their causes, and then propose the remedies in such a language and manner that the sincere modern inquirer will consider and even accept them. But this again demands that Catholic philosophers studiously examine the various phenomena that touch the lives of people. Catholic intellectuals must know more than how their philosophical system differs from those of their fellow citizens. And if Catholic philosophers are true seekers after wisdom, they should be prepared to seek the grain of truth which exists everywhere. Moreover, they must do so with a sympathetic candor "so apparent as to convince others of its presence." In this regard Father Virgil observed in 1921 that too many Catholic teachers of philosophy "have lived entirely in the past"; they have been catholic neither in outlook nor approach.

Why must the Scholastic philosopher cultivate a critical spirit in his own regard but a spirit of humble open-mindedness towards thinkers not of his faith? The answer was simple. Completely apart from rethinking and refining his own philosophical principles and convictions, philosophy, like all else in life, was an apostolate, and in a befuddled, disintegrating world, a most important one. Here are Michel's words:

If we refuse to see the standpoint of others, or ignore their sincerity, we are not only shutting off all possibility of assisting them, but we are actually building a wall around ourselves and closing to them all avenues of approach.[67]

And that is why Father Virgil always sought a common ground with non-Catholic intellectuals and stirred up discussion with them on vital issues of the day whenever possible.

As a consequence of this attitude, he insisted that the professor of philosophy in the Catholic school does not prepare his students for such discussion by verbally transliterating or slavishly repeating Scholastic teaching, often even as found in inadequate textbooks. Nor may he treat the *philosophia perennis* as if his ideal were to fondle a precious mummy. Modern man cannot be convinced by a heaping up of Scholastic terminology, phrases, and adages. And we do the Angelic Doctor no honor, Michel said, by merely adapting his thought as if he had said the last word on all things, past and present. It was precisely this feature which Michel severely criticized in reviewing the Dominican Walter Farrell's doctoral dissertation.[68] There would be less danger of merely restating the thought of Aquinas if the teacher experienced the refreshing stimulus and challenge of analyzing books of contemporary philosophy, of sifting out elements of truth, and if, moreover, he grappled with the problems they raised. Had not Leo XIII, in his encyclical *Aeterni Patris* of 1879, inaugurating the neo-Scholastic movement, urged Catholic philosophers to "accept willingly and gratefully anything that was wisely said or usefully discovered or thought from whatever source it came"? In this connection Dom Virgil once stressed that, if Aquinas were writing his *Summa* today, the objections in it would be the errors of modern thought. To point out these errors — or better, to lead his students to their discovery — was the task of the alert teacher. The living message and spirit of St. Thomas, which he had first made his own, must provide requisite norms. Only such a teacher could suitably equip his students for intelligent action. Dom Michel's repeated pleas for a vital philosophy remind one of Lacordaire's famous observation, "St. Thomas is a beacon, not a barrier."

In the light of the foregoing, it is easy to understand Michel's words to the editor of the symposium, *Essays in Thomism*, which he helped to plan and which was subsequently dedicated to him and to his friend, Dom Augustine Walsh. The first essay was written by Father Virgil and edited by Robert E. Brennan, O.P. To this Dominican he wrote concerning the projected volume:

I think our presentation

should reflect modern problems and language in its outlook even when we oppose these directly. I am positively overwhelmed by the fear that we may give occasion to outsiders to feel that we are slavish followers of past leaders in the field of human thought.[69]

Actually, what was needed was a truly living philosophy. In "Towards a Vital Philosophy" Michel described the three stages by which such a philosophy could gradually be built up, not by one thinker only, but by the cooperative work of many. This article was a critique, a ringing indictment of the decade-old American neo-Scholastic movement; it caused soul-searching among some philosophers. Concerning this article, Gerald Phelan noted in 1939, "The task confronting Catholic philosophers today has never been more clearly stated." [70] In his article Father Virgil observed that one could count on the fingers of one hand the books of a vital character by American Thomists. In philosophy, as in other fields, he seemed to know what was being done and what needed doing. Thus in his favorable review of Etienne Gilson's *The Spirit of Medieval Philosophy*, Michel took occasion in 1937 to observe concerning Catholic philosophical works in English:

Far too many works, certainly the great majority, that propose to give a summary of Thomistic thought fail even to mention the ideas that come under the general heading of social ethics or social philosophy. In our day, when vital thinking is concerned above all with this question, the lacuna is as self-condemnatory in professed works of synthesis as it is unintelligible. Just for this reason a chapter on the common good, the purpose of civil authority and organization, the place of ownership in human life, its rights as well as its duties, its social aspects above all, the duties of rulers towards their subjects, the purpose of economic activity in individual life and in public social life, would have been almost a unique contribution.[71]

By articles and pamphlets Father Virgil had begun to supply this need.

But what were Michel's prescriptions for the development of a vital philosophy? First, because of the vicissitudes suffered by the Scholastic synthesis in past centuries, the great minds of the past must be studied anew. This entailed much historical research and criticism and first-rate scientific investigation. Although much had been accomplished in this necessarily first step, much more needed to be done. However, for one engaged in this task, scientific training and research ability were not sufficient: he must also be a philosopher and a theologian. This first and indispensable task performed, the fruit thereof was by no means as yet a vital philosophy. Hence the work must go on to a second phase, from which must come an intelligent, convincing, and sympathetic exposition of medieval philosophical thinking as vital then. This could be accomplished either by way of an over-all synthesis or by way of monographs. But even such scholarship in no way constituted the vital philosophy so needed in the modern world. Therefore, the culminating third stage must produce the essence of any vital philosophy: sympathetic, critical, vigorous, original, and constructive philosophizing on urgent present problems in the light of mastered traditional principles. This was the way and spirit of Aquinas. And this is the hardest task because it entails incisive and creative, penetrating and personal thinking.

Such fruitful thinking, however, can begin only with the recognition of existing problems. In a striking passage Dom Virgil described the vital process of a mind grappling with such a problem:

The Scholastic who was trained to be a philosopher in the schoolroom or textbook atmosphere . . . is inclined to see problems not as stimulants to virile mental research, but rather as so many occasions for drawing upon already-mastered solutions. Problems are then solved by approaching them from without and surrounding and smothering them with blanket phrases and conclusions hoary with tradition. A true philosophical problem is like a thicket or a jungle. Its bearings cannot be solved from without, but only by a plunge into its heart. One must be as it were, lost in it, and then by careful searching and staking off get one's bearings from the center out, gradually working the whole plot until one reaches the edge and sees the light of day and familiar terrain. No one who fails to see genuine problems as such is going to philosophize about them in a sympathetic and convincing way. In fact, the treatment of all problems as nothing but pseudo-problems which only ignorance of past wisdom prevents a man from seeing in their pseudo-problematic character can only result in pseudo-philosophy.[72]

But because there was so little mental wrestling with real problems, philosophers as a group — like, as he said, "idle spectators on the sidelines, interested perhaps in watching the tide of events" — had contributed little to "stem the tide of chaos that has come upon our world, including the world of thought, in the past generations in particular."[73] With a final jab at philosophical smugness and the academic formalism of "textbook philosophy," he remarked:

What is needed now is not a blind conservation of philosophical rightness, but a revolt of the right remaining within the limits and the spirit of the general tradition, but otherwise radical in the sense of a person plumbing down to the roots of our system with a new and critical and vigorous constructive activity accompanied by an eradication of everything that is not of the nature and the spirit of the genuine philosophical temper.[74]

No better summary and description could be given of Dom Virgil's ideas as to a living philosophy and of Michel the philosopher than by citing his edited words:

[A living Thomism] is nothing less than a complete modernization of the thought of Aquinas. By this I mean that if we are to be true Thomists we must think and speak and write in terms of the problems of our age. We must consider seriously the intellectual needs of the times, the confusion and chaos with which our generation has been afflicted. We have the tools to do constructive work, because we have the principles on which all straight thinking is grounded. This discussion of contemporary problems must be wrought with the same spirit and balanced temper that distinguished Aquinas in his dealings with his own age. It must be accomplished by men who, on the one hand, are thoroughly sympathetic with the *Zeitgeist* and its peculiarities, and who, on the other, are keen enough in philosophic insight to discern its fundamental errors, and strong enough in philosophic virtue to apply the remedial measures. Only those thinkers who, like Aquinas, are vibrating with the life-pulse of their age, can lead profitable discussion at the roundtable, from the lecture platform, in the literary circle. For these are the marks of a vital and personalistic philosophy: when it becomes the food and very sustenance of the mind; when it presents reasonable answers to our difficulties; when it fortifies us against the mistakes of the past; when it gives us an earnest of peace and harmonious living for the future. With a wisdom such as this we shall be protected against our own selfish inversions which would shut us off from communication with our own fellow men. . . . If our thinking is vital and responsive to the needs of the times, if it is penetrating and developed from the wells of knowledge within us, it is hardly too much to expect that our diction will largely take care of itself. In any event, the thing of capital import is the precious deposit of truth which we possess and which, to be effective, must be critically expounded and developed with insight and originality.[75]

Ever conscious of the problems before the modern scientific mind, Father Michel never really abandoned his cherished plan of writing several manuals. His reviews of current philosophical texts, Scholastic and non-Scholastic, show that he was very dissatisfied with them.

Especially was this true of textbooks on ethics. On the one hand, Scholastic manuals, he emphasized, contained theological presuppositions in a world that had in large part rejected the supernatural. In a word, they were not truly or exclusively philosophical, and thus had little appeal to the modern, non-Catholic intellectual who believed Catholics began from theological premises. Nor did they meet pressing problems in a changing world — as if these did not exist. For instance, they said nothing of labor as a title to ownership.

Furthermore, nearly all of these textbooks in ethics were based on the second part of the *Summa Theologica*. But St. Thomas had not written a strictly philosophical treatise on human conduct. In a time when religion permeated culture and life, such a treatise was unnecessary. "Such is decidedly not the case in our day," Father Virgil wrote in 1928. "Today a philosophical ethics is one of the most acute needs of the Scholastic synthesis." [76] On the other hand, manuals of ethical science by those who had more or less abandoned the supernatural often amounted to "merely a statistical or otherwise descriptive study of how men act." [77] Having read the works of his secular contemporaries and employed from these what would strengthen his own position, he composed his *Philosophy of Human Conduct*,[78] an attempt at a purely rational ethics for senior college students. This was a distinct effort to meet the modern mind in terms of the theories and philosophies of life of the past and especially of the present. Michel discussed the basic obligations of human conduct in a way that leads up to, rather than presupposes, theism. He quoted non-Scholastic philosophers almost exclusively, often with approval, always with sympathy. His procedure was original and truly philosophical.

Similarly unhappy about texts in rational psychology, he wrote a 258-page manuscript, but he died before he could revise it for publication.[79] While at Louvain he had seriously begun a similar effort in cosmology. His classmate, Gerald Phelan, who knew its plan, remarked, "What a pity that the project could not have been brought to fruition!" [80]

Pleading for more articles in 1936, John K. Ryan, editor of *New Scholasticism,* wrote to Michel, "Your articles in the earlier volumes were very well received when they appeared." [81] Some remarks, therefore, should be made about the more important ones.

Because John Dewey was, in Father Virgil's words of 1929, "the philosophical spokesman of the civilization of today and tomorrow" and the "acknowledged dean of American philosophers, an outstanding liberal," and an ultra-modern, it is not surprising that he should have periodically analyzed Dewey's thought. He read him avidly and aimed to show how that philosopher-educator's "thought must be of interest to every Scholastic." In 1930 Dom Virgil called attention to a growing "Dewey-cult" among a certain group of educators who engaged in a "most artless ipse-dixitism" which was itself quite unlike Dewey. On the other hand, Michel considered Dewey's insistence that being aware of problems initiated thought, a basic and fertile principle of educational theory. He endorsed Dewey's statement, "Creative activity is our great need; but criticism, self-criticism, is the road to its release." [82] He noted Dewey's change from being an almost complete reactionary to turning to a more positive attitude, even a constructive one. Precisely the challenging work of moderns like Dewey made self-criticism in philosophical and educational thought most necessary for Catholics. While pointing out Dewey's errors and shortcomings, Dom Michel warned Catholic philosophers and educators not to underestimate the sage of Columbia. Dewey was not to be refuted by pat answers to pat questions found in Catholic textbooks of the day. Father Virgil concluded one article with a familiar appeal: Leading thinkers of the day must never be ignored; that was why one must approach "a vigorous and bold thinker" such as Dewey, like all others, "without a pre-formed attitude of either sympathy or antipathy, in order to gain from them the grain of truth that is ever the united quest of all." [83]

"Why Scholastic Philosophy Lives," published in the *Philosophical Review* in 1927, was a closely reasoned argument to win the attention of secular philosophers to the value of the *philosophia perennis*. Michel took pains to distinguish the *philosophia perennis* from the decadent and discredited Scholasticism of the fourteenth and following centuries. He reviewed the Scholastic and Aristotelian revival in in the various countries. Admitting an "almost complete absence" of such a revival in English-speaking countries until very recent years, he tried to show how a sound Scholasticism was only then showing signs of life in these countries. While defending the values of such a renaissance, he refuted the common charge or facile assumption in vogue, namely that Scholasticism was to be equated with "philosophical authoritarianism." Such authoritarianism, he contended, is anything but Thomistic:

> Scholasticism, if true to its principles, is the growth of life. . . . Because of such vitality, it is supremely adaptable

to different times and interests. Having a place for every question, it can enter into the investigation of any problem. . . . True scholasticism cannot but vibrate with the zest of the tried explorer. Problems along the whole front! When was there ever greater incentive? How like the situation in which a true Scholastic spirit six or seven centuries ago wrought and fought! [84]

As has already been shown in connection with his article "Towards a Vital Philosophy" written a decade later, American Thomists apparently did not take up the challenge Father Virgil set before them in 1927.

But Virgil Michel, the philosopher wrestling with modern problems, was at his best in a lengthy essay, "Liberalism Yesterday and Tomorrow," written in 1937 but published posthumously in *Ethics*.[85] With a cogent logic he traced the origin, nature, and evolution, as well as the social, economic, political, and spiritual effects of classical liberalism. He came to this conclusion: liberalism is morally bankrupt. It had indeed been tried and found wanting. Could there be greater proof than the confusion of modern thought and the general chaotic conditions in contemporary society? But there was more proof. By his characteristic way of quoting past and contemporary philosophers, including the prime leader, Dewey, Dom Virgil demonstrated how inconsistent they were. For instance, during the depression they advocated what previously they had vociferously and apodictically deplored in the name of the same liberalism. Formerly the liberal gospel was: government, hands-off business; now they spoke for government intervention in economic life, and some so-called liberals went so far as to counsel putting business into the hands of government with hardly a thought of the ultimate repercussions on human freedom. The naively assumed pre-established harmony of social life (going back to Rousseau, Smith, *et al.*) had called for each individual's "freedom" to seek only his own enlightened and unfettered self-interest; in the final analysis this would automatically assure a maximum of good for all. Actually, Michel explained, this had led ultimately to a maximum of exploitation of all by each. What better witness for this was there than the obvious maldistribution of wealth, the pyramiding of holding companies, the presumed absolute right of ownership over human rights, the millions of unemployed, the poverty and suffering in the midst of a potential plenty for all? Meanwhile the communists — to say nothing of the fascists — were quietly preparing to snuff out all human values and freedom. Indeed, the old style liberalism was dying—or rather it was already dead.

Again, freedom and equality had been liberalism's watchwords, never more employed than in the field of politics. Father Michel observed:

Here, however, a fundamental error was committed whose effects came to light only in the course of time. The political enfranchisement of the individual, it was thought, would *ipso facto* guarantee his freedom in every way. And yet it was precisely in the political field that the artificial abstractionism, so to say, of individualistic liberalism tended to dehumanize and depersonalize man most completely. The individual became an abstract citizen, a political animal in separation from all the other aspects of his being, his family relations, economic, and the like, divorced from his traditional culture. As a citizen with a vote he counted simply as a mathematical unit. Thus a concept of man that was both artificial and unnatural was basic to the new political liberalism. Man is properly not an isolated individual but a man living in a society of his fellowmen, a member of a family, of a community, of an economic order or profession, etc., with abundant cultural and religious interests and interrelations. He is in a multiple manner a functional being in society. All these relations were ignored and he was *de facto* considered simply a numerical but very abstract individual. . . . Is there any wonder that recently the plea could be made from on high and pressure brought to bear in order to have honorable United States senators bury their differences and their intelligence on a significant public question such as support of, or opposition to, the President's court plan merely in order to show a unified party front, the so-called "party loyalty?" Why not, indeed, unite politically in spite of differences of conviction if the citizen is merely an abstract political animal, a sort of neutral atom as far as all higher values go?[86]

He went on to show, among other things, how freedom without responsibility and moral obligation was illusory and contradictory. Exploitative capitalism was "distinctly the child of liberalism." The latter had falsely hoped to achieve an attitude or ideal (freedom of man) with a materialistic philosophy of life. So too the rationalism, individualism, and naturalism of liberalism had swept moral and religious values out of home, school, and society, thus secularizing them. Now that the assumption of the pre-established harmony of individual and social interests had been exploded, Father Virgil indicated that human life must be anchored in moral and positive values and ideals; that the currently recommended governmental regulation of socio-economic life entailed a scale and system of values, a philosophy of life; that actually every man — and laissez-faire liberals not the least — acts in view of a philosophy of life and a metaphysic of cosmic existence and finally, that communism, in its philosophical ideal at least, had retained the "unspoken philosophy of the original state of perfection of human nature" of nineteenth century individualism and liberalism, while — like bankrupt liberalism — looking "forward to an earthly paradise of anarchic individuals." He explained, moreover, the folly of belief in an inevitable social progress; the falsity of the Cartesian antithesis between matter and spirit, and the harm it had done. Personalism and the Christian ideal were elucidated as the mean between the extreme of individualism of past liberalism on the one hand, and of threatening impersonal collectivism on the other. The true nature and purpose of human liberty, the purpose of material things in human life were likewise clarified.

Was it not time for all men of good will to reconsider, to admit the mistakes of the past, to seek out the true nature of present problems and to work out together by laborious and constructive thinking a philosophy of human values based on commonly accepted moral principles and spiritual ideals? The liberals had boasted that human intelligence can and must direct human affairs; well and good, but only after liberal thinkers rid themselves of their fashionable philosophical idols, among them the denial of free will, the contempt for the past, the notion that thinking was hopelessly "conditioned or determined by blind impulse, feeling, the will-to-power, the unconscious, the subconscious, the libido, or what have you. . . ." Life is not truly human without liberty. And if the human mind cannot direct human affairs in the world, Dom Virgil reiterated, then obviously all is hopeless.

Speaking of communism and the enormous allied problem of human freedom in the modern world, Dom Virgil observed in 1937 that "never was it more incumbent upon all who share the liberal and Christian hope in human freedom and intelligent endeavor to give full thought to as big a problem as has ever confronted men in the course of history." Compared to the problem of communism and of the preservation of human freedom, he believed, all other philosophical problems shrank into insignificance. Yet, after reading current philosophical literature, Michel concluded, there seemed to him "no sign more indicative of philosophical sterility than the fact that the great majority of professional philosophers do not seem to think of even attacking the problem." [87]

"Liberalism Yesterday and Tomorrow" was one of Michel's finest pieces of writing. This article is a synthesis of his economic, political, and social philosophy. It demonstrates, as none other, his power to synthesize, the grasp he had of the temper of his times, and the effort he made to refute the errors of modern thinkers on their own grounds, while also appealing for their cooperation.

Bare mention can be made of other topics treated in Father Michel's philosophical writings. There was an interesting disquisition on pragmatism; [88] he dealt explicitly with the Aristotelian theory of matter and form; [89] he attempted to show the unsoundness of the idea of an organic superpersonality; [90] he concerned himself with the relations between religion, philosophy, and science.[91] His book reviews often contained his philosophical convictions and thinking on certain points as well as criticisms of the errors and inadequacies of current Scholastic textbooks. The reviews contain some of his best philosophical insights. In these reviews, furthermore, one can see him salvaging the elements of truth from secular philosophical books. There was no blind denunciation. Where refutation was necessary, it was always kindly — as one would expect from a Catholic philosopher for whom philosophy was an apostolate and who was forever looking for common ground.

Only his earlier mentioned and proposed speech to the American Philosophical Association, "Philosophy at the End of an Era" needs comment. Recalling Plato's definition of philosophy as the love and continuous seeking after wisdom, that is, an all-embracing synthesis including life-values, Dom Virgil indicated how, in the very name of modern philosophy, this concept of the philosopher as lover and guide to wisdom had been abandoned. Such was, in part, the fruit of rationalism. The trend of limiting the subject-matter of philosophy and of increasing analysis without the corresponding synthesis was only accentuated by the advent of positivism. The latter called for the mere application of intelligence to scientific data of immediate experience. After all, according to positivists, nothing else existed. Thus was shelved the whole realm of religious speculation, abstract metaphysics, a theory of values. Not only did the triumph of positivism limit the subject matter of traditional philosophy; modern philosophy aped scientific specialization to the extent of adopting the methods of empirical science. In this way modern scientists and philosophers lost perspective, closed their minds to many things and invited a death blow to the acquisition of wisdom. Philosophy, in fact, became in the minds of many "nothing more than a fringe of vague guesswork surrounding the natural sciences."

Again, positivistic philosophy had abandoned human values. How can there be truth and human values without permanent principles and a metaphysic of the universe? Due to the intense specialization of science without the safeguard of a wider synthesis, Dom Michel stated, the modern philosophical mentality is characterized 1) by the bland settling of age-old problems of philosophy by recourse to authority, e.g. Kant, Mill, Dewey, Aquinas, etc.; 2) by a vicious abstractionism and by the subsequent ridicule of philosophers who refuse to engage in such abstractionism; 3) by the employment of negative evidence as a basis to deny positive ideals; and not least, 4) by the prime vice of naturalism and materialism, twin fruits of positivistic rationalism. In this way must be explained the muddle of modern philosophy, the futility of discussions at formal meetings, and the philosophical bankruptcy best demonstrated by the lack of constructive suggestions and ideas for the solution of vexing problems in the world.

Michel did not undervalue the contribution and methods of empirical science. He defined the nature and the role of scientific method. But he emphasized that the processes by which facts are gathered do not contain the explanation and interpretation of these facts; such explanation and interpretation can be the fruit only of a wider synthesis; science should prepare the materials for a deeper and wider speculation. However, such speculation fell within the purview of philosophers with a reasoned synthesis. Their task it is to interpret intelligently the findings of science. In view of prevailing conditions, was there any wonder, he asked, that philosophy had lost almost all contact with life as men live it?

Hence, too, came the disparagement of philosophy in the universities and of the philosopher himself as a "professional crank," the prevalence of modern cynicism, pessimism, agnosticism, skepticism, the absence of faith in the supernatural, in reason, in self, in mankind. Philosophy has "lost its birthright as the liberator of man," he said, and in surrendering to science, "it is guilty of practically all that is now so often being laid to the blame of science by a disillusioned world," because philosophers gave up all leadership of living thought. Meanwhile science continued without guidance to forge the instruments of an ever greater chaos in modern society. Thus he concluded the manuscript, written in 1936:

The choice before philosophy is

either to enlighten by its wisdom the chaos of our life or else to follow subserviently the new lead of events as in the totalitarian states. In either case it now stands at the end of an era.[92]

In evaluating his philosophical thought, one can readily agree with his insistence that the whole Catholic intellectual apostolate suffers from poor philosophizing by Catholics, that the first requirement for the necessary internal reconstruction of society was clarity of correct thinking, that philosophy has missionary aspects, that no one really understands the temper of his age until he has grasped its thought-climate. But in his efforts to stimulate a revival of sound thought, to make the voice of reason heard in the anarchy and confusion of contemporary philosophy and to meet the modern mind, he was perhaps at times too "pragmatic" in his approach.

His writings touching the relation of philosophy to science do not assure one that he completely grasped the relation in all its ramifications.

One might say he relied too much on philosophy. However, if he did not always turn up the right answers to all the problems he uncovered, the reason was not that he failed to make bold, creative attempts by lifelong study inspired by the profound conviction that the hope of mankind, naturally speaking, lay only in the intelligent guidance of life as far as that is possible. Looking into the future in 1932, he predicted, "Such guidance is an imperative task today, and one that will tax to the utmost all the energies and patience the human race can muster." [93] No one will deny that this is still an imperative task at the present time. Michel's own efforts in this regard prompted Leo R. Ward, C.S.C., to observe in 1945:

To keep making and re-making a map of a truly human order fit for man's nature and his life in Christ — that is the task of every social philosopher worth his salt and of every social scientist. Of course, that was Virgil Michel's task, the bold attempt to work out such an order in theory and at the same time to keep his mind and hand not far removed from practice. I cannot easily name persons in this country who were more zealous at the work or more effective in doing something toward its realization."[94]

NOTES TO CHAPTER 10

[1] "Liturgy and Catholic Life," p. 129.

[2] *St. Thomas and Today* (St. Paul: Wanderer, 1936) , p. 9.

[3] Obviously this was not the *Christian Front* of the semi-fascist, Jew-baiting organization which later usurped the original title of the monthly magazine dedicated to Christian social reconstruction. The *Christian Front,* growing out of the ferment created by the Catholic Worker movement, began in January, 1936, changed its title to *Christian Social Action* in 1939, and ceased publication in July, 1942. The nine pamphlets on the social question first appeared as a column in the *Wanderer,* from May 10, 1934, to September 10, 1936. The *Wanderer,* a Catholic weekly published in St. Paul, was certainly one of the leading Catholic publications dealing with social action in the 1930's.

[4] *Christian Social Reconstruction* went through two editions and was chosen book of the week by the London *Catholic Herald.* Michel's series of nine pamphlets, like his other writings on the social question, enjoyed a considerable influence, as can be seen from these excerpts from his letters: "I looked through the copies and I think you have done excellent work! It is somewhat in the way the German *Volksverein* has spread our ideas through the Catholic and non-Catholic population. As things are at the present time — complicated, confused, without an outlet — it is necessary to come back to first principles, to state them in plain language, and to start afresh from them. That's what you have done. I think this is a great merit" (Goetz Briefs to Michel, Washington, Dec. 12, 1935). "I read some of them and like them so much that I took the whole set to a book binder to be bound in permanent form so that I might enjoy reading the entire series at my leisure. As I expected, the pamphlets are an excellent philosophical exposition of a decent society. In contrast to some parallel publications, they are not afraid to face fundamental issues. I think they are the best thing of their sort I have seen" (Furfey to Michel, Washington, Jan. 27, 1937). "I sincerely believe these pamphlets have done more to wake up an intelligent discussion of basic social concepts in small Catholic circles than volumes of heavy dissertations could have accomplished" (Alphonse Matt to Michel, St. Paul, Dec. 2, 1937). "They have been a great help to me in many ways, particularly in preparing certain

points in a little book on *Interracial Justice* which I hope to have out shortly" (LaFarge to Michel, New York, Jan. 21, 1937). "His pamphlets . . . were my Bible in those days" (Owen Rice to the present writer, Natona, Pa., Apr. 5, 1954). Maritain and Emannuel Mounier considered their translation into French (Mounier to Michel, Paris, Dec. 19, 1938).

[5] What called forth articles from Michel on key concepts was the frequent glib use of terminology by many without exact definition. Thus, in surveying periodical literature in 1936, he found only one attempt at a definition of social justice, that of John A. Ryan (cf. Michel, "Defining Social Justice," *Commonweal*, XXIII [1936], 425–426). Nor did Michel have much patience with loose statements such as this appearing in the *Catholic World*, "Christ was the first preacher of capitalism as a most workable thesis for society" (cf. Michel, "What Is Capitalism?" *Commonweal*, XXVIII [1938], 6–9).

[6] Cf. *Social Regeneration*, Social Justice Leaflet No. 9, n.p.g.

[7] "Mission of Catholic Thought," *American Catholic Quarterly Review*, XLVI (1921) 657, 662.

[8] "The Seed of Thought," *Central-Blatt and Social Justice*, XXX (1938), 371.

[9] Cf. Michel's keen analysis of the flush predepression period, especially of the impact of science and technology on civilization and human living as well as of his recommendations and warnings in a series of nine articles under the general title, "Modern Civilization," in the *Acolyte* from June 1 to September 21, 1929.

[10] *Human Rights* (St. Paul: Wanderer, 1935), 7.

[11] "What Is Capitalism," *Christian Front*, I (1936), 12. In this chapter references will be selective, in no way exhaustive; the reader will have no trouble finding additional references in Michel's bibliography. Cf. Michel's disagreements with O. Nell-Breuning on certain capitalist practices in "The Ethics of Exchange," *Central-Blatt and Social Justice*, XXI (1928), 235–237.

[12] Cf. *The Nature of Capitalism* and *Critique of Capitalism* (St. Paul: Wanderer, 1936). Michel defined the essence of the liberal, capitalist system "to be the unrestricted acquisition or accumulation of material wealth, to which all other relations and considerations are subservient" ("What is Capitalism?" *Commonweal*, XXVIII [1938], 7).

[13] *Christian Social Reconstruction*, p. 58.

[14] In this connection Michel quoted Keynes (*A Treatise on Money*, II, 405): "In recent years most people have become dissatisfied with the way in which the world manages its monetary affairs. Yet they distrust the remedies which are suggested. We do badly; but we do not know how to do better. I do not think that practical bankers are primarily blameworthy for this" (*Christian Social Reconstruction*, p. 60).

[15] *Ibid.*, pp. 45–61, and bibliography. For Michel's critique of Charles E. Coughlin's Union for Social Justice, cf. *Reconstruction Schemes* (St. Paul: *Wanderer*, 1936), pp. 37–43. Michel criticized Coughlin, among other reasons, for failing to make the elementary distinction between the corporative order and the corporative state ("The Corporative Order," *Christian Front*, III [1938], 155–157).

[16] "Capitalism, Ownership and Finance," in *Economics and Finance* (Collegeville: St. John's Abbey, 1936), p. 32.

[17] Cf. bibliography, but esp. *St. Thomas and Today* and *Ownership* (St. Paul: *Wanderer*, 1935), "Ownership and the Human Person," *Review of Politics,* I (1939) 155–178.

[18] "Ownership and Finance," *Christian Front,* I (1936), 77. On distributism, cf., e.g., *Reconstruction Schemes* (St. Paul: *Wanderer*, 1936), pp. 21–24.

[19] "Individualism and Its Social Effects," in *Social Concepts and Problems* (Collegeville: St. John's Abbey, 1936), p. 17.

[20] "The Labor Movement," *Commonweal*, XXVIII (1938), 148; cf. "What is Capitalism?" *Commonweal*, XXVIII (1938), 6–9. Michel's letters show that his provocative articles were well received, e.g., "I met many here who liked your article on capitalism. The formidable Dr. Gurian has required all his students to read it; and . . . he has said . . . that your work on *Christian Social Reconstruction* is the best book on that subject, not excepting anything in German" (Leo R. Ward, C.S.C., to Michel, Notre Dame, May 6, 1938). But they also brought him more work, e.g., "I am sending you a copy of my mimeographed economics text, *Economics and Society*. Knowing your reputation for realistic analysis, I should welcome your opinion on the contents" (John F. Cronin, S.S., to Michel, Baltimore, May 28, 1936).

[21] "The Labor Movement," *Commonweal*, XXVIII (1938), 148.

[22] *Critique of Capitalism,* p. 8. "Our future lies . . . not in a literal return to the past," Michel said before the onset of the depression, "but in the welding of the best of the present and of the past into a new civilization. And the best of the present has been its technological and scientific advance, while the best of the past [middle ages] is its spiritual and ideal outlook upon life, its universal grasp of the meaning of life" ("The Church on the Morrow," *Acolyte*, June 1, 1929).

[23] "The Spirit of Capitalism," *Christian Front,* I (1936), 23.

[24] "What is Capitalism?" *Commonweal*, XXVIII (1938), 9.

[25] *Christian Social Reconstruction,* p. 91.

[26] Cf. *ibid.,* pp. 91–108, *passim,* and articles in bibliography: "I am glad you are going to print my article on the corporative order soon, since there is practically nothing like it in print so far" (Michel to Norman McKenna, Collegeville, Jan. 1, 1937); cf. McKenna to Michel, New York, Sept. 9, 1937; for John A. Ryan's writings on the subject, cf. Gearty, *op. cit.,* p. 287.

[27] Cf. G. J. Schnepp, S.M., "Let's Call it the Industry Council Plan," *America,* LXXVIII (1948), 572–574.

[28] "The Social Thought of Virgil Michel, O.S.B.," *American Catholic Sociological Review,* I (1940), 176.

[29] (New York: Longmans, 1938). Mounier was the founder of *L'esprit* in 1932 and the leader of a group of French intellectuals, Catholic and non-Catholic, who emphasized the primacy of human and spiritual values in human life; cf. Michel's introduction. Mounier and Michel became fast friends. Thus the French thinker wrote: "I don't know

what value this small book *(A Personalist Manifesto)* may have, but I believe it capable of awakening, beyond itself, some inner voices confronted by which its author would bow in humility. . . . Pray for us, for this Christian world gives us so many worries today. And what right have we to judge it? Being more conscious of its problems is not being better." After the translation of the *Manifesto:* "It is quite an imposing volume. I enjoy the linguistic alchemy of you Americans. . . . I look upon it not merely as a book but more as a brotherly message from friends scarcely known or guessed who have spent much labor on the work. . . . It seems to me that these pages, full as they are of insufficiencies, for which I must bear the responsibility, have now, as it were, been baptized by these hours spent in translating them, work interlaced with hours of prayer. . . . Shall I some day have the joy of thanking you by word of mouth? . . . Will you keep me posted concerning your success or failure? I have noticed some brochures and a book of yours. . . . They seem quite a venture and full of interest. We are considering the project of translating them. . . . Who is this Furfey whose article on 'Catholic Extremism' I am reading? Our great opportunity is to know that we shall bring the Christian idea to the forefront of the modern world, not by compromise and liberalism, as our fathers attempted . . . but by an undiluted Christianity and by our own searching into its depths" (from Mounier's letters Dec. 18, 1936, to Dec. 19, 1938). Shocked by Michel's death, Mounier wrote, "He offered benevolent friendship to me, and his ever more cordial letters made him as present to me as if I had always known him. This same Nov. 26, when he rendered his soul to God, there came from him a charming work, a souvenir for my little girl, who this same day gave us such anguish because of meningitis. . . . I hope that the loss of my friend will not interrupt the spiritual bond which links me to your abbey" (Mounier to Deutsch, Paris, Dec. 27, 1938).

[30] "The Corporative Order I," *Christian Front,* II (1937), 75.

[31] "The Corporative Order II," *ibid.,* 96–97.

[32] "The Corporative Order," *Christian Social Action,* V (1940), 144. In this posthumously published article, Michel revealed the nature and aim of much of his social writings: "Here all we can do is to emphasize some of these ideas and principles in the hope that they may be firmly implanted in the minds of many young Christian apostles and may germinate and grow in due time" *(idem).*

[33] *Social Regeneration,* Social Justice Leaflet No. 9, n.p.g.

[34] "The Corporative Order III," *Christian Front,* III (1938), 157.

[35] "The Corporative Order II," *Christian Front,* II (1937), 96–97.

[36] "Ownership and the Human Person," *Review of Politics,* I (1939), 156.

[37] Cf., e.g., Michel's articles in the 1920's and the social question series — *passim* — with books, dates, and findings in Delbert C. Miller and William H. Form, *Industrial Sociology* (New York: Harper, 1951), pp. 3–85. It seems to have taken industrial sociologists a long time to discover that man is a social being whether he recreates, works, or worships.

[38] *A Personalist Manifesto,* xv-xvi.

[39] Cf., e.g., "The Corporative Order," *Christian Social Action*, V (1940) 144–145; "Liberalism Yesterday and Tomorrow," *Ethics*, XLVIII (1939), 417–434, *passim;* "Facts About Capitalism," *Commonweal*, XXV (1937), 541–543. By the distinction between "individual" and "person" Michel meant that a human being is never just an individual nor merely a member of a society or community, but both.

[40] P. xi.

[41] "Dehumanization of Property," *Free America*, II (1938), 16.

[42] *A Personalist Manifesto*, p. 277.

[43] Hynes, *op. cit.*, p. 179.

[44] The title of the manuscript was "Catholics and the Catholic Spirit," rejected because the editors had just accepted a similar one by Prince Hubertus Loewenstein (Joseph Barber, Jr., to Michel, Boston, July 18, 1938); cf. Loewenstein, "Catholicism at the Crossroads," *Atlantic Monthly*, CLXII (1938), 325–330; this article gives a good picture of the confusion existing in the political world at the time and is much less favorable towards the Church than Michel's. In citing examples of gross errors about the Church appearing in prominent literature, Michel mentions one in *Ethics*, five in the *New Republic*, and more from prominent books, including Dr. Franz Alexander's ridiculous statement about Scholasticism in his introduction to Mortimer Adler's *What Man Has Made of Man* (p. xvi). Concerning Alexander's remarks, Michel observed: "Should not a university whose honored faculty member makes such completely obscurantist statements cry out in anguish against him? Worst of all, this statement also was made in the very name of scientific truth. If that is our modern enlightenment, then 'Good Night' indeed, for the new dark ages are upon us!" (p. 5).

[45] "Catholics and the Catholic Spirit," pp. 26–27. In defense of the Church Michel said: "I venture to say that there is no large body of people today in which there is so much frank and articulate self-criticism as within the body of Catholics" *(idem).*

[46] "Surely, the pro-Franco Catholic of mature thought should be able at this stage of the war to put in a demurer to the Franco policy which refused regional autonomy to the Basques and Catalans from the very beginning, insisting instead on complete national unity, and which lately has begun to suppress the Basque language. This is in every way contrary to Catholic ideals. Likewise must he demur at the shooting of so many Basque priests by Franco in the earlier part of the war, the use of churches as military defenses, the bombing behind the lines (which elicited a plea from the Pope), the juxtaposition in public places of the trinitarian pictures of Franco, Mussolini, and Hitler, political executions like that of the prominent Catholic democrat and intellectual, Carrasco Formiguera, after thirteen months of imprisonment and in spite of the many requests for reprieve also from members of the hierarchy." Michel believed the Swiss (cf. London *Catholic Herald,* Jan. 21, 1938) and French hierarchies' policy of neutrality a wise one *(ibid.,* p. 25).

[47] *Ibid.*, pp. 22–23. Michel believed that the majority of Catholics outside of Spain were anti-Franco at the beginning of the war and then

(uncritical of Franco tactics) swung over when the butchery of nuns and priests began, a brutal fact, he pointed out, scandalously unreported by the secular press.

[48] *Ibid.*, p. 32; cf. "Political Catholicism," *OF*, XIII (1938), 79–81. This view of Church-state relations had been more or less outlined in Maritain's *Freedom in the Modern World* (New York: Scribner, 1936), which Michel quoted and by which he was most likely influenced; certainly Michel's views on Church and state presented in "Catholics and the Catholic Spirit" represented a development in his thinking, for earlier — e.g. *The Christian in the World,* pp. 154–167 — he gives the more traditional view. However, cf. his advanced ideas of a decade earlier in "The Church in Time," *Placidian*, IV (1927), 247–250; 313–316.

[49] "Catholics and the Catholic Spirit," pp. 33–34.

[50] In 1938 Michel asked, "Was there an indirect rebuke of emotional Catholic anti-communists in the Pope's words to Cardinal Verdier, repeated in the latter's [sic] Christmas message, in which the Pope told the communists that Catholics could not join with them because of fundamental doctrinal differences, but that they would exercise towards them the charity of Christ? 'In the name of Christ, who loves you, we greet you!'" ("Catholics and the Catholic Spirit," p. 13).

[51] "The Fight against Communism," *OF*, XI (1936), 125–126.

[52] Michel to Skillin, Collegeville, July 11, 1938, copy; cf. also, *The Christian in the World*, pp. 167–196, esp. 178–185; "War or Peace," *Acolyte*, August 10, 1929. The pacifist atmosphere prevailing in the 1930's can perhaps best be seen from an excerpt in Archbishop John T. McNicholas' lenten pastoral of 1938 which Michel quoted for consideration: "There is the very practical question of informed Christians who acknowledge the supreme domination of God and the divine toleration of governments that reject and ignore God: Will such Christians in our country form a mighty league of conscientious non-combatants? The organization of such a league deserves the serious consideration of all informed Christians who have the best interests of America at heart" (*The Christian in the World*, p. 185).

[53] Cf. *The Christian in the World*, pp. 167–196. "Internationalism," in *Political Theories and Forms* (Collegeville: St. John's Abbey, 1937), pp. 82–88; in the light of what happened after Michel's death in 1938, the reader will find in these pages some prophetic observations.

[54] *The Christian in the World*, pp. 171–172; "Internationalism," in *Political Theories and Forms* (Collegeville: St. John's Abbey, 1937), pp. 83–88.

[55] "Social Injustices," *OF*, XI (1936), 79.

[56] Foreword to *A Personalist Manifesto*, p. xii.

[57] "Will Anti-Clericalism Increase in the United States?" *Ecclesiastical Review*, XCVI (1937), 284–290. Michel (anonymously) tried to indicate how secularism had infiltrated even into the ranks of the clergy in "Secular Culture Capturing Christian Minds," *ibid.*, pp. 65–66.

[58] *Ideals of Reconstruction* (St. Paul: Wanderer, 1936), p. 43.

[59] *Ibid.*, p. 44.

[60] Cf. e.g., *American Catholic Sociological Review*, I and II (1938–41).

[61] "The Seed of Thought," *Central-Blatt and Social Justice*, XXX (1938), 371–373.

[62] Collegeville, Jan. 23, 1936, copy; Perry's answer was not found.

[63] *The Church Today* (Chicago: Fides, 1953), p. 139; cf. Michel, "A New Manual of the History of Philosophy," *Fortnightly Review*, XXXIV (1927), 412.

[64] *American Catholic Quarterly Review*, XLVI (1921), 657–661.

[65] *New Scholasticism*, XI (1937), 128–139.

[66] "Mission of Catholic Thought," *American Catholic Quarterly Review*, XLVI (1921), 657, 661. Written before the American neo-Scholastic movement was organized, this article presents a good picture of the status of philosophy in Catholic schools at that time, etc.

[67] *Ibid.*, p. 662; cf. "Intellectual Confusion Today and Philosophia Perennis," *Fortnightly Review*, XXXIII (1926), 211.

[68] *The Natural Law, According to St. Thomas and Suarez* (Sussex: St. Dominic's Press, 1930), in *New Scholasticism*, VI (1952), 72–76.

[69] Collegeville, Nov. 11, 1938, copy; Michel had entitled his essay "Thomas of Aquin: Then and Now," but it appeared as "Troubadour of Truth," *Essays in Thomism* (New York: Sheed & Ward, 1942), pp. 1–24; the first draft of this essay is in the Michel Papers; Michel had submitted his final copy for Brennan's editing before November 15, 1938: "You have been good in replying so promptly with your excellent chapter . . ." (Brennan to Michel, Providence, Nov. 15, 1938). The exchange of letters between Brennan and Michel began February 11, 1938, and ended with Michel's death.

[70] "Father Virgil the Philosopher," *OF*, XIII (1939), p. 121.

[71] *University of Toronto Quarterly*, VI (1937), 280–281; this was a passing observation, not a criticism of Gilson's book. Cf. Michel's interesting remarks concerning Gilson's concept of a Christian philosophy.

[72] "Towards a Vital Philosophy," p. 136. "Examine the textbooks of ethics that have come out in the past years under the rising star of neo-scholastic thought, and the smugness of conviction, the lack of fathoming difficulties and problems or rather the total absence of any suspicion that problems exist, the facile marshalling of arguments that are supposed to be devastating in their telling force, will tell their own tale" (*idem*, p. 133).

[73] *Ibid.*, 132. Michel in this article cited philosophical errors from current books by Catholics, especially from *Liberty, Its Use and Abuse* by Ignatius Cox, S.J. Michel and Cox exchanged several heated letters over the affair.

[74] *Ibid.*, p. 139; Michel cited two books by Maritain as examples of a vital philosophy and Gilson's *The Spirit of Medieval Philosophy* as convincingly presenting medieval thought.

[75] *Essays in Thomism*, pp. 20–22.

[76] "Reflections on a Scholastic Synthesis," *New Scholasticism*, II (1928), 17. In this article Michel presented his ideas as to the order in which the various branches of philosophy might be taught.

[77] "Some Fundamentals of Ethics," *New Scholasticism,* IV (1930), 242. In this article, in "The Metaphysical Foundations of Moral Obligation," American Catholic Philosophical Association: *Proceedings* (1928), pp. 29–44, in the article mentioned in the preceding footnote, and in a number of book reviews Michel spells out his ideas of the needed manual of rational ethics.

[78] (Minneapolis: Burgess, 1936); unfortunately not finding time to complete a definitive edition, he had to be satisfied with lithoprinted copies; cf. John A. Ryan's criticism of this when it first appeared in the form of notes: *New Scholasticism,* II (1928), 189–191.

[79] Cf. "Page the Psychologist," *Fortnightly Review,* XXXVI (1927), 22–23.

[80] *Op. cit.,* p. 118; Phelan gave a brief description of the proposed volume. In 1929 Michel noted that the editors of the Stonyhurst Series of popular philosophical manuals included no volume on cosmology since they thought it unnecessary: "And that in the heyday of controversy about evolution! Shades of Huxley and Mivart! The truth is that at that time — in the late nineties of the last century — the problems of cosmology were in an inextricable mess" ("Some Thoughts on Cosmology," *Fortnightly Review,* XXXVI [1929], 187).

[81] Ryan to Michel, Washington, Oct. 27, 1936. Thus Notre Dame's Professor Willis D. Nutting wrote to the present writer: "When I first came into the Church, twenty-three years ago, I was studying philosophy in the University of Iowa, and I used to read the back volumes of *New Scholasticism.* The articles by Virgil Michel that I found seemed to be about the only ones that attempted to be more than a rehashing of St. Thomas, and so I read them avidly. He seemed a person that dared to innovate, which was refreshing. . . . I think what I gained from him that I value most was the sense of the great freedom that exists in the Church. He seemed so perfectly willing to say he disagreed if he did. . . . I am sure that I would place Virgil Michel very high in the list of my masters. And I am very proud to claim to be his disciple in that part of his teaching that I knew" (South Bend, Oct. 18, 1953). The late Ignatius Smith, O.P., observed, "At meetings Father Michel always showed considerable originality and was a daring fellow; all wished he'd write more, but we knew he was too busy with other things" (interview, Washington, Dec. 4, 1952).

[82] Michel reviewing Dewey's *Construction and Criticism* (New York: Columbia, 1930), in *New Scholasticism,* VI (1932), 78.

[83] "Some Thoughts on Professor Dewey," *New Scholasticism,* II (1928), p. 341; cf. "Philosophy at Sea," *Acolyte,* Sept. 21, 1929, and "The Philosophy of John Dewey"; the latter is a twenty-six page manuscript on the first page of which Michel has the note, "Accepted by *Rivista neoscolastica* — never published?"; it was not found in the latter publication.

[84] Cf. "Why Scholastic Philosophy Lives," *Philosophical Review,* XXXVI (1927), 166–173. Realizing that Michel aimed this article at non-Catholic philosophers, one of his philosophical friend-critics remarked concerning it, "I am sure you are doing well. But do not let

adaptability and relativity make you forget the anchorage in necessity. What is needed today is simply metaphysics. You cannot give them too much of it. They are actually thirsting for it" (O'Mahoney to Michel, Louvain, n.d.).

[85] XLIX (1939), 417–434. The liberalism here condemned was not the non-philosophical, political and social liberalism frequently found in America.

[86] *Ibid.*, pp. 425–427.

[87] *Ibid.*, p. 428; cf. also "Ownership and the Human Person," *Review of Politics*, I (1939), 155–178, and Michel's review of Joad, *Matter, Life and Value* (New York: Oxford, 1929), in *New Scholasticism*, VI (1932), 144–154.

[88] "Christian Social Reconstruction," *Ethics*, XLVIII (1938), 444–446; cf. book reviews in the bibliography.

[89] "On the Theory of Matter and Form," *Ecclesiastical Review*, LXXIII (1925), 241–263.

[90] "Organic Superpersonality," *Philosophical Review*, XXXVI (1927), 178–180.

[91] Cf. nine articles under the general title of "Modern Civilization," in *Acolyte*, June 1 to Sept. 27, 1929; *The Christian in the World*, pp. 197–220. In the late 1920's Michel had been asked to give a paper on the relation of philosophy to science at a meeting of the American Catholic (?) Philosophical Association; he seems to have turned it down: "You have been invited to a very difficult task in being offered the Relations of Philosophy and Science. I must confess that for the moment I should not care to be asked to give the last word on it. But then I know your long experience and knowledge of the two sides — of science as well as of philosophy — would be an incomparable advantage. And your intellectual courage is not lacking" (O'Mahoney to Michel, Louvain, n.d.).

[92] "Philosophy at the End of an Era," p. 7; this manuscript was rejected by the *Philosophical Review* as "too hortatory" (G. Watts Cunningham to Michel, Ithaca, April 14, 1936).

[93] Michel reviewing Joad, *Matter, Life and Value* in *New Scholasticism*, VI (1932), 154.

[94] *Ourselves, Inc.* (New York: Harper, 1945), 71.

CHAPTER 11

IT ALL FITS TOGETHER

SO VARIED was Virgil Michel's thought and activity that it is difficult to gather even the major facets into an orderly whole. Before proceeding to outline his various apostolic activities, several preliminary observations are necessary. In the 1930's some prominent persons condemned abuses and called for reform while quietly remaining in their studies and doing little or nothing to implement in a practical way what they so eloquently preached. This was spoken of as "sanctified detachment." Such detachment hardly characterized Virgil Michel. In him knowledge, vision, and action seemed to be one. In 1928 he told the National Catholic Women's Union:

It has been stated that we Catholics are without zeal and initiative, that even in our external Catholic activities we are greatly imitative. We organize societies, scout movements, and the like in imitation of non-Catholic activities, instead of leading in all good work.[1]

Instead of copying, he urged, Catholics should lead, create, produce in all areas of activity — for God. The words, written in 1936, are a familiar refrain in his writings: "The besetting sin of our age has been a self-complacent apathy and inaction."[2] Michel's conception of the role Catholics should play in a pluralistic society is best stated in his own words; these words — among his last — may also explain his own diverse activities:

In a turning point of history so gigantic as ours is, there must needs be an era of fumbling and of experimentation, of

347

many individual currents all seeking to flow into the right direction. The Christian of today should condemn no movement that is not against Christian ideals. On the contrary he should take an interest in every such movement and do his part towards trying to bring the Christian principles in it to greater consciousness. This is the least, and for the present perhaps also the most, that the ordinary Christian can do towards contributing to the reconstruction of the social order that is the imperative task of the day.[3]

If, as Father Virgil frequently stressed, a vital understanding of the liturgy as the essential work of the Mystical Body tends to bring with it spiritual awakening and a social outlook; and if the liturgy also lends the strength to live and work for Christ in God's world — in short, to be apostles — one must investigate whether these assertions proved true, first in his own life, and then in the lives of those to whom he brought a similar spirit and vision.

In summarizing Michel's educational ideas, Mortimer J. Adler observed in 1939:
> He saw that upon the right reform of education depended the reconstruction of the social order. Educational matters were for him never merely academic questions. He knew that the rottenness of existing education reflected the decadence of modern culture itself.[4]

Certainly, as a personalist, Michel considered education one of the most vital factors in social change and betterment. Before attempting to describe his activities, a cursory examination of his philosophy of education is imperative. Education was truly a lifelong interest. And perhaps not the least of his contributions was his intelligent criticism of educational institutions. His appraisal of religious instruction as inadequate at all levels has already been considered and, too, his theological (liturgical) analysis of possible reasons why Catholic colleges failed to produce needed Catholic lay leadership.

Little has been said about Father Virgil's concept of the Benedictine vocation of prayer and work. His ideas on education stand out best perhaps against the background of what he believed to be an essential task for monks in the modern world. The stress of monastic pioneer days well-nigh ended, he detailed in 1929 for the National Benedictine Educational Association a long-range program of education and scholarship aiming at the rechristianization of society. For Michel the Benedictine abbey was anything but a relic or symbol of a better past. Each community should be a dynamo generating a genuine Christian spirituality; furthermore, it should be the center of a truly Christian culture and scholarship. The monks must frequently look beyond the monastic walls into the rest of God's world. Failure to do so could easily engender self-complacency.

The Benedictines, he admitted, had no special work — except that which was most needed in the Church at any particular time. In the previous fourteen centuries this had generally been a work of rechristianization, as was evidenced by the early missionary labors in Europe, by the Christian and agricultural education of the newly converted, by the process of christianizing the institutions of the Middle Ages, by the scholarly and literary endeavors of the Maurists. And what was the great need of the Church in the chaotic modern world? He answered: realistic efforts to build a Christian culture and society through education and scholarship suffused with the Christian spirit in all its comprehensiveness and perfection. Had not the Order of St. Benedict emerged, he asked, just as the primitive Christian spirit was being dissipated in the declining days of pagan Rome, as if the monks were providentially "to be the guardians of it in a changing world?"

The Benedictines were in a unique position to formulate a liberal arts program. Not only had they fourteen centuries of rich Christian tradition to fall back on, he reminded his fellow religious, but rooted in a community through the vow of stability, they could, by intelligently looking into the future, establish first-rate faculties. They had this added advantage: Living in community, being largely an on-campus, democratic family group all but perpetually in meeting and functioning as a committee of the whole, a Benedictine college faculty was in a unique position to realize Newman's ideal of a community of scholars.

Michel next outlined in terms of prevailing conditions the task before the Catholic educator. He analyzed the typical attitudes of the collegian of 1929 who had imbibed the naturalism, the Menckenism, and the paganism of the day.[5] As for the collegian's good qualities, Michel said, he was amiable and frank; if he was somewhat bold, he was also eager for knowledge, even though he was not quite prepared to do the necessary hard work of acquiring it. Having a good deal of worldly wisdom, he wanted "not merely to be told, but also to be shown." The questions he asked, the doubts and skepticism he expressed — these were evidence of the culture he had absorbed. Because he lacks a thorough knowledge of his faith, the Mass and spiritual exercises were largely matters of routine; they seemed formalistic to him and so affected him for the most part only externally; hence he often lived his life "not necessarily opposed to, but somewhat apart from, his religion." He exemplified the general pagan philosophy of life as found in literature, magazines, and movies of the day. And even if the collegians had not been affected by a false philosophy of life and a pagan atmosphere, the Catholic college had to cope with the latter, for its graduates would certainly meet them later.

More specifically, Michel continued, the social environment of 1929 was "frankly naturalistic," materialistic, indifferent to religion if not hostile, exemplifying an unbridled individualism. The Church appeared outmoded; she had failed. In a time of cutthroat competition there was little social responsibility. Self-realization was the ideal; unrestricted and individualistic self-expression, the means. Nevertheless, a certain reaction to the customary ideas of the past had also brought a degree of cynicism. But in any case, the main aim in life was to be unreservedly free in having a good time. Nor was this ever to be checked or measured in terms of a moral code or authority, for these would restrict liberty.

All these attitudes — and many more that he described — were found in varying degrees in the minds of Catholic college men. No longer, therefore, were the old educational methods sufficient, and certainly not the content of current education. The former compartmental knowledge resulting from so many hours of English, religion, science, classics was wholly inadequate. Religion, for instance, must not be left to religion classes as if the other classes were "non-religious classes" or "classes in non-religion"; it was necessary that Catholic principles and values of life pervade the whole student atmosphere and be brought to bear upon "*every* activity" of student life. Speaking of instilling an apostolic Christian mentality, Michel insisted, "Anything that separates action from knowledge is inadequate today, even more so than in the past."

And in this regard the modern Catholic student, he emphasized, must be shown not only *what* the Church teaches, but *why* — and why what she teaches is right, true, and good *today*. "New conditions of today," Dom Virgil reminded his fellow Benedictines, "also call for a new type of Catholic in the world." The graduate of current education he depicted as

the Catholic self-satisfied in his internal aloofness. External conditions of life do not disturb him because he does not reason about his life and his faith and he has no need of doing so. He is close to being egoistic in his self-righteousness. He is mentally intolerant of every non-Catholic and refuses even to find out anything further about his own faith. He is satisfied to believe what he has been authoritatively told to believe and to do what he has been told it is his duty to do. To go further than that in thought or action never enters his mind. Still less has he any social responsibility in regard to the truths of life he possesses. He is in no sense an apostle. As to the world about him — *videant consules!* And there is no sense whatever in which he wishes to be up-to-date.[6]

On the other hand, the Catholic college should aim to produce as an ideal product

the Catholic who is filled with apostolic zeal for a world bleeding out of many wounds — the lay apostle, the man of Catholic Action. He is fired with inspiration for the service of Christ. He carries the image of God truly in his heart, reflecting even the supremely divine principle that *bonum est diffusivum sui.* He partakes of Christ's own sympathy and charity for all mankind, and Christ's desire and willingness to help all others. For him the treasure of his Catholic faith is also a social responsibility. He keenly feels the need of being up-to-date in a very proper sense of the term.[7]

Obviously the next question was how to implement such an ideal. The first essential was a balanced and vitalized Catholic thought exhibiting the universal sympathy of Christ, even the Savior's attractiveness. Such a vital thought would not allow Catholic teachers to meet the general accusations launched against the Church by ridiculing them and then by "unqualifiedly extolling Catholic truth in terms of unbounded enthusiasm." Patiently and charitably the falsity of these objections must be faced and explained. And this, in turn, would demand a careful distinction between the divine and the human, the natural and the supernatural, the temporal and the eternal, elements in the Church. Human failings and mistakes in the history of the Church must be frankly admitted; it would not be enough, as in the past, only to explain her divine character and to overlook her human aspects. Then also the Catholic view of life should be presented against the background of modern materialism as the only way of satisfying both present and eternal needs of individual and social man; as the best answer to the needs and aspirations of human nature; as the only practicable and sensible philosophy of life for all men who desire a good life in this world as well as eternal salvation in the next.

The Catholic college teacher ought to be perspicacious and sympathetic enough to show how the supernatural fulfills, and takes into itself, and ennobles the best in the natural and human order. Grace builds on nature. Everything that exists has some good. Therefore, the faculty of a Catholic college must be ready to accept the best that the modern world of education and culture has to offer. Members of an alert college faculty will be in touch with life because they have a warm sympathy for all things human; they will be intelligently immersed in the problems of an ever-changing world; they will know its spirit, its errors, and aspirations, just as they will know the present and future needs of their students. Only then will they be able to show convincingly how the Christian plan of life includes in an harmonious whole the best that natural humanists and the world of science and technology have to offer — and incomparably more. The fruit of such enlightened teaching will be well-formed and integral Christians characterized by prudence, self-direction, and activity, by rational choice and a sense of values to meet and to measure the values of an unchristian world. Armed "with a charitably militant Catholic philosophy of life and an ideal of Catholic personality," such Catholic graduates will understand the necessity and reasonableness of order, obedience, and authority.

Again, every subject in the curriculum, whether cultural or vocational, and every teacher, whether lay or religious, must contribute to this educational work and environment. Any course which cannot be fitted into such a Catholic philosophy of liberal arts education should be dropped. Any teacher who cannot further such an ideal should be dismissed. Speaking of the manner in which even purely technical courses should be related to Christian values, Michel stated:

A Catholic's vocation is always something more than the narrow profession he is preparing for, i.e., more than mere technical knowledge as prescribed by the needs of that profession. Every Catholic also has the general profession and calling of being not only a citizen in this republic, but a member in the fellowship of souls, the Church, called the Mystical Body of Christ. And these three aspects are not so many separate compartments of the entire man, unrelated among themselves. They together make up the one man, and are strictly inseparable in him. His very profession must also be a service to his fellow-citizens and a service to God. Precisely therein lies some of the grandeur of the Catholic conception of life.[8]

But not only must every course aim at this ideal; not only is it necessary that every staff-member know thoroughly his role in the

whole educational plan as well as know his subject "from a to z"; he himself must live the Christian ideas and ideals he professes:
One of the characteristics of our age is that the good advice a man gives to others, or the ideals he tries to inculcate, will have a chance of acceptance only if he exemplifies them in his own person.[9]

Such goals for Catholic college education Virgil Michel held out to the National Benedictine Educational Association in 1929. He invited the members to the "gigantic" task of formulating "a vital philosophy of education — one that is in full sympathy with all the aspirations of human nature, and of our time, but also full of the true Christian spirit." This, he said, was "one of the most urgent works in the Church today." The job of working out a fully Catholic philosophy of education in terms also of curriculum and method was admittedly an enormous one; it called for a critical analysis of modern civilization and culture as well as the Catholic response, to say nothing of a rigorous re-examination of old and new methods. It demanded laborious work, detailed scientific studies, research, and scholarship "contributed bit by bit and gradually growing into what we are ultimately aiming at."

Certainly this was not the work of one monk nor even of one abbey, but of all spontaneously collaborating and cooperating in the typically Benedictine family spirit. The Association could be the forum for discussion; the frequently discussed Benedictine quarterly could publish the results of studies by specialists; it could circulate first within the various monastic families, and then, having achieved a degree of excellence, it could be offered to the wider public as a traditional Benedictine work. If American Benedictines have been remiss in contributing to Catholic higher education and scholarship and to the intellectual apostolate generally, it has not been due to the fact that one of their own did not outline almost thirty years ago a feasible program to remedy the situation. Meanwhile, the quarterly known as the *American Benedictine Review* established in 1950 continues to limp.

According to Michel, education must always grapple with actual problems. Consequently, educators must keep their ear close to "the ground of human life" to catch and interpret the significance of events. Only then can they make constructive suggestions and modifications to meet future as well as present problems in terms of the experience and wisdom of the past. Precisely because effective education must be forward-looking, complacency in educators can be disastrous.[10] Accordingly, in 1926, in two installments of an article entitled "Utopia Rediviva," [11] Father Virgil set down in some detail his ideas of liberal arts or general education, its content and method. In so doing he anticipated some of the ideas and ideals — especially as to method — propounded during the 1930's in the philosophy of education by President Robert Hutchins and associates at the University of Chicago.[12] "Utopia Rediviva" was really a critique of the whole educational system, from grade school through university. As usual, he offered criticism, both destructive and constructive, although his suggestions, particularly in regard to methods, were tentative and, therefore, open to debate. Only some highlights, intermeshed with bits from other articles, can be given here.

He began, characteristically, by examining the conditions and tendencies of the time. He noted that it was admittedly a period of transition, in which the ideas and standards of the past were questioned, while much of life was in an unsettled state. Naturally there was a certain curiosity as to what the future would bring. The undoubted theoretical and practical achievements of the natural sciences in the past two generations were, he said, "epoch-making," and they "*did* correct many past notions and ways of living." [13] A decade before, Dom Virgil observed, the past had been despised and the millenium awaited. Meanwhile, as the scientific method became gospel and philosophy of life for many, government and industry and even education became intensely organized and specialized. Because a few did the thinking, the many were spared this difficult mental operation. At least so it was assumed by some. But already there was a reaction among the more discerning. And reactions, unless halted, often beget extremes. There is a familiar ring in the words of the author whom Michel quoted:

> We have bottled and tinned and canned not merely our foods but in a subtle and sensitive machinery our labor and to a startling extent our very culture, our music, our drama. These are all provided for us vicariously.[14]

In view of the detailed mechanization and intense specialization of the educational process, Michel speculated as to how the liberal arts college might play its proper role in the transition then definitely in progress. Although he emphasized that the two are intimately related, he took up curriculum first and then methods.

Discerning a decided swing from the purely utilitarian to the cultural and humanistic in education, he asked whether a return to the more humanistic education could be reconciled with the modern growth of the natural sciences and the related mathematics. The answer, he said, depended on whether one lived in the past or in the present, or, in other words, it was a matter of one's definition of culture. He quoted this definition approvingly:

The worthy fruit of academic culture is an open mind, trained to careful thinking, instructed in the methods of philosophic investigation, acquainted in a general way with the accumulated thought of past generations, and penetrated with humility.[15]

To have an "open mind" one must have some appreciation of science. In Michel's words, "Science today has become such an intimate element of daily life, that without it no well-balanced cultural curriculum can be constructed. And this would be true even if scientific progress from this day forward were to cease."[16] To his mind, science definitely has cultural value, and he gave his reasons. But then, why had science in the college curriculum been taught from the purely utilitarian point of view? Had scientists become the victims of their method? Michel offered this explanation:

May the reason not, apart from the enormous practical utility of science, be this, that the scientists are as human as the rest of us and are as much as we the children of their generation? . . . We all have been affected by this atmosphere, and it may be for this reason that the cultural possibilities of the sciences were not better realized. Is not the very same true of the classics?[17]

A liberal arts curriculum, therefore, should include a certain amount of the natural sciences and mathematics without which one could hardly know "what is talked about in the educated world today." It must also contain history "in all its wider human aspects embracing everything that is included under social studies," even if in the name of a balanced culture some of the older classics would have to be dropped. Finally, the integrating principle, giving a synthetic grasp of the whole, could come only from the revival of philosophy. In this connection Michel's words may indicate not only how philosophy was taught in 1926 but also his own conception of its essential part in general education:

Nor can we any longer consider philosophy to be exhausted by logic, ethics, or an introductory course in problems, or an historical survey. . . . But this philosophy cannot be a mere memory exercise on a definite number of cut and dried theses, as has at times been the case, even in our seminaries. Such a course produces an undue self-satisfaction at the end of the course (for various reasons!), the attitude of having finished *something*. We might call philosophy the educated mentality in concentrated form, just as all higher education must be philosophical in the wider sense of the term.

Hence, like education, philosophy can never be really finished; it must go on forever. Philosophy in that sense might best be defined in terms of the mentality it is to engender, and it would then imply (1) an attitude of inquiry, as a natural "state" of mind: (2) ability to inquire, and some initial practice in method of inquiry over against uncritical study; (3) a synthesis of solutions to the problems of life that are, quantitatively, more or less tentative. Any one of these characteristics taken by itself hardly defines philosophy. Unfortunately philosophy often means only a definite set of solutions, a *Weltanschauung*, accepted in all its details once for all. . . . If the three are taken together, the essential relation between philosophy and higher education is at once apparent, as well as the relation of philosophy to life.[18]

This introduced the question of educational methods, which Father Virgil maintained had been very much neglected. Thus, in a time of transition, and despite considerable discussion on the inadequacy of educational procedures, he asserted that there were not five colleges in 1926 that were boldly experimenting in this regard. Education was the transmission to future generations of the wisdom and achievements of the past. These, however, may be transmitted either as "a living tradition, as a dynamic inspiration; or else as a collection of dead fossils, as products of the creative energies of the past"; or, what is worse, as "dead debris of the past as if it were the vitalizing inspiration of the present and the future." But this becomes "calamitous" when teachers are not even suspicious of the fact that they are "merely echoing a swan song of the dead or dying."[19] Rigid submission to system, specialization, quantitative standards, standardized routine, and slavish adherence to textbooks and manuals — to these Michel objected in "Utopia Rediviva" and in other articles. Certainly there was need of specialization, but to call it education was shortsighted. The elective system was no solution. For after choosing from a bewildering assortment of courses, the student fell into the hands of specialists for "scientific feeding" which often amounted to "spoon-feeding" — so many facts gathered, categorized, memorized, and mechanically returned in examinations. This was "education" by accretion rather than by inner growth and assimilation, by an active reliving and rethinking of the best of the past with an eye also on present life-problems.

Nor were students the only victims; the mechanistic educational system had the teachers also in its strangling mesh. Thus upper class teachers, owing to the requirements of specialization, were often shut up within the narrow confines of their own speciality. The broader aspects of life they could neither interpret nor judge; and if they did, they did so in terms of their specialty. Again, they might overlook or deny all else, make unwarranted judgments, or blindly repeat the opinions of others.[20] Hence, if education was an apprenticeship for life, if students were to be motivated to spontaneous activity and to acquire depth and perspective, a shake-up in the educational system was imperative. But Dom Virgil was realistic enough to see that "the changes cannot come without great difficulties, since we pride ourselves on our standardization."[21] Nonetheless, he sketched his "dream" college, quoting Cardinal Newman to buttress his arguments. Only a bare outline of this plan can be given here.

In the first two years of college, the student would be given the fundamental principles of English, language, history, science, and mathematics. Having acquired sufficient mental training and a general orientation, the student would continue his education in the final two years by self-activity in his field of concentration. Teachers would function as guides and consultors. Only one regular course would be offered in the last two years: a general course in the various branches of philosophy; other courses would be taught as needed, and the students would choose which courses to attend and under which professors to work. There would be no enforced class attendance; the privilege of remaining in college would be dependent on self-application, for as Michel stated, "ultimately real education must be self-propelled, and self-impelled to the greatest extent possible." But the program called for public disputations, for much informal association and discussion between students and teachers with kindred interests, for "in the realm of the mind communion as well as spontaneity is of the order of things." Incidentally, the college staff would have to include "broadly cultured teachers of wide sympathy and human understanding" as well as of a "wider experience in the things of mind and soul, possessing the optimism of a sound faith in God and man." The four years completed, degrees would be awarded after the student had proved in public defense that he had acquired sufficient wisdom to meet the problems of life. After working out the details, answering several objections, and showing what results a program like this produced in the universities of the Middle Ages, Father Michel admitted in 1926:

Our scheme must seem utopian to the average mind of today, and the objection naturally presents itself: it may be ideal but. . . . To which we may answer: Precisely so, and the prevalent system is *not* ideal. . . . It is however true that not all men are spiritual in their temperament; some are quite mechanical and very willing to take everything at second hand and without effort of their own. Still, if among the many that are attending our colleges there is only a small percentage that would eagerly welcome some such scheme as the above for satisfying their intellectual appetites, would there not be room somewhere for at least one college or for a few to try to measure up to such an ideal? [22]

In the 1930's much soul-searching took place among educators. As Father Virgil observed in 1936, "Today we are becoming frank even about the colossal failure of the gigantic and highly efficient system of modern education." [23] Nowhere was self-criticism more needed than in education, Michel thought, for education, too, had been depersonalized and become stifled by system.

In the 1930's the National Catholic Educational Association (NCEA) attempted to improve and re-accredit Catholic colleges already on its accredited list. Some Catholic educators then suggested that this be done more or less on the basis of criteria set up by secular regional accrediting agencies. In the case of the school of which Michel was dean, this would be the North Central Association of Colleges and Secondary Schools (NCA). Michel then wrote a critique of that procedure — "Let's Examine Ourselves" — [24] an address to the Minnesota Conference of Catholic Colleges, which he had helped to found and of which he was president at the time of his death.

Previously, in noting the evidence showing why graduates of Catholic colleges had lost their faith, Father Virgil offered as one explanation the observation that their Catholic teachers had imbibed secular values and views in secular (and even some Catholic) graduate schools. Speaking of such instructors in Catholic colleges, he explained:

Their faith is in one airtight compartment and their erudition in another, and never do the twain meet. Only thus can one understand the ardor with which some Catholic colleges have seemed to pursue only one aim, that of aping the secular institutions of learning in everything as much as possible.[25]

After stating that he was not criticizing persons but rather standards, he analyzed the questionnaires sent out by the NCEA in its program for the re-accreditation of Catholic colleges. These colleges had to reply to questionnaires and submit to an inspectional survey or be struck off the list of approved schools. If in general the material and quantitative ideals of the NCA were to be the measuring stick of Catholic education, then why have the NCEA or a Catholic college at all, he asked. And he went on to show that the NCA itself had become dissatisfied with its mechanical standards, and that even after revisions, some members of that Association were still dissatisfied. Yet here were Catholic educators relying on such standards as a gauge. To Dom Virgil it was "an assumption, almost monstrous . . . that the common denominator of standards accepted for a group of colleges of whom some are quite secular and others denominationally Christian is adequate for us." [26] Does not Catholic college education have specific and unique qualities that must permeate the whole educational system?

Nor could he accept the bland assumption by the NCEA that Catholic schools which had refused to join the NCA because of its predominantly material standards were for that reason inferior.

He pointed out the enormous, impersonal administrative problems, the mechanical, inhuman efficiency, of huge educational "plants." Big business methods in such institutions, the frequent absence of smaller self-determining and self-functioning units, dictation from above and blind conformism from below — these spell "the death of real education."

These institutions and their "efficient" methods the smaller colleges were expected to imitate. Unfortunately all too many of the latter were eager to do so, he said, whereas the ideal was the small college with its spontaneously cooperating faculty, in which educational goals were democratically discussed and commonly accepted and furthered throughout the whole educational process. But, he asked, was it not

typical of the age to act bigger than you were and to trample underfoot
human and personal values, which could be best cultivated and preserved in the small family college? In large, centralized institutions
criticism of method and ideals often spelled "sabotage of effective
machinery." And yet, "if educational ideals have anything at all to
do with mental and moral improvement, with intellectual and spiritual stimulation, then a healthy and vigorous questioning of accepted
methods and ideals is imperative." [27] The small college had a mission
all its own; but unfortunately the general educational tone was
largely set by the mechanistic pattern of impersonal educational cor-
porations specializing in mass education.

Of the questions in one questionnaire dealing with faculty competence, Michel believed only two had a direct bearing on the Catholic
college, while all the rest applied to secular institutions. But even
these two did not touch vital issues of Catholic education. Many of
the questions could have been asked twenty or thirty years ago. That
is, they failed to take into account the serious skepticism about past
educational ideals, methods, and mechanical standards, the existing
chaotic conditions in the world, the beginnings of a Catholic revival
spearheaded by the liturgical apostolate and its subsequent Catholic
Action. Nor did the authors of the questionnaire seem aware that
education must be forward-looking. As for hiring teachers, it was
implied that if they were Catholic, all was well, no matter what kind
of Catholics they might be. He then recalled how a teacher-friend
discovered that he had been teaching naturalism in a Catholic college
for ten years; how in a large midwestern Catholic university instructors of economics had been told not to become specific about *Quadragesimo anno* in class lest financial friends of the school should be
embarrassed. Should such a university have been struck off the list
of approved schools by the NCEA? Michel wanted to know. Further,
qualitative teaching was more or less overlooked, except for questions on supervision of teaching. Father Virgil thought methodic
supervision for a qualified college teacher beneath the dignity of
that profession.[28] Indeed, the questionnaires fitted the unwieldly
educational giants, not the "democratic family group" that had been
Newman's ideal, and which should be the ideal of every small Catholic college.

Again, a questionnaire had asked about the number of degrees, not
about graduate study. "Is it merely a personal quirk of mine," Michel
confessed, "that I have been fond of saying a person only begins to

deserve his degree (or not) after he has attained it? Do not many degreed persons show *post factum* that they never deserved a degree at all?" [29] This question was called forth by the assumption that good teaching is to be measured *per se* by degrees, theses, teachers' publications, and scholarship. Indeed, scholarship and command of subject are essential for good teaching; yet they constitute only a general condition *sine qua non*. They do not prove ability to teach; more than one scholar has failed in the classroom as teacher. In a word, faculty competence is also to be measured by genuine enthusiasm, personal interest, initiative, and constructive suggestions shown and given by teachers whose teaching is not just a job but a vocation. Or were teachers to be treated like supervised "hired servants" instead of "intelligent cooperators stimulated by one another and fully free to express their opinions and convictions" to administrators? Were teacher-loads such as to allow the faculty to read and to reflect?

Michel mentioned other questions that might have appeared in the questionnaire. As for religion classes: Were they still taught in the same old way, consisting in large part of apologetics or advanced catechism despite papal pleas for a revival of the liturgy and the training of lay leaders for Catholic Action? What schools were making intelligent efforts to revive the much-needed vital philosophy? Building a Catholic culture — that was the great need, and what educators had set themselves consciously to this task? In view of recent discussions about making Christian culture the core of the liberal arts course, it is worthwhile to record Michel's words of twenty years ago: "To what extent are we trying to develop a common background of Catholic culture in the face of modern paganism, a Christian synthesis shared in by every member of the faculty?" [30] Only a few schools, he implied, were boldly and creatively coming to grips with vexing current problems of an unjust social order. The NCEA questionnaires, he said, were further evidence that the number was small.

Finally, in scrutinizing the questionnaire on adequacy of library facilities Father Virgil found similar shortcomings. Here, too, real issues were ignored and a generally complacent copying of past secular standards was evidenced. It touched only externals. With the help of confrere Father Oliver Kapsner he was able to show that ninety per cent of the questionnaire had been lifted out of one prepared by the American Library Association, a questionnaire the NCA had found unsatisfactory and had rejected for more qualitative criteria. Yet, Catholic librarians were to gauge themselves by the discarded quan-

titative standards of the NCA. Michel concluded his discussion with
the following:

> If there is one thing we have ignored more than others
in our education, it seems to me to be the very obvious but also all-
important truth that education, both teaching and learning, is specifically a matter of the spirit. If we ignore that vital truth, then not
only will the phrase "Christian Education" contain a superfluous
qualifying adjective, but the very word *education* will cease to have
human significance.[31]

After reading Michel's published address and referring to the
Minnesota Conference of Catholic Colleges, the president of a well-
known Lutheran college in Minnesota wrote to him:

> I take my hat
off in admiration for what you Catholics are doing both in a church
way and in education. I only wish that we Lutherans could walk
in your footsteps in presenting our Lutheran philosophy of education,
if any. In the face of modern paganism, we that believe in Jesus
Christ and His Gospel will have to find ways in which we can stand
together, shoulder to shoulder, without necessarily sacrificing the convictions that we have as to particular truth.[32]

Under Michel's deanship, St. John's at Collegeville was accredited
to the University of Minnesota in 1938.[33]

Only some remarks can be made about Virgil Michel's other articles
and addresses on education. Speaking to the Minnesota Conference of
Colleges in 1927 on the subject of "Stimulating Intellectual Independence in Senior College Students," he defined the nature of
intellectual independence. Certainly a general and broad understanding of human problems, their various aspects and implications, is
essential. Then, against the background of the latest educational
theories, he described the methods by which independent personal
thinking can be cultivated. He remarked:

> Now I would submit that
the educated man, such as we expect the senior college graduate to
be, must be aware of this welter of confusing opinions and problems
of today and must see them in their present implications, in terms
of the life-values claimed for them; and again must see them in
their historical settings, in their antecedents and effects — and that
without losing his mental poise in the din of contradicting voices.
To achieve this poise, without which true intellectual independence
is not possible, unassisted, would seem to require years of intellectual
digesting.[34]

He mentioned, moreover, five broad courses of synthesis, and the changes in method that were necessary if an unbalanced judgment of the problems of life and a sense of narrow self-sufficiency were to be avoided. Instructors should not impose their opinions and solutions upon the students; it is much better to analyze with them pertinent issues in all their breadth and depth. For Michel believed that in the classroom as in other areas of life there must be active and intelligent participation. The vital teacher should present thought-situations that elicit a creative search for answers — but answers, again, which lead to more questions and more investigation. Dom Virgil came to the conclusion that intellectual independence results "chiefly from contact with minds possessed by it." These words describe Michel the teacher:

The teacher must not compel by the force of magnetic personality or hypnotize by the momentum of one-sided enthusiasm, but lead on, as it were, by silent example, in so far as he will lead mainly by how he does things and by the atmosphere he diffuses.[35]

In an essay on "The Role of Authority" Michel admits that "discipline is of the very essence of education . . . it strikes at the very heart of the purpose of education."[36] But genuine, human discipline is the fruit of good teaching. He depicted the role of the teacher in various impersonations of authority and traced the effects of such impersonations on the students in the classroom and in later life. Like Christ the effective teacher has a sympathy for all things human and creates an atmosphere of winning reasonableness.

"Are we Educating Moral Parasites?" written in 1927, was the application of the philosophy of personalism to the training and education of the human being in an enticing, secularized culture, from the necessary dependency of childhood, through the inevitable unsteadiness of adolescence, to the rich and responsible personality of adulthood. Sound education, he wrote, is not indoctrination nor is it "a struggle for overlordship." To educate is more than merely to instruct:

Our training of youth often seems quite ignorant of the fact that the aim of the training must be the development of persons, men that are exercised in the use of reason and will, that have become accustomed to controlling their other tendencies by their higher ideals and faculties.[37]

Early and frequently Dom Virgil warned of the worldwide swing toward totalitarianism as an inevitable reaction to selfish individualism. In 1935 he maintained that the world's problems for a long time to come would be predominantly political; that is to say, while they were basically spiritual, they would have to be solved by and large in the political arena. After tracing the great political changes since 1918 and their significance, he remarked that while the present trend of events would seem to be obvious, "yet the best of intellects seem to be entirely ignorant of the goal towards which we are rushing. What is worse, they no longer profess to know the goal to which we should be traveling." Hence the imperative need for strengthened political science courses in Catholic colleges. He concluded:

Today it is necessary, above all, not merely to espouse or champion a solution, but to be grounded more than ever in the principles underlying any solution. We need to go back to the first principles of all sound political philosophy to separate them from their historical settings, so that we can view them again in their original purity. Only then can we hope to re-digest them as we must, and apply them with more chance of success and accuracy to the new conditions of our social life of today. . . . Such principles are by no means confined to the sphere of revealed religious truth. They include all the Christian heritage of human wisdom and thought — and are rooted in the traditional personal and social values and ideals that have been the growing achievement of the best thinkers of the Christian past. In these we must ground our students firmly. The college graduate of today must emerge secure in his possession and in a knowledge of the conditions of life today such as is adequate to allow him to enter with other men of thought upon the momentous task of applying these principles to these conditions. Without this attainment, the education of the college graduate of today is incomplete. And the attainment is incomplete today without a good knowledge of political science, of the present political set-up, of the historical developments that led up to it, and of the fundamental principles of social philosophy or social ethics.[38]

"Education for Tomorrow" was among the last of Michel's articles on a favorite subject. If a narrow specialization — the primary characteristic of all higher education — was not the greatest evil of modern education, it was at least responsible in part for removing the educative process from what he termed life as a whole. Speaking in 1938 of higher education in general, he maintained:

Our present education is distinctly the product of our bourgeois mind, of extreme self-complacency above all else. . . . We are at the end of an era. . . . Yet our educational efforts of today, and the predominant body of educators today, are still transmitting the cultural attitudes they learned in their own generation, the materialistic liberalism and individualism, with which our curricula and textbooks are completely imbued. In other words, our schools are but intermittent museums in which ideals and facts of a dead past are held to view. They are as little vital and inspirational as our art museums, when these become the normal burial places to which art is relegated.[39]

He went on to deplore the fact that curricula, in village and country, were completely "citified"; such curricula tended to make all students city-minded and nostalgic for the good old, easy-money, predepression days, which, he said, were neither good nor old. The fact was obvious to thinking men that highly centralized and mechanized city living is not conducive to the best ideals of traditional Christianity and family life.

Must all big city dwellers then strike out for the country and start plowing? No; but it was a fact that in decentralized urban-rural communities there could now be fostered and preserved — thanks to science and technology — all the material and cultural values formerly associated with highly concentrated populations.[40] "In so far as schools do not take this prime fact of modern progress into account," he said, "they are definite burial places of the . . . fossils of an irreversible past." And the devitalization of education would continue so long as teachers failed to make the best of the past and present their own, so that they could hand it on as a living tradition — indeed rooted in the past but always refined and transformed by present human experience — in schools vitally in contact with their environment as well as with the peculiarities and trends of current civilization and culture. Only in this way could educators be inspirationally forward-looking and in touch with life and life's problems, and therefore also — in so far as humanly possible — provide for an uncertain future. And then also the school would creatively mould culture rather than be, as he said many were, "an isolated curio in the neighborhood or a temporary refuge from life."[41]

If Virgil Michel had been satisfied with doing no more than enunciating criticism of the educational system, he might, perhaps, be charged with a sort of sanctified detachment. But, as in other matters, so in education, he translated his ideas into action. A word must be said, therefore, concerning a two-year seminar, which he began in the fall of 1936 and which he called "Catholic Backgrounds and

Current Social Theory." The experiment would seem to have been unique for that time. In any case, it was a practical illustration of Michel's educational method. Conducted entirely on the basis of mutual cooperation and exchange according to the ideal pattern set down by Cardinal Newman for a true university, this seminar for select senior college students was meant to arouse and to form active Catholic laymen by having them inquire into the nature and function of a living Catholic culture vis-à-vis modern secularism. Besides scrutinizing current socio-economic theory and analyzing the true nature of modern civilization and its antecedents, members of the seminar studied the writings of thinkers like Mounier, Dawson, and Maritain. They reviewed books by prominent non-Catholics in order to develop a sympathetic understanding for their point of view. Moreover, they examined the various branches of the Jocist movement, the cooperative movement, the *Catholic Worker*, the Catholic Rural Life Conference, and the personalist and liturgical aims and endeavors. Into the round table discussion Michel inserted the pertinent principles of Aquinas and of other Christian thinkers. Under his guidance (not dictation) the students wrote reviews, summaries, and reports of books and articles in Catholic and secular periodicals. With the help of seminar members he edited the best of these reports, appended bibliographies, translated articles on personalism and on the corporative order from foreign journals, added his commentary on classroom procedure, and then mimeographed the whole in two syllabi. Hundreds of these were sold or distributed in various parts of the country.[42] His correspondence indicates that the seminar was a preliminary step to establishing a small institute in which Catholic graduates from secular colleges and universities could study Catholic culture, theology, philosophy, liturgy, and social science.

That Michel became intensely interested in the educational philosophy propounded at the University of Chicago during the 1930's is hardly surprising. These educational policies (along with Thomistic philosophy) were frequently discussed with his friend, Mortimer J. Adler, and others connected with the Chicago program. Father Virgil went to St. John's College at Annapolis to consult Dean Scott Buchanan and to see the program in operation. As dean at Collegeville, Father Virgil had held one or two faculty meetings preliminary to working out a modified Catholic version of the Great Books idea at his own St. John's University. But he died before the plan could take tangible shape.[43]

In his public addresses to students he frequently spoke of the chaotic world situation and of the need for an active and intelligent Catholic laity; he publicly asked students not to accept indoctrination blindly but to suggest "changes in educational policies to members of the faculty in an effort to shape the educational system into an instrument for the development of self-reliance and personal responsibility." As graduates, he said, he wanted alert, well-formed, and responsible persons to become citizens and apostles, leaders with initiative, not conformists and blind followers.[44] As dean he is remembered for stirring up discussion on the vital issues of the day among the faculty and for recommending and passing out periodicals and books on various current problems. This latter activity was pursued to such an extent as to cause some annoyance at times. According to a lay faculty member, Michel attempted by personal discussion to bring to the few lay members of the faculty trained in secular universities an understanding of Catholic thought and philosophy.

Adler correctly observed that for Michel education was never just an academic affair. In 1938 Father Virgil wrote:

Where education remains more specifically intellectual, as it must in many instances, the ideal of the educated man must nevertheless include in a high degree the social responsibility of the intellectual aristocrat in a democracy. . . . But education must also make haste to extend itself beyond the more esoteric domain of abstract intellectualism.[45]

Pointing to the triumphs of the Antigonish cooperative movement of St. Francis Xavier University in Nova Scotia, which had succeeded through adult education, and to the folk-school movement in Denmark, he observed that educators in the past had concentrated too exclusively on the young. An ardent exponent of adult education, he pointed out in another connection that "there is no longer any doubt that adult education in one form or another is with us to stay."[46]

In the fall of 1934 he and Alphonse Matt had founded at St. John's in conjunction with the Central Verein, the Institute for Social Study or the Social Institute as it was also known. This was an adult education project designed to train lay leaders in Catholic social principles. Unfortunately, an initial misunderstanding concerning the Institute arose with the Most Reverend Joseph F. Busch, Bishop of St. Cloud, who accused Michel of furthering Catholic Action without a mandate. The latter explained that the Institute was an academic venture and thus an extension of the university's educational work. For a time this adult education program seemed doomed, but eventually the matter was peaceably settled. When in June, 1936, an extensive Catholic Action program was inaugurated in the Diocese of St. Cloud, the Social Institute was incorporated into the diocesan program and the bishop became one of its strongest supporters. Thereafter the Institute also began to promote practical projects of social reconstruction.

Later, this adult education project was again threatened. Several Catholic, well-to-do, and conservative business men, thinking Father Virgil was promoting a kind of socialism or even communism, resented the Institute's studying and fostering cooperatives. They attacked the Institute through parish societies which were sending delegates to the weekend conferences. Then Bishop Busch came to the defense of the Institute.[47]

St. John's Abbey had stood at the cradle of the Central Verein in Minnesota and had always cooperated in its work. So, in collaborating with Frederick Kenkel in various Central Verein programs and conventions since the middle twenties, Michel merely fell in line with his abbey's traditions. Under his direction the Institute for Social Study conducted monthly week-end conferences to which chosen delegates from various parish societies in Minnesota were invited for lectures and discussions on a wide range of subjects, including the many phases of the social question, the encyclicals, Christian culture, Catholic Action and socio-liturgical activities. The conferences were always attended by a number of seminarians and students at Michel's urging. Incidentally, one of the latter is today the Honorable Eugene McCarthy, United States Representative from Minnesota's fourth district.

The lectures for the Institute were given mainly by the faculty of St. John's University but also by invited guest-speakers. Dom Virgil gave many of them himself. Speaking of him as the discussion leader for these conferences, Alphonse Matt observed:

He could propose remote ideas for discussion and criticism, and wait for them to yield fruit. . . . He could discuss a problem in all its ramifications almost to infinity, smilingly admitting that he was also a learner, even while he was endeavoring to teach. He did succeed in giving to the Minnesota Central Verein, and therewith to the Catholic Church in this state, a staunch group of believers in the organic union between the Mystical Body and social justice.[48]

A unique feature of the Institute was the exclusively spiritual conference on Saturday night devoted to some phase of the doctrine of the Mystical Body or of the liturgy, especially emphasizing the active participation in the Mass on Sunday morning.

This adult education project in time brought enquiries from all parts of the country and from Canada, occasioned a large correspondence, and inspired similar projects locally and nationally. As a matter of fact, Kenkel, speaking at state and national conventions of the Central Verein, held it up as a model to be imitated. In the fall of 1935 the Institute was extended to the City Federation of Parish Societies (Minneapolis-St. Paul), to which Michel gave a series of lectures on *Quadragesimo anno* and related subjects.[49] At first some of the lectures of the Social Institute at St. John's were mimeographed and distributed. But beginning in 1936 the best lectures were published in four brochures averaging 100 pages as the Social Problem Series: I: *Social Concepts and Problems*; II: *Economics and Finance*; III: *Political Theories and Forms*; IV: *The Mystical Body and Social Justice*. Of these more than 10,000 were sold, chiefly to study clubs, in the United States and Canada.[50]

In connection with the Institute for Social Study, Dom Virgil advocated and fostered cooperatives and credit unions. He invited the leaders of cooperative groups to lecture at the Institute and worked and corresponded freely with them. He frequently deplored the fact that Catholics had not assumed leadership of the cooperative movement in the United States and had not imbued it with a Christian philosophy of cooperation, social justice, and charity. He disagreed with Kenkel and the officers of the Minnesota Branch of the Central Verein when they proposed forming a separate federation of parish credit unions in the state, and subsequently in the nation. Father Virgil wanted them to join the existing secular federation and there bring to bear a Christian influence. That he should have thought the Central Verein policy in this case "smug Catholic exclusivism" possibly harming the whole Catholic social apostolate was, as Kenkel noted, typical of him.[51] While he never considered the cooperatives a panacea but only one instrument of christianization, he did say that "no Catholic interested in the principles of *Quadragesimo anno* can afford to neglect the cooperative movement." And again: "There are few movements or ideals in our day that harmonize so well with the ideals of Christianity as do the cooperatives."[52]

Speaking to Protestants and Catholics on the relation between the liturgical and cooperative movements at the National Catholic Rural Life Conference (NCRLC) at Fargo in 1936, Michel pointed out that both movements were reactions to the same selfish and exaggerated individualism: the cooperative, in economic life; the liturgical, in the spiritual life. He remarked:

The cooperative movement as a purely economic movement, as something side by side with, but still separate from, the Christian movement, would be a movement in the domain of pure nature; it would be a movement supported by the natural powers of men, without the assistance of the grace of God. It would indeed be in the domain of nature a counterpart of the supernatural program of Christianity; but it would function in terms of the naturalistic philosophy of our neo-pagan civilization, which says man is sufficient for himself and there is no need of God.

Now this is fundamentally unchristian. . . . To achieve Christian results, our natural efforts need the guidance and the assistance of Christ, of the grace of God. And for that reason it is eminently true that the cooperative movement, which in the domain of nature seeks to realize the ideals of Christ, needs the support and the help of the Christian spiritual movement that seeks to realize the ideals of Christ more fully in the supernatural domain of our spiritual lives. For us Catholics, this means in particular that the cooperative movement needs the help and inspiration of the liturgical movement, and it necessarily means that the liturgical movement, under pain of remaining sterile, needs to flower out into ever-increasing Christian cooperation in all the things of life. . . . The lesson of history is that any movement towards Christian ideals, when fostered apart from all relation to Christ, will soon decline: it will, in spite of its manifest idealism, be of the earth earthly and will go the way of the flesh. . . . For the Catholic then, the liturgical movement . . . must be both the inspiration and the model of the cooperative movement in economic life. . . . Not only is the Mystical Body the model at which the organization and functioning of the economic body must aim, but the proper restoration of the latter is possible only under the inspiration of the former.[53]

This speech contained one of Michel's many explanations of the way in which material and spiritual, natural and supernatural, must be intimately fused in man; of the need for any effective and realistic apostolate to take into consideration both the natural and supernatural, the individual and social, elements of man's life. Lucid and consistent presentation of this integral view was perhaps the most convincing aspect of his socio-liturgical writings. In spiritual conferences to members of the Institute he used to elucidate his assertion that the greatest act of cooperation in the world is the Mass, where

Catholics cooperate spiritually with one another in and with Christ — man with God, God with man. And this spirit of cooperation, he emphasized, should suffuse the whole of the Christian's life. "Without the ethical principles and the religious ideals of the Christian religion," he said in another connection, "cooperatives will become close-knit oligarchies, actuated by selfish and monopolistic policies." [54]

But despite such protestations, Michel's correspondence seems to indicate that he was blind, at least for a time, to the exploitative possibilities of *consumer* cooperatives. On the other hand, in his last statement on the cooperative movement he wrote:

Cooperatives can be perverted to false ends as well as any other movement. Today it is important for us to keep a balanced view of them because all sorts of cranks are trying to edge in on them. It is necessary therefore to keep our minds centered on their essential principles, and not to forget that the fundamental idea of cooperation is — in contrast with cutthroat individualistic competition or with totalitarian collective regimentation — the basic Christian technique of life. [55]

Father Virgil's convictions concerning the role of cooperatives, credit unions, and adult education as instruments of economic reform were considerably bolstered by three weeks of personal study of the Antigonish movement in Nova Scotia. Here he met the pioneer promoter of cooperatives, Father James Tompkins. [56] Fortunately, he kept a diary during his visit. In this maritime province he saw his idea of social reform at work: a movement of, by, and for the people, from the bottom up: the people studying, cooperating, and solving their own problems through adult education and by intelligent effort. Here he witnessed the downtrodden, drunkards, and paupers learn to read, study, work together under cultivated lay leadership and clerical direction and to become "human" beings and fervent Christians again; non-Catholics cooperating with Catholics, with the latter taking the lead; Christians rescued from communists, and communism effectively countered. [57] Michel and Tompkins were two of a kind, seeing eye to eye. Together they traveled, discussed, observed, talked with the men, and saw the program work. Indeed, as Tompkins had said, "Ideas have hands and feet." Like Tompkins, Michel was always ready to "Trust the little fellow."

Over the Sydney radio, in the churches, at meetings, to small groups — to all who would listen — Michel explained the liturgy, the need for Catholic Action, the relation between the liturgical and cooperative movements. He resolved, with the consent of his superior, to set up an Extension Service at St. John's and to petition the Carnegie Foundation for an endowment. A number of cooperatives had sprung up under his inspiration. But before the Extension Service came into reality, he died. Seven months before his death, when E. R. Bowen, Executive Secretary of the Cooperative League, looked for a Catholic leader in this country who might rally Catholic forces to the Cooperative League, he turned to Dom Virgil at the suggestion of Tompkins.[58]

Later Tompkins told Dorothy Day: "Father Virgil taught me more than any priest I ever met. I got more from his visit to Nova Scotia than I have received from anyone for many, many years." [59] Stunned by Michel's sudden death, the inspirer of the Antigonish movement wrote to Abbot Alcuin:

To us all in America it is an irreparable loss. . . . He made a wonderful impression on the people here — priests and people. Many priests came to listen to him and thought his message was wonderful. . . . I hope St. John's will go into this Extension work head on. . . . You will have the benediction from heaven of our dear separated Father and lover of his fellowmen.[60]

Turning now to his interest in the rural life movement, we find this comment written by Dom Virgil in 1938:

I know now that it is indeed very often a misfortune to be born in a larger city; and subsequent experience and contacts have convinced me that it may become almost an irreparable spiritual calamity to be born in some of our largest metropolitan areas.[61]

This embodied the main reason why he was active in the NCRLC. This was one of his favorite projects in the apostolate. One feature of the Conference that particularly appealed to him was its happy cooperation with men of other faiths who had similar ideals as to sound Christian rural living. Thus Michel freely collaborated with non-Catholic agrarian and decentralist forces and, as one of his students has noted, "soon had Ralph Borsodi, for instance, reconsidering the anti-clerical and anti-religious notions which marred his *This Ugly Civilization*." [62]

Even to record from his correspondence the rural projects and programs in which he had a hand would take up considerable space. Yet one should note his speech on the Christian philosophy of rural life at a symposium on the integral society at Northwestern University in 1937. Here he also acted as chairman for a panel on the "Church and the Social Question." [63]

Father Virgil frequently described the regrettable human and spiritual effects of the "mechanization even of Christian religious life and practice" in huge impersonal city parish "plants." In this regard he remarked:

> There is no question primarily of turning as many city dwellers as possible into "dirt" farmers. . . . The question is first of all one of decentralization of the present artificial city congestions, of bringing people back closer to nature, regardless of their professions in life. It is not first of all a question of city or farm, but of unnatural life as against a normal life close to nature. [64]

The NCRLC is not concerned merely, he said, with an economic question but ultimately with a spiritual one. Needed were a Catholic rural or rural-urban culture and also adult education programs conducted by sympathetic teachers in rural and village schools to lay the groundwork for such a culture. To meet this need at the Catholic college level he was in the process of drawing up a four-year curriculum for St. John's at the time of his death. [65]

He also had made preliminary plans for a model, self-supporting, rural Christian community. There is no reason to believe that he would have succeeded where others have failed.

He wrote for the NCRLC publications, lectured at its forums and meetings throughout the country, and had a voluminous correspondence with its leaders. With these he planned the *Manifesto on Rural Life*. He collaborated with Father LaFarge in contributing to it the chapter on cooperatives. With the help of Monsignor Vincent J. Ryan (later Bishop of Bismarck), Father William T. Mulloy (now Bishop of Covington), and Bishop Aloisius J. Muench of Fargo (now Apostolic Nuncio to Germany), Michel and his confrere Father Marcellus Leisen reworked the final draft before its official adoption. [66] Finally, with Bishop Muench and others, he also planned the first Catholic Rural Life School at Collegeville in the summer of 1938. For unexplained reasons this school was postponed at the last moment; two years later Martin Schirber, O.S.B., organized the school, which became the model of many others held throughout the country. [67] In the words of the late Archbishop Edwin V. O'Hara, founder of the movement, "The NCRLC is indebted to Dom Virgil Michel for sharing with its founders a broad vision of the rural apostolate." [68]

To assess Michel's role in the various movements in which he took part is not easy. He often worked quietly behind the scenes of action. Not given to black or white thinking, he participated even when he could not accept all that was propounded. What he approved, he furthered; what he could not accept, he tried to change. As the sympathetic adviser of a number of "radical" lay Catholics he had the gift to temper where necessary their misguided zeal without killing their spirit. He encouraged and defended a small flock of "little people" who, he thought, had the right spirit of Christian social reform, and contributed to their magazines. Only a few of these many persons can be mentioned and only a few of their journals.

To describe Father Virgil's part in the NCRLC is comparatively simple; to outline his role in the Catholic Worker (CW) and kindred movements is more difficult. Writing in the *American Catholic Sociological Review* for June, 1952, Father Daniel Cantwell remarked that the *Catholic Worker's* initial significant contribution to American Catholic life has been obscured by the *Catholic Worker's* later adoption of pacifism and an anti-industrial ideology.

Peter Maurin and Dorothy Day founded the first Catholic labor (then) paper in the United States, the *Catholic Worker*, in May, 1933. The first House of Hospitality was established at the end of that year, just as Michel returned from the Indian Missions. From Abbot Alcuin, who had called Michel's attention to the *Catholic Worker*, he secured permission to send the editors gratis all the publications of the Liturgical Press, so that they might integrate the liturgy more fully into their program of social action. This gesture brought the following response:

> We are overwhelmed with gratitude at your generosity. . . . The office staff has been sitting around ever since devouring them eagerly and profitably. Nearly all our friends who were interested in social justice from a Catholic point of view, from the very beginning of the paper, have been people equally interested in the liturgical movement — a fact which rather surprised us at first, as we hadn't realized that the relation between the two was so widely appreciated. But by now we are well accustomed to having most of the all-day discussions in our office come around eventually to the doctrine of the Mystical Body of Christ.[69]

Thereafter the *Catholic Worker* contained an increasing emphasis on the liturgy as the inspiration of social action. One of the avowed aims of Dorothy Day was to bring the doctrine of the Mystical Body to the man in the street. And while it would be hazardous to estimate to what extent the CW movement spread an understanding of this doctrine and of the liturgy as a whole along with the social teachings of the Church, it is safe to say the influence was considerable. In May, 1938, the New York CW group alone distributed 165,000 copies of the paper. This was read in all parts of the world. At that time there were more than twenty CW Houses of Hospitality and cells in the United States.

Ever since Dorothy Day carried the first of 2,500 copies of the initial *Catholic Worker* into Union Square, where 200,000 communists and their sympathizers held a rally on May 1, 1933, the paper has either edified or angered its readers. The communists, who claimed to profess the ideal of social justice and human brotherhood, called the Catholic Workers fascists, while many Catholics called them communists, fellow-travelers, revolutionaries, idealists, crackpots—and other names. The nation-wide battle of the CW movement with communists between the years 1933–38—the only years with which we are concerned here—has been partially told in several books by Dorothy Day. A critical history of the movement with full contemporary background remains to be written. At this time the story is perhaps best told in the back issues of the *Catholic Worker*, especially when contrasted with much of the contemporary Catholic press, which often fought the influential *Daily Worker* and communist bookstores, as well as communist unemployment councils and propaganda, with a combination of negativism, condemnation, and hysteria rather than with a positive program of intelligent criticism and action based on the social encyclicals.[70] As John A. Ryan remarked in the *Catholic Worker* of June, 1936, "America is in far less danger from the preaching of Communists than from certain professedly anti-Communist propaganda, which is in reality directed against social justice." According to an editorial in the *Catholic Worker*, Patrick Cardinal Hayes remarked from the first that the *Catholic Worker* in its pioneer work could not help but make mistakes but that the thing to do was not to persist in them.[71] As in other pioneer projects, mistakes were certainly made. Many believe that there was and has been even a persistence in some of them.

Virgil Michel's part in the CW movement was one of strong support and of friendly criticism. To a Franciscan who questioned the wisdom of such support, Michel wrote after pleading for patience with a movement just in its beginnings: "As far as I know, there is no more successful antagonist against Communism in this country than the *Catholic Worker*."[72]

To Dom Virgil, Dorothy Day was one of those martyr-spirits and lay apostles so much needed in extreme times and so often called for by him. But he was too much a man of order to countenance the general disorder he found whenever he visited the New York House of Hospitality, and this he told Miss Day, among other things. Besides deprecating lack of organization, he urged a more positive and constructive program. He cautioned against extremist tendencies and urged prudence and an unfailing charity in meeting what was often fierce opposition. Of course, Dorothy Day needed no Virgil Michel to teach her the virtue of charity. Needless to say, however, she did not always agree with his suggestions.[73]

Michel believed that the *Catholic Worker* possessed a great potential for good, and that it was awakening many. So he wrote to her: "Keep up the good work, no matter what slanderous tongues may say. That is the way Christ Himself did it." [74]

Late into the night Michel discussed current issues with Peter Maurin whenever they met. It is not necessary to elaborate on the statement that Father Virgil could not agree that round table discussions, Houses of Hospitality, farming communes (the basic program), and other CW projects were the whole answer to the social question.

A number of publications devoted to Christian social reconstruction grew out of the CW ferment, or broke away from the parent-publication. Chief among these were the *Christian Front* and the *Social Forum*, English-speaking Canada's first labor paper. The *Christian Front* was a more intellectual approach to the solution of social ills and was based largely on the social encyclicals. Besides contributing articles, Dom Virgil was the chief adviser to the editors, Norman McKenna and Richard Deverall.[75] Much the same was true of his relations with the *Social Forum*, whose editors wrote in their issue for December, 1938, "The announcement of Dom Virgil's death was a sudden blow. Throughout our relationship with him, which was continuous since the paper's beginning, we have placed him always among the most courteous and kindest of our benefactors." [76]   He was likewise the inspiration of a small group of apostolic laymen in St. Louis who held liturgical days and spread the social doctrines of the Church through lectures and other activities as well as through their quarterly bulletin, the *Catholic Alliance*.[77] "Won't you please criticize . . . and make any comments which you think fit?" Michael O'Shaughnessy, founder of the League for Social Justice and editor of the *Social Justice Bulletin*, asked Michel in one of his letters.[78] Father Virgil had a continuing correspondence with the various editors of the *Commonweal*, for which he had a special predilection.[79] He contributed articles to India's *Social Order*.[80]

Dom Virgil was also one of the guiding spirits behind *Liturgy and Sociology*, a periodical issued by the Campion Propaganda Committee of New York. The Campions were affiliated members of the CW movement, younger men and women who in various cities organized into small apostolic bands. With "Prayer-Action-Sacrifice" as their watchword, they studied the liturgy, techniques of Catholic Action, and the social encyclicals. He worked out a tentative constitution with the Campions. They engaged in various forms of apostolic work.[81]

Dom Virgil's last "Timely Tract," published after his death, was a vigorous defense of the lay apostolate in general and the CW movement in particular. On a lecture tour in late 1938 some nuns had asked him whether the Catholic Workers were "a bunch of communists," while some priests assured him they were. After having promoted and guided the work of these various lay groups, Michel must have found it difficult to contain himself when he heard such assertions. Having reviewed CW and other apostolic lay activities, he ended his "Timely Tract" by stating:

Catholic Workers and apostles! You have your faults and your shortcomings. But who among us on earth is not burdened with them? If people slander and calumniate you, so did they Christ. You are indeed an eyesore and a scandal even to Catholics, but usually only to such as revel in their self-complacency, whose religion is one of asking from God and knows not the blessedness of giving. If you are a stone of scandal to the self-righteous, so was Christ. And He told us that it was not the Pharisee but the Publican who went away justified. If there is a Judas among you, he is still unknown and undiscovered. But even if such a one should be found, there was also a Judas among the Twelve and you are now many times twelve. Blessed are you if you are among those who suffer persecution for justice's sake, since "theirs is the kingdom of heaven." [82]

Michel carried on a large correspondence with these Catholic Worker and allied groups who sought his advice and support. They spread his pamphlets, brochures, reprints of his articles, and the publications of the Liturgical Press and the Social Institute far and wide. His talks to the various Houses of Hospitality and other affiliated lay groups invariably dealt with the Mystical Body, the liturgy, social action, and the social teachings of the Church.

Were this a history of the CW movement, one would have to mention all the bishops and other prominent priests who rose to its defense. But it would be an injustice not to record at least briefly the work of Father Paul Hanly Furfey, who furthered the movement by his lectures, articles, week-end retreats, encouragement, and advice. His *Fire on the Earth*, dedicated to the Campions and published in 1937, stirred many into thinking and action at a time of widespread self-complacency. His *Three Theories of Society* published in the same year was a more scholarly contribution. After the first colloquium on social Catholicism in Washington in March, 1937, there were a few more such meetings of priests and laity, largely the inspiration of Father Furfey. His courses in advanced Catholic social thought, introduced into the graduate school at the Catholic University of America as early as 1935, seemed to have been among the first in this country.[83] Their letters show that Father Furfey and Michel discussed liturgy and social action and personalism in Washington and at Collegeville. One cannot say that their approaches to Catholic social action and their concepts of personalism were entirely the same. But it is not necessary to treat of their differences here. Suffice it to say that Father Furfey's emphasis — before 1938 at least — lay more exclusively on the spiritual and the supernatural, as his words to Michel in 1937 seem to indicate:

. . . I find you approach the problems of society from two different aspects, namely, the natural and the supernatural. Of course this dual approach is legitimate and even inevitable, but the question remains, "What should be the relative emphasis of each of the two treatments?" This is a question which I have been thinking over very seriously myself and which I cannot solve to my complete satisfaction. It seems clear, however, that the supernatural approach should take precedence and should receive the greater emphasis. This, as you remember, was the thesis of my paper at Chicago. If you have the time, perhaps you might sometime jot down your views on this matter and send them to me. There is no one person whose opinion I would value more.[84]

Another lay venture in the social apostolate, Friendship House, engaged Michel's sympathetic interest. Catherine De Hueck with four others started the first Friendship House in the slums of Toronto in the early 1930's. Although she had the full support and official approbation of Archbishop Neil McNeil, there was strong opposition from both clergy and laity, as well as much ridicule and misunderstanding. Destitute, desperate, and lonely, they faced a wall of indifference and suspicion, while living and working among the unemployed poor and communists. As yet they had no idea of a vocation as lay apostles. They were ready to quit when Father Michel, sometime in 1934 or 1935, stepped into the bare room of the empty storefront on Portland Street. He sat down on an old broken chair, and seeing their plight, he began as one who understood:

How fortunate you are. . . . This is what I have been dreaming about. You are discouraged. You need the Mass. You must persevere by all means. You have a vocation. Study the Mass, live the Mass. Between two Masses you can bear everything.[85]

He said much more then and in the correspondence that followed about the apostolic vocation of the laity and about the liturgical life as the basis of Catholic social action. As usual, he sent literature on the liturgy and social justice. In this way, the foundress of the Friendship House movement has said, the liturgy came to be the heart of the movement. On June 30, 1938, she wrote to Michel:

I value your letters very much as I value your friendship and interest in my work. . . . So when I write about all these things to you, it is because in my human weakness I hope for just such a letter as you have written, for it helps me and gives me courage to go on. . . . As to the liturgy, you are right again. . . . I often wonder how it is that Catholics, good, pious Catholics, prefer novenas to Mass. How is it that the children of light do not seem to need the source of all light daily? How is it that we speak of Catholic Action, and any other Christian action, going forth into the heat of the battle without Him who is the very reason for our battle?

In Catherine De Hueck's opinion, "Father Virgil foresaw the laity as the spearhead of the Church in coming times. . . . Without him there may not have been a Friendship House movement at all." When she went to Rome in 1951 as the official delegate of her diocese to the International Congress of Lay Apostles, Pius XII's words to her in a private audience, she recalled, were strikingly similar to words she had heard from Virgil Michel almost twenty years before: "Persevere in your vocation at all costs; the Church needs lay apostles." [86]

No large city in this country has a fuller and more varied Catholic Action program than Chicago. Today much of it is rooted chiefly in the liturgical life of the Mystical Body. This happy situation is the fruit of the apostolic labors of many, both past and present.[87] The first articles on the liturgy in this movement appeared in 1929 in

Ciscora News, and were written mostly by Sister Estelle Cullings, O.S.B., at the behest of Virgil Michel.[88] Later, with the active cooperation of the magnanimous Father Martin Carrabine, S.J., but chiefly through Sister Cecilia Himebaugh, O.S.B., Michel played a large role in helping to launch the very successful re-organized Chicago Inter-Student Catholic Action (Cisca) on a study of the liturgy and the Mystical Body as the foundation of apostolic work. With its leaders Dom Virgil planned study days, helped in preparing study outlines, and other literature for their various meetings. This story is told in Sister Cecilia's more than thirty letters, some of great length, to Virgil Michel, and in his replies.[89] Thus she wrote to him before Cisca officially embarked on a study of the liturgy:

> Father Carrabine is really very much interested in the project, though he sees even more clearly than I the innumerable obstacles in our path. The idea is going to be a difficult thing to sell to hard-shelled Ciscans, to many of whom the doctrine of the Mystical Body is like a heresy that we are trying to promulgate in opposition to the good old-fashioned teachings of their pastor and teachers. Father is now in retreat, and I am praying much that God will let him know His will about what is to be done this coming year.[90]

Dennis Geaney, O.S.A., observed correctly in 1955, "Lay activity has a respectability in Chicago due to those who braved the loneliness of the trail-blazer." [91]

Somewhat apart from the social apostolate but still directed toward unity in Christ was another of Father Michel's interests, the ecumenical movement. While in Europe in 1924–25, Dom Virgil had acquired from his mentor, Dom Lambert Beauduin, an interest in the ecumenical apostolate for Christian unity. Michel's ecumenical interest is reflected in his correspondence [92] from the first days of the American liturgical movement as well as in the first volumes of *Orate Fratres.* Commenting in 1927 on the possibilities and efforts at reunion made in various parts of the world, he stated:

> If a reunion of East and West is ever to come about, a necessary preliminary will be a rapprochement in the field of ideas, sincere exchange of views. Often that alone greatly diminishes psychological obstacles, to speak of no others; often it is a most difficult step, like all beginnings of big things. . . . The time of bitter personal feeling between our separated Catholic brethren and us is rapidly ending, and relations henceforth should be more completely in the spirit of Christ's charity. . . . Again, the chief

differences and grievances stressed by the Eastern Orthodox Catholic Church against us are liturgical, in the true sense of that term, which goes beyond the meaning of *rubrical*. Hence, too, the hope of a better understanding on our part by reason of the growing liturgical movement among us.[93]

Readers of *Orate Fratres* were kept informed of developments. How former Anglicans, Ellen Gates Starr in the United States and Dr. K. F. McMurtrie in Africa, aided in spreading the liturgical apostolate has been told. There were others. Virgil Michel sympathized with the sense of loss experienced by converts from Anglicanism who — accustomed to active participation in the vernacular Anglican liturgy — now had to worship passively in the silence of Catholic churches. He was in contact with "High Church" or "liturgical movements" among various non-Catholic communions as well as with Anglican and Orthodox religious communities. In the 1930's he read avidly the works of a group of Anglicans in England interested in a Christian social reconstruction of society inspired by sacramental, corporate worship and Christian solidarity in the Mystical Body. Father Virgil spoke of the providential role which the liturgy and the doctrine of the Mystical Body could play in drawing Christians into the oneness of Christ. As he said, the problem of Christian unity is fundamentally a problem of the doctrine of the Church. On February 22, 1937, he addressed a small group of Catholics and Anglicans in New York, interested in social regeneration based on the encyclicals. His subject was the necessity of social and religious unity.[94]

Another activity which attracted Father Michel's support was the movement to make the divine office once again the prayer of the people. As early as 1926 Fathers William Busch and Virgil Michel discussed ways and means of accomplishing this. But they decided to work first for a better understanding of the Mass through the intelligent use of the vernacular missal, then little used. In late 1935 these two priests initiated plans to organize the League of the Divine Office. The League was one of the many original suggestions of Father Busch, than whom Michel had no better adviser and guide. Modeled after the Society of the Magnificat founded in England in 1927, the loosely organized League was formed with headquarters at Collegeville to promote the recitation of the divine office, in whole or part, in groups or individually, by the laity. In May, 1938, Dom Virgil estimated that approximately 1,000 persons in the United States and Canada were carrying on the work of this laymen's association.[95] As early as 1928 Fathers Busch and Michel had considered publishing a shortened version of the breviary for the laity. This was published as *A Short Breviary* by the Liturgical Press in 1941. It was compiled by Collegeville monks Basil Stegmann, Paschal Botz, and William Heidt.

A specialized field of Catholic Action, the apostolate carried on by college graduates, was aided by Father Virgil in the 1930's. For instance, he played a considerable part in the apostolic work of the Catholic Laymen's League of Orange and Rockland Counties in New York organized in 1933 and mandated by Patrick Cardinal Hayes, in the work of the Alumni Committee on Catholic Action of Manhattan College, and in that of similar apostolic activities in various parts of the country. He outlined a lecture-course in Catholic Action for Manhattan College, and other apostolic programs for its active alumni and the Laymen's League. A prominent Catholic lawyer in New York, Arthur T. O'Leary, wrote under Michel's guidance several hundred articles on the liturgy over four years for five daily and some weekly suburban secular newspapers. Of him Michel said, "We know of no Catholic layman more zealous in bringing others to an active appreciation of the treasures of the liturgy of the Church." [96]

One could go on for pages citing the groups and individuals, movements and apostolic activities which Dom Virgil initiated, inspired, encouraged, or guided. This widespread and varied apostolate was well summarized by Joseph Matt, who for years was closely associated with Michel's work, when he said:

He was apparently never too busy to lend assistance to the little groups of idealists and workers wherever he found them during his frequent travels. It mattered little to him whether the group was large or small, whether their activities were far developed or just emerging from the planning stage — as long as he discovered the spark of Catholicity he stood ready to help, to encourage, to inspire. And he possessed the rare talent to gather every manifestation of Catholic thought and life into a coordinated whole, until a veritable network of somehow related movements went out from the monastery cell of Father Virgil at St. John's to well-nigh every section of the United States and Canada. And everywhere the name of Virgil Michel was mentioned with respect and gratitude. . . . His enthusiasm and his irenic personality may have influenced him, at times, to judge certain personalities and movements according to their good intention rather than according to their works, may have persuaded him to waste valuable time and effort at times on ephemeral things. But those who saw him surrounded by students who came from all classes and professions seeking guidance and knowledge were unable to resist the charm of his logic and the persuasive power of his unflinching activity in the service of social justice.[97]

Obviously this farflung activity entailed an immense correspondence. Writing letters was his way of contacting, uniting, and guiding the various groups and individuals; his correspondents, in turn, kept him informed. These letters indicate a great charity. Writing to him were university professors and students, young intellectuals and writers, educators, editors, bishops, abbots, seminarians, wavering converts, men with causes, extremists, anti-clericals, agnostics, farmers, workers, and artists. In his files are many letters from non-Catholics, whose confidence he enjoyed because he respected their sincerity and, whenever possible, participated in their non-religious projects. He was forever looking for common ground, whether between conflicting philosophies or social action programs, and especially between Catholics and non-Catholics. The *Commonweal* did not exaggerate when it stated of Michel editorially on December 9, 1938, "His generous personality will be missed by men of all faiths."

Father Michel carried on a lengthy correspondence with a communist in labor circles and tried to convince him that the Church had an effective social program despite the negativism and blind condemnation expressed in much of the Catholic press. Some of his most interesting letters are those in which he tried to make more members of other religious orders apostles of the liturgy. Nor did he always fail. To one and all went replies, at times very long ones, sometimes including reprints of his articles, outlines for the recipient's activities, pamphlets, bibliography, and even books. Obviously the whole story of this correspondence cannot yet be told.

As a lecturer Virgil Michel became a traveling participant observer. He addressed many and varied groups. He took part in symposia, many of which were conducted under secular auspices. The itinerary he submitted to Abbot Alcuin was planned by the hour. In these travels he hunted out leaders and contacted lay apostles.[98] On such trips he was never without a file of letters to be answered should there be a spare moment. The subject-matter on which he lectured was as varied as the subjects about which he wrote. But his favorite topics were the basic ideas of the liturgical apostolate and the consequent Catholic Action, the encyclicals, the nature of vital education, a living philosophy, and the role of Christian womanhood in the modern world. His ability to quote at any given moment from all parts of the liturgy indicated to what extent the rich thought of the Church's public prayer had become a part of himself.

While never at a loss for an idea or word, he was by no means an eloquent speaker; the message of the calm philosopher poured out in monotone, with somewhat annoying exactitude of enunciation, almost without a trace of emotion. If a sense of humor was not one of his gifts, clarity of expression certainly was. While it was not in his power to move the emotions, those who came to think with him were rarely disappointed. He was listened to for what he had to say, not for the way he said it. He gave retreats to diocesan clergy, religious, lay and youth groups, and to Indians. Testimony to his success as a retreatmaster varies sharply from high praise to its opposite. As far as religious communities were concerned, success seemed to depend on the extent to which they were ready for his liturgical message. However, his letters indicate that, both as lecturer and retreatmaster, he was much in demand. It should be added that he was never more effective than in private conversation or in small discussion groups — "talkfests," he called them. And such talkfests, by the way, constituted his idea of recreation.

For Michel, writing was never harder than sitting down to a typewriter. To produce several articles on different topics at one sitting was not unusual for him. After finishing a philosophical treatise, he could turn to editing things like *Simple Mass Prayers*, which went into the hands of more than 500,000 grade-school children. Rare was the day, even when traveling, that he did not write. Translations aside, he wrote the equivalent of six or seven volumes of his own, collaborated in ten more, produced at least a dozen pamphlets and more than 300 articles — not counting editorials, unpublished manuscripts, and book reviews — scattered through more than thirty periodicals.

However, his was not a fluent pen. He never took the time to polish a phrase. His writings were not literary; they were often heavy, at times academic and abstract, philosophical, yet in their way convincing, concise, and lucid. His socio-liturgical writings often combined liturgy and social philosophy. His articles were avidly read because they faced current issues or even controversial subjects and because they were written by a man constantly in touch with contemporary civilization. While he urged other writers to popularize the liturgy, he himself never aimed at being a "popularizer." He avowedly wrote

for the thoughtful and for leaders, and it was to them that he geared
Orate Fratres and his articles as the most effective way of spreading
ideas, always his primary concern. He often said that the apostolate
requires spirit, quality, and leadership, not numbers — for the latter
will come if the first are assured. In 1936 he wrote:

Everywhere the
good Christian spirit is propagated by small bands or even individuals
who are alive with the zeal of God. These are the true leaven of God
among the people, and none better exists in our opinion than our
devoted friends and followers in the liturgical cause.[99]

Again, he wrote with intellectual generosity and a courteous logic.
He was fond of understatement. As he said, every exaggeration is a
kind of lie. A continuing nightmare awaits anyone who attempts an
accurate restatement of Michel's thought with his numerous distinctions and qualifications, if's and but's. He possessed the gift of striking
at the heart of things and of clarifying the middle way. And if he
found fault with much, there was, nevertheless, always the note of
Christian confidence and optimism. Taken all together, his writings
constituted a kind of Christian synthesis. As he said, an integral Catholicism embraces all things.

However, the most surprising aspect of his literary work is the fact
that he could keep himself out of controversies, especially since in his
pioneer labors and in much that he wrote he found himself off the
beaten track and thus in his time considered far to the left by some.
But it may also be due to the stark reasonableness of his presentation
and approach.

Constructive self-criticism, he maintained, is the mark of maturity
and the indispensable condition for spiritual and social progress. Personalism, Mounier had written, begins by disquieting persons. Michel
disquieted not a few. As he wrote to a friend at Georgetown University in 1936, "There should never have been a period in which ardent
Catholics were not really eager to be told where mistakes and faults
lay and how they might improve themselves and come nearer to
Christ." [100] Not only was Michel highly critical of his age and its
defects, but he also spoke out frankly about his fellow Catholics. And
yet, this was usually done in a humble, kindly, prudent, and impersonal way. John LaFarge, S.J., whom Dom Virgil called "our fellow
apostle," wrote editorially after Michel's death:

He gave his life . . .
to a difficult, controversial cause. But strenuous and incisive as was

Father Virgil's literary warfare, he was a man who steadfastly refused to quarrel. God's cause and not his own was at his heart, and his critics became his warmest friends. . . . He developed that gift for lucid exposition of intricate subjects that made his numberless articles prized by the Catholic Press of this country. To be a college educator, an editor and writer and lecturer, an organizer in the field of adult education, is a stiff program for a scholar who is also a monk and man of prayer. The causes he represented are still in too great need of worthy advocates to allow us to suffer lightly the passing of Father Virgil Michel.[101]

On the other hand, Patrick Scanlon wrote editorially in the Brooklyn *Tablet* for December 10, 1938:

Virgil Michel had many critics. They did not agree with him in dozens of ways. But all admired him as a thoroughly Christian gentleman, a noble priest, a scholar of rare ability and a zealous promoter of the Christian cause on many fields.

Did Dom Virgil achieve more by his personal influence than by his literary labors? Both in and out of the abbey he displayed an unusual gift of organizing and persuading others, of winning their cooperation, yet of respecting their personalities and opinions. In general, he wanted no one to go his way who was not intellectually convinced that it was the proper direction. Sister Cecilia, O.S.B., spoke for many when she wrote of Michel's connections with Cisca:

Brimming over as he was with vast and irrepressible ideas, he yet possessed that rarest of qualities in a leader — namely, the power to draw out and implement the initiative of others. . . . This must have required a self-effacement that was heroic in view of his intellectual stature and breadth of vision. . . . Only when we showed signs of getting lost in some theological fog did he relax that self-imposed restraint of an adviser; it is impossible to think of him as a dictator or intellectual bully. So sure was his counsel and so unflagging his interest in every detail of our projects that we always submitted our plans to him and ever received, not just approval, but an enthusiastic and stimulating response.[102]

However, his many disciples, lay and clerical, outside the abbey will find it hard to believe that at home Michel at times gave the impression of being too busy to have time for students and sometimes even for his brother religious. To know him was to work. While much loved by most of his fellow monks, a few thought of him as a dehumanized intellect. Because he was somewhat unimaginative and al-

*Dom Virgil and Indian par-
ishioners at St. Mary's Mission,
Red Lake, Minnesota.*

*A liturgist shocks corn, while confreres Damian
Baker and Florian Locnikar pose.*

Mr. Mortimer J. Adler.

Rev. Paul Hanly Furfey, at Collegeville, 1937.

Rev. Irmin Vitry, O.S.B.

Sister Jane Marie Murray, O.P.

Rev. Paul Bussard.

Sister Cecilia Himebaugh, O.S.B.

Mr. Maurice Lavanoux.

Institute of Social Study.

Ready for the hunt in northern Minnesota.

Mrs. Catherine De Hueck.

Dom Virgil, Miss Janet Kalven, and Mr. Jerome Kerwin.

St. John's Abbey — Home of the Liturgical Press.

*Dom Virgil's collaborator, Basil Steg-
mann, O.S.B.*

*Dom Virgil's collaborator and successor,
Godfrey L. Diekmann, O.S.B.*

most completely unsentimental, some of his brethren considered him cold, heartless, even mechanistic, as he went about planning his day's work to the minute. He seemed aware of his cold exterior. Once, when others were impressed and he remained unmoved, he recorded the situation in his Diary, adding, "Am I really so inhuman?"

He rarely spoke of inconsequential things. All who knew him were amazed by the range, comprehension, and speed of his reading. Even while brushing his teeth, his eyes were riveted to a periodical.

Not all the monks, however, cared to discuss the liturgical movement, educational theory, the social question, or the subtleties of modern philosophy during the time set aside for recreation. Once gently told by a confrere that some considered him heartless, he was hurt beyond words. However, those who knew him intimately insist that he was anything but a robot apostle. The enemy of all pretense, he at times could be blunt. About this all are agreed: Virgil Michel never worked for himself. And it must also be said in his favor that the many who collaborated with him at St. John's and elsewhere, never felt that they were working for another man's cause. He almost never spoke about himself or his own work. A confrere has stated that, although Dom Virgil did not talk about his sacrifices and asceticism, one could nevertheless perceive them. At Louvain he kept his mail for reading in the evening not to gain time for study one suspects, but say classmates, to mortify himself. He carried the observance of poverty to the extreme of picking up used and cast-away student papers on which to write his research notes. After his death his superior found in Michel's room the barest essentials.

Perhaps only Abbot Alcuin knew the full extent of his work outside the abbey. A year before his death the abbot forbade him to take on any more work and begged him to conserve his health. In referring to this when turning down a task, Michel once wrote a friend, "I know in my heart that the abbot is right." But it was too late to extricate himself from burdens too heavy even for a man of boundless energy. As he confided to another friend, "It seems to me that the rush of modern life is beginning to overwhelm us even in the monastery."

There was another side to the man. He loved to talk and play with children. It was not beneath him to offer to baby-sit in the homes that he visited. Once, when parents came home to their children, they found Michel under a couch, playing a game of hide-and-seek with the youngsters. Each fall in his last years, after a retreat to the Indians, he reportedly shot deer with the best of them. One of the last things he did before his final illness was to spend two hours with a lonely colored girl from New York City who had come to him from the neighboring College of St. Benedict. The many who came to Collegeville to consult him seem never to have forgotten his gentle kindness. He was equally at home with the learned and the unlettered. He was always interested in everyone's opinion.

For St. John's Abbey the relation between Abbot Alcuin and Dom Virgil was a significant one. To describe this relation accurately, however, presents no small challenge. That both had so many characteristics and convictions in common makes the task no easier. In his answers to the many letters of condolence after Father Virgil's death, Abbot Alcuin praised his monastic spirit and the example of zeal, initiative, and leadership that Father Virgil set for his fellow monks. For his initiative and leadership he would be missed most of all, the abbot said. The superior had a strong confidence in his subject's judgment and acted upon many of his welcomed suggestions. But it cannot at all be said that they saw eye to eye in every matter. Abbot Alcuin once remarked, "I had to stand up to him as Peter did to Paul." Father Virgil was an exceedingly independent thinker and his abbot hardly less so. Several times Abbot Alcuin told Michel that he was too ambitious and that his zeal was too impatient. While in Europe Dom Virgil confessed to the abbot that he was persecuted with ideas. In later years the brunt of that persecution sometimes fell on the Abbot of St. John's when Dom Virgil urged the promotion of projects and ideas endlessly hatching in his fertile mind. Father Paul Bussard's observation is entirely to the point:

I remember walking around the lake with him one afternoon and being completely astounded at the projects for work he brought up in those two hours. I suppose it would have taken a small army to get all of them done.[103]

Perhaps it should be added that Father Virgil tried to dispel what he considered the indifference of Abbot Alcuin to the systematic building up of a first-rate college faculty. The superior at Collegeville was convinced that the community there was becoming too large. When a group of monks including Father Virgil suggested a small building program in 1936, the abbot stated that any new construction was a source of anxiety to him. He explained:

I am conscious that the future of the community is thereby more or less fixed. But I shrink from fixing its future, when I consider the things that come to my mind in connection with its future. I would rather see less magnitude, so that there might be more flexibility and ready facility to go into other lines of work where the cause of God may be promoted. A school like ours, in these days of severe and changing demands, is in a sense a millstone around our neck and drags us down and prevents the unfolding to the best advantage of the powers that lie in us as priests and religious. We are compelled to do too much work and to spend too much money for purposes that only promote the material and are perhaps not at all conducive to the spread of God's kingdom, which in these days stands greatly in need of men and money.[104]

The college enrollment stood then at 300. To supply adequate educational facilities was the obligation of bishops, the abbot told his monks. When in the next decade opportunity came for establishing new monastic foundations, Abbot Alcuin was ready with both men and money. It was when Father Michel as dean pressed for development of the school, both its faculty and its material equipment, that he received responses like this from Abbot Alcuin:

I hope this my reply to your propositions will satisfy you for the present and dispel whatever temptation to pessimism may come upon you. . . . How easy it is to preach to others (I mean this for myself, too) to enter into the sacrificial spirit of Christ and submit to the will of the Father! It has often occurred to me that all participation in the liturgy is but external and superficial if it does not lead to this sacrificial submission. This is not meant unkindly, but with affectionate appreciation of your good will.[105]

Father Virgil also harbored the fear that Abbot Alcuin, with all his broad vision, did not grasp fully the future proportions of the evolving popular liturgical movement in the United States and the magnitude of the work necessary for its proper promotion. He therefore frequently asked for more trained help. Michel was obsessed with the notion that the proper flowering of the liturgical apostolate in the future would require that St. John's Abbey become a center of liturgical research and of a living Catholic culture to shore up the work of liturgical popularization. In Michel's opinion, Abbot Alcuin never assigned a sufficient number of monks to prepare men for this expanding future educational and liturgical apostolate. Whether the abbot had the manpower for this is quite another question. This much is certain: In sending 101 monks to graduate school in 29 years of abbatial office, Abbot Alcuin did not neglect the educational development of his community, although in this he was often yielding to the repeated urging of monks like Severin Gertken, Virgil Michel, Mark Braun, Walter Reger, and Martin Schirber.

On the other hand, Abbot Alcuin told Michel that the bishops would resent it if St. John's Abbey pushed the liturgical movement too obviously. For this reason he at times refused to consider Michel's plans for current and future liturgical promotion. And it was for the same reason, perhaps, that the abbot was never particularly interested in the organic development of the Liturgical Press. Abbot Alcuin, like Michel, expressed the hope that the hierarchy would sponsor the liturgical apostolate. The hierarchy of several countries of Europe had done this years before. With the official blessing and guidance of the bishops the liturgical revival would progress more surely and safely. In 1942 the administrative board of the National Catholic Welfare Conference declined the invitation to sponsor the annual Liturgical Week through the Conference. At the strong suggestion of Deutsch, the Benedictine Liturgical Conference as the sponsoring body of the Week was then dissolved.

In the spring and summer of 1938 Father Michel gave eight retreats besides lecturing for a week to a group of clergy and sisters of the Archdiocese of Indianapolis on the Christ-Life Series. Before starting the retreat for the Basilian Fathers in Toronto, August 15, 1938, he wrote to Abbot Deutsch:

My eyes are quite granular again and sleep is very spasmodic. I'll surely need a good rest and vacation by the time October comes; but I'll not be able to enjoy that much since you voiced your disapproval of it so strongly. And physical change and rest without mental relaxation will not do much good. . . . I really haven't much heart for the retreat. . . . I feel mentally all used up. . . . The Lord will surely have to supply abundantly.

The Lord did provide. But for Virgil Michel it was the beginning of the end. With Maritain, Adler, and other leaders he took part in the Philosophical Symposium at the University of Notre Dame, November 4–5, discussing the social, economic, and political conditions in the United States. Here Dom Virgil gave a masterly address on one of his favorite subjects, "Ownership and the Human Person." It later seemed to the hearers that, believing himself soon to pass on, he was giving his philosophy of life. Waldemar Gurian, about to found the *Review of Politics,* heard the speech and invited Michel to join his board of advisers.[106]

Two weeks afterwards, however, worn out by labor and over-whelmed by an avalanche of correspondence and requests for articles and advice, Father Virgil fell victim to pleural pneumonia. A strep-tococcic infection set in. With complete resignation he passed to the Lord in his forty-ninth year on November 26, 1938, in the infirmary of St. John's Abbey, still with too many ideas for a large Benedictine Abbey and a small army of lay and clerical apostles to carry out. In life he had always been logical and systematic in his work; even his death followed that pattern. It was the last day of the liturgical year, shortly after midnight, while some students and a few confreres kept an all-night vigil and offered themselves in his place, if it were God's will. An eye-witness told the writer that Abbot Alcuin broke down and wept when word of Father Virgil's death came to him on the following morning.

At the time of his death, besides working on a four-year college curriculum for rural living and on a modified, Catholic version of the so-called Annapolis Plan, and also preparing the way for setting up an Extension Service, he had just finished his contribution to *Essays in Thomism*. A paper on agriculture was on his desk for the *Commonweal*. He had begun work on an article, "The Dynamic Character of Reality," for the first issue of the *Thomist* at the invita-tion of Walter Farrell, O.P. He was revising his *Life in Christ* and *The Christian in the World* for Benziger, and planning a book on "Liturgy and Culture." He was also outlining a series of lectures to be given that winter at the University of Wisconsin.

Letters and telegrams poured in from all over the country, eloquent proof that he had spread his message far. Thus he had written to Abbot Peter Engel before returning home from the Catholic Uni-versity of America in 1918 to begin his life's work: "I think the best thing for us, especially with the nervous American spirit, is to see ahead of ourselves at all times at least double the work we can man-age." [107] Associates have said that Virgil Michel had a way of practic-ing what he preached. But in the end he worked himself to death. Men from all walks of life, from university professors to Indians, came to the large funeral.

Of the many who wrote to Abbot Alcuin perhaps none so well summarized Michel's life as did Mortimer Adler, whose words will be a summary to this chapter:

It was a great loss, not only to you, but to all of us who knew Father Virgil, however slightly. His mental and spiritual qualities made him a gentle guide and an understanding friend. For me he was in addition, a companion in philosophy, in whose clear vision I trusted so much, because it combined undeviating regard for the truth with unswerving courage in pursuit. I learned much from him, particularly in the field of social philosophy, the field of justice. His little pamphlets on social questions and his exposition of the doctrine of the great social encyclicals will always remain reservoirs for me. They abound richly in the basic principles, boldly stated, rightly interpreted, and applied to the contemporary scene with a sound reckoning of the main currents of our times. . . .

. . . His was a voice crying out in what was almost a wilderness of silence and conformity and complacency. He dared always to be true to the principles of Christianity, first and foremost, and to regard the authority of merely human sources as secondary. He never allowed himself to betray these principles by an uncalled for compliance to local prejudices or institutional shibboleths. He would not become party to any cause which was not the cause of all good men. For him Christianity required more than lip-service. It required daily practice. . . .

In the crisis of our times, he saw the need to go straight to the point, leaning neither to the right nor to the left. He was almost alone, — in this country, — in his Christian understanding of the position the Church must take toward fascism and communism in the struggle for a good society; or, if not alone in such vision, he was certainly eminent and singular in the courage with which he expressed and reiterated the basic truths, plainly, frankly, and with impeccable honesty. He did this at great expense of time and labor, never saving himself if there was an opportunity to reach other minds through one or another vehicle of communication. He had many readers, through many channels, the country over, and these will realize how much his death has cost them in leadership and inspiration.[108]

NOTES TO CHAPTER 11

[1] "The Liturgical Movement and the Catholic Woman," in Catholic Central Verein of America: *Annual Report* (1929), p. 59.

[2] "Back to the Liturgy," *OF*, XI (1936), p. 11.

[3] "Social Reconstruction," *Michaelman*, IV (1939), p. 23.

[4] "A Christian Education," *OF*, XIII (1939), 128.

[5] "The Basic Need of Christian Education Today," National Benedictine Educational Association: *Proceedings*, XII (1929), 34–35; an adaptation of this address appeared in the *Catholic Educational Review*, XXVIII (1930), 3–12; the well-known anthropologist, John Cooper, was impressed by Michel's analysis of the age and wrote to ask whether the observations were the fruit of a formal survey, and if not, whether he would undertake such a survey; Michel answered that the analysis was "the result of ordinary observation here and elsewhere . . ." and also that "making such a survey is entirely outside of my work." Then he asked Cooper whether the Catholic University could not undertake it (Michel to Cooper, Collegeville, Jan. 29, 1930, copy).

[6] "The Basic Need of Christian Education Today," NBEA: *Proceedings*, XII (1929) 38; cf. pp. 34–38.

[7] *Ibid.*, p. 38.

[8] *Ibid.*, p. 40; "The staff of the Christian college today must be, not a well-drilled army of technicians, but a well-unified cooperative family spontaneously breathing out a common atmosphere" (*idem*, p. 41).

[9] *Ibid.*, p. 41.

[10] Cf. "Education for Tomorrow," *Free America*, II (1938), 13–14.

[11] "Utopia Rediviva," *Catholic Educational Review*, XXIV (1926), 257–264; 356–364. Note the strong cultural emphasis in this and in other articles on education by Michel.

[12] Actually the University of Chicago began its examination of the undergraduate program in 1925, but the new curriculum was inaugurated only in 1931. Hutchins' *Higher Learning in America* appeared in 1936. Cf. Michel, "Religion for Credit," *Catholic Educational Review*, XXI (1923), 465–470. W. F. Cunningham, C.S.C., in "Christian Culture in General Education," *America*, XCIII (1955), 63–65, gives a summary of the history of general education in the United States; this article throws Michel's educational ideas and endeavors into proper perspective.

[13] "Utopia Rediviva," *Catholic Educational Review*, XXIV (1926), 258; italics, Michel's.

[14] Alfred H. Lloyd, "The Time of Day," *Scientific Monthly*, XVII (1923), 571, as quoted in "Utopia Rediviva," pp. 259–260.

[15] *Ibid.*, 263; the definition was that of Charles W. Eliot and quoted from Horne, *The Philosophy of Education*, p. 244.

[16] "Utopia Rediviva," p. 258. Cf. "Science and Its Hopes," *Acolyte*, June 29, 1929.

[17] "Utopia Rediviva," p. 264; Michel of course elaborates the points only mentioned in this section.

[18] *Ibid.*, pp. 356–357; italics, Michel's; note how Hutchins made more or less the same point eleven years later in "The Integrating Principle of Catholic Higher Education," *College Newsletter, Midwest Region Unit, NCEA*, (May, 1937).

[19] "Utopia Rediviva," p. 357; cf. "Education for Tomorrow," *Free America*, II (1938), 13.

[20] Cf. "Stimulating Intellectual Independence in Senior College Students," *Catholic Educational Review*, XXV (1927), 524–533.

[21] "Utopia Rediviva," p. 358.

[22] *Ibid.*, pp. 363–364.

[23] "Liturgy and Catholic Life," p. 189; references to education can be found throughout Michel's writings and correspondence.

[24] *Catholic Educational Review*, XXXVI (1938), 65–77. Cf. *College Newsletter, Midwest Regional Unit, NCEA* (May and Oct., 1937). The second anonymous letter in the October issue on how the NCEA might improve and make the Catholic college more Catholic is Michel's. The Minnesota Conference of Catholic Colleges was founded in 1935 to promote Catholic educational ideals; it is now defunct.

[25] "Infidelity in the Church," *OF*, IX (1935), 493. According to Michel's correspondence, one Catholic college even numbered its courses according to those in a secular university; students of commerce in a famous Catholic university were required to take three hours of ethics per week for the first time in 1938, etc. He cited athleticism in some Catholic colleges as concrete evidence of a false sense of values.

[26] "Let's Examine Ourselves," *Catholic Educational Review*, XXXVI (1938), 65; that there was much dissatisfaction with the NCA among the officials of the denominational and Catholic colleges in Minnesota is evident from the Michel Papers. Hence the anomaly of being faced by NCA standards. Speaking of the unique character of Catholic education, Michel explained: "By religion I do not here mean the isolated thing that is sometimes taught in specialized departments of religion, but rather the whole ensemble of Christian truths and ideals as these should inspire and permeate a complete philosophy of life — a philosophy of life, in turn, that must inspire and permeate every element and activity that is subsumed under the phrase of Christian education or, for us here, of the Catholic college" (*ibid.*, p. 66).

[27] *Ibid.*, p. 69. Speaking to the American College of Hospital Administrators in October, 1955, Dr. Hutchins observed that, as President of the

University of Chicago, he did not fully realize the urgent need for carrying on education on a small, personal, truly human scale (cf. Russell Kirk, "From the Academy," *National Review*, I [1955], 25).

[28] "Let's Examine Ourselves," p. 71. Cf. "Supervision," National Benedictine Educational Association: *Proceedings*, VI (1923), 67–74.

[29] "Let's Examine Ourselves," 74. Faculty competence, Michel believed, could be best achieved if the graduate student — unhampered by residence requirements at one school and not constrained into a narrowly specialized field of study and research — could for a few years choose the courses he needed and the best professors anywhere in the country instead of "spending many hours at what is frequently a wasteful make-believe of creative work disguised under the high-sounding title of a doctoral thesis" (*idem*). A school, he said, should be "a short-cut" to years of private study and application.

[30] *Ibid.*, p. 76.

[31] *Ibid.*, p. 77; italics, Michel's.

[32] Documentation withheld; italics, of the president quoted.

[33] Did Michel favor the entrance of St. John's into the NCA in his last years? There is no agreement among his confreres, and the writer finds the question impossible to answer adequately. Considerable evidence from Michel's articles and letters could be marshalled in support of the view that in the late 1930's he seems to have abandoned all hope that secular accrediting agencies like the NCA or even the NCEA would lead the way to a vital higher education; and for this reason he may have come to the conclusion that St. John's should strike out on its own educationally and prove itself by its graduates. Yet, this would have been a complete reversal of his thinking in the 1920's. Abbot Alcuin, who suggested a Catholic accrediting agency, had always considered acceptance of secular accreditation as dictation by secular standards; even in 1950 he accepted membership in the NCA most reluctantly. On the other hand, Michel believed that an accrediting agency, after insisting on certain basic standards, should allow for the individual character and aims of each institution. Eventually the NCA came to this. In view of the fact that Catholic education after Michel's death made notable progress along the lines he had suggested (cf. Cunningham, *op. cit.*) and in view also of the decided swing by the NCA to more qualitative standards, it is safe to say that Michel would have urged joining the NCA.

[34] "Stimulating Intellectual Independence in Senior College Students," *Catholic Educational Review*, XXV (1927), 531. "Real intellectual independence, therefore, seems to include a general broad knowledge of the problems of life and of their various aspects and implications" (*idem*, p. 529). Otherwise a one-sided, self-sufficient point of view cannot be avoided. In this article there is a good description of the dangers and pitfalls of intense specialization; and it contains many stimulating suggestions for teacher and student.

[35] *Ibid.*, p. 532.

[36] *Ibid.*, XXII (1924), 267. Cf. "Smith-Towner Bill Again," *Educational Review*, LXI (1921), 70–79.

[37] *Catholic Educational Review*, XXV (1927), 147–155; *The Christian in the World*, pp. 112–121.

[38] "The Need Today of College Courses in Political Science," National Benedictine Educational Association: *Proceedings*, XVIII (1935), 26–27.

[39] "Education for Tomorrow," *Free America*, II (1938), p. 13.

[40] Cf. "City or Farm," *OF*, XII (1938), 367–389. Since Michel's time many suburban communities have sprung up, hardly what he called for; today suburbia is not without its critics.

[41] "Education for Tomorrow," *Free America*, II (1938), p. 14.

[42] Michel's intention, of course, was to work out some kind of model for similar courses in other schools and to furnish study club materials for various lay groups with which he was in contact.

[43] The exchange of letters with Adler ran from January 27, 1937, to November 22, 1938. On September 13, 1938, Adler submitted at Michel's request and according to the latter's general specifications a ten-page memorandum for the Great Books program to be inaugurated at St. John's. Michel's plan was to begin experimentally with twenty freshmen, and then on the basis of experience, to build up the program further, if warranted. Initially there were to be one seminar, one formal lecture with discussion, and three tutorials: 1) reading and writing; 2) study of the classics; 3) mathematics and science — amounting to twelve hours of class weekly. Students were expected to put in twice this amount of time in preparation; planned in addition to this were six hours of classes in a major field taught in the traditional way. The program was to begin in the fall of 1939. "I am sure that your plan of spending next year in preparation to begin the actual teaching program the year after is well advised. . . ." "I am delighted that your first meeting [with the faculty] was so successful" (Adler to Michel, Chicago, June 15 and Nov. 22, 1938). Adler, "A Christian Educator," *OF*, XIII (1939), 123–129, summarizes Michel's plans. Great Books programs went into operation at Manhattan College and Notre Dame in 1949 and 1950, respectively (cf. Cunningham, *op. cit.*).

[44] Cf., e.g., St. John's *Record*, Jan. 17, Feb. 14, 1935; May 14, 28, and Sept. 24, 1936; May 6, 1937.

[45] "Education for Tomorrow," *Free America*, II (1938), p. 14.

[46] "Christian Education for Rural Living," *Catholic Rural Life Bulletin*, I (1938), 21.

[47] Cf. Bishop Busch — A. Matt — Boerger — Blenker — Michel Letters. "The bishop [Busch of St. Cloud] is taking the stand that . . . under all circumstances the Institute and the Catholic Action Program are to go on anyhow" (Michel to A. Matt, Collegeville, Feb. 5, 1937, copy).

[48] "Father Virgil and the Social Institute," *OF*, XIII (1939), 137–138; besides this description of the Institute, cf. also John Giesen, "A Cooperative Study," *Catholic Action*, XIX (1937), 9–10; Michel, "An Institute for Social Study," *Central-Blatt and Social Justice*, XXIX (1936), 170–171 and 211–212. Beginning its first conference in January, 1935, it became a war casualty in 1942. Peter E. Dietz organized the first such institute in 1909: cf. Fox, *Peter E. Dietz Labor Priest*, pp. 32–34. Cf. Exchange

of letters between Kenkel and Michel concerning the Institute, May 14, 1935, to Feb. 2, 1938.

[49] It is impossible to mention the activities the Institute inspired or in which it took part beyond these two: Dom Virgil planned and gave with Busch and other priests a series of lectures to a unit of the National Catholic Women's Union in St. Paul in the winters of 1936–38 inclusive; and he planned with the help of Father Ferdinand Falque, director of Catholic Action for the Diocese of St. Cloud, the series of lectures given by himself, confreres, and diocesan priests for the Catholic Action and Catholic Family Institutes in St. Cloud in 1936 and 1937. Michel's topical outlines for all three series are in the Michel Papers. Cf. Letters of Falque to Michel, Dec. 5, 1936, to May 21, 1938. "The bishop likewise approves of the idea that you should preside at all the sessions, as we agreed yesterday" (Falque to Michel, St. Cloud, Dec. 5, 1936).

[50] Statements like these are common in the Michel Papers: "May I compliment you on the fine publications which appear from your university. I do not understand how you can put out such fine works at the low price you charge. I shall show the work on political forms to our political science professor. It would be much better than the semi-pagan works out for general use. My best wishes for your success in your many excellent enterprises." "Permit me to congratulate you on the excellent work you are turning out on all sides. It is a real pleasure to see your name appended to a book or article" (John Cronin, S.S., to Michel, Baltimore, Mar. 21, 1938, and Apr. 2, 1936). "I have been following with a great deal of interest the work of the Institute. . . . It appears to me that St. John's is leading the way in the field of social reconstruction as it has so magnificently in the liturgical movement. Personally I feel a great debt of gratitude to you for the numerous excellent publications and pamphlets which you have given us" (Thomas Manning, O.M.I., to Michel, Ottawa, Dec. 9, 1937).

[51] Cf. A. Matt to Michel, St. Paul, Oct. 23, 1936. Kenkel strongly disagreed with Michel's view and wrote to Matt of Michel that "this is characteristic of the man" (Central Verein Archives in St. Louis: A. Matt to Kenkel, St. Paul, Oct. 23, 1936; Kenkel to Matt, St. Louis, Oct. 26, 1936, copy). The Central Verein began advocating credit unions in 1913 without much success. The first Federal Credit Union Act was passed only in 1934; at about that time the Credit Union National Association was formed, the majority of its members now being Catholic parishes. Cf. J. T. Croteau, "The Parish Credit Union in the Federal Credit Union System," *American Ecclesiastical Review*, CXXV (1951), 293–302, and the Denver *Register*, January 28, 1955. Note how Dietz warned Kenkel as early as 1910 of the dangers of Central Verein self-isolation (cf. Fox, *op. cit.*, p. 34).

[52] *Christian Social Reconstruiction*, pp. 122–123. Cf. *Social Forum*, May, 1938.

[53] "The Cooperative Movement and the Liturgical Movement," in *Catholic Rural Life Objectives* (St. Paul: NCRLC, n.d.), pp. 16–18. This article was widely reprinted; also in *OF*, XIV (1940), 152–160.

⁵⁴ LaFarge and Michel, "Farmer Cooperatives," in *Manifesto on Rural Life* (Milwaukee: Bruce, 1939), p. 58.

⁵⁵ "Social Reconstruction," *Michaelman*, IV (1939), 23; but cf. Michel "The Small Shopkeeper," *Free America*, II (1938), 7; Michel, "Coopera- tion in a Distributist Society," *G. K.'s Weekly*, XXVI (1938), 352. Ed- ward Koch, "Injudicious Support of Cooperation," *Guildsman*, V (1937), 3–6, is an answer, requested by Michel to his own, "The Basic Soundness of Cooperation," *Christian Front*, II (1937), 5–6.

⁵⁶ Actually the main reason for going to Nova Scotia was to spread the liturgical apostolate; Michel sent Father James Tompkins twenty topics and asked him on which he would like to have him lecture. Tompkins answered: "You have guessed aright — we want to 'pick your brains' on this liturgical movement, to give you a chance to tell us all about it. . . . Priests in these parts will be glad to talk with you and meet you." After Michel's tour, Tompkins invited him back and wrote, "Your name is indeed in benediction down here and will be so remembered." "Your tribe will increase in these parts and beyond." "Your article in the *Com- monweal* (April 29, 1938) hits the bull's eye. Some of your capitalist friends will have lock-jaw when they read the *Commonweal*." "I have been reading — sometimes at 3 A.M. — your little blue books. . . . They are wonderful. How have you succeeded in keeping your light under a bushel? You have a message for the whole world. I am fast becoming *your* disciple. You should be *free* to write and explain in popular form your amazing messages" (to Michel, Reserve Mines, Feb. 23, April 29, May 13 and June 14, 1938; italics, Tompkins'). Michel had been in con- tact with the real liturgical pioneer in the Maritime Provinces, Monsignor Charles Curran (cf. "Monsignor Curran," *Worship*, XXVIII [1954], 532–533). Inviting Michel to give retreats to his clergy, Bishop J. H. MacDonald wrote to him, "It takes time to make our priests social-minded in the true sense of the term, but I know it can be done. I was very pleased with reports of your visit to Antigonish, where the influence of your ad- dress will be felt for years to come" (Edmonton, Alberta, June 3, 1938).

⁵⁷ From Michel's Diary, Apr. 10 and 19: "Reserve Mines once a regular hobo place, drunkenness galore. Cooperatives, credit unions, study clubs did the work. Adult education is the backbone and background of the whole business. . . . Biggest feature of movement is the education pro- gram and reading done by simple folks. From these the ideas and the doing come of themselves." "Actual projects among people often start after three or four months of study; sometimes after a year. . . . One man learned to read after sixty years of age."

⁵⁸ "Father Tompkins feels that you are destined to do a great work in the United States" (Bowen to Michel, Chicago, May 12, 1938).

⁵⁹ Day, "Fellow Worker in Christ," *OF*, XII (1939), 139. But Michel never failed to say how much he learned from Tompkins.

⁶⁰ Reserve Mines, Dec. 1, 1938. There is a brief description of Michel's preliminary plans in "Rural Life Notes," *Free America*, II (1938), 13. Abbot Alcuin had given Michel permission to establish this Extension Service. Besides promoting cooperatives and credit unions and "a number

of practical reconstruction programs, first of all, within our own neighborhood," the Service was to conduct a small, year-round folk-school, and various adult education programs, including a training center for Catholic rural leaders. (Michel to Walter Sturges, Oct. 31, 1938, copy). The over-all aim was to build a Catholic rural culture exemplified in a self-sustaining rural community (cf. *Wanderer*, Oct. 23, 1941).

[61] "City or Farm," *OF*, XII (1938), 367.

[62] Hynes, *op. cit.*, p. 175. Thus Borsodi wrote to Michel, "My trip to St. John's gave me a new perspective on what we are doing here, and I cannot thank you enough for the inspiration" (Suffern, Nov. 11, 1938). After Michel's death: "We have lost a wonderful friend. The movement has lost a wonderful leader" (Borsodi to Deutsch, Suffern, n.d.).

[63] The sponsoring professor told this writer: "Fr. Virgil impressed me greatly with his quietness and confidence. He made an excellent talk and a fine impression at the Conference. The group felt then and I still feel that his written work, although not extensive, is an important contribution to the literature on the integral life" (Baker Brownell, Evanston, Feb. 18, 1953).

[64] "City or Farm," *OF*, XII (1938), 368.

[65] He summarized the discussion of such a curriculum and methods in "The Christian Education for Rural Living," *The Catholic Rural Life Bulletin*, I (1938), 19–21. This, his last article on education, is also his best on methods: "Again, the educational activity itself is not to be confined to formal courses of instruction, to the accepted methods of the past, in which the teacher quite spontaneously does a maximum and the student a minimum in the expenditure of effort. . . . Unless education again resumes its noble task of 'drawing out' the student self-activity, instead of suppressing and dulling his thirst for knowledge, we are not even beginning to get out of our present bad way" (*ibid.*, p. 20).

[66] "We are asking you to do two things; first, to suggest revisions of or additions to the Manifesto proper, and secondly, to supply us with the factual materials and pertinent references for the annotations. . . . Kindly let me have your report not later than August 28" (Muench to Michel, Aug. 6, 1938; cf. Bruce to Deutsch, Milwaukee, Dec. 2, 1938. Cf. *Manifesto on Rural Life* (Milwaukee: Bruce, 1939), pp. 73–74. *Twenty-Five Years of Crusading* (Des Moines: NCRLC, 1948), by Raymond Witte, is a history of the NCRLC.

[67] Cf. Luigi Ligutti to Michel, Granger, Jan. 3, 1938; Michel to Walter Sturges, Collegeville, Oct. 31, 1938, copy; Franz Mueller to Michel, St. Louis, Mar. 30, 1938. Witte, *op. cit.*, pp. 199–200, has wrong dates in his account.

[68] To the writer, Kansas City, Feb. 18, 1953. Cf. Muench, "A Friend of Rural Life," *OF*, XIII (1939), 130–134. The Executive Secretary of the NCRLC, Father James Byrnes, with whom Michel corresponded from August 18, 1935, to November 7, 1938, wrote: "Father Virgil's gifts of mind and heart are matched but rarely. . . . He shared them with reckless generosity whenever and wherever he sensed the prospect of profit to Church and society. We of the Conference drew heavily upon the great

good will of Father Virgil. On innumerable occasions we disturbed him at his studies, or summoned him from his monastic seclusion, often to points distant from St. John's, to give of the richness of his knowledge and judgment. Not once did he hesitate to lend himself to our undertakings" (editorial, *The Catholic Rural Life Bulletin*, II [1939], 15).

69 Cf. Apostolate, *OF*, VIII (1934), 284, 277; Michel to Day, Collegeville, Feb. 14, 1934, copy; *Catholic Worker*, May, 1934; Bussard, "The Source of Christian Spirit," *OF* (1936), 323–326.

70 Lack of space prevents citing many examples from the Catholic press. "I remember that it was not easy to get Catholics to join (unions). And I remember too . . . that there were only a handful of priests in the diocese who were willing to get out and assure hesitant Catholics that they had the papal encyclicals on their side" (James O'Gara, "Communism in the Thirties," *Commonweal* [1955], 425); O'Gara (p. 424) cites a statistic from *Report on the American Communist* that 700,000 Americans left the Communist Party in 1930–50. The *Daily Worker* in January, 1934 (the year of the United Front), boasted that it had spread 250,000 copies over the United States, and that the communists were organized in 500 cities (*Daily Worker*, January, 1934; cf. *Catholic Worker*, February, May, 1934, and May, 1937). Allowing for bias, one could perhaps find no better account of communist activities and much Catholic indifference and inaction in the 1930's than in the *Catholic Worker*. Back issues are on microfilm at the Catholic University of America.

71 Cf. *Catholic Worker*, October, 1934; the communist line was that the Church, not having a social program, would suppress the *Catholic Worker*. But the officials of the New York chancery office were, of course, fully aware of the true situation and of CW activities from the beginning and through authorities suggested to the editors to choose a priest-adviser to be approved by them. Chosen was Joseph McSorley, C.S.P.

72 Michel to Adalbert Callahan, O.F.M., Collegeville, Feb. 6, 1936, copy; "Our Fathers here generally have been viewing the 'Workers' with a certain sense of suspicion for reasons which I cannot elaborate upon here, but are nevertheless well grounded" (Callahan to Michel, New York, Jan. 18, 1936).

73 E.g., "Thank you for your continued support of our work." "Thank you very much for both your kind letters. . . . We are certainly glad for your friendly criticism and will do our best to work as Christians (this as members of the Mystical Body), and with love rather than animosity. . . . We do indeed realize our responsibilities. . . . The one thing I do not agree with you at all about was your feeling that perhaps 'each one is willing to let the other one assume the burden of assistance in the general work.' I am very careful at this time to do nothing without the advice of Father McSorley, our approved advisor, so there will be as much united front as he sees fit. He has been in touch with the work since the beginning and I thank God that we have a priest who is on hand always to tell us what sides to take" (Day to Michel, New York, Apr. 16, Oct. 5, 1936). Cf. Day, "Fellow Worker in Christ," *OF*, XIII (1939), 139–141, for her account of Michel's relations with the *Catholic Worker*.

⁷⁴ Cf. *Catholic Worker*, Oct., 1938.

⁷⁵ "We read the New York *Times* last Sunday with consternation, for it brought to us news of the death of our inspiration and leader, Dom Virgil Michel. I could hardly believe it at first. . . . We cannot tell you what an inspiration Dom Virgil was to us. I am certain that our lives bear the impress of the work which he started. A missal and a Divine Office before me on my desk are fruit, in a small measure, of the work he carried on. Certainly there are thousands of other young Catholic men who owe their inspiration to the unceasing and Christian labors of Dom Virgil" (Deverall to Deutsch, Villanova, Nov. 28, 1938). Norman McKenna kindly submitted files of letters from Michel and from Furfey, and his own replies. The *Christian Front* began in January, 1936.

⁷⁶ The *Social Forum*, a first class labor paper clarifying Catholic social thought and fighting the communists, was founded by Smith Sullivan, O.M.I., in March, 1936; eventually it came into the hands of various laymen with whom Michel corresponded, among them: John Connolley, Robert Fay, Olga LaPlante, etc.

⁷⁷ Cf. Bolen Carter to Michel, East St. Louis, Mar. 26, 1936, and Mar. 8, 1938; *Catholic Alliance*, February, 1939.

⁷⁸ O'Shaughnessy to Michel, New Canaan, Feb. 12, 1936. This league and publication are not to be confused with those founded by Father Coughlin.

⁷⁹ "His articles were always well received. When we had something from Virgil Michel, we know we had something substantial. He encouraged us through 1938 when we were in a most precarious position" (Skillin to the writer in an interview, New York, Dec. 19, 1952).

⁸⁰ E.g., the editor of *Social Order*, B. S. Gilani, of Alahabad, U.P., India, wrote to Michel on April 28, 1938: "I published a series of your articles some months ago, and am now hoping that you will kindly help us again. My paper will have given you some idea of the Indian economic conditions. We are in a state of serfdom with some 250,000,000 of our masses who have never had a day's whole meal, any day for years on end. How would St. Thomas view such a distress; what he would say to the people who have driven us to this state and what he would do to set matters right—these are some of the questions, the replies of which will interest Indian non-Catholics."

⁸¹ The Campions—nationally about 400 strong in 1936—published a Parish Liturgical Bulletin that at one time had a circulation of 4,000; they battled the communists and scattered thousands of leaflets on the liturgy and the social teachings of the Church. *Liturgy and Sociology* began in February, 1936, and after building up more than 3,000 subscriptions, failed financially in January, 1938 (cf. Michel-Albert Coddington letters, Feb. 4, 1936, to Feb. 17, 1938). Coddington wrote much on the liturgy for the *Catholic Worker*.

⁸² "Catholic Workers and Apostles," *OF*, XIII (1938), 71.

⁸³ In reviewing Dr. Mary Elizabeth Walsh's *The Saints and Social Work*, Michel remarked, "Dr. Walsh is assistant to Father Furfey, and both deserve hearty congratulations for the true spirit of Christianity they

are injecting into the Department of Sociology at the Catholic University and far beyond" (*OF*, XI [1937], 335).

⁸⁴ Furfey to Michel, Washington, Jan. 27, 1937. The address referred to was given to the American Catholic Philosophical Association meeting in Chicago: "The Challenge of Modern Social Thought to Neo-Scholasticism," *Proceedings*, XII (1936), 45–58. "Did Father Martin show you the letter that I wrote to him immediately after the Chicago meeting? . . . I at once expressed my opinion of your stand as I saw it, to Father Martin in the hopes that he would show my letter to you. This was not meant that you should become convinced of my view, but rather that we would understand one another's attitudes better and could more readily enter into frank discussion and exchange of opinions" (Michel to Furfey, Collegeville, Jan. 30, 1937, copy). For Furfey's concept of personalism, cf. *Fire on the Earth*, pp. 92–97; for a critique, cf. Cronin, *Catholic Social Principles* (Milwaukee: Bruce, 1950), 684–692. Father Furfey graciously made available a file of letters.

⁸⁵ Interview with Catherine De Hueck, Washington, Feb. 5, 1953; cf. *Restoration*, April, 1953.

⁸⁶ *Ibid*. "It was to him that my mind instinctively turned when I was troubled, to him that I went for counsel and advice. . . . His last letter was so full of courage, advice, and help" (De Hueck to Deutsch, New York, n.d.). Cf. *Social Forum*, March, 1936, April, 1937; Friendship House *Monthly Letter* (Chicago), March, 1946; Furfey to McKenna, Washington, April 12, 1937. It was through the encouragement of the priests George Ford, Michael Mulvoy, and John LaFarge, S.J., that the Friendship House in Harlem was established in February, 1938. No one has done more for the inter-racial apostolate than Father LaFarge.

⁸⁷ Cf. Vincent J. Giese, "The Lay Apostolate in Chicago," in Louis J. Putz (ed.), *Catholic Church, U.S.A.* (Chicago: Fides, 1956), 358–374. Dennis J. Geaney, O.S.A., "The Chicago Story," *Today*, X (1955), 10–11, gives an account of the beginnings and of the leading personalities in the various phases of this apostolic lay movement. But one should also mention the pioneer work of Jesuits Gerald Ellard, William Puetter and Daniel Lord and the sodalities: cf. Michel's correspondence with these, starting in 1926.

⁸⁸ "In these papers (*Ciscora News, Raven*) I have checked the articles on the liturgy. We would like very much to make an impression some place, but whether we are succeeding or not we cannot tell" (Sister Estelle to Michel, Chicago, Dec. 15, 1929). A small contingent of nuns from St. Scholastica's Convent in Chicago had attended the liturgical summer school at St. John's Abbey in 1929 and 1930, and thereafter began liturgical activity on a small scale in connection with the sodality.

⁸⁹ Cf. Michel-Sister Cecilia letters, Dec. 24, 1934, to Oct. 24, 1938; "It looks as though we shall have well over a thousand for our two Catholic Action Institutes based on the Dogma of the Mystical Body" (Carrabine to Michel, Oct. 22, 1935). There was also a healthy collaboration between the Chicago *Catholic Worker* and Cisca, involving among others Ed Marciniak, James O'Gara, Tom Sullivan, and John Cogley: cf. Michel-

Dr. Arthur Falls correspondence, May 21, 1935, to Mar. 7, 1938. "We are deeply grieved by the death of Father Virgil. His life and labors were an inspiration to us in our work, and we shall always remember him gratefully" (Cogley to Deutsch, Chicago, Nov. 28, 1938).

[90] Chicago, Aug. 6, 1935. To Michel's examination she submitted all her writings. Cf. "The Cisca Plan," OF, X (1935), 68–77; Apostolate, 80–82. The detailed plan contained about 200 pages; Michel had the fond hope that the Cisca Plan might be the beginning of a nation-wide, apostolic, youth movement, an American adaptation of the Jocist movement in Europe. In an interview with the writer, Chicago, August 26, 1953, Father Carrabine said of Michel: "After the encyclicals, he was my greatest inspiration in directing Cisca and in teaching in the classroom."

[91] Op cit., p. 11.

[92] The amount of Michel's correspondence touching this area is incredible: cf., e.g., his letters to and from Donald Attwater, Norman McKenna, Serge Bolshakoff, Maurice B. Reckitt, editor of the Anglican quarterly, Christendom, Dom Bede Winslow, editor of Eastern Churches Quarterly, and many others.

[93] Apostolate, OF, II (1927), 58; italics, Michel's; cf. Theodore Vermilye, "Father Virgil and Church Unity," OF, XIII (1939), 113–116.

[94] According to his correspondence, this address was published in Christendom, not available to the writer. Working with Father George Ford of New York and Theodore Vermilye — then executive secretary of the Anglican Church Unity Octave Council — and others, Michel tried to arrange unofficial and entirely informal round table discussions between twelve Catholic priests and twelve Anglican clergymen to discuss points of agreement and disagreement with a view to promoting better understanding and to preparing the ground for possible future reunion. The bishop of Ogdensberg was in favor of such meetings and even offered himself as chairman; diocesan authorities of New York, when consulted, were not in favor; the bishop of Brooklyn said he would need the approval of the Apostolic Delegate; the Apostolic Delegate disclaimed jurisdiction. Nothing came of the attempts. In this Michel was not the initiator, but as so often, the strong encourager; he was offered the chairmanship but declined because of distance, but he did work out preliminary procedures and topics for getting the discussions under way, should bishops approve (cf. Michel-Vermilye letters, Feb. 23, 1937 to Nov. 16, 1938). According to Michel's letters from Europe, such unofficial and informal discussions between Anglicans, Catholics, and Orthodox were going on there with episcopal blessing.

[95] Cf. Busch-Michel letters; the history of the League is recorded in successive issues of Orate Fratres, starting in January, 1936. In 1935 the Society of the Magnificat had two members in the United States out of a total of 160 (Kathleen Pond to Busch, Oct. 24, 1935). The first known organized attempt by laymen to recite the Church's prayer was that of the Approved Workmen of New York, who began in 1924 under the leadership of Eugene McSweeney (cf. Liturgical Week: Proceedings [1940], pp. 153–157; McSweeney to Michel, New York, Sept. 10, 1928). Cf. Michel,

404 VIRGIL MICHEL AND THE LITURGICAL MOVEMENT

"Campions and the League of the Divine Office," *Liturgy and Sociology*, I (1936), 14–15, 18. In 1952 Godfrey Diekmann, O.S.B., estimated that "several hundred thousand of the laity are more or less regularly praying at least part of the Divine Office" ("The Primary Apostolate," in *American Apostolate*, p. 37).

96 "First Rate Catholic Action," *OF*, XII (1937), 35. Cf. Brother Cornelius Justin to Michel, New York, April 4, 1936; Feb. 2, 1937, and the O'Leary-Michel correspondence. Spiritual director of the League was Rt. Rev. Henry O'Carroll, V.F. Participating in the newspaper work were seminarians of St. Joseph's Seminary, Dunwoodie, under the direction of Michel's close friend, Father Jeremiah Toomey. Both the Laymen's League and the Alumni Committee on Catholic Action were founded by O'Leary, while Brother Cornelius Justin, F.S.C., moderated the alumni group. "The course at Manhattan is starting this semester. It is called Social Ethics and will be properly accredited. Brother Justin is conducting it, and will have some of the alumni give a few classes during the year, to make a connection with contemporary movements. Fordham is rumored to be starting a Catholic Workers College. Are we becoming social minded!" (McKenna to Michel, New York, Sept. 24, 1937); cf. Apostolate, *OF*, XI (1937), 512–515.

97 *Wanderer*, Dec. 1, 1938.

98 E.g., according to his Diary he spoke on April 5, 1938, to the following groups on the following subjects: to Franciscan seminarians: "The Liturgical Movement and the Franciscan Idea"; Marygrove collegians: "The Apostolate of the Christian Woman Today"; over radio station CKLW (Windsor): "The Corporative Order"; Assumption College: "The Social Question." On the train he met a Franciscan retreatmaster and learned that he had "evidently no suspicion of the liturgical movement or of the social question"; from two lads returning from an Anglican boarding school and drinking liquor in the "wash apartment" he wheedles their views on school-life, religion, and their pessimistic outlook for the future. (Such conversations were typical of his way of familiarizing himself with all things human.) "At Toronto met by John, Pat & Elmer & two others. . . . Talked till 12:00, then one hour discussion on plans & ideals of *Social Forum*." "At Montreal met by J. T. O'Connor, friend of J. G. Connolley, together with five other gentlemen all keen on liturgy and social question. Most delightful meeting around supper table and discussion" (Diary, April 4–8, 1938). Cf. *Social Forum*, May, 1938.

99 Apostolate, *OF*, XI (1936), 30.

100 Michel to William F. Sands, Collegeville, May 20, 1936, copy.

101 *America*, LX (1938), 218.

102 To the present writer, Chicago, Oct. 10, 1954.

103 Bussard to the writer, New York, Mar. 31, 1954.

104 July 23, 1936, Collegeville.

105 January 30, 1936, Collegeville. Within a decade of Michel's death, Abbot Alcuin shocked two monks with the statement that the Liturgical Press and *Orate Fratres* could gradually cease operations since they had done their work. Could he have been serious?

[106] The speech is found in *Review of Politics*, I (1939), 155–178. "Father Virgil was one of the most open-minded priests whom I have ever met and a man of admirable intellectual interests in the most varied fields" (Gurian to Deutsch, Notre Dame, Nov. 28, 1938).

[107] Washington, Mar. 3, 1918.

[108] Chicago, Nov. 27, 1938.

CHAPTER 12

SUMMARY AND EVALUATION

Thirty years ago Father Virgil Michel told his confreres at home and collaborators elsewhere that the liturgical movement was, from a human standpoint, a hopeless case. However, he hardly had a doubt that it would succeed. If they planted "prayerfully, prudently, and patiently," God in His own time and way would give the increase. For the liturgical apostolate was God's work, he said, and the Holy Spirit was its promoter.

Actually, the cause for the revival of the liturgy has progressed beyond Dom Virgil's most sanguine hopes. Compared with conditions in the 1920's, liturgical renewal has in many ways been notable.

At once Pius XII's words of last year to the International Congress on Pastoral Liturgy suggest themselves:

If one compares the present state of the liturgical movement with what it was thirty years ago, it is obvious that undeniable progress has been made both in extent and in depth. . . . The liturgical movement is thus shown forth as a sign of the providential dispositions of God and for the present time, of the movement of the Holy Ghost in the Church, to draw men more closely to the mysteries of the faith and the riches of grace which flow from the active participation of the faithful in the liturgical life. . . . We express the wish that this new sowing, together with the work of the past, will bring forth a rich harvest, to the benefit of the individual members as well as the Church as a whole.[1]

Nevertheless, to assess the strength of a leaven is difficult, if not impossible. Who would presume to measure the work of the Holy Spirit? Add to this the difficulty of evaluating the varied thought and activity of a man who never sought the limelight and who preferred to work behind the scenes, and a perilous task is at hand.

In one of his first editorials Dom Virgil instructed his co-workers that they might never see the full fruit of their labors. Certainly he himself did not see the results of his own. On December 18, 1938, the scholarly Jesuit collaborator, Father Ellard, wrote to Abbot Alcuin concerning Michel's death:

We have lost a great leader. In the cause of the liturgical apostolate in America, with which Dom Virgil was most closely associated, he was surely the most clear-sighted observer, the most articulate voice, the readiest, most gifted all-around worker. His removal comes just when, the long and pioneer work fairly well over, a nation-wide response seemed to be at hand.

In attempting to evaluate the liturgical renaissance it would seem best to do so in terms of the progressive liturgical evolution which Michel foresaw and set in organized motion. In 1925 the vernacular daily missal enjoyed only a limited use. Even in 1928, as has been pointed out, there were fewer than 50,000 such missals in the United States. Today many millions of copies of the nineteen editions of English daily missals are in the hands of the faithful. According to Michel's correspondence, even priests at first considered the idea of lay recitation of parts of the divine office wholly unrealistic. Today hundreds of thousands are familiar with at least a part of the Church's prayer as a regular portion of their prayer-life. The Liturgical Press has sold more than 300,000 copies of its Prime and Compline booklets. *A Short Breviary*, first issued by the same Press in 1941, has gone through several editions, the latest revision having sold 25,000 copies in its first year. In 1956 the Collegeville Press alone sold 1,600,000 copies of its seasonal missal, *The Masses of Holy Week and the Easter Vigil*, and could have sold double that number except for the shortage of paper. The Liturgical Press distributes an annually increasing volume of liturgical literature to all parts of the English-speaking world.

In 1926 *Orate Fratres* began with 800 subscribers; in 1938 it had only 4,000; today *Worship* has approximately 10,000. As the editor of the *Catholic Journalist* wrote for November, 1950, "In proportion to its circulation, no Catholic magazine ever exercised so great an influence on American Catholic life." Meanwhile, other liturgical journals have come into the field.

Perhaps the greatest indication of progress — especially when contrasted with what was available in the 1920's — is, however, the content of current spiritual literature and periodicals. This literature is emphasizing more and more the heart of Christianity: Mass, sacraments, sacramentals, and the divine office. The auxiliary movement for the restoration of chant has likewise made much headway.

Since 1940 the Liturgical Week has drawn large numbers annually from all parts of the country.

When *Orate Fratres* began publication in 1926, the spiritual nature of the Church as the Mystical Body of Christ seems to have been given little attention in seminaries, to say nothing of being almost unknown among even informed and intelligent Catholic laymen. The very term "Mystical Body" was for a time suspect. Today the doctrine of the Mystical Body is much better understood and lived.

Three encyclicals, *Mystici Corporis, Mediator Dei,* and *De musicae sacrae disciplina,* the letter *Menti nostrae,* the American English Ritual, international liturgical congresses sponsored by the Sacred Congregation of Rites, evening Mass, the new psalter, change in the regulations concerning the communion fast and in the liturgy of Holy Week, simplification of the rubrics and calendar, as well as other liturgical innovations aimed at restoring a usable and living liturgy — these have confirmed what a small group of forward-looking apostles had pleaded or prepared for since the mid-1920's. Pius XII's message to the international liturgical congress at Assisi in 1956 constitutes the latest stamp of approval of the liturgical renaissance:

The present-day attitude of liturgical milieux towards the past seems to Us in general to be entirely sound: there is investigation, serious study, attachment to that which truly deserves it, without, moreover, a falling into excess. . . . We sincerely desire that the liturgical movement progress and We wish to help it; but it is Our office also to anticipate anything which would be a source of error and danger. It is, however, a consolation and a joy for Us to know that We can rely on your help and your understanding in these matters.[2]

In the United States more than in any other country has the liturgical apostolate enjoyed a peaceful evolution and development. One reason for this may be that Father Virgil did not confuse liturgical revival with liturgical reform. The pages of *Orate Fratres* were never open to those writers more interested in winning an argument than in promoting a spiritual cause.

If Virgil Michel had done nothing else than to organize the liturgical movement, his name would be enshrined among American Catholic leaders of this century. *Orate Fratres* and the Liturgical Press were his inspiration. But one should not fail to mention those who shared with him the burdens, the misunderstanding, and the loneliness that constitute the cross of pioneers. The first name is that of Abbot Alcuin Deutsch, whose initial vision allowed the work to start. Then there was Michel's forerunner, close friend and consultor, Father William Busch, as well as the priests Hellriegel, Ellard, Power, Cummins, and many others, clergy and laity. At Collegeville during Michel's time the liturgical work was always a family affair. However, if the whole family cannot be mentioned, one must at least mention Fathers Basil Stegmann, Cuthbert Goeb, Joseph Kreuter, Godfrey Diekmann, and William Heidt. Father Virgil's successor as editor-in-chief, Father Godfrey, has led *Worship* to its present maturity and status. However, there are those who think that *Worship* has lost some of the breadth of view found in the older *Orate Fratres*. On the other hand, the current greater concentration on scriptural and theological aspects of the liturgy rather than on its immediate and practical implications for Christian culture and the social apostolate may have been a healthy, natural evolution, especially since other semi-liturgical journals have come into the field and are stressing the social apostolate. It should be added that under Father William the Liturgical Press has broadened its influence in recent years.

Father Virgil once concluded an article that summarized a decade of liturgical progress by saying, "Much has been accomplished under God; yet almost everything needs yet to be done; we must start all over again." By and large, these words still apply, even if the liturgical leaven has in some way penetrated into every area of the Church's life. If the hopes of the promoters of the liturgical apostolate were somewhat shaken by the failure of some to understand — even in high places — the logic behind Pius XII's recent changes in the liturgy of Holy Week, they were perhaps restored by the response on the part of the faithful. However, the term "liturgical movement" still conjures up in the minds of many sincere priests thoughts of spiritually irrelevant, ceremonial perfectionism. This fact alone suggests that the liturgical apostolate is still more hope than reality. A movement may be said to have realized its purpose when its ideals become general practice. If the misunderstanding associated with the liturgical apostolate even today only proves its great need, then indeed, the movement has much work to do.

In the foreword to *Orate Fratres* Dom Virgil wrote that the liturgy is a veritable mine of the widest cultural life. In the brief life-span that was his, he quarried much and well. His unique contribution to American Catholic social thought and action was the integration of the liturgy with all phases of social action. It may not be too much to say that he, his confreres, and collaborators remedied, in part at least, "the spiritual lag" in the American Catholic social movement.

He was convinced that sound liturgical living could not but flower into apostolic action, individual and social, for reconstruction of an atomized and secularized society. Genuine Catholic social action begins when the Christian realizes from his membership in Christ that the gifts of nature and grace belong to the whole of mankind, that he fulfills the law of Christ to the extent that he bears another's burden.

If, therefore, the liturgical apostolate remained true to its nature, he held, it would gradually produce a living Catholic culture and a vital Christian art. Such a living Catholic culture would confirm at every turn the Christian as an apostle of Christ. Formed and inspired by the liturgical life, competent artists could create true works of sacred art, and thus restore the arts to the service of God and man.

Michel was interested in every new movement, in everything which might serve to bring the good tidings of the redemption into all activities of human life. In his own person he brought together the liturgical apostolate, different lay movements, the rural life and the Antigonish cooperative movements, the neo-Scholastic movement, the apostolate for improved religious education, the Hutchins-Adler educational ideas, encyclicals, and other vital currents.

Michel's was an integrated view of all the aspects of Christian living, natural and supernatural, individual and social. For him the Mystical Body had to be the unifying basis of all Catholic social endeavors, for in Christ all have one life, one work, and one goal: the extension of His kingdom. Christian life is an apostolate rooted in the Mass and the sacramental life. This living in Christ should affect in some way all of the Christian's acts, thoughts, words, and affections. In short, he who would effectively work with the Church must think and pray with her.

Father Virgil pondered deeply on the role of the Church in the modern world. He conceived the Church as a living organism, as

Christ continuing his redemptive life and action through the liturgy and in His incorporated members. The priest must "convert" the laity into being apostolic by leading them into active and intelligent contact with Christ in the liturgy; in turn, apostolic Christians in all spheres of life must win the world back to Christ. What if every Catholic layman really understood that he is a part of the Church, that Christ truly lives in him and wills to work through him, that because of the organic oneness of Christ's Body, the whole Body is rendered more or less effective by the way he lives his life and uses his apostolic opportunities? What if every family and parish were corporately so motivated? What if every priest, intensely living this great truth, brought this vision, to the Christian woman, to the layman, and to the parish-community, and then treated the laity as having such responsibilities in their proper sphere? Such were some of the questions the organizer of the liturgical movement asked himself, talked and wrote about in spreading the doctrine of the Mystical Body. Only the man who has grasped the true nature of the liturgy can fully comprehend, he believed, the role of the laity in the Church.

It was impossible for Dom Virgil to think of a genuine Catholicism which was not by its very nature apostolic. There is no sincere Catholic, he repeated again and again, who cannot do something in an apostolic way for the Church. In the early centuries the life of the Church was spread from one to another by men who knew their faith and lived it. To this mission he tried to awaken as many Catholics as possible. When the history of the lay apostolate in the United States is written, Virgil Michel's name will occupy a prominent place in it.

The American liturgical movement has been weak in producing first-rate liturgical scholarship. Certainly Michel never produced any beyond some preliminary work on the doctrine of the Mystical Body. Gerald Ellard, S.J., has done commendable work in this regard. Nor should the contribution of the European scholar at the Catholic University of America, Dr. Johannes Quasten, be overlooked. Father Virgil several times warned Abbot Alcuin that the popularizing phase of the liturgical apostolate would pass; that monks trained in liturgical research could then properly anchor the movement. Perhaps if this ideal could have been realized at St. John's Abbey, the monks of Collegeville would not have been so dependent over the years — perhaps, at times, even slavishly — on European liturgical research. To be sure, it is no credit to the American liturgical movement that each year the faculty of Notre Dame's Liturgical Summer School, founded in 1947 by Michael Mathis, C.S.C., is made up almost entirely of European scholars.

Liturgical participation cannot alone furnish the total basis for an integral Christian life. Last year in Rome the Pope told the delegates to the congress at Assisi, "The liturgy is not, however, *the whole Church*; it does not exhaust the scope of her activities. . . . All the faithful as members of the Mystical Body should love it [liturgy], value it, and take their part in it, understanding none the less that the tasks of the Church extend beyond it." [3] In their efforts to win a hearing, proponents of the liturgical apostolate have at times left the impression that the restoration of the liturgy would alone solve most modern ills. Father Virgil deplored the short-sightedness which caused such false impressions, even if a few times he himself left such impressions. Active sharing in the liturgy does not absolutely guarantee a general social mentality, even if this is often its fruit. Writing in *America* for October 12, 1935, Father Virgil warned that the faithful might conceivably achieve a social consciousness in their liturgical participation without thereby greatly affecting their social outlook upon life as a whole. He perhaps should have added that some have acquired a social consciousness from other sources than the liturgy.

Be that as it may he himself was never without a keen awareness of how the economic, social, and cultural system impinges on re-deemed man living in Christ. That is why he organized the liturgical apostolate on such a broad base, touching all of human activity. He carefully distinguished between theology, philosophy, and science, between the natural and the supernatural.[4] That is why, too, he was active on many fronts. As His Holiness implied, the liturgy cannot solve all our problems.

For Michel the liturgical and social apostolates were one in the sense that they needed each other for a vital, total approach. It would not do, for instance, to make a general admission that social problems are ultimately spiritual problems, and then to live, speak, write, and work as if this were not so. Nevertheless, he was interested in socio-economic and political problems from the viewpoint of the philos-opher and the apostle and not that of the empirical scientist. Inherent in the Christian vocation, he emphasized, is always the task of doing all in one's power to bring the social framework into right order so that men can live a fully human and Christian life. And if there is no Christian social order without the redeeming grace of Christ working through dedicated Christians, so there can be no sound social movement without the clarity of thought which makes possible the intelligent application of the principles of social philosophy and the encyclicals.

While Michel pointed out the great need for economic reform, he was not specific beyond calling for such things as cooperatives, decentralization, labor unions, a broader spread of private and responsible ownership of property, and general social legislation after the spirit of the encyclicals.

In an age of rapid change and transition, there is need for reconsidering fundamental principles. With the clarification, propagation, and implications of these he mainly occupied himself. For he was convinced that even the theoretical economist crosses over into the area of social philosophy when, moving beyond fact and theory, he enters the field of policy to implement his thinking in the practical world. In so doing, he has already, consciously or unconsciously, chosen a *Weltanschauung*, an attitude toward material things, values, goals touching the purpose of human existence. Men, therefore, hope in vain for permanent social betterment from a mere external change of social institutions if the false philosophy inhering in and vitiating these institutions is not also changed. In this regard Michel observed: "Try as we may, as long as we accept and nurse the root evils of a materialistic civilization, the matured evil of it will come to the surface." [5] To expose and to destroy these root evils stemming from the false ideas in the minds of men was one of the chief aims of his socio-economic writings.

On the other hand, while one has to resist the temptation to criticize his social writings in terms of what has developed and matured in socio-economic theory since his death in 1938, it nevertheless ought to be said that his grasp of theoretical economics was inadequate. At times he had trouble reconciling economic facts with ethical and social principles. He was sometimes too easily impressed. In social science he often had to feel his way and sometimes lost his direction. Much as he studied the theory and function of money, for instance, his knowledge was not such as to enable him to evaluate theories unerringly. He made no empirical studies, he carried out no systematic social experiments, he worked out no social system. For empirical social facts he was dependent on the work of others. In a time of social unrest, amidst many proposed solutions, he was a coordinator who sifted and saved what was of value in these by presenting an integral social outlook which was basic and which took into account both natural and supernatural elements of human existence. Finally, this social outlook was presented in such a way as to admit new plans. Michel would have been the first to admit that a new socio-economic situation demands a new appraisal. No one in his right mind, this modern monk used to say, would want to go back to the Middle Ages. In every age men must creatively rethink, restate, and re-apply unchanging principles of a sound social philosophy with a view to current realities. But convincing restatement and realistic re-application are impossible without knowing thoroughly the kind of world in which men live. Careful studies can tell them what their problems are. Hence the need for a continuing re-examination of modern civilization, coupled with a courageous readiness to experiment, with positive efforts at social reconstruction, zeal compelling, prudence restraining, experience guiding. Often there can be only small beginnings gradually growing into long-range, flexible programs.

In short, philosophy clarifies the ends for a Catholic social movement and gives it direction. Social science works out the possible empirical means to realize these ends. Liturgy gives such a movement life.

Accordingly, if forming a truly human social order is the work of enlightened and apostolic Catholics first of all, it is likewise also the task of men of all religions, of all men of good will. The common meeting ground for these is the philosophy of personalism. The latter recognizes the supreme dignity of each human personality with all its individual rights, but not apart from its social duties in an organic and communitarian society. Dom Virgil, like all personalists, saw the reform of society from the bottom up, from the free and responsible person up to the social institutions serving the human being, for whose development and welfare all else in the material order exists. It is not enough to know and point out what is wrong, to indicate what is right. Enlightened and aroused persons must act personally and in groups to set things aright, if human and Christian social structures are to be formed and society gradually regenerated. Personal reform first, but without neglecting social reform. If Father Virgil in his efforts to stir up voluntary programs of social action always showed great respect for the human person and expected much from each, he gave his own reason for this: "Not to accord any responsibility to a human person is to show disrespect to human personality." [6]

In philosophy, too, he stood ready for new growth. Much of modern scholarship in the field of thought, especially in philosophy, consisted in the systematic cataloging of the thoughts, events, facts, and opinions of the past. Yet, this is only the prelude to vigorous, creative thinking. A vital philosophizing begins when the mind of the philosopher, having made the principles and the spirit of the Scholastic tradition his own, meets head on the real and vexing problems of the day. Such an alert mind is not satisfied with the intellectual achievements of a bygone age, with the mechanical recitation of past solutions and Scholastic phrases, with repetition of the borrowed thoughts of others — as if today no unique problems existed. Indeed, a living philosophical thought is much more than scholarship. "It is above all creative thinking," Michel explained. And this original, personal thinking, he said, "cannot be done by mere observance of the canons of scientific or scholarly study methods or even the laws of logic, important as all these may be as supplementary to the real philosophizing." [7] Again:

The views of Aquinas must be studied in the light of their own day, and the basic permanent principles separated from the changeable conditions of his time; only then can these principles be properly applied to the conditions of our own day in the spirit of St. Thomas. [8]

In this way was the thought of St. Thomas reborn in the writings of one who always cultivated a refreshingly creative attitude toward the whole of life.

That Virgil Michel never found the time, that he did not live long enough, to produce the philosophical manuals he had envisioned is regrettable. At an early date he called for a neo-Scholastic movement in this country. He clearly pointed out the directions it should take and the tasks it should perform. He outlined steps by which a vital philosophy could be constructed and how it could help in the solution of current difficulties. His friendly relations with non-Catholic intellectuals enabled him to put them in touch with a sound philosophical tradition which they might otherwise have overlooked.

From the early 1920's Dom Virgil pleaded for educational reform. He condemned narrow and unbalanced specialization. True education was not to be measured by mere numbers, credits, hours of enforced class attendance, formal and often passive subjection to textbooks and lectures. The educational system had by and large taken on the impersonality of modern life. Because depersonalized, mass-education had, to his mind, in many cases led to dangerous conformism.

Ideally, genuine education is the fruit of active contact and interplay of minds enriched as much as possible with the heritage of the race. The mind is a well. One primes a pump to bring forth a stream. Similarly in the classroom, the vital teacher arms his students with minimum study and research techniques. But at the same time he awakens and challenges the living mind, makes it inquisitive — and so leads it on by guided self-activity to the sources of knowledge. From these sources the true student draws the treasures of wisdom. He does not slavishly memorize and categorize unrelated facts and data. Rather the various items are revitalized into a mental pattern and refined by active reflection, discussion, and present experience by one who has also been coached to keep an eye on the problems of contemporary life. Having been led on to think for himself by being confronted with problems with which he must wrestle instead of being forcibly subjected to an assembly-line procedure of fact-and-credit gathering, such a student will not have the impression after four years of college that "schooling" has ended. Such a graduate can think and discuss, read and write, speak and listen. And to produce such persons is the task of liberal education, whose content and methodology must themselves be constantly rethought and re-aligned to meet the changing needs of a never static world.

When the school in question is a Catholic liberal arts college, it has failed if its graduates do not see their life, their fellow men, and their world with the eyes of Christ. Here the total cultivation of human nature is in itself the best preparation for the working of God's grace. Such a task of vital education, however, can be accomplished only through a faculty whose own grasp of the Christian message has made each member personally apostolic, along with having acquired professional competence. The ideal faculty is a close-knit, democratic, family group in which each member is aware of the whole scholastic program or curriculum, and because he knows his part in it, can creatively contribute to it. Such an ideal educational community — with smaller, self-functioning units if necessary — has assimilated the wisdom of the past, is in active contact with the living present, and so can intelligently anticipate the future.

This total program would entail a revitalized religious instruction from the first grade through college. Through the *With Mother Church* manuals, the Christ Life and Christian Religion Series, Michel and his associates had hoped to supply the books for such instruction. Religious education must not only produce religious knowledge but also spiritual growth. Here the liturgy itself, as dogma prayed and experienced in worship, is a kind of model teacher. Again the Pope's recent words are fitting: "It would be difficult to find a truth of the Christian faith which is not somehow expressed in the liturgy. . . . The solemn liturgical ceremonies are, besides, a profession of faith in action." [9] According to Dom Virgil, unless religious education led to active and intelligent participation in the grace and prayer-action of the Mystical Body, Catholic colleges would continue to graduate for the most part "practical Catholics" who knew the precepts of the Church, perhaps, but who were not Catholic in heart, mind, and life, and certainly not, in an apostolic way.

In education as in other things Michel was presenting ideals or goals to be striven after even if in time they could not be fully realized. In the 1920's he was ready to carry out educational experiments, but only at the end of his life did he succeed in convincing his superior of the feasibility of such experimentation. Then it was too late. The treatment of Michel's philosophy of education in this volume has nevertheless shown reason for the judgment of Leo R. Ward, C.S.C., and Emerson Hynes, namely, "that Virgil Michel was one of the outstanding educators of our time . . ." [10]

Father Virgil had only twenty-two years of priestly life. But they were fruitful ones. His was not a rigidly determined plan but rather a flexible program of living ideas and ideals. Essentially a leader of his contemporaries, he achieved eminence by stimulating others. Alert to his age and highly critical of its defects, he planted the seeds which others would cultivate. He prepared the way for others to advance. It was precisely in neglected areas that he often inspired or organized others and set to work, tongue articulate, pen in hand.

Karl Jung once remarked that the number of persons in touch with contemporary civilization and culture is always minute. Father Virgil was one of these. From the early 1920's he repeatedly warned that the world was at the turning of the ways, that a new world was in the making, that the old liberalism and individualism were dying or already dead, that a moralistic Christianity could never meet the inevitable crisis. But precisely because the world was in a stage of transition it was essential that apostolic Catholics be active in the world's refashioning. To scatter right ideas and spiritual ideals, to prepare the needed apostles, clerical and lay, he spent himself.

About two years before World War II, and some years before the onset of the atomic age, he observed

that we are living in extraordinarily important times; that our days are in a special sense big with the human destinies of the future, and that we are witnessing the complete breakdown of the ideals of a civilization that had been building up for a whole period of history.[11]

Woodrow Wilson wrote that "our slow world spends its time catching up with the ideas of its best minds." As should be evident, much that Father Virgil advocated has become commonplace, while some of his ideas seek implementation.

In coming times, he insisted, the heart of the needed Catholic revival will be the liturgical life and its accompanying Catholic Action. To be a Christian is to live and work for Christ in God's world. "We live in God with Christ who works in and through us; we must lose ourselves in Him": that was the message he gave to one lay apostle in the world. And to another: "To know and to live the liturgical life, to understand the Church as the Body of Christ, to realize the full implications of being an apostle of Christ is to have a sympathy for all men and for all things human, together with a realization that all belongs to God, we above all." Needed was "*action* based on *knowing,* and both on *being.*" He explained:

First the inner conversion, and a tested and tried conversion at that, and then the external apostolate. Even then not too much action at once, not action for action's sake, but action out of the abundance of the inner life, under pressure of the supernatural *élan vital* of the true Christian.[12]

Nor did he underestimate the magnitude of the work and anguish before the truly apostolic Christian in a secularized culture. As he wrote on June 22, 1938, to Catherine De Hueck, when she was trying to establish a Christian beachhead in Harlem, "Live the liturgy . . . and you will realize the need of sharing in Christ's calvaries to have a share also in His resurrections." Thus, all his far-flung activities always began at and always led back to the fountainhead of the Christ-life and to the central truth of Christianity: that all things must be restored in Christ through the redemption as continued in the liturgy. To achieve this end, art, philosophy, education, scholarship, cooperatives, labor unions, contacts with non-Catholics, and all the rest were but means. The words of a kindred spirit and collaborator, written in 1951, are appropriate:

There are three great movements of our time, the theological movement, the liturgical movement, the apostolate movement . . . which vitalize the Church today, and these three are organically one. Their synthesis was the vision of Father Virgil Michel. Whether or not he ever expressed this ideal in these precise words, it was the ideal which governed his thought and his writings.[13]

Cardinal Suhard once gave a beautiful description of a zealous priest:

Like Christ, the priest brings mankind a priceless good, that of worrying it. He must be the "minister of restlessness," the dispenser of a new thirst and a new hunger. . . . The revolt which the priest must advocate is the insurrection of consciences, the order which he comes to disturb is the apparent calm which covers up disorders and hatreds. . . . Eternally unsatisfied . . . he rejects the calm . . . to start a ferment.[13]

Dom Virgil Michel, it seems, was this kind of priest and caused this kind of ferment.

NOTES TO CHAPTER 12

[1] "The International Congress on Pastoral Liturgy (Assisi)," *Irish Ecclesiastical Record*, LXXXVI (1956), 344–345.

[2] *Ibid.*, p. 356.

[3] *Ibid.*, p. 348.

[4] It is interesting to note Michel's careful distinction between religion, philosophy, and the science of sociology: Cf. Michel to Serge Bolshakoff, New York, Feb. 25, 1937. Only twice in his formal writings, and then each time in book reviews, did he use the term "Christian sociology." Cf. Eva Ross — Michel letters.

[5] Michel, Foreword to Mounier, *op. cit.*, p. xv.

[6] *The Christian in the World*, p. 77.

[7] "Towards a Vital Philosophy," *New Scholasticism*, XI (1937), 132.

[8] *St. Thomas and Today*, p. 35. "The greater part of philosophy by far is the application of principles — it is here that philosophy or philosophizing does all its good and all its harm. The permanent 'principles' are relatively few, and even here we grow in knowledge and understanding of them. The Scholastics of the thirteenth century did not say the last word on these" (Michel, "A New Manual of the History of Philosophy," *Fortnightly Review*, XXXIV [1927], 412).

[9] "The International Congress on Pastoral Liturgy (Assisi)," p. 346.

[10] "Virgil Michel," *Commonweal*, XXIX (1938), 238.

[11] Foreword to Mounier, *op. cit.*, p. xi.

[12] "A New Parish: The Apostolate," *OF*, XII (1938), 561.

[13] Busch, "Past, Present, Future," *OF*, XXV (1951), 488. Michel did express, and more than once, the ideal to which Busch referred: cf., e.g., "Liturgy and Catholic Life," p. 33, and "The Scope of the Liturgical Movement," *OF*, X (1936), 485–490.

[14] *Priests Among Men* (Chicago: Fides, n.d.), p. 32.

APPENDIX 1
BIBLIOGRAPHY OF VIRGIL MICHEL

Because Virgil Michel wrote in so many fields, it was thought best to divide his writings topically into six categories in which the items were alphabetically arranged. This arrangement will show how he drew his inspiration primarily from the liturgy; in writing about human affairs and current problems he again and again came back to some phase of the Church's official worship. In many instances it was hard to decide to which section an article belonged. Thus paragraphs on art, social philosophy, and other subjects are to be found throughout his "liturgical" writings. Whatever pertained in any way to the liturgy was put in the classification, "Liturgy — Social Action — Catholic Action." That is why, for example, the reader will find articles on education, apologetics, etc., in this section. Anyone interested in Michel's philosophy of religious education should also consult his writings on general education.

The bibliography lists in order books, pamphlets, articles and finally translations. It does not include Michel's preseminary writings; nor have there been added "The Editor's Corner," "Liturgical Briefs," and editorials in the "Apostolate" section of *Orate Fratres* during the time of his editorship; Liturgical Press publications on which he worked with his confreres and others were likewise not mentioned; the Michel Papers indicate that he wrote unsigned articles, book reviews, letters to editors, etc., for American and foreign journals — and these will likewise not be found in this bibliography. Had it been feasible or possible to incorporate all of Michel's pen work, the list of his writings would have been lengthened considerably.

The nucleus of this bibliography had been collected by the library staff of St. John's University, thanks to the inspiration of the indefatigable Oliver Kapsner, O.S.B. The writer failed to secure bibliographical data on some articles in a few obscure or unavailable publications.

421

The references cited throughout the bibliography are the works of Virgil Michel, O.S.B., with the exception of the collaborations which are specifically noted.

I. LITURGY — SOCIAL ACTION — CATHOLIC ACTION

BOOKS:

In collaboration with Basil Stegmann, O.S.B., and the Sisters of the Order of St. Dominic, Marywood, Grand Rapids, Michigan. *The Christ-Life Series*: (Eight volumes, one for each grade) New York: Macmillan, 1934–1935:

> *God Our Father*, 69p.
> *Jesus Our Savior*, 134p.
> *The Story of God's Love*, 170p.
> *A Child of God*, 192p.
> *The Redeeming Sacrifice*, 228p.
> *The Kingdom of God*, 263p.
> *With Mother Church*, 295p.
> *Through Christ Our Lord*, 274p.
> *Teacher's Manual*, two volumes: 141p., 206p.

in collaboration with Sister Jane Marie Murray, O.P.: *The Christian Religion Series for High School*: Milwaukee: Bruce:

> *The Life of Our Lord*, 1938 (revised 1945), 370p.
> *Christ in His Church*, 1952, 656p.

in collaboration with monks of St. John's Abbey, Collegeville, Minnesota, and Sisters of the Order of St. Dominic, Marywood, Grand Rapids, Michigan: *The Christian Religion Series for College*: Collegeville: Liturgical Press:

> *Our Life in Christ*, 1939, 240p.
> *The Christian in the World*, 1939, 241p.

The Liturgy of the Church, New York: Macmillan Co., 1937, 369p.
My Sacrifice and Yours, Collegeville: Liturgical Press, 1926, 62p.
and the Sisters of the Order of St. Dominic, Marywood, Grand Rapids, Michigan, *With Mother Church*: (Five volumes, known as "Laboratory Manuals" for grades three to twelve, and meant to be supplementary to other religion textbooks) Collegeville: Liturgical Press, 1929.

PAMPHLETS:

The Liturgical Apostolate, Collegeville: Liturgical Press, 1926, 19p.
and Martin B. Hellriegel: *The Liturgical Movement*, Collegeville: Liturgical Press, 1930, 29p.
in collaboration with the Sisters of the Order of St. Dominic, Marywood, Grand Rapids, Michigan: *Simple Mass Prayers*, 1938, 32p.
and Louis Traufler, O.S.B.: *Why Do Catholics Attend Mass?* Collegeville: Liturgical Press, 1926 (revised and published as *Why The Mass?* 1928), 33p.

ARTICLES:

"Adequate Preparation for Teaching the Mass," *Journal of Religious Instruction*, VIII, 594–598, 1938.

"Advertising our Wares," *OF*, IV, 122–126, 1930.
"Again: Religion — Or What?" *OF*, XI, 555–558, 1937.
"Announcing Baptisms," *OF*, II, 404–407, 1928.
"Are We One in Christ?" *Ecclesiastical Review* XCI, 395–401, 1934.
"At Peoria," *OF*, IX, 566–569, 1935.
"Back To The Liturgy," *OF*, XI, 9–14, 1936.
"Baptismal Consciousness," *OF*, I, 309–313, 1927.
"Benediction of the Blessed Sacrament," *OF, VIII*, 490–495, 1934.
"Blessing of Holy Water," *OF*, XIII, 326–327, 1939.
"Bourgeois Spirit and the Christian Renewal," *OF*, XIV, 253–260; 302–308, 1940.
"Campions and the League of the Divine Office," *Liturgy and Sociology* I, 14–15, 18, 1936.
and Parsch, "Care of Souls Today," *OF*, XIII, 534–539, 1939.
"A Case for Private Piety," *OF*, XIII, 354–360, 1939.
"Catholic Leadership and the College," *OF*, X, 22–27, 1935.
"Catholic Workers and Apostles," *OF*, XIII, 28–30, 1938.
"The Chant of the Church," *OF*, XI, 363–365, 1937.
and Godfrey Diekmann, O.S.B., "Check List of Liturgical Periodicals," *Liturgical Arts* IV, 160–162, 1935.
"Christianity and Cooperation," *Beacon*, April, 1938.
"Christian Christmas Cheer," *OF*, X, 82–83, 1935.
"Christian Culture," *OF*, XIII, 296–304, 1939.
"Christian Woman," *OF*, XIII, 248–256, 1939.
"Christmas Again," *Wanderer*, December 20, 1934.
"A Christmas Homily," *OF*, III, 46–49, 1928.
"The Church in Time," *Placidian*, IV, 247–250; 313–316, 1927.
"The Church in the Morrow," *Acolyte*, V, 5–6, 1929.
"The Church Unity Octave," *OF*, XI, 131–133, 1937.
"Cisca Plan," *OF*, X, 80–82, 1935.
"City or Farm," *OF*, XII, 367–369, 1938.
"Communion at Mass: Effect of Communion," *OF*, IV, 311–315; 364–368; 412–416, 1930.
"Confirmation: Call to Battle," *OF*, II, 234–239, 1928.
"Confirmation: Its Divine Powers," *OF*, II, 199–204, 1928.
"Confirmation: Our Apathy," *OF*, II, 167–171, 1928.
"Confraternity Meeting at St. Louis," *OF*, XII, 36–38, 1937.
"The Co-operative Movement and the Liturgical Movement," in *Catholic Rural Life Objectives* (2nd Series), St. Paul: NCRLC, n.d.; *OF*, XIV, 152–160, 1940.
"Correction and Approbation," *OF*, IX, 228–230, 1935.
"A Daniel Comes to Judgment," *OF*, XI, 274, 1937.
"The Divine Purge," *OF*, X, 273–275, 1936.
"The Effect of Communion," *OF*, XI, 157–162, 1937.
"Emphasizing Essentials," *OF*, IV, 170–174, 1930.
"Eucharistische Kongresse in den Vereinigten Staaten," *Wanderer*, March 11, 1926.
"The Evening Mass," *OF*, IV, 90–91, 1929.

424 VIRGIL MICHEL AND THE LITURGICAL MOVEMENT

"Examining Our Conscience," *OF*, X, 367–369. 1936.
"Faith without Understanding," *OF*, X, 413–415, 1936.
"Faith without Charity," *OF*, X, 462–464, 1936.
"The Family and the Mystical Body," *OF*, XI, 295–299, 1937.
"The Family and the Liturgy," *OF*, XI, 393–396, 1937.
"The Fight Against Communism," *OF*, XI, 125–128, 1937.
"The Great Apostasy," *OF*, XI, 31–32, 1936.
"First National Liturgical Day in the United States," *OF*, III, 324–330, 1929.
"First Rate Catholic Action," *OF*, XII, 34–36, 1937.
"Frequent Communion and Social Regeneration," *OF*, X, 198–202, 1936.
"Full Life," *OF*, XIV, 111–116, 1940.
"Home Religious Instruction," *OF*, XI, 316–318, 1937.
"If I Were Satan," *OF*, XII, 76–78, 1937.
"Infidelity in the Church," *OF*, IX, 492–496, 1935.
"Knowledge Requirement for Teaching the Mass," *Journal of Religious Instruction*, VIII, 765–770, 1938.
"Layman in the Church," *Commonweal*, XII, 123–125, 1930.
"A Layman's Lament," *OF*, XII, 80–84, 1937.
"A League of the Divine Office," *OF*, X, 177–181, 468–470, 1936; XI, 33–34, 83–84, 1936; XI, 133–134, 224–226, 1937; XII, 136–137, 274–275, 324–327, 1938.
"The Liturgical Apostolate," *Catholic Educational Review*, XXV, 3–6, 1927.
"The Liturgical Movement," *Ecclesiastical Review*, LXXVIII, 136–142, 1928.
"The Liturgical Movement," *Fortnightly Review*, XXXIII, 108, 1926.
"The Liturgical Movement," *Irish Catholic*, XLII, 8f, 1929.
"The Liturgical Movement and the Catholic Woman," Central Verein of America: *Annual Report*, 57–62, 1929.
"The Liturgical Movement and the Future," *America*, LIV, 6–7, 1935.
"The Liturgical Movement and the Retreat Movement," *America*, XLIII, 71, 1930.
"Liturgical Parish Missions," *OF*, XII, 219–222, 1938.
"Liturgical Religious Education," *OF*, XI, 267–269, 1937.
"The Liturgical Spirit in France," *OF*, XII, 515–517, 1938.
"Liturgical Worship," *Pax*, 88, 238–247, 1928.
"The Liturgy and Catholic Women," *OF*, III, 270–276, 1929.
"Liturgy and Labor," *Social Forum*, March 6, 1938.
"Liturgy and the Changing World," *OF*, XII, 1–7, 1937.
"Liturgy and Modern Thought," *OF*, XIII, 205–212, 1939.
"The Liturgy in the Vernacular," *OF*, XII, 172–174, 1938.
"The Liturgy the Basis of Social Regeneration," *OF*, IX, 536–545, 1935.
"Making Converts to the Liturgy," *OF*, IV, 18–21, 1929.
"The Mass and the Life of Christ," *OF*, IV, 72–77, 1929.
and Louis Traufler, O.S.B., "Mass as the People's Sacrifice," *OF*, I, 208–214, 1927.
"The Meaning of the Church's Liturgy," *America*, XXXIV, 586–587, 1926.

"Modern Greed and the Mass," *OF*, XI, 322–324, 1937.
"Modernism and the Chant," *OF*, XI, 463–465, 1937.
"The Mystical Body," *Commonweal*, XXIX, 18, 1938.
"The Mystical Body," *OF*, X, 419–421, 1936.
"The Mystical Body and Economic Justice," in *The Mystical Body and Social Justice*, (The Social Problem IV), Collegeville: St. John's Abbey, 53–61, 1938.
"The Mystical Body at Prayer and Work in Summer Schools of Catholic Action, 1938," *OF*, XII, 513–515, 1938.
"Mysticism and Normal Christianity: The Place of Liturgy in Mysticism," *OF*, XIII, 545–548, 1939.
"Natural and Supernatural Society," *OF*, X, 243–247; 293–296; 338–342; 394–398; 434–438, 1936.
"A New Parish: Building Up," *OF*, XII, 507–510, 1938.
"A New Parish: The Apostolate," *OF*, XII, 561–564, 1938.
"Nine Years After," *OF*, X, 2–7, 1935.
"On Pentecost," *OF*, III, 193–197, 1929.
"Our Social Environment," *OF*, XII, 318–320, 1938.
"Outline of a Week-end Retreat for Laymen," *OF*, XII, 445–455, 1938.
"The Parish, Cell of Christian Life," *OF*, XI, 433–440, 1937.
"A Parish in Action," *OF*, XIII, 83–85, 1938.
"Participation in the Mass," *Ecclesiastical Review*, LXXXI, 395–397, 1929.
"Participation in the Mass," *OF*, I, 17–20, 1926.
"Personality and Liturgy," *OF*, XIII, 156–159, 1939.
"Polacy a Liturgia," *Sodalis*, XVIII, 6–8, 1936.
"Political Catholicism," *OF*, XIII, 79–81, 1938.
"Preface to Religion," *OF*, X, 208–212, 1936.
"The Priest and the Liturgy," *Acolyte* IV, 6–7; 8–9; 11; 7–8; 8–9, 1928.
"The Problem of Religious Education," *Fortnightly Review*, XXXIII, 262, 1926.
"A Program for a Liturgical Movement," *America*, XXXIV, 614–615, 1926.
"Public Baptism," *OF*, XIII, 180–181, 1939.
"Rediscovering the Obvious: Liturgy and the Psychology of Education," *OF*, XIV, 529–532, 1940.
"Religion Today," *Acolyte*, V, 8–9, 1929.
"Religion — Or What?" *OF*, XI, 506–508; 555–558, 1937.
"Religious Education," *OF*, XI, 218–220, 1937.
"Religious Experience: Liturgy Depersonalizes Piety?" *OF*, XIII, 493–496, 1939.
"Sacramenta Propter Homines," *OF*, XI, 84–85, 1936.
"Sacramental System," *OF*, IX, 114–119; 156–161, 1935.
"Sacraments for the People," *OF*, XII, 261–263, 1938.
and Louis Traufler, O.S.B., "The Sacrifice of Christ," *OF*, I, 76–81, 1927.
"Sanctity and Dignity," *OF*, IV, 265–269, 1930.
"The Scope of the Liturgical Movement," *OF*, X, 485–490, 1936.
"Secular Culture Capturing Christian Minds," *Ecclesiastical Review*, XCVI, 65–66, 1937.

"Sermon or Meditation Thoughts," (Advent), *OF*, XIII, 1–4, 1938.
"Sermon or Meditation Thoughts," (Christmas), *OF*, XIII, 50–53, 1938.
"Significance of the Liturgical Movement," *NCWC Bulletin*, X, 6–8, 26, 1929.
"Social Aspects of the Liturgy," *Catholic Action*, XVI, 9–11, 1934.
"Social Injustices," *OF*, XI, 78–80, 1936.
"Social Justice," *OF*, XII, 129–132, 1938.
"The Social Nature of Communion," in *The Mystical Body and Social Justice*, (The Social Problem IV), Collegeville: St. John's Abbey, 1938, 11–16.
"The Social Nature of the Offertory," in *The Mystical Body and Social Justice*, (The Social Problem IV) Collegeville: St. John's Abbey, 1938, 5–10.
"Solesmes Centenary," *OF*, XI, 422–423, 1937.
"Something New in Altar Missals," *Fortnightly Review, XXXVII*, 13–14, 1930.
Basil Stegmann, O.S.B., and the Sisters of the Order of St. Dominic, Marywood, Grand Rapids, Michigan, "Some Pedagogical Features of the Christ-Life Series in Religion," *Journal of Religious Instruction*, VI, 583–588, 1935.
"Spiritual Nuptials," *OF*, XI, 537–542, 1937.
"Teaching the Life in Christ," *OF*, XV, 12–17, 1940.
"Terrible But True!" *OF*, XI, 174–176, 1937.
"Thanksgiving and Communion," *OF*, XI, 98–102, 1937.
"Thanksgiving in the Eucharistic Life," *OF*, IV, 412–416, 1930.
"Third Order of St. Francis," *OF*, X, 130–133, 1936.
"Through Human Persons," *Catholic Worker*, April, 1936.
"Timely Tracts: Introductory," *OF*, X, 265–267, 1936.
"True Christian Spirit," *Ecclesiastical Review*, LXXXII, 128–142, 1930.
"Traditional Catechesis," *OF*, XIV, 492–495, 1940.
"The Vernacular in the Liturgy," *OF*, X, 182–183, 1936.
"Volume X," *OF*, X, 467–468, 1936.
"Von der Bedeutung der liturgischen Bewegung," *Wanderer*, January 14, 21, 28, 1926.
"What is to Be Done?" *OF*, X, 306–308, 1936.
"Why Do We Do It?" *OF*, IX, 63–67, 1934.
"Why Not the Evening Mass?" *OF*, XII, 29–31, 1937.
"Will Anti-Clericalism Increase in the United States?" *Ecclesiastical Review*, XCVI, 284–290, 1937.
"A Youth Sunday," *OF*, XI, 412–414, 1937.
Editor, *Orate Fratres*, A Review devoted to the liturgical apostolate: 1926–30; 1935–1938.

BOOK REVIEWS:

"Aedificatio Corporis Christi," (Noppel), *OF*, XII, 334, 1938; "The Angel Teacher," (Reuter), *OF*, XII, 383, 1938; "Bete mit der Kirche," (Kramp), *OF*, XII, 383, 1938; "The Breviary and the Laity," (Hoorndaert), *Liturgical Arts*, V, 152–153, 1936; "Call on God," (Reuter), *OF*, XII, 141, 1938; "Calvary and the Mass," (Sheen), *OF*, X, 477–478,

1936; "Catholic Art," (Hennig), *OF*, IX, 380–381, 1935; "Catholic Central-Verein of America, *Official Report*, 73d Annual Convention," *OF*, IV, 287, 1930; "Catholic Truth Survey," (*Falque*), *OF*, XII, 332, 1938; "Charismes de vie sacerdotale," (Bertram), *OF*, XII, 527, 1938; "The Christ-Life Series in Religion," (Michel, et al), *OF*, X, 92–94, 1935; "Christus in Unserer Mitte," (Lang), *OF*, XI, 189, 1937; "Christus und die Kirche," (Tyciak), *OF*, XI, 525, 1937; "The Church and the Catholic" and "The Spirit of the Liturgy," (Guardini), *OF*, X, 236–38, 1936; "Church Property and its Management," (Frommelt), *OF*, XI, 234–235, 1937; "Confirmation in the Modern World," (Laros), *OF*, XII, 572–573, 1938; "Creative Revolution," (Prince), *OF*, XII, 142–143, 1938; "An Essay on Catholic Action," (LeClercq), *OF*, XI, 189–90, 1937; "Fire on the Earth," (Furfey), *OF*, XI, 45, 1937; "From Holy Communion to the Blessed Trinity," (Bernadot), *Fortnightly Review*, XXXV, 144, 1928; "The Fullness of Christ," (Sheen), *OF*, X, 281–285, 1936; "Gottesgeheimnisse der Gnade," (Tyciak), *OF*, XI, 479–480, 1937; "The Holy Ghost," (Leen), *OF*, XII, 239–240, 1938; "How To Build a Church," (Williamson), *OF*, X, 238, 1936; "I Go To Mass," (Sr. M. Alphonsus), *Fortnightly Review*, XXXVII, 145–146, 1930; "Jahr des Herrn," (Loehr), *OF*, IX, 140–141, 1935; "Lent and the Mass," (Burke), *OF*, X, 285, 1936; "Life in Christ," (Tyciak), *OF*, XI, 479–480, 1937; "Liturgy and Society," (Hebert), *OF*, XI, 92–94, 1937; "The Liturgical Sacrifice of the New Law," (Kramp), *Fortnightly Review*, XXXIII, 312, 1926; "Maria Schutzherrin der Kirche," (Scheeben), *OF*, XII, 240, 1938; "The Mass Explained," (McDonald), *Catholic Educational Review*, XXVIII, 306, 1930; "Mass Prayers for the First Grade," *OF*, IX, 141–142, 1935; "The Mind of the Missal," (Martindale), *Catholic Educational Review*, XXVII, 630–631, 1929; "The Mystery of the Church," (Clerissac), *OF*, XI, 573, 1937; "The Mystical Body of Christ," (Sheen), *OF*, X, 281–285, 1936; "The Mystical Body of Christ in the Modern World," (Fahey), *OF*, XI, 236, 1937; "Der Mystische Leib Christi," (Juergensmeier), *OF*, VIII, 525–526, 1934; "A New Catholic Dictionary," (Pallen and Wynne), *OF*, IV, 238–240, 1930; "The New Roman Missal," (Lasance and Walsh), *OF*, XII, 283–285, 1938; "Participation Active à la Messe," (Francois), *OF*, XI, 190, 1937; "Pfingstgeist ueber Uns," (Laros), *OF*, X, 140–141, 1936; "Pray Always," (Sausen), *OF*, XI, 190–191, 1937; "Praying the Mass," (Butler and Clendenin), *OF*, IX, 143–144, 1935; "La prière des églises de rite byzantin," (Mercenier and Paris), *OF*, XIII, 575–576, 1939; "Radiating Christ," (Plus), *OF*, XII, 285, 1938; "Readings and Reflections on the Gospels," (Herbst), *OF*, XII, 383, 1938; "The Sacrament of Catholic Action," (Lord), *OF*, XI, 191, 1937; "Sententiae Florianensis," *Fortnightly Review*, XXXVII, 50–51, 1930; "Tales of the Blessed Sacrament in Devotion, Figure and Symbol," (Murray), *OF*, XII, 143–144, 1938.

TRANSLATIONS:

Liturgy the Life of the Church, from the French of Dom Lambert Beauduin. Collegeville: Liturgical Press, 1926, 111p.

The Spirit of the Liturgy, from the Italian of Abbot Emmanuele Caronti, Collegeville: Liturgical Press, 1926, 123p.

II. SOCIOLOGY — ECONOMICS — POLITICS

BOOKS:

Christian Social Reconstruction, Milwaukee: Bruce, 1937, 137p.

Editor of *Catholic Backgrounds and Social Current Theory*, two mimeographed syllabi, compiled by students of Sociology 47–48, Collegeville: Institute for Social Study, 1937–1938, 43p.; 55p.

PAMPHLETS:

Critique of Capitalism, St. Paul: Wanderer Printing Co., 1936, 48p.

Human Rights, St. Paul: Wanderer Printing Co., 1936, 45p.

Ideals of Reconstruction, St. Paul: Wanderer Printing Co., 1936, 56p.

Labor and Industry, St. Paul: Wanderer Printing Co., 1936, 45p.

Modern Individualism and Its Effects, St. Louis: Central Bureau, 1936, 15p.

Money and the Common Good, St. Paul: Wanderer Printing Co., 1936, 52p.

The Nature of Capitalism, St. Paul: Wanderer Printing Co., 1936, 46p.

Ownership, St. Paul: Wanderer Printing Co., 1936, 44p.

Purpose and Duty of Ownership According to Thomas Aquinas, St. Louis: Central Bureau, 1935, 17p.

Reconstruction Schemes, St. Paul: Wanderer Printing Co., 1936, 78p.

St. Thomas and Today, St. Paul: Wanderer Printing Co., 1936, 78p.

The Theory of State, St. Paul: Wanderer Printing Co., 1936, 44p.

ARTICLES:

"Agriculture and Reconstruction," *Commonweal*, XXIX, 317–318, 1939.

"The Basic Soundness of Cooperation," *Christian Front*, II, 5–6, 1937.

"Basis of Human Rights," in *Social Concepts and Problems* (The Social Problem I), Collegeville: St. John's Abbey, 1936, 33–38.

"Birth Control," in *Social Concepts and Problems* (The Social Problem I), Collegeville: St. John's Abbey, 1936, 114–120.

"Brownson, A Man of Men," *Catholic World*, CXXV, 755–762, 1927.

"Brownson's Political Philosophy and Today," *American Catholic Quarterly Review*, XXXXIV, 193–202, 1919.

"Capitalism and Ownership," *Christian Front*, I, 54–55, 1936.

"Capitalism, Ownership and Finance," in *Economics and Finance*, (The Social Problem II), Collegeville: St. John's Abbey, 1936, 28–35.

"Catholics and Lynching," *OF*, XI, 184–185, 1937.

"Christian Reconstruction Cells," *OF*, XI, 179–182, 1937.

"Christian Social Reconstruction," *Ethics*, XLVIII, 444–446, 1938.

"Christian Sociology," *OF*, X, 275–276, 1936.

"The Common Good," *Commonweal*, XXIII, 511–512, 1936.

"Cooperation in a Distributist Society," *G. K.'s Weekly*, XXVI, 352, 1938.

"The Corporative Order," *Christian Front*, II, 74–75; 95–97, 1937.

"The Corporative Order," *Christian Front*, III, 155–157, 1938.

"The Corporative Order," *Social Justice Leaflet*, no. 10.

"The Corporative Order," *Christian Social Action*, V, 144–147, 1940.

"The Corporative Order," in *Political Theories and Forms* (The Social Problem III), Collegeville: St. John's Abbey, 1936, 74–81.

"The Daimon of Business," *Acolyte*, V, 7–8, 1929.

"Defining Social Justice," *Commonweal*, XXIII, 425–426, 1936.

"The Dehumanization of Property," *Free America*, II, 7, 16, 1938.

"The Ethics of Exchange," *Central-Blatt and Social Justice*, XXI, 235–237, 1928.

"Facts About Capitalism," *Commonweal*, XXV, 541–543, 1937.

"Farm Tenancy — Its Causes and Remedies as Suggested in the Papal Encyclical," National Conference of Catholic Charities: *Proceedings* (1937), 281–286.

and John LaFarge, S.J., "Farmer Cooperatives," in *Manifesto on Rural Life*, Milwaukee: Bruce, 1939, 55–59.

"Father Michel Protests," *Catholic Worker*, March, 1937.

"The Fine Basis of Human Rights," *Wanderer*, March 14, 1935.

"Government Regulation of Business," in *Political Theories and Forms*, (The Social Problem III), Collegeville: St. John's Abbey, 1937, 29–32.

"How Old Is Capitalism?" *Commonweal*, XXVII, 21–22, 1937.

"Humpty Dumpty," *OF*, X, 40–42, 1935.

"Individualism and Its Social Effects," in *Social Concepts and Problems* (The Social Problem I), Collegeville: St. John's Abbey, 1936, 12–20.

"An Institute for Social Study," *Central-Blatt and Social Justice*, XXIX, 1936, 170–171; 211–212.

"Internationalism," in *Political Theories and Forms* (The Social Problem III), Collegeville: St. John's Abbey, 1937, 82–88.

"The Labor Millennium," *Acolyte*, V, 9–10, 1929.

"The Labor Movement," *Commonweal*, XXVIII, 146–148, 1938.

"Labor Unions and Quadragesimo Anno," in *Economics and Finance* (The Social Problem II), Collegeville: St. John's Abbey, 1936, 51–57.

"Money and Civilization," *Christian Front*, III, 10–12, 1938.

"National Catholic Social Action Conference," *OF*, XII, 273–274, 1938.

"Nature and Purpose of Money," in *Economics and Finance* (The Social Problem II), Collegeville: St. John's Abbey, 1936. 73–78.

"Nature of Capitalism," in *Economics and Finance* (The Social Problem II) Collegeville: St. John's Abbey, 1936, 14–20.

"Orestes A. Brownson," *Catholic World*, CXXV, 499–505, 1927.

"Origin and Basis of Civil Power," in *Political Theories and Forms* (The Social Problem III), Collegeville: St. John's Abbey, 1927, 11–18.

"Our Modern Civilization: Medieval and Modern," *Acolyte*, V, 5, 1929.

"Ownership and Finance," *Christian Front*, I, 76–77, 1936.

"Ownership and the Human Person," *Review of Politics*, I, 155–178, 1939.

"Profit Motive Necessary to Man," *Social Forum*, January 13, 1939.

"Purpose and Duty of Ownership," in *Social Concepts and Problems* (The Social Problem I), Collegeville: St. John's Abbey, 73–79, 1936.

"The Seed of Thought," *Central-Blatt and Social Justice*, XXX, 371–372, 1938.

"The Small Shopkeeper," *Free America,* II, 7, 1938.
"Social Justice," *Wanderer,* December 31, 1936.
"Social Reconstruction: Between Communism and Fascism Lies the Christian Plan for Social Reconstruction," *Michaelman,* IV, 2–3, 23, 1939.
"Social Regeneration," *Social Justice Leaflet,* no. 9.
"Spirit of Capitalism," *Christian Front,* I, 22–23, 1936.
"War or Peace?" *Acolyte,* V, 9, 1929.
"What is Capitalism?" *Christian Front,* I, 5, 12, 1936.
"What is Capitalism?" *Commonweal,* XXVIII, 6–9, 1938.
"What of the Family?" *Acolyte,* V, 8–9, 1929.
BOOK REVIEWS:
"A Catholic Looks at His World," (Bell), *OF,* X, 430, 1936; "Church, Community and State," (Oldham), *OF,* X, 478, 1936; "Die Christlichen Soziallehren," (Der Katholische Gedanke XVI), *Fortnightly Review* XXXIV, 43, 1927; "Economic Planning and International Order," (Robbins), *Liturgical Arts,* VI, 160–161, 1938; "Efficiency Expert," (Converse), *OF,* XI, 141, 1937; "Interracial Justice," (LaFarge), *OF,* XI, 332, 1937; "The Lord Helps Those," (Fowler), *Journal of Adult Education,* XI, 82–83, 1939; "Medieval Socialism," (Jarrett), *OF,* X, 140, 1936; "Mind and the Mystery," (Eustace), *OF,* XI, 379–380, 1937; "Our Promised Land," (Neuberger), *Commonweal,* XXIX, 165, 1938; "Peace and the Clergy," (Bonacina, Tr.), *OF,* XI, 334, 1937; "The Religious Education of the Negro," (Walsh), *OF,* XII, 383, 1938; "The Saints and Social Work," (Walsh), *OF,* XI, 335, 1937; "Social Message of the New Testament," (Schumacher), *Commonweal,* XXVI, 108, 1937; "The Suicide Problem in the U.S.," (Frenay), *Fortnightly Review,* XXXV, 35, 1928; "Three Theories of Society," (Furfey), *Liturgical Arts,* VI, 161–162, 1938.

III. EDUCATION

ARTICLES:
"Are We Educating Moral Parasites?" *Catholic Educational Review,* XXV, 147–155, 1927.
"The Basic Need of Christian Education Today," National Benedictine Educational Association, *Proceedings:* XII, 34–44, 1929.
"The Basic Need of Christian Education Today," *Catholic Educational Review,* XXVIII, 3–12, 1930.
"Christian Education for Rural Living," *Catholic Rural Life Bulletin,* I, 19–21, 1938.
"Controversy on Accrediting Resolution," (To the Editor — second letter), Midwest Regional Unit, NCEA: *College Newsletter,* October, 1937.
"Education for Tomorrow," *Free America,* II, 13–14, 1938.
"Facility in Expression," *Catholic Educational Review,* XV, 410–415, 1918.
"A High School Course in Religion," *Catholic Educational Review,* XXII, 408–419; 472–486, 1924.

"Let's Examine Ourselves," *Catholic Educational Review*, XXXVI, 65–77, 1938.
"The Need Today of College Courses in Political Science," National Benedictine Educational Association, *Proceedings*, XVIII, 23–27, 1935.
"Reconstructing the Latin Curriculum," *Classical Bulletin*, XIII, 61, 1937.
"Religion for Credit," *Catholic Educational Review*, XXI, 465–470, 1923.
"Religious Instruction Again," *OF*, XI, 321–322, 1937.
"A Religious Need of the Day," *Catholic Educational Review*, XXIII, 449–456, 1925.
"The Role of Authority," *Catholic Educational Review*, XXII, 267–271, 1924.
"Smith-Towner Bill Again," *Educational Review*, LXI, 70–79, 1921.
"Stimulating Intellectual Independence in Senior College Students," *Catholic Educational Review*, XXV, 524–533, 1927.
"Supervision," National Benedictine Educational Association, *Proceedings*, VI, 67–74, 1923.
"To Father Wilson," *College Newsletter*, (Adrian, Michigan), October, 1937.
"Utopia Rediviva," *Catholic Educational Review*, XXIV, 257–264; 356–364, 1926.

BOOK REVIEWS:
"Catalogue," (Central Catholic Library), *OF*, XI, 525, 1937.

IV. PHILOSOPHY

BOOKS:
The Critical Principles of Orestes A. Brownson, Washington: privately published, 1918, 106p.
Notes on Epistemology, Collegeville: The Order of St. Benedict, 1929, 95p.
Philosophy of Human Conduct, Minneapolis: Burgess, 1936, 138p.

ARTICLES:
"Intellectual Confusion Today and Philosophia Perennis," *Fortnightly Review*, XXXIII, 211–212, 1926.
"The International Philosophical Congress," *Fortnightly Review*, XXXIII, 459, 1926.
"Liberalism Yesterday and Tomorrow," *Ethics*, XLIX, 417–434, 1939.
"Metaphysical Foundations of Moral Obligation," American Catholic Philosophical Association: *Proceedings*, IV, 29–44, 1938.
"The Mind-Body Problem," *Philosophical Review*, XLV, 611, 1936.
"Mission of Catholic Thought," *American Catholic Quarterly Review*, XLVI, 657–664, 1921.
"A New Manual of the History of Philosophy," *Fortnightly Review*, XXXIV, 412, 1927.
"On the Theory of Matter and Form," *Ecclesiastical Review*, LXXIII, 241–263, 1925.
"Organic Superpersonality?" *Philosophical Review*, XXXVI, 178–180, 1927.

"Page the Psychologist," *Fortnightly Review*, XXXVI, 22–23, 1929.

"Philosophy at Sea," *Acolyte*, VIII, 8–9, 1929.

"Progress of Neo-Scholasticism," *Fortnightly Review*, XXXIV, 472, 1927.

"Psychoanalysis and the Catholic World-View," *Fortnightly Review*, XXXIII, 333–334, 1926.

"Psychological Data," *New Scholasticism*, III, 185–188, 1929.

"Quest for God," *Fortnightly Review*, XXXIII, 271, 1926.

"Reflections on a Scholastic Synthesis," *New Scholasticism*, II, 1–17, 1928.

"Science and Its Hopes," *Acolyte*, V, 5–6, 1929.

"Some Fundamentals of Ethics," *New Scholasticism*, IV, 241–260, 1930.

"Some Thoughts on Cosmology," *Fortnightly Review*, XXXVI, 187–188, 1929.

"Some Thoughts on John Dewey" *New Scholasticism*, II, 327–341, 1928.

"Towards a Vital Philosophy," *New Scholasticism*, XI, 128–139, 1937.

"Troubadour of Truth," in Robert Brennan (ed.), *Essays in Thomism*, New York: Sheed & Ward, 1942, 3–24.

"Whither Does Imagism Tend?" *Catholic World*, CVII, 620–627, 1918.

"Why Scholastic Philosophy Lives," *Philosophical Review*, XXXVI, 166–173, 1927.

Foreword to Mounier, *A Personalist Manifesto*, New York: Longmans, Green Co., 1938, xi–xx.

BOOK REVIEWS:

"The Aim of Human Existence," (Rignano), *New Scholasticism*, III, 443–447, 1929; "Approximaciones a la Doctrina Tradicional," (Teran), *New Scholasticism*, XII, 414–415, 1928; "Archives de Philosophie," (Beauchesne) *New Scholasticism*, II, 392–393, 1928; "Construction and Criticism," (Dewey), *New Scholasticism*, VI, 76–78, 1932; "Cosmology," (Colligan), *OF*, XI, 431, 1937; "Die Ethik des Hl. Thomas Von Aquin," (Wittmann), *New Scholasticism*, VIII, 174–176, 1934; "The Growth of Philosophic Radicalism," (Halevy), *New Scholasticism*, III, 451–453, 1929; "History of Philosophy," (Glenn), *Fortnightly Review*, XXXVI, 297, 1929; "Inside Experience," (Hart), *New Scholasticism*, II, 179–180, 1928; "Introduction to the Theological Summa of St. Thomas," (Grabmann), *OF*, VI, 95, 1931; "Liberty Its Use and Abuse," (Cox), *OF*, XI, 431, 1937; "John Dewey, the Man and His Philosophy," *New Scholasticism*, VI, 76–78, 1932; "Matter, Life and Value," (Joad), *New Scholasticism*, VI, 144–154, 1932; "The Metaphysics of Pragmatism," (Hook), *New Scholasticism*, II, 294–296, 1928; "Moral Values and the Moral Life," (Gilson), *OF*, VI, 96, 1931; "Movements of Thought in the Nineteenth Century," (Mead), *New Scholasticism*, XI, 162–167, 1937; "The Natural Law, According to St. Thomas and Suarez," (Farrell), *New Scholasticism*, VI, 73–76, 1932; "Power," (Russell), *Commonweal*, XXIX, 133, 1938; "A Preface to Life," (James), *OF*, XI, 191, 1937; "Progressive Scholasticism," (Bruni), *Fortnightly Review*, XXXVI, 76–77, 1929; "Psychologia Sensitiva," (Froebes), *Fortnightly Review*, XXXIV, 472, 1927; "La raison règle de la moralité d'après Saint Thomas," (Lehu), *New Scholasticism*, VI,

70–71, 1932; "The Spirit of Medieval Philosophy," (Gilson), *University of Toronto Quarterly*, VI, 278–282, 1937–38; "Die Tiefen der Seele," (Klug), *Fortnightly Review*, XXXV, 121, 1928; "Untergang des Abendlandes, Christentum und Sozialismus," (Briefs), *Fortnightly Review*, XXXIV, 117–118, 1927.

TRANSLATIONS:

Thomas Aquinas: His Personality and Thought, from the German of Dr. Martin Grabmann, New York: Longmans, Green and Co., 1928, 191p.

and monks of St. John's Abbey, *A Personalist Manifesto*, from the French of Emmanuel Mounier, New York: Longmans, Green and Co., 1938, 298p.

V. ART AND ARCHITECTURE

ARTICLES:

"Architecture and the Liturgy," *Liturgical Arts*, V, 13–18, 1936.
"Art and the Christ-Life," *Catholic Art Quarterly*, V, 2–5, 1941.
"Artist and Saint," *OF*, XI, 419–420, 1937.
"A Cardinal Speaks," *OF*, XII, 167–171; 208–211;250–254, 1938.
"A Church Goods Journal," *OF*, XIII, 41–43, 1938.
"The Liturgical Arts Society," *OF*, XI, 182–184, 1937.
"Religion in Pictures," *OF*, IV, 223–226, 1930.
"Sacred Art For Everyone," *OF*, X, 272–273, 1936.
"Our Running Head Designs," *OF*, IV, 458–461, 1930.
"Unless the Lord Build The House . . ." *Liturgical Arts* VI, 65–68, 1937.

BOOK REVIEWS:

"Catholic Art," (magazine) *OF*, IX, 380–381, 1935; "Modern Sacred Art" (International Annual Review), *OF*, XII, 379–380, 1938.

VI. MISCELLANEOUS

ARTICLES:

"Catholic Opinion," *Atlantic Monthly*, CXLI, 396–397, 1928.
"The Challenge of Rhythm and Rime," *Fortnightly Review*, XXVI, 356, 1919.
"Chippewa a Music Language," *Indian Sentinel*, XIII, 3, 137, 1933.
"Chippewa Catholic Indian Congress," *Indian Sentinel*, XIV, 4, 84, 1934.
"Chippewa Congress of Minnesota," *Indian Sentinel*, XIII, 4, 174, 1933.
"A Diocesan Confraternity Program," *OF*, XII, 421–423, 1938.
"First You Catch Your Rabbit," *Indian Sentinel*, XIII, 2, 85, 1933.
"Glimpses From Our Bahama Missions," *Benedictine Forum*, I, 36–37, 1917.
"I Would Steal a Dog," *Indian Sentinel*, XIII, 2, 73, 1933.
"Modernes Deutsch," *Wanderer*, March 11, 1926.
"On the Road to Mahnomen," *Indian Sentinel*, XIII, 3, 129, 1933.
"Pig to End Depression," *Indian Sentinel*, XIII, 30, 1932–33.
"St. Paul's Guild," *OF*, XI, 367–369, 1937.
"Streifzüge in Spanien," *Wanderer*, December 2, 1926, — August 4, 1927.
A series of thirty-six articles describing his trips through, and impres-

sions of, Spain and Europe in general; translated into German by
Joseph Matt.

BOOK REVIEWS:

"Rutherford Uncovered," (Felix), *OF*, XI, 480, 1927; "Think and Live,"
(Morrison and Rueve), *OF*, XII, 335, 1938; "Benediktinisches Kloster-
leben in Deutschland," (Monks of Maria Laach), *OF*, IV, 95–96, 1929;
"Geschichte des Benediktinischen Moenchtums," (Hilpisch), *OF*, IV,
95, 1929.

APPENDIX 2
BIBLIOGRAPHICAL ESSAY

The complete bibliography of Virgil Michel's writings and the bibliographical data given in the footnotes make unnecessary mentioning these items again. To comment on the significant sources of information is of greater relevance and importance here.

Chief among these were the Michel Papers. For the years 1925–38 the letters he received are preserved as well as copies of the letters he wrote, dictated to three different secretaries. Besides these Father Virgil personally typed many of his own letters, and of these he seems to have retained copies of only important ones, while he kept first drafts of significant letters. Always systematic, he had the habit of writing notes on letters while he read them to aid him in composing his replies. His correspondence for the years 1925–30 was tightly packed into nine bundles, each about two inches thick. It seems that either Michel or someone else took these to an abandoned corner in a basement before going to the Indian missions in 1930, for it was in this basement corner that the archivist of St. John's Abbey accidently discovered them some years after Michel's death. The archivist was just in time, for he snatched them up just as water seeping through a wall had begun to eat away the edges of one bundle. In these letters is the account of the organized beginnings and development of the liturgical movement in the English-speaking world. There is reason to believe that important letters for these years are missing. For example, while it is apparent that Michel corresponded with Dom Beauduin and a few others at this time, there is no such evidence in this group of letters. Of great value for this study were the letters to Michel of the associate editors of *Orate Fratres* and of many others, as well as Dom Virgil's replies.

The correspondence for the years 1933–38 is in well-nigh perfect alphabetical order. Father Virgil kept separate files for the letters of those many persons with whom he was continually in touch. Except for those in his active file at the time of his death, it is clear from other sources that he destroyed many letters bearing on matters of conscience. According to the archivist at St. John's, Abbot Alcuin destroyed at least six large bundles of letters after Michel's death. There were six files of letters dealing with the Social Institute. Valuable also were large files of correspondence with publishing firms such as Burgess, Bruce, Macmillan, Lohmann, Benziger Brothers and the Wanderer — correspondence for the last named three going back to 1926. The Michel Papers are also interlarded with numerous programs for meetings and conventions and with clippings from newspapers and periodicals saved by him or sent to him by his many friends. These often furnished the key to the clarification of difficulties that could not be solved in any other way. Similarly helpful were copies and drafts of outlines for action programs sent by Michel to various members of the laity and to organizations.

Dom Virgil enjoyed the confidence of both Abbots Peter and Alcuin. It is safe to say that nothing important happened at St. John's Abbey in the years 1916–38 which is not reflected in the communications that passed between the abbots and their subject. These letters were invaluable, therefore, in reconstructing the story of Michel's role in the various activities, as well as in the spiritual, liturgical, social, and educational evolution of his community for these years. Hardly less valuable for this purpose were the letters from his confreres, many of which Michel saved after 1923. An aid also were the many telegrams and letters of condolence addressed to Abbot Alcuin after Michel's death, and the copies of the abbot's replies. These messages revealed the broad scope of Father Virgil's work and the esteem in which he was held by many, a fact which seems to have come as somewhat of a surprise to Abbot Alcuin.

Among the Michel Papers were found copious outlines for retreats, unpublished manuscripts, and some research and lecture notes. The outlines for his lectures on the Christ-Life Series were an aid in restating his philosophy of religious education. Outlines for the Christ-Life and Christian Religion Series of textbooks were also among his Papers, as well as a number of drafts of articles, published and unpublished. An index of liturgical articles appearing in American and European Catholic periodicals for the years 1925–30 was compiled by confreres under Michel's direction. Sister Jane Marie

Murray, O.P., had typed Dom Virgil's personal Liturgical Index, a reference guide to ideas in all parts of the liturgy. The individual items had been written by Michel on discarded paper slips of various forms and kinds. Unfortunately there is no trace of what must have been a large collection of philosophical notes, nor has Michel's diary for his days with the Indians been found.

The following persons graciously submitted letters from Father Virgil for this study: Fathers Paul Hanly Furfey, William Busch and Martin Schirber, O.S.B.; the Anglican Serge Bolshakoff, Catherine De Hueck Doherty, Norman McKenna, Edward Skillin, and Clare Fontanini; Sisters Cecilia Himebaugh, O.S.B., Virgil and Eleanore Michel, C.S.J. The last two also gathered family documents for the writer. Sister Eleanore retrieved Father Virgil's written sermons from a priest in North Dakota who had been using them. Going back to the first days of Michel's priesthood, these afforded insights into the liturgical evolution of his thinking. Father Paul Bussard generously contributed four files of letters covering the early history of the *Leaflet Missal* and other subjects, while Abbot Patrick unhesitatingly made available correspondence and documents from the Archives of St. Mary's Abbey, Newark, dealing with the first and subsequent Liturgical Weeks. The writer is also indebted to Norman McKenna for a file of documents, pictures, and clippings dealing with communist and Campion activities during the 1930's.

A complete file of *Liturgy and Sociology* is available only in the New York Public Library. Most of Canada's *Social Forum* had been saved by Father Furfey, and the missing issues supplied by Catherine De Hueck. Like the New York *Catholic Worker*, this will soon be on microfilm at the Mullen Library of the Catholic University of America. Except for the kindness of Edward Marciniak, the writer would not have seen the Chicago *Catholic Worker*. Bolen Carter kindly contributed bulletins of the *Catholic Alliance*. The St. John's *Record*, organ of the students and alumni of St. John's University, yielded valuable information on Michel's premonastic student life and on his talks and activities as a lecturer, retreatmaster, and dean of Prep School and college. Archivists of St. John's Abbey clipped many articles and editorials of appreciation as these appeared in periodicals and newspapers throughout the country after Michel's death. From the beginning Father Virgil intended the Apostolate section of *Orate Fratres* to record the growth of the liturgical movement in the world generally, but especially in the English-speaking world. Also appearing therein are occasional items of interests and activities concerning the liturgy before the organized liturgical apostolate had begun. The back numbers of *Liturgical Arts* were a further fruitful source of information.

One fortunate circumstance in writing the life and work of Virgil Michel was the fact that so many Benedictine confreres and other associates were still living and so could be interviewed. It was an unforgettable experience to discuss for many hours the origins, early efforts, the opposition, and development of the liturgical movement with pioneers like the priests William Busch, Martin Hellriegel, Gerald Ellard, S.J., and several others. Sister Jane Marie was always a sure source of accurate information on obscure points in connection with Michel's work in the field of religious education. Many hours of conversation were passed with Sister Cecilia concerning Cisca and the Chicago *Catholic Worker*. Much time for valuable consultation was given by Dorothy Day and by Dorothy Weston Coddington, at one time co-editors of the *Catholic Worker* in New York. The latter was also one of the editors of *Liturgy and Sociology*. Sister Eleanore and John Schmitz, a boyhood friend, knew most about Father Virgil's pre-high school years. The writer learned much from the various members of the Matt family in St. Paul, as well as from discussion with Catherine De Hueck. Among the many members of his own community who were helpful, the following should be singled out: Joseph Kreuter, Walter Reger, Damian Baker, Basil Stegmann, Godfrey Diekmann, Hilary Thimmesh, Roger Schoenbechler, Eric Buermann, Ronald Roloff, William Heidt, and a former member of the community, Abbot Severin Gertken. The following were generous in granting interviews: Bishops Francis J. Haas and Bernard J. Sheil; Monsignors Reynold Hillenbrand, Luigi Ligutti, William H. Russell; Fathers Paul Bussard, James Byrnes, Daniel Cantwell, Vincent Donovan, O.P., George Ford, Charles Hart, John LaFarge, S.J., H. A. Reinhold, Damasus Winzen, O.S.B., Ermin Vitry, O.S.B., Gerald Phelan, Robert Kothen, Martin Carrabine, S.J., Joseph Collins, S.S.; and members of the laity: Edward S. Skillin, John O'Connor, Emerson Hynes, Eva J. Ross, John Cogley, Edward Marciniak, Ewald Michel, Ade Bethune, Maurice Lavanoux, Justine B. Ward, and many others.

APPENDIX 3
THE SCOPE OF THE LITURGICAL MOVEMENT[1]

Ten years of active apostolate in the cause of the liturgical revival have undoubtedly brought about a better understanding in our country of the full scope of the liturgical movement. The primary objective of the latter must always be to bring the faithful to a better appreciation of what the Church's liturgy is in the life of the Church and therefore in the life of every member of the Church. It goes without saying that this better appreciation must be more than merely intellectual, and that it must lead to a better participation of the members in the corporate worship of the Church. The more wholeheartedly and intelligently the member of the Mystical Body enters into this corporate worship of the Church, the more should the divine life and the spirit there imbibed affect his daily conduct and thus transform this conduct and all its instruments into a truly Christian environment. If the first purpose of the liturgical movement is to lead the faithful into more intimate participation in the liturgy of the Church, then the further objective must also be that of getting the liturgical spirit to radiate forth from the altar of Christ into every aspect of the daily life of the Christian.

This twofold objective or scope of the liturgical movement derives naturally from the very nature of the liturgy as the life of the Church. That the liturgy, as the official worship of the Church, calls for active participation by all the faithful has been abundantly emphasized wherever the liturgical apostolate has been promoted. The very texts of the liturgy, as well as the ancient tradition of the Church, call for this active participation in it by the faithful. At the same time the very texts, which use the sublime truths of Christ's revelation as the bases and means of prayer and worship, likewise give constant inspiration and direction for the carrying over of this spirit from the actual worship into the daily life of the Christian, whether he be at home or at work or at play. Everywhere the liturgy urges to constant fidelity in living true to the sublime action of dedication to God that takes place in the sacrificial worship, everywhere it urges to the full transfer of the spirit of the divine service enacted at the altar from thence into all the contacts of daily life. All these must likewise reflect the true Christian spirit that is properly derived from the sacrifice of the altar

[1] Virgil Michel, O.S.B., *OF*, X (1936), 485–490.

439

as the source and center of the life of the whole Mystical Body of Christ and of every single member. If it is true that the liturgy has as its primary purpose the glorification of God and the sanctification of man, it is also true that both this glorification and this sanctification must be realized not only in the concentrated worship of the altar but likewise in every thought, word, and action of the day. That is why the saintly Pius X called for a reflowering of the true Christian spirit "among all the faithful in every way" and pointed out as the foremost and indispensable source of this true Christian spirit the active and intelligent participation of the faithful in the solemn and public worship of the Church.

Many persons, even some professing interest in the liturgical movement, have continued to look upon the liturgy rather in its external aspects than as the inner worship of soul and the divine action of Christ and of God that is enacted through the visible elements of the liturgical rites. It is under this mistaken emphasis that the aim of the liturgical movement was by them narrowed down to an external participation of the faithful in the Mass, say, by means of the *Missa recitata* drilled conscientiously but with no attempt to gain a real understanding of the inner action of the Mass and of the supernatural relation of the individual member to the corporate sacrifice of the Mystical Body. Obviously such a participation may be quite purely mechanical and not really intelligent at all. Intelligent participation of the faithful in the Mass means primarily a participation by understanding and will according to the capacity of the member. Just as a sin carries with it inner guilt only if the evil deed was knowingly and willingly performed, so a Christian participation in the Mass is the more meritorious the more it is done with an understanding of the true nature of the prayer-action of the Mass and with the willing joining of heart and soul in that action as it unfolds itself before the senses. And for each member of the Mystical Body at least that degree of intelligence and of will should be applied to his participation in the Mass which he employs in his other serious labors and actions. To lead back to such a degree of intelligent participation of the faithful in the liturgical worship of the Church is the primary objective of the liturgical movement. But that once attained, the liturgy urges to ever greater assimilation with Christ the divine head, so that the member should continue to grow spiritually and supernaturally in his participation in the divine action of Christ enacted in the liturgy.

The whole aim of the liturgical apostolate can therefore also be expressed as that of the constant growth in Christ by ever drinking deep at the source of the Christ-life, the sacrifice of the altar and the sacraments: it means a continuation and ever greater realization of the divine seed of life implanted in the sacrament of baptism. As far as understanding goes, it means a better realization of the status of the Christian as a member of Christ, of his part in the corporate worship of the Mystical Body, of his dignity as a temple of the Holy Ghost, of the divine law of the love of God and of man as well as the service of God directly in worship and indirectly in the service of fellowmen, and especially of the twofold truth that in the supernatural life of the Christian it is always Christ who is acting and producing the effects of the supernatural value, but that the abundance of such fruitful actions, even while they are Christ's, is directly proportionate also to the good will and effort put forth by the Christian himself.

As far as the will is concerned, the true Christian spirit means a constant putting into effect of these sublime truths of membership in Christ, it means the will to live for the glory of God above all, to give oneself over wholly to the service of God and His children, in other words, to seek above all the kingdom of heaven, and to relate and coordinate all else properly to this supreme aim of the Christian life. This will unto living fully as "another Christ," as a regenerated child of God and member of Christ, is fundamentally dynamic and it can continue only if it is given ample opportunity to function. In the very nature of the liturgical or the Christian spirit, it cannot function only in the inner recesses of the soul, but must show itself wholeheartedly in every action of the day. In terms of the liturgical spirit, then, there is no place left for the kind of negative Christianity so frequent in our day, which does a minimum for God and a maximum for self, which measures its service of God by the rule of minimum obligation, only to give itself over all the more to a secular life in a secular way and to a maximum extent.

The Christian who drinks deep at the liturgical sources of the Christ-life will appreciate the seal of Christ with which he was indelibly marked at his baptism, and he will endeavor to put this same seal on everything with which he comes in contact throughout his daily life. Far from willingly giving himself over to a secular and un-Christian environment he will spare no effort to Christianize his environment and thus fulfil his function as "another Christ" over against the world in which he lives. Even as all creation below man partook of the effects of the fall of man and was through man in a way separated from God, so the regenerated Christian will always function as a mediator through Christ in making use of all this same creation in the service of God and of his fellows in Christ, unto a true flourishing of the true Christian spirit among all the faithful in every way. This should mean a Christian revitalizing of all human activities and therefore a true reflourishing of Christian culture, of the arts and literature, of social institutions formed after the mind of Christ, e.a.

The general flourishing of the true Christian spirit should show itself in a growing understanding of the truths of the Christian dispensation. That it will give new vitality to the science of theology is even now abundantly clear. The relatively short period of the Christian revival that is the liturgical movement has seen a renewed interest in the fundamental truths of the Christian dispensation, especially as these should affect the life and the status of the members of Christ. The renewed interest in the sacrifice of the Mass and in the entire nature of the Church and of the Christ-life will mean a renewed *approfondissement* of the fundamental truths of our faith, the Trinity, the indwelling of the Holy Ghost, the Mystical Body of Christ, the Communion of Saints, the priesthood of the faithful, etc., at least in so far as these are basic to the liturgical life of the Church. And intelligent participation of the faithful in the liturgy will restore to them their native right to a share in this theological knowledge and understanding, in place of the relegation of theology to an abstract science for experts, such as it has been until recently.

There are many other ways in which a reflourishing of the true Christian spirit will affect our entire culture and life. We have just gone through several centuries of individualism, in which the individual man was taught to seek his own interest and advantage in disregard of that of his brethren. The chaos of the resultant disruption has ushered in the reaction of a totalitarian collectivism in which the social body is given exclusive value to the suppression of all individual personality. We are today facing anew the great problem of the relation of the individual to the fellowship, the problem of personality. Our present chaos is the result of the violent rejection of the Christian tradition of the golden mean between a disintegrating individualism and an all-devouring totalitarianism. We must return to the traditional concepts in order to develop them further in terms of our past experiences. Here the liturgy has an important part to play since it has preserved intact the supernatural model of all human fellowship in full harmony with the complete responsibility of all individual members. Having learned again from the liturgy the harmonious relation of responsible personalities and their voluntary cooperation in the common life of the fellowship, we must apply these Christian concepts to all the forms of our social life, the family, the community, the state, and thus build up anew a Christian social order of life. The basic notions of duty and right must be given new vitality by a right understanding of human responsibility, of the human person and not the individual as the basic element of the social fellowship.

Through the materialistic and naturalistic philosophy of our times men have come to look upon all material riches as so many instruments of personal pleasure and aggrandizement. Here a flourishing of the true Christian spirit will help us to see all material goods as destined for the fulfilment of the purposes of God's creation, as instruments of man in the service of God. Thus the possession of material goods will change from a mere means of individual privilege and enjoyment into one of service of God in his fellowmen, and the social duty of wealth will again function in the society of mankind. The will to perfection engendered in the Christian filled with the zeal of Christ will show itself in all his relations to his environment, both social and material, and the true Christian spirit will thus be the source of a culture that is built up on the eternal values of life in God.

That all of this must bring notable changes in education, in the concept of parental responsibility, in the Christian functioning of authority, in a fruitful concept of obedience, in our educational methods and procedures, goes without saying. Our entire educational mechanism and set-up is the result of the individualism and materialism that have dominated our life. It is in many ways thoroughly unchristian. What the full changes in education are that a reflourishing of the Christian spirit among the faithful would bring about can only be vaguely envisioned at present, but that they would be immense no one can doubt.

Today the entire world is at the turning of the ways. Either the dechristianizing trend of the past centuries must go on to its bitter conclusions, or else a change must come in terms of a reflourishing of the true Christian spirit. The latter can happen only through an intelligent return to the primary and indispensable source of this spirit, as the vicars of Christ have repeatedly pointed out. But the new trend cannot remain there, as it were, in idle self-complacency. To live, as it should, it must needs blossom forth in rich fruits of human achievement by bringing new spirit to all man's activities and efforts, unto the flourishing of a new Christian culture and civilization — else its new life will be but as the temporary glow of a dying ember.

INDEX

ABBEY, the Church in miniature, 7
Abbots, 7
Accreditation, 358–62, 395 (n. 33)
Acolyte (periodical), 91, 92, 156, 160
Adler, Mortimer J., 321, 348, 366, 391–92
Adult education, 367
Advertising, 287
    in *Orate Fratres*, 135 (n.53)
Aesthetics
    Brownson's philosophy of, 12
    Michel's theory of, 274
Alexander, Franz, 342 (n.44)
Altar
    church architecture and, 282
    rubrical, 142–43
Altar and Home (periodical) 149
Altar builders, 142
Alter, Karl J., Abp.
    on social action, 197
Alumni Committee on Catholic Action, 382
America (periodical), 110
American Benedictine Review (periodical), 353
American Catholic Philosophical Association, 36, 161
American Catholic Sociological Society, 298, 308
American Library Association, 361
American Philosophical Association, 161, 324
Angelicanism, converts from, 381
Anti-Catholicism
    American history, 84
    Atlantic Monthly article, 161
Anti-clericalism
    signs of, 320
    in Spain, 30
Antigonish cooperative movement, 367, 371
Apathy, 60, 112, 193, 347

Apologetics
    Catholic college teachers, 351
    inadequate proofs, 240
    methods; Christian living, 240
    value of the liturgy, 239
Apostolate
    American, 411
    Christian culture, 261
    duty of all Christians, 188
    laity and social justice, 184
    liturgical life and, 138, 139, 348
    method, 167 (n.6)
    Pius XI on, 193
    Pius XII to Roman pastors, 214 (n.45)
    qualities for, 385
    sacramental characters and, 214 (n.46)
    See also Catholic Action
Approved Workmen (association), 403 (n.95)
Architecture
    bibliography of Michel's writings, 433
    unifying idea of, 280
    See also Church architecture
Art
    bibliography of Michel's writings, 433
    Brownson's philosophy of, 12
    Catholic revival, 142
    Christian, 410
    culture and, 273
    every man an artist, 284–85
    idea and meaning in, 274
    liturgical, 142, 275ff
    liturgical, lectures on, 143
    Liturgical Press and, 126
    living, 280
    love and, 276–77
    modern secular, 276
    practical, 296 (n.80)
    purpose of liturgical, 278

Date Due

JAN 2 2 '60			
JY 1 1 '60			
Feb. 1 '61			
FE 24 '61			
JE 30 '62			
JY 6 '62			
JY 21 '62			
	PRINTED	IN U. S. A.	